FISH FOR LIFE

MARE PUBLICATION SERIES

MARE is an interdisciplinary social-science institute studying the use and management of marine resources. It was established in 2000 by the University of Amsterdam and Wageningen University in the Netherlands.

MARE's mandate is to generate innovative, policy-relevant research on marine and coastal issues that is applicable to both North and South. Its programme is guided by four core themes: fisheries governance, maritime work worlds, integrated coastal zone management (ICZM), and maritime risk.

In addition to the publication series, MARE organises conferences and workshops and publishes a social-science journal called *Maritime Studies (MAST)*. Visit the MARE website at http://www.marecentre.nl.

SERIES EDITORS

Svein Jentoft, University of Tromsø, Norway
Maarten Bavinck, University of Amsterdam, the Netherlands

PREVIOUSLY PUBLISHED

Leontine E. Visser (ed.), *Challenging Coasts. Transdisciplinary Excursions into Integrated Coastal Zone Development*, 2004 (ISBN 90 5356 682 1)

Jeremy Boissevain and Tom Selwyn (eds.), *Contesting the Foreshore. Tourism, Society, and Politics on the Coast*, 2004 (ISBN 90 5356 694 5)

FISH FOR LIFE

Interactive Governance for Fisheries

Edited by Jan Kooiman, Maarten Bavinck,
Svein Jentoft and Roger Pullin

MARE Publication Series No. 3

Centre for Maritime Research

AMSTERDAM UNIVERSITY PRESS

Cover illustration: Steef Meyknecht

Cover design: Sabine Mannel / NAP, Amsterdam
Lay-out: JAPES, Amsterdam

ISBN 90 5356 686 4
NUR 741

Contents

Preface

This volume on fisheries governance is the result of collaboration between academics and practitioners from around the world. For over three years, thirty fisheries professionals from a wide variety of disciplinary backgrounds shared their experiences, ideas and concerns, and gathered together at regular intervals to develop what they felt was a new approach to the problems and opportunities that beset fisheries and aquaculture. This endeavour was generously supported by the European Commission by way of its programme for development cooperation (INCODEV, project number ICA4-CT-2001-10038).

The FISHGOVFOOD network, as it came to be known, was particularly concerned with the situation of countries in the South. Not only are substantial parts of their populations dependent on capture fisheries and aquaculture for a living, fish also play an important role in their food security. While recognising the special status of fisheries in the South, the network also took care to emphasise basic similarities in the workings of the 'fish chain' in North and South, and in the governance of fisheries, in various geographical regions.

Basing itself on an understanding of developments in the fisheries field, the network's source of intellectual inspiration lay elsewhere. One of the newly elaborated perspectives in governance theory – known as interactive governance – appeared particularly relevant. First, its two points of departure – the increasing diversity, complexity, dynamics and differences of scale among the fisheries systems-to-be-governed, and the notion that governance is not a task of government alone – matched with the network members' understanding of developments in fisheries. More fundamentally, however, they felt that interactive governance theory provided an alternative framework for understanding the current state of affairs, and the new directions that could be explored.

One of the conditions for making a conceptual advance is the integration of social, economic, and ecological insights and the bridging of disciplinary gaps. This requires a propensity for what Wilson (1998:8) has called consilience, 'a "jumping together" of knowledge by the linking of facts and fact-based theory across disciplines to create a common groundwork of explanation'. One of the fact-based concepts utilized by the FISHGOVFOOD network for this purpose is the 'fish chain'.

Sensitivity for what Aristotle in his discourse on ethics described as the 'phronetic' (value-based) approach to knowledge, in contrast to 'episteme' (scientific), and 'techne' (craft) approaches, is another condition for making a conceptual advance (see Flyvbjerg 2001). According to this viewpoint, principles and values cannot be disconnected from governance practice, and must be brought out into the open. In phronetic discourse, one asks questions like: Where are we going? Is this desirable? And, what should be done? Interactive governance theory follows a similar route by highlighting the importance of articulated principles and values.

This, in brief, was the network's compass at the inception of the project. The explorations that followed, which are chronicled in this book, were necessarily intense. The network devised the book's chapter outline after intensive meetings and discussions in Amsterdam and Dakar. Chapters were subsequently drafted through substantial collaboration among network members, and were rewritten many times over, as the overall framework developed and chapters were tuned to comprise the whole volume. The result stands somewhere between an academic monograph and a multi-author, edited volume on the topic in question. While various author groups hold responsibility for their respective chapters, and these chapters can also be read independently, the book is meant to be a composite whole. Accordingly, each chapter exercises a function in the larger argument, and chapters should, ideally, be read in sequence.

This academic volume is accompanied by a policy workbook on the same topic entitled Interactive Governance for Fisheries – a Guide to Better Practice, which summarizes the findings of this volume and explores avenues to strengthen existing governance practices. More information on this policy workbook is available at the following website: www.marecentre.nl. The reader is also alerted to the continuing existence of an interactive fisheries governance network, which can be contacted at www.fishgovnet.org.

Many individuals and organisations have contributed to the realisation of this volume. SISWO/Institute for Social Policy and the Centre for Maritime Research (MARE) hosted the project and provided essential facilities. From Brussels, Cornelia Nauen provided constant encouragement and advice. Maarten Bavinck coordinated the project, receiving assistance at various stages from Marja Harms, Marloes Kraan, Iris Monnereau, and Jeroen Dijk. Peter de Kroon designed the figures. Sheila Gogol and Ann Holleman are responsible for the English language editing. Finally, we thank two anonymous referees for their comments, and Vanessa Nijweide and Jaap Wagenaar of Amsterdam University Press (AUP) for their care in publishing the manuscript.

The Editors

PART I

Governance:
A new Perspective for Fisheries

I

The Governance Perspective

Jan Kooiman and Maarten Bavinck

Background

Capture fisheries are in crisis. Documents and figures on the state of global fisheries that have appeared since the 1990s point out a strongly negative trend, with three related components. The first is the decline or collapse of fish stocks, the world over. The degradation of aquatic ecosystems is reflected in the levelling off of the total world catch in the 1990s (FAO 2002a), and in the declining catches of individual fishers. The second component of crisis is fishing overcapacity. There are simply too many vessels and too many people fishing. Their aggregate activity is the main cause of the collapse of fish stocks. The third aspect of crisis relates to management. Despite signals that things were going terribly wrong, fisheries managers have been unable to reverse the trend. Thus, the foundations of fisheries management theory and practice have been called into question.

New economic players have been quick to fill in the gap. As cod stocks in the North Atlantic during 2002 reached deleterious levels, and the European Commission suggested a total ban on cod fishing, the first cod farms opened up in the Norwegian fjords. Scientists and policymakers often view aquaculture as a solution to problems faced by capture fisheries. Figures would seem to confirm their points of view: as capture fisheries went into decline, global aquaculture entered a period of strong growth, meeting an ever-increasing proportion of the demand for fish.

Capture fisheries and aquaculture would thus seem to reflect different conditions of crisis and opportunity. Whether the situation is as black-and-white as this would suggest – and indeed we believe it is not – the comparison highlights societal phenomena that play an important part in this book. Crises and opportunities occur, in differing mixes, in all sectors and societies, and at all times. Their governance is therefore a matter of great concern.

Food security is another matter demanding attention. Five decades of development effort have not significantly impacted the incidence of poverty, particularly, but not exclusively, in the South. According to the World Bank (2001), a fifth of the world's population lives on less than US$1 a day. They constitute the world's poor. One of the multiple deprivations they suffer is a lack of food security. Fisheries and aquaculture have often been singled out as making a meaningful contribution to the alleviation of hunger and malnutrition. Fish and other aquatic produce are highly nutritious and often affordable to low-income households. This applies to coastal and landlocked states.

The aim of the fisheries governance network (FISHGOVFOOD), of which this volume is a result, was to develop and to share a new, interactive perspective on the governance of fisheries and aquaculture. The reason for the initiative was that we, the participants, believe that the crisis that is currently affecting the sector cannot be resolved by conventional methods. There is a need for creative thinking, which means crossing boundaries between disciplinary understandings and routine approaches. This implies a shift from a problem-solving approach to one that emphasises opportunity-creation and the effective handling of tensions.

Two general assumptions underlie policymaking. One is that governments, researchers or user groups possess, or can develop, sufficient knowledge on their own to form the basis for policy. The second assumption is that the world in which we live can be represented in simple models. We find both assumptions untenable. Academics, policymakers and users have to interact 'to get the picture right'. In addition, they have to put the diversity, complexity and dynamics of governance issues right on the table.

Four bodies of literature have informed our views. Governance literature considers problem solving and opportunity-creation as a joint and interactive responsibility of all parties – state, market and civil society (Kooiman 2003). According to this perception, public responsibilities are handled with an eye for private needs and capabilities, while private tasks are fulfilled with a concern for public needs and capabilities. The literature on food security is our second source. It emphasises access to food as a moral and a practical issue, and concentrates on the situation of the poor in developing countries. It is concerned with questions of food quality and safety as well as quantity (Kurien 2004). Third, socio-economic literature highlights the intricacy and interconnectedness of capture, processing and marketing activities, and the role of institutions in regulating the usage of natural resources (cf. Schlager and Ostrom 1993; Platteau and Baland 1998; Hersoug, Jentoft and Degnbol 2004). Finally, the aquatic life sciences highlight that well-functioning ecosystems underlie the capture and culture of seafood, and hence that durable fisheries and aquaculture depend upon their conservation (Abramovitz 1996; Boyd 1999a; Pauly and Maclean 2003). Without the ecosystems that produce them, there are no fish. Without social and economic circumstances that support the people who catch and farm fish, there are no fisheries and aquaculture.

Besides drawing on different literature sources, we use various scientific methods – deductive reasoning, empirical observation and interactive learning. The latter includes a step-by-step focused dialogue between academics from different disciplinary backgrounds and professionals in fisheries and aquaculture. We believe that the process of knowledge development proceeds in stages, and rests on elements such as professional self-reflection, peer review, dialogue and integration.

Any new approach to fisheries needs to be cognisant of, and adaptive to the characteristics of its particular field. In the following section, we highlight two important features of fisheries. The first is a time trend toward greater diversity, complexity and dynamics. The second is scale. Both have important consequences for our case for bringing governance into fisheries.

Diversity, Complexity, Dynamics, and Scale

The globalised fisheries are highly *diverse*.

> Diversity is a characteristic of the entities that form fisheries systems and it points to the nature and degree in which they vary.

Catalogues of fishing technology point out that fishers and fish farmers exercise their professions in widely divergent ways. They hunt or farm different fish, using varying methods and techniques, resources and bodies of knowledge. Their understandings of, and meanings attributed to, fishing and farming differ from one location to another (see chap. 4). Globalisation, a process that has intensified over many centuries and recently accelerated, has tended to further the existing division of labour, creating a rich plethora of specialised niches and activities (see chap. 2).

Globalisation has also affected the *complexity* of fisheries and aquaculture the world over by lengthening the chains of interaction.

> Complexity is a function of the architecture of the relations among the parts of a system, and between a system and its environment. Interactions are exchanges that take place in a context of interdependency, and also affect the partners involved. One speaks of lengthening chains of interaction when more actors become involved, and/or when the geographical distance between them extends.

Thorpe and Bennett (2001) distinguish three forms of globalisation in capture fisheries: the globalisation of production, trade, and regulation. The globalisation of production refers to extensions in the range of fishing operations, and the globalisation of trade has connected more fishers to larger markets. The globalisation of regulatory control has resulted in a burgeoning body of rules and guidelines affecting the fisheries at all governing levels creating complicated, and often confusing, regulatory patterns. All three forms of globalisation contribute in different ways to the complexity of fisheries and their governance.

Diversity and complexity are reinforced by *dynamics*.

> Dynamics apply to the tensions within a system and between systems. They are associated with the incidence of, or propensity towards, change.

The dynamics affecting fisheries derive from various sources, affecting disparate moments in the fish chain. The origin of change may be the aquatic ecosystem, the market, the wider social, cultural and political environment, or the regulatory regime. We argue that dynamics are increasing because of the vigour of modern society, in combination with a lengthening of the chains of interaction. When chains extend and include more actors, changes in any one aspect have a broad series of consequences.

Up to now we have discussed diversity, complexity and dynamics as societal phenomena, traversing the realms of the economic, the social, the political, and the regulatory. In recent years the same characteristics are, however, recognised as applying to ecosystems, and imposing limits on human control (see chap. 3).

We have argued above that globalisation and the lengthening of interaction chains have increased diversity, complexity and dynamics in fisheries and aquaculture. This is our first main premise. We also recognise *scale* of phenomena, events and structures, as their other major characteristic.

> Scale refers to time and space dimensions of systems to be governed as well as to governing systems.

The concept of scale is easily illustrated. Some fish species, and some kinds of aquatic ecosystems, have a geographically limited range, whereas others traverse the globe. The same holds true for types of fisheries and fish farming and for types of markets for aquatic produce. Spatial scale plays a role on all these fronts, as well as in any attempt at governance. Time scales play a role in ecology (e.g., the life cycle of a fish species, or the time needed to destroy or rebuild an ecosystem), as well as in capturing, trade, and societal processes in general. They also include the time perspective of human actors involved – the periods over which they assess, judge, plan, and expect things to happen. In governance, time scales are important.

This still sounds quite neat and tidy. In real life, the contrary is actually the case. If all governance efforts, at various scale levels, were to be diagrammed, the resulting picture would resemble a large, tangled and constantly changing spider's web. For ordinary citizens, the web in which they are entangled is sometimes very confusing, and even frightening. Next to diversity, complexity and dynamics, scale becomes a major factor in governance, the subject of the next section.

Governance Approaches

Governance has become a catchword in the social sciences as well as in the policy world. The term was in use even before it became widely known at the beginning of the 1990s, when the World Bank introduced the norm of 'good governance' to international development. Concurrently, it became a focal concept in more scholarly literature stressing the importance of other actors besides the state in governing at the local, the national, and the international level.

As is the case with other terms that have become part of the popular vocabulary, the term 'governance' has different meanings for different people. In many cases, these differences revolve around the perceived role of the state. Governments have often failed to live up to expectations. This has resulted in analyses of weak, unstable, collapsing or failed states. Unable to rely on the state to carry out governing tasks, other actors move forward into prominent positions. Some authors thus argue for a minimal or limited state, as expressed in the often-quoted phrase 'less government and more governance'. Others view governance as 'self-organising networks', whereas in the field of international relations authors speak of 'global governance'.

'Good governance' and 'global governance' are relevant branches of enquiry for those interested in the governance of natural resources. Good governance is a concept closely connected with the World Bank's efforts to couch political renewal in terms of increasing political legitimacy as a precondition for sustainable development (World Bank 1989). Although the term good governance has been broadly applied and has become a major issue in developmental literature and practice, the Bank itself now seems to have narrowed down its original ideas on the subject. In a recent report on governance of fisheries the concept refers mainly to – in the opinion of the Bank – good practices (World Bank 2004). The rise of the concept of global governance in international relations followed from dissatisfaction with theories that limited themselves mainly to relations between states. Governance theory opened up this field to non-state actors. In this usage of governance, it becomes clear that private actors (market parties and non-governmental-organisations (NGOs) often play a much more important informal role than states, nationally and internationally.

For all their variations, however, governance perspectives have three common features. The first is the conviction that 'governing' is a matter of public as well as private actors. Traditionally, governance is viewed as the task of government – it is government, at various levels, that enjoys responsibility for the public good. Indeed, governments are equipped with laws and procedures, money, and staff – in short, with power – to undertake many kinds of action in the public realm. Governments, however, are not the only actors capable of addressing societal problems and opportunities. The range is myriad: individuals, voluntary associations, companies, NGOs, village councils, international organisations, political parties, and militant groups in a variety of roles and circumstances are engaged in shaping societal futures. Just as in a game of football, the interactions among players determine what actually happens, whether it is a goal, a fierce competition, or a boring match.

Second, governance approaches emphasise that the dividing lines between public and private sectors are blurred, and that interests cannot be assumed to be either public or private, but are frequently shared. In this connection, it is generally more appropriate to speak of shifting, rather than shrinking, roles of government. A reshuffling of government tasks and a greater awareness of the role of other societal actors does not render government obsolete. It implies a growing awareness, not only of the limitations of the command-and-control form of governing, but also of the fact that many societal problems and opportunities require the commitments of a broader set of actors and approaches.

This brings us to a third common element, namely, the realisation that governance has a basis in societal developments, and constitutes a reflection thereof. The state of contemporary governance reflects in particular the growth of social, economic and political interdependencies, and trends such as differentiation, integration, globalisation and localisation. These processes result in lengthening chains of interaction, stretching across different scale levels and sectors. In addition to other effects, the lengthening of chains increases the numbers of parties participating in them, while interactions among these parties also multiply.

Governance approaches also suggest that there are important differences between management, policymaking and governance. These differences are not straightforward and unequivocal, and may vary with culture and language. Thus what is termed 'policy' in Anglo-Saxon political culture may be termed 'gouvernance' in the Francophone tradition; American authors, on the other hand, may label the same phenomenon as 'management'. In this volume, we take the view that governance is the more inclusive term, followed by policy, and finally by management. In comparison with managers and policymakers, governors take a step back, and broaden the view in various ways. Governance thus goes beyond the problems at hand to consider longer-term societal trends and needs. In addition, it does not limit itself to one particular sector, such as fisheries, but considers sectoral issues as a reflection of more widely prevalent circumstances.

Governance is not considered here to be the natural prerogative of government or of fisheries managers, but rather a widely practiced activity and a broad responsibility. Governance transcends a problem-and-solution focus and brings an interest for the creation and exploitation of opportunities. It balances a concern for troubles and quandaries with an eye for fresh and promising chances. Governance pays systematic attention to institutional arrangements for governing activities and to the normative principles guiding them.

Finally, an important distinction to be made in discussing governance is that between an analytical and a normative perspective. Governance is both what is and what should be, reality as well as potential. It is in both senses that we use the concept in this volume, with the normative aspect surfacing most strongly in the latter part. In the first part, we are primarily interested in governing as a real-life phenomenon. After all, problems and opportunities emerge all the time, and are tackled, more or less successfully, by people and by institutions.

All of the above indicate that the governing system, the framework of actors engaged in governing, is often as diverse, complex, and dynamic as is the system-to-be-governed. There is no reason to assume that fisheries and aquaculture are exceptions.

Our Governance Perspective

We use the following definition of governance:

> *Governance is the whole of public as well as private interactions taken to solve societal problems and create societal opportunities. It includes the formulation and application of principles guiding those interactions and care for institutions that enable them.*

The most important element of the above definition is the term *interactions*, which stands at the heart of the proposed new interactive governance perspective. For the moment it is sufficient to understand an interaction as a specific form of action, undertaken by actors in order to remove obstacles and tread new pathways. The definition of what constitutes a 'problem' or 'opportunity' depends on the issue and the position and understanding of the viewer in question. The adjective *'societal'* is best understood by way of its opposite, *'private'*, and is often replaced by the word *'public'*. 'Societal' is everything that has a common, social, and collective component. The definition refers also to the importance of *institutions* in governance. Institutions offer structure, order and predictability in human relations such that social actors would know how to interact, what is expected of them, and what they can expect from others. Thus caring for institutions is a part of governance. The same applies to *principles*. Without basic principles, no human relation or governing interaction can last. When governors try to solve problems or create opportunities, they inevitably bring to surface fundamental assumptions, world-views and ethical values for discussion and examination.

In our view, governance is made up of various components. Fig. 1.1 presents a schematic overview.

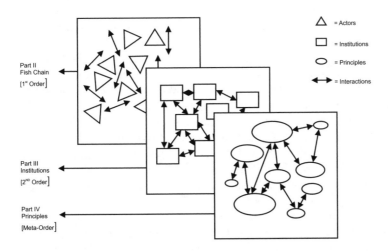

Fig. 1.1 The governance scheme.

In the following section, we discuss the various components one by one, starting with 'interaction'.

Governance as Interaction

The governance concept proposed in this volume has its basis in the social sciences. Its proponents recognise that society is made up of a large number of *actors*, who are constrained or enabled in their actions by *structures*. Actors, in this perspective, are any social unit possessing agency or power of action. These include individuals, but also households, associations, leaders, firms, departments, and international organisations. Structure, on the other hand, refers to the frameworks within which actors operate, and which they take into account. These include culture, law, agreements, material and technical possibilities, and the many other dimensions of that which we inherit from our birth, and which constitutes the world we live in. According to sociological reason, actors are continuously making changes to structure while at the same time being subjected to its influence.

It is a truism to note that actors in society interact. People communicate with each other in a large variety of settings, join up or compete, feel included or excluded, and deliver and demand services to and from one another. In the course of these interactions they often change their minds, adapt their strategies, and take or withdraw from responsibilities. The innumerable interactions that occur determine, in their totality, the courses that societies take. Interactions among actors are partly based on social interdependencies. In contemporary societies with a highly developed division of labour and which operate at a multitude of scales, and people rely on one another to a great extent. No single actor, public or private, has the knowledge and information required to solve complex, dynamic, and diversified problems; no actor has an overview sufficient to make the needed instruments effective; no single actor has sufficient action potential to dominate unilaterally.

Interaction is central in our governance approach. It is an essential part of the system-to-be-governed as well as of the governing system. An interaction is a mutually influencing relation between two or more actors, possessing an intentional and a structural dimension. The actors involved aim for a certain result; at the same time, the interactions in which they engage are constrained by what we established above as structures. It is important to note that interactions have intended as well as unintended consequences. The latter result from tensions between the goals, interests and purposes of actors, as well as between actors and their structural environment.

Governance, from this point of view, emanates from many sources, as a large number of actors strive to address the issues that emerge along their path. As society does not pause, and is never in equilibrium, the totality of these governance efforts is like a multiplicity of hands moulding the clay on a potter's wheel. Some hands have an advantage over others, but never such that they completely determine the shape of the pot being created. Moreover, unlike a potter's clay, the actors being governed react to the hands moulding them. Governance therefore is not merely something governors do, but a quality of the totality of the interactions between those governing and those governed – it is itself an interaction.

It has been noted that many actors, in different positions and levels of society, are involved in governance. This is a statement of fact. But there is also a normative side to it, an understanding that participation in governance is an expression of democracy and therefore a desirable state of affairs. From the normative point of view the goal is to maximise participation and to structure it according to democratic principles. In this volume we are advocating the necessity of broad participation in governance from a normative and from a practical standpoint. The latter follows from the realisation, discussed in a previous section, that societies all over the globe are becoming more and more diverse, complex, and dynamic. Under these circumstances, governance is effective only when the approach is well-structured, open, and flexible.

Orders

The second aspect of our theoretical framework relates to orders of governance. The issue here is not one of geographical or temporal scale, but levels or rings, as in the construction of an onion. We distinguish three concentric circles: first-order, second-order, and meta-governance.

The outer ring deals with day-to-day affairs, and is termed *first-order governing*. First-order governing takes place wherever people, and their organisations, interact in order to solve societal problems and create new opportunities. In the context of this volume, first-order governing means solving the constant stream of problems which surface in the fish chain – problems of supply, price, market, employment, work satisfaction, etc. First-order governing is the nitty-gritty of governance activity. In diverse, complex and dynamic societies first-order governing faces special challenges. It starts with the identification of problems. After all, problems are not an objective reality, they become such only in the minds of societal actors. The first step in the governance process is therefore the localisation and formulation of societal problems, whereby the latter are distinguished from private problems by their scale and shared nature. Once problems, and problem systems, have been identified, attention shifts to the solution space. It is important throughout the analysis to retain the diversity, complexity, and dynamics of situations, as only then will images remain close to reality.

In the preceding paragraph, the term 'opportunity' may be substituted for 'problem', as the processes of identification and response are basically the same. Risk is an important issue in the handling of problems and opportunities. What are the risks involved in a certain course of action, to whom do they pertain, and what level of risk is actually termed acceptable?

This topic has come to the forefront in fisheries science with the ecosystem approach and the precautionary principle.

Second-order governing focuses on the institutional arrangements within which first-order governing takes place. Here we use the term 'institution' to denote the systems of agreements, rules, rights, laws, norms, beliefs, roles, procedures and organisations that are applied by first-order governors to make decisions. Institutions provide the framework within which first-order governance takes place, and constitute the meeting ground of those being governed and those governing. They provide the criteria against which success and failure are measured. Second-order governing implies the reconsideration and adaptation of the parameters of first-order governance. It includes, for example, creating new quality standards, labour laws, and rules on limiting bycatch.

Third-order, or *meta-governance*, takes us to the centre of the onion that feeds, binds, and evaluates the entire governing exercise. One of the core principles of meta-governance is rationality – the idea that governing must be based upon verifiable facts, a logical choice of instruments, and a defendable strategy. Other core principles include responsiveness and performance. In meta-governance, governors and the governed alike take each other's measure in formulating the norms by which they want to judge each other and the measuring process itself.

Elements

Interactive governance, as an intentional activity, consists of three components: images, instruments and action. *Images* constitute the guiding lights as to the how and why of governance. Images come in many types: visions, knowledge, facts, judgements, presuppositions, hypotheses, convictions, ends and goals. They not only relate to the specific issue at hand, such as fisheries or food security, but also contain assumptions on fundamental matters such as the relation between society and nature, the essence of humankind, and the role of government. The main question is not whether actors involved in governance possess images – because everyone does – but how explicit and systematic they have been and will be made.

One of the most influential images in fisheries management in the last decades has been the 'tragedy of the commons', as expressed by Hardin (1968). His suggestions that humans are relatively short-sighted, non-communicative and profit-maximising beings have exerted substantial influence on management theory and practice, and have provided an impetus towards privatisation of fishing rights.

Instruments constitute the second – and intermediary – element of interactive governance. They link images to action. Other than the toolkit metaphor suggests, however, instruments are not a neutral medium – in fact, their design, choice and application frequently elicit strife.

The range of instruments available to influence societal interactions is extremely wide. Instruments may be 'soft' in nature, such as in the case of information, bribes, or peer pressure. They may also have roots in the legal or financial realms, and involve court cases, taxes, permits, or fines. Finally there are the 'hard' instruments of physical force. It is clear that the choice of instruments is not free; one's position in society determines the range available. In addition, instruments have a varying range of applicability, some being general and others specific.

The last element of interactive governance is _action_, or, putting the instruments into effect. This includes the implementation of policies according to set guidelines, which is a relatively dry and routine affair. Action may also, however, consist of mobilising other actors in a new and uncharted direction. In this case, the actors rely upon convincing and socially penetrating images and sufficient social-political will or support. The interactive aspect of governance emerges succinctly.

These three elements of interactive governance are closely connected and not always easily distinguishable. Moreover, they generally do not present themselves in an orderly sequence.

Modes or Styles

Governance theory distinguishes modes of governance that differ according to their locus. There are three ideal types: hierarchical governance, self-governance, and co-governance. All societies demonstrate, and require, mixes of these three modes or styles.

Hierarchical governance is the most classical of the governance modes, characteristic for the interactions between a state and its citizens. It is a top-down style of intervention, which expresses itself in policies and in law. Steering and control are key concepts in this approach. Although the metaphor 'steering the ship of state' has now become old-fashioned, the act of steering societal dynamics is still commonplace. The need for control and steering is not in doubt; its practice is more intricate than often imagined. As modern society is diverse, complex, and dynamic, the controlling or steering authority requires complementary abilities. In addition to top-down governance there are many other arrangements providing for checks and balances in modern societies. In recent years, our perceptions of hierarchical governance have become redefined. The commanding state has been transformed into a regulatory one, the procuring state activities into enabling ones, and benevolent into activating roles. The state nonetheless remains the central governing unit in modern society.

Self-governance in modern society refers to the situation in which actors take care of themselves, outside the purview of government. This is a ubiquitous phenomenon, quite distinct from government intention or policy. Liberal governments will highlight societal self-governing capacities, and socialist ones may downplay them. Governments may choose to deregulate or privatise, withdrawing from the public sector or incorporating self-regulatory capacities in their governance frameworks. We emphasise, however, that self-governance is not a government-created capacity, but comes about of its own accord. In fact, without sustaining a capacity for self-governance, societal governance is an impossible task. The collective action school has made the most systematic analysis of self-regulation with regard to the exploitation of common-pool natural resources, such as capture fisheries.

The third mode is termed _co-governance._ The essential element of this governance mode is that societal parties join hands with a common purpose in mind, and stake their identity and autonomy in the process. Much attention has been devoted to co-governance and to the opportunities it opens. In fisheries, the form of co-governance called co-management is particularly influential. We discuss so-called 'fisheries co-management' in this volume as an expression of co-governance. Co-governance is much broader than the other governance modes and implies the use of organised forms of interaction for governing purposes. A key assumption is that no one actor is in control; instead, interactions are of a horizontal kind.

Governance theory contains numerous manifestations of co-governance, including communicative governance, public-private partnerships, networks, regimes and co-management. We believe that co-governance, in its varying forms, is well equipped to deal with diverse, complex, and dynamic situations. No society, however, operates solely along the lines of co-governance, or, for that matter, of self- or hierarchical governance. Instead, mixes of various modes inevitably prevail. Their design is of special concern.

Governance in the North and South

We aim in this volume to develop an approach to fisheries governance and food security that is of relevance to the South as well as to the North. This expectation is premised on the existence of similarities as well as on interconnectedness. Thus, although there are important differences between aquatic ecosystems in tropical and temperate waters, the ecological principles ordering life and conditioning fishing and fish farming are identical. This is true for the human side as well: markets, politics, and social intercourse are underpinned and triggered by the same human condition.

Not only does life on this planet develop according to identical principles, it is also highly connected. Some fish undertake extensive migrations, affecting the fishers of many nations. Environmental changes in one region impact others, often in unpredictable ways. Finally, the globalisation process, with its economic, political and cultural ramifications, ties countries and people more tightly together than ever before. These are good reasons to take a universal approach. And indeed, many scholars addressing the governance of fisheries and food security, either from an analytical or a prescriptive perspective, do so.

At the same time, there are manifold differences between North and South, most prominently perhaps in the human dimension. Some years ago a scientist pointed out that fisheries management is largely identical to people management, as it is only through influencing people that one reaches the fish (Symes 1996). As societies within and between the North and the South vary substantially, this is bound to affect the practice of governing. It is for this reason that variations must receive more attention.

In the 1960s, Myrdal (1968) suggested that nations in the South are 'weak states'. This description has made way for other normative nomenclature, such as 'collapsing states' or even 'failed states', and, not to forget, 'authoritarian' and 'dictatorial' states. Compared to the states of Europe and North America, the states of the South are sometimes unstable, and either have a deficiency or an overload of authority. They are also often less 'democratic'. There are, in the parlance of today's policymakers, inadequate traditions of good governance, insufficient transparency, and an overdose of corruption. Moreover, in many developing countries institutions making up civil society are underdeveloped.

We cannot escape from evaluating governance styles according to their effectiveness in the face of trends such as increasing societal diversity, complexity and dynamics. Some styles apparently have greater capacities to handle such changes than others do. Generally speaking, the more successful are those of a co-governing kind, in which participation of societal actors is encouraged, rather than hampered.

Food security and safety concerns are intimately related to poverty in North and South. However, in the North, fisheries governance has stronger connections with employment of fishers and fish processors, and with supplying luxury markets, where fish is only one of a range of affordable animal protein sources, and not generally with food security per se.

The socio-economic literature on fisheries and aquaculture points out other differences between North and South. The FAO (2002a), for example, notes that in 2000, an estimated 36 million people were directly engaged in fishing and fish farming. A stunning 94% of marine fishers live and work in Asia, Africa, and Latin America. The dimensions of employment and income-generation clearly need to be included in the governance of fisheries, particularly in the South. In addition, employment figures bear a direct connection with governance. Some fisheries management instruments, such as the Individual Transferable Quotas currently propagated to regulate northern fisheries, clearly lack relevance for many southern fisheries, where landing points are many, employment levels high, and quotas impractical. Here other solutions must be found.

The Outline for this Volume

This volume has five parts, organised according to the orders of governance.

Part I presents the governance perspective (chap. 1) and identifies the overarching challenges and concerns in fisheries (chap. 2).

Part II is devoted to the first order of governance and an analysis of the fish chain. In consecutive chapters, we deal with the ecological basis of fish production (chap. 3), capture fisheries (chap. 4), aquaculture (chap. 5), post-harvest systems (chap. 6), and a number of crosscutting issues (chap. 7).

Part III turns to the second order of governance, and the topic of institutions in fisheries governance. In three substantive chapters, we highlight the roles of local institutions (chap. 8), national-level institutions (chap. 9), and international institutions (chap. 10). Chapter 11 presents an analysis of institutional linkages.

Part IV reviews the principles of fisheries governance, and introduces a normative perspective. Chapter 12 presents a review of principles underlying current governance in fisheries, drawn from international sources. The following chapter (chap. 13) goes on to propose a set of meta-principles based upon the governance approach proposed here. Chapter 14 discusses hard choices and values that emerge from the contradictions.

Part V sums up and expands upon our arguments. Chapter 15 returns to the challenges and concerns of chapter 2 and reviews the current state of governance in their light. Chapter 16 is more theoretical in nature, and confronts the insights of earlier chapters with the governance approach described in chapter 1. Chapter 17, finally, considers how the governance approach can be put into action in fisheries.

2

Challenges and Concerns in Capture Fisheries and Aquaculture

Ratana Chuenpagdee, Poul Degnbol, Maarten Bavinck, Svein Jentoft, Derek Johnson, Roger Pullin, and Stella Williams

Introduction

Fish, taken here to mean all living aquatic products harvested by humans, are a critical source of protein, lipids and micro-nutrients in people's diets in the North and South alike. Fish are often part of the staple diet in developing and less-developed countries, and consumption of fish in developed countries has increased with its heavy promotion as healthy food and up-market food sources. Global concerns about fish harvests, fish stocks, and the health of aquatic ecosystems are directly related to the increasing demand for fish as food and to the potentially short supply, due largely to overfishing and unsustainable fishing practices. Because fish are such an important part of the human diet, these concerns intertwine with social concerns such as fair allocation, improved livelihood and social well-being, and secure access to a safe food supply.

Fish are not only food for human consumption – they also serve ecosystem functions. From an anthropocentric point of view, fish as food for people is the central concern, reflecting management actions and goals. Recently, the importance of fish in their natural ecosystems has been recognised, resulting in the adoption of a more comprehensive approach to fisheries management. Challenges are thus based on acknowledgement of the interconnectivity of concerns for ecosystem health, social justice, livelihoods and food security and food safety.

The health of ecosystems determines their productivity. In capture fisheries, target species are often overexploited to the point where other parts of the aquatic ecosystem are affected. In the past, this problem was mainly addressed from the perspective of the overexploitation of single fish stocks. However, there is increasing awareness that the productivity of capture fisheries should be seen in the context of the overall health of the ecosystem and that ecosystem-based management of fisheries should be employed. Such a management approach aims also to address the problems of bycatch (including incidental catches and discards), and habitat damage caused by fishing gear.

Social justice is a key issue in fisheries, since the distribution of power and income and the allocation of rights change in relation to access to resources. The changes often tend towards greater concentration in the North, and in the South the distribution is centred on those with ample economic and political power. The issue of social justice thus plays an important role in fisheries decision-making and policy development.

Closely related to ecosystem health and social justice are the livelihoods of people in coastal communities who rely directly or indirectly on fisheries as their major source of employment and income. Many members of these communities have long traditions and cultural ties to fisheries livelihoods, which are being threatened by various activities taking place in the coastal areas. Coastal sprawl, for example, is spreading all across the globe, turning coastal lands into urban centres and expensive residential areas in some cases and industrialised zones in others. Yet in many places in the South, living along the coast is often a necessity and the quality of life is not always high, particularly for unskilled workers who migrate from the inland areas. These coastal communities are marginalised and have very little bargaining power when it comes to access to resources or participation in management.

Lastly, fisheries play an important role as a provider of food. In many developing countries, fisheries products are the main source of animal protein and some micronutrients. The use of 'low value' fish for fishmeal production, which is then used as feed in aquaculture production of 'high value' fish, is an example of the competition in fish consumption and food safety between the North and South. Overall, changed productivity and the redistribution of fisheries products on the market will greatly impact the poor. Therefore, in the discussion on food security and fisheries governance, it is important to include issues related to the history of the human use of aquatic ecosystems, which has witnessed major changes. As societies change, so do their perceptions of the constraints and opportunities provided by their natural capital, in particular the aquatic ecosystems they depend on for their livelihood.

Given these basic concerns, does the management of fisheries resources face greater challenges than the management of other food production systems such as poultry farming? In the domain of fish as food, fish do not differ from anything else in their potential for industrialisation and technological advancement to increase productivity or in their vulnerability to environmental consequences. Mad cow disease in Europe and North America and the recent incidence of avian influenza affecting millions of chickens in many countries in Asia are just two examples of the price of intensive agricultural systems that parallel the recent study showing the high level of toxins in farmed salmon (Hites et al. 2004). Stories like this and various scientific findings generate grave public concern about food security and food safety and have direct effects on ecosystem health, social justice, and livelihoods.

The aspect distinguishing fish from other food products lies in its origin as a common pool resource with free access for all. Since the early development of human societies, capture fisheries have been managed under various systems world-wide. Traditional fisheries management based on customary and territorial user rights as in the Pacific Islands was perhaps one of the oldest, and in the context of a widespread modern discourse favouring property rights, it might seem the most advanced. Thus, Hardin's *tragedy of the commons* metaphor (1968) not only fails to capture the real governance issue in fisheries, its implication that the property right system is a remedy is also misleading. In the former, the issue is not that governance is absent in dealing with the commons. The problem is that new driving forces have developed, surpassing the capacity of the old management systems and putting new pressures on the natural and social systems. In the latter, the essence of property is the right to exclude others and reserve for oneself the benefits to be drawn from the resources.

The immediate external driving forces for increased exploitation of fisheries are multifarious, including over-investment in fishing fleets, the influx of people to coastal areas, the expanding demand due to population increase and better market access, and more efficient capture technologies and vessels. These immediate driving forces reflect the more fundamental forces such as globalisation. What follows is the presentation of the driving forces and the process of globalisation, with an emphasis on its relation to fisheries and the challenges it poses to fisheries governance. Concerns about ecosystem health, social justice, livelihoods, food security and food safety are then described in their own right and as results of globalisation.

Globalisation and Fisheries

Although globalisation is often considered a good thing for the world, it all depends on what drives it, and in regard to fisheries, how it drives the development of fisheries, and more importantly, how it affects ecosystems, allocation, employment and food supplies. Changes induced by globalisation occurred in the major world fisheries prior to the mid-twentieth century (e.g., Innis 1954; McEvoy 1986), but the global transition to capitalism and modern fisheries with all its intended effects did not arise until the second half of the twentieth century. Trends in global production and trade in fisheries since 1950 illustrate the massive scale of that transition.

At the beginning of the 1950s, less than 5% of the global marine fisheries resources were maximally exploited or overexploited. By 1994, 60% of global marine fisheries had reached that condition and total marine production was at a plateau (FAO 1999a). The strength of the global demand over the period from 1961 to 1999 is indicated by the rate of growth of fish product exports. Export quantities increased almost five and a half times, while production only a little more than doubled (FAO 2003a). Growth in global production and trade was fed by huge increases in effort, notably in industrialised fisheries. According to the Food and Agriculture Organization (FAO) estimates, the global number of fishers increased from 12.5 million to 36 million from 1970 to 1998 (FAO 1999a). From 1970 to 1995, the number of non-decked fishing vessels grew by roughly 55% and decked vessels more than doubled in number (FAO 1998). These data do not even include the significant advances in the technological sophistication of fishing craft and gear over the same period, which resulted in the changing patterns of fishing grounds as shown by Pauly et al. (2003).

Another important point to note in the changing picture of global fisheries has been the increasing prominence of aquaculture. As capture fisheries production stagnated in the 1990s, aquaculture production picked up the slack. Aquaculture accounted for 18.5% of the total fish production in 1990 and 26.3% by 2000 (FAO 2002a). As in fisheries, modern aquaculture, with its intensive operations and high yield, is driven by capitalism and modernity, and with similar consequences to ecosystem health and other concerns, as described below.

At the heart of the transformation in fisheries since 1950 is the growth in demand driven by several factors related to an intensification of capitalist production globally. The first is the increasing wealth and size of the population in the dominant economic regions of the world and major areas of fish consumption: Europe, North America, and Japan. The second is the demand diversification in these regions. The third is the increasing importance of demand sources in other regions as populations there experience economic growth. Increasing global demand raised international fish prices, intensified effort, and expanded commodification to hitherto untapped supply sources in the form of fishing areas and fish species not previously linked to the global market. Regional examples of fisheries globalisation are presented by Arbo and Hersoug (1997), Johnson (2002) and Thorpe and Bennett (2001).

The dominant framework for developments in the 1950s to the 1970s was modernisation theory, as exemplified by the countries of Western Europe and North America. It holds that judicious intervention by the state and the international community, as informed by scientific understanding, can propel poorer regions and nations through the stages of growth leading to development. Several observers of fisheries have adopted the analytical label of Fordism to describe the particular process of fisheries modernisation (Bonanno and Constance 1996; Apostle et al. 1998). Fordism describes the ideal organisation of production and implies a perception of the relationship between humans and the sea. Production under Fordism is based on product standardisation, production process decomposition, technological intensity, relatively inflexible production designs and large production volumes (Harvey 1989). It shares with high modernity a basic belief in people's ability to understand and manage their environment to achieve predictable and consistent results. We have learned – though far too late – that in many cases, such as fisheries, this is simply not true.

The mass capture techniques and efficient high-speed production of the industrial fishing sector are the fullest expressions of Fordism in fisheries. During the heydays of state-led fisheries development from the 1960s to the 1980s, Fordist industrial fishing was the ideal in both the North and the South because it was felt to maximise production for national consumption and international exchange. Bailey and Jentoft (1990) present a critique of fisheries development strategies in an effort to achieve these two objectives. The shift towards industrial production was to be achieved through the state-sponsored creation of industrial fishing fleets and processing plants and the professionalisation of existing small-scale fisheries sectors. While many countries have established industrial fisheries sectors and small-scale fisheries have changed in dramatic and differing ways to reflect new technological and market opportunities, the promise of the Fordist model turned out to be illusory and, indeed, has had catastrophic effects for global fisheries.

The destructive effects of the Fordist model on fisheries can be expressed in terms of a primary effect and secondary effect. The main problem with the Fordist model is its fundamental conflict with the natural conditions to which it is applied. Fish stocks fluctuate according to a range of natural factors whose interaction is poorly understood. In addition, fishing adds to the unpredictability of aquatic ecosystems. The underlying assumption of Fordist fishing, that constant high volumes of fish can be extracted from an ecosystem, fails to account for these natural conditions (Apostle and Barrett 1992). The effect of applying the industrial model to fisheries is then to exacerbate instability and hasten resource collapse world-wide, as shown by Pauly, Christensen, Froese and Palomares (2000) and Pauly et al. (2002).

A critical secondary effect of Fordism in capture fisheries is the conflict between industrial and small-scale sectors. The richest available fishing grounds are generally in coastal waters and are generally exploited by small-scale fisheries. If there are no area restrictions on fishing or if there is weak enforcement, as in many places in the South, industrial fishing vessels move into inshore waters and disrupt small-scale fishing. Despite strong measures that exclude industrial fishing from the inshore zone, industrial fisheries may still have an impact on migratory stocks fished by both sectors and on critical habitats of many species that are economically important to large and small-scale fishing.

By the 1990s, conditions for global capture fisheries had changed. Most importantly, the increasing intensity of fisheries crises made it obvious that the Fordist model of fisheries industrialisation was destroying global fisheries. Two solutions are commonly presented as remedies to this state of affairs. The first argues that only complete rationalisation of production on an international scale can solve the global fisheries crisis. Systems of full fish stock privatisation should be worked out, fishing fleets rationalised, employment in fisheries slashed, and market mechanisms of stock allocation and disposition put in place – in short, the full capitalisation of fisheries. The alternative proposes that the industrial model of fisheries production is grossly unsuited to the sustainable exploitation of fisheries. Instead, a much more flexible, even co-management model should be implemented with management responsibility devolved in such a way as to incorporate local expertise, recognise distinct local conditions, and empower local participation (Pinkerton 1989a; Collet 2002).

Regardless of the particular combination of responses to the current global fisheries crisis, they need to grapple with four clear consequences of globalisation and the legacy of the Fordist model of development: (1) aquatic ecosystem health is globally threatened by the massive intensification of fishing efforts; (2) the capitalist development of fisheries is resulting in social changes that have profound implications for social justice; (3) coastal livelihoods, employment and social relations are threatened by the transformations of fisheries due to capitalist development; and (4) the expansion of the international fish market and intensification of local links to it have raised the spectre of food insecurity and food safety for poor populations that historically depended on fish as an inexpensive source of protein.

Ecosystem Health

The most widely accepted definition of an ecosystem is the one formulated by the Convention on Biological Diversity (CBD 1994): '*Ecosystem* means a dynamic complex of plant, animal and micro-organism communities and their non-living environment interacting as a functional unit'. This definition suggests that fishing grounds and fish farms are ecosystems, as are components of the nested structures of larger and smaller ecosystems: entire oceans, coastal zones, watersheds and so forth. In order to function well and adapt to present and future challenges (including exploitation by humans and climate change), an ecosystem has to be healthy. Some definitions of ecosystem health are based on the absence of ecosystem stress, for example: 'An ecosystem is healthy and free from "distress syndrome" if it is stable and sustainable – that is, if it is active and maintains its organization and autonomy over time and is resilient to stress' (Haskell et al. 1992). Costanza (1992), however, describes ecosystem health as 'a normative concept: a bottom line', and includes the following concept definitions of ecosystem health: homeostasis, absence of disease, diversity or complexity, stability or resilience, vigour or scope for growth and balance among the system components (see chap. 3).

The numerous parameters of ecosystem health invite the use of multiple criteria and reliable indicators at all levels of biological organisation from genes through species, populations and communities to whole ecosystems. Christensen (2000) explores two categories of indicators for marine fisheries, one based on 24 classical ecosystem attributes (Odum 1969), and the other on a fishing-in-balance index. Further works on sustainability indicators for marine capture fisheries, some of which emphasise ecosystem-based governance, are reviewed by Garcia and Staples (2000a, b). For aquaculture and its supportive ecosystems, Pullin et al. (forthcoming) suggest sustainability indicators for aquaculture and emphasise those related to ecosystem health: ecological footprints, emissions and escapes from fish farms, and the ecological implications of competition vs. sharing of resources among food production and other sectors. Costa-Pierce's (2002) paradigm shift to ecological aquaculture amplifies the same theme.

Assessments of the health of natural resource systems and the effects of fishing on ecosystems largely depend on the assessor's perspective. The historical dimension and shifting baseline that lead each new generation to accept its own observations as the norm (Pauly 1995, 2001) apply in particular to fisheries and environmental assessment. Many of the world's capture fisheries are undoubtedly in poor shape (e.g., Hutchings 2000; Pauly, Christensen, Froese and Palomares 2000; Jackson et al. 2001; Ellis 2003; Pauly and Maclean 2003). Kempf et al. (1996) describe the 'fisheries crisis that transcends political boundaries and affects north and south alike'. From an ecosystem-based perspective, the effect of fishing on fisheries ecosystem health is high, particularly if gears that result in a high level of bycatch and habitat damage are employed (Chuenpagdee et al. 2003).

Aquaculture has witnessed a similar historical technological development, and in some cases a boom-and-bust period. Many aquaculture industry techniques, particularly those involving herbivorous species and less intensive systems, can be sustainable, but many intensive coastal aquaculture techniques pose serious concerns for ecosystem health (e.g., Chuenpagdee and Pauly 2004). Environmental problems caused by intensive aquaculture include water pollution from effluents and the conversion of large areas of wetlands; for example, mangroves (Dierberg and Kiattisimkul 1996).

The points made by Naylor et al. (1998, 2000) regarding nature's subsidies for salmon and shrimp farming, the loss of top predator species such as sharks as presented by Myers and Worm (2003), and the global crisis in fisheries as revealed by Pauly, Christensen, Froese and Palomares (2000) naturally provoke various defences (e.g., Roth et al. 2001, Lomborg 2001). Capture fisheries, aquaculture, and other sectors have an impact on each other ecologically, especially when they are mismanaged. For example, it was the extraction of water, principally for irrigation, that destroyed the Aral Sea and its fisheries. Another example is the use of synthetic fertilisers on land, which is expected to result in a doubling in the level of nitrogen run-offs between 1990 levels and 2050 (Seitzinger and Kroeze 1998).

One measure used to assess the health of ecosystems is the ecological footprint introduced by Wackernagel (1994). In principle, food production as well as its processing, distribution, and consumption all have ecological footprints because of the consequent waste processing. The utility of ecological footprints in natural resource management is controversial (e.g., Ferguson 1999; Van den Bergh and Verbruggen 1999; Wackernagel 1999). However, non-negotiable natural laws and area-specific limits to productivity always set the bottom lines around which humans can negotiate their economic and social options. The bottom lines for capture fisheries and aquaculture are primary production (Pauly and Christensen 1995) and ecosystem carrying capacities (e.g., Christensen and Pauly 1998).

Social Justice

Fisheries in the North and South are relevant to both the rich and the poor, the privileged and the unprivileged, the organised and the disorganised, and those with varying degrees of political and other bargaining powers. Considering the problems of distribution that emerge around every corner, the issues of trade within the fish chain and the rights of property and access to common fish resources, fisheries are perhaps more prone to justice discourses (Armstrong and Clark 1997; Sumaila and Bawimia 2000; Hernes et al. 2005;). Clearly, social justice – with its many elements – is something a governance approach cannot ignore.

A measure commonly used for fisheries allocation is the total allowable catch (TAC). In principle, once it has been determined, managers first need to take into consideration that there are several heterogeneous user groups, and then establish rules to ensure a fair distribution among them. Allocation thus raises issues of social justice. What criteria should be used to decide which groups should get how much? How do users qualify and what should be required of those who obtain access?

Some nations, especially in the North, consider Individual Transferable Quotas (ITQs) an effective way to distribute the TAC (Apostle et al. 2002; Arnason 1995). This practice is based on a different set of justice principles, since ITQs are tradable commodities and the entitlement is based on the ability to pay. Here, rights are only loosely coupled with dependency, if at all, which is a major reason why there are so many objections to ITQs. In general, justice principles tend to be different in the market than in the public sector, where equal treatment is required, and in civil society, where individual needs are key, although the boundaries between them are not necessarily closed (Walzer 1983). Similarly, as the market and the state penetrate civil society, perhaps adopting some of its functions and responsibilities, they replace the justice principles of one sphere with those of the other. Since fisheries involve all three spheres, the challenge of fisheries governance is that so many inherently contradictory principles all need to be reconciled at the same time.

In the South, justice issues concerning the market and trade are not focused around ITQs. Rather, they are concentrated on the daily marketing and trading of fish and seafood products with direct power implications (Bailey and Jentoft 1990). Fishers are typically in a weak bargaining position. With a perishable product that cannot be stored for long, people who fish often have few alternatives than to sell to the buyer at the price that is offered. Relations between fishers and buyers and/or middle-persons are further complicated as they engage in informal loans. In such cases, fishers often have no choice but to sell their catch to a particular middle-person as part of their debt payments.

Social justice is of a completely different form and scale when it follows the market chains from fishers and their communities to the processors, wholesalers, retailers, and consumers around the world. Kaczynski and Fluharty's study (2002) clearly demonstrates how the fisheries of Sub-Saharan West African coastal countries are heavily exploited by European fishing fleets, albeit under bilateral fishing cooperation agreements. The economic and political inequalities between the North and South are crucial to this fisheries issue.

Social justice is directly related to power and poverty and indirectly to resource conservation. To make a living when no alternative sources of employment are available and one's bargaining position is weak, the only response to falling prices is for fishers to increase their fishing efforts. It is true that overfishing ruins the resource base and is a source of poverty, but poverty may also be what makes people overexploit (Béné 2003). Encouraging fishers to organise or otherwise helping to shield them from a dismal situation is a strategy for empowerment, since it can strengthen their position vis-à-vis middle-persons. It is also a way of relieving the pressure on the resource.

Gender equity is another aspect of social justice, and is usually left out when planning development programmes, especially regarding resource management (Mehra and Esim 1998). A critical examination reveals that many resource management programmes and initiatives often target the male members of the community, the fisher*men*, who are considered the direct harvesters of the fisheries resources. Women are assumed to be secondary in terms of development interventions and are generally given a lower priority (Lokshin and Yemtsov 2000; Williams 2000). This is despite the important role that women in many traditional and modern societies play in the marketing, and, to a lesser extent, the capturing, of fisheries products. In many societies, women occupy lower positions in the hierarchies of command and control and in the households (Cadigan 1991; Binkley 1995; Connelly and MacDonald 1995; Begossi 1996). The advantaged position of men in the division of labour contributes to male dominance in decision-making. The inequalities have major implications in the social justice debate.

Livelihood and Employment

The importance of fisheries for people's livelihood is reflected in figures as well as in the political discussions on the restructuring of the sector. It is widely recognised that if fisheries are not properly managed, the fishers' abilities to obtain income or food from them diminish. This is a problem in the South as well as in fisheries-dependent regions of the North, since alternative employment opportunities are frequently unavailable.

Many fishing populations are joined by new entrants, some of whom end up with better access to market shares and economic activities than the existing local communities. Globalisation and local developments outside the coastal areas have important positive or negative impacts on the livelihoods of fishing communities. Despite the important impact on their livelihoods, coastal communities are often excluded from decision-making processes and debates on their livelihood options, such as access to the resources they depend on.

How many people in the world are employed in fisheries? FAO data suggest there are 36 million fishers in capture fisheries and aquaculture worldwide (FAO 2002a). Garcia and Moreno (2003) estimate that more than 100 million people depend on fisheries and Berkes et al. (2001) put this figure even higher, with 50 million people currently directly engaged in fish capture and as many as another 200 million dependent on their activities. The exact number is not known, but millions of people fish and depend on fishing and their livelihood security is increasingly under threat. The technological intensification of fish capture places unsustainable pressure on resources and increasing export market dependence creates economic instability (McGoodwin 2001). An important consequence of globalisation is that pre-existing arrangements that regulate access to marine resources are challenged and undermined, resulting in increased competition and livelihood insecurity. If the experience of the Organisation for Economic Co-operation and Development countries, excluding Iceland and Portugal, is any guide for the future, this trend has already begun. The countries with the most industrialised fisheries in the world saw employment in fisheries decline by a third between 1970 and 1996 (Mathew 2003).

Livelihood is not only a matter of quantity; it also involves the quality of employment. Maritime anthropologists often note the specific nature of capture fishing and emphasise similarities in work worlds in disparate places (Acheson 1981; McGoodwin 1990). They include egalitarian relationships among crew members, a tendency to spread the risks of fishing by sharing systems of remuneration, and a strong sense of competition among fishers. There are also considerable differences between sub-sectors, particularly between the moral economy of small-scale production and the market basis of industrial fish capture. The view of capture fishing as hunting and gathering as opposed to aquaculture as a form of agriculture portrays another dimension of quality in employment associated with personal and financial risks, seasonal variations and lifestyle patterns.

Fishing is known for its division of labour by gender. In all parts of the world, women perform land-based activities ranging from shoreline or tidal pool fishing or gleaning of other aquatic organisms to fish culture, fish processing and marketing. Several studies note increasing instances of women participating in actual fish capture, predominantly in riverine and lagoon aquatic ecosystems (Begossi 2002). Women also engage in pre-fishing activities such as preparing and mending nets as well as preparing bait and post-fishing activities including processing, distributing and marketing. Women's involvement in fisheries generally lowers the operational costs and overhead expenses of the household (Storey and Smith 1995; Grzetic et al. 1996; Ostrove and Adler 1998).

Food Security and Food Safety

The most general definition of food security is the one formulated by the World Bank (1986): 'Food security is access by all people at all times to enough food for an active healthy life'. There are, however, many definitions of food security, depending on the context (see reviews by Maxwell

1996; Kurien 2004). Some definitions include elements of food choice, like the one formulated by the UN:

> Food security exists when all people at all times have physical and economic access to sufficient, safe and nutritious food to meet their dietary needs and food preferences for an active and healthy life .... The right to food is the right to have regular, permanent and unobstructed access, either directly or by means of financial purchases, to quantitatively and qualitatively adequate and sufficient food corresponding to the cultural traditions of the people to whom the consumer belongs and which ensures a physical, mental, individual and collective fulfilling and dignified life free from anxiety .... (UN 2001b).

Emphasising the key role of women in intra-household food security, Gillespie and Haddad (2001) encourage an expanded concept of food security across agricultural and nutritional development efforts and a strengthening of the human rights paradigm in the field of human nutrition. Indeed, the Universal Declaration of Human Rights (Article 25) and subsequent international agreements emphasise people's basic right to adequate food (see chap. 13). In a recent publication, Kurien (2004) argues that food security has three dimensions, or A's: accessibility, affordability, and absorption. Accessibility and affordability describe an individual's capacity to obtain sufficient foodstuffs and connect to the incidence of poverty. The last dimension – absorption – refers to the conditions of hygiene and health needed for food to be absorbed by the human body. This aspect is otherwise known as food safety.

Fish has long been recognised as a healthy food. It is rich in high quality protein and in vitamins, minerals, and essential fatty acids (e.g., Steyn et al. 1995; Elvevoll and James 2000). Many rural communities in the South rely heavily on fish as part of their diet. As reported by Thilsted et al. (1997) and Roos (2001), small indigenous fish contribute significantly to the nutrition of the rural poor in Bangladesh as an extremely important source of calcium, iron, and vitamin A. Fish is regularly consumed in the South, is a traditional food choice in some countries in the North and in many others fish consumption is widely promoted as a healthy food choice.

The increase in the demand for fish has heightened the interest in the important contributions of aquaculture to food security. The review by Ahmed and Lorica (2002) of Asian experiences shows the increasing roles of aquaculture as nutrition supplier to poor households and contributor to poverty reduction. The integration of freshwater aquaculture into smallholder farming systems can increase the availability and affordability of fish in the diets of the rural and peri-urban poor (e.g., Edwards et al. 1988; Ruddle 1996; Prein and Ahmed 2000), especially when vegetables are raised around fishponds.

A food can be deemed safe if its production does not present its producers (in this case fishers and farmers) with unreasonable risks and its consumption does not harm consumers. In determining whether a food is safe to eat, there are many important variables in the features of consumers, including age (babies, adolescents, and adults), gender and status (e.g., special needs of pregnant women and lactating mothers), state of health and tolerances (e.g., diabetics, acclimation to local micro-organisms, and so forth). The amounts consumed and consumption frequency of a given food, whether by choice or by force of circumstances, are also important variables.

Aquatic animals and plants are also capable of harming people who handle or consume them by transmitting pathogens and parasites. They may also contain harmful substances such as heavy metals, toxins, and a wide range of organic chemicals. Some groups of aquatic animals are inherently more risky as human food because of their propensity to accumulate pathogens and chemical contaminants. The most risky groups are the filter feeders, especially bivalve molluscs such as mussels and oysters, which have long been used as indicators of marine pollution and risks to seafood consumers. The risk associated with consuming bivalve molluscs increases if there are harmful algal blooms (Maclean 1993). Landsbergh (2002) gives a comprehensive review of the effects of algal blooms on aquatic organisms and ecosystems, covering about 200 species of harmful or potentially harmful micro-algal or ciliate species and showing that the problems are much wider than the phenomenon commonly called *red tide*.

Another risk to human food safety is the ciguatera poisoning in tropical fin fish, especially in the Caribbean and the South Pacific. Ciguatera poisoning comes from eating reef fish such as barracuda, snappers, or groupers that contain ciguatoxins from *Gambierdiscus toxicus,* an epiphytic dinoflagellate growing on algae and coral rubble. Since 1990, records of ciguatera poisoning in the South Pacific have been collected in the FishBase data collection now managed by the Secretariat of the Pacific Community (www.fishbase.org). The database includes detailed records of the prevalence and distribution (geographical and by species) of ciguatera poisoning.

To summarise, food security, food safety and quality assurance are essential if developed and developing countries are to exercise options regarding fish for export as well as for their domestic consumption.

Challenges and Concerns in Governance

Globalisation, ecosystem health, social justice, livelihood, food security, and food safety are fisheries challenges and concerns that should be primarily addressed by people who are directly and indirectly involved. A governance approach is seen as conducive to efforts to address these concerns and is thus a prerequisite for positive outcomes in terms of healthy ecosystems, better justice, improved livelihoods, and better food security and safety.

Fisheries governance has not kept pace, however, with the deep and rapid changes in fisheries, resulting globally in a complex ecological, social, and economic crisis. As the demand for fish products grows world-wide and the productive capacity of the world's aquatic ecosystems decreases, governance responses should also be global. Developing and implementing governance systems to effectively address fundamental concerns has thus become a global challenge that requires thorough and comprehensive efforts from both North and South. One of the existing initiatives along this line is the Sustainable Livelihoods Approach (SLA), which offers an alternative way to consider development priorities by putting people at the centre. SLA uses an analytical framework that integrates natural, social, physical, financial and human components in the formulation of policy, institutions and processes, based on sustainability concepts and within the context of vulnerability and poverty (see chaps. 15 and 17). This, and the governance approach presented in this volume, ultimately support the United Nations Millennium Development Goals, as declared in September 2000, particularly those pertaining to environmental sustainability, gender equality and empowerment.

PART II

The System to be Governed

Introduction

Andy Thorpe, Derek Johnson, and Maarten Bavinck

The challenge for fisheries governance is to resolve, as effectively and equitably as possible, the conflicts that result from seeking to simultaneously
pursue the goals of maintaining a healthy ecosystem whilst continuing to
derive social benefits from it. Social benefits from the ecosystem include
the preservation of sustainable livelihoods and social justice for those associated with the sector, and meeting income and food security requirements
for the wider community. A basic requirement for resolving conflicts over
the use of aquatic ecosystems is understanding the context in which they
are played out. This part of the volume concerns the aspect of that context
that we label the 'fish chain': the production, distribution, and consumption of aquatic products. Part III focuses on the human institutions that
organise and regulate the human interactions around the chain.

Although the term 'fish chain' has been used elsewhere (most notably
Kooiman et al. 1999) its scope has, nonetheless, not been clearly defined
in the extant literature. We use the term 'chain' to suggest connectedness –
one link fits in with, and influences, the next in sequence, as it is itself
affected by the preceding link. It is generally conceived of in a 'vertical'
sense, following a resource from the marine ecosystem, through capturing,
processing and marketing phases, to the consumer. Figure 1 is a simplified
depiction of the chain as a vertical series of linkages, showing changes in
monetary values and resource transformation with each link. Key characteristics of the various stages of this fish chain exert influence on the whole.
Consumer preferences may therefore come to affect fisher strategies, di-
recting capturing activity towards certain target species. Likewise, the introduction of preservation schemes may determine whether a certain market
can be serviced and a fish chain comes about or not. Finally, the particular
characteristics of an ecosystem also influence whether a fishery emerges in
a certain locality.

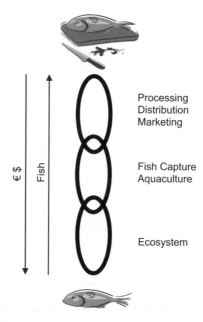

Fig. 1 The fish chain (1).

While a vertical notion of the fish chain is a useful tool for visualising the series of connections that link the ocean and the fish farm to the dining table, it may also be depicted in a manner that emphasises the interactions that underpin the chain. Figure 2 was drawn according to this idea of the chain.

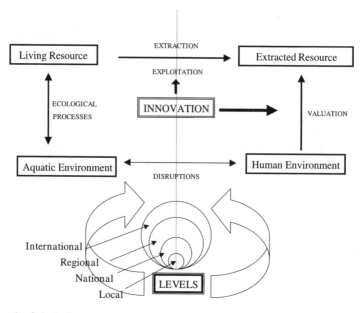

Fig. 2 The fish chain (2)

Living resources – whether free roaming or captive – are a product of, and interact with, their natural environment. Resources are abstracted into the human domain or environment, either by *extracting* the resource from its natural environment or by *exploiting* the resource within the context of its natural environment. Fishing is a case of extraction, while marine reef eco-tourism is an example of exploitation. As the living resource is part of a natural environment, its abstraction results in impacts upon the environment. The overexploitation of certain species in the ecosystem can trigger ecosystem change, allowing other species to move into the vacant niche. Extraction methods may also change the marine environment. The clearest example is bottom trawling, which severely affects the constitution of the seabed, and thereby the whole marine ecosystem. Furthermore, as human and natural environments are interdependent, process outcomes in the human domain, such as pollution, have an impact upon the natural environment and thereby feed through to affect the potential extractive mass of the underlying natural resource.

The precise nature of the extraction process is conditioned by the operation of cultural and economic value systems and/or regulatory initiatives. If the system places high values on resources, this will encourage technological innovations designed to accelerate their extraction. The economic integration characteristic of contemporary globalisation, for example, has raised the economic values of numerous aquatic resources, leading to intensified pressure upon them. At the same time, collective institutions at different scales of human interaction and responding to a wide range of interests influence the pace of extraction. Some, like Marine Protected Areas (MPA), could well serve to dampen the pace of extraction.

Aquaculture is the farming of aquatic animals and plants, notably seaweeds. It is a sector very similar to agriculture in terms of its organisations, structures and interrelationships, including those with the natural environment. Aquaculture supplies about one-third of the world's fish, and its contribution continues to increase. Therefore, aquaculture is a major player in the fish chain.

The natural and human elements of the fish chain operate at varying dimensions, or what we choose to refer to as *scales*, and thereby complicate interactions within the chain. Space and time are the most important scales for the fish chain. As the spatial scale across which different species range varies enormously, from the captive environment of the cultured shrimp, to the global migratory patterns of the high-seas tuna, so too does the reach of markets. Fishers also have different ranges: many artisanal fishers limit their operations to adjacent sea territories, whereas distant-water fleets roam the globe.

Time scales also affect institutions and people. The pledges of elected governments and the objectives of departments are broken down into targets, outputs, and deadlines, and modified accordingly as time progresses. Scientists make risk assessments, into which they factor temporal disturbances such as the El Niño events which occur every two to seven years. The same is true for fishing enterprises and facilitating institutions such as banks, which calculate economic recovery rates along predefined time scales.

Scale is also important with regard to the nature of the extraction and, albeit to a lesser extent, the exploitative process itself. At one end of the technological scale we encounter an individual fishing part-time on the beach with a hand-line to supplement his or her income, whilst at the other extreme we come across the Atlantic Dawn, the largest fishing vessel in the world, with nets the size of four football stadiums, fishing off West Africa. Shaping, or channelling, the process of technological change across the chain is therefore likely to be a crucial governance task if ecosystem health and/or social benefits are to be realised.

The historic emphasis on bio-economic modelling which dominated fisheries management, served to focus attention on the extractive phase of the chain, looking particularly at how extraction rates affected underlying fish stocks. More recently, the recognition that fisheries resources interact and that the strength of that interaction may, in fact, be more profound than the impact of extraction has changed the analytical entry point to the ecosystem. Equally, recognition has increased concerning the notion that perhaps the consumer is not at the end of the chain, but rather at the beginning; with growing consumer demand for high-quality, safe, and sustainably-captured fish causing a fundamental restructuring in the way that aquatic resources are being cultivated (in the case of aquaculture), extracted, and processed.

Rather than adopt just one of these perspectives (ecosystem, extractive, or consumer-driven), however, and thus run the risk of conferring undue importance upon that particular analytical entry point, Part II elects to give roughly equal weight to each approach. Chapter 3 examines the pre-capture segment of the chain – that is to say, how the living resource acts and reacts within its natural environment (the 'ecosystem' approach). Chapter 4 deals with the extraction (extractive approach) of aquatic resources in capture fisheries. The following chapter considers the special characteristics of aquaculture, whilst chapter 6 evaluates the post-capture supply chain in order to discover the extent to which it is consumer-driven. A last chapter discusses the dynamics of interaction between segments of the chain and the forces that propel them.

3

Aquatic Ecologies

Michel Kulbicki

Introduction

The ecology of fish resources is part of a larger picture defined as the fish chain. Diversity is at the base of most ecological processes involving resources and its alteration is viewed as a major source of large ecological and societal changes (Chapin et al. 2000). In addition, diversity is easy to define and conceptualise and is probably the best-studied ecological variable. Differences in the diversity of exploited species are extremely important, for example, the approximately thirty species commonly exploited in the Northeast Atlantic as compared with well over two hundred species in the tropical Western Pacific. Consequences may be numerous at any level of the fish chain, as is illustrated in fig. 3.1.

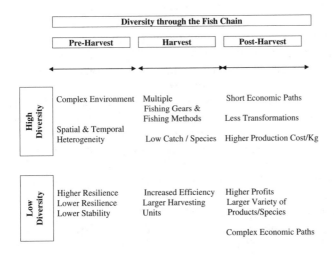

Fig. 3.1 Possible consequences of diversity for fish chains.

Diversity has many meanings in marine ecology (Steele 1991). It can apply to a continuum of organisation levels ranging from genetic diversity to ecosystem and landscape diversity. All these levels may be viewed as linked and the factors affecting one level of diversity usually affect the other ones as well (fig. 3.2). In this chapter, the diversity is mainly considered from the genetic to the functional levels.

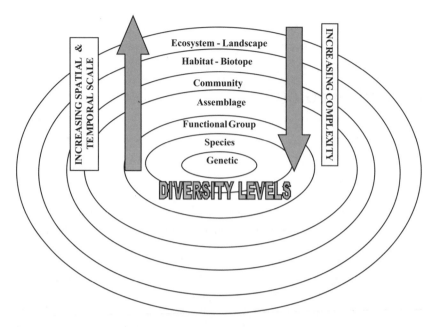

Fig. 3.2 Diversity with increasing levels of organisation. The ascending arrow indicates that, moving from the genetic to the ecosystem level, changes in diversity depend on larger spatial scales and lo9nger time scales. The descending arrow shows that the total number of components increases as the organisation level decreases.

The ascending arrow indicates that, moving from the genetic to the ecosystem level, changes in diversity depend on larger spatial scales and longer time scales. The descending arrow shows that the total number of components increases as the organisation level decreases.

Diversity can be essentially approached from three perspectives. The first is composition; e.g., of the species or functional groups in an assemblage. The second is the relative abundance of species in an area, as is usually expressed by indices related to the evenness of the distribution of individuals among the total number of species (Legendre and Legendre 1998). The indices make it possible to compare populations or assemblages through time for the same or different areas. The third perspective is the number of items at any organisational level (fig. 3.2), e.g., the number of species in an assemblage. This is often referred to as richness and can be considered at various spatial scales. In this chapter we are interested in the following:

– *Regional diversity*: the number of species known in a region. At the taxonomic level, it usually refers to a species checklist, but can also be considered at the functional group, genetic, or other levels.
– *Island or province diversity*: the number of taxa known for a sub-region, often called a province in ecology, or an island.

- *Local diversity*: the number of taxa (or functional groups or genetic varieties) in a specific habitat, e.g., the number of fish species at a specific reef, mangrove area or trawling ground.
- S*pecies density or richness*: the number of taxa in each standard sampling unit, e.g., transect or trawl.

Regional diversity is at the base of the concept of a regional meta-community, i.e., the pool of species at the regional level. From this pool, island or province, meta-communities are derived, which are the species pools the species assemblages are drawn from in a specific habitat, e.g., the fish assemblage at a particular reef.

Factors and Scales Affecting Diversity

Types of Factors and Scale Range

In all three of its meanings, diversity is affected by a range of factors at all the spatial and temporal scales. It might be convenient to split the factors into large-scale and local-scale groups and recognise a continuum between them. Large-scale spatial factors may be linked to physical phenomena such as regional upwellings, island size, island type, connectivity between islands, or regions or evolutionary phenomena such as biodiversity centres of origin or dispersal routes. These factors are not linked to human influence. Local-scale spatial factors include physical factors (e.g., depth, coastal configuration, and terrestrial input) as well as ecological factors such as biotope type (e.g., mangrove, reef, soft bottom), habitat (e.g., reef flat, reef slope, and back reef), components of the habitat (e.g., mangrove height, coral cover, and sea-grass density), and human factors such as fishing level and pollution. With the exception of some factors such as depth, most local factors are susceptible to human influence.

Time scales usually refer to perturbations. Short-term perturbations may involve cyclical changes (e.g., seasons) as well as acute pollution, catastrophic climatic events such as storms or floods, coral bleaching and temperature disruption. Mid-term perturbations cover events that are usually less intense but have a longer duration such as fishing, chronic pollution, invasive species, climatic events such as El Niño and their consequences (droughts, temperature, and salinity changes). Long-term perturbations are less easy to perceive and represent events such as sea level rise, long-term temperature shifts, and their consequences (e.g., current patterns), changes in land use (e.g., deforestation of the Amazon basin, construction of major dams, long-term effects of fishing). Even though the role of humans is not always clearly established, there is usually some anthropogenic influence in most time-related factors acting on diversity.

Factors and Scale Interaction

It is important to note that spatial and temporal factors interact. In particular, large-scale spatial factors are mainly affected by long-term perturbations and all the time-scale levels influence local-scale factors. All these factors essentially have two effects on diversity. Firstly, they induce perturbations so that composition, richness, and evenness may be affected at all the organisational levels. Secondly, these factors structure diversity, with the changes depending on the factors and their intensity.

There is a relation between the scale where factors intervene and the organisational level where they act (Sale and Guy 1992). In general, the higher the organisational level, the larger the spatial and time scales (fig. 3.2, see also Hatcher 1997 for coral reefs). To understand the variations observed at the level of a single specimen, the scale is limited to the immediate environment of this fish and its life span. At higher organisational levels, the spatial and time scales necessary to comprehend changes become larger. The major problem facing the ecologist is that the larger the scale, the less information is available. The paradox, however, is that at the higher scales the crucial factors are easier to detect and measure. If we are interested in reef fish, measuring the effects of local factors such as coral cover, habitat complexity, perturbations due to fishing, pollution, and so forth may be very complex. Conversely, when considering the regional scale, the major factors are island size, island type (high or low island, opening of the lagoon to oceanic influence), the connectivity between islands (function of the distance and size of nearby islands) and so forth, factors that are easy to measure and can be rather simply integrated into models.

Diversity at Various Scales

Species have particular habitat needs. This means that on a local scale, species are found under specific conditions. A basic law of ecology states that there is a strong relation between the number of habitats and the total number of species in an area. Furthermore, species diversity tends to increase with habitat complexity or heterogeneity. Habitat complexity can be scaled for the major coastal marine biotopes (fig. 3.3). Many factors act on habitat complexity or heterogeneity. Firstly, there are regional factors such as latitude, biogeographical region, regional climate, large-scale geomorphology, and geology or island size. In comparing North-South situations, habitats are usually more complex in warm climates, e.g., more complex in the Indo-Pacific than in the Atlantic. This large-scale component is often overlooked when examining fisheries management, since most models do not take into account such regional factors even though they can play major roles in diversity and consequently in resource levels. There are also local factors regarding habitat heterogeneity, in particular depth, salinity, and temperature as well as perturbations, especially fishing and pollution.

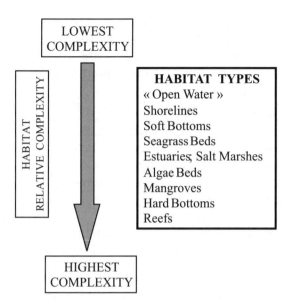

Fig. 3.3 Classification of some major coastal marine habitats according to complexity.

Humans have little power to increase habitat diversity (number of habitats in an area). The method most frequently used to try to increase marine habitat diversity is the creation of artificial reefs. This is often, though not always, a minor change compared to the huge adverse impacts on habitat diversity caused by coastal works, pollution, certain types of fishing (in particular trawling), the introduction of alien species and so forth. However, humans can restore habitat complexity and heterogeneity to some extent by limiting the perturbation levels of these factors.

Why do we think diversity is so important to the fish chain? After all, fishers do not sell species, they sell fish and usually the more fish they sell, the better (though this is debatable as fish size and quality come into play). The fact is that there is a strong correlation between diversity and fish density (fish/m²) or fish biomass (weight of fish/m²). This type of relation has a theoretical background (Hubbell 2001) indicating that the higher the number of species in an area, the larger the number of species with large densities or large biomasses.

Diversity and Ecological Functioning

Ecosystem functioning is based mainly on the variability of diversity in the broadest sense of the word. In particular, diversity is instrumental in three important characteristics of ecosystems: stability, resistance and resilience (McCann 2000). An ecosystem is stable if it does not deviate from an average state. An ecosystem is resistant if it requires a great deal of perturbation to make it deviate from this stable state. Resilience is the ease with which an ecosystem returns to its former stable state. It is important to note that a stable state does not necessarily mean equilibrium, since ecosystems are admittedly never in equilibrium for long, but perpetually change from one state to another, depending on their environment.

If a fish assemblage is submitted to a perturbation, it tends to change. Once the conditions return to their initial state, the assemblage should as well. Ecological theory formulates the hypothesis that systems with high diversity have more resistance but less resilience than systems with fewer species (McCann 2000). In other words, fish assemblages such as those on reefs with very high numbers of species tend to resist perturbations for a long time but once they start changing, a return to their initial state is slow and may be impossible. Conversely, simple fish assemblages such as those on soft bottoms are less resistant to perturbations but more apt to return quickly to their initial state once the disturbance is over. In the real world, things are not that simple and there are various examples of non-resilient fish in simple assemblages and low-resistance fish in highly complex assemblages. The variations are due in part to the existence of keystone species (see below) and the scales at which disturbances occur. Functional groups do not all operate at the same scale; some are localised and others act over very large areas. Since disturbances are limited to specific scales, functions that operate at other scales may not be affected.

When it comes to fish chains, this has several consequences. Firstly, the number of ways a fish assemblage may recover depends on its functional groups. The impact on large fish species is of particular significance in this connection. Indeed, these fish are often unique in their functional groups, which may be very important to the system, e.g., because they prey on grazers or transform the substrate. The elimination or reduction of these species can change the entire system (Jackson et al. 2001; Bellwood et al. 2003). This is referred to as the ecological inactivation of the species. It is not, however, the only lesson. Within a functional group, ecological functions are unevenly distributed among the species, with driver species making a large ecological impact and passenger species a minimal one. The addition of drivers increases the stability of the system, while passengers have little or no direct effect (Peterson et al. 1998). One of the goals in a fish chain is to increase the yield per species and to achieve this goal, passenger species are often either intentionally or unintentionally eliminated from the system. This reduces the resistance of the system and increases its vulnerability. It may become more resilient but less productive on an all-species basis.

The concepts of stability, resistance and resilience are a matter of scale. It is usually the case that the larger the scale and the larger the stability and resistance, the smaller the resilience. Historical changes are interesting from this perspective. They show that the numbers of fish species in marine ecosystems have not changed much over time, but that some disappearing species have induced drastic changes in the structure of the ecosystems (Jackson et al. 2001; Pauly et al. 2002). These changes usually take a long time, indicating that on a large scale, resistance may be important. Unfortunately, once the changes have taken place, there is very little chance of a return to the initial state (low resilience). On the local scale, however, if some catastrophic event disrupts the state of an ecosystem, in many cases, the system bounces back. Catastrophic events may even be a necessity to some systems with high diversity such as coral reefs and tropical estuaries (Connell 1978; Blaber 1997). On the same local scale, slow but constant perturbations often cause more damage than catastrophic events because environmental conditions such as pollution, increasing fishing or major land use changes prevent the system from bouncing back.

Perturbations are necessary to maintain diversity and ecosystems maintain their diversity as long as perturbation levels and types stay within a given range. The problem facing most ecosystems nowadays is a change in the perturbation patterns and levels that have the potential of inducing long-term changes called *phase shifts*. This is due to the increasing actions of humans that affect nature. It has become increasingly difficult to separate natural from human-induced disturbances. This is illustrated by the synergistic effects of overfishing and a natural disease affecting an algae-grazing urchin in the Caribbean (Hughes 1994). This has resulted in a complete change in the benthic landscape, which is transformed from coral-dominated to algae-dominated, the results of which can be potentially disastrous for the reef fish community

Types of Diversity Change and their Consequences

Diversity may change in various ways. There can be species losses or gains usually associated with changes in evenness and variations in the functioning of fish assemblages. In a system undisturbed by humans, there may be species gains resulting from migration or speciation, both occurring on longtime scales. In systems influenced by humans, alien species can be introduced, some of which may become invasive. We consider a species invasive in an area if it is known to be new there and its abundance or ecological roles are such that the system in the area is modified. Not all introduced alien species become invasive (Kolar and Lodge 2002) and not all invasive species are introduced by humans. However, the emergence of most documented invasive species follows their deliberate or accidental introduction by humans.

Migration and speciation are natural phenomena that seldom occur at time scales that affect fisheries. Their effects on ecosystems may be very important but the changes are usually gradual. Conversely, the introductions and invasions of alien species may occur over short time scales and have drastic effects on ecosystems. Most invasive alien species are initially introduced by humans either deliberately (e.g., Nile perch in Lake Victoria, common carp in the USA and Australia) or accidentally (e.g., lamprey in the Great Lakes). There are also cases of natural invasions, e.g., triggerfish (*Balistes carolinensis*) in West Africa (Caverivière et al. 1981). Invasive species may have dramatic effects on ecosystem structures. This is well illu-strated for freshwater species (e.g., tilapias in many Asian and Pacific coun-tries, Nile perch in Lake Victoria). Introductions of alien marine organisms are increasing. They include deliberate introductions such as *Cephalopholis argus* and *Lutjanus kasmira* in Hawaii (Randall 1985) and the unintentional results of human interventions such as Lessepsian species in the Red Sea and the Southeast Mediterranean and introductions through ballast water (Wonham et al. 2000). The effects of these introductions can be devastat-ing, for example for the *L. kasmira* in Hawaii (Randall 1987), jellyfish in the Black Sea (Shiganova and Bulgakova 2000) and sea-stars in southern Aus-tralia (Ross et al. 2004). However, not all introduced alien species become invasive. Most Lessepsian species have become integrated into the South-east Mediterranean basin fish community without generating any impor-tant changes. The major problem with the introduction of alien species in the marine environment is that once they have become established or inva-sive, they are almost impossible to control or eradicate.

Species loss is as important to diversity and ecosystem functioning as species gain. In general, species loss is associated with extinction or extirpa-tion, which are *true losses*. Extinction means the species no longer exists on Earth. Like speciation, extinction is a natural phenomenon, but man can cause extinction rates far beyond the average ones found in nature. Extirpa-tion is the loss of a species over part of its native range. There is also spe-cies inactivation, which means that even though it is still present, the spe-cies has reached such a low abundance or biomass that it no longer plays a significant ecological role. Inactivation is considered a natural process be-cause within a functional group, species tend to replace one another over time depending on the environmental and species history. However, hu-mans may induce rates of species inactivation that are higher than normal and thus unbalance fish communities or their ecosystems.

A number of studies (Jackson 2001; Jackson et al. 2001) indicate that before human intervention, coastal ecosystems had structures very differ-ent than the present ones. Although very few marine fish have disappeared so far due to human disturbances, the number of extinctions may increase dramatically in the near future for species with a restricted range (Hawkins et al. 2000). The consequences of the disappearance of a species in a sys-tem depend on its functional group and its role in the ecosystem. The first species to disappear are usually the ones that are of high commercial or subsistence interest. These species are often large predators that play very important roles in the ecosystem. Their disappearance may irreversibly un-balance the system (Jackson et al. 2001). Species losses of marine fish are usually extirpations, and very few cases of total extinction have been docu-mented up to now. However, extirpation can have very serious conse-quences, in particular if the distribution is patchy (Hanski as cited by Côté and Reynolds 2002). In the Caribbean, the disappearance of the Nassau grouper (*Epinephelus striatus*) and other large groupers of the genus *Mycter-operca* over most of their range has had numerous direct and indirect ecolo-gical impacts (Sadovy 1993; Roberts 1997). Direct impacts are reductions in the preying on small reef fish that may play an important role in structuring the reef landscape and thus, indirectly, the reef-fish assemblages. Indirect impacts include shifts of fishers towards other large carnivorous fish, further depleting this functional group.

This brings us to the role of rare and endemic species in the functioning of coastal marine ecosystems. There are driver and passenger species in a functional group and the dominance of species there may change in time and space. A species' rarity is a combination of geographical range and density, since a species may be rare in one place and abundant somewhere else and its role in the system will change accordingly (Jones et al. 2002). In the marine environment, most fish species have the potential to disperse over large geographical areas. This generates lower endemism rates (Mora et al. 2003) than in terrestrial systems, even on remote islands. There is an endemism rate gradient in the tropical Pacific, with the highest rates in the central Pacific (Hawaii, Marquesas, Easter Island) and the lowest ones in the western part (Robertson 2001). Similarly, endemic species tend to be larger and more abundant in the central Pacific than the rest of the Pacific. This could be due to different causes depending on the region. In isolated areas, endemism may be the result of local speciation and in areas close to a biodiversity centre, endemic species may be relic species that used to have a wider geographical distribution. This suggests that the roles of endemic species in the functioning of fish communities probably differs from one region to another. Unfortunately, very little is known about the causes and effects of rarity or the relations between endemism and abundance among marine fish (Robertson 2001; Jones et al. 2002).

In general, there is a much higher percentage of undescribed marine species in the tropics than in temperate or cold regions. In addition, the geographical range of species is far less known in tropical than in temperate or cold areas. There are more than 6,100 taxa of coastal fish in the Pacific, more than 14% of which are undescribed. Most of the undescribed species are small and usually have little ecological impact. However, some large and even commercial species have yet to be described. Moreover, there is no checklist available for various regions in the Indo-Pacific. This is particularly true of a number of the Pacific island states such as the Solomon Islands, Vanuatu or Tuvalu. The situation is even worse in eastern Africa. In Eritrea, Somalia, Tanzania and Mozambique, little is known on the distribution of coastal fishes. These gaps are obstacles to understanding the status of coastal marine fish in these countries because there is a link between regional diversity and local diversity and local diversity is usually an important factor in fish density and biomass.

In addition to inadequate taxonomy, we are faced with many problems in sampling local diversity. Without going into the details of the numerous sampling technique biases, it is clear that no method can give a precise image of fish diversity (richness and evenness) in coastal waters. In general, the precision of the methods decreases with increasing diversity, since each species presents a different response to the sampling method. The biases are usually impossible to assess correctly because we have no access to what the *true* community is. In addition, most sampling techniques are adapted to one type of biotope. Since the tropics have more biotope types and habitat heterogeneity than temperate or cold regions, multifarious sampling methods are needed to get a correct sample in the tropics. Many tropical countries have neither the means to conduct intricate sampling nor the specialists to interpret them, generally leading to less adequate knowledge of the fish diversity in many coastal tropical fisheries than in their temperate counterparts. The notable exceptions are shallow coral reef fisheries, where clear waters allow underwater visual censuses that can record a high proportion of the species present, even though the reefs support the most diverse marine fish assemblages known to man.

In addition to recording species and their relative abundance, knowledge is called for on the biology and ecology of the fish in a fish assemblage to understand how the assemblage is structured and functions. Here the knowledge gap between temperate and tropical systems is similarly sizeable. There are far more species in the tropics and far less has been invested in studying the biology and ecology of tropical fish than temperate ones. There is a lack of basic information on the growth, reproduction, mortality and movement of most tropical species. This is an obstacle for the management of tropical fisheries.

Large-Scale Variations in Fish Diversity

It is surprisingly difficult to get reliable information on the world-wide distribution of coastal marine fish. The data presented here were extracted from FishBase (Froese and Pauly 1998). However, a number of problems were encountered in defining coastal marine species and getting information on their size and diet. That is why the data are indicative of major trends but need to be refined for further analyses. The distribution of coastal marine fish diversity on a world-wide scale (fig. 3.4) indicates huge differences in diversity from one region to another (nearly ten-fold between the Northwest Pacific and the tropical West Pacific). These differences are not randomly distributed. The highest diversities are found in the tropical Pacific and Indian Ocean and the lowest in the northern parts of the Atlantic and Pacific oceans. This spatial distribution of diversity is very probably a major source of the differences in landings. In highly diverse regions, it is likely that the first 25% of the landings is composed of many species and in regions with low diversity, the same 25% probably consists of a restricted number of species. This difference could historically explain why fisheries management started by addressing the species as a management goal rather than the ecosystem. If your catch is composed of only a few species, you tend to think that by controlling these few species you can master the whole community. Because this was the situation observed in the North, where most fisheries science was initiated, it became the basis used for most fisheries management. Had fisheries scientists been confronted from the start with a very mixed catch as in the Indo-Pacific, they probably would have taken the same attitude as the local people and proposed management based on a community approach. It is not surprising that the concept of marine protected areas (MPAs) arose precisely in regions with very high fish diversity, where management on a species basis may not have been profitable.

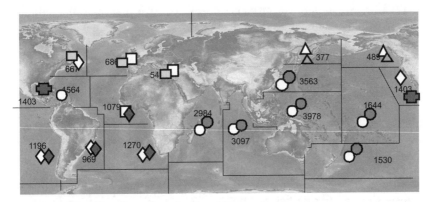

Fig. 3.4a Distribution of coastal marine fish diversity.

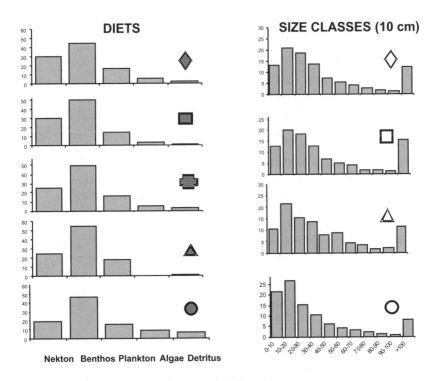

Fig. 3.4b Distribution of coastal marine fish diversity.

Despite its low level of precision, the available information (fig. 3.4) clearly indicates that, even at large regional scales, there are major differences in the characteristics of coastal fish species. This undoubtedly has important consequences as regards resource use and management. Regions where herbivorous species are diverse and large (e.g., western Pacific) are not apt to have the same response to a change in primary production as regions with a few small herbivorous species (eastern Africa) at the same latitude. There would certainly be a great deal to learn from a more detailed analysis of this regional distribution. In particular, there are probably interesting correlations between these broad-scale structures and primary production, habitat type, and the nature and level of the catch. Unfortunately, the extensive data needed for this type of analysis are not easily available because, until recently, they were not recognised as a priority in understanding fisheries.

The numbers in fig. 3.4a indicate how many species are known in each region. Regions are grouped according to the size distribution or diets of their species, the symbols are as in (fig. 3.4b). Regions were re-grouped according to a cluster analysis using Ward's method and Euclidian distance. Coastal marine fish are defined as any fish living within less than 100 metres and represent 11,280 species. The data were extracted from FishBase 2000 (Froese and Pauly 1998) and were completed by analogy, allocating the same diet to species in the same genus and of similar size.

Virgin Systems

There are no longer any virgin marine systems. Even the most remote areas are either exploited themselves or are facing the consequences of exploitation in nearby regions. There are, however, numerous accounts of what pristine marine systems used to be like (e.g., Jackson 2001; Jackson et al. 2001). The accounts have several points in common:
- large marine organisms such as turtles, manatees, or large predatory fish used to be common and at times abundant in many systems;
- the loss of these large animals induced major ecological changes such as very heavy mortality in sea-grass beds, coral or kelp;
- some of these systems have undergone phase shifts and no longer resemble the initial systems (e.g., Caribbean reefs, Northeast Atlantic kelp forests, Chesapeake Bay) and are unlikely to have the potential to return to their initial state in the foreseeable future;
- huge natural fluctuations also occur in the absence of human intervention;
- there is often a long time lag between the start of the perturbations and their major ecological consequences;
- as fishing proceeds there is a reduction in the size of the targeted species as well as a shift from species high in the trophic organisation to species from lower trophic levels.

The most targeted large fish species in marine systems are long-lived carnivores that reproduce late in life and, in the case of sharks, bear small clutches of live young (Stevens et al. 2000). Many of these species congregate to spawn (e.g., Sadovy 1996) and are thus very vulnerable to modern fishing methods. Their features render these species very sensitive to exploitation and they are thus slow to recover (Jennings et al. 1999). They often play an important role in controlling lower trophic levels and their collapse may generate long-term changes in their marine systems (Jackson et al. 2001). However, large animals are not the only ones responsible for maintaining the major characteristics of an ecosystem. The loss of features such as coral on reefs, oyster beds in estuaries, sea-grass or algae beds can induce major ecological shifts (Jackson et al. 2001). The losses may be due to direct capturing and mechanical damage from fishing gear (Hughes 1994 on reefs; Jackson et al. 2001 on sea-grass beds and oyster beds). Disease and the loss of keystone species are also major contributors to change. Habitat-constructing organisms often need to be in high densities to maintain themselves. Once they get past a certain threshold, they quickly disappear with little chance of return. Irreversible changes or phase shifts have probably been more common than we think, since we know so little about the initial status in many areas. Even major systems such as coral reefs were barely documented before 1960. Major events occurring today on reefs such as invasions of crown of thorns starfish or coral bleaching thus have barely any historical references.

There is often a long time lag before major events start occurring. It took two centuries for cod fishing to collapse in the Northern Atlantic. The major problem is that nowadays, with the advent of increasingly sophisticated gear, collapses of this kind could accelerate. In addition, interactions at large geographical scales are occurring that we did not think possible even in recent times. The large decrease in many spawning stocks around the Caribbean islands could thus have major influences on the recruitment levels of islands far from these spawning grounds and result in a domino effect of successive collapses (Roberts 1997).

There have been a number of reviews on the effects of fishing on marine systems (e.g., Jennings and Kaiser 1998; Hall 1999; Hollingworth 2000). It is, however, essential to look at some of the major effects and how they may intervene in an ecosystem-based approach to fisheries in a North-South perspective. Fishing down the food web and catching smaller and smaller fish are common to most marine systems. However, the scale of these changes is often difficult to assess without historical documentation. There are very few places where long time series can be observed and we all too often look at the existing system as the reference point and analyse changes from a short-term perspective.

Direct Impacts

Direct Impact on Substrate and Benthos

Most fishing gear has some impact on the environment. Trawl nets and dredges are probably the most widely studied gear in this respect (e.g., Moran and Stephenson 2000). The effects of trawl nets on soft or rocky bottoms can be devastating, especially if the gear is fitted with tickler chains or rock-hoppers. Studies on the northwest shelf of Australia (Sainsbury 1987; Hutchings 1990) indicate that most of the epifauna that initially harboured prime target species were destroyed by a few years of trawling, resulting in a shift of fish species and a large decrease in the epifaunal diversity. In addition to killing sessile epifauna, trawls and dredges kill invertebrates (echinoderms, molluscs, worms, crustaceans and so forth) that are food for fish and they have a mechanical effect on the sediment (bioturbation). Several studies show a compacting effect (e.g., Schwinghamer et al. 1996). This results in a loss of diversity and major changes in the structure of the benthic fauna (Hall 1994) as well as a homogenisation of the fauna, flora and their substrate (Brand et al. 1991). The gear also increases water turbidity and re-suspends sediment, which can modify the primary production with multifarious potential effects on the epifauna and their predators (Caddy 2000). Sea-grass beds can be affected by both the mechanical effects of the gear and the increased turbidity (Fonseca et al. 1984).

There may be recovery from the gear and the rate of recovery is a function of the natural rate of disturbance. In areas where the sediment is often naturally disturbed (e.g., estuaries), the effects of trawling may not be drastic. Conversely, trawling over deep-water sea-mounts may have very long-term effects. Slow-growing and late-reproducing organisms are more affected than short-living ones which, as several studies indicate, can recover in less than a year. However, especially in deep waters, recovery can take a very long time for long-living organisms, in some cases decades or more. The lengthy recovery time for large epifaunal organisms may be a major problem, since they are often at the base of microcosms that drastically increase the diversity in otherwise poorly diversified habitats. Despite the effects of trawling on the abundance, species composition and size structure of benthic invertebrate communities, their trophic structure seems rather stable (Jennings et al. 2001). In the tropics, several specific fishing techniques are known to damage habitats and their fauna or flora, e.g., drive nets, poison and explosives (Maragos et al. 1996), brush parks or juvenile shrimp nets (Blaber et al. 2000).

Direct Impact on Fish

The direct effects of fishing on fish or other resources start at the species level with a decrease in abundance and biomass, a shift towards smaller sizes, increased mortality and growth and reproduction alterations. These variations have been mainly studied at the population rather than the community level. Fishing and pollution are the major causes of fish diversity change (Jennings and Kaiser 1998). As is noted above, there are very few cases of documented extinction among marine fish (Powles et al. 2000). There are, however, many examples of extirpation and ecological inactivation. Fishing can also significantly reduce species density in tropical fisheries (e.g., Roberts and Polunin 1992, 1993; Watson and Ormond 1994; Jennings and Polunin 1997). Decreases in diversity in temperate waters are not easily demonstrated (e.g., Greenstreet and Hall 1996). The differences may stem from the type of biotopes analysed. On tropical reefs, many species are site-attached and long-lived and have restricted adaptation to change. They may thus be quite sensitive to fishing or its indirect effects. The temperate fisheries tested for changes in diversity are all trawling grounds where most species are migratory to some extent, their life span is usually short in comparison with tropical reef fish and they adapt quickly to new environmental conditions. It is likely that a survey of tropical trawling grounds would produce similar findings, i.e., relatively minor changes of diversity over time despite intense fishing as suggested by data presented by Bianchi et al. (2000). This suggests that perhaps we should not base our judgement of the effects of fishing on diversity on a stable versus variable environment gradient rather than a tropical versus temperate to cold gradient.

In stable environments, species are expected to be rather long-lived, have limited flexibility in their life-history traits and form part of diversified functional groups with high functional similarity (Martinez 1996). In the tropics, reefs are the typical stable environment. At all latitudes, sea-mounts are also candidates, as are rocky shores or deep-water coral banks in temperate and cold climates. Conversely, variable environments such as the open ocean (pelagic fish communities), estuaries and to a lesser extent soft-bottom continental shelves can be found at any latitude, with of course an increasing diversity in warmer climates. In these environments, most species have shorter life cycles and more adaptable life histories and on average functional groups have fewer species. Stable environments tend to resist but to have little resilience. In extremely stable environments such as sea-mounts or deep water fisheries, resistance may be weak since recruitment, growth and production are very low because of very low input in these systems. Diversity loss in terms of species density can be rapid and the system can be very slow to recover (Koslow et al. 2000). The opposite holds true for the least stable environments (e.g., pelagic systems in upwelling regions), where resilience is usually very important.

The impact of fishing on density or biomass is drastic at the species level but not necessarily at the community level. The total fish production of the

North Sea was fairly stable over time (before 1980), even if most species exhibited wide temporal fluctuations in their landings (Ursin 1982). In other words, global fish production remains approximately the same from year to year but the species involved may change. It is likely that fishing is not the only cause of fluctuation in many species, and in many cases recruitment variations are probably just as important. This hypothesis of rather stable global production needs to be better substantiated and many fisheries seem to point the other way, i.e., to a decrease of global production beyond a certain level of fishing effort. This reasoning has to go along with the notion of fishing down the food web. In a mature system, production is minimal and the highest trophic levels make an important contribution to the total biomass. Once exploitation starts, the largest and often least productive individuals are taken out first. As exploitation increases, the community consists of younger individuals and gradually of species at lower trophic levels. As a consequence, global production should increase. However, the system reaches a point where individuals are caught at their minimum capturable size and only the lowest trophic levels remain in sizeable quantities. With further exploitation, either the system collapses or the production remains rather stable. In heavily exploited systems, another likely consequence is the possible dominance of the catch by fewer and fewer species as suggested by the data presented by Bianchi et al. (2000).

The effects of fishing on the structure of fish communities also need to be considered. Their structure is usually stratified into several components, the two most common ones being trophic and size structures. However, this view is simplistic, just as trophic chains are a simplistic view of trophic webs. Structure comprises many other aspects such as behaviour or reproduction. The various components interact. A large piscivore with a wide home range bears very little resemblance to a small sedentary piscivore, even though they share the same trophic level. The two species do not have the same impact on the system, nor are they affected by the same factors. Until recently though, they were often pooled together in the analysis of community structures. Several authors address this problem (Kulbicki 1992; Thiebaux and Dickie 1993; Duplisea and Kerr 1995; Garrison and Link 2000 (see www.ird.sn/activites/sih/symposium/Programme.htm)).

As most fishing gear is size-selective, fishing induces a decrease in size in many species. This decrease is more acute in large long-lived species than small short-cycle ones (e.g., Zwanenburg 2000). Do the changes result in an increase in total production and thus in potential yield? Does the system stabilise after sufficiently long and intense exploitation? Comparison with terrestrial ecosystems gives the impression that production should increase as trophic level drops and size structures evolve towards smaller specimens. However, marine systems have several specificities, including the link between recruitment and environmental conditions. As Jennings and Kaiser (1998) conclude in their review, 'Most of the marked effects of fishing on diversity and community structure occur at relatively low levels of fishing intensity. However, once systems enter a fished state, diversity and overall production may often remain relatively stable despite further changes in fishing intensity'.

Fishing may also affect the life-history strategies of species. Fishing eliminates the largest specimens in a population, which can have drastic effects on genetic diversity, growth, reproduction, behaviour and mortality. There is still very little information on the genetic changes induced by fishing at the population level (Law 2000), the best studied cases being the anadromous salmonids (Ryman et al. 1995). Fishing tends to reduce heterozygosity, but there are few documented cases of the impact of fishing on genotypic diversity, one exception being the study by Smith et al. (1991) on the orange roughy (*Hoplostethus atlanticus*) found off New Zealand. These authors demonstrate that even after a relatively short exposure to fishing, the heterozygosity of fished populations of this species is strongly reduced. Responses of fish to fishing can be genotypic as well as phenotypic and it is usually difficult to separate the two sides of life-history traits (Stokes et al. 1993). In heavily fished areas, growth can be phenotypically enhanced for small fish since the larger individuals are no longer at the top of the pecking order and food availability is higher. Similarly, fishing may genetically select in favour of faster growing fish since they reach their full size and maturity earlier and are more likely to reproduce than slower-growing, later-reproducing individuals. Rijnsdorp (1993) demonstrates that changes of this kind observed in plaice in the North Sea are more likely to result from genotypic than phenotypic variation linked to fishing. More recently, Conover and Munch (2002) demonstrate experimentally that fishing significantly affects growth on a genetic basis. The ramifications of their results are debated (Malakoff 2002), but they suggest that management measures such as MPAs directed separately at juvenile and adult phases could be effective.

In many tropical species, there is a change of sex with size, some species being first female and then male (e.g., wrasses, parrot fish, groupers) and others vice versa (e.g., *Centropomidae, Synodontidae*). Traits like this are also observed in temperate or cold-water species but to a much lesser extent. Fishing for larger individuals can thus modify the sex ratio in populations of these species and sometimes to a dangerous level (Thompson and Munro 1983; Sadovy 1996).

Beyond the effects of fishing on the genetic characteristics of the resource, there is an increasing awareness of the importance of genetics in fisheries and related fields. Bowen (1999) discusses the policy implications of conservation at gene, species and ecosystem levels. The American Fisheries Society's publication on evolution and the aquatic ecosystem (Nielsen and Powers 1995) is a milestone in its provision of information on the application of genetics in fisheries management. Since then, applied genetics in fisheries management has expanded very rapidly, accompanied by expanding recognition of the need to fill gaps in fish genetic resource policy and take appropriate action (e.g., Harvey et al. 1998; Pullin et al. 1999). In addition, changes in genetic diversity are becoming easier and cheaper to monitor and the genetics of exploited fish populations and living components of their supportive ecosystems are likely to be the focus of far more attention in fisheries management. This should make it possible to carry out the proposed efforts towards more effective management of fish genetic resources (Pullin 2000).

Indirect Impacts

Fishing can have numerous indirect effects on marine habitat structure, fauna and flora (e.g., Blaber et al. 2000). In temperate regions, the most well-known changes are the ones affecting sea urchin densities (Tegner and Dayton 2000). In Alaska, changes of this kind have been correlated with killer whales preying on sea otters, and on the Northwest Atlantic coast they were first attributed to the reduction of predation by lobsters (Mann 1982). Subsequent studies demonstrate that lobsters are probably not sufficient enough to control the urchins and other causes such as variations in urchin recruitment can explain the changes (Hart and Scheibling 1988). In tropical regions, the most illustrative examples are linked to the decrease in predation on urchins generated by fishing for urchin predators (McClanahan 1994). In Kenya, fish that feed on urchins are removed by fishing to the point where urchins proliferate and decrease algae by grazing. However, the same causes do not necessarily have the same effects. Recent studies in the South Pacific fail to show any correlation between fishing intensity and urchin abundance at various spatial scales, even though fishing is intense in several places and the species composition exhibits many similarities with the Indian Ocean ichthyofauna found in Kenya. There are many other unexpected and indirect impacts of fishing, e.g., the increase of litter in mangroves next to crab fisheries and changes in the trophic structure of West African estuaries next to brush parks (Blaber et al. 2000).

In temperate regions, many studies investigate the relations between fishing and the top predators represented by sea birds (Tasker et al. 2000) and marine mammals (Jennings and Kaiser 1998). The reproductive success of some sea birds is heavily dependent on the abundance of small coastal pelagic fishes. The fish are dependent on combinations of environmental conditions and fishing mortality. Where these fish populations have markedly declined, so have the sea bird populations, e.g., in Peru, South Africa and the northern Atlantic. The rejection of trash fish and other by-catch has however boosted populations of scavenging sea birds, mainly sea gulls. Declines in several seal populations have coincided with increases in fishing efforts or changes in the target species by fishers, with corresponding declines in seal prey, e.g., in Alaska, Peru and northern Europe. In tropical countries, this concern for sea birds or mammals may at first seem trivial. Neither sea birds nor marine mammals are abundant in most of the tropics and fisheries managers usually do not devote a great deal of attention to them. For several reasons though, this is likely to change. Firstly, there is an ever-growing increase in the import of marine products from tropical countries by temperate developed ones. Public opinion in developed countries is increasingly sensitive to animal rights, particularly those of charismatic species including sea turtles, marine mammals and some sea birds. Products from countries where no attention is devoted to these animals might be boycotted, as was the case with Mexican tuna when the Mexican tuna fishing industry failed to comply with US regulations on porpoises. Secondly, these top predators may play an unforeseen ecological role in the functioning of the systems. Thirdly, some marine mammals, in particular whales, are extremely valuable for tourism. Taking the ecological needs of these animals into account could enhance tourism in places where it is an important source of external revenue (e.g., Tonga, Fiji, and New Caledonia in the Pacific).

Huge quantities of fishing bycatch are discarded every year, an estimated 27% of the world's total catch (see Britton and Morton 1994 for a review). In addition, many kinds of fishing gear, for example trawling, blast and poison fishing, kill fish and benthic organisms that are not brought to the surface (side-kills). Bycatch and side-kills are eaten by sea birds, marine mammals, and bottom-dwelling organisms. Numerous studies show that bottom-feeding fish and crustaceans feed on these food sources, with at times huge increases in abundance. Changes like this in densities may unbalance the systems they occur in. Very little research has been conducted on bycatch and side-kills in tropical countries. For several reasons, they could play a different role than in temperate or cold systems. Firstly, bycatch is usually minimal in tropical countries, where people find a use for most marine products. Secondly, sea bird and marine mammal populations are usually less abundant there (except in coastal upwelling systems such as Peru) than in temperate countries, so that a higher percentage of the discarded catch should reach the bottom. Along with side-kills, this material becomes prey for a much higher diversity of benthic scavenger organisms on the bottom than in temperate or cold regions. Its availability per scavenger species should thus be lower in the tropics. Moreover, decomposition is faster in the tropics and tropical carrion feeders, sharks excepted, tend to be smaller than in cold and temperate waters.

Interaction of Fishing with other Disturbances

Large-Scale Disturbances

Very few studies have been conducted on the possible consequences of global change and capture fishing. Zwanenburg (2000) considers the potential effect of bottom-water temperature rises off the Scotian shelf (NW Atlantic), which might be linked to global changes. There are also numerous reports of warm-water species recently observed out of their usual range, such as the trigger fish *Balistes carolinensis* in the northeastern Atlantic. Conversely, some cold-water species have begun to disappear from the warmest parts of their distribution ranges. Temperature shifts associated with global warming are believed to be potentially important in changing some major current patterns such as the Gulf Stream and in raising the sea level. Changes in current patterns could have huge and unforeseen effects on the recruitment of most types of fish with either pelagic eggs or larvae. Changes of this kind are well documented along the coast of Peru where El Niño, a natural phenomenon, causes drastic changes in the recruitment patterns of small pelagic fish with multifarious effects on their predators and on fisheries. The rise of the sea level could have dramatic effects on many estuarine systems and coral reefs. However, it should be noted that if such a rise occurs, it would probably be rather slow. Some corals and mangroves would have time to adapt to this type of change. The apparent increase in catastrophic events such as tropical storms (Done 1999), crown of thorns starfish infestations and coral bleaching is a matter of greater concern in the tropics. The variation in the frequency of these events is thought to be linked to global change. Tropical storms are known to destroy coral over large expanses (Scoffin 1993; Dollar and Tribble 1993) and to be major factors in coastal systems associated with estuaries (Blabler 1997). Coral bleaching and crown of thorns starfish infestations can similarly lead to the mass destruction of coral (Hoegh-Guldberg 1999; Nyström et al. 2000). The consequences are still not well understood, but it is likely that reef- or estuarine-associated fish diversity will decrease (McManus et al. 2000), with a probable increase of herbivores in reef communities. There could also be phase shifts on small isolated islands where recolonisation by coral may be slow.

Local Disturbances

Local disturbances are likely to change coastal marine resource systems. The changes can be drastic and are not necessarily limited to the immediate disturbance area. As indicated by Caddy (2000), the effects of high nutrient inputs from rivers in the Mediterranean region extend far beyond the river mouths. Similar effects are observed on a large-scale in the Baltic Sea, where the overall fish biomass is thought to have increased four-fold in the twentieth century (Thurow 1997) due to terrestrial nutrient inputs. This demonstrates that disturbances can have even more profound effects than intense fishing. The opposite effects are observed in the Black Sea, where the deep anoxic layer is gradually becoming shallower due to the inputs of rivers such as the Danube, the Don and Dniepr and is jeopardising the entire ecosystem (Caddy 2000). Another infamous case is the slow death of the entire Aral Sea from the pumping of the Amou-Daria drainage system water as a result of the cotton culture. In the tropics, similar effects can be expected from the extensive logging in many areas (e.g., Central Africa, Amazonia, Indonesia, Papua New Guinea, Solomon Islands) or open pit mining (e.g., Indonesia, New Caledonia, Fiji).

A recent addition to the localised coastal disturbances is the advent of intensive aquaculture in coastal zones. Shrimp farms have destroyed huge areas of mangroves in Southeast Asia and Ecuador and the high quantities of nutrients in their wastes have led to sizeable amounts of pollution (e.g., Suvapepun 1997). The destruction of wetlands and mangroves is a major concern in many countries around the world. These areas are often of paramount importance in the cycling of many coastal resources (Blaber 1997; Blaber et al. 2000). However, the importance of mangrove areas for reef or soft-bottom fish species is variable from one region to the next (Thollot 1992). In particular, the Caribbean and southwestern Pacific mangrove systems play very different ecological roles as regards reef fishes.

Urban development and coastal zoning may have important impacts on coastal resources by modifying a number of cycles and recruitment, as well as increasing pollution and nutrient inputs. In most cases, this results in a decrease in the habitat quality and a subsequent decrease in the diversity of the resource and non-target species, with subsequent decreased resistance and often with increases of r-selected species. Tourism also exerts a substantial influence on coastal resources (e.g., Maragos et al. 1996). It increases the demand for marine products, especially those that fetch high prices (e.g., crustaceans, large carnivorous fish). It also emphasises the need for pristine areas (e.g., marine parks) and the need to protect charismatic species (e.g., turtles, seals, whales and porpoises). Tourists can cause direct damage to marine habitats by trampling on corals fringing reefs, turning over rocks in search of shells and so forth.

This chapter highlights the roles of diversity and environmental factors in marine fisheries. As regards diversity, we have changed our philosophy of sampling for the purposes of understanding and governing fisheries. Most of the historical data have only been collected for target species. The taxonomy of non-target species is problematic, even in areas such as the North Sea (Bianchi et al. 2000; Vecchione et al. 2000). Diversity assessment is very sensitive to the methods and it is important that standardised methods be used. As Bianchi et al. (2000) note in their conclusions, 'Efforts should be put into standardising data collection and developing appropriate sampling design to satisfy requirements of comparative studies'. Standardisation is often possible on small scales if only a few collectors are involved. However, it is a much greater problem on a regional scale, since there is no international standard. Efforts are currently underway in the South Pacific to standardise reef fish sampling procedures (Kulbicki et al. 2004), but it is difficult. It becomes even more difficult if the species to be surveyed are not accessible by the same method or there are huge interspecific biases within the method. In an ecological approach, we might for instance wish to consider all the fish in a lagoon with mangroves, soft bottoms, and reefs. At present, there is no method that can sample all three biotopes accurately because each biotope requires its own specific method.

Diversity can also be considered at higher levels than taxa. Functional groups can play a major role in improving our understanding of ecological processes, since species replacement in a functional group is not uncommon (Jennings and Kaiser 1998). This approach requires that functional groups be clearly defined and that we have enough information to classify taxa properly. At present the concept of the functional group is still fuzzy and there is no unequivocal definition of what it is or is not. This is probably not a problem in simple systems, but in complex ones as in most tropical coastal marine environments, the issue can quickly become difficult. This is even more so due to the lack of information on the life-history traits of species. There is less and less incentive for scientists to publish work on basic traits such as diet, reproduction (behaviour, sex ratio, size at first maturity and so forth). This type of work is increasingly regarded as descriptive and is thus not well accepted by many scientific journals. This kind of information is however essential to defining functional groups and to trophic analyses, which are increasingly considered an essential step in understanding ecological processes for management purposes (Jennings and Kaiser 1998; Pauly, Christensen and Walters 2000).

Environmental factors should also be better integrated into fisheries governance. It is not so much that more environmental measurements are needed as that they need to be more effectively used to better understand ecological processes. The environment has a paramount influence on the ecological processes governing coastal marine resources. Of course we need to improve the ways we acquire and process environmental data, but that should not be the most important point. We need to relate more accurately resource and environmental data sets to the appropriate time and spatial scales.

One important point that is clear from a review of the current literature on the ecological aspects of fisheries is that there are so few possible control areas for comparison. In most regions, fishing has been going on for so long and so intensively that there are no control areas against which to compare their current status. Jennings and Kaiser (1998) suggest creating reserves to give us an idea of the status reached by resources in undisturbed or less-disturbed areas. The study of islands, especially in the Pacific, may in part solve this problem for reef resources since there is an entire gradient in the disturbance level of islands to allow a comparative approach.

From a North-South perspective, it is important to note that diversity and complexity tend to be greater in southern ecosystems. Sampling the higher diversity and complexity of ecosystems in the South is problematic. In addition to the inadequate taxonomy and information on biological traits in the South compared to the North, coastal marine resources in the South exhibit greater spatial and temporal heterogeneity. One consequence of this heterogeneity is a need for better sampling strategies and higher sampling efforts to achieve approximately the same power of analysis as in the North. There is also far less historical and reliable data for the South, which is a problem when it comes to understanding the role that is played by present perturbations and natural phenomena. Acquiring data on a regular basis (observatories) is often a problem for countries in the South due to political and economical instability, the lack of permanent structures, and rapid turnover of qualified staff. These difficulties have raised the question of the minimum data needed for management decisions (Johannes 1978; Walters 1998).

Perspectives

Collecting data is at one end of the decision chain and management decisions at the other. This indicates a need for a framework. Until recently the approach was based on population dynamics, with target species as the focus of management decisions. The focus is now shifting from the species to the ecosystem level (Botsford et al. 1997; Beamish and Mahnken 1999; Maltby 1999; Prins 1999). At the moment, however, we do not have a unifying theory to enable us to understand the functioning of these coastal marine ecosystems. We are still at more or less a descriptive stage, trying to link ecological processes with a whole range of factors. Our lack of historical data, the problems related to controls in an experimental or comparative approach and the huge complexity of marine systems, especially in the tropics, do not make the task any easier. In addition, even if we do understand the functioning of these systems, management will not necessarily follow. The general state of an ecosystem, the level of its fish populations, fishing efforts (number of fishers and amount of gear in use, number of boats) and economic factors do not operate at the same time scales. Fishing fleets tend to increase when fishing conditions are good, but they do not diminish at a similar rate when the yields drop or market conditions are unfavourable.

Even if we think we understand ecological processes (e.g., Cury et al. 2003 for a recent classification) or if keystone species are identified, we may not be able to manage an ecosystem sufficiently to achieve the desired results. There are also major North-South differences, since increasing fishing activity to maximise the yield is less and less of a priority in the North now that other uses mainly related to conservation and recreation are becoming more important. In the South, subsistence fishing is still paramount in many places and conservation issues may seem trivial unless people can be convinced they are essential. This brings up the problem of education and understanding measures. A measure is more apt to be accepted if its consequences are understood. Basic education in ecology can prevent some tragic errors. Local people usually have ample knowledge of their own environment, but may ignore key information or have erroneous ideas about major ecological processes in their fishing area. So it is essential to include local people in the protection of their resources and take their traditional knowledge into account. This might require a specific kind of education to enable the local people to better understand the consequences of modern fishing in a monetary economy.

Promoting diversity from a governance point of view is a difficult task that involves several decision levels. It ranges from direct promotion, enhancing the juvenile survival of fish, reducing the fishing pressure on spawning grounds or limiting the use of non-selective gear, to indirect action ruling out destructive fishing methods, encouraging habitat restoration (wetlands, mangroves, near-shore reefs) or increasing habitat diversity (e.g., artificial reefs). If regulations are to be accepted, it is also necessary to promote the ecological education of various resource users. This is usually a long and costly process. Teaching governance with an ecological perspective means helping people understand that ecosystems are complex and preserving only part of them is often less efficient than protecting an array of biotopes. The interaction between ecosystem parts or between whole ecosystems may be geographically huge, and in order to integrate the various spatial and temporal scales of interaction, governance will have to adapt from the local level all the way to the international level.

MPAs may illustrate the need to expand from the local to the regional level. This concept was initially a protective measure addressing local problems. The question was soon posed as to the size, shape and ecological complexity (i.e., number of biotopes) MPAs should have. This responds to several governance problems: 1. What do we need to protect? 2. How much can we protect without affecting other users? 3. Who is involved in the decision-making process? The size of the proposed MPAs has grown with the awareness of multiple-interactions in ecosystems and there are now even proposals for MPAs crossing international boundaries.

It is essential for improved governance to involve various resource users in the decision chain. For users to take part and accept decisions, it is essential that they understand the consequences. This means that educating people and demonstrating the effects of governance should be part of governance. In particular, education should include basic ecological information. For example, fishers usually want to increase their catch value. They can do so in several ways, by catching more fish, catching fewer but larger fish or catching more valuable species. These strategies have different governance implications. A larger number of fish means an increase in production and usually in fishing effort. This increase is easier if the number of available species is low, but low diversity systems are usually more vulnerable to perturbation. This is the problem facing most coastal pelagic fisheries, where misunderstanding the ecological processes involved in increased production has led to numerous fisheries collapses. Catching fewer but larger fish means fish are allowed to grow and juveniles and the reproduction and habitats for juveniles and reproductive stocks are protected. In many Pacific island countries, the expansion of the live reef fish trade and aquarium fish trade is an example of catching more valuable species. This implies difficult choices. Destructive fishing methods bring fast cash over a short time period, though better fishing practices yield fewer but better fish and allow a longer exploitation of the resources, even if the immediate cash flow is lower.

Making decisions and evaluating the consequences of governance decisions require measurements that can be easily understood by all the actors. Developing indicators is in part a solution to this problem and a great deal of research is currently being conducted in this field. The present trend is to propose an array of indicators ranging from ecological to socio-economic aspects of fisheries and bridge the various indicators into warning systems with a capacity to focus on the potential interaction between the various aspects.

The parties responsible for fisheries governance face some environmental factors they may directly influence and others they should take into account but have little or no influence on. Handling the two kinds of environmental factors can be viewed as *active* and *passive* governance. The climate and region largely determine the diversity, habitat types and the characteristics of the resources. Taking regional or climatic differences into account is very important but is a passive decision. Conversely, one may act directly on many factors such as fishing levels and gear, pollution, coastal and land management and so forth, but this active governance requires recognition of the consequences of intervention that can result in drastic ecosystem changes. In highly diverse systems, mainly tropical ones, resistance to change is generally high but resilience is low, whereas the opposite is often true in less diverse systems. This means changes in governance take longer to be effective in diverse systems but their effects last longer as well. In highly degraded but still diverse systems, this could mean some governance issues are hard to accept because users may not detect rapid changes. Similarly the scales involved in diverse and non-diverse systems may be different and the spatial patchiness of many diverse systems can render them less sensitive to changes than less diverse but more homogeneous systems.

Two approaches to ecosystem governance are currently recognised, a holistic one addressing the system as a whole, and a reductionist one considering each species separately and just viewing the ecosystem as a support for the species of interest. The second view has prevailed to date, but there is increasing awareness that the first approach can be fruitful and that a combination of the two with a balance of active and passive governance might be preferable. Lastly, one should consider time and space interaction with top-down governance decisions that extend from long-term and large-scale issues to shorter-term and smaller-scale issues and bottom-up governance decisions that extend from local to regional issues.

4

Fish Capture

Derek Johnson, Maarten Bavinck, and Joeli Veitayaki

Introduction

Fish capture and aquaculture are the central articulating links of the fish chain, connecting consumer demand to ecosystem impact through the social organisation and technologies of resource extraction (and input, in the case of aquaculture). This chapter is concerned with the capture of wild marine resources; that which follows focuses on fish culture.

Capture is the complex of social and technological factors that forms the immediate context for the extraction of fish and their transport to landing sites. Matching its linking position in the fish chain, fish capture is also central to fisheries governance as the set of practices that connects humans most directly to their marine environments. In the early 21st century, human interaction with the sea has become troubled. It has now been conclusively demonstrated that anthropogenic pressure on marine ecosystems through fishing has severely degraded the world's marine ecosystems (Pauly et al. 2002). The degradation of marine ecosystems in turn threatens the livelihoods of coastal populations. As part of a sustained attempt to build more positive and enduring connections between people and the sea, governance of fisheries has to challenge the incentives and institutions that have contributed to human overuse and abuse of marine ecosystems.

This chapter portrays fish capture in two parts. First, it presents a 'global' view of capture fisheries as ordered by the academic lens. Second, it presents one facet of the 'local' view: the livelihood rationality that shapes small-scale fisheries. While a useful way of organising the representation of capture fisheries, this expository division of global and local does not rest on mutually exclusive categories. The global academic view on the dynamic of resource degradation in capture fisheries, for example, necessarily owes much to the observations of local fisher informants while having its own disciplinary, paradigmatic, and purely chauvinistic 'subjective' biases. Similarly, an analysis of livelihoods could be just as well made from an external standpoint that classifies and orders for simplicity rather than listening for complexity. One of the key governance lessons of this chapter is that it is necessary to be able to move between the global and local positions, while recognising their interactions and overlaps, in order to grasp the diversity, complexity, and dynamics of fish capture and its governance.

Scales and the Representation of Fish Capture

The central challenge of this chapter is to represent the diversity, complexity, and dynamics of global capture fisheries and the governance challenges that they face. We meet that challenge through recourse to this book's guiding argument about the impact of globalisation on capture fisheries and through reference to the notion of scales as a conceptual tool for the ordering of diversity and complexity in fish capture.

In this chapter, we employ two approaches to scales. The first is the 'objective' approach to scales, one that reduces the diversity, complexity, and dynamics of capture fisheries to their key components. This approach facilitates the representation of capture fisheries as a whole that we undertake in the first section. In this sense, scales are representational tools. Scales are composed of a series of attributes or levels, of quality or quantity that can be ordered or ranked and that have a conceptual logic. Fisheries, like other socio-economic phenomena, however, vary according to many different scales and the attributes of these scales are themselves often scales that have their own attributes (Strathern 1991). How these scales and sub-scales are prioritised and deemed to interact are therefore fundamental representational, methodological, and political problems. A considerable literature has recently developed that has begun to engage with these issues around the discussion of how to appropriately scale responses in natural resource management (Cash and Moser 2000; Gibson, et al. 2000; Berkes 2002).

The complexity of using scales for representation leads, however, to difficulty in maintaining the fixed subject position that most natural resource management approaches imply. It is impossible to maintain simultaneously awareness of a multiplicity of different scales and their dimensions when representing objects and their interactions. Feminist and anthropological approaches have suggested that one solution to this difficulty is to allow for different subject positions. Thus, instead of seeking a single reference point from which to characterise fish capture, representation attempts to move between different subject positions. This approach to scales has important implications. The particular scale or arrangement of scales that we choose to privilege influences what we see, highlighting some things and obscuring others. This means that a representation can never be all encompassing, but is a particular position among many possibilities (Strathern 1991; Haraway 1994). Important methodological exercises for the academic observer are thus the attempt to understand the scalar limitations of one's view and the attempt to understand the positions and perspectives of others, while recognising the limitations that one's own point of view places on the attempt. This second approach to scales is well suited to representing the complexity of different perspectives.

One of the challenges for governance, in the interactive sense, is to retain an awareness of the contingency of the positions we assume so that we can be open to alternative ways of perceiving reality. In the second section of this chapter, we show how social science has attempted to understand and represent the rationality of small-scale fishers through focus on their livelihoods. This is one attempt by social science to capture the 'subjectivity' of small-scale fishing. The movement between the objective position from which global challenges to fish capture can be discerned and the subjective positions sensitive to local complexity and diversity is one potential lesson for fisheries governance from the scales approach.

Industrial versus Small-Scale Fish Capture

While there are various categorisations of fisheries, underlying most, if not all, is the opposition between small-scale and industrial fisheries. We accept the utility of this distinction but are concerned that it is often employed with little or no explanation on the presumption that definitions of the two categories are self-evident or commonly accepted. Frequently scholars distinguish the two categories according to a list of attributes (Roest et al. 1995; Berkes et al. 2001; Charles 2001) without acknowledging that the categories are simplifications of changing diversity and complexity of fish capture. Thus, for example, small-scale fishing encompasses a range of fish capture systems from those that are largely subsistence based to those that are highly connected to the global market. While the attempt to provide a comprehensive set of distinctions among small-scale and industrial fisheries and their variants is valuable, the power of the distinction is increased by conceptually linking the various attributes and thereby providing a guideline for understanding diversity, dynamics, and complexity in fish capture. The first step in formulating the conceptual underpinnings of the small-scale-industrial scale of fish capture is the identification of key factors that differentiates them from one another.

In our view, three characteristics are particularly important for representing fish capture and the diversity of fish capture systems. These are the social organisation of production, the technological intensity of fishing, and the closely related attributes of space and time. Each of these characteristics is analogous to a scale in the sense that it encompasses a range of attributes. Those attributes are themselves scales. The dynamics of fish capture are evident in shifts in social organisation, technological intensity of fishing, and speed and coverage of operation. The complexities of fish capture lie in the interaction among these characteristics over time.

A second element of the conceptual distinction of small-scale and industrial categories of fish capture is their divergent historical origins. This is clear from the term industrial fisheries itself. Industrial fisheries are self-evidently those that grew out of the advances in production triggered by the development of the factory system and the international mass market during the industrial revolution. The stimulus for the development of steam-powered trawler technology in 1880s Britain was the growing demand for low-cost fish by the new industrial working classes (Kurlansky 1997). The continued intensification of industrial capture capacity has been a response to the steady growth of the world demand in fish products.

Box 4.1 Change and sectoral diversity in the fisheries of Gujarat, India

The recent history of development in the Gujarat fisheries is an example of the scale changes in global fish capture presented in the first part of this chapter. From the early 1960s, the fishers of Gujarat began to rapidly adopt new technologies and techniques in response to state efforts and international market opportunities. At the same time, they began a process of spatial expansion from a narrow coastal band into deeper waters and into under-exploited zones in the state's coastal waters. In recent years, with the expansion of the trawler sector and the export market, the most successful of Gujarat's fishing operators have begun increasingly to rely on hired non-local crew. All of these trends have had interesting classificatory implications for fish capture in Gujarat.

Development in Gujarat's fishery has led to the coexistence of numerous sectors, the most important divisions being between trawlers, gill netters, and bag netters. All have been engaged in a process of technological innovation and modification of their fishing strategies, although a minor non-mechanised sector still exists. Trawlers are the economic basis for the local fishing elite, the wealthiest elements of which also control processing factories and other ancillary industries.

There are several aspects of the Gujarat fisheries that are particularly interesting for our concern in this chapter for the classification of fish capture. First, the socio-economic and technological divisions that have stratified the fisheries have arisen indigenously, although stimulated by connection to the global market for fish products. This is different from the frequent case in developing country contexts where outsiders control the most capital-intensive sector. Second, the capture practices of the trawler sector and the gill net sector are so much a product of globalisation that it would be nonsensical to label them as 'artisanal' but for the fact that they are led by members of local fishing castes. Nonetheless, third, if we put the Gujarat fisheries into a global comparative perspective, a good argument could be made that all three of the major sectors that we identify in the preceding paragraph are small-scale. The argument is easiest for the gill net sector, which remains organised by a share system embedded in the social practice of Gujarat fishing communities. Even though production on trawler boats is organised on a wage labour basis, technologically, spatially, and organisationally the sector is still far simpler and more locally rooted than what is generally considered industrial in discussions of fish capture internationally. It might most appropriately be labelled semi-industrial in character. The Gujarat example demonstrates that scale categorisations vary quite considerably by context, something that has to be recognised when trying to make classifications of fish capture.

Author: Derek Johnson

Small-scale is frequently used synonymously with artisanal in studies of fisheries. Neither term is ideal in representing the non-industrial sector of fish capture. Artisanal fishing is problematic, because it focuses attention on the local fabrication of gear, which is less and less the case in a world of global product markets, even for small-scale fishers (McGoodwin 2001). While we have chosen to use small-scale in this chapter for its concision, we also recognise that the term is relative. The small-scale craft and gear of one area would be considered large-scale in other areas (Mathew 2003). In contrast with industrial capture, small-scale fish capture originates as part of livelihood strategies by human groups in areas adjacent to aquatic resources. As such, it long predates industrial fisheries. This does not mean, however, that small-scale fisheries are largely subsistence based. Trade in fish products produced by small-scale community-based fisheries has been common for millennia. Since the development of mass markets for fish, small-scale fisheries have become increasingly linked to global commodity networks and have taken advantage of technological innovations to increase their productivity. Like the industrial sector, therefore, they have also steadily increased their catch capacity.

A crucial topic for consideration in assessing the industrial versus small-scale division from an historical perspective is whether there is an increasing convergence between small-scale and industrial fish capture systems. Whether, in other words, small-scale fisheries are increasingly becoming industrial in their organisation. This would certainly be the prediction of classical Marxist analysis, judging from work done in the agriculture sector (Lenin 1964; Thorner 1966). It is the case that small-scale fisheries are changing under the influence of globalisation and are becoming more integrated into global markets. Nonetheless, there is a considerable literature in fisheries that highlights their resilience, adaptability, and continued distinctiveness from the industrial sector (Platteau 1989a; Apostle and Barrett 1992; Chauveau and Jul-Larsen 2000). In many situations, it may make more sense to talk about the transition from small-scale fishing to semi-industrial fishing, reflecting the very great impact of mechanisation but the persistence of non-capitalist relations of production. This ambiguity of change is reflected in the dotting of the line at the bottom of table 4.1 that represents the directionality of change in fish capture.

In table 4.1, we represent the key elements of our conceptualisation of fish capture in relation to diversity, complexity, and dynamics. The table is divided according to the generally accepted distinction between small-scale and industrial fish capture. It leaves a blank central column for those adaptations that are between the two, including those small-scale fish capture systems that have adopted industrial techniques or other attributes of industrial fishing. Each of the three main scales by which we represent the difference between the two sectors is divided into sub-scales. As is indicated at the margins of the table, varying combinations of these sub-scales constitute diversity in small-scale capture fisheries and industrial capture fisheries. Complexity is the actual interactions between the different sub-scales of each diverse combination. As is noted below the table, there is a general trend for capture fisheries to experience a shift from left to right. This movement reflects the influence of the globalisation of technologies and markets. Note, however, that we are not arguing that the shift from left to right in the table means a transition from small-scale to industrial fisheries. As we state in the previous paragraph, there is not a great deal of evidence for this. Rather, small-scale fisheries are adopting more efficient techniques and technologies of production while preserving their social-institutional distinctiveness. The addition of explicit reference to diversity, complexity, and dynamics in the table is a deliberate attempt to emphasise that the scales and sub-scales within it are contingent representations. Or, in other words, the representations of small-scale and industrial in the table are ideal typical simplifications of complex, diverse, and changing realities.

Table 4.1 Attributes of small-scale and industrial fish capture

	Small-scale	Intermediate (semi-industrial)	Industrial	
			National fleets	Distant water fleets
Social-institutional				
	Less market based		More market based	
	Affective relations key		Wage-based key	
	More employment		Less employment	
	Locally relevant complex systems of access regulation		Greater importance of state systems of access regulation	
Technology				
	Less capital intensive		More capital intensive	
	Less catch capacity		Greater catch capacity	
	More diverse gears		Less diverse gears	
	Smaller craft		Larger craft	
Space and time				
	Slower resource exhaustion		Rapid resource exhaustion	
	Shorter seasons		Longer seasons	
	Shorter time at sea		Longer time at sea	
	Closer to shore		Further from shore	

Diversity arises from particular combinations of these sub-scales across space and time

Complexity rests in the interactions among combinations of these

- ->>

At a global scale, the dynamic of change in fish capture has been from the left to right side of this table but this has not generally meant the conversion of small-scale fishing to industrial fishing (see text above)

The remainder of this section offers a more detailed discussion of these key scales of the capture sector.

The Social-Institutional Scale of Fish Capture

The social relations that organise the capture of fish define the social-institutional scale of fish capture. The two extremes of the social forms organising fish capture are production that is organised entirely around affective relations in the small-scale sector and that which is organised purely on a commodity basis in the industrial sector. In the purest version of the latter form, individual labourers are perfectly substitutable for each other through the medium of cash. Fish harvesters are hired as wage labourers and are reduced to interchangeable inputs in the operating costs of fish capture. In fish capture based on affective relations, in contrast, participation is defined by social characteristics deemed appropriate to fishing. Such characteristics are foremost kinship and gender based, but ethnicity, social-occupational groupings like caste, and religious grounds are also often important. These two categories are idealised end points on the social scale of fish capture. Virtually all contemporary cases of the social organisation of fish capture fall between these extremes. In general, there has been growth in wage-based relations in fish capture due to the expansion of industrial fishing and increasing differentiation into owners of capital and hired crew in some small-scale fisheries (see box 4.1 on the Gujarat fishery).

The key scale category in discussing the social-institutional scale of fish capture is the community-based sector because this is the site at which the tension between social and wage-based relations of production is most acutely felt. There is an enormous degree of variation in the combination of these two forms within this sector. Analysis of this mix in the small-scale sector has been one of the dominant themes in the social study of fisheries with much debate over the importance and persistence of affective relations for the resilience of the sector. Sinclair (1985), for example, has argued that the mix of household and commodity relations in small-scale fishing should be highlighted with a term like domestic commodity production. The key social institution of importance in this debate is the household, with proponents of the resilience of the small-scale sector arguing that the household allows small-scale fishing to persist under conditions that would drive commercial fishers out of the fisheries. We define commercial fishers here in the sense of those who operate on a strict profit-loss rationality and include financially valued labour costs in their accounting. Household-based small-scale fisheries can continue to operate in conditions where economic return from fishing is consistently below operating costs because of the self-exploiting capacities of household labour. This form of fish capture can operate without factoring in labour costs. Social contracts organising fish capture at the community scale may similarly reduce the impact of labour costs through share system institutions. The household and community contexts of small-scale fishing often also anchor complex systems of locally adapted knowledge of fish and fish capture and institutions for restriction of access to fish resources. These attributes, under conditions of non-catastrophic change and relatively strong institutional cohesion, also provide a potentially strong comparative advantage over commercially based fishing.

Industrial fish capture is organised foremost according to a market-based logic and is almost exclusively the domain of multinational corporations and state fishing fleets. The bottom line for industrial fish capture is profitability. Efficiency of operation based on maximising the ratio of harvest quality and quantity relative to costs is central to the rationality of this production type. The social relations around fish capture in the industrial sector are thus those of the firm, although the particular and dangerous conditions of work on industrial fishing vessels make them a very different work environment than other forms of factory employment. Labour is valued as an input in production. Share-based systems of remuneration are present in industrial capture fishing, but wage labour is its predominant form. Systems of remuneration are chosen to maximise productivity, reinforcing the idea of the crewmember as an input into the production process.

Between small-scale and industrial fisheries lies a classificatory grey area that we label as intermediate or semi-industrial since the organisation of production is based on a mix of community and industrial attributes. Key to this sector is the nature of ownership and relations between owners and labourers. Generally, ownership of boats and gears is concentrated in a single owner or family but not in a corporate firm. The titular owner manages the boat or, usually, boats, and does not engage in fishing although his or her kin may be designated as captains of the vessels to monitor crew. These latter may be recruited through local kinship, ethnic, religious or other networks or may be recruited according to a more impersonal hiring system. Crewmembers are frequently employed on a wage labour basis, although wages may be combined with shares as an incentive to raise production.

The Technological Scale of Fish Capture

There are instances where fishing has been practiced without the support of fishing gears, with fish being caught by hand or with the assistance of animals, but these are unusual cases (Brandt 1984; Van Duijn 2004). Normally, technology is required in fishing to facilitate the capture of fish and other marine organisms. A variety of classificatory schemes have been proposed to order the technological scale in fishing. One of the simplest of these and one which has a high degree of currency in literature on fisheries turns on the distinction between passive and active fishing gears. Passive gears are those that the target species moves into itself while active gears pursue fish in order to entrap them. Gill nets, hooks and lines, and fish traps are thus passive gear, while trawling and seining are active gear.

A fuller representation of fish capture, however, would be grounded in a more detailed technological classification. The most complete scale which still retains a manageable summary form is that proposed by Brandt (1984). His classification into sixteen categories according to the *'principle of how the fish is caught'* (italics in the original) has the advantage of not requiring a residual category of 'other' technological types (Charles 2001) and includes non-commercial gears, unlike Sainsbury (1996).

An important point evident in Brandt's work is that industrial fishing techniques of dragged gears, seine nets, surround nets, and gill nets all had small-scale precursors, reflecting human ingenuity in capturing diverse species of fish in varied coastal and marine settings (Sainsbury 1996). Modification and mechanisation of these techniques in the industrial sector, however, have had a reciprocal influence in small-scale fishing with the introduction of motorised fishing equipment, sophisticated electronics such as fish finders, echo and depth sounders, and new materials and techniques. This is indicative of the long-term trend in both sectors of technological innovation and intensification in order to increase productivity (Garcia and Moreno 2003; Mathew 2003). It also means that while in general small-scale, and particularly subsistence fishing, are still associated with the most labour intensive, technically simple, and low-cost fishing methods, in many parts of the world small-scale fishing has growing technological similarities with industrial fishing. One of the most important of these is that small-scale fishing increasingly has the capacity to overcome natural limitations on fishing such as the vagaries of tides, weather conditions, seasons, and phases of the moon.

As technological complexity increases and small-scale fishers are less restrained by natural limitations on their efforts, particular locally adapted forms of knowledge change, placing mounting pressure on marine ecosystems. This is an important qualifier to the tendency to romanticise small-scale fishing in writing on fisheries sustainability. Firstly, although simple, some traditional fish capture practices are very destructive to the environment. Fish drives, the use of fish poison and stupefacients, and various fish gleaning and collecting methods not only result in the collection of all resources in a given fishing spot but also cause extensive, long-term physical damage. Fortunately, these methods are relatively rare and generally cause only localised effects. Secondly, a larger scale trend and one that is much more worrying is the increasing adoption of more efficient technologies by small-scale fishers. In parts of the world such as Atlantic Canada, the small-scale inshore fishery has intensified technologically to the point where it would be considered semi-industrial or industrial in a developing country context.

Despite the foregoing, the global industrial sector remains by far the most capital intensive, captures the lion's share of the global catch, and thus makes the most serious contribution to global overfishing. Indeed, while decision making in the small-scale and industrial sectors is motivated by maximising economic benefit, this tendency is counterbalanced to some degree in the small-scale sector by social obligations that place limits on the degree of capital intensity. Labour-saving technological innovations will thus tend to be adopted much more readily in the industrial sector. The capital intensity and relative ecological impact of the industrial versus the small-scale sector are evident in box 4.2.

Box 4.2 Comparisons of Small-scale and Large-scale Fish Capture

An often-repeated tool for comparing small-scale and large-scale fishing has been a table with two columns of data comparing the sectors on a series of attributes. Data from two such exercises are presented below. The first table is the model which has inspired many subsequent graphical comparisons (e.g., Berkes et al. in this box and those in Maclean 1988; Le Sann 1998; and Pauly and Maclean 2003). The second table gives a more recent estimate of the same attributes.

Attributes	Large-scale	Small-scale
Number of fishers employed	ca. 450,000	Over 8,000,000
Marine fish caught for human consumption	ca. 24 million metric tonnes (mt) annually	ca. 20 million mt annually
Capital cost of each job on fishing vessels	$10,000 – $100,000	$100 – $1,000
Marine fish caught for industrial reduction to meal and oil, etc.	ca. 19 million mt annually	Almost none
Fuel oil consumption	10 – 14 million mt annually	1 – 2 million mt annually
Fish caught per mt of fish consumed	2 – 5 mt	10 – 20 mt
Fishers employed for each $1 million invested in fishing vessels	10 – 100	1,000 – 10,000

Source: Thomson (1980)

Attributes	Large-scale	Small-scale
Direct employment in Fishing	500,000 people	50,000,000 people
Fisheries-related occupations	–	150,000,000 people
Fishing households and dependents	–	250,000,000 people
Capital cost per fishing job	US$30,000 – $300,000	US$20 – $300
Annual catch for food	15 – 40 million mt	20 – 30 million mt
Annual fish bycatch	5 – 20 million mt	<1 million mt
Annual fuel oil consumption	14 – 19 milion mt	1 – 2.5 million mt
Catch per mt of oil used	2 – 5 mt	10 – 20 mt

Source: Berkes et al. (2001)

Unfortunately, neither of these sources shows how it obtained its figures. A methodology for doing so is given by Sumaila et al. (2001), whose work also shows that the comparison of the two sectors at the regional level can lead to very different local balances between the sectors.

Changes in the Space and Time of Fish Capture

An alternative scale frequently used for the categorisation of fish capture is its spatial range. Following this scale, fisheries can be grouped into inshore, midshore, offshore, and distant water fisheries. Spatial scale is closely related to technological intensification. Innovations in technology, besides intensifying pressure in the most productive coastal zone, tend generally to provoke fisheries expansion further offshore. Consequently, except where strictly delimited by state regulation, the boundaries between zones, particularly inshore and offshore, tend to shift. The delimitation of fishing zones by states is generally part of regulatory activities that assign specific zones to specific fishing adaptations. In most parts of the world, such zonal regulations either do not exist or are ignored (Bavinck 2001). This may lead to situations where, within inshore waters, small-scale fishers, industrial fishers, recreational fishers, and aquaculturists compete for the same spaces and resources. One of the critical dynamics in fish capture has been the challenges to local systems of access rights that technological change generates, a governance issue that we address in more detail in the second section of this chapter. Despite the ambiguity of spatial zones in many parts of the world, they are often used as a convenient scale for labelling groups of fishers. Subsistence and small-scale fishing are thus defined as inshore fishing and industrial fishing is labelled as offshore or distant water fishing.

The spatial scale of small-scale fisheries has changed with the improvement of existing technologies or adoption of new technologies and techniques and the consequent increased pressure on resources. The introduction of powered motorboats and the adoption of inboard storage facilities has allowed fishers to access formerly remote fishing locations. This tendency has been encouraged by new and more efficient fishing gear such as monofilament nets, floats and buoys, and positioning devices such as the Global Positioning System. In many developing countries, technological innovation resulting in the expansion of spatial scale has been instigated by states and international development agencies in deliberate attempts at economic modernisation in order improve living conditions (Kurien 1985; Johnson 2001). Financial packages and incentives such as training and technical assistance have been offered to stimulate the creation and extension of industrial fishing sectors and to intensify production and range in the small-scale sector.

Midshore and offshore fisheries indicate relative distances beyond the inshore area but still generally within national exclusive economic zones. While small-scale fishers and recreational fishers increasingly penetrate into mid-shore areas, the offshore still remains largely the preserve of industrial fishing. Operation in offshore areas is capital intensive and requires sophisticated technology due to the depth at which fishing takes place and the distance that must be travelled to fish in that zone. Fishing methods employed in these areas include trolling, longlining, purse seining, trawling, and pole and line fishing.

Box 4.3 Local and global scales in Fiji's fishing sector

Fiji is home to the extremes of global fishing practices. Many Fijian coastal communities are heavily dependent on the resources from their customary fishing grounds adjacent to their villages and fishing remains a main source of subsistence, livelihood, and traditional obligations. At the same time, the Fijian state-owned Pacific Fishing Company (PAFCO) is the local processing hub for catches from a Taiwanese fishing contractor, Fong Chen Formosa, which supplies Bumble Bee Seafoods, one of the world's largest seafood corporations.

Recent studies conducted in Fiji have demonstrated the continued importance of fishing as a source of protein and employment. They have also demonstrated, however, that small-scale fishing in Fiji has been subject to a wide range of state-sponsored and market driven changes, including the spread of mechanised boats and intensification of gill net fishing. These have had significant social impacts, including growth in the number of women leading fishing trips. They have also resulted in a high degree of pressure on marine resources and considerable local concern about the effects of overfishing.

The opposite extreme of the global fishing industry is represented in Fiji by the operations of PAFCO and its connection to Bumble Bee Seafoods through a toll-pack agreement signed in 1999. Under the agreement, Bumble Bee supplies raw tuna and markets to PAFCO. PAFCO, in return, supplies the physical facilities and labour, for which it is paid toll-pack fees to do the preliminary processing of tuna prior to export to the USA. Bumble Bee has engaged PAFCO to do the most labour intensive 'loining' phase of processing, while reserving the final packing for its California plant. It does this because tariffs charged on loin imports into USA are much lower than the tariffs charged on canned tuna imports (0.2% versus 12.5% respectively). PAFCO earns about US$40 million per year from this arrangement and employs about 1,000 people, which makes it a large player by Pacific standards. PAFCO's revenue pales in comparison to Bumble Bee's turnover of US$1 billion per year, which reflects its position as the largest supplier of canned albacore tuna to the USA and the second largest supplier of canned tuna in the world.

Authors: Mecky Kronen and Joeli Veitayaki

Distant water fish capture is the domain of states and multinational companies, which operate large fleets and have bases in many countries around the world. Large capital requirements are the key limiting factor in this sector. The largest players in distant water fishing have been the USSR and, more recently, the states of the Russian Federation, Japan, Spain, South Korea, Poland, Taiwan, Portugal, and Germany (Bonfil et al. 1998). European Union vessels fish off the coasts of Africa and in the Indian Ocean while Russian, Japanese, Taiwanese, and South Korean factory vessels, including mother and supply ships, fish in the Pacific and Southern Oceans. Distant water fleets operate in international waters such as the North Pacific 'Donut Hole' but also in national waters, particularly those of developing countries. In countries such as Senegal and India they have pro-voked considerable resentment by indigenous fishers. In other cases, they may provide temporary or long-term benefits to countries that have insuffi-cient capacity for or interest in fishing their own resources. Such benefits have to be weighed against less than perfect control over foreign fleets in national waters and possible related consequences for ecological sustain-ability (Bonfil et al. 1998).

Integral with the shrinking of space due to technological innovation in fish capture has been a changing perception of time. The adoption of active gear as the norm in industrial fisheries is an example of this change. Rather than waiting for the fish to come, industrial trawlers and purse seiners go to the fish, thereby reducing capture time. Motorisation has also reduced the time it takes to reach fishing grounds, while onboard freezing and pro-cessing technologies have sped up processing. Communications technolo-gies have allowed highly market sensitive fishing, where boats are dis-patched to target particular species only when prices reach a certain level (Apostle et al. 2002).

Ensuring a Livelihood from Fishing

While the preceding section made an argument for a way to understand capture fisheries at a global scale, with emphasis on the generalised influ-ence of globalisation, this section looks at the complexity, diversity, and dy-namics of capture fisheries from the local scale. We attempt here as much as possible to take the subject position, that is a view receptive to the per-spectives and priorities of those involved in and influenced by fish capture. Our perspective is further deliberately limited by excluding the experience of industrial fishing in order to concentrate on the largest group of people involved in fish capture. In our approach, we bring together an ethno-graphic sensitivity and a livelihoods approach to emphasise the point, so important to fisheries governance, that diversity, complexity, and dynamics look very different from below. Rather than seeking to make overarching statements in this section, then, we draw upon a number of case studies. These reveal that the activities and goals of those involved in capture fish-eries are multiple and changing, reflecting the diversity and complexity of their livelihoods. Fisheries governance has to bear these different and pos-sibly inconsistent objectives in mind because they may conflict with the strict, scientifically based objectives of fisheries managers.

The livelihoods approach has become a standard tool in interventions aimed at poverty alleviation for human groups dependent on natural re-sources (see chap. 2 and FAO/DFID 2004). It is now beginning to be ap-plied in coastal settings with communities that rely on marine resources. The key thrust of the livelihoods approach is the attempt to understand the assets, activities, and access conditions that shape how individuals and households make their livings (Ellis 2000). The approach is attractive for its emphasis on the diversity and complexity of the ways in which people attempt to reduce their livelihood vulnerability within the particular constraints of their situation. It pushes fisheries researchers to examine the degree to which fishers depend on fishing for their livelihoods and the social and political divisions that make co-management contentious.

When looking at capture fisheries as a livelihood it becomes apparent that a strict division between the taking and landing of fish and other aspects of life is hard to maintain. As anthropological studies have long shown, the maintenance of livelihoods in capture fisheries involves recourse to a wide range of interrelated activities, of which the catching of fish is just one. And, while fish capture may be of central importance to fisher livelihoods, it depends on the other activities that buffer it and support it.

Work and Employment in Capture Fisheries

Studies of coastal communities by ethnologists, sociologists, and historians have long emphasised the diversity of work, including fishing, that people undertake to make a living. Boas and Malinowski, two of the founders of ethnography who studied coastal hunting and gathering peoples on opposite sides of the Pacific in the early decades of the 20th century, both wrote about diverse livelihoods using different terminology. Boas showed this most clearly in his descriptions of how the complex social system of the Kwakiutl depended on an array of activities based on coastal resources (Boas 1966; Stewart 1977). But while the artistic sophistication and societal complexity of the Kwakiutl was attributable at least in part to surpluses offered by their rich marine environment, they were also engaged in a wide range of terrestrial activities including gathering plants and building materials, and conducting long-range trade with peoples deep inland and up and down the western coast of North America. Below the surface of Malinowski's research in the Trobriand Islands is evidence of an equally multi-faceted coastal economy, where harvesting molluscs and fishing co-existed with horticulture and farming of yams and pigs, and with highly ritualised long-distance trading (Malinowski 1922).

Raymond Firth, another classic figure in 20th-century ethnography, carried on the tradition of coastal studies in the 1940s and early 1960s with his research on Malay fisher-peasants. His work demonstrated the social, technological, and market complexity of Malay small-scale fishing while revealing that fishers had a wide range of livelihood patterns ranging from considerable dependence on capture fishing to much more mixed adaptations where fishing was combined with rice and vegetable agriculture, trade, and other economic activities. Firth makes the important point that full-time engagement in fishing tends to require the existence of an exchange economy so that fishers can exchange their fish for other products, as fish alone does not make a balanced diet (Firth 1966).

A fundamental institution in which the diversity of small-scale fishing economies is anchored that does not come across strongly in these early studies is the household. The importance of the household as a core institution for fisheries is examined in chapter 8. For the moment, we introduce the household in order to emphasise how it articulates capture fishing and other livelihood activities into larger social and economic arrangements. This livelihood complexity and diversity, anchored in the household, shapes fisher interests and thus has to be accounted for in fisheries governance.

The centrality of the household as the link between diverse elements of livelihoods for fishers has been amply illustrated in the case of Atlantic Canada (e.g., Sider 1986; Ommer 1989; MacDonald and Connelly 1990). In the Acadian Peninsula of northern New Brunswick, for example, capture fisheries were historically one part of a larger system of household production organised by gender and age (Johnson 1999). Acadian men worked aboard lobster boats and cod dories while women worked in the lobster canneries and on the cod flakes. Every member of the household gathered clams at low tide, while men fished for eels in the autumn and smelts through the ice in the winter. These fishing related activities were complemented by summer work on garden plots primarily by women and the elderly and the gathering of berries (especially blueberries) for subsistence and for cash by women. The wealthier households that owned land and traction animals devoted a greater amount of time to agriculture, some even to the exclusion of fishing. In the fall, men hunted geese, ducks, and moose, while women canned vegetables, fish and berries and tended domestic animals. In the winter, many men, particularly those from poorer households, departed for logging camps while women stayed back to look after the children and the aged.

This Acadian example shows how capture fisheries are often only part of a larger system of household organisation by which people make ends meet. Obligations to others within the household and the necessities induced by household involvement in a diversity of livelihood activities condition the receptivity of those actually involved in capture fishing to changes in its governance.

Risk and Rationality in Capture Fisheries

An important explanation for the diversity of activities undertaken by the household, including engagement with the exchange economy, is the rational mitigation of the high degree of risk that characterises capture fishing. Diversity in the household, and in fishing economies more broadly, thus reflects the key importance of strategies to reduce livelihood uncertainty. The implication of risk adverse behaviour by fishers is that they do not necessarily react as predictable self-interested economic maximisers, as they bear the broader interests of their households in mind (Durrenberger 1996).

Risk in capture fishing comes from two sources: the marine environment and the market. The most obvious risk of fishing is personal: the sea and the weather at sea are physically enormously risky. Marine fishing is still the most deadly of occupations. Storms, rogue waves, cyclones, fatigue, and the cold all threaten the lives of fishers. Risk in the marine environment also comes from the uncertainty of capture that pervades fishing, much as it does in hunting (Pálsson 1991). While knowledge and skill are very important preconditions for successful fishing, fishers always run the risk of a meagre catch or a lean season, with implications for the income and subsistence of themselves and their families. Market risk relates to price, which is determined by factors as much out of the control of individual fishers as the weather at sea. Fishers can be hurt by low prices for their catch or by high prices for inputs into the production process that they cannot provide themselves. As fisheries become ever more integrated into the global market, such economic risks become increasingly powerful.

Besides the household, there are several recurrent risk reduction strategies in capture fisheries. On the market side, these are credit arrangements, often administered by a dominant merchant elite (Firth 1966; Ommer 1989; Johnson 1999). On the environmental side, these are ritual and share systems. Fishing rituals often involve propitiating deities in order to assure personal safety and good catches. Thus, for example, fishers in Hong Kong have a particularly strong relationship with Tianhou for whom they burn incense and make offerings of pork and steamed buns at New Year and on other ritually significant days during the year (Ward 1985). Similarly, Hindu fishers in Gujarat begin the fishing season at the end of the monsoon with a festival called *narial poonam*, in which they throw coconuts into the sea after having called upon a Brahman priest to make prayers for a successful year of fishing. Muslim fishers offer coconuts at the graves, or *dargas*, of saints for their blessing of the fishing effort (Johnson 2002).

Share systems in capture fishing have engendered a considerable literature (Platteau and Nugent 1992). These authors have argued that they are a response to the high-risk natural and market environments of fishing and to the need to restrain opportunistic behaviour in contracts between owners of fishing craft and gears and crew. In terms of abating risk, they meet the requirements of the crew for their subsistence and broader livelihood needs while giving the owner of capital the assurance that his or her equipment will be used efficiently and carefully. Share systems often include a basic provision of fish to crew for their household subsistence needs. This small share of the catch is separated out first, before any other divisions are made, indicating its importance. Accordingly, in the Philippines, it is known as the 'share for the body' of the catch (Russell and Alexander 2000), while in Malaya it was known as the *makan lau'* or 'flesh component' of a meal (Firth 1966). The secondary division of the catch occurs according to a variety of complex and somewhat malleable rules that allocate shares according to perceived contribution to the fishing effort. The share going to the owner of the principal means of production varies according to the degree to which the technology contributes to the catch quantity and accounts for the risk of loss and depreciation.

Livelihoods as Shaped by Access Institutions

Access restrictions are a second component of fishing adaptations common in many parts of the world that have significant implications for how livelihood strategies are realised. Access restrictions limit use rights to certain areas, species, technologies, or activities, possibly at limited times, for certain groups or individuals. Here we provide first an overview of the complexity and diversity of access systems at a group level before changing the focus to the experience of access restrictions at the individual level. Access rights constrain the livelihood options of some but protect those of others.

The first category of restrictions on access has become perhaps the driving force of fisheries management discussions in recent years. In situations of resource depletion, the standard response is to turn to mechanisms by which access can be restricted so as to reduce pressure on resources. Initial access management interventions that came to prominence in the 1960s were founded on the notion that the seas were open access and drew upon that most famous metaphor of Hardin, 'the tragedy of the commons' (1968). They proposed that the appropriate response to the problem of open access resources was state regulation (Scott 1999). From this perspective, the core of resource degradation problems lay in 'the fisherman's problem' where 'every harvester knows that if he or she leaves a fish in the water someone else will get it, and the profit, instead' (McEvoy 1986: 10). The state thus had to respond by imposing quotas, licenses, or other such limitations on the ability of individuals to maximise their share of a limited resource.

While this approach might make sense in fisheries where open access conditions do indeed pertain, social scientists rapidly began to point out that most fisheries in the world were already regulated by indigenous systems of access management (Berkes 1985). To ignore these in the implementation of sweeping new state limitations on access was at best to overlook locally appropriate resource management tools. At worst, state regulation could make things significantly worse (Finlayson 1994).

In many of the world's capture fisheries, particularly in developing countries, the state is not the dominant party and much access regulation emanates from other sources. The classic work on community-based restrictions on access is Acheson's work on the Maine lobster fishery where he showed how groups of Maine lobster fishers prevent non-local entry into their areas of control (Acheson 1975; Acheson 1988). The extent of such semi-formalised systems has been illustrated in a wide variety of locations around the world (e.g., Alexander 1977; Berkes 1987; Carrier 1987). As box 4.4 shows, access restrictions may be imposed directly on fishing grounds or on marketing channels and landing facilities. It is important to recognise that not all fisheries have clear access regimes of this order (e.g., Russell and Alexander 2000) and that sea-tenure systems are not static. Sometimes they deteriorate (Anderson 1987; Meltzoff 2000) or are introduced or enhanced in response to new conditions (Lobe and Berkes 2004).

Box 4.4 The attempts of trawler fishers in South India to restrict access to the fisheries

In the mid-1990s, about 1,000 small trawlers were based in the fishing harbour of Chennai on the south eastern coast of India. By that time, trawler owners had become interested in restricting access to the profession as the continued growth of the trawler fleet was leading to overfishing, overstrained shore facilities, and gluts of supply leading to low prices. The problem, as many fishers and their trawler association perceived it, was that outsiders were able to acquire boats and enter the fisheries much too easily.

One of the key problems of the Chennai trawler fisher community in restricting access was how to define outsiders and insiders. In disputes, caste and kin links to fishing and residence in Chennai were most frequently cited as support for insider status. Although these criteria excluded, at least in theory, a segment of outsider investors, there were many borderline cases. What to do, for example, with a fisher born outside of Chennai, but who had married locally? What about a person who had not been born in Chennai, but had lived there for many years?

Complicating access criteria were murkier layers of cheating and abuse of power. Senior officials in the trawler owners' association were suspected of acting as fronts for outsider fishers under an arrangement known as *benami*, and taking selective action only. These officials defended themselves by emphasising their limited capacity to enforce decisions on access to fisheries. Most significant were the cases in which so-called outsiders, who were ordered by the association to discontinue their operations, had taken the matter to court. On the basis of Indian law, which provides for equal opportunity for all citizens, the judge had ruled against the order, and permitted the outsiders to take up fishing again. Having become wary of putting their orders to paper, and risking being taken to court, the officials of the association began to make use of informal sanctions like slander and violence against outsiders.

In spite of the flurry of emotion and action, the net result of fishers' attempts to regulate access to the Chennai trawler sector was apparently limited. They were not able to agree on a set of rules for access to trawler fishing and no outsiders with investments in trawler fishing decided to withdraw. It is possible, though, that newcomers were discouraged by the antagonistic climate.

Author: Maarten Bavinck

Unlike the putative goal of state intervention for fisheries management, not all 'sea-tenure' systems are oriented towards resource conservation (Bavinck 2001). They might instead reflect other factors like status ranking or the organisation of capture. Individual attributes also have access limiting or enhancing effects. The variety of resources necessary for capture fishing, including access to sea space, capital, technology, fishing skill, and knowledge of marine ecology, flow from an individual's social identity (McGoodwin 1990) as determined by one's position in a social group – whether it is a harbour gang or village community, a fishing caste, or citizenship in a nation state – through residence, kinship, and history. These allegiances convey rights or, as in many of the world's fisheries, access to the skills and knowledge that are passed on in non-formal, on-site apprenticeships. These are phenomena Schlager and Ostrom (1993) subsume under the heading 'boundary rules'. Boundary rules include the cultural ascription of gender roles, which are noted to be particularly strong in fishing. The world over, men are generally assigned the task of fish catching, whereas women are more strongly involved in marketing and processing (Acheson 1981; Ram 1992). On occasion, however, these roles are reversed, as Cole has illustrated in a Portuguese case (Cole 1991). Access to the profession of marine capture fishing, and the niche one comes to occupy, thus depends on a variety of factors, only part of which is captured in the term 'property rights'.

Diversity, Complexity, Dynamics, and Governance in Capture Fisheries

This chapter began with a discussion of representation under the assumption that the image by which we depict a phenomenon has a guiding influence on how we react to it. In this case, the phenomenon in question is capture fisheries, which we have argued are diverse, complex, and dynamic. From this chapter a number of governance responses to such a characterisation of capture fisheries emerge. The broadest of these responses is that the basic variability and changeability of capture fisheries necessitates a way of looking that is flexible and creative. We argue that one model that fisheries governors might look to that stimulates these capacities is our distinctively defined scales approach. While scales do represent dimensions of a phenomenon, they also constitute positions that shape the way we see. Thus a movement between scales when considering capture fisheries affects our image of capture fishing and the nature of the problems it faces. The governance practices of fisheries governors might better reflect the diversity, complexity and dynamics of fish capture if it internalised a conscious shifting between scales, understood as positions or points of view. It would certainly prompt the realisation that fishers and other coastal stakeholders have perspectives and priorities regarding fish capture that will not match those of the governors.

Two pairs of scales structure this chapter and are key reference points in the governance of fish capture. The first pair is the external, global view of the first part of the chapter and the internal, local view of the second part. The second pair is composed of small-scale and industrial fish capture. The dynamism of the scales approach is reflected in the tension within the oppositions. This is a tension of conflict in the lived reality of fishing but also a conceptual tension between the imperfection of the categories.

Beyond the general methodological approach to governance that the chapter seeks to convey, a number of more specific governance implications arise from it. The first and determinative of these is the importance we place on globalisation as the driving force of change within capture fisheries. While the globalisation of fish capture in different places produces distinctive sets of interactions, the spread and intensification of market links and the introduction of new technologies and methods of production, among other factors, are transforming fisheries everywhere. Globalisation is a binding force. Governance of fish capture has to face the basic reality that the dynamism of change comes from interactions across multiple scales, many of the points of which transcend local capacities of knowledge and power of influence. New global alliances of fishers, fishworkers, governors, and their supporters such as the World Forum of Fisher Peoples (WFFP 2004) and the International Coalition in Support of Fishworkers (ICSF 2004) are required to promote local interests for sustainability of ecosystems and livelihoods.

A number of insights for the governance of capture fishing arise out of the external view of fish capture from earlier in this chapter. First, a consideration of the social-institutional scale of fish capture reveals that different rationalities underpin large-scale and small-scale fishing. Governance of the two sectors will likely take different approaches. Second, as the dynamism of globalisation operates on the space and time of fishing, conflicts between and within these sectors are increasing. A key challenge of governance is thus to mediate the interests of different groups in the context of an increasingly diminished and degraded resource. In this resource context, the continued trend to the technological intensification of effort in all sectors is pernicious. Fisheries governors have to challenge incentives to increasing capital intensity, particularly in the form of ill-conceived subsidies.

In the second part of this chapter, we looked at fish capture from the perspective of the smaller scale sectors, deliberately excluding the industrial sector. As with the conclusions of chapter 3, we argue that attempts to sustain and promote diversity are fundamental to governance. In fish capture, this relates particularly to livelihood diversity but also includes diversity within fish capture itself. Diversity in both of these areas acts to reduce risk in capture fishing and thus creates conditions militating against the race for fish. One of the most important reasons for the destructiveness of industrial and industrialising fish capture is just this loss of diversity as effort becomes focused on a few species of high value for global market niches. The consideration of fish capture from the fishers' perspective also reveals the frequency of indigenous resource allocation systems. While this is now a widely accepted notion within common property resource management, a generation ago it was little acknowledged. Current research cautions us, however, not to romanticise such systems, which may be ineffective, in decline, or oriented towards priorities other than resource conservation.

This chapter has refrained from being explicitly normative, adhering instead to its mandate of representing fish capture. As a final conclusion, however, we would highlight that one of the principal hard choices in governance of fish capture is how to divide up the stagnant or dwindling pool of living wild resources in the sea. The implication of the chapter and these final governance reflections is one that favours the small-scale sector. As has been argued for a long time, small-scale fisheries support the larger group of fishers, yet industrial fisheries take the larger share of the world's resources in a much more energy-intensive fashion (Thomson 1980). At present the trend in capture fisheries continues to be the industrialisation of fish capture, although now perhaps more in terms of technological intensification of small-scale fishing than the building of new distant-fleet capacity. Slowing or diverting this industrialisation is the most pressing challenge of the governance of fish capture.

We have sought in this chapter to restrict our discussion as much as possible to the issue of fish capture. Clearly, when talking about the importance of globalisation or the impact of increased fishing effort, we are indicating the links in the chain that bind this chapter to the others in this section. The global market, after all, drives globalisation, and local responses are conditioned by ecosystem characteristics. The governance of fish capture likewise has to make the connections to the market, to the ecosystem, and to other sectors, particularly that of its closest relative, aquaculture.

5

Aquaculture

Roger S.V. Pullin and U. Rashid Sumaila

Diversity, Complexity, and Dynamics in Aquaculture

Aquaculture, the farming of aquatic plants and animals (finfish, crustaceans, molluscs and other invertebrates), in fresh-, brackish, and seawater, is very diverse (Stickney 2000). Aquaculture statistics reported to the FAO from its member countries in 2000 covered 210 different species (Tacon 2003). Aquaculture systems are commonly classified according to their nutrient inputs. Extensive aquaculture involves no intentional fertilisation or feeding; e.g., the capturing of naturally settled mussels and oysters. Semi-intensive aquaculture comprises the farming of fish and invertebrates in ponds, pens and cages with supplementary fertilisation and/or feeding. Intensive aquaculture is entirely reliant on added feeds (e.g., salmon cages, eel tanks and raceways) and resembles feedlot systems for livestock. Fish farmers are also diverse. They range from poor smallholders in developing countries to the world's largest corporations. Their operations range in scale from backyard ponds of less than 100 m², operated by rural and peri-urban households, to enterprises that cover thousands of hectares of land and water with ponds, pens and cages. Aquaculture is as diverse as agriculture.

Aquaculture, like agriculture, is also a highly complex sector, comprised of sub-sectors (breeding, hatchery and nursery operations, grow-out and marketing, etc.) and interdependent with a wide range of associated industries; e.g., feeds, fertilisers, medication, and equipment. The diversity and complexity of aquaculture inevitably make it a very dynamic sector. Its dynamics include its rapid growth, as a new frontier for food production in many countries, and its necessary coexistence with other longer established sectors. The intersectoral relationships of aquaculture with agriculture, capture fisheries and other sectors are often areas of conflict and it is a major future challenge for aquaculture and those other sectors to resolve their conflicts and to pursue co-operation, especially in the sharing of land, water, and other natural resources (Sumaila 1999). Aquaculture has great scope for integration with other food production sectors. Fishponds in mixed farming systems and aquaculture integrated with wastewater reuse also have long histories and huge potential (e.g., Edwards 2000; FAO 2000a; Edwards et al. 2002). A governance approach to aquaculture is just beginning (Van der Schans 1999).

Global Aquaculture Production and Trade

From 1984 to 1998, the contributions of developing countries to global aquaculture production increased from about 73% to 90%; the remainder came from developed countries. In 1998, about 82% of total aquaculture production came from Low-Income Food-Deficit Countries (LIFDCs), and the total production from all developing countries was 35.5 million metric tonnes (mt) Over the same period, aquaculture production in LIFDCs grew five times faster than that of developing countries in general (Tacon 2001).

Asia contributes most of global aquaculture production. In 1998, about 90% of total global production by weight was produced in the People's Republic of China (PRC), by far the leading producer, accounting for nearly 70% of total global production. PRC aquaculture data are often considered separately from those of the rest of the world (e.g., New 2003; Tacon 2003). Other regions remain minor contributors to global aquaculture production: Europe, about 5%; South America, less than 2%; and Africa and Oceania, around 0.5 % each (FAO 2000a; Tacon 2001). In 2000, this picture had not changed much but global aquaculture production had risen to 45.7 million mt, valued at US$56.5 billion (FAO 2002a). Total aquaculture production in 1998 comprised by weight over 50% finfish, 23% molluscs and 22% aquatic plants (FAO 2000a).

Aquaculture occupies and uses large tracts of land and water. In 1999, marine aquaculture in the PRC covered an area of 1.1 million ha: 71,000 ha for finfish, 238,000 ha for crustaceans, 711,000 ha for molluscs, and 55,000 ha for seaweeds (http://www.fao.org/fi/fcp/en/CHN/profile.htm). In India, the estimated area of brackish water available for aquaculture in 1998-99 was 1.19 million ha, of which 135,660 ha was devoted to shrimp culture (http://www.fao.org/fi/fcp/en/IND/ profile.htm). At the same time, aquaculture in Indonesia occupied 507,513 ha (60% brackish water ponds, 28% integrated rice-fish farming and 12% freshwater ponds; http://www.fao.org/fi/fcp/en/IDN/profile.htm), and in the Philippines brackish water ponds covered about 143,197 ha (94% of the total aquaculture area; http://www.fao.org/fi/fcp/en/PHL/profile.htm). In 1996, there were 23,413 tiger shrimp (*Penaeus monodon*) farms in Thailand with a total area of 72,663 ha, supplying 241,000 metric tons of shrimp worth US$1,250 million, with freshwater aquaculture widely practiced, particularly in the central and northeastern regions, comprising 154,000 freshwater fish farms (ponds, cages and rice-fish systems), with a total area of 63,000 ha (http://www.fao.org/fi/fcp/en/THA/profile.htm). Farmed fish products are widely traded internationally, the main trade products are shrimp and prawns, salmon, and molluscs. Farmed tilapias, seabass, and sea breams are growing in importance as products for international trade. The major markets for farmed fish are Japan, the United States and the European Union. Major exporting countries are Thailand, Ecuador, Indonesia, India, Mexico, Bangladesh and Vietnam (FAO 2002a).

According to the FAO (2002a), the numbers of fish farmers in the world increased from 7.07 million in 1998 to 7.47 million in 2000. The corresponding numbers for 1998 (and 2000) by region were: Asia, 6.76 (7.13) million; North and Central America, 191,000 (190,000); Africa 56,000 (75,000); South America, 41,000 (41,000); Europe, 27,000 (27,000) and Oceania, 5,000 (5,000). It is difficult to collect accurate data on the numbers of fish farmers in developing regions, where fish are sometimes farmed as a part-time occupation and in remote areas. Therefore, some of the data above are probably underestimated.

Aquaculture and Capture Fisheries Products in Capture and Post-Harvest Chains

It has been argued that aquaculture enjoys both supply and product advantages over capture fisheries (Muir and Young 1998; Eagle et al. 2004). This is because markets assign high value to consistency and predictability of production, and fish farms generally have far more control over the timing, consistency, and quantity of production than capture fisheries. The latter face a number of constraints, including the fact that production is usually variable, uncertain, and cannot be increased at will. These constraints have impacts on the quality and supply of fish from capture fisheries to the supply chain. The ultimate effect of this is that the price per unit weight of capture fish is usually low while the cost of storage, transportation, and processing of capture fish can be high compared to those for farmed fish (Eagle et al. 2004).

Markets demand consistent products that are aesthetically pleasing, easy to prepare, traceable, and inexpensive (Eagle et al. 2004). Fish farmers are better positioned to achieve all of the above than fishers because they can control the characteristics and diets of the fish they raise. Fish farmers can also time the growth of their fish to ensure that they enter the fish supply chain at optimal times, thereby allowing for shorter times between when the fish is captured and when it enters the supply chain. Fish farmers, unlike many fishers, can also choose the size of the fish that they harvest, to allow for lower processing costs due to increased mechanisation (Naylor et al. 2003; Eagle et al. 2004).

Expansion of Aquaculture: Limits to Growth and Governance Implications

With many of the world's capture fisheries in decline or collapsing, the big question is – how much more can aquaculture contribute to world fish supply? Attempting an answer is exceedingly difficult because of complex and interrelated factors. There are limits to the expansion as well as to the productivity of aquaculture systems, as there are for any system based on availability and efficiency of natural resource use. There are also the issues of resource ownership, access and equity, biosafety and other environmental safeguards, markets, competition, etc. Analysis of these factors and of their many interactions is difficult and those who make forecasts for the potential growth of aquaculture tend to focus on one or a few factors, especially the availability of suitable land, water, and feeds, rather than taking a more holistic, governance approach. It is widely believed that aquaculture will contribute an increasing proportion of world fish supply. For example, Ackefors (1999) stated that the: '... *aquaculture yield of 26 million metric tonnes (mmt) in 1996 must increase to about 55 mmt by 2025 to meet the demand of fishery products*'. By using economic models, Delgado et al. (2002) projected that the contribution of aquaculture to total world fish production would rise to 41% by 2020. *The Economist* (Anon 2003) confidently reported predictions that aquaculture will supply the majority of the world's supply of fish by 2030. Are such forecasts realistic? Are optimistic economic models for the future of aquaculture consonant with the likely ecological and economic realities? This is a huge debate with a wide literature, and no consensus has yet emerged – although there is increasing acceptance that ecosystem-based aquaculture is the key to the sector becoming more sustainable, productive, efficient, and environment-friendly (e.g., Costa-Pierce 2002).

Pullin et al. (forthcoming) used 1984-95 FAO data and estimated 1950-1983 data to show the astonishing historical expansion of aquaculture (fig. 5.1). Note, however, that the rates of increase for all of the major commodity groups are slowing.

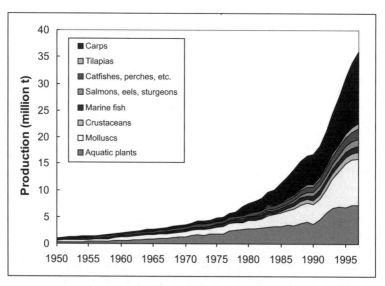

Fig. 5.1 Contributions of major commodity groups to aquatic production from 1950-1995. For 1984-1995, the data used were FAO aquaculture statistics. The FAO did not separate aquaculture production statistics before 1984. For the period 1984 to 1987, FAO catch and aquaculture data, for species, countries and FAO areas, were used to determine aquaculture total production ratios and these were then applied to over 1,600 cases to generate 1980-1983 data. Source: Pullin et al. (forthcoming).

Box 5.1 Milkfish (*Chanos chanos*) pen culture in Laguna de Bay, Philippines: An example of entrepreneurial aquaculture that boomed and then declined

Milkfish *(Chanos chanos)* has long been one of the Philippines' most popular food fishes. Its herbivorous feeding habits (filtering phytoplankton and grazing on benthic algal felts) made it an ideal species for pen culture in Laguna de Bay, a shallow eutrophic lake of 90,000 ha., adjacent to Metropolitan Manila. Following the success of a single experimental bamboo pen in 1970, entrepreneurs constructed over 7,000 ha of pens by 1976, yielding about 7 mt.ha^{-1}.yr^{-1} (Pullin 1981). This began as truly low-input, extensive aquaculture, growing fish mainly on natural feeds. Rapid over-expansion and intensification followed, with huge pens (some around 50 ha) resembling aquatic ranches. These were mostly owned by the rich and powerful, while poor traditional fishers were excluded from more and more of the lake. The pen area peaked at around 34,000 ha and by 1992 had declined to about 2,800 ha; with yields down to about 3.8mt.ha^{-1}.yr^{-1}, mainly because of water pollution and turbidity problems (Pullin 1993).

Author: Roger Pullin

Box 5.2 Cage culture in Indonesian reservoirs: An example of donor-driven aquaculture development, with unforeseen social and environmental consequences

From 1985 to 1988, the construction of the two new reservoirs (Saguling and Cirata), near Bandung, W. Java, Indonesia, displaced over 40,000 families. This development was part of a World Bank project. Cage and land-based aquaculture were explored as potential livelihoods for 3,000 resettled families. Production of carps and tilapias from the reservoirs grew rapidly, reaching 24,500 mt in 1996. However, the very success of this reservoir cage culture resulted in it being taken away from the displaced families, who were the intended beneficiaries, by rich urban operators. Government and local regulations failed to prevent this. For example, a permit system restricting access to *bona fide* displaced families to 4 cages per family was not enforced. Overexpansion and intensification followed. In 1992, 7,933 mt of fish were produced, compared to a plan that called for 6,390 mt. By 1996, there were 25,588 fish cages, compared to the reservoirs' calculated maximum carrying capacity of 10,600, and the cages were concentrated into a few convenient areas. Serious environmental fish kills caused by oxygen depletion began in 1993, with losses of 500 mt between 1994 and 1995.

Source: Summarized from Costa-Pierce (1998)

The expansion of aquaculture has been typified by boom-and-bust development, with new ventures constantly emerging (see boxes 1-3). This complicates production forecasting based on the past. Moreover, despite its overall long history, aquaculture is still very new in many countries (including most of Africa and Latin America) and, contrary to popular belief, in large areas of most Asian countries.

Governance Issues in Aquaculture

The track record of aquaculture development to date reflects the fact that a governance approach has been generally lacking. A comprehensive listing of major governance issues in aquaculture has yet to be attempted, but most current opinions suggest that it would include the following:
- lessening adverse ecological effects;
- focusing on the net social benefit of aquaculture rather than private profits to private fish farmers;
- taking into account the income distribution and poverty alleviation effects of aquaculture;
- giving due consideration to long-term net benefits rather than short-term benefits.

These and other issues that affect the growth and sustainability of aquaculture are all diverse, complex, and dynamic. This is illustrated here by brief reviews on the feeding of farmed fish; environmental impacts and biosafety; equity and ethics; what and where to farm; and intersectoral relationships.

Feeding Farmed Fish

In intensive aquaculture, the cost of feeding is almost always about 60-70% of the total variable costs of production. Feed costs and feed conversion are the main determinants of profitability. An intense debate continues about the extent to which the availability and cost of fish feed ingredients (particularly fishmeal and fish oil) will limit expansion and sustainability of aquaculture. The basic question is whether aquaculture that consumes fish and other animal protein is augmenting fisheries production, thereby lessening pressures on aquatic ecosystems, or actually increasing those pressures? There is an extensive literature on this (e.g., Naylor et al. 1998, 2000; Roth et al. 2001; New and Wijkström 2002; Tidwell and Allan 2002; Tuominen and Esmark 2003) and general agreement that fish feed manufacturers will have to reduce their reliance on fishmeal and fish oil. According to New and Wijkström (2002), the global fish feed industry has the potential to utilise 70% of the average historical fishmeal supply by the year 2015, thereby putting it in increasingly severe competition with livestock feeds and other uses, with consequent price increases. For fish oil, New and Wijkström (2002) found that the global fish feed industry could require more than its average historical supply before 2010.

One approach to reducing fishmeal and fish oil requirements is to farm fish that are naturally herbivorous or omnivorous – as are all the major livestock that are farmed on land. Fish and other farmed aquatic organisms can be categorised according to their trophic levels, which are calculated by estimating the proportions of their diets that are derived from plant and animal sources. Primary producer organisms (plants, phytoplankton, detritus and its associated micro-organisms) eaten by fish are assigned a level of 1, zooplankton a level of 2, and so on up the food chain. Trophic levels and their applications are fully explained in FishBase (Froese and Pauly 1999; www.fishbase.org).

Given the diversity of farmed finfish, Pullin et al. (forthcoming) tracked their historical (1950-1995) mean trophic levels by region, based upon information on their natural feeding habits. Their analysis suggested little change in the overall trophic levels of farmed fish, but increasing levels for aquaculture in Europe and the Americas. By reviewing FAO data to 2000, Tacon (2003) found that aquaculture in the developed countries comprised: 2.4% filter feeders (mainly bighead and silver carps), 50,602 mt; 20.7% omnivores/herbivores, 489,390 mt; and 73.8% carnivores, 1,521,781 mt. The developing country equivalents were: 27.2% filter feeders, 5,712,512; 65.7% omnivores/herbivores, 13,811,585 mt; and 7% carnivores, 1,631,729 mt. This suggests broad differences between aquaculture in the South and the North, with the former still less dependent upon fishmeal- and fish oil-based feeds than the latter. However, farmed fish often feed at higher trophic levels than wild fish of the same species, and intensification has raised the trophic levels of most farmed herbivorous/omnivorous fish. For example, intensive cage culture of Nile tilapia (*Oreochromis niloticus*) in the Philippines uses feeds that resemble chicken feeds, often with higher protein contents. Such fish feeds contain fishmeal and fish oil, as do almost all fish feeds to varying extents. Farming the world's most widely farmed freshwater fish, common carp (*Cyprinus carpio*), which is omnivorous, consumed 64,000 mt of fishmeal and 13,000 mt of fish oil in 1999 and could require 117,000 and 58,000 mt, respectively, by 2015 (New and Wijkström 2002).

There are many diverse plant, animal, and microbial proteins that can be used to replace fishmeal in feeds. Despite constraints such as anti-nutritional factors, availability cost, feed palatability, and flavour (e.g., Hardy and Green 1999; New and Wijkström 2002), some fish feed manufacturers have been able to reduce their reliance on fishmeal. Tidwell and Allan (2002) pointed to a decrease of the fishmeal content of feeds for channel catfish (*Ictalurus punctatus*) (not a strict carnivore) from 8-10% in 1990 to less than 3% in 2002. El-Saidy and Gaber (2002) succeeded in complete replacement of fishmeal in Nile tilapia feed with soybean meal and L-lysine supplementation. Parallel to this work, there was an attempt to incorporate a legume meal as a protein source for rainbow trout (*Oncorhynchus mykiss*) in sea cages (Glencross et al. 2002). There are numerous similar studies – the aims being to push farmed carnivorous fish towards what is for them unnatural herbivory, and intensively farmed herbivorous fish back towards their natural herbivory, with varying success.

The replacement of fish oils with alternative lipid sources in fish feeds is much more difficult than replacing fishmeal with alternative protein sources, which is essentially just substituting sources of the same amino acids, with extra supplementation where necessary. Changing the lipid profile and overall lipid content of fish feeds can have marked effects on product composition and flavour, as well as on feed energy content and consequent growth (New and Wijkström 2002). Research continues on replacement of fish oils with diverse plant and animal fats and the use of some of the latter would have problems of acceptability for some consumers. For example, the 'white fat' used in experimental fish feeds by Martino et al. (2003) is pig lard.

Current overall opinion appears to be that research to replace fish oils in fish feeds will be significantly successful, but that fish oils will always be needed to some extent. The likely natural sources of an increased supply of marine oils include the same sources to be targeted for increased fishmeal production; e.g., deep-sea fish species, krill (*Euphausia superba*), and fish and crustacean processing wastes (New and Wijkström 2002). Capture fisheries and aquaculture are becoming increasingly interdependent.

Research on and utilisation of livestock and fish by-products in fish feeds continues to grow (e.g., Bureau 2000; Bharadwaj et al. 2002) and the EU has recently reviewed the possible risks and necessary safeguards (European Commission 2003). The complexity of governing this has become very clear in recent years. Changing the natural nutritional regimes of farmed species can have negative consequences. Intensification of feedlot farming systems implies least cost formulation of feeds, using all available ingredients. Wrong choices here can have negative consequences for product quality and for fish health and public health. The same applies in agriculture. Cattle are herbivores. Bovine Spongivorm Encyphalopathy BSE in cattle arose from feeds containing inadequately processed livestock offal. Dioxins in feeds have been another serious problem and the EU has proposed dioxin limits in fishmeal, fish oil, and fish feeds (New and Wikström 2002).

Environmental Impacts and Biosafety

Aquaculture has been much criticised for adverse environmental impacts. Some of this criticism is unfair when seen in the context of the environmental impacts of other sectors, particularly those of agriculture, capture fisheries and forestry. However, aquaculture does have a flawed environmental track record, mostly from circumstances where its rapid expansion has overridden environmental safeguards. Folke and Kautsky (1992: 6) summarised the problems thus:

> The recent expansion of intensive aquaculture world-wide has caused severe environmental damage to coastal ecosystems. Rapid-growth (sic) and mono-culturing methods have led to socio-economic and environmental problems.

Pullin et al. (1993) compiled reviews on the wide diversity and dynamics of environmental issues in developing-country aquaculture. These include: pollution by waste feeds and fish excreta; overuse of antibiotics and other chemicals; changes to and losses of natural habitats; displacement of traditional fishers; alien species; and genetic impacts on wild stocks, etc. A recent compilation of ecological issues in aquaculture, with more emphasis on northern examples (Davenport et al. 2003) covers essentially the same range of issues, showing that there are many common issues and problems, North and South. They also apply across all aquaculture subsectors: inland and coastal; fresh-, brackish and seawater; extensive, semi-intensive and intensive; hatchery, nursery and grow-out.

The complexity of some biosafety issues in aquaculture can be illustrated by the example of the ongoing debate on genetically modified organisms (GMOs). The Convention on Biological Diversity (CBD 1994) and its Cartagena Protocol (CBD 2000) take a narrow perspective on biosafety, as meaning essentially the safe use of so-called Living Modified Organisms (LMOs). These are organisms engineered by gene transfer. The public usually calls them GMOs. Aquatic GMOs are under development, though none have yet entered the human food chain. GM crops command most of the world's attention, with far less given to biosafety in a broader sense, especially in the aquatic realm, where it requires a broader perspective.

The current narrow perspective on GMOs ignores the obvious fact that hybridisation is a form of genetic modification. Hybrid fish are obviously novel organisms: genetically altered, by comparison with their parents. Some hybrid fish (including probably all interspecific tilapia hybrids) are fertile. According to most current definitions and perceptions, however, hybrid fish are not LMOs or GMOs. Hybrids, like alien aquatic species (whether genetically altered or not) and indeed *all* farmed fish that have been altered genetically from their wild relatives by any procedure (not just gene transfer) can have impacts upon wild fish and ecosystems. Their impacts may include: predation; competition for food, shelter and breeding sites; transmission of diseases and parasites; and direct genetic impacts through interbreeding. In terms of biosafety and of responsible development of aquaculture together with conservation of wild genetic resources, prior appraisal of the potential impacts of movement of farmed fish across watersheds and other ecological boundaries is as important as that for movements across national and other political boundaries. Moreover, the precaution needed applies to all alien and genetically altered fish, not just to GMOs in the narrow sense. The Consensus Statement from an ICLARM-FAO Bellagio Conference 'Towards Policies for Conservation and Sustainable Use of Aquatic Genetic Resources' (Pullin et al. 1999) included the following (p. 253):

> (We) recognise that in the formulation of biosafety policy and regulations for living modified organisms, the characteristics of the organisms and of potentially accessible environments are more important considerations than the processes used to produce those organisms.

A governance approach would help to address the diversity, complexity, and dynamics of biosafety in aquaculture, broadening the perspectives of its many actors and stakeholders and facilitating institutional and policy development.

Equity and Ethics

In agriculture, ownership of and access to biodiversity, genetic resources, biotechnology and related information are equity and ethical issues that have become increasingly controversial, especially over plant genetic resources, biotechnology and related information (e.g., Crucible Group 2000; Pardey et al. 2003). Concerns range from the rights of Parties to the CBD over their national genetic resources and the rights of indigenous peoples to the resources of their lands and waters and their traditional knowledge, to private and corporate intellectual property rights on genetically enhanced material. The same concerns arise in aquaculture (Pullin

1998; Bartley and Pullin 1999). Ownership of and access to lands and waters for aquaculture are often highly conflictual, with outcomes generally detrimental to the poor and to the natural resources upon which they depend (see boxes 5.1 and 5.2 above). A governance approach would help to limit and to resolve such conflicts. Ownership of and access to natural resources, biotechnology, and related information for aquaculture are governance issues.

The rights and welfare of farmed animals are considered important ethical concerns and affect the public's acceptance of farming methods and of farmed produce, especially in the North. Recent contributions to the relevance of this for aquaculture were reviewed by New (2003), who cited a European Parliament Resolution (2003) that recognises fish welfare concerns in aquaculture. This area of aquaculture ethics is, however, relatively new and is at present dominated by issues such as the ethics of feeding fish to fish in an increasingly fish-poor world and to the use of GM fish, rather than on fish welfare and avoidance of cruelty.

What to Farm and Where to Farm?

At the husbandry and public acceptability levels, the future of aquaculture will depend upon developing good domesticated breeds that can be farmed profitably and equitably, without unacceptable environmental impacts. The huge diversity of potentially farmable aquatic species might appear more of an asset here than a constraint – but things are not that simple. The domestication of any aquatic species is a lengthy and costly undertaking, involving the development of captive breeding, hatchery and nursery technology, husbandry, disease control, etc. Moreover, there is the fundamental question of whether it is worth investing in the domestication of species whose farming might not be profitable for long (for example, because of high feed costs) or permissible on a wide scale because of biosafety and other environmental concerns. For example, Bridger et al. (2001) described the prospects for offshore mariculture in the Gulf of Mexico. All of the species considered are undomesticated, strict carnivores: red drum (*Sciaenops ocellatus*), red snapper (*Lutjanus campechanus*), and cobia (*Rachycentron canadum*). To farm these species means high costs for feeds and hurricane-proof containment facilities. On the other hand, the increasing market prices of some predatory fish favour such enterprises. For example, fillets of cod (*Gadus morhua*) (also a carnivore) were retailing at 5 Pounds Sterling per pound in London at the end of 2002. Cod farming commenced in Norway in 1987 and production had risen to 167 mt by 2000 (FAO 2003b).

Another area of debate is what to do when there are no obvious native species that fit available farming sites. For example, there are many thousands of hectares of underutilised brackish water coastal ponds in Southeast Asia in which farmers would like to grow fish as well as or instead of shrimp. The only obvious candidates among native species are: the Asian seabass (*Lates calcarifer*), a strict carnivore; the milkfish (*Chanos chanos*), a herbivore with no significant markets beyond Indonesia, the Philippines and Taiwan; and the mullets (*Mugilidae*), also herbivores but with limited markets and underdeveloped hatchery technology. This has led to research and development using alien species, especially brackishwater tilapias (e.g., Tayamen et al. 2002) some of which has been done without prior appraisal of possible environmental impacts. The same applies in freshwater aquaculture, where common carp and Nile tilapia have become widely farmed as alien species, sometimes (e.g., Nile tilapia in the Philippines) where there are no good native equivalent species for aquaculture. Where aquaculture uses, out of genuine necessity and lack of native alternatives, alien species and genetically altered organisms, parallel and effective programmes for the conservation of natural biodiversity and genetic resources are essential. In many cases this will mean allowing aquaculture in some waters and prohibiting it in others. These are complex situations. What and where to farm are governance issues – hard choices for policymakers and investors.

Intersectoral Relationships

The future of aquaculture will also depend upon the extent to which not only its diversity but also its interdependence and scope for synergy with other sectors are recognised. If policymakers, legislators and developers fail to recognise the diversity of aquaculture and treat it as a separate food production sector, many opportunities for synergy in improving food security and the environmental and socioeconomic aspects of food production will be missed. The costs and benefits of different aquaculture operations can be compared with each other and with other methods of food production. For example, Folke and Kautsky (1992) compared fossil fuel energy needs (table 5.1).

The intersectoral needs and opportunities for aquaculture (especially freshwater aquaculture, have led to the concept of 'integrated aquaculture' (e.g., Lightfoot et al. 1993; Edwards 1998). Here, the key intersectoral resource is water itself. Aquaculture is obviously a potential partner in water resources management and multiple use/reuse of water, but has not yet received adequate consideration in the large and expanding programme of the Global Water Partnership (GWP) and others. The water resources sector is in crisis: 'a crisis of governance' (GWP 2002a). The water resources sector has made claims to be gearing up for 'integrated water resources management' (e.g., GWP 2002a), but the potential for food production in water itself has not yet been recognised sufficiently (e.g., Zalewski et al. 1997). Rather, integration is still envisaged largely in terms of securing domestic and industrial supply and crop irrigation (maximizing 'crop per drop'; e.g., GWP 2002b). Large opportunities to farm fish in waters that are managed for other purposes (e.g., crop irrigation, waste treatment) are being missed.

Table 5.1 Estimates of inputs of fossil fuel energy for the production of various foods

Food type	Kilocalories of fossil energy input per kilocalorie of protein output
Seaweed culturing	1
Vegetable crops	2-4
Mussel rearing	10
Sheep farming	10
Cod fisheries	20
Broiler farming	22
Cage-farming of rainbow trout	24
Atlantic salmon fisheries	29
Pacific salmon fisheries	18-30
Pig raising	35
King salmon fisheries	40
Cage-farming of Atlantic salmon	50
Feedlot beef production	20-78
Lobster fisheries	192
Shrimp fisheries	3-198

Source: Condensed from Folke and Kautsky (1992), omitting entries on ranching, original sources and assumptions.

The intersectoral relationships of aquaculture will depend mostly upon the 'ecological soundness' of aquaculture operations, as described by Lightfoot and Noble (2001) for farming systems. The two main attributes of ecological soundness in an integrated farming system are high diversity of enterprises and extensive recycling through bioresource flows. Lightfoot and Noble (2001) included diversity and recycling, along with profitability and productivity, as their four main indicators for sustainability. McIntosh (2002) pointed out that achieving productivity, profitability, and good environmental relations for aquaculture will succeed because of 'technical solutions'. Costa-Pierce (2002) is optimistic for the evolution of 'ecological aquaculture' and for its coexistence and synergy with other sectors.

Governance in Aquaculture: Interactions are the Key

The development of responsible and sustainable aquaculture is high on the agendas of many actors at the international, regional, national, and local levels (e.g., Creswell and Flos 2002) and is being accompanied by high investment. The FAO (1997a, 2003b) and the NACA/FAO (2000) provide codes of practice and guidelines for aquaculture. Numerous frameworks, flowcharts and aids for responsible and sustainable aquaculture are also available (e.g., NTAS 1998; Ackefors and White 2002; Des Clers and

Nauen 2002; Pullin et al. forthcoming). Boyd (2003) has reviewed emerging best management practices in aquaculture. The Joint Group of Experts on the Scientific Aspects of Marine Environmental Protection is working on new guidelines for environmental risk assessment and communication in coastal aquaculture (www.fao.org/fi/publ/report/gesamp). The International Council for the Exploration of the Sea has a Working Group on 'Mariculture-Environment Interactions'. As an example at the national level, the US Environmental Protection Agency has introduced a new 'water quality trading policy' as a mechanism for cleaning up watercourses (http://www.epa.gov/owow/watershed/trading.htm). Organic aquaculture is also gaining strength and is being defined broadly, encompassing not only exclusion of the use of chemicals but also promotion of low-trophic level species (www.fw.umn.edu/isees/Organic/Aquaculture/Workshop/finalrep.pdf).

The diversity, complexity, and dynamics of the above-mentioned scenarios, and of the many other actors, institutions, mechanisms, organisations, and stakeholders concerned with aquaculture, suggest a governance approach. At all levels, the main elements that require strengthening are adequate and effective *interactions*. For example, at the sectoral level, conflicts between aquaculture development and natural resources conservation will persist until both are conceived, planned, adequately financed and administered interactively. The same applies to the interrelationships among aquaculture, agriculture, navigation, tourism, waste treatment, water supply, and other sectors that use land and water. Many of the conflicts among these sectors could be lessened or avoided by interactions. Many opportunities for intersectoral partnerships and synergy are being missed because of the lack of effective interactions. Aquaculture is as legitimate a user of land, water, and other resources as any of the above-mentioned sectors but is, in most cases, a relative newcomer compared to their long histories. Interactive governance of water space and of water itself (especially freshwater) is crucial for aquaculture to play an increasing and responsible role in supplying fish for food security, in concert with other resource users.

A recent special issue of *Marine Resource Economics* (vol. 17, no. 2, 2002) is entirely devoted to aquaculture. In its Introduction, Asche and Tveteras (2002: 73) stated the following:

> During the last 25 years, aquaculture production has changed from a minor, relatively unimportant contributor to the world's seafood supply (about 7% in 1975) to constituting about one third of supply in 2000. This has of course changed seafood consumption patterns substantially, and therefore market structure.

In the same volume, Anderson (2002) imagined a group of fisheries experts sitting down to dine on salmon and shrimp and discussing ongoing problems in open access fisheries, etc. He suggested (while acknowledging that this was a bit unfair) that they would be oblivious to the fact that they were eating the produce of the *future* of fisheries (aquaculture) while continuing to focus on its *past* (the irretrievable yields of capture fisheries). So, here is the hard choice for policymakers, researchers, educators, entrepreneurs, and regulators – how to strike a balance between investments in aquaculture development and fisheries rehabilitation? Both are, of course, vital to the future of fisheries governance for food security.

6

The Post-Harvest Chain

Andy Thorpe, Stella Williams, and Jacques van Zyl

Introduction

The journey from trawler to table (or farm to fridge in the case of aquaculture) can be swift or extended. In many developing countries the path is usually short with the catch being sold fresh either from the quay-side or beach or in an adjacent market. However, the fish chain is extended when processing – curing, smoking, pickling, salting, drying, freezing or burying – is undertaken, although the destination of the final transformed product may remain local. Canning – preserving and protecting the product – affords additional commercial opportunities, while the despatch of fish to inland or overseas markets further lengthens the chain.

As humans consume over one thousand species of fish extracted from a variety of ecological habitats and geographic quarters across the world – the ensuing fish chains are inevitably disparate, being a reflection (to varying degrees) of local, national, regional and global market arrangements and the socio-cultural settings in which harvesting, processing, distributing and consuming take place. Moreover, the complexity of the chain has evolved over time. One of the consequences of the creation of Exclusive Economic zones, and with it the establishment of Extended Fisheries Jurisdiction, has been a marked growth in the national fleet of coastal nations, often aided and abetted by a favourable macroeconomic policy environment, particularly regarding subsidies (Thorpe et al. 2000; Milazzo 1998). The recent exponential growth of aquaculture production has added to this complexity, whilst the increased global integration of fish markets has contributed to a dramatic growth in the international fish trade, up from 4.5 million metric tonnes (mt) in 1960 (export value US$1.3 billion) to 42.9 million mt (export value US$52.9 billion) in 1999 (Ruckes 1995; FAO 1999b).

This growth has highlighted the relationship between fisheries management decisions and events in seafood markets (Johnston and Wilson 1987). While regulatory policies may be associated with lost market opportunities if fishers are prevented or dissuaded from extracting high-quality products (as is the case with the growth of 'no-take' reserves, for example), it is equally true that changes in market conditions may have undesirable implications for those boat owners, shellfish collectors or aquaculturists at the beginning of the supply chain (as was the case with the US embargos on Mexican tuna imports during the eighties). In other words, as market-occasioned disruptions may reverberate throughout the chain in the same detrimental way that a collapse in fish stocks will, it is as necessary to understand both market organisation and the governance measures operating in the post-harvest supply chain as it is those at the point of resource capture.

An understanding of post-harvest fish chains and the way they function is imperative then in the context of the fundamental concerns highlighted earlier (see chap. 2), specifically with regard to:

– *Livelihoods and Employment:* Macfadyen (2002) estimates that while the numbers directly involved in marine and inland capture fisheries was in the order of 5.8 million in 2001, this figure was overshadowed by the 64.2 million individuals employed in either post-harvest operations and/or the input supply chain. Consequently, governance measures affecting the post-harvest sector have the potential of having an impact on significantly more livelihoods than measures whose effects are restricted to just the harvesting process.

– *Social Justice:* Concerns that market arrangements are neither free nor fair are frequently expressed in fisheries texts (Reid 2000). However, effective governance measures designed to redress such post-harvest inequities will need to acknowledge existing market arrangements, seeking to moderate exploitative chain relationships whilst not alienating those middlemen (or women) whose current market power could allow them to frustrate or undermine the proposed changes.

– *Food Security and Food Quality:* Fish can be a key component in a country's national food security strategy. The FAO (2003c) notes that fish protein accounted for 82% of animal protein intake on the Solomon Islands in 1997-9, and its contribution to total animal protein intake was over 40% in another 15 developing countries. Governance measures that impinge on chain direction then (for example, tariffs on imported fish products), can have profound effects upon trade patterns and, consequently, national – or local – food security objectives. Moreover, given the highly perishable and fragile nature of the product, quality considerations are also an imperative part of the distribution equation. As spoilage is an irreversible process, quality control and assurance systems are important safeguards (providing they function effectively), in ensuring fish products of an acceptable standard for human consumption.

In light of these concerns, this chapter seeks to document the complexity of contemporary fish chains, and how market arrangements and governance measures may vary across such chains. The paper commences by proposing a framework, derived from the work of Folkerts and Koehorst (1998), which permits the analysis of the organisational structure of fish chains. Second, it documents how such chains have evolved over time. Recourse to a continuum of spatially (local, national, regional, and international) differentiated African fish chains allows us to illustrate how the highlighted concerns manifest themselves in practice. Finally, the fourth section examines specifically how issues relating to food quality are incorporated into these chains, and it reviews the governance measures entrusted with improving/upholding these standards.

The Fish Supply Chain

The management of the supply process has provoked an enormous general supply chain literature (Handfield and Nichols Jr. 1996; Copesino 1997; Poirier 1999; Simchi-Levi and Philip-Kaminsky 1999), a literature which principally focuses on managing the logistics of the process (Hahn and Ribeiro 1999; Shein 2000; Hoffman and Mehra 2000; Van der Voorst et al. 2000). However, such literature invariably takes for granted that, by conceptualising the process as a chain, the interdependence of the constituent parts (or links) is implicitly recognised, the idea being that no participant in the chain is an island but that their livelihoods are determined by the actions of others within the chain as much as, if not more than by their own individual actions. Consequently, as trading relationships grow and supply chains are progressively fine-tuned, the emergence of governance measures are evermore important to ensure that profits/returns are maximised at the chain level. Moreover, particularly within the food sector, ethical and health concerns are ensuring that these governance measures are becoming increasingly consumer-driven, as the recent furore over both Bovine Spongiform Encephalopathy (BSE) and Genetically Modified Organisms (GMOs) foods has only too clearly demonstrated.

Folkerts and Koehorst (1998) embrace the consumer-driven supply chain ('chain reversal' as they term it) thesis in advocating an approach to chain management which focuses on improved governance of chain strategy and activities. They identify nine key fields of interest, distinguishing between the participants involved, the activities undertaken, and the final outcome (fig. 6.1).

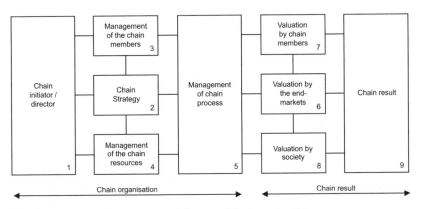

Fig. 6.1 The supply chain. *Source: Folkerts and Koehorst (1998).*

The chain strategy (fig. 6.1 [2]) can be determined exclusively by an individual, company or association, or in conjunction with other chain members (the chain 'director', fig. 6.1 [1]). Management of the chain process (fig. 6.1 [5]) and members and resources therein (fig. 6.1 [3, 4]) can be somewhat restrictive – with a regulatory body emerging to ensure that participants adhere to certain agreed rules, or relatively autonomous – where chain members are largely at liberty to make their own decisions or pursue their own goals. The consequence of these decisions – the chain outcome – can be evaluated in both monetary (valuation by end-markets, fig. 6.1 [6]) and non-monetary (valuation by chain members and society, fig. 6.1 [6,7]) terms. More effective chain integration, perhaps via the introduction of new institutional arrangements, affords the opportunity to augment market, participant or societal returns (fig. 6.1 [6-8]). Marsden et al. (2000), for example, show how beef farmers in the Llyn Peninsula in Wales elected to form a cooperative to improve the collective strength of farmers in the supply chain and, by a more judicious marketing of the product's origin in line with consumer demands for naturally-reared beef, increase produced returns. This new organisation, the Llyn Beef Producers Cooperative (LBPC), also enhanced chain governance by building up a closer relationship with retailers and securing a contract with a major wholesaler. Chain reorganisation in this way resulted in LBPC beef generating a £24 per head price premium (£108 compared to £84) in the end-market (fig. 6.1 [6]), almost doubled producer margins and local abattoir returns (fig. 6.1 [7]) and led to greater customer satisfaction (fig. 6.1 [8]).

Folkerts and Koehorst's model is a potentially useful tool, then, for analysing the myriad of fish supply chains that prevail across the globe. Past work on the theme is certainly sparse, with most fisheries researchers electing to focus on consumer demand for fish products (Wessells and Anderson 1992; Kirman 1994; Graham et al. 1998; Young and Muir 2002 [on tilapia]) or processing techniques (Ali 1964; FAO 1985; Essuman 1992) rather than the underlying supply chain that both conveys and transforms the commodity between trawler and table. The exceptions are the now somewhat outdated studies by Kazmierski and Formela (1964), who examined the organisational set-up behind the distribution of fish in Poland; an article by Ruckes (1972) that details some of the major [dis]similiarities in marketing fresh and frozen fish across five countries with a view to improving the planning of fish marketing systems in developing countries; a TPI Conference report (1977) on fish marketing in developing countries; and a conference paper by Young (1986) that surveyed developments in the UK fish marketing environment since the 1970s. More recently – while reviews of the fish marketing systems in Guinea, Togo, the South West province of Cameroon, the Solomon Islands and France (Kamphorst 1994; JICA 1994; Amegavie 1995; Diallo et al. 1996; Mariojouls and de Lesquen 1997) have been published – no schematic attempt to synthesise the findings of such research, much less derive an appropriate analytical framework for understanding how fish supply chains function, has been undertaken. It is this lacuna in the literature that this paper seeks to address.

The Temporal Evolution of Fish Supply Chains

While fish chains date from early human history, Zohar et al. (2001) documented how coastal archaeological sites have disclosed evidence of Neolithic man (8140-7550 BC) gutting and processing grey triggerfish with a view to future consumption or trade, detailed information on the chain itself is of more modern origin. Kowaleski (2000) notes how the sale of fish in England was one of the most heavily regulated medieval trades, as local and national authorities intervened in an attempt to shorten the chain by encouraging fishers to sell directly to the consumers.

The relative failure of such governance measures was consequently superseded by the delegation of control over the chain to sanctioned fishmongers or fish-traders. The Guild of Fishmongers in London, for example, attempted to assert its authority over the whole chain process (fig. 6.1 [5]) in London by decreeing that fish could only be sold wholesale from vessels, with only Guild members being permitted to purchase fish for resale (Kowaleski 2000) in the mid-thirteenth century. Although the objective of such arrangements was to guarantee reasonable prices to consumers (fig. 6.1 [8]), in practice the delegation of regulatory powers allowed price manipulation and, from the 13th century onwards, various reform measures designed to lower prices were introduced. National legislation to oversee the activities of foreign merchants had been introduced by the early fifteenth century, while the London monopoly was (unsuccessfully) challenged by a reformist mayor in the late 14th century. Many towns and boroughs also began to appoint inspectors to oversee the operation of local fish markets, investing in such inspectors the duty to uphold quality standards and regulate prices, although the great fairs of the day in Exeter, Scarborough, Saltfleethaven, and Great Yarmouth, amongst others, were generally less supervised.

While the supply of fresh fish had a limited spatial distribution due to the innate perishability of the product, lengthier fish chains emerged temporarily in times of high seasonal demand (between Advent and Lent) when the higher returns available offset the probability of greater spoilage rates, and/or in instances where the product had been cured. Curing contributed to the development and expansion of an international fish chain from the mid-thirteenth century onwards as English merchants journeyed to Skånia (Sweden) to purchase salted herring, Norwegian skippers brought dried and salted cod to the east coast of Britain, and Irish vessels supplied the south and west with salted herring, salmon and hake (Childs 2000). International market arrangements were in constant flux as different states made periodic attempts to wrest management of the chain to advantage domestic stakeholders. Childs (2000), for example, notes how Hansard merchants successfully petitioned for the enactment of legislation that prohibited English merchants from setting up salting and barrelling stations in Skånia in 1369. Sometimes, however, policies were conceived with different ends in mind – and domestic participants in the chain were penalised over their foreign counterparts. The British salt tax was a case in point. Introduced with a view to help fund domestic and international military endeavours, the *ad valorem* tax rose from 5% in the 1600s to 1,500% in 1815 and, by effectively ensuring that British fishers could not compete with foreign competitors in producing Icelandic salted cod, forced both domestic fleet and merchants out of the Anglo-Icelandic fish chain (Jones 2000).

Box 6.1 Technological change and its impact on the UK post-harvest herring chain

The evolution of post-harvest herring processing in the UK exemplifies the 'triumph' of modern capital-intensive production over traditional artisanal organisation and products, the effects of changing patterns of trade and consumption, and the decline of a way of life. After centuries of attempting to emulate Dutch success in this trade, the trade 'took off' in early nineteenth century Scotland, stimulated by the repeal of punitive salt taxes, abolition of subsidies that perversely discouraged investment, and strict quality controls (Coull, 1996). Britain had become Europe's leading producer of cured herring by 1914, Scottish production rising on average by some 3% per annum in the century to 1913 to around 275,000 mt. Curing was overwhelmingly labour-intensive, undertaken by small artisanal firms mainly employing women gutters and packers. Together they constituted an itinerant community following the fishing, endlessly romanticised by contemporaries and historians (Thompson, 1983). The trade was, however, severely disrupted by the inter-war trade depression and changing consumer tastes. Following the axiom of 'the maximum of maximum production', the Herring Industry Board supported the introduction of mechanisation, quick-freezing and fishmeal production after 1945 (Reid, 1998), a tendency towards capital-intensity evident elsewhere in the British fish processing trades (Reid and Robinson, forthcoming). This reflected the consumer's ever-increasing desire for more highly processed fish products (Reid, forthcoming) and the difficulties of recruiting labour to the trade in competition with cleaner and more remunerative employment alternatives. The effect of new technology was quick and irreversible: traditional artisanal herring processing had been reduced to about one-tenth of herring processing by the late 1950s. When the North Sea herring fisheries collapsed in the mid-1970s traditional herring products had long been replaced by mass-produced alternatives and an occupational community had ceased to exist.

Author: Chris Reid

The complexity and sensitivity of the fish chain has been heightened in more recent times by technological change (both curing and transportation practices), sometimes with devastating effects upon traditional artisanal processors (see box 6.1). The invention (in 1809) and subsequent commercial utilisation of canning techniques increased fish trade, as did the advent of freezing methods at the turn of the subsequent century (Asche and Bernard 2000). However, as both frozen and canned fish are imperfect substitutes for the fresh variety, the impact of such developments was to introduce new niche markets, thereby creating a more complex web of interlocking fish chains, rather than increasing the organisational complexity of existing fish chains. Improved transportation options, most notably the use of air-freight, has not only permitted the spatial expansion of fish trade (fresh, frozen and cured) into relatively remote areas, but has also increased chain sensitivity – a sudden and unexpected rise in fish prices in London for example, is likely to be reflected in rapid upward price movements for the same fish on European, and perhaps even global, markets. Nevertheless, while the overall complexity and sensitivity of the aggregate fish chain has increased, the underlying route from trawler to table remains the same (fig. 6.2).

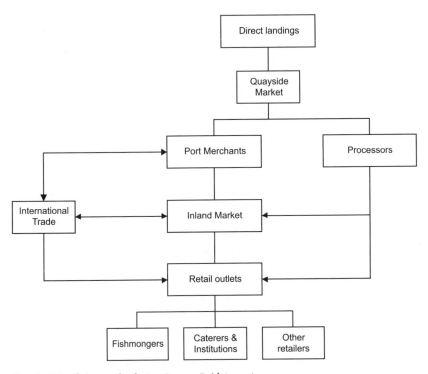

Fig. 6.2 The fish supply chain. *Source: Reid (2000).*

What has changed is simply the number of individuals, organisations, operations, and processes contained in the boxes (and the institutional arrangements governing the interaction between them). Historically, as Zohar et al. (2001) note, processing was undertaken at the household level using rudimentary gutting and preservation techniques. Although Young (1986) suggests the UK fish processing industry encompassed 2,095 plants deploying a variety of equipment and techniques and spread across the fresh, canned and frozen processing sectors in 1983, nevertheless, the underlying processing objective is the same; to transform the product into a commodity with a longer shelf-life that remains attractive to the purchaser.

Equally, the preoccupations expressed regarding the chain's operation remain the same, namely that, (i) fish markets are neither free nor fair, (ii) returns to the trade's participants are excessive, and (iii) quality considerations have been disregarded (Reid 2000). Yet such preoccupations clearly relate to the market arrangements and governance measures embedded within the different fish chains and so, for the purposes of this chapter, we prefer to reformulate such preoccupations slightly so as to reconcile them with the fundamental concerns highlighted in chapter 2. First, as regards to market valuation (fig. 6.1 [6]) – *are fish markets free and fair? Are the returns on offer sufficient to sustain the livelihoods and employment of current and future participants – or is there a tendency for post-harvest operations to become more concentrated over time? Equally important, is the market valuation process tending to reinforce food security or to undermine it?* Second, social justice demands that benefits should primarily reach the most impoverished within the post-harvesting sector. This requires 'active participation of the rural poor ... as both agents and beneficiaries' (FAO 2002c:1.4), so *how do chain members view their involvement in the post-harvest process (fig. 6.1 [7])? In other words, is the chain a participatory one, or do certain stakeholders exert undue pressure over organisation of the chain, division of the spoils, etc. (fig. 6.1 [5])?* Finally, given that society places a high value on food safety (fig. 6.1 [8]), *how is product quality maintained/improved within the chain? What quality assurance mechanisms exist, or are planned, and are they sufficient to safeguard human health and/or ethical concerns?* The next section addresses the first two of these concerns, the quality assurance issue being dealt with separately in the subsequent section.

Competition and Participation in Contemporary Fish Supply Chains

One obvious failing of many analyses of seafood markets is the underlying assumption that such markets are perfectly competitive (Johnston 1995; Neilsen 2000). Yet DeVorets and Salvanes (1993) and Steen (1995) find that Norwegian salmon farmers are capable of exerting an undue influence over the supply chain in parts of Europe, while research by Skytte and Blunch (1998) indicates that large retail traders can potentially exercise market power through their fish buying behaviour. Furthermore, as information technology developments have allowed retailers to capture more detailed information about consumer preferences and desires, the chain reversal alluded to by Folkerts and Koehorst (1998) is perhaps coming increasingly to the fore. It is imperative, then, to comprehend how participants in the fish chain interact with each other, not only in organising the chain but also in harvesting the benefits of participation. As Neilsen (2000: 62) says;

> ... it is of relevance to know whether seafood consumers now pay more, whether fishmongers face increasing competition from retail sales regard-

ing the sale of fresh fish, whether primary producers [fishers and aquaculture producers] attain lower prices, or whether fish processors may absorb these lower prices caused by retailer's possible use of market power, and whether the establishment of food corporations affect supply and demand.

Sadly, little research into market structures and arrangements within the post-harvest supply chain has been undertaken to date, a deficit this chapter seeks to redress by recourse to illustrative case studies indicating the degree of competitiveness and participation across short and extended African fish supply chains. The first two case studies comment upon the organisation and management of the national fish chain(s), while the third and fourth cases focus on transborder fish chains.

Case 1: The Creek Road, Apapa Fish Market, Lagos (A Short Local Fish Supply Chain)

Nigeria is one of the leading maritime countries in West Africa with several southern coastal states stretching from Lagos Lagoon in Lagos State to the southwest across to the southeast state of Akwa Ibom (Tobor 1984). The most important demersal species landed are croakers (*Pseudotolithus elongatus, P. typus*), catfish (*Chrysichthys nigrodigitatus, Arius* spp.), sole or flatfish (*Cynoglossus*), shinynose (*Polydactylus quadrifilis*), and snapper (*Pomadasys*). Pelagic species most commonly caught are bonga (*Ethmalosa fimbriata*) and shad or long finned herring (*Ilisha africana*). Lagos has historically handled both fresh and frozen fish products from the local trawling industry as well as fisheries products from artisanal fishers from fishing villages around the Lagos Lagoon. The Creek Road, Apapa fish market functions as an outlet for both the Lagos-based Nigerian industrial fishing companies as well as motorized artisanal fishers (Tobor and Ajayi 1979). Here, local-based fish distributors (wholesalers) buy fish products in bulk, 'fish importing companies' act as a clearing-house for the industrial fleet (selling fresh fish on ice to retailers) and retailers, who can pick up as much fish as they are financially able to purchase.

Although a variety of species are sold, the main fish chains involve the sale of fresh fish on ice landed daily by local trawlers to wholesalers and fish importing companies for onward transmission to both linked and independent retailers, and fresh fish/fresh fish on ice landed by the artisanal fishers whose product is sold by retailers through the nightly fresh fish markets across Lagos. The fish products are preserved on ice blocks to retain the freshness of the fish because heat and high temperature can cause deterioration of the fish before the retailer gets to the night markets. Some wholesalers also have distribution centres in the urban markets where the fish products are stored and sold in small quantities to retailers and local consumers who buy the fish products from such centres at posted prices (Williams 1998).

At the fresh fish retail markets (both daytime and night-time), there are no posted prices. Wholesale buyers negotiate prices as fish products are not sold by auction in Nigeria. Fish prices are very competitive (fig. 6.1 [6]) – although prices of frozen fish products (imported 'trash fish') are lower compared to the fresh fish marketed by the artisanal fishers. Yet although prices are determined in a transparent and open manner, there are indications that the returns on offer may be inadequate to sustain operations in the industrial sector. Only 10% of Nigeria's domestic fish production is presently sourced from the commercial sea-trawling fleet with the number of fish trawlers operating in southern coastal waters now reduced to just 34 vessels employing only a few hundred Nigerians. High operating costs (in hard currency) for an ageing trawling fleet and depleted offshore stocks have been the main reasons for downsizing – with a concomitant impact upon livelihoods and employment in the sector. The industrial sector pales into insignificance beside the artisanal fleet, however – where more than 1.1 million fishers are to be found. Moreover, there is a clear gender bias in the Creek Road fish chains. Fishing activities are restricted to men – in both the industrial and artisanal sectors, the chain strategy (fig. 6.1 [2]) in the Creek Road fish market is largely dictated by the owners of the industrial fishing companies (who are 98% male) and the wholesalers who purchase the fish products off-loaded at the fish port/market (95% are males). In contrast, retailers who come to the fishing port/market are exclusively female.

Tobor (1990) reviewed the fishing industry in Nigeria in terms of its status and potential for food security in fish production. He found serious nutritional deficiencies related to fish protein, suggesting that food security goals may well have been sacrificed. One consequence of this has been an increased interest in aquaculture development which, according to Satia (1990) and Afolabi and Fagbenro (1998), is viewed as a means of increasing fish production, and thereby supplementing currently inadequate animal protein supply. Unfortunately, even though there are considerable prospects and potential for commercial aquaculture in Lagos state, to date the results have been poor. Reasons are linked to local ignorance of the production process allied to the difficulties of ensuring an adequate access to working capital (Fagbenro 1997).

Management of the chain process (fig. 6.1 [5]) appears participatory in the sense that the chain functions as a consequence of the interplay of the demands of the different fisheries unions (wholesalers, retailers, fishing companies), each intenton pursuing their own economic interests. Consequently, the wholesalers market their products on the basis of union-agreed prices that are regularly re-negotiated using the tariffs decreed by the federal government (from whom the industrial companies get the recommended prices for the fish products) as a reference point. Wholesalers have their union's permission to sell directly to the retailers registered/ linked with their companies and, occasionally, to any buyer willing to purchase the fish at the recommended price tags. Retailers are precluded from buying directly from the fishing companies, being obliged to buy from the representative of the wholesalers who is always at the port to supervise the quay-side sales of fish products. While these institutional arrangements generate a degree of income stability for all concerned, it is questionable whether such arrangements truly empower those at the consumptive end of the chain – the female fishmongers, and/or the eventual consumer.

Case 2: South Africa (A National Fish Supply Chain)

As we extend the spatial domain, the variety and complexity of fish chains increase. In Japan, for example, there were 2,118 fishers' cooperative associations and 1,077 wholesale fish markets trading a plethora of domestically caught and imported sea-food products (Miki and Yamamoto 1992; Odaka and Yamamoto 1992). In comparison to the Japanese supply chain, the South African fish chain is both more oligopolistic and, as is increasingly the case in the developing world, more geared towards the satisfaction of international demand. Historically, with South Africans not traditionally great fish eaters (annual consumption of fish protein is less than 0.5 kg per capita), fish and fish product exports have been a lucrative foreign exchange earner, generating US$271 million in foreign exchange receipts in 2000.

The South African fish chain is dominated by two large, vertically integrated, demersal fishing companies who catch, process and market fresh and frozen fish products (nationally and internationally) and employ in the region of 20,000 employees (Branch et al. 2002a,b). The fresh fish chain is relatively short, the larger 'prime quality' fish are landed by the companies in a gutted head-on form, packed into special containers surrounded by ice packs, and exported fresh to the key European markets. A secondary chain sees the trawler fleet tie up directly alongside the processing factory, landing the fish in headed and gutted form, in a special soft ice. After washing and grading, the fish are stored in chilled tanks, and then transformed into a range of products – headed and gutted fish, skin-on and deep-skinned fillets, folded fillets, paired fillets, skinless steaks and loins, and fish blocks – destined for all the major white fish markets of the world. A more complex processing chain produces a wide range of coated, battered, crumbed and char-grilled products made from either block, shaped or natural fillets, depending on the customer's requirements and specifications. Fish fingers and fish cakes form an important part of this range. A fourth chain has emerged since the late 1970s, as the trawling companies have moved from operating a number of frozen at sea processing trawlers to deploying ships capable of filleting at sea (early 1980s), deep skinning and de-boning fillets (1989) and producing individually quick frozen and graded fillets (1990s). All frozen sea production is presently exported, with the key markets being the US, Canada, Australia, and the UK. The highly integrated nature of these supply chains where strategy (fig. 6.1 [2]) is determined in an oligopolistic fashion by two companies (fig. 6.1 [1]), and management of the chain process (fig. 6.1 [5]) is delegated to the sales and marketing divisions that take charge of all selling and marketing, both domestically and (more generally) internationally, through a network of associations and agents, makes discussion of end-market valuation being free and fair and the chain process being a participatory one rather redundant. While there is some evidence of sectoral de-concentration since 1994, chain management remains the domain of the two leading companies that fish for demersal species.

Nevertheless, there are also a further series of fish chains in South Africa, which are small-scale, and exclusively local in both origin and destination. Only granted legislative recognition following the 1998 Marine Living Resources Act, the small-scale fisheries sector is estimated to encompass 29,233 fishers, the majority (more than 75%) being based in the Kwazulu-Natal region between East London and Durban (Branch et al. 2002a,b; Clark et. al 2002). Although small-scale catches of commercial species such as abalone and rock lobster are generally sold given the premium prices paid, almost 75% of the artisanal fish catch in Kwazulu-Natal (35% in the south, under 25% in the western region) is destined for home consumption. The preponderance of subsistence fishers in the Kwazulu-Natal region indicates that the returns on offer from fishing activity are unlikely to guarantee noticeably improved livelihood opportunities through an immediate redefinition of fish chain strategies – as the majority of landings recorded by this group fail to enter the chain at all. Instead, efforts to reduce food insecurity in poor fisher households (defined as those who spend more than 60% of their household income on food), estimated at more than 43% of all artisanal fishing households (Branch et al. 2002a,b), need to focus on providing alternative non-fishing income opportunities, while ensuring that food prices do not move against this vulnerable group.

Case 3: West Africa (A Regional Fish Supply Chain)

Since the mid-1980s many coastal African countries have sought to augment their export earnings by prioritising fish exports, exports from the region rising from US$700 million in 1981 to US$8.7 billion in 1999, producing a substantial foreign exchange surplus of US$6.4 billion in the process (Globefish 1994; FAO 1999b). While the major portion of this trade is with the developed economies, regional fish supply chains have evolved. In West Africa, the most notable trade flows are between the resource rich northern East Central Atlantic (ECF) fishing nations and the more densely populated southern ECF states. Two principal fish chains can be identified. A frozen pelagic chain links Senegal and Mauritania (and to a lesser extent Guinea, Guinea-Bissau and Sierra Leone) to markets in Nigeria, the Ivory Coast, the Democratic Republic of the Congo, Cameroon, Ghana, Togo, and the Congo, although such exports pale in comparison to the corresponding volumes imported by the same countries from cheaper European sources. Nevertheless, sourcing from Africa has increased over time. From 1995 to 1997, the bulk of West Africa's US$145 million annual fish imports were sourced from the EU (50.6%) rather than other West African countries

(24.5%). Between 1997 and 1999, West African imports had risen to US $277.5 million, with the West African share climbing to 39.1% and the EU share slipping to 46.9%. By far the biggest change over the period, however, was the elimination of the Soviet share, which was 17.5% from 1995 to 1997, but had fallen to almost zero by 1999 (FAO 1999b).

There is also a significant, though largely undocumented and unquantified, intra-regional trade in cured fish products (Tall 2002). Although curing is undertaken at the local artisanal level, the curers either sell wholesale to traders or hire representatives and/or family members for onward despatch of the product to other markets in the region (Jallow 1994). The principal regional trade flows – and the commodities in question – are identified in table 6.1. These flows also seem to transcend regional, political, and social unrest, if past disruption in Sierra Leone-Guinea/Liberia and Ghana-Togo/Benin trade is anything to go by (Globefish 1994).

Table 6.1 Principal regional fish trade flows (West Africa)

Exporter	Importer	Main Products Traded
Ghana	Togo/Benin	smoked sardinella and anchovy
Ivory Coast	Burkina Faso	smoked sardinella
Sierra Leone	Guinea/Liberia	smoked sardinella and bonga
Gambia	Guinea/Sénégal	smoked bonga and skates
	Ghana	dried shark products
Mali	Burkina Faso/Ivory Coast/Niger/Nigeria	cured freshwater fish
Sénégal	Cameroon/Congo/Ivory Coast/Mali/ Gabon/Ghana/Nigeria/Togo/Benin/ Democratic Republic of the Congo	smoked/dried-salted marine fish
Benin	Nigeria	smoked catfish and *bonga*

Source: constructed from Globefish (1994).

While a small canned fish trade concentrated on sardines and pilchards (tuna is canned in the region but traded outside) also exists, it is either oriented almost exclusively to the internal market (in the case of Nigerian, Angolan, Namibian and Ghanaian canneries) or imports are drawn from outside the immediate West African region (principally from Morocco and South Africa).

At a regional level, the evolution of a more extensive network of fish chains was hampered by three factors. First, the relatively small scale of operations of many fish traders ensured that transport costs per unit of product exported accounted for a high proportion of the final end-market price. Furthermore, such traders were also generally unable to access credit to allow the expansion or development of their operations. Second, poor handling, storage, and distribution facilities in a number of the African states militated against any immediate trade expansion. Finally, although preferential trade regimes can facilitate the emergence/expansion of regional fish chains – Mauritania and Senegal benefited markedly from the tax concessions offered on fish traded within the *Communaute Economique de L'Afrique de L'Ouest* (CEAO) during the 1980s – in practice, foreign exchange scarcities have all too often inhibited the development of regional fish chains. In Nigeria (1985) and Ghana (1986), for example, economic problems led to the temporary banning of imported canned and frozen fish respectively, whilst tariffs hindered the export of Kenyan Nile perch to Zaire (now the Democratic Republic of the Congo), Moroccan canned sardine to Ghana and Namibian frozen horse mackerel to Nigeria (Globefish 1994).

The Globefish (1994) report highlighted a series of problems in the reviewed regional fish chains. Once more the major preoccupation appeared to be volatile end-market prices (fig. 6.1 [6]), although in this instance the price instability was occasioned by the activities of new external suppliers (mainly Las Palmas based) whose sporadic incursions into West African markets drove down prices. While this ensured a more competitive atmosphere and temporarily improved food security prospects for local consumers (Fig. 6.1 [8]), it eroded local wholesaler margins. The unpredictability of these incursions, and their adverse impact upon wholesaler livelihoods manifested into '... an environment of nostalgia for the well-organised, co-ordinated supply system of the past' (Globefish 1994).

One attempt to improve the returns on offer to chain participants in West Africa has been the launch of government programmes to reduce wastage rates by remedying inadequacies in national handling, storage and distribution facilities. In a regional context, regionally-oriented organisations (such as CEAO or the Economic Community of West African States) were expected to become more pro-active in not only harmonising, and thus reducing, the prevailing discriminatory tariff regimes (vis-à-vis fish products), but also in preventing external suppliers from dumping their catch within the regional market. More stable markets, with lower equilibrium prices in the wake of tariff harmonisation, were likely to contribute to food security prospects in the region. Equally, chain members were not precluded from developing new, more participatory, institutional arrangements so as to enhance the returns they derived from the chain process (fig. 6.1 [7]). For example, in Gambia, the Ivory Coast, and Kenya traders pooled their resources and embarked on a strategy (fig. 6.1 [2]) of exporting larger consignments to their historic markets in Guinea, Burkina Faso and the Democratic Republic of the Congo, respectively. The consequence – a dramatic slashing in transport costs – saw the benefits shared between chain members and the final consumer, thereby enhancing both the livelihoods of chain members and local food security objectives.

Case 4: Nile Perch Exports from Lake Victoria (A Global Fish Supply Chain)

Although African nations export a variety of fish (ranging from low-value pelagic species to high-value tuna and swordfish) to global markets, details on the nature of these extended supply chains are sparse. The exception relates to exports of Nile perch from the Lake Victoria region. While the introduction of the perch into the lake triggered dramatic changes in the lake's ecosystem (Achieng 1990; Kaufman 1992; Witte et al. 1992), it also spawned a whole new industry related to the capture, processing and subsequent export of perch fillets. By the end of the 1990s, the three countries bordering the lake (Uganda, Tanzania, and Kenya) were extracting an estimated 300,000 mt annually which generated between US$280-400 million in export revenues (Revenga et al., 2000). This boom brought profound changes in both the fishery itself and the structure and organisation of the post-harvesting sector.

While fishing activities flourished, the number of fishers swelled from 11,000 in 1971 to around 30,000 in 1995, with an estimated 8,000 fishing boats in operation on the lake in the same year. There was also significant investment in nets and associated technology (Reynolds and Greboval 1988; Jansen et al. 1999), and there was a major structural transformation within the post-harvest sector. Although the initial boom enhanced the earnings and livelihoods of those involved in historic processing activities, encouraging a sharp influx of individuals – principally women – into the sector (Jansen et al. 1999), this began to change after the first processing factories were established along the Kenyan shoreline in the early 1980s. The fresh and frozen perch fillets produced by these factories were airfreighted to overseas markets in the EU, Israel, Australia and Japan – rather than directed to the domestic market. By the late 1990s, there were 34 factories scattered around the lake (12 based at Kisumu in Kenya, the historic centre of the trade, 12 in Uganda, and 10 around Mwanza in Tanzania), with strong national industrial processing organisations emerging to lobby governments on behalf of the processors (Megapesca 1997). Ownership of the factories was concentrated within a small local elite (Gibbon 1997), an elite whose control was determined by their access to financial capital and international trading circuits rather than any underlying or historic interest in the fishery itself. Excess industrial capacity spawned competition between processors for the underlying unprocessed resource and, as local perch prices rose, many local fishmongers and traditional processors were squeezed out of the chain as post-harvest operations became more concentrated over time (Jansen 1999; Henson et al. 2000). Abila and Jansen (1997), for example, have suggested that every one job created in the factory sector led to the loss of six to eight jobs in the traditional sector.

Furthermore, such competition provoked vertical integration as factories strove to establish greater control over chain resources (fig. 6.1 [4]). Initially, the chosen strategy (fig. 6.1 [3]) was to acquire trawlers which could deliver large quantities (500-1,500 kg per trip) of perch to the quay from whence they were directly transported by factory-owned trucks to the processing plant. After regional authorities moved to ban trawler fishing due to its adverse ecological effects at the end of 1995, the factories adopted a new strategy. Now factories elected to 'sponsor' artisanal *matajiri* (fishing vessel proprietors), generally by supplying nets and engines, the *matajiri* in return were obliged to deliver their catch to the factory. Gibbon (1997) suggests that as many as 600 of the lake's vessels were tied in this manner (one factory having 113 tied vessels), with the precise nature of the agreement also serving to exacerbate concentration in the harvesting sector over time. Factories supplemented tied supplies through a decentralised collection system of agents, field agents and sub-agents. The agent was generally based at the company jetty and was responsible for strategic co-ordination of the supply network and price-setting. Field agents operated from the different fishing ports and were often equipped with large collector boats and ice. Sub-agents were responsible for directly procuring the catch from both tied and non-tied vessels. Factory processed fillets were either transported to Mombasa (Kenya) or Dar-es-Salaam (Tanzania) by refrigerated road transport for onward shipment to external markets or were air-freighted out from Nairobi, Mwanza, or Entebbe.

The Nile perch supply chain is probably one of the best fisheries exemplars of Folkerts and Koehorst's 'chain reversal' thesis – whereby consumer demands exert a strong influence over chain structure and operation (Van Vliet and Friis 1999). Not only have burgeoning Western consumer demands for whitefish fillets supported the establishment of perch processing factories in East Africa, but subtle differences in consumers' tastes are reflected in the plant operations. Fillets destined for the Japanese market are despatched skin-on and scaled whilst those delivered to the North European, US, and Australian markets are deeply skinned and have the dark flesh removed (Megapesca 1997).

This external dynamism is also, paradoxically, the Achilles heel of the chain insofar as a dependence upon external markets can have unpleasant implications for the livelihoods of some chain participants if trade is unexpectedly curtailed (either due to an abrupt change in consumers tastes and/ or due to governmental edicts) – we elaborate on this point in the subsequent section. Furthermore, whilst the chain does exhibit a degree of oligopolistic competitiveness, the chain management structure that has evolved is extremely exclusionary – 34 factories have, by capturing over 90% of perch landings, provoked the demise of many local fishmongers and traditional processors and hastened concentration at the harvesting level via the propagation of tied contracts. This has also had negative local food security implications by removing the perch from domestic dinner plates. Although a sub-industry processing skeletons and other waste discarded by the factories did subsequently evolve with a domestic market focus, local food insecurities are being further exacerbated as even this sub-industry is now being squeezed out, as such discards are increasingly being diverted into newly constructed fish meal plants.

These four case studies serve to illustrate the dynamic and constantly evolving nature of fish supply chains – with new chain strategies emerging endogenously to overcome identified chain deficiencies, as in the cases of resource pooling between traders in the West African case or tied-contracts in the Lake Victoria Case. Improved vertical co-ordination of the chain, whether state- or privately-driven, can allow profits to be maximised at the chain level, and returns to chain members and/or societal benefits (in the form of enhanced food security through reduced product prices) can improve through the promotion of more open, quay-side, auctions (case 4) or via direct negotiations (case 1). A very real danger however, is that entry barriers (the *tembea* boat preferred by participants in the Nile perch fishery can cost up to US$10,000, according to Jansen et al. (1999)) and the oligopolistic behaviour of some current chain members, as around the case of factories in Lake Victoria, can ensure that these aggregate benefits are disproportionately distributed within the chain. One possible remedy to this is to establish counter-veiling governance measures, the banning of trawlers on Lake Victoria is one instance of this, which induce a more equitable participation in the chain without necessarily compromising its operational effectiveness. In some cases too, notably with regard to the Nile perch in Lake Victoria, there has been a redirection of chain activities, with domestic consumption of the catch (food self-sufficiency) being sacrificed for the goal of increased export earnings. Governance measures are not simply limited to issues of social justice, ensuring domestic food security and the livelihoods of those involved in the post-harvest sector, however. Their presence may be equally warranted if other concerns – such as food safety – are considered imperative.

Governance Measures to Ensure Quality Standards in Fish Supply Chains

While traditional sensory inspection of gill coloration, colour, shine and texture of skin/flesh, thickness and colour of the slime on the skin, and smell affords a consumer some indication as to freshness (Fraser and Sumar 1998), such inspection is unable to necessarily discern the initial breakdown of various components present in the fish which trigger its subsequent decomposition (see Plahar et al. 1999; Poli et al. 2001). Equally, sensory inspection is unlikely to disclose whether the product is contaminated with bio-toxins and heavy metals, residues of veterinary medicines (aquaculture products), *salmonellae*, etc., or if it has been irradiated (Woolston 2000) – although subsequent consumer awareness of the fact is likely to have a similar impact upon market demand as consumer's sensory perceptions over product freshness. In instances where products are of poor quality, or have questionable credibility in the consumers' eyes, then spoilage rates will be high and chain returns are markedly reduced. The issue of quality assurance/control consequently encompasses the entire post-harvest chain; 'fishermen take care to land fresh and undamaged fish'

(Van Vliet and Friis 1999: 208), whilst caterers, fishmongers, and other retail outlets expect their suppliers to meet exigent quality standards. A failure to do so results in visible deterioration/contamination of the commodity to the detriment of downstream chain participants/consumers (see box 6.2), for quality assurance failings early on in the distributional process cannot be rectified at a later stage (Van der Schans et al. 1999).

Box 6.2 Histamine poisoning from poorly handled tuna and other scombroid species

Histamine is a product of normal food spoiling bacteria. In high quantities it can cause food poisoning, resembling hyperallergic reactions. Fish from the family Scombridae (which includes tuna) are the main culprits.

In the Solomon Islands, most of the tuna bycatch from longliners is dumped at sea, but some is left in the sun on the decks of transshipment vessels in Honiara harbour, where by law they cannot be dumped. Villagers collect these poor quality tuna for free in their dugout canoes and sell them in the local fishing village market, which is squeezed between a busy road and the beach. Vendors are crowded together in an area of about 60 m by 10 m. There is no concrete slab, the site is bare dirt and gravel, dusty, and exposed to road dust and fumes. There is no source of fresh water. Some vendors sprinkle their fish with seawater taken up from the beach. Most stalls are made of bare wood or plywood (non-cleanable surfaces). Some have cloth roofs, others are not shaded at all and there are no shade trees. The tuna are not iced at any stage from the deck of the transshipment vessel to the point of sale or even to consumption. The tuna here sell quickly for SI$5 a piece. The consumers seem not to care about quality, they are mostly influenced by price. No testing for histamine levels has been carried out, unstructured interviews with staff from Honiara Central Hospital have revealed cases of histamine poisoning each year, typically involving several people who had all eaten the same fish. There is no provision for categorising the cause of the poisoning in hospital records.

In Kiribati, Joseph is a tuna fisher and his wife, Peria, a tuna trader. Peria sells her husband's catch by the roadside in Bairiki, Tarawa. A number of skipjack tuna are on a wheelbarrow on the edge of the main road, in the shade of a tree. There is no icebox or ice. Peria has a scale to weigh the fish, and brushes flies away with a branch. Joseph fishes close to Maiana Island, heading out at around 5:30 a.m. and coming back about 10:00 a.m. Fish are gutted and gilled when they reach shore. Peria has never known any fish to be spoiled on arrival, everything is in saleable condition. The fish are never on ice either on the boat or while displayed for sale. At the end of the day, about 5:30 p.m., Peria puts any unsold fish on ice in a Styrofoam box. She does not have a freezer. She has never had to throw fish away. Their family eats any fish which is not sold. They have never known anyone to get sick from eating fish. The histamine level in a sample of skipjack taken from Peria's wheelbarrow was 67 ppm. Safe limits are usually regarded as 50 ppm (USA) to 100 ppm (EU).

Source: Tony Chamberlain

Self-interest then, encourages the emergence of endogenous policing/governance measures whereby it may be in the interest of chain participants to cooperate, so as to ensure the product meets mutually agreed quality norms as it transits its way down the supply chain. In the wake of the UK BSE crisis for example, the strategic response of the sector was to introduce retailer- and manufacturer-led assurance schemes intended to reduce product category and product specific risk and thereby return consumers' overall risk perceptions related to the consumption of beef to pre-crisis level (Fearne et al. 2001). Equally, Van der Schans et al. (1999) have indicated that producers' organisations in Vigo (Spain), Peterhead and Lerwick (Scotland), and the Netherlands are well-placed to assume rather higher, pro-active quality control roles vis-à-vis the fish captured by their members.

Yet endogenous control mechanisms, whether in the form of trade/producer associations or proprietary quality control schemes, may be insufficient to allay consumer preoccupations/fears over the safety or origins of a particular product. In such instances, exogenously implanted assurance or quality improvement mechanisms may be necessary. These may be either national in character – as with the US Food and Drug Act, 'which assures consumers that the products of a nation are produced in a prescribed manner' (Zaibet 2000: 313), or global. Global standards can emerge following the deliberations of global organisations, such as the Hazard Analysis and Critical Control Point (HACCP) scheme which seeks to identify and control hygiene risks at distinct points in the processing chain. Similarly, the derivation of a set of international standards enabling the traceability of seafood products (capture or farmed) from catcher through to retailer is another example currently gaining greater legal currency, given that it will become a mandatory requirement of EU food law in 2005 (Graz 2002; *Fishing News*, 2003). Because failure to conform to HACCP standards can lead to product rejection, HACCP is 'a powerful weapon in the pursuit of improved international hygiene levels' (Thorpe and Bennett 2001: 157). It is equally plausible too, that, in cases where the chain is strongly consumer-driven, consumers' ethical preferences can be marshalled at the global/national level to demand participants conform to other non-hygiene based standards. In the fisheries domain, this has most commonly manifested itself in moves which affect the nature of the international trade in fish-based products, either in voluntary cases (for example, the case of the Marine Stewardship Council's 'eco-labelling' certification scheme – see box 6.3) or enforced cases (as in the case of the US government's 1990-1992 embargo on the import of 'non-dolphin safe' tuna from Latin America).

Box 6.3 Eco-labelling and the Marine Stewardship Council (MSC)

Over the last decade, different eco-labelling schemes have emerged with the objective of informing consumers what processes have been used in the production of the designated good. Some, like the MSC initiative for example, assure the customer that the product they are buying has been produced in accordance with sustainable development principles. There are many different products that display an eco-label on their packaging, however, the problem is that it can be difficult for consumers to judge whether the different schemes are delivering what they are promising.

Labelling schemes can be divided into three types; first, second, and third party labelling. First party labelling relies on self-declaration, with the producer themselves guaranteeing the particular merits of the good. In second party labelling, labelling standards are laid down and enforced by the industry concerned (or alternatively by an external certifying company hired by the industry). The third party scheme sees the certification and labelling process overseen by an independent organisation or body (Deere, 1999a). The MSC, an example of the latter type, was created in 1996 by the World Wildlife Fund and Unilever and 'rewards' environmentally responsible fisheries management and practices by permitting products emanating from such fisheries to bear the MSC logo. By 2002, over 105 product lines in ten countries across the world carried the MSC logo (Roheim, 2003).

Developing countries are somewhat wary, however, about the growth of the MSC's labelling programme and eco-labelling of fisheries products generally, seeing such certification processes acting as a non-tariff barrier and limiting access to high-value markets in developed countries (Vitalis, 2002). Equally, as membership of such schemes requires the production process to meet standards set by the evaluating body, the costs of compliance may be high for fisheries in the developing world, as they are often artisanal, and do not have sufficient technical knowledge (or are too small) to participate fully in such schemes.

Source: Øyvind Kvie

Governance Issues: Quality Control

How have governance measures, both endogenous and exogenous, operated to assure/improve product quality within each of the four cases alluded to in the previous section of this paper then? In Creek Road, Apapa in Lagos quality was less of an issue given the shortness (geographic and temporal) of the supply chain. However, endogenous action by boat-owners and retailers saw ice blocks used to retard the deterioration process and extend the product's shelf life. The application of quality assurance mechanisms in the South African fish chain is facilitated by the oligopolistic and highly integrated nature of the demersal fishery. Quality assurance procedures start on board the ships and follow right through until the product is despatched to the market. Corporate quality control mechanisms are reinforced by a plethora of exogenous (state-determined) quality edicts including: minimum hygiene requirements for the processing and transport of goods intended for human consumption (Public Health Act 63, 1977), microbiological and chemical content limits for certain fish products (Foodstuffs and Disinfectants Act 54, 1972), compulsory and voluntary standard specifications for frozen and canned fisheries products (Standards Act 29, 1993) and, in the case of all fish exports, the South African Bureau of Standards certifies facilities to ensure they meet HACCP and US standards.

Presently, there are few quality considerations affecting West African fish trade, despite the fact that such transactions need to pass across national borders, a convenient point for the imposition of more stringent quality requirements. Yet while the EU and US exploit this opportunity to extend domestic food safety and quality standards to trade partners, in the West African context trade, intervention is presently based almost exclusively on economic considerations – with the value of import surcharges as a generator of government revenue being balanced against the national desire to conserve foreign exchange (Globefish 1994) – rather than food quality considerations. Here it seems that individualistic responses largely continue to determine quality – or the lack of it – as the products pass up the chain.

Quality controls are most stringent in those instances when the commodity is intended for the international market, in particular, US or European markets. Such trade requires compliance with exogenously-set basic hygiene standards, standards which are increasingly focused upon the conditions of production – the vessels engaged, the landing facilities used, the export processing plants employed – rather than analysis and certification of the end product. The most common of these standards is HACCP, and potential exporting countries are best advised to ensure that all local chain members have implemented HACCP-acceptable hygiene standards. In the case of the EU, if such compliance is certified by the (EU-designated) national competent authority then approved exporters can freely export to the EU (Henson et al. 2000; Goulding 2002). Nile perch exports are no exception to these procedures and ineffectual Kenyan domestic hygiene systems saw both the Spanish and Italian governments prohibit perch imports from Kenya amidst fears of *salmonellae* in November 1996 – causing Kenya's foreign exchange earnings to drop by 13.1% (total exports to Spain fell by 86%). A year later, in December 1997, a further EU-wide ban – this time following an outbreak of cholera in East Africa – saw perch exports to the EU fall by 66% while Kenya's forex fisheries earnings fell by 32%. National inability to challenge the latter embargo on technical/scientific grounds was only remedied by the intervention of another external agency, the World Health Organization (WHO), and the ensuing incorporation of new wording on plant employees' medical certificates, which ensured the embargo was removed in June 1998 (Henson et al. 2000; CUTS 2001).

Significantly, the national governance failings exposed by the above embargoes on the quality control front prompted a more timely, pro-active, response to subsequent exogenous threats. The governance measure employed to counter a new March 1999 EU embargo grounded in the belief that chemicals were being used to capture fish in lake Victoria was blunt and taken without consulting domestic chain participants. The national government simply banned all fishing activity for a period of two weeks. While this drastic action failed to win immediate EU approval, it did, however, make all domestic participants in the chain acutely aware of the urgent necessity of establishing acceptable quality norms if the export door was to be re-opened. This manifested itself in a number of ways. Firstly, it triggered the formation of a new producer's organisation, the Kenyan Association of Fish Exporters and Processors, to represent the collective interest of members in discussions with both national government and the EU on quality (and other) issues. Secondly, it encouraged an individualistic response by each processor to raise quality standards within their own supply chain. Investment in cold stores on the landing beaches and the provision of ice were two of the more common elements – measures which tied the fishers ever more closely to their upstream processor (Henson et al. 2000). These enhanced endogenous control mechanisms were complemented by exogenous schemes, in particular, the government's commitment to: (i) establish 511 beach management committees that were to be entrusted with ensuring beach cleanliness and sanitation (in conjunction with the Lake Victoria Environmental Management Project), (ii) provide instruction for chain participants on improved fish handling and processing techniques, whilst fisheries inspectors were scheduled to receive advanced training in quality control issues, and (iii) approve new legislation designed to harmonise hygiene requirements in the processing factories with EU guidelines (Hoza 1999). This bipartite assault on deficiencies in local quality control proved sufficient to overturn the ban and exports to the EU resumed in March 2000.

The episode also shows how a complex web of interlocking governance measures (re-designed national legislation, new lobby groups to promote the interests of certain stakeholder groups within the chain, development of extended clientelistic relationships between chain members, etc.) may emerge/evolve if the opportunities likely to be foregone through not upgrading quality standards are marked. Contrarily, in instances where 'chain reversal' has not arisen, and consumer pressures for improved quality standards are weak, there is much less compunction for chain members to either collectively or individually impose strictures to raise product quality. Although new institutional arrangements may still evolve within such fish chains, they are unlikely to be motivated primarily by quality considerations.

Conclusion

This chapter has explored the post-harvest nature of fish chains, illustrating how the journey from 'trawler to table' involves a series of stakeholders who have both competing and complementary interests. The chain strategy that emerges as a consequence will reflect the relative numbers and/or relative strength of the stakeholders located at each individual point in the chain: a small number of industrial processors may disproportionately determine and manage the chain strategy in one instance, whilst a cartel of fishmongers could dictate chain organisation and outcomes in another. Consequently, efforts to comprehend: (i) if fish markets are free and fair and the returns on offer are sufficient to sustain livelihoods and employment, (ii) if the market valuation process contributes to food security or undermines it, (iii) if a perceived sense of participatory involvement is both a necessary and sufficient condition for social justice, and (iv) if prevailing quality mechanisms are sufficient to guarantee an 'acceptable' level of food safety, demand a more detailed understanding of each individual chain. Also, an analysis of the economic, social, and cultural factors that intercede to influence the arrangements by which the commodity passes from hand to hand up the chain, is essential. Such an analysis serves to highlight the potential governance measures by which stakeholders are able to act so as to influence the conditions or context within which chain activities take place. It also allows external agents, such as national governments and NGOs, who aspire to modify chain strategy and outcomes to identify optimal entry points vis-à-vis intervention.

As the chain is extended spatially to the global plane, as the preceding case studies have shown, more intermediaries are involved and chain organisation and management become correspondingly complex. However, such global fish chains are also more consumer-driven than their local counterparts and consequently more vulnerable to 'top-down' pressures to restructure the chain in a particular way. Nowhere is this more evident than in the area of quality control. Around 60% of international fish markets presently require imported fish and fish products to conform to HACCP standards (Lupin 1999), and a failure to introduce appropriate governance measures at the local level to ensure compliance with this standard can lead to the sudden loss of export markets. The Nile perch example is a case in point. The 1998 EU Nile perch embargo had severe macroeconomic repercussions for Kenya, Tanzania and Uganda, repercussions that reverberated back down the chain to devastate the livelihoods of both fishers and ancillary workers in the local lakeside communities. Paradoxically, however, this catastrophe – beach prices for perch in Tanzania fell from Tanzanian shillings 306.3 per kg in 1998 to 126.3 per kg in 1999 after the ban was implemented (Hoza 1999) – served to make chain participants more receptive to chain re-organisation in order to meet HACCP standards. The panoply of governance measures applied in response to the supposed use of poisons to capture fish in East Africa served to modify existing institutional arrangements sufficiently so as to ensure HACCP compliance, compliance that led to the EU embargo being subsequently rescinded. In this instance, successful chain strategy modification occurred as a consequence of the disastrous short-term effects on livelihoods and employment following the ban, effects which prompted broad stakeholder agreement regarding the appropriate response measures required to meet the designated international consumption standards.

7

Links in the Fish Chain

Derek Johnson, Andy Thorpe, Maarten Bavinck, and Michel Kulbicki

As the preceding chapters of this section have demonstrated, resource regulation has not been the strong suit of fisheries. Each chapter has identified serious problems of, or challenges to, governance in the world's fisheries: overfishing, human-induced ecosystem shifts, threats to livelihoods, pollution, over-dependence on marine sources of fish feed, and quality control. These are well-known problems that have in recent years prompted increasing recognition that fisheries governance has been inadequate to the challenge of maintaining sustainability and livelihoods in maritime areas.

While not excusing governance failures, the preceding chapters have provided a major reason for them: the diversity, complexity, and dynamics of the main segments of the fish chain that we identify militate against the establishment of straightforward, effective governance mechanisms. This task is rendered even more complex when the attempt is made to incorporate all of the segments of the chain into a whole. The intent of this chapter is to reflect on the constitution of the fish chain or, really, the multiple intertwined fish chains that extend from the world's fisheries, and then to assess the governance challenges specific to governing the interactions within entire fish chains. Both of these tasks have been anticipated in the introductory chapters to this volume and in this section of the book. We begin this chapter with a short reflection on the representation of the chain.

How Should the Fish Chain Be Viewed?

Two explicit approaches and one implicit approach to representing the fish chain have been taken thus far. The first of these, most consistent with the metaphorical image of the chain, is the notion of a vertical, interlinked sequence of interactions that brings an aquatic organism from its ecosystem to the consumer's dining table (fig. 1 in the introduction to Part II). The second is the more complex, multi-layered image of the chain represented in the diagram in fig. 2 (in the introduction to Part II). For now, we will content ourselves with the descriptions of approaches one and two as presented in the introductory chapter to this section. Later in this chapter, we will return to their importance as images for understanding the chain.

The third, implicit, approach is that, in order to grasp the complexity of the chain one has to break it into constituent segments in order to view each more closely. Two aspects of the breaking up of the chain merit particular attention: how it is divided and the lessons that become apparent from its division. The logic by which the chain was divided is clear from the chapter breakdown and from the affiliation of the authors. We divided the chain largely according to disciplinary expertise. A biologist thus wrote on ecology, sociologists and anthropologists on the organisation of fish capture, another biologist led the chapter on aquaculture, and a team led by an economist produced the chapter on post-extraction processes. Such a division matches the typical arrangement of studies of fisheries and fish chains. The implication of dividing the chain disciplinarily gets less attention in fisheries studies. Each of the disciplines involved in the study of fisheries has particular perspectives and emphases associated with it. These are evident to a degree in the four contributions to this part of the book. Beyond highlighting these disciplinary tendencies below, but also showing their limitations, we wish to emphasise the comparative advantages of so closely juxtaposing the disciplinary approaches for understanding the fish chain.

Decoupling the Fish Chain

The task of breaking and reassembling the chain was anticipated in the assignment to the chapter authors who were instructed to incorporate a concern with diversity, complexity, and dynamics. How individual authors responded to that challenge is a good indication of disciplinary predilections and overlaps.

Kulbicki (see chap. 3) focuses on diversity– at either the spatial or species level – and how this impacts on the stability, resistance, and resilience of aquatic ecosystems. Yet, as the author notes, ecosystems are not static and the diversity 'mix' can change either naturally, through migration and speciation, or through human intervention, with species loss just as, if not more, important to diversity and ecosystem functioning as species gain. The complexity and dynamics of such ecosystems inhibit the development of effective governance, more so when the full range of parameters are unknown – these include the presence of presently *undescribed* species within the system, particularly in the tropics, and how widely or narrowly concentrated their habitats are.

Yet species diversity is inextricably linked to habitat diversity – and so the promotion of the latter will also benefit the former. The implications, in terms of governance with an ecosystem health objective in mind, will range from the ban or regulatory restriction of certain gears that reduce habitat diversity such as bottom trawling, dynamite fishing, use of poisons, and mangrove destruction, to the promotion of habitat enhancement through the construction of artificial reefs, the restoration of degraded areas of coastal wetlands, the delineation of marine protected areas, effluent controls, etc. Equally, ecosystem health-oriented governance could address the direct promotion of resource diversity through such measures as enhancing juvenile survival of fish, reducing the fishing pressure on spawning aggregations, and limiting the use of gears that are not selective in terms of size or species catch composition.

Evidently Kulbicki's main points of reference are biological and physical parameters of the ecosystem: fish species and ecosystem boundaries and interactions respectively. Human interventions are seen from the perspective of the fish, with the most immediate threats, fishing and other direct anthropogenic pressures, looming largest. Markets and other factors conditioning human effort are in the distant background. Following from this orientation, the chapter's governance recommendations are directed at measures to ensure the basic conditions for maintaining ecosystems and the species diversity they contain.

As Johnson et al. (see chap. 4) note, from the *capture* point of view, the most important dimensions of diversity are the social organisation of production, technological intensity, and the space and time involved in the extraction process. The technological intensity of production will grow as the spatial sphere of operations is extended – with subsistence fishers who fish inshore coastal waters tending to use local knowledge and locally produced, low-cost gear while the distant water fleets of multinational companies make recourse to global positioning devices, monofilament nets, and state-of-the-art fishing vessels. The overall historical dynamic of capture fishing has been in the direction of technological intensification, the increasing importance of large-scale industrial production, and changes in the space and time of fish capture.

Yet, even within small-scale and large-scale fisheries, there is a rich complexity of extraction strategies that reflect local livelihood conditions and institutional priorities. In inshore coastal fisheries, for example, if fishers target a single species they generally use a limited range of gears – adapted according to fish size and/or fish behaviour. Most fishers in these single species fisheries tend to adopt one specific gear as this reduces costs and may optimise efficiency. However, in a coastal fishery with several commercial species, the fisher has to decide which species to target, in the belief that (if everything goes according to plan) he or she will get a mixed catch, albeit dominated by the target species. Moreover, depending on the dynamics of the underlying ecosystem, he or she may well have to – or choose to – shift from one target species to another depending on the season, the market or other factors; so it is probable that he or she retains a portfolio of gears, or at least has gears that can either adapt to different situations or deliver a broad spectrum of catch. In very diverse coastal fisheries, in which the catch is necessarily varied, the choice is explicit: either have many different gears selected according to target species or invest in the minimum of gear giving the maximum spectra of catch. The first choice implies either having enough capital to buy and maintain several gear types and, perhaps, the corresponding vessels, or splitting the investment between various members of a fishing community. The second is usually the 'poor person's choice' insofar as it reduces both the investment and the returns, since broad-spectrum gears do not necessarily catch the most commercial species.

The nature of the capture process has a number of implications in terms of governance then, particularly with regard to the objectives of social justice and livelihoods/employment. If a capturing 'free-for-all' is permitted, inequities in the stocks of fishing capital will likely be translated into inequities in catch levels. If governance mechanisms are sought instead to regulate resource access, more latitude is available to pursue social equity and ecosystem health objectives. If the regulatory approach is chosen, a decision has to be taken about whether to apportion stocks between competing fishers, or to control effort through gear restrictions and the like. Variations on these alternatives have different implications for social equity and the maintenance of diversity in fish capture.

At the centre of the sociological approach to fish capture are the social relations and institutions that organise the extraction of fish. Ecosystem variables are seen as one factor among many which influence how fish are captured. To the degree to which the market is viewed as a collection of social actors, it may be internalised into the organisation of fish extraction. Johnson et al. deliberately left an implicit external influence, as the authors were aware that discussion of the market would be left for exclusive treatment by Thorpe et al. (see chap. 6). Following from Johnson et al.'s social focus, key governance priorities for fisheries sociology are the degree to which fisheries interventions and governance influence livelihoods, employment, and the quality of social relations.

Pullin and Sumaila's chapter on aquaculture (see chap. 5) diverges from the model of the other chapters in the fish chain section because it was written by a biologist, with significant input from an economist. This cross-disciplinary collaboration matches the anomalous status of the topic of aquaculture in terms of the disciplinary division of the fish chain we have made here; aquaculture includes interactions among a range of ecological, social, organisational, and marketing segments of the entire chain. And, while it would be quite feasible to devote disciplinary chapters to each of those elements in another context, the single chapter devoted to aquaculture in this volume meant their integration. In the context of the exponential growth of aquaculture, Pullin and Sumaila here emphasise the cross-sector impacts of aquaculture development. A central concern of the chapter is the (over) reliance of aquaculture on fish-meal and fish-oil as feed inputs – diverting a substantive proportion of the global fisheries catch – around thirty percent according to recent figures – into the mouths of captive fish rather than humankind (Tuominen and Esmark 2003). The governance challenges facing aquaculture relate to the complexity of its ecological and social interactions and its market links, which have generated a dynamic of rapid growth. Aquaculture also involves a highly diverse set of operations ranging from a fisher-farmer using a local water resource to raise fish so as to supplement household consumption and, often, income to large, capital-intensive, foreign-owned salmon farms in Chile and shrimp farms in India (Barrett et al. 2002).

Governance strategies for aquaculture have to reflect these conditions. The land-based activities of some aquaculture operations, for example, necessitate mediating mechanisms to reconcile relevant objectives like ecosystem health and social justice with those of coastal and/or riverine zone management. The cross-sector linkages in aquaculture governance include its impact on local ecosystems, whether through the introduction of alien species, the generation of effluents and eutrophication, the destruction of local habitats, or the influence of vested interests and power structures, which can often override the establishment and enforcement of environmental safeguards. Governance strategies for aquaculture also need to arbitrate on issues of social justice; how, for example, should access to water bodies and/or coastal regions suitable for aquaculture activities be governed? Equally, as the genetic aquatic treadmill of selective breeding, hybridisation, and gene transfer gathers pace, multiple issues of 'justice' arise – from the sovereign rights of states over all their native genetic resources (Eberlee 2003), to private intellectual property rights on genetically enhanced aquatic resources.

Governance in the extraction process, as in post-extraction activities – whether capture or aquaculture – is not solely confined to the processes themselves, but has a far wider remit in terms of the fundamental concerns identified in chapter 1. The markedly higher occupational incidence of mortality in the fishing industry, for example, offers a compelling reason for the implementation of exigent and ongoing safeguards to protect lives, and not just livelihoods, in the sector (cf. US Bureau of Labor Statistics 1998). Equally, governance arrangements such as formal and informal share arrangements among crewmembers, or community mechanisms to support disabled mariners and the families of drowned or disappeared seamen, can contribute significantly towards norms of social justice.

The final chapter on the fish chain details the nature and organisation of historic and contemporary *supply* chains, using African cases for illustration. They comment on the extent to which such chains are both competitive and participatory, and illustrate how quality considerations are becoming a major driving force underpinning the chain. While they recognise the diversity within, and complexity of, fish supply chains, they also contend that such variations do not invalidate the Folkerts-Koehorst thesis of consumer-driven supply chains (see chap. 6).

Consumer-driven supply chains in a plainly unequal world (UC Atlas 2003) have profound implications in terms of the objectives of food security and safety, social justice, and livelihoods, as Northern agendas orient fish chains that originate in the developing world to the market and quality edicts of the global fish trade. The Nile perch trade, like that of the South African demersal trade, bypasses local markets and, with ecosystems capable of delivering finite fish resources, impacts adversely upon local consumption levels. Food insecurity is compounded by the limited local employment opportunities offered in such global food chains, as the drive for efficiency in processing and capturing and the need to meet exacting quality standards merely serves to aid the concentration and integration of fishing capital, to the detriment of other stakeholders. Small-scale fishers face reduced stocks of fish; paid labour loses employment on increasingly capi-

tal-intensive and often foreign-owned fleets; and market traders have reduced stocks available for sale.

Governance in the post-extraction sector can take many forms; from a
laissez-faire market approach that allows market participants to determine
the structure of the resulting chain, to an approach where the state directs
the chain strategy, controls participation, and determines the competition
therein. Furthermore, a plethora of potential governance tools exists. These
include, among others: the imposition of tariffs and quotas to protect domestic markets from cheap imports or to guarantee domestic consumption
levels; restrictions on foreign investment to prevent excessive foreign intervention; measures to forestall restrictive practices, particularly closed auctions; and the derivation and enforcement of chain quality standards,
whether on food safety or other grounds.

Thorpe et al.'s starting point (see chap. 6) is the nature of post-extraction
supply chains. These vary enormously, reflecting their length and the number of stakeholders involved. Thorpe et al. make clear the very direct impact
that market chains have on local populations and on local environmental
conditions. They argue that markets are increasingly consumer-driven, and
that consumers in the North have undue power to influence the priorities
of the supply chain, which have deleterious impacts on the South. Chains
are becoming longer and more complex, with a corresponding loss of local
control over them. While the focus of the chapter is on changing flows of
supply and demand, and the institutions that structure fish chains, it also
deals explicitly, like Johnson et al. (see chap. 4) with topics such as equity
and social organisation.

This last point illustrates that the division of the fish chain into disciplinary components for ease of presentation cannot avoid overlap between
them. Areas of linkage are most pronounced in the chapters by Johnson et
al., Pullin and Sumaila, and Thorpe et al. (see chaps. 4, 5, and 6), while the
difference is greatest between them and Kulbicki (see chap. 3). This reflects
the relative inter-disciplinary distances between the chapters, with that between the natural and social science showing the largest gulf. The difference between Kulbicki and the other authors can also be demonstrated by
the different emphases given to diversity, complexity, and dynamics. Diversity comes across most strongly in Kulbicki's chapter, while the other
authors pay as much if not more attention to complexity and dynamics.
Even between chapter 3 and the other chapters in the section, however, the
connections are sufficiently important to point to ways of reconstituting the
chain.

Reassembling the Fish Chain

The advantage of disassembling the chain, besides allowing for a more detailed examination of its components, is that doing so gives a better sense
of how the chain looks from the perspectives of different places within it.
When coming back to view the chain as a whole, the visits to each part of

the chain bring an altered perspective. This process of immersion in the parts and then return to the whole is the scales approach advocated in chapter 4. The contention of this approach is that a perfect, complete view of the fish chain is impossible. Any view of the fish chain represents choices and loss of detail in certain areas. But, at the same time, the movement between different perspectives and scales within the chain can allow for a more appropriate approximation of the diversity, complexity, and dynamics of the global fish chain and its constituent fish chains. Such an adaptive approach to understanding the chain mirrors the dynamics of the interactive approach advocated in this book. It also furnishes the basis for a reflexive interdisciplinary approach that recognises the advantages of the understandings available from each disciplinary position without trying to synthesise them.

These rather abstract comments will be better understood by bringing them back to the content of this section's chapters and how each anticipates the work of reassembling the whole of the chain while preserving its own particular emphasis. Kulbicki (see chap. 3) draws the connection between the ecological and human spheres primarily in terms of human fishing pressure on ecosystems. The view of the chapter from the fish's perspective is an interesting place to put oneself as a social scientist. Social scientists are used to seeing the ecosystem as a mysterious other, at best defined through the indigenous classifications of the people with whom they work and visible through the landed species on the beach. The impression from Kulbicki's chapter is quite the opposite; the ecosystem is the rich subject and the motivations and behaviour of fishers the mysterious other. While the market is much more clearly conceivable as a human creation than the human-influenced ecosystem, it too can take an agency of its own when viewed in abstract terms. Yet, while Thorpe et al.'s emphasis is on the market and participants in the supply chain, the latter could equally be viewed from a biological, species-based, perspective. Indeed, doing so serves to reinforce the notion of chain connectedness between the living resource in its aquatic environment and the extracted resource in the human environment.

Pullin and Sumaila's (see chap. 5) analysis of aquaculture provides a useful point of reference on the section as a whole. First, chapter 5 was written from a more synthetic approach, in that it comes closest among the discussed chapters to covering an entire fish chain. Yet, in the limited space of the chapter, that synthesis emphasised the inter-sector effects of growth in aquaculture, particularly in terms of ecological impact. It would be just as reasonable to imagine a chapter on aquaculture that prioritised social impacts and equity concerns in terms of changing market control. Second, aquaculture has a great deal of overlap with and influence on capture fisheries and the ecosystems and markets within which they are embedded, yet is nonetheless subject to very different market and production logics. Given the connections of aquaculture to capture fisheries, its importance for the future of aquatic foods, and its partial resemblance to capture fisheries chains, the combination of similarities and differences of aquaculture comprise a stimulating alternative vantage point.

In the foregoing paragraphs, we have shown how a scales approach provides a way of viewing the relationship among the different segments of the fish chain in an interactive, dynamic way. The advantage of such an approach is that it offers a flexibility useful for its recognition of the value of the positions and inputs of different stakeholders. The approach could well provide epistemological support to the argument for, and methodology of, co-management. At the same time, this book argues that governance is more than just getting the methodology right, although that is fundamental. Governance, as Kooiman and Jentoft (see chap. 14) will emphasise, is also about having to make choices according to normative frameworks. In the governance of the fish chain, these are choices of inclusion and exclusion and of allocation. One of the important choices with normative implications in discussing the fish chain is what holds it together. In the next section we show that the assessment of the drivers of interconnection and change in the fish chain varies, again to some degree according to discipline. After summarising some of the key theoretical models of the glue that holds the chain together, we return to the argument presented by Kooiman and Bavinck (see chap. 1): that globalisation encapsulates the most useful set of forces for understanding the interactions of the chain as a whole.

What Drives the Fish Chain?

Propositions about what binds the chain together are an essential part of knowing what the chain is because they explain how the fish chain can be internally diverse, complex, dynamic, and yet can still be considered a distinct whole. The degrees to which different propositions about the chain's drivers can account for diversity, complexity, and dynamics also provide a measure of their explanatory power.

The basic candidates for the dynamics of the chain that emerge from the discussion of the fish chain in this part of the book are natural forces, the individual, or social constructions. Each has an important influence on the chain and its specific manifestations. We argue, however, that the determinative factor is the social.

As Kulbicki's comprehensive treatment of the ecology of fisheries in a North-South perspective demonstrates, ecosystems are highly complex and subject to a wide range of factors, the effects and interactions of which are very imperfectly understood. Nonetheless, prior to intensive human intervention, permanent ecosystem shifts generally were gradual, occurring over long time scales. As the chapter notes, historical ecosystems even tended to be able to incorporate catastrophic events. It seems probable that for small-scale fishing for local consumption that developed over long time periods, the ecosystem was determinant in terms of influencing fishing gear and fishing strategies, which were diverse and complex in reflection of the ecosystems they depended on. Small-scale fishing for which the time depth is great, however, is the only case in which natural factors can be said to be primary in shaping the fish chain.

Kulbicki (see chap. 3) clearly acknowledges the current unprecedented power of direct and indirect human effects on marine ecosystems, with marine ecosystems changing in ways that biologists are unable to predict and that are having permanent effects. The weight of causality within the fish chain can be said to have reversed, with the anthropogenic now ascendant over the natural in the dynamic of the fish chain. While the primary force for change is now human, this does not imply increased predictability of ecosystem change. On the contrary, there is considerable evidence that human interventions are creating greater instability and more dramatic shifts within ecosystems. In all modern fisheries, human agency and institutions are far more important in shaping the character of the fish chain, although such a move from the environmental context has implications for the long-term sustainability of the modern fish chain in that it is less receptive to ecosystem feedback.

If we accept that human agency has come to assume the dominant position in the fish chain, we need to define what drives that agency. One option is to invest the source of agency in individual self-interest, as does neo-classical economics. In the case of fisheries, individuals are free agents who seek to maximise their shares of the rent available for the given resources. Under the assumptions of a perfect market, ecosystem health will be maintained because cost of effort equals price at the point of maximum sustainable yield (MSY). Hardin's *Tragedy of the Commons* hypothesis is grounded equally in individuals seeking to maximise their shares of a common-pool resource. Unlike the neo-classical view, however, he did not hold that the market would restrain over-exploitation of available resources. Rather, he argued that exploitation of the resource would continue to the point of exhaustion as resource extractors devote ever-more effort into trying to maximise their resource share unless mutually agreed upon coercive measures could be adopted (Hardin 1968).

Critics of these approaches – the present authors among them – argue that it is erroneous to look strictly to the individual as the source of agency. Individual action has to be considered in its social-cultural-political – and ecological – context, which informs action even as it is influenced by it. On the one hand, political-economic imperatives may skew incentives such that MSY may be overshot. On the other hand, tragedies of the commons may not arise despite considerable population pressure when collective institutions restrain individual interest. We do not deny the importance of individual agency as a key source of dynamics within fisheries. Our point is rather that individual agency is strongly conditioned by collective incentives and restraints, which have a determinative role in guiding change. The dynamics of the fish chain comes thus not from a single source, but from a complex series of interactions which at present may best be summarised as globalisation, as a way of describing the general shift in the scale of the context shaping coastal and fisheries populations.

Over the past several centuries, globalisation has meant that the sources of influence on individual decision-making have becoming increasingly distant from local experience. The dynamic of change in fisheries is due to an increasingly complex interaction of events, many of which occur in far-removed regions of the world. Perhaps the most critical force is the evolution of the global economy itself in terms of the development of new or intensified demand, growing market linkages, and the global spread of technological innovations. Growing importance also has to be attributed to the attractions of modernity through media and interaction with members of one's own kin or cultural group who have made good abroad. The pressures of globalisation on local environments are felt through such forces as more efficient vessels and capturing/processing technologies, fleet subsidies driven by international models of fisheries development, in-migration to seaboard regions including the expansion of coastal-based tourism, and requirements imposed by organisations tracing and regulating the international fish trade.

These and other impacts of globalisation are felt and translated into local experience and the actions of individuals in diverse and complex ways, reflecting particular local contexts. Nonetheless, they put the sources of change at a distant and largely unreachable remove from local perception. While the idea of governance has advanced by recognising the socially situated nature of individual agency, and the need thus for collective institutions to manage individual action and harness collective power, it also has to face the new global reality that much of the sphere of locally-important decision-making capacity lies outside of the local realm.

Images of the Fish Chain Re-examined

While fig. 1 (see p. 42) is useful as a simplification of the market process that links consumers world-wide with ecosystems and producers in specific fisheries, it gives a misleading sense of the verticality and unity of international fish production chains. As the decomposition of the chain in this section of the book has demonstrated, fig. 3.1 conceals an enormous depth of variation and complexity of the chain. That depth cannot be appreciated except through immersion in each of the segments of the chain, an effort that alters the perception of the chain as a whole.

Fig. 2 (see p. 42) conveys more effectively the interactive dynamic of the chain. It illustrates how market valuation influences the resources targeted for extraction from the natural environment. Innovation provides constant stimulus to means by which resources are extracted and to the kinds of resources targeted. Human extraction of a series of target living resources is the primary among many disruptions of the natural environment emanating from the human environment. The ecological processes by which valued species are created in the natural environment are indirectly influenced by human disruptions. An indication that these processes occur across different scales is evident from the lower part of the diagram.

Each of these figures thus captures only aspects of the forces driving the chain. Fig. 1 (in the introduction to Part II) shows that the chain is now global while fig. 2 (in the introduction to Part II) gives a sense of the complexity of the interactions propelling it. Yet neither of the figures captures fully what drives the chain. Fig. 2 does provide a source for the chain's dynamics in the innovation box. Yet innovation is itself dependent on the deeper incentives provided by the international economy and the attractions of modern life, the inclusion of which would necessitate adding another dimension to the diagram. Additionally, neither of the chains acknowledge the diversity and complexity of local conditions or the ongoing change to them that globalisation brings.

Governance Implications

The main challenge of the governance of the entire chain is that its diversity, complexity, and dynamics inhibit the construction of universally applicable models of governance. Rather, governance solutions need to be multiple and able to work at different spatial, institutional, and disciplinary scales. This is all the more urgent with globalisation, which is causing fish chains to lengthen, diversify, and become more complex. Thus, there is a need to work on governance approaches that are consciously interactive in the sense of involving multiple disciplines and stakeholders and in the sense of being able to adapt to rapidly changing situations. This is not new ground; there are longstanding disciplinary and cross-disciplinary attempts to meet these challenges.

Johnson et al. (see chap. 4), for example, connect to a large literature that tries to link social and ecological systems (Berkes and Folke 1998). This reflects the acceptance among natural scientists of the importance of human activities on natural systems, which has led to increasing attempts to incorporate humans into ecosystem models. Granted, some proposals from biological scientists simply advocate the exclusion of humans from ecological zones, but others recognise the importance of involving local people and communities in the management of natural refugia. From the social sciences, there are many initiatives that address the difficulties of human organisation for natural resource management, such as collective action theory, institutional economics, cultural materialism, and legal pluralism.

The consideration of diversity, dynamics, and complexity of the fish chain in this part of the book has raised the importance of choice as a key issue for governance. Governance of the fish chain requires making hard choices between alternatives that will result in potentially negative consequences for individuals, groups, or the natural environment. Such choices are embedded in the social, political, and economic dynamics of fisheries and are constrained by the uncertainty of knowledge of the fish chain, and thus the associated unpredictability of intervention in it. The social nature of choice and the contingency of knowledge mean that fish chain governance necessarily has to engage with its epistemological and normative foundations. We have made an important start in that direction in this chapter with the discussion of the images of the fish chain. The methodological outcome of that discussion, the advantages of decomposing and re-composing the fish chain with multi-disciplinary input, reaffirms the importance of multi-stakeholder involvement in fish chain governance. It also reaffirms the importance of precaution in decision-making, for the sake of the natural environment, and the importance of social equity considerations as a normative guide.

It is apparent from the preceding chapters that the context in which governance occurs – what we choose to term the 'fish chain', is diverse, complex, and changing rapidly. Equally clear is that a multitude of governance tools/instruments can be deployed to resolve the fundamental concerns identified by Chuenpagdee et al. (see chap. 2). The task is to identify the most appropriate governance tools given particular local conditions. It falls to state, market, and civil society institutions, as the following part of this volume shows, to determine and implement the most effective instruments and resources for the resolution or remediation of concerns and then to oversee their operation. We have suggested in this chapter, however, that those approaches which are flexible, interdisciplinary, multi-sector, and self-aware will most likely be able to adapt to the demands of globalisation on the fish chain while achieving key objectives of resource and livelihood sustainability, food safety, and food security.

PART III

Institutions for
Fisheries Governance

Introduction Part III

Svein Jentoft

The four chapters in Part III depict institutional mechanisms and challenges in fisheries at the global, national, and local level and their interconnections. Fisheries governance and food security involve institutions at all levels and require vertically and horizontally co-ordinated and structured linkages. The diversity, complexity, and dynamics of fisheries institutions provide targets that are obscure and moving. Fisheries governance is thus a never-ending process that requires institutions that are robust and flexible. What these institutions should be like is in itself an important governance issue with no easy answers. But what are institutions? What exactly do they do?

Institutions are the instrument through which the formation and execution of fisheries governance occurs. The design and workings of institutions are key issues. As instruments they can be effective, fitting, legitimate, and socially just to various extents. From a governance perspective, they need to be continually evaluated and adapted to changing circumstances. Governors should always relate to institutions, as should the stakeholders who experience their impact. Institutions are obviously social constructs and they are the outcome of human experience, foresight and ingenuity. They introduce structure, order, and predictability into human relations and interactions. Without institutions, social actors would not know how to interact and would not know what is expected of them or what they can expect of others. As March and Olsen (1995) argue, institutions provide 'a logic of appropriateness' that comes with rights, routines, roles, responsibilities, agendas, standards, and practices that enable the people confronted with them to distinguish between right and wrong, good and evil, normal and abnormal, and natural and unnatural. Since they need to be recognised by everyone affected by them, institutions also come with meanings and interpretations.

Among academics, the institution is a concept with many definitions. It is one of the terms used by scholars and the general public alike and the two do not always perceive it in quite the same way. Perceptions of what institutions do and what their potentials are can vary. In a sense, how we perceive these specific institutions determines what fisheries governors can and should do. If institutions are narrowly defined, the ideas on what they can do are similarly narrow, and a broad perception of institutions includes a more comprehensive repertoire of mechanisms, incentives, and designs. If institutions are defined as 'rules' of conduct (cf. North 1990), governors emphasise the legal aspects of institutions. Institutional design then only means rules. If institutions are perceived to be more generally about norms, their design includes whatever mechanisms, such as moral standards and upbringing, that make people obey rules. If the definition of institutions is even broader so that it includes cognition, as Scott (1995) notes, the action frame of institution-building is further expanded. Institutional design then covers all the information, knowledge, learning, and validation processes that determine which perceptions of reality are taken for granted and which are not, what or whose knowledge is reliable and relevant and what or whose is not.

We argue that a governance approach to fisheries should adopt a broad, rather than a narrow, definition of institutions. A governance perspective on institutions needs to emphasise their regulatory, normative, and cognitive attributes. It also needs to emphasise their social and cultural underpinnings and the idea that institutions never operate in a vacuum but are always embedded in social networks, which are often institutions themselves. In other words, institutions not only work at micro, meso and macro levels of society, at a lower level they are often contained within institutions at a higher level – like a Chinese Box, as it were. The relationships that structure the environment of institutions should also be within the governance realm. In other words, governance is not only about institutional designs, it is also about institutional environments that cannot always be 'negotiated' (Cyert and March 1963) but need to be taken as a given.

Fisheries governance should employ a broad perspective. Obviously, fisheries systems may not work well because of deficiencies in their internal institutional design or because their institutional environment is not supportive. Market and community failure both imply incompatibilities in the institutional environment of fisheries systems and both provide an impetus to the well-known 'tragedy of the commons' (cf. McCay and Jentoft 1998). This is also why we hold that a governance approach to fisheries cannot only focus on the state, the market, and civil society individually; it should also take into account how the three interact (Kooiman 2003). It is a classical thesis in social science that civil society provides essential inputs to the working of the market and the state. As Wolfe points out (Wolfe 1989: 39), 'Civil society, if understood as the place where people pause to reflect on the moral dilemmas they face, is necessary if individuals are to possess those capacities of agency that will enable them to make rules as well as follow them'. The users of common property resources are typically caught in a dilemma where the only way out is agency in terms of rule formation and compliance. It follows from Wolfe's observation that civil society is essential to sustainable fisheries resource use. In fisheries, civil society involves the community, the family, user groups, and religious groups – all institutions that are typically left out and regarded as irrelevant to fisheries management, which currently tends to overemphasise the state and the market and the interaction between them.

Wolfe also hints at the enabling role of institutions. Institutions keep social actors in check, but in so doing they also provide opportunities for problem solving. Institutions allow social actors to accomplish things and without institutions they would be handicapped, some things would simply be beyond their reach. Institutions that curb the fishing effort give actors instruments to help them realise what is in their common interest – a healthy resource. Institutions also make social actors trust each other more. They can often trust institutions more than individuals. Institutions supply the stability, order, and predictability that make fisheries systems work. This is why we believe it is essential to employ a concept of institution that transcends rules. Cognition is clearly among the factors that make institutions play their enabling roles. As institutions validate knowledge, social actors can operate with less uncertainty. For instance, fisheries research institutions relieve management agencies from some of the political pressure they would otherwise be exposed to. Knowledge validated by the institution of science makes the state more confident and less vulnerable when controversial management measures are implemented.

Institutions fail if the rules that regulate behaviour are underdeveloped or poorly enforced. They also fall short if their normative standards provide inadequate incentives and guidance on how to interact. The same occurs if the knowledge they build on or generate is insufficient or nonsensical. Any governance approach to fisheries systems should alleviate the weak points of the three institutions – state, market, and civil society. The diagnosis of the problems and opportunities of institutions should start here. The next step should highlight the contributions of institutional environments. Institutional designs are adapted to the environment to varying extents. In real life, they are not always developed and implemented via a thorough analysis of the situations they are supposed to work in. Instead, they are adopted for reasons that may be external to the problem structure of a particular fishery. Sometimes solutions even generate problems rather than the other way around. We know that institutional forms often spread by imitation in much the same way as fashions do.

Institutions are supposed to be robust, stable and lasting, but they sometimes need to be reformed or totally overhauled. However, despite the need for change, they remain entrenched. Institutions come with vested interests and the status quo may be preferable to change. Management systems tend to produce winners and losers, and while the latter might be expected to favour change, the former would prefer management to stay the same. Institutional reform often has to be backed by power, but it risks opposition if the power is not legitimate. What makes institutions and power legitimate is an important issue in fisheries governance (Jentoft 2000a). Fisheries governance effectiveness relies on legitimacy. As Max Weber noted in his classic treatise (Roth and Wittich 1978), legitimacy can have various sources such as tradition, charisma, or legal/bureaucratic rationality, but his list is not complete. Parsons (1968) adds professional, functional knowledge as a fourth source, as is the case with research institutions. It is generally assumed that legitimacy can be attributed to political process and that, *ceteris paribus,* a management regime that works according to democratic principles has a greater degree of legitimacy than a regime that does not. This is a central assumption as to the feasibility of user group participation in fisheries management (Jentoft and McCay 1995).

As Kooiman argues in a similar vein, 'In diverse, dynamic and complex areas of societal activity, no single governing agency is able to realise legitimate and effective governing by itself. Such governance is achieved by the creation of interactive, social-political structures and processes stimulating communication between the actors involved and the creation of common responsibilities in addition to individual and separate ones' (Kooiman 2003: 3-4).

Which institutional formations in fisheries can bring about this kind of interaction is a key governance issue. Institutions display great variety. They operate at all levels and are interconnected in complex ways. With regard to socio-political governance, Kooiman concludes that governing interactions and their institutional settings vary enormously from 'the "street corners" at local communities, via public-private partnership to institutionalising regimes governing international political-economic global arenas' (Kooiman 2003: 156). As is stated above, the chapters in this section attempt to grasp what governing interactions occur within institutional settings that range from the local to the global village level. Fisheries governance is played out within, and regulated or affected by, institutions that have a global focus, such as the World Trade Organization, the International Council for the Exploration of the Sea and the Food and Agriculture Organization of the UN. Since fisheries have increasingly become a global enterprise where problems are exported from one geographical area to another as fish stocks become exhausted, these institutions have become more and more important. Global governance has a much weaker institutional foundation than nation-state governance. But what nations can and cannot do is increasingly influenced by global institutions, such as international conventions on biodiversity or the human rights of oppressed indigenous peoples (ILO Convention 169, see Jentoft et al. 2003).

The nation-state nonetheless should and does play a role in fisheries governance and not only as a representative within global institutions, but also as a regulator and facilitator in domestic fisheries affairs. Most governance reforms are either initiated by or target state fisheries agencies and legislation. The theory of fisheries often holds the state responsible for mismanagement (Hannesson 1996; Indicello et al. 1999). State inducements are felt to be largely to blame for the fleets' massive harvesting capacity that globally puts most fish stocks in jeopardy. Any solution to this problem would require an institutional response by the nation-states individually and in concert. In fisheries governance, the state is part of the problem as well as the solution. We should not forget, though, that state authorities are frequently subject to pressure from powerful private interests and lobbying groups, making governance a highly political affair. As Pauly and MacLean argue, 'Politics often dilutes the best management schemes at the national level as well as at the intergovernmental level' (Pauly and MacLean 2003: 79). Governance is also about how political processes affect and are affected by institutional arrangements such as resource management regimes.

At the end of the day, institutional processes at the global and national levels are also felt at the level of the local community. As Giddens points out, 'Modern organisations are able to connect the local and the global in ways which would have been unthinkable in more traditional societies and in so doing routinely affect the lives of many millions of people' (Giddens 1990: 20). It is the fisher people who have to live with the consequences of national and global organisations at these higher levels, often without any influence on their creation or operation. Fishers and fish workers are thus often the primary victims of mismanagement at a higher institutional level. A tragedy of the commons easily turns into a tragedy for the commoners. The community and its institutions are a central governance issue that is largely ignored in the state governance approach to fisheries. Instead, communities find themselves at the receiving end of the chain of command (Jentoft 2000b). Yet we know that communities are the buffer against external pressures of globalisation. The community plays an important role in shaping people's lives and fisheries activities are usually rooted in communities. It is within the community and its sub-institutions that fishers and fish workers are socialised and acquire their values, morality, and worldviews. Social research demonstrates that because of the social capital embedded in them, communities often play a very constructive role in managing common pool resources (Ostrom 1990). Fisheries authorities should draw on the capacity of communities to become responsible co-governors of fisheries systems and regimes. Communities are, however, not isolated entities. They are connected to each other and to institutions at higher levels. As Agrawal and Gibson hold, 'Community-based natural resource conservation initiatives must be founded on images of community that recognise their internal differences and processes, their relations with external actors, and the institutions that affect both' (Agrawal and Gibson 2001: 2). The local and vertical linkages of communities need co-ordination in one way or another, but since linkages do not always have to rely on hierarchical steering, there is still an opportunity for a bottom-up governance approach.

8

Local Institutions

José J. Pascual-Fernández, Katia Frangoudes, and Stella Williams

Fishers and Communities

There are many definitions of a community. Community studies have played an important role in the social sciences, such as anthropology, since the early twentieth century. In this sense, functionalist studies by Malinowski and Radcliffe Brown served as models for studying communities as a strategy for analysing culture as a whole. Even precursors like Tönnies with his concept of Gemeinschaft and his positivist organicism can be quoted. Culture was conceptualised as consisting of functionally interrelated parts, creating a model of analysis that was to pattern the standard in social anthropology (Redfield 1971 [1955-6]). The studies depended on a community concept characterised by isolation, homogeneity and shared values or culture. Redfield identified four essential characteristics in communities: a small or reduced social scale, homogeneity regarding their members' activities and state of mind, a consciousness of distinctiveness and a certain self-sufficiency over time (Redfield 1971; Rapport 1996).

In the 1950s, Hillery found 94 alternative definitions of this concept and the features most commonly shared were 'interaction' and 'ties of interest' followed by 'geographical proximity', with the only substantive overlap being 'all dealt with people' (Hillery 1955: 117). In the same decade, a generally critical tendency of the models in community studies led to the partial demise of this concept in anthropology. It was replaced by alternative notions (such as population) with fewer connotations. However, in recent years the role of communities in conservation has been rediscovered as the locus of conservationist thinking. After a long history of failed top-down development programmes, international agencies from the World Bank or USAID to the International Union for Conservation of Nature (IUCN) have turned to programmes that implement or reinforce community-based conservation policies (Agrawal and Gibson 2001: 4). This process is linked to the emphasis on the participation of local populations after the recognition of state policy limitations in designing and enforcing adequate measures to achieve the sustainable use of natural resources.

Communities are more diverse, heterogeneous and unstable than Redfield and other authors assume. To summarise, we use a definition formulated by Agrawal and Gibson (2001: 1): 'Communities are complex entities containing individuals differentiated by status, political and economic power, religion and social prestige, and intentions. Although some may operate harmoniously, others do not. Some see nature or the environment as something to be protected; others care only for nature's short-term use. Some have effective traditional norms; others have few. Some community members seek refuge from the government and market; others quickly embrace both. And sometimes communities come into existence only as a result of their interactions with governments and markets'. The emphasis here is on intra-community diversity related to power, wealth, status or culture. Consequently, the characteristics of community life or behaviour in relation to resource management can be quite different in each concrete case. However, in contrast with this position, three elements have been relevant in the analysis of communities in literature: the small spatial dimension, a social structure that is supposedly homogeneous and a global set of shared norms (Agrawal and Gibson 2001: 2). We note that the social and cultural systems of contemporary fishing peoples should always be analysed taking their linkages into account with regional, national and international processes.

Small Spatial Units

The idea of communities as small spatial units is associated with isolation and images contrasting with our globalised contemporary world. Since Wilmsen's (1989) analyses of the Kalahari Bushmen – considered the archetype of pristine hunter-gatherers ever since the 1960s – demonstrating their close link to different populations through deep historical commercial bonds and a rich history of associations, the myth of the isolated community or isolated societies has been in question. As regards fishing populations, the geographical dimension of a community is also an issue that poses problems. In Europe, Japan, and other areas, there are fishing communities that occupy definite geographical boundaries. However, in other cultural contexts such as the migrating fishers of West Africa, who move from one place to another, even in neighbouring nation states, all the while maintaining ties with their country and co-ethnics back home in the village, geographical boundaries are practically non-existent (Ruffier 1999; Cormier-Salem 2000; Jul-Larsen 2000).

The geographical limits of the communities and the resource management they may accomplish in these areas are also relevant. Through their institutions, communities manage a limited maritime territory. This territory may extend over the borders of a community or even a country. These examples show that geographical limits are not the main basis of the definition of local coastal communities and the institutions devised to locally manage the resources may not fit with local settlement boundaries and can control a wider area.

Homogeneous Composition

The concept of community is linked to a supposedly homogeneous composition. However, inequalities of wealth, gender, power or knowledge may lead to very different positions in a community. Communities are usually stratified and completely egalitarian societies are as yet unknown. Perhaps the assumption of a single economic activity is one of the most pervasive stereotypes conferred upon fishing communities, even though the combination of fishing, agriculture, commerce or even tourism and service-related activities is much more widespread. In many South Pacific or Greek islands and the fishing-farming societies of Africa, local communities practice fishing and agriculture simultaneously and these activities are even combined within the same household. Many authors describe how migrating fishers in West Africa engage in different activities at different times of the year or of their lives, combining fishing with navigation in cargo boats, trade or even agriculture (Bouju 1994; Chauveau et al. 2000).

Shared Norms

This is essentially the third dominant meaning of the concept of the community in literature: the community as common interests and shared norms. To Agrawal and Gibson (2001: 10), all communities are imagined communities that depend upon the perceptions of their members. The self-ascription of individuals and their feelings of membership may be similar to the criteria in the definitions of concepts such as the ethnic group. As members of communities, individuals give up some of their selfish interests in favour of community or group interests. Some authors claim the roots of local communities lie in a common culture, since fishers in a community generally share the same values and perception of nature. Fishers and fishing practices are guided by the values, norms and knowledge shared in each community (Jentoft 2000a: 54). This view depends of course on a specific concept of culture.

Every culture is enmeshed in processes of change, and conflicts may arise between alternative patterns of behaviour in certain areas. Enculturation processes of different kinds and strengths are used to transfer values and models of thinking or behaviour from the older to the younger generations and problems may arise in the course of the process. The values and norms or patterns of prestige may vary quickly in areas undergoing rapid development processes. For example, European or African fishers of a certain age may be unable to envision themselves in any other occupation than the one they learned from their fathers. However, it is not rare nowadays for young men born into fishing families to prefer alternative occupations in societies where the alternatives exist. These are problems many fishing communities in Europe are faced with today. In this sense, the transmission and inheritance of the fishing culture and the related specific knowledge, techniques or abilities may be in danger in many areas, where it can be increasingly difficult to find young members for a fishing crew. For instance, French fishing vessels, having difficulties in finding local fishers, employed Spanish or Portuguese for years, but had to shift recently to Polish ones because they had trouble finding crew members. Greek, Italian or Norwegian ships are having similar problems (Sagdahl 2000).

These and many other processes of change indicate that not all communities exhibit the same characteristics and not even the same community at different historical moments. The ideal community with shared beliefs, a homogeneous composition, stability, and clear ties is a myth. As Jentoft indicates, communities are often characterised by social fissures, conflicts, inequities and power differentials (Jentoft 2000a: 58), and by diversity, fluidity, and change processes, as are cultures as a whole. In fact, in the real world, communities usually consist of subgroups with different interests and variable access to capital, knowledge or power. Local politics in the communities may be complex and changing, but always present.

Pluri-Activity and Migration Patterns

Theoretical approaches defining fishing communities as composed of people who mainly live off fishing are no longer valid in many areas of the globe where fishers, at the same or different moments, also engage in other economic activities. On many South Pacific islands, people engage in fishing as well as farming and are as much fishers as farmers (e.g., Bataille-Benguigui 1999). The examples of fisher-farmers given by Cormier-Salem (2000) show that people who do both also live in some parts of West Africa. In the Casamance, the fishing territory may be a lagoon close to the coast where fishers manage their piscatorial territories in much the same way as they manage their agricultural fields. For years, fishing far off the coast was practiced by ethnic groups specialised in it. But for historical reasons, fishing is no longer an exclusive activity of these ethnic groups. The famine that affected peasant populations in the 1970s in many parts of Africa drew them to the coast to fish (Cormier-Salem 2000).

Diversified or pluri-activity strategies characterise the societies of fisher-farmers and are also present among migrating fishers in West Africa. Most of the migrating fishers there engage in various supplementary economic activities and it is often doubtful whether fishing is their main productive activity. To them, fishing is merely one of many means of livelihood and people choose and often combine their productive activities with others not always linked to a fishing-related identity (Chauveau and Jul-Larsen 2000; Chauveau et al. 2000).

Box 8.1 Peasants/farmers/fishers: early adaptations in Nordic countries

For pre-industrial Sweden (1700-1900) Lögfren (1979) describes four different adaptations (ecotypes) among the coastal and fishing populations:

1. *Farmer-fishers* who balanced various activities linked to land (agriculture, raising cattle) and sea exploitation (fishing, hunting, gathering) in their household economy in a continuum from farming fishers to fishing farmers.

2. *Mobile deep-sea fishers* with an economy based on intensive fishing linked to herring captures that mainly developed in specific areas of Sweden. The captures were exchanged for cash or agricultural products. Few farming activities were combined with fisheries.

3. *Fisher-burghers* who combined living in town with summer fishing in distant archipelagos, enjoying exclusive rights granted by the king and combining fishing with coastal trading. The catch was salted and sold in the cities at the end of the summer.

4. *Landless or crofter fishers* who came from the poorest strata in the coastal peasant communities, frequently because population growth outpaced the demand for farm workers. They practiced subsistence fishing combined with small-scale exploitation of marginal lands.

These four ecotypes depict an image clearly different from the stereotype of fishers who only engage in extractive activities. In fact, most of them, especially the fourth category, are the by-product of lengthy population growth from 1750 to 1850 that expelled landless peasants, transforming them into proletarians who tried to exploit marginal land in coastal areas with permission from the landowners and combined farming and fishing activities. As Lögfren indicates, 'before the introduction of deep-sea fishing the demarcation between maritime and agrarian adaptations was indistinct. Many coastal farmers carried out some subsistence fishing while most peasant fishers supplemented their meagre marine living by developing small-scale gardening and farming activities' (Lögfren 1979: 91). This pattern began to change in the twentieth century in Sweden due to increasing labour specialisation and new market characteristics.

Source: Lögfren (1979)

As in many other areas of Europe, similar patterns were observed in northern Europe centuries ago with different adaptations to specific constraints. In the Canary Islands, mid-way between the North and South, fishing populations exhibited multi-activity patterns until the twentieth century. For centuries, fishing around the coasts of the islands was of meagre importance. In many areas, fishers migrated from one side of the island to the other, depending on the seasons and weather conditions (Pascual-Fernández 1991). Even nowadays there are many examples of shifting or combined occupations, especially if we consider all the economic activities carried out in the household. In the domestic units involved in artisanal fishing in the Canary Islands, women and young people work in alternative jobs: hotels and restaurants, commerce and construction. This strategy of combining economic activities is not new. Since the fifteenth century, littoral communities have survived via a complex matrix of interconnected labour in different sectors. Until recently, transportation services, agriculture and fishing in the fleet that worked the Saharan banks were the alternatives frequently engaged in by the fishers themselves, shifting occupations in some periods of their life or simply from season to season, especially in winter, a pattern that continues today (Pascual-Fernández 2004).

Fishing, Communities and Institutional Arrangements

Communities can contribute to fisheries management in multifarious ways or pose insurmountable obstacles. Institutional arrangements providing sustainable use of marine resources have been developed in different ways, shapes, and forms in many areas of the world. Because of the subtractive character of the resources related to fishing or gathering, management in this area requires a collective dimension: the use by one individual may affect the actual or future use by other individuals of the same or different resources. This is more evident in fisheries than in many agricultural adaptations, except in the use of water resources, which usually also presents subtractive patterns. For this reason, institutional arrangements to manage sea resources are nothing new. Examples of historical overfishing are increasingly evident (Pauly et al. 2002) and in this sense, human societies and local communities have had to find solutions to these problems, although institutional arrangements are not always successful.

In some areas, high levels of organising the local use of these resources have emerged and in other places, processes of institutional innovation have either failed or are non-existent. The design of these institutional arrangements is faced with several limitations. Firstly, there is the internal diversity of communities that may present important problems for collective action in the event of organised groups with opposing interests. Secondly, there is the complexity of the relations between individuals and groups inside the community and in a wider context that may influence their institutional viability. Thirdly, there are the dynamics, a factor that is now crucial in many local scenarios where changes induced by the market, demographic transformations, tourism, and so forth may alter the preconditions for local institutions. Lastly, the possibility of controlling fishing activities in a territory depends to some extent on spatial or even temporal scales that may affect the feasibility of local institutional arrangements.

Box 8.2 Preconditions of collective action

A particularly interesting area of inquiry are the preconditions of collective action. In other words, what factors explain the differences between dissimilar communities in their capacities to design, implement, and enforce successful autonomous institutions for resource management. A general rule used by economists and political scientists is the net benefit of these institutional arrangements. All innovation processes in these areas imply organisational costs, and large amounts of time invested in making the necessary arrangements, attending meetings, convincing other users, and supporting the institutional arrangements once in force. The perceived benefits of these institutions may or may not compensate for all these costs, and the perception that users have of the balance between both elements in the equation may affect their decision to support or not those institutional buildings or maintenance processes (Wade 1987; Gibson et al. 2000). This perception may be influenced by many factors, and past experiences of local management of resources can help decisively in the process.

The development of local or folk management is neither automatic nor inevitable, and any assumption in this sense is unrealistic. Pinkerton (1994: 318) suggests that a long period of stable population size, location, and resource use is required for local populations to experiment, learn and adapt to local environments, in a process of trial and error. Sometimes it may be very difficult to develop folk management practices in situations of industrial development, multiple use conflicts, migratory patterns, and so forth. The existence of different groups inside a community may lead to all these issues, as groups and individuals negotiate the use, management and conservation of resources. At the local level they attempt to implement the negotiated rules and try to solve the disputes that arise in the whole process (Agrawal and Gibson 2001: 13). The power structure at the local level or the benefits to gain by different subgroups or individuals may also influence this process. Several authors have tried to systematise the preconditions of collective action in this area (Wade 1987; Pinkerton 1989b, 1994; Mitchell 1999; Gibson et al. 2000).

Source: Authors of this chapter

Many variables may affect the behaviour and strategies of resource users, facilitating or hindering the building or maintenance of local institutions in charge of resource conservation. These processes are linked to more general patterns at the societal level. Some authors cite the relevance of a well-functioning civil society as a prerequisite for co-management since in many areas, residents are poorly organised beyond the household and their experience of working institutions within the communities may be limited (Sandersen 1999; Jentoft 2000a). From among a multiplicity of contradictory conceptions of civil society (Rodríguez Guerra 2000), we take this concept as referring to an entity basically complementing the state, a social sphere between the economy and the area of political power (identified with the state). It is on the periphery of political power in modern states and comprised of a multiplicity of private entities (organisations, associations, interest groups and so forth) that make up the associative scheme of the public sphere. In local communities, these entities may be varied and powerful. The causes of the differences may be in different areas of social reality, such as political history, migration patterns, dictatorships, heavily centralised states and so on, but can obviously affect the possibilities of co-management and self-organisation in local scenarios.

Fishing communities depend on certain resources and areas of maritime space, developing management strategies throughout history to secure these resources. It is necessary to manage the activity of their members to avoid conflicts among them and avoid resource exhaustion, and frequently to exclude foreign fishers from their territory. Local management of the fishing activities in a territory hopes to guarantee peaceful co-existence among the members of the community and a fair sharing, if possible, of the resources by its members. This heavy responsibility may rest on an organisation (cofradia, prud'homie) or an individual (water master). For example, the aim of French prud'homies (fishing organisations in the French Mediterranean) is to ensure a decent income for all their members. The members of the prud'homie are elected by the whole community and the first prud'homme is an experienced fisher. The members of the organisation follow its rules, which are designed to avoid conflicts between different fishing fleets or gear. If the rules are not respected, the first prud'homme can judge and inflict penalties. In the event of recidivism, fishers can be excluded from the prud'homie and in a sense from the community (Tempier 1986; Féral 1990; Frangoudes 1997). The membership in prud'homies results in shared values and norms and similar attitudes to resources. They respect the rules set by the institutions that generally regroup fishers of various neighbouring ports, although each may also have separate specific rules. The institutions are able to regulate the fishing activity under their jurisdiction, and their strength derives from the large number of members and from being long-standing institutions.

In southern Europe, there are the cofradias, which have channelled fishers' participation in marine resource management in Spain for centuries. In some regions of the country, they can be traced back to the Middle Ages (Erkoreka Gervasio 1991; Alegret 1999) but in other parts, and the Canaries are a good example, they have a more recent history along with reduced institutionalisation (Pascual-Fernández 1999). These non-profit organisations have a special legal status as corporations with public rights, similar in some aspects to local councils. The cofradias depended on the central government until the creation of autonomous communities in Spain. From then on, several communities began to receive specific competences in these areas and to issue specific legislation about cofradias. In the Canary Islands, Decreto 109 of 26 June 1997 regulates fishers' cofradias. This is why there are now some relevant differences in how these institutions are organised in different areas of Spain. They represent the interests of the fishing sector as a whole and serve as consultative and cooperative bodies for the administration in multiple duties related to promoting the sector. Moreover, they perform economic, administrative and commercial management tasks. They frequently also cooperate in regulating access to the resources and informing about infractions in their territory. To summarise, they try to manage the activities and in some senses the resources, together with the state, and reduce conflicts in the fishing sector between different fleets, fishing techniques and so on.

Box 8.3 General features of cofradias

The aim of the cofradias is to integrate everyone in the sector – fishers, ship-owners and even shellfish gatherers – in their area of influence (one or more harbours). Sometimes different interest groups or associations co-exist in the cofradias. In the case of shellfish gathering, there are special associations within the cofradia in Galicia that are in charge of organising this activity, usually carried out by women. Ship-owners and crew members have equal representation in the governing bodies of the cofradias, except for the role of Patrón Mayor (president of the organisation), which is in the hands of one individual. In fact, in some cofradias, the position of Patrón Mayor has considerable influence and great authority. The person in this position, elected by the members, is in charge of management and also obeys the rules issued by the cofradia and enforces its agreements. Two additional governing bodies of the cofradia are the General Committee (Junta General), and the Cabildo (12 to 48 elected members) as an administrative and management body.

In many areas of the mainland, the cofradias manage the first sell of the produce (Pascual-Fernández 1999) and are beginning to organise more complex commercialisation schemes, even using the Internet as the main commercialisation channel (see www.lonxanet.com). Like the prud'homies they issue rules that their members have to respect, such as timetables for departing or returning to the port in Catalonia, or propose changes in the techniques to be used in their area of influence, changes the government usually accepts, as in the Canary Islands (Pascual-Fernández 1999). They do not have the same prerogatives as the prud'homies to judge, but they may impose sanctions in some senses if users do not respect the rules. They also perform other tasks such as the management of first-sell auctions, the accounting of ships or their bureaucratic management and so forth. These functions are what has enabled the cofradias to survive, as opposed to the prud'homies, whose role has weakened (Franquesa 1993; Alegret 1995, 1996; Pascual-Fernández 1999). That does not mean these institutions have not had problems in recent years. Ship-owners' associations, fish merchants' associations or producer organisations have begun, e.g., in Catalonia, to reclaim some of their traditional political and bargaining space and this 'is provoking a significant loss of bargaining power, an increase in transaction costs and institutional change in all the fishery sector of Catalonia, with unforeseen consequences for the future of the management system currently in place', since until now the cofradias have been the main link between the fishing sector and the state (Alegret 2000: 183).

Source: José J. Pascual-Fernández

Local Institutions and Conflicts with the State

These models of traditional institutional arrangements within communities sharing the same culture and values are not always accepted by the administration. In some cases, the administration considers these organisations archaic or obsolete and replaceable by new ones that appear to be modern or more egalitarian. The public powers frequently do not hesitate to destroy them even if the fishers are overtly opposed. In France the establishment of local fisheries committees (comités locaux de pêches) since 1945 has weakened the role of the prud'homies. Some fishers consider the prud'homies useless now that the local committees decree rules concerning resource management. Nowadays, producers' organisations (POs) recognised by the EC have the capacity to establish fisheries plans for different species. The aim is to regulate fish markets, thus avoiding price decreases. But the majority of French fishers are not members of these organisations. The power of the POs to manage the resource is directly granted by the EU and is added to the two already-existing fishers' organisations.

In West Africa the water master used to play an important role in the management of local fishing resources. The oldest in the local group, he had the responsibility of issuing rules such as geographical or seasonal prohibitions and had to be the first to start each fishing campaign, after which the other fishers could follow suit (Kassibo 2000: 203). The colonial administration considered these local institutions too archaic for the management of the fishing territory. After gaining independence, the national administrations adopted the same position. For them as well, water masters and their rules were considered feudal. However, in the past the rules enacted by water masters and their decisions were respected by all (Fay 2000). To the Mali administration, traditional law represents feudalism because it overlooks equity, since foreign fishers are excluded from local fishing grounds. In this case, state management erodes traditional strategies and institutions that local communities have developed to cope with and benefit from fluctuating resource availability (Sarch and Allison 2000).

In the course of modernisation in Mali, state regulations abolished the role of the water master in fisheries, promising that the new Fisheries Law would take into account the traditional rules exercised by the water master. This attention devoted by legislators to traditional rules can be interpreted as meaning they were aware that modern law could not destroy the traditional customary law still practiced in the communities. In Chad as well, public authorities had to allow the water master to regain some of his powers in the context of local fishing communities. In other words, in some places in Africa the official disappearance of the water masters has not meant their informal fading, since they still retain ample power in the local communities and all migrant fishers have to be presented to these water masters. They have to learn the local rules and practices and their behaviour at sea has to comply with them (Jul-Larsen 2000).

Even if the authorities want some of these institutions to disappear without a trace in the name of modernity, traditional rules do not vanish overnight. Not violating the customary rules is a well-established custom among community fishers in many areas of the world and strangers who want to fish in their territories have to comply with these rules if they want to remain undisturbed. The administration can set up new rules, but they do not have the same social acceptance – they are not the product of the community but imposed from outside – and no one respects them. Platteau (1993) explains that the economic growth of traditional fishing in Kayar (Senegal) is linked to the fact that the economic organisations have not been modernised. They remain traditional, which is precisely why they are efficient. Traditional institutional models are efficient because they remain integrated into a traditional institutional environment and are rooted in the local identity and strict moral patterns. However, in a context of fragile states that compromise their implementation, many of the new regulations issued to manage the fisheries in a modern way barely get any support from the local populations.

In many countries where the state is weak, fishers' compliance with rules mainly depends on the social control exercised by individuals on their neighbours who do not comply. The community's punishment can be stronger than the authorities'. It can even mean the exclusion of fishers from the community. Social ostracism in a context of mutual dependence and cooperation for many daily tasks can be a strong argument against free-rider behaviour.

Regulating conflicts in a local fishing community does not necessarily require an organisation, as is clear from a case in the north of Greece. At the end of the 1970s, a trawler fleet destroyed numerous nets that belonged to inshore fishers in the area, causing a serious conflict. The inshore fishers asked the authorities to forbid trawling in the Bay of Thessaloniki. Despite the opposition, an agreement was reached with the trawlers and the gear was banned in the area. The explanation given by local fishers was as follows: 'We could not walk freely in the village!' It was necessary to find a solution because the trawler crewmembers and the inshore fishers were members of the same community and sometimes of the same family. The social peace of the community was at risk and this could not be accepted (Frangoudes 1997).

Threats to local institutions do not solely come from state intervention. Industrial fishing frequently causes difficulties for fishers' organisations, jeopardising the cohesion of the community. Basque ship-owners in Spain may leave the traditional organisations and create their own. However, French industrial fishers may participate in the same organisations as small-scale boats, although effectively they are more powerful and in some cases promote their own interests to the detriment of the smaller boats. According to the preconditions of collective action, these differences add complexity to the institutions of local management. Even in potentially adverse conditions though, as the French case shows, they may survive.

As a general rule that is frequently emphasised in the literature about local institutions focused on resource management, wherever possible, the state should support the pre-existing institutional framework instead of imposing a new one imported from another country or institutional context. Compliance with externally-imposed norms is usually more costly to enforce and more subject to questioning than if users in a sense self-impose the rules, even if they are exactly the same. As is suggested above, the development of these institutions is not feasible in every situation, but wherever possible it may be wise to support their development and stability. However, local institutions are not always able to adapt to new and changing situations. Inertia and resistance to change are observed in national bureaucracies as well as in local scenarios. For instance, the problems women have entering many local institutions with equal rights may demonstrate the shortcomings of these institutional arrangements and the necessity to adapt them and the local culture to new situations.

Even in the numerous cases where the state or supranational bodies have destroyed these local institutions or replaced them with centralised management schemes, returning the responsibilities to the local populations and reconstructing local institutions capable of assuming these tasks is becoming a political priority: the devolution of responsibilities. The reversal of control and accountability is an essential element of devolvement, the process of giving back management responsibilities to local populations or communities (see chaps. 9 and 11). In this area, co-management (Jentoft 1989) is a strategy characterised by involving stakeholders in policy formulation through consultation and delegating management responsibilities for implementation processes to these stakeholders to provide legitimacy and consensus in the eyes of user groups (Symes 1998).

This practice implies decentralising and creating institutions that assume the tasks, breaking down the centralised structures of management, coping with the inertia and resistance of bureaucracies and locating decision-making processes closer to the reality to be managed. In this process, sharing responsibilities with users is a key factor and their participation in the management process a precondition. Building these special relationships requires time to reach reciprocal commitment and trust between the government and the user groups and compliance with the ethical principles that evolve as this relationship develops (Symes 1998: 70). These processes also mean regionalising management and broadly defining stakeholder groups in the current situation of multiple use conflicts in many coastal areas. These scenarios are linked to the recognition that where there is a certain degree of parity in the relationships and interactions between the participating entities, co-governance is better adapted to complex, diverse, and dynamic situations than top-down models.

Gender, Fisheries, and Institutions

The term *gender* refers to the socially defined roles, resources and responsibilities of men and women as they relate to one another (Davis and Nadel-Klein 1992). These roles are not given. Rather, they are socially constructed and vary across different times and places according to changing values, practices and technologies (Oyewumi 1997; Williams et al. 2002). It is these socially constructed roles and responsibilities that are responsible for the structure employed to organise women's and men's differential relationships with their environments, their resource utilisation patterns and strategies, their experiences with environmental degradation and their perceptions of the environment.

Images of fishing tend to be male in many cultures, especially Western ones. The men are in charge of building and managing boats and coping with the perils and risks of navigating and fishing, and they get all the prestige associated with the activity. The literature has minimised or overlooked the role of women in this area, as in many others, for years and even gives them a negative role as carriers of bad luck at sea (Nadel-Klein and Davis 1988b). For decades in many areas of social sciences a male bias, remarking the relevance of activities developed by men and disregarding those developed by women has been too common.

In economy, for instance, the neo-classic paradigm verges towards the concept of economic man (Cohen 1989), using a methodology that usually discards women's activities, excluding a large percentage of their work from the calculus of Gross National Product and all their domestic labour. In anthropology during the 1960s, seminal works such as *Man the Hunter* (Lee and DeVore 1969) concentrated on men's activities, in this case hunting, although women were not completely omitted. However, at the end of the decade this bias was increasingly contested, and some years later another seminal work in the field (*Woman the Gatherer*) remarked precisely what the latter had omitted: the activities developed by women in foraging societies, especially gathering, assuming new theories, developed during the 1970s, about the evolution of mankind that highlighted the women's role in this process (Dahlberg 1981).

This new perspective was related to the emergence of feminism in social sciences, forcing a reconsideration of what had been anthropological 'truths' with a male bias. For instance, key concepts such as the household or domestic group and the different economic roles and status positions inside it now receive detailed attention (Narotzky 1988). In sum, the gender perspective, as a necessary instrument and a central problem in all the research areas, was consolidated in the 1980s and 1990s (Narotzky 1995), around the analysis of the social construction of the differences. This issue can be associated with the concept of *work*, which frequently is related to an androcentric and capitalist perspective that restricts this concept to *paid* work, dismissing many of the complex and essential tasks developed by women all around the world. The division of work in a society is the product of social and power relations between its members. Each society creates a specific representation of sex differences, and because of these assumptions about abilities and skills, the activities are distributed with a gender bias (Yanagisako and Collier 1987). The socialisation and education processes reinforce these patterns of social division of work and roles and drive people to accept what the society devises for them. In this sense, each society may associate certain tasks with specific gender roles in a specific moment of its history, changing the linkages in a historical process. These patterns may be completely different between diverse societies, and even in the same society in different historical periods (Comas d'Argemir 1995).

In the fisheries arena, since the 1980s, a similar re-analysis has been developed, starting with the seminal compilation of Nadel-Klein and Davis (1988a), which emphasises some specific biases. For instance, the previous invisibility of women's activities within the communities, on board, in commercialisation, in the reproduction of groups and their culture, or even in local or supra-local management organisations, is now receiving detailed attention. In this sense, the relevance of their roles in many of these areas has been remarked, without completely separating this perspective from the study of men's activities or other social problems, stressing the dynamic interplay of gender roles with gender identity (Nadel-Klein and Davis 1988b).

The historical focus of fisheries research on fishing vessels and gear has probably contributed to the invisibility of women in fishing economies. However, since the 1980s, an increasing number of studies note the relevance of women in the economic realms of fishing populations, e.g., by demystifying their absence on board and acknowledging how, in many cases, they join the crews (as in some areas of Portugal). In addition, many fishing societies acknowledge that the purpose of their activity is to earn a living and not per se to fish, and in this realm the social analysis of the division of labour needs a broader perspective going further than the activities on board. The diversity of women's subsistence and work roles is more complex than is usually assumed, ranging from collaborating spouses in France to ship-owners in Spain, crewmembers in Portugal (Cole 1991), scuba-fishing divers in Galicia or Japan, fish plant labourers, fish processors, fish sellers, financial managers, or political agents like the patronas mayores in Galician cofradias. These patterns of work distribution are flexible, dependent on circumstances, and less rigid and stereotyped than is usually presumed.

Of course the economic roles are related to variable status positions that are rapidly changing in many areas of the world. In fishing communities, men usually predominate in the public spheres, although the role of women is far from marginal. Besides, women of the North and South also rarely play a role in local fishing institutions. However, even in long-standing institutions like the Galician cofradias in Spain, their status and power have increased enormously in recent years as a result of their professionalisation as shellfish gatherers (mariscadoras), and they now have the same rights as men and control political positions in some of these organisations. In France, women's fisheries organisations have also gained social relevance. All these processes are changing the prestige rankings of men and women in public spaces and their role in household economies as a result of social and economic transformations in the North and South alike. In short, like men, women play a number of specialised roles in fishing-related populations all across the globe and an active role in household adaptive strategies, and their contribution should not be underestimated.

In development arenas, as Boserup analysed decades ago (1970), these patterns of social division of work and roles should be carefully taken into account in designing proper development programmes, although it may require more research on the causes and effects of gender roles in specific fishing adaptations (Williams 2002). However, gender as an important concept is usually left out as a variable strategy when planning development programmes, especially those on resource management (Mehra and Esim 1998). Most of the literature in community resource management (CRM) implies or cites the community as the primary participants, movers, and beneficiaries of resource management activities. A critical examination reveals, however, that in reality, these resource management programmes and initiatives often target the male members of the community – the fishermen – assumed and identified as the direct capturers of the fisheries resources (Horemans and Jallow 1997). Women, on the other hand, are assumed to be secondary to men, in terms of development interventions, and generally receive low priority (FAO 2001b). More recently, women's roles in fisheries are gaining recognition, and women are given the attention they deserve. Yet, the genuine involvement of women in resource management activities, as well as their access to benefits derived from CRM programmes, has yet to be clearly defined and accepted.

The roles played by women in the North and South alike frequently have the same objective – the economic survival of the family – even if it may play out in different ways. Without the support of their wives, the households of French fishers cannot go on, because during the fishing trips the women are in charge of the family and many fishing-related tasks on land. Their households are 'between the sea and the land' (the name of one Breton fisher-women's association) and women are responsible for multifarious tasks related to the fishing business; accounting, sales, and administrative work. This work carried out by women in the EU member states is rarely recognised and never remunerated. If European fisher-women play an increasingly important role within fishing enterprises, it is because their households need their contribution to save money and assure their reproduction and autonomy. However, according to the statistics of the European fisheries production only 3.2% of the women are apparently involved (MacAlister 2002), and in the aquaculture sector they only constitute 3% of the total workforce. In some countries, like Spain, we have detected that the numbers are higher than those detailed in MacAlister's report, which confirms the invisibility of women's work in fisheries.

It is possible, though, to understand this reduced participation by taking into account how difficult it is to combine household tasks and other activities. Since the men are away from home, the women bear the sole responsibility for bringing up the children. Added to old taboos, this explains why only a few women in Europe work on board. Fisheries do not have office hours and the kindergartens and schools are closed when the boats leave or come back to harbour. Women have to use different social networks to take care of their children. Relatives and neighbours may often help out and even replace the schools in some situations. Their contribution is one way to save household income. If women do as much as they can on their own, the family does not need to pay for these services.

However, especially in southern countries, several studies point to increasing instances of women participating in actual fish capture, predominantly in riverine and lagoon aquatic ecosystems. Women in the South Pacific islands contribute directly to production and are not prohibited or kept in any way from using the same fishing gear as men. According to Kronen (2002), the women of Tonga fish to satisfy family consumption needs and fishing is abandoned once the needs are filled. The only major difference between fishermen and fisher-women is the number of landings and the species captured. This difference can be explained by the fact that women do not use boats and thus fish in different areas than men. Bataille-Benguigui (1999) explains that in Tonga 'collecting is a female activity' and this may be why fisher-women do not use boats. This author notes that women and children only exploit the shore (sand reef) where they gather. High-sea fishing is reserved for men. In other Pacific islands, women use boats and are involved in fisheries extractive activities. Further, women are involved in pre-fishing activities such as preparing and mending nets as well as preparing baits, and post-fishing activities including processing, distributing and marketing of the fish. Women's involvement in fisheries generally results in lower operational costs and overhead expenses of the household (Grzetic et al. 1996).

In some West African countries, women's role in fisheries is more structured and seems to have a heavy impact on the local communities and their social structure. In Ghana or Togo, women are the main fish merchants. In Ghana, where pirogue fisheries constitute an exclusively male task, women are in charge of selling and processing fish and have a sizeable amount of capital, which is used for credit. It was the women who believed in using outboard engines for catching the pirogues and provided the fishers with credit to install them (Overaa 2000). The fishers increased their production and the women who loaned them the capital for the engines got preferential access to the captures. This is why some of the women have considerable wealth and social prestige. This ethnic group is matrilineal and women see to the children and household responsibilities alone. This could be one factor encouraging women to be efficient fish merchants. Their capacity to manage and control their money allows them to join the world of men (Overaa 2000). In Togo, a group of women call *nana Benz* also controls fish commercialisation and provides credit for the fishers. Their name comes from the French word *nana* (girls) and *Benz* because they drive Mercedes-Benz cars (Weigel 1987). *Nana Benz* women are the main actors of the fisheries sector in Togo because they control the fish commercialisation as well as the credit.

In Abidjan (Ivory Coast), Ghanaian women control the fish smoking industry. 'We don't become *fumeuses* (smoking workers) by choice, we are born *fumeuses*'. All of them learn their job from their mothers when they are only children. When they reach the marriageable age, they marry fishers and continue to practice the same job. The labour force that does the smoking consists of young girls from Ghana, who work for four or five years without a salary but with free accommodations and clothes. After five years, their boss (also a woman) takes them back to Ghana and gives them money to pay for their wedding. The female fish smokers need initial start-up capital to build an oven and buy the fish. The way they get access to the raw material (fish) is interesting. Not all women have access to fish even if they have the necessary money. Fish supplying is based on the solidarity of individuals of the same ethnic group. Fanti fishers sell their fish to Fanti women and Awlan fishers to Awlan women. A Fanti fisherman would never sell his fish to an Awlan woman and vice versa (Ruffier 1999).

Since the end of colonial rule, national and local governments in developing countries have been responsible for the establishment of associations/organisations. Because more men hold government positions, their representation in these organisations is higher. Not surprisingly, the majority of members of fish workers' associations are men. The disadvantage to women is that they are left out of the information loop about fisheries interventions, marketing, and bank loans. Furthermore, despite the stark realities of women's involvement and their contributions to the fishing economy, most of the organising activities by national government agencies, non-governmental organisations, churches, and academic institutions are of the strong view that fishery first and foremost implies catching and capturing. This assumption narrowed down the principal targets of organising efforts to include only male members in the community, thus paving the way for the formation of organisations that are exclusively male. Even in the North, although French women have their own organisations, until now they have not been given the chance to be elected to positions in the general fisheries organisations. Women participated for the first time in the elections for the local fisheries committees in January 2003, but via the trade unions the fishers tried to restrict the women's participation. This was done in several ways. The women were not informed until the last moment about whether they could participate or not and the administration did not issue its interpretation of the law until after the deadline for submitting the electoral list. In fact, the fishers' trade unions did not want women in their organisations because 'women have bad habits', 'they want to know everything' and this 'disturbs the tranquillity' of the trade unions (Frangoudes 2002). From a governance perspective, women's rights, voice, and equal treatment in the fishing-related organisations are a must.

Box 8.4 Successful collective action of *Mariscadoras*: a long and winding path

In Galicia, Spain, the regrouping of *mariscadoras*, women who earn a living collecting shellfish along the shore, was the culmination of a defeat. In the 1990s, shellfish beds declined along the shoreline and income levels fell. To salvage a future that had been compromised by the decline in shellfish stocks, biologists worked alongside the mariscadoras. As a result, the women gained an overall perspective of production and marketing. Every October, they plan together how to work the beaches the following year. From collective awareness to the control of their sector, women have gone through various stages in the process of obtaining autonomy:

First step, collective action: The mariscadoras realised they had problems in common and shared the same objectives. These shallow-water fisherwomen got together to found professional associations. Their goals were to gain entry to men's organisations, participate in stock management and be represented before the administration.

Second step, make capturing professional: Training was the best way to gain recognition. The women collaborated with the authorities to monitor the natural beaches and prevent poaching.

Third step, gaining financial independence: The women got funding and subsidies to launch clam production operations and planned their savings to purchase spats.

Fourth step, mastering marine farming: They mastered all the production processes to breed their own spats so they would be less dependent on private hatcheries.

Fifth step, promotion and development: They promoted their products regionally using a Protected Geographical Indication. They gathered the producers' stock at the same site to set prices at a similar level. They safeguarded their concessions, saw to stock regeneration and did unpaid work for the improvement and upkeep of the beaches.

Solid results: The results match the scale of the efforts. The standard of living has increased even though the business activity is seasonal. Sales prices are also rising. The percentage of workers making social security contributions has gone from 10% to almost 100%. This increase shows that these women have become true professionals.

And now what? There are twenty-four associations in Galicia in 2004, almost half of whom are grouped under the name AREAL (Confederation of Galician Mariscadora Associations). They are very active and play a significant role in the independence of these women.

Source: Aktea no. 2 (2003)

At the same time, women are the ones responsible for transmitting the culture to their children. The culture and values of fishing communities are passed on through the mothers, especially in industrial fisheries where the absence of fathers for lengthy periods justifies this argument; women are the pillars of the culture and see to the continuity of the fisheries. In Europe, if a mother does not want her son to work in the fisheries sector, she can always encourage him to go to school and find a job outside fishing.

It is clear from these examples that the role of women in fisheries is extremely diverse around the world. There is probably barely a job in fisheries that is not done by women somewhere, although taboos and prejudices may keep them from joining a fishing crew in many countries. However, cultural and economic changes are modifying traditions. Perhaps the main challenge in this area is women's admission to fishing-related institutions with the same rights and duties as men.

Conclusion

Throughout history, fishing populations world-wide have developed diverse institutional arrangements to avoid conflicts and manage resources. More than in agricultural adaptations, in fisheries the subtractive nature of the resources generates a need to devise institutions for minimising competitive conflicts or managing resource exploitation. These institutional arrangements generate various measures to control the behaviour at sea, the gear allowed, closed seasons and so forth, and in many cases regulate the phases of product commercialisation.

These arrangements have neither been infallible nor free of difficulties, and technological development and the advance of capitalism in the past few centuries have often endangered their survival. With various obstacles or even interruptions, some arrangements have lasted for centuries in the North and South alike. However, these institutions were not created everywhere, since in situations where there is not much conflict for the resources, the costs of building and maintaining specific institutional arrangements to limit this kind of conflict would surpass the benefits. There are also cases where local management has been inefficient or non-existent, as is witnessed by the global rise in overfishing (Pauly et al. 2002).

To manage marine resources, local institutions usually depend on traditional knowledge, shared and accumulated through the generations using trial and error strategies. This knowledge, especially in the twentieth century, started to compete with various areas of scientific research. Marine biology or economic discourses began to propose new perspectives for fisheries management that first affected the management patterns of industrial fisheries and later transformed all the fisheries, including artisanal or small-scale ones. These scientific models were supported by Western states that frequently created specific institutions to assess fisheries management or take direct control of these processes in top-down schemes. Specific images were developed to support these new institutions that denied the possibility of governance models in local scenarios.

Evidently, this plan often deliberately marginalised the local institutions and even made them disappear as outmoded solutions to a problem with a scientific answer. However, the scientific models could not provide solutions to every problem, nor could their recommendations always gain political support. In a sense the dramatic failures of some of the new top-down systems have changed the perspective in the analysis of local institutions. In some areas of inquiry, the costs of top-down management schemes and the misfit with local circumstances, enforcement, compliance and so forth have led to models that emphasise the participation of local populations and the co-management or local management of resources. However, after the destruction of many long-standing institutions, it is extremely difficult to go back and rebuild them.

In this context, the support for existing local institutions, the possibility of creating or recreating others and the devolution towards local control of resources managed in top-down schemes now constitute especially interesting areas of research. Many top-down schemes of management were designed to manage fish, not people, although it is essentially the fishers who are managed and rarely the fish stocks. This is why the institutional arrangements devised to improve the situation should be primarily designed to manage people and to manage the fish stocks through them. There are circumstances that favour building or maintaining local institutions linked to communal resource management, but if one crucial aspect is to be highlighted, perhaps it is the decisive role of the state in supporting, or at least not weakening, the long-standing local fisheries institutions all across the globe.

In the context of gender analysis in fisheries, governance issues are related to equitable access to resources and banking institutions, which should be linked with gender empowerment through training and projects on alternative sustainable livelihood and income-generating activities. In the same way, it is necessary to strengthen women's bargaining and negotiating positions, not only in the decision-making of the day-to-day operations but also on issues that concern personal choices on sexuality, fertility and contraception. This is related to encouraging changes in gender stereotyping within coastal communities and directly addresses issues concerning population, gender violence, and body politics. In sum, development agendas must include programmes to promote women's productive potentials with appropriate support systems.

9

National Institutions

Svein Jentoft, Jan Kooiman, and Ratana Chuenpagdee

Introduction

In this chapter the focus is on fisheries governance at the national level. Here the state is a key actor and will, accordingly, be an important focus in what follows. Although there is much discussion about the proper role of the state as a societal institution, even the strongest advocates of a 'minimal' state would not deny that the state must be the one responsible for a number of essential functions in every society. Therefore the question is not so much 'if' but 'how' the state should perform its role, in fisheries as well as in other sectors.

We begin this chapter with a discussion of the role of the state in modern society in general and fisheries in particular, and how it interacts with markets and civil society. Using three case studies from France, Thailand and the Philippines, we illustrate that in governing fisheries, trends are towards dealing with the diversity, complexity, and dynamics in new and more appropriate ways than those of the past. Currently in many countries, the state seeks to relieve some of its responsibilities by devolving authority to lower levels of governance by building public/private partnerships involving the market and civil society. This is also a key emphasis in governance theory, which starts with the assumption that given today's diversity, complexity, and dynamics, the state cannot govern alone but needs the active support of the market and civil society. The creation of functioning working relationships between these three institutions is an important governance issue in itself, as it is ridden with problems and dilemmas as well as challenging opportunities and hard choices.

The next section draws on state governance experiences from three countries in the South: Mozambique, Nicaragua, and Senegal. These cases show that state involvement in fisheries is not always a happy story. In many places around the world, the situations have been quite the contrary. State fisheries governance has been riddled with failures, caused by mismanagement, negligence, or sheer incompetence. But we should not for a moment believe that these are characteristics only of state governance in the South. In fact, if we compare the North and the South with regard to successes and failures, it is not clear that the North would serve as a better example. The state has been part of the problem, and yet it has to be part of the solution.

Next, we revisit some of the issues related to national institutions that characterise ways towards a new governance approach. Finally, in the concluding section, we identify what we believe are the important fisheries governance issues and challenges at the national level and how they should be addressed. Again, the relationship between the state, market, and civil society is the focus. We call for constructive partnerships, but we also emphasise the need for more research, institutional experimentation, and interactive learning as an integral part of the new governance approach at the national level.

State, Market and Civil Society: Roles, Interactions and Reforms

As the central authority with legislative powers and the resources to back them up, few would dispute that the state plays an important role in fisheries. However, in reality, the role of the state in fisheries was always, and still is, highly contested. Some see the state as part of the problem; others see it as part of the solution. Thus, there are always some who want more state interference and some who want less. Whenever there is a crisis – and in fisheries they are rampant – the state takes the blame. When times are good, the state seldom gets any credit. Sometimes the state is regarded as an ally and sometimes as an adversary. Perceptions of state involvement in fisheries, as in society as a whole, are usually ideologically tainted. What the state should be and do are among the issues that divide politics into left and right wing.

The state has been a key promoter of fisheries development by preparing the ground for industrialisation and by providing the infrastructure and training (Platteau 1989b). But as Hersoug notes, the role of the state in fisheries development varies according to established structures (Hersoug 2004: 34): 'In countries with a strong trading bourgeoisie, such as India and Nigeria, private operators are in charge of catching, processing, and export. In other countries, with a weaker class of traders and a shorter tradition of commercial fisheries, the state undertakes important functions related to the actual catching, processing and market'. Thus, there is hardly a standard state role that would be considered appropriate, regardless of context, time, and ideology. It will typically vary according to the prevailing situation in a particular country and industry. The governance of the state, or any other institutions, could always be different from what it is, because it is in essence a human artefact. Governance can also be expressed in terms of power; it is always what those in power want it to be. From the Marxist perspective, the state in capitalist societies is the instrument of the ruling class, never one of the poor and disenfranchised. True emancipation would therefore require a major state-institutional overhaul, and in some cases would require its abandonment and then reconstruction in a new form.

One should not view the state from a purely rationalist perspective. Rationality is also 'bounded' for the state. Despite the best of intentions, the state may fail. Therefore, negative impacts of state policies often come as a surprise, as crises in fisheries often do (Apostle et al. 1998). The management of fisheries was never a straightforward exercise but one full of complexities and uncertainties. In some instances, overfishing is a by-product of laudable policies, such as subsidy schemes to alleviate unemployment and rural poverty. But now and then, government agencies and their representatives engage in illegitimate activities. Governance failure may result from blatant mismanagement. Writing on the African situation, Cooper (2002) talks about the 'gatekeeper state'; referring to the fact that in many instances the political and bureaucratic elite controls the flow of resources in and out of the country. In this situation, opportunity may very well make a thief.

Typically the state apparatus is not a streamlined organisation with clearly defined internal and external boundaries, mandates, and standardised working procedures. Rather, it is an amorphous system, often developing in ways that would contradict notions of what constitutes proper governance. Consequently, state policies and practices are often incoherent and contradictory. Good governance would require the state to be concerned about how policies in one area affect another area. Good governors would strive to make such external effects positive so that various sectors of society may support each other. However, departmental boundaries often impede the broad vision necessary to make this happen. As a result, state policies might be counterproductive. Moreover, the state would sometimes employ quite different governance principles for fisheries than for other industries, despite its relative importance for the national economy. If fisheries are economically important, they get special treatment. Even if their importance is marginal, attention is paid to them for their social and cultural significance. Yet, in some instances, they suffer from government neglect. Sometimes differing governance approaches are due to the traditions, routines, cultures, and competencies within a particular state agency. As fisheries tend to be among the traditional industries, the sector carries institutional baggage from the past that may restrict healthy reform.

A good example of this is the French fishery (box 9.1), with its deep history of fisheries management institutions that are now centuries old. The restructuring of the French institutional framework for fisheries management illustrates the complexities that occur horizontally and vertically in the chain of governance. The mandates of various organisations at the local, regional and national levels are not always clearly defined and overlaps are a cause of constant conflict. Institutional change in countries like France provides opportunities and problems in the current situation where there is more proactive fisheries policy co-ordination at the European Union level, which directly interferes with deep-seated institutional patterns. Interestingly, in the French case, the devolution of management functions to lower-level institutions is not entirely new, but more a matter of rediscovering and recycling management institutions that have existed for a very long time. Institutional reform does not and perhaps should not always start from scratch as if a void has to be filled. It should address the weaknesses and fill the gaps in the framework that already exist. Sometimes more fine-tuning is all it takes, and a total overhaul of something that works is not always worth the effort.

Box 9.1 France – fisheries governance with a deep history

In France, fisheries fall under the administrative authority of the Maritime Affairs Administration (MAA). The MAA corps is a military structure in charge of many functions related to the maritime public domain and maritime activities in the coastal zone. The MAA is at all levels under the authority of the port admirals for coastal navigation of the regions and prefects for fisheries and aquaculture. The MAA serves many roles and functions in fisheries, including policing, participating in fisheries management, education, and preparing statistical reports. Although the MAA is organised at the national, regional, and local levels, it is at the latter level that management has been the most prominent. The local level MAA is based on the geographical division of the coastline into maritime quarters. Each quarter is under the complete authority of an administrator who deals with problems arising within his/her jurisdiction.

The concentration of legislative and juridical powers at the state level, the development of the national organisational structure of offshore fisheries, and the expansion of the EU Common Fisheries Policy (CFP) in the Mediterranean have challenged the traditional institutions for local management, in terms of rules and organisations. Rules have been reinterpreted or changed, while the organisations and decision-making processes have also been modified. One notable example is the prud'homies (proud men), which have existed as fisher organisations for almost a thousand years, and with official recognition and legal status since the seventeenth century. The prud'homies were subjected to the state decision to dissolve all the guilds during the French Revolution, and to develop a national professional organisation after the Second World War. Although they did not disappear after the French Revolution as most guilds did – due to their major attributes, such as territory, elective legitimacy, and governance principles – their authority has been progressively reduced.

In addition to the prud'homies, local fisheries management has also been a function of the Comité Loceaux de Pêches, which has existed side-by-side and in competition and conflict since 1945. The CLPs' mandate is to propose fisheries regulations, give social aid to skippers and financial help in training young recruits. Although the present composition of the CLPs includes many prud'homie leaders, their functions are distinguished by the fishers. The fishers generally feel that prud'homie leaders are closer to the field than the representatives of the CLP. Yet they are generally supportive of the idea of complementarity between the two.

In 1991, the French government once again reformed the structure of the entire professional organisation at the local, regional, and national levels. One of the main modifications was the direct election of CLP representatives. The legal framework is, however, very imprecise on how the elections should be organised. As is typical of the French socio-political context, the possibility of individuals serving as representatives of the fishers was not considered before the first election was organised in 1992. In the old system, the national unions used to nominate candidate representatives. Under the pressure of the unions, it was decided that the

In some countries, fisheries have a prominent position within the state administration, typically with a separate fisheries ministry, whereas in other countries fisheries fall under agriculture, commerce, industry, or environmental state administration. As with the Thai experience (box 9.2), there is every reason to believe that the way fisheries are integrated into the state machinery has a significant bearing on how fisheries problems are defined, policies are determined and how management is carried out. In any case, fisheries always have to find a place within the existing institutional governance structures that may or may not promote or inhibit effective fisheries management agendas. Therefore, governors never start with a clean slate, even if the problem they are facing is of recent origin, as when they are experiencing marine resource degradation for the first time. Rather, decision-makers and stakeholders tend to interpret new challenges based on existing conceptual frameworks.

Their approaches follow familiar trajectories. They look for new solutions in the proximity of the old ones, and they prefer marginal rather than drastic reform (Jentoft 2004a). Neither should it be forgotten, however, that governors have their own interests, which may determine their agendas in concrete governing situations. As Cicin-Sain and Knecht observe (1998: 217), 'It is well known that agencies jealously guard their missions and the responsibilities and resources that accompany them. Indeed, survival of the agency depends on it, keeping the mission and resources intact (or better yet, expanding them). Anything that threatens the mission or the resource base tends to be resisted with great vigour and tenacity'. On a similar note Berkes et al. (2001: 210) hold that fisheries administrators 'may be reluctant to relinquish their authority or parts of it, fearing infringement by local fishers and their representatives upon what they consider their professional and scientific turf'.

Box 9.2 Thailand – fisheries institutions restructured

The Gulf of Thailand (GoT) is a classic example of over-fishing due largely to the rapid development of trawl fisheries, with studies showing a strong form of 'fishing down marine food webs' (Christensen 1998; Pauly and Chuenpagdee 2003). Other causes of overfishing that have not been adequately addressed include inappropriate incentives provided by the state, the lack of alternative jobs for fishers, and the lack of interest in ecosystem-based management.

Fisheries management in Thailand had long been a responsibility of the Department of Fisheries (DOF). Until late last year, it operated under the Ministry of Agriculture and Co-operatives. The roles and responsibilities of the DOF include enforcement of fisheries laws pertaining to fishing rights in the Thai Exclusive Economic Zone, research on the development of aquaculture, stock enhancement, feed development, animal health and fishing gear, and surveying of fishing grounds in the Thai and distant waters. The DOF generally develops a five-year plan for fisheries policies, corresponding to the National Economic and Social Development Plan. The plan for 1997-2001 explicitly indicated the government intention to address problems of overfishing and degraded habitats and to resolve conflicts within fisheries. Although several measures were put in place, such as controlling the number of fishing boats and the gear, protecting fish spawning and nursery areas and implementing seasonal closure of the fisheries, they were not effective in protecting and restoring fisheries resources and marine ecosystems. The state effort to limit the number of trawlers resulted in a fleet size decrease from about 10,500 units in 1980 to 7,000 in 1988 (Phasuk 1994). However, the current number of registered trawlers, reported at 8,000 units (DOF 2002), is still what will produce the maximum sustainable yield or even maximum employment in the industry (Christensen and Walters 2002). Since not all the trawlers operating in the GoT have licenses, it is apparent that much more work is required to reduce the capacity of this fishing sector.

Since December 2002, fisheries have been managed by the new Ministry of Natural Resources and Environment (MNRE). This arrangement suggests a major shift from managing fisheries as agricultural resources to managing them as natural resources. This implies a change from the sole focus on managing fisheries for maximum harvests to conservation and protection of fisheries resources. Ecosystem-based management approaches and precautionary principles are explored as ways to achieve a balance between maintaining ecosystem integrity and providing viable livelihoods for the fishing and coastal communities. Moreover, a certain extent of the division of the DOF under the MNRE makes it possible to manage fisheries in combination with other coastal activities that impact coastal resources under the protection of the MNRE. This includes, in particular, strong support for a participatory approach to fisheries management by setting up small-scale fishers groups, fisheries market cooperatives, and education and capacity-building programmes to provide training in production and marketing, and environmental awareness. Small-scale fishers can use their fishing boats to take tourists to the islands, caves, and other tourist destinations. Many fishers also host tourists in their home, as in 'homestay', and charge them for accommodations, meals, and boat tours.

Lastly, the new institution will support the Thai government, a member of the Association of Southeast Asian Nations, by endorsing various regional fisheries agreements and international treaties and conventions, such as the United Nations Convention on the Law of the Seas, the UN Agreement on Conservation and Management of Straddling Stocks and Highly Migratory Fish Stocks and the FAO Code of Conduct for Responsible Fisheries. A positive outlook can be observed in the fisheries policies for 2002-2006 that focus on involving all the stakeholder groups in the management and development of fisheries, integrating scientific and traditional knowledge, and promoting the export of fisheries products through quality control and health and safety regulations. Some of the challenges faced in this institutional reform are the overlapping of jurisdiction and responsibility, limited human capacity and capabilities to serve in the new administrative roles, lack of consistency in national policy and legislation, and insufficient financial support to implement innovative programmes .

Author: Ratana Chuenpagdee

Although state administrators rarely applaud such reforms, in a number of countries, devolution of management authority to lower-level public or civic institutions takes place. In fisheries management literature, co-management is the label frequently employed for such reforms (Wilson et al. 2003). The Philippines provides a vivid example of such a country where a large step in this direction has been taken (box 9.3). Here the effort is to make fisheries management more adept to local situations and to spread responsibilities to a broader partnership of institutions with the aim of increasing the legitimacy and effectiveness of fisheries management. In most coastal developing countries, the state has limited capacity to fulfil a comprehensive role in fisheries governance. Sharing the burden of management with markets and civil society may therefore be a way out. In many situations, however, this option is ruled out. Rather than working with industry or non-governmental organisations, the state attempts to contain them. As Paulson (1999) reports from Africa, the strong emphasis on state-led development, while overlooking or suppressing the private sector, has had mixed results. We believe that there are important lessons to learn from countries such as the Philippines that in recent years have taken a different route.

The World Bank, in its report *The State in a Changing World* (1997), notices a growing gap between the demands on states and their capacities to meet those demands. In the Bank's opinion it does not make sense to reduce or dilute the role of the state as such, but to aim at reforms in which demands and capacities are better matched. This means, among other things, designing effective rules and restraints, checking arbitrary state actions and combating entrenched corruption, increasing the performance of state institutions, and making the state more responsive to people's needs. But it also means focusing on the first jobs of states, entailing five fundamental tasks: establishing a foundation of law; sustaining a benign policy

Box 9.3 The Philippines – fisheries governance decentralised

In the Philippines, the national territory (land and municipal waters) is divided into political areas called local government units (LGUs). Fisheries management is one of the functions devolved by the state to its subsidiaries, mainly cities and municipalities, along with other basic functions such as health services and education. The devolution of fisheries management reflects the main objectives of the controlling legislation, the Local Government Code of 1991 (LGC), which focuses on the key features of political autonomy and decentralisation, as well as resource generation and mobilisation. The principles of autonomy and decentralisation are embodied in provisions that refer to sharing LGU responsibilities with the state for maintaining the ecological balance, the right of LGUs to collaborate for purposes commonly beneficial to them, and the need for the state to consult with LGUs on specific projects that may cause environmental harm. Moreover, the LGUs are vested with corporate powers entitling them to create revenues, levy taxes, fees and other charges, share in the proceeds from the development and utilisation of the national wealth in their territories, and share in the collection of national taxes.

The law concerning decentralisation and autonomy caused drastic changes in the institutional design of fisheries management, and a structural shift in power that placed coastal local governments at the forefront of resource management. Prior to the enactment of this law, fisheries programmes emanated from national agencies. The programmes were transmitted to the LGU clients in the implementation phase. Under the LGC, the process has been reversed. The people's direct participation in planning and implementation has been reinforced and is now considered an inherent strategy of all fisheries management activities.

The fisheries management functions of the LGUs include protection and conservation, regulation, enforcement, and legislation, with the latter being the most salient manifestation of local autonomy. Unlike in the past, when ordinances had to be approved by the Secretary of Agriculture and Natural Resources, the LGUs have been given full autonomy in fisheries management, to the extent that they are free to legislate on their own laws in the absence of national ones. This new design also results in LGUs becoming the focal point of all the technical assistance with academic institutions.

There are advantages and disadvantages to the devolution of fisheries management. From a practical standpoint, the decentralisation augurs well for fisheries management having local governments at the forefront. They are well aware of the issues, are in touch with the stakeholders, and have a better grasp of practical and workable solutions. Further, fisheries issues tend to be very area-specific and the dynamics among the various stakeholders differ from one locality to another. Local officials are thus in the best position to appreciate these dynamics and cultural sensitivities. Finally, since LGU officials are elected officials, the impact of what they do or how the stakeholders perceive them is reflected at the next elections. Bureaucrats from national agencies are not locally accountable.

The success of devolution did not happen without any problems. The devolution of functions did not automatically accompany the devolution of information and budgets. Coastal local governments state that the major problems with reenvironment; investing in people and infrastructure; protecting the vulnerable, and protecting the environment. In the cases presented in this chapter, all these basic tasks are reviewed in some way.

National governments affect societal resources and social, economic, and cultural activities in major ways. Thus, they necessarily interfere with the lives of individuals, groups, and communities and become part of the resources and frameworks of the strategies these actors develop (cf. Long 2001). At their disposal, governments have whole sets of tools, instruments, and measures usually in the hands of a political, an administrative, and a juridical branch. The distinctions between these branches are not always clear, and major issues are raised about the ways these branches of the state operate separately and together. It is often said that the political branch does not give the necessary directions, that the administrative branch is ineffective, and that the juridical branch is becoming impenetrable. Much of this applies also to the way governments in the North and the South deal with fisheries, as is illustrated in this chapter. Although examples are harder to find, there are also instances where a balance between political directions, administrative action, and juridical oversight has been found. In any case, whether one is in favour of a minimum, medium, or maximum role of the state, the question of what exactly the state's responsibility should be is a pertinent one. Regardless of time, context and ideology, there is hardly a standard answer to any of these questions. The role of the state will typically vary in accordance with the prevailing situation in a particular country and a specific industry. Although government agencies can learn from each other and from those of other countries, to be effective they must relate to, and be able to learn from, the particular situation that prevails within the concrete context in which government agencies operate.

As the governance perspective maintains, socio-political governance is not solely a state function, it is also a function of the market and civil society. Central to the governance approach is the awareness that when diversity, complexity, and dynamics reign, markets and civil society have important contributions to make and should become more involved than they now are. In a 2001 White Paper on European Governance delivered by the

European Commission, non-governmental organisations are viewed as positive contributors to the definition and implementation of European policies (Schutter 2002). Their participation is seen as a way of broadening the democratic process. The same position is articulated in the EU Nice Treaty, which refers to the input of 'organised civil society' (Article 257). In fisheries, as expressed in the 2001 Green Paper on the Future of the Common Fisheries Policy, there are the regional advisory committees of stakeholders in policy-making. From the governance perspective advanced in this book, these developments are a step in the right direction.

A properly functioning market and civil society, which Walzer (2003: 64) calls 'the space of uncoerced human association and also the set of relational networks – formed for the sake of family, faith, interest, and ideology – that fills this space', will support the governance process. The market and civil society may also relieve the state of some of its burdens. There are social functions the state cannot take on, at least not alone, as efficiently as market and civil society actors can. Obviously, it is not the job of the state to socialise fisher-recruits, operate fishing vessels or run a business enterprise. There are also limitations to what the state can do in building communities. If, as Offe (2000) claims, the state is driven by 'reason', the market by 'interest', and civil society by 'passion', one institution cannot easily replace another. The consequences of replacing the logic of one institution by those of another may also be detrimental. Good governance should draw on all three institutions, help them become more effective and smooth out their differences.

The interaction between the state, the market and civil society is a major governance issue, but raises some serious questions. What exactly should be the division of labour? Will socio-political governance be improved if responsibilities shift among them? What partnership arrangements involving the state, the market, and civil society are suited as governance instruments in concrete fisheries situations? The conclusion can be made that the governance of the interaction between the state, the market, and civil society is and probably always should be diverse, complex, and dynamic. The structure, role, and performance of state institutions should be responsive to these characteristics and should largely be a manifestation of them. For instance, the move towards ecosystem-based management is adding new complexities to the management task. The same is true of the increased awareness of cooperation at the supranational level and the need for fisheries administrators to build partnerships with stakeholders and non-governmental organisations (cf. Berkes et al. 2001).

Some authors question the state's ability to meet these demands, arguing that bureaucratic structures inevitably cause inertia and dysfunction (cf. Crozier 1964; Leeuw et al. 1994). Jentoft and Mikalsen (2004) also discuss the problems complex institutional designs in fisheries management may cause for users who have to cope with them. They can simply become too difficult to comprehend, which affects their legitimacy and workability. We argue that a great deal depends on how institutions bridge the boundaries between the state, the market and civil society (Kooiman et al. 1999). Good governance in fisheries should always strive for simplicity within the parameters this industry provides.

If it is true, as is argued in our governance approach, that the state cannot do it all alone and needs to draw on the contributions of the market and civil society to handle diversity, complexity, and dynamics, the co-management institutions are of great interest. Again, the institutional design of co-management arrangements cannot start from a *tabula rasa*, it should draw on existing institutional patterns and cultures to avoid misfit and conflict.

The state operates at various levels of the chain of governance – at the overall societal level and at the structural level within a particular industry like fisheries. The state can play an enabling or a restricting role pertaining to societal interactions among actors within the market and civil society. The *modus operandi* tends to differ from one level to the other, e.g., using interference, interplay, and intervention depending on the particular societal interaction and institutional framework, and utilising self- or co-management or hierarchical modes of governance at the structural level. Countries differ as to which state modes of operation are common, which may explain why the state is more effective in some instances than in others.

The state adapts to the specific circumstances it is operating in and the demands confronting it. Since these circumstances and demands change, so does the state. This is why the state apparatus has to be flexible, able to respond in a timely fashion, and be willing and able to learn from experience and to change its ways accordingly. However, as in most coastal developing countries, the capacity to fulfil a comprehensive state role in fisheries may be limited or non-existent. In developed countries, where state authorities have financial freedom to exercise a proactive role, current neo-liberal ideologies favour a leaner and a reformed state apparatus as well as a larger market function. Thus, the role of the state in fisheries as well as in other societal sectors cannot be determined independently of other governance institutions, including those of civil society.

Governance Experiences of Fisheries Institutions

The previous section describes the many state institutions in terms of their roles, responsibilities, accountability, and how they are perceived, i.e., their 'images'. Several attributes of the state can contribute to enhancing their performance, given that it can be judged against a set of criteria based on well-defined goals. This implies, however, that there is no single formula on what constitutes a high-performance state. Yet lessons can be learned about governance based on experiences of various fisheries institutions.

We present three case studies to suggest some of the challenges faced by governing institutions dealing with current pressures in the fisheries sector. The case of Mozambique (box 9.4) is typical of multi-sector fisheries, with a large number of people depending on resources, but with a depleting resource situation. Although supported by foreign aid for the implementation of parts of the fisheries plan, the formulation of the plan was done by the government. Such hierarchical governance not only has limitations in terms of achieving stated objectives, but it can also lead to more conflicts between various sectors and to social-economic hardship.

In some instances, the governments are well-equipped with laws and legislation to protect the benefits and interests of stakeholders across sectors. The problem arises, however, when they are not consistently applied. This is illustrated by the case of Nicaragua lobster diving fisheries (box 9.5), which involve a large number of indigenous people, the Miskito, whose health is greatly affected by this dangerous occupation. The legal system that protects their health and their welfare is not used to their benefit, but instead to the benefit of others, especially foreign-owned seafood export companies. In addition to dealing with this constraint through increasing government accountability, programmes to increase public awareness are required.

The final case of Senegal (box 9.6) offers a timely discussion about fisheries governance in relation to the current trend of resource exploitation policy through fisheries agreements. The Senegalese government took pride in being the pioneer in signing agreements with other states, which resulted in certain benefits such as increased export incomes and local employment. An extensive evaluation of their experience, as reported by Kaczynski and Fluharty (2002), suggests that local fisheries resources are being heavily exploited through these agreements, and that the food security of the local population has become increasingly threatened, with the majority of fish and seafood being exported mainly to European markets. The government is re-thinking its policy and considering trade-offs between foreign earnings and the local food supply, among other things.

Limitations of Hierarchical Governance

The rationalised, bureaucratic, vertically organised or hierarchical state so well depicted by Max Weber (1964 [1925]) is still very present, and very much alive, despite critical voices about its performance. Hierarchical governance may have lost some of its classical glory, but in many areas of socio-political life, it is still a major governing approach. This top-down governing mode is conceptualised by the process of steering and control.

Steering is a powerful metaphor for (public) governing in the traditional sense, as well as for modern society with all its dynamics. The key element of steering is direction, which implies that governors have a general idea where they want to go, i.e., have an image of a future state they prefer above the existing one. Since steering is a way of intervening, it looks uni-directional and top-down, such as expressed in goal setting. However, as all governing activities, steering is also an interactive process between governors and those governed, upon whom setting the right course relies. For this reason, it is preferable to speak of goal seeking rather than goal setting.

Traditionally, control in the public sector is considered a matter of political accountability and/or a matter of political-bureaucratic relations. In the

Weberian tradition, both were 'insured' by proper legal/constitutional and bureaucratic rules. While this 'insurance' as norm is not in doubt, serious questions have been raised about the practice of such rules. Modern public organisations are so highly complex and diverse that controlling them demands abilities to 'mirror' these traits. It should be noted, however, that while in modern (public) governance top-down control is still an important mode of controlling complex activities, other arrangements with checks and balances, and even bottom-up control are also widespread. Further, controlling diversity within the public sector is not only expressed in the variety of institutions with specific control functions (e.g., audit offices, courts, management controls), but also by the plurality of instruments available to and used by these offices. Trying to master diversity in the ways mentioned is a characteristic of modern (public) governance, but we also have to mention that many of these controlling efforts are at odds with each other, in substance, scope, time, and sanctions attached to them.

In the traditional hierarchical, instrumental approaches, states rely on laws, rules, and regulations to intervene in whatever societal activity they want to influence. More recently, as policy becomes a major hierarchical means that states govern with, specific goals are set and combinations of means are developed as strategies to influence, control, or steer societal activities in pursuit of the goals. In what has developed most recently as (public) management approaches, the state tries to influence developments closer to the scene. For this purpose, managers are allotted roles and tasks often with considerable amounts of discretionary power and means. In fisheries, this is a model receiving more and more attention and practice.

The case study of Mozambique (box 9.4) illustrates this point. It describes efforts by the Mozambican administration to develop a Master Plan for fisheries, with a set of objectives that are difficult to attain. In particular, the government chose to support the artisanal sector at the expense of the industrial sector, since it perceived the former to be more effective in providing subsistence and employment for the local population. The plan has only been partly successful. The harvesting capacity has not been reduced and land-based jobs not created as desired. The case of Mozambique thus reveals some of the limitations and dilemmas of hierarchical state steering and control in fisheries. Even though the numerous stated goals of its Master Plan for fisheries are all laudable, they are also in conflict with each other.

Box 9.4 Mozambique – government facing a hard choice

Mozambique's fisheries are of crucial importance to its people in terms of food, economic activity, and export revenues (Degnbol et al. 2002). Some 80,000 Mozambicans engage mainly in fisheries-related activities and communities all along the coast rely on fisheries as one of their main economic activities. In 1999, 40% of Mozambique's exports came from fisheries, with an export value of US$76 million.

The overall strategic perspective of the fisheries sector in Mozambique is represented by the Master Plan approved in 1995 (State Secretariat of Fisheries 1995), with an accompanying Action Plan. The Master Plan focuses on three main objectives: an improved domestic food supply, an improved national income, and an increased standard of living in the fishing communities. These objectives have caused serious dilemmas for the Mozambican fisheries policy.

The Mozambican government aimed to achieve these objectives by enhancing its national income via export earnings and improving the conditions in the fishing communities by developing semi-industrial shrimp fishing and onshore processing. The underlying agenda was to develop the sector with the most jobs for Mozambicans while maintaining the export earnings. The Master Plan was accompanied by initiatives to fund projects to develop the infrastructure needed for the semi-industrial fleet (e.g., harbours, quality control services, onshore processing capacity), encourage investments through credit lines, and prioritise the allocation of quotas to this sector. The number of industrial vessels was to be reduced and the state was to develop greater management capacity, primarily in relation to the shallow water shrimp resource.

A major fisheries development programme was initiated to follow up on the Master Plan. The main donor, DANIDA, supported the development of onshore processing, quality control, and capacity development in the Ministry of Fisheries, while NORAD supported capacity development in relation to fisheries management in the research institute and the Ministry. The programmes have largely been successful in attaining their immediate aims.

The developments since 1995 illustrate the limits to state intervention. It has not been possible to reduce the industrial fishing effort and move the utilisation of the resource to the semi-industrial segment. On the contrary, the industrial fisheries effort has continued to increase. Furthermore, instead of building up the semi-industrial sector and the land-based fish processing plants, ice-carrying semi-industrial trawlers were introduced and were regarded as implementing the plan, and thus undermining its main idea. Although parts of the industrial fleet were downsized to meet the formal requirements, they still maintain the more profitable on-board processing capacity. The net result is that capacity development has not created land-based jobs and the overcapacity in the shrimp fisheries only grew. The problem of overcapacity has not been solved and may seriously affect the chance of future profitability for the companies and the state.

The Mozambican government is faced with a dilemma it shares with many other countries. In retrospect, the strategy of developing an industry with maximum economic opportunities in local communities and with Mozambican ownership may imply a technology and a type of industrial organisation that is not the

National Institutions

most competitive on the global market, especially if it tries to simultaneously address wider social concerns that its competitors are not subjected to. The pressure to shift towards industrial operations with few local jobs is not entirely driven, however, by the global market. There are indications that the industrial fleet operates with profits beyond what would be expected on a competitive market. This indicates that the state infrastructure for fisheries management, which amounts to an indirect subsidy to the industry, could become economically sustainable without government funding and the production from Mozambique's major natural resource could benefit the people of Mozambique better than it does today. At least for the time being, it may also be economically viable to prioritise solutions that might not be the most competitive on the global market but create other social benefits. The real dilemma is whether that is the road to take or whether the value of the shallow-water shrimp resources should be fully realised on the global market and put to use for Mozambican society through its treasury.

Author: Poul Degnbol

Constraints on Legal Governance

The relation between the state and the rule of law is close, but not exclusive. All modern states engage in comprehensive legal actions, and by doing so influence many aspects of the private lives of citizens, individually and organised. Through legal instruments, the state intervenes, governs, and provides protection to all entities in society, as well as protection against the state itself. The more penetratingly the state intervenes in the private sphere, the more formal guarantees, such as equality before the law, legal security, unity of the law, and due care are required.

It should be noted that many of these legal interventions have a broad coordinating, modifying, controlling, or steering purpose, and thus almost by necessity, are based partly on legal norms and partly on policy. In other words, modern lawmaking is directed at the setting of norms (legal) as well as bringing about changes (policies). In the course of extending steering and control by legal and administrative means, as interconnection between law and administration grows, the limitations and disadvantages of hierarchical governance become more evident.

The continuous amplification of governing by law and other legal instruments, however, is unavoidable given increasing societal diversity, complexity, and dynamics. The key question is whether the legal and administrative systems can handle this, or even more crucially, if they themselves may have become roadblocks. As often observed, deregulation may result as a way to cope with expected or unexpected side-effects in these complex situations. Refinement of legal interventions may take place to deal with diversity, while hierarchical governance is affected by dynamics. The time it takes to fulfil all juridical, political, and administrative requirements means that many of these interventions may become outdated by the time they are enacted. More often than not, the effort is spent on legal updates and re-pair.

The difficulties mentioned above not only diminish the effectiveness of legal-administrative rule making, but also its legitimacy. At the structural level, hierarchical governance loses its meaning, resulting in a sense of powerlessness, a growing alienation from the legal state, and the erosion of the obeisance of the law. Resistance against the state as a distant and omni-present, but not interacting legal machine, seems to be growing. While counter-moves in terms of guarantees, publicity, participation and other forms of citizen involvement are not lacking, in practice they are restricted to special groups or interests and to issues of a 'not-in-my-backyard' (NIMBY) character. As shown in the case of the Miskito lobster divers in Nicaragua (box 9.5), these indigenous people are the victims of political and social discrimination, even though Nicaragua has advanced legislation on labour welfare and indigenous people's rights. Instead of addressing the growing number of accidents, injuries, and deaths of these divers due to their fishing practices, the government sides with the industrial corpora-tions, which are often foreign-owned. Clearly, the state is not working for the common interest, but is steered, in this case in the interest of the pri-vate interests of the few and powerful.

Box 9.5 Nicaragua – legal instruments ineffective

Seafood is Nicaragua's second most important export product after coffee, with dramatic increases in production in the 1990s. In 2001, the Ministry of Support for Industry and Commerce had 41 registered diver ships. The ships deposit the catch in storage space that belongs to domestic and foreign companies in Puerto Cabezas, Bluefields, Corn Island, and Pearl and Miskitos Cays. The increase in production, while good for Nicaragua's export earnings, has taken a considerable human toll, as divers frequently suffer injuries that are often fatal (Acosta 2002). Although exporters pay the divers US$2.50 for a pound of lobster tails that sell for US$12.50, they do not see it as their responsibility to assist the divers when acci-dents occur. If lobsters are scarce, divers feel the impact, since they have to dive for longer periods of time and at greater depths. Between 1988 and 1998, the depth they had to dive increased from 30 to 120 feet. In the 1980s they used five oxygen tanks a day and now they use fifteen. Diving for lobster is a common job for young men of the indigenous Miskito population. It is estimated that 98% of the 2,500 to 3,000 divers are Miskito. There are many boat drivers (cayuqueros) under the age of 18 who work alongside the divers. This suggests that due to the conditions of lobster diving, the underage cayuquero's work is a violation of the International Labour Organizations Covenant no. 182 of the Worst Forms of Child Labor, 1999.

The impact of large-scale commercial diving has increased occupational risks such as embolisms, paraplegia, and hemiplegia, produced by the decompression syndrome, the bends. Frequent accidents among divers have left many of them physically handicapped, missing, or dead. The lack of awareness, training, proper equipment, and economic alternatives combined with the indigenous cultural characteristics can be considered immediate triggers for this situation. The physical and social consequences of this activity can only be compared to the situation of indigenous miners in other Latin American countries.

In Nicaragua, there is abundant constitutional legislation that protects the health, labour, and social conditions of the divers. There are also laws defending environmental sustainability and regulating the commercialisation of lobster fishing. Moreover, there are several state institutions that play major roles in regulating commercial diving. The National Fishing and Aquaculture Administration (AdPESCA) regulates and controls lobster catch. The Ministerio del Trabajo (MITRAB) has the authority to inspect and guarantee safety regulations in the work place, while the Ministerio de Salud establishes a clear policy to prevent decompression syndrome, and the National Institute for Social Security can oblige employers to pay for insurance to cover the illness, injury, retirement, or death of divers. Finally, the Ministry of Natural Resources and the Environment regulates environmental sustainability. Sadly, when it comes to the Miskito divers, instead of complying with their legal duties, these state institutions completely distort their roles.

In general, state institutions are passive and usually negligent about enforcing the laws. For example, the MITRAB is aware of the problems concerning Miskito divers but instead of protecting them, it protects the companies' interests. This is why the Procurator for Human Rights in Nicaragua held regional MITRAB officials responsible for violating the divers' human rights (mainly the rights to life and social security). The Procurator's pronouncement failed to generate any changes in the MITRAB. Instead, the MITRAB's Minister tried to excuse its negligence by noting that diving is an informal activity, that divers consume drugs and alcohol, and although labour conditions are precarious, employers promise to obey the law in the future.

The MITRAB's attitude is due in part to its own frailty. It is also due to the isolation of the divers' communities, which is undoubtedly related to the divers' indigenous background. Indigenous peoples do not have economic or political power to influence state agencies. Factors like cultural and linguistic differences and lack of awareness about the law, social security and national institutions make the enforcement of labour guarantees for divers all the more difficult.

Author: Maria Luisa Acosta

Fisheries Governance Under Pressure

For a long time, policies have been considered one of the major instruments governments have at their disposal to bring about politically preferred societal changes. Notwithstanding the many different ways in which policies have been and are defined, most of them have distinguished stages or phases. There is a stage that is mainly concerned with translating a problem into a subject for policy; a stage in which alternatives are considered and choices made; and finally a stage in which the chosen policy is implemented and executed. In most policy theories, the perspective is from the governmental or public side of policy processes, but recent developments emphasise the institutional framework in which policies are prepared and implemented, with an open interest in social aspects. As the latter implies that more players are involved in pursuing specific goals and interests, it may bring about resistance, evasion and improper implementation.

The above challenges can be addressed using a framework with two levels of governing interactions, the intentional and the structural, and three government elements: image, instrument, and action. At the intentional level of policy interactions, we look primarily at variables such as information exchange, communication and discourse, knowledge creation and learning; in other words, the formation of policy images. Secondly, there is choice and selection of policy instruments, which can vary from formal to informal, from broad to specific, and from those with short-term or long-term effects. Finally, there is the action component, where we consider aspects such as political will to act on the governors' part and mobilisation to support or resist on the part of the governed. The structural level of policy images is based on existing bodies of knowledge or ideological sensitivities. For the instrumental element, its structure consists of the distribution of material and immaterial resources available for the choice of instrumentation. At the structural level of the action, we can think of capacities to collectively act or resist as in the mobilisation of social capital.

The shift of focus from the more intentional or actor-oriented notions of policy processes to structural aspects has grown in relation to broader societal processes. Along the way, positivist, neo-positivist, modernist and postmodernist, analytical, and constructivist tendencies in policy studies have appeared, flourished, and shrivelled. Unfortunately there is not much debate between them, making it difficult to suggest that much progress in the overall understanding of policies as a means of public intervention has been made. As shown in the case of Senegalese fisheries (box 9.6), it is often a question of taking your pick and using what is on offer. Fisheries problems in Senegal are related to the interactions between an industrial, foreign (mostly European) fishing fleet, and a huge domestic artisanal sector. While facing internal pressure, such as increasing exploitation of resources, weak enforcement, lack of research funding, and few employment alternatives, Senegal engages in fisheries agreements with other states. Policies for sustainable fisheries governance have to be reconsidered to deal with all the sectors, inside and outside fisheries, as well as the external pressure through foreign fishing fleets.

Box 9.6 Senegal – rethinking fisheries policies

Fishing in Senegal is composed of numerous sectors with distinct and traceable histories. The industrial fishing sector targets high commercial value demersal species, large pelagic fish and increasingly at present, small pelagic fish that are the staple of the national fleet because of its weak technical capacity. Senegal's very dynamic artisanal fisheries target a multitude of species using a diverse range of gear. The fisheries have experienced generally uncontrolled growth and supply approximately thirty offloading points along the coast. The sector's catches grew very rapidly until recently, when they began to stagnate. At present, the artisanal sector contributes about 80% of the country's total annual catch (at approximately 350,000 tonnes). Artisanal and industrial fisheries share the same space but often target different segments of the same species populations. The problems between these sectors arise mainly as a result of lack of access regulations for artisanal fishing and an ineffective system of control and surveillance.

The system is further challenged by the fisheries agreements that Senegal signs with states in the sub-region and in Europe. As a pioneer in this type of fisheries situation, the state has received foreign aid and gained valuable experience. On the positive side, the fisheries have contributed to increasing export income, meeting the people's food needs and creating local employment. Acknowledging the social, economic, and nutritional importance of the fisheries, the state was quick to establish an institutional framework and monitoring and regulatory mechanisms for fishing. Furthermore, the state assists the sector through extraction and export subsidies to lower costs, boost exports and improve its competitiveness in external markets. It has also arranged a maritime credit programme exclusively for the industrial sector. These various measures have been implemented and evaluated by the government and external experts. The conclusion is that, despite these efforts, the state faces several institutional, structural, and organisational constraints.

One of the main problems with the fisheries agreements stems from the inappropriate national system to regulate access to resources for national and foreign industrial fisheries. A new arrangement is needed to respect the laws and regulations at the national level, while conforming to international law. This includes creation of local equitable partnerships to replace the commercial fishing agreements currently in force for almost all fish-producing nations with the nations of the North. It is acknowledged, however, that existing fishing agreements that maximise public and private benefits should be maintained. Clearly, the strengthening of regional discussion forums focusing on communal resources to realise scale economies, and reinforcing regional trends is required. In addition, capacity building, financial means, infrastructure, and human resources need to be sufficiently allocated to strengthen research. Stakeholder capacities can be reinforced through the provision of pertinent information and through appropriate training to enhance stakeholders' organisational capacities, as well as to transfer fishing labour to other sectors.

Author: Taïb Diouf

Towards More Interactive Governing at the National Level

A basic expectation related to state involvement in fisheries is that if left alone, fishers would destroy the resource and squander the rent. If the state does not regulate it, no one else will, and hence the tragedy of the commons and the commoners is inevitable. They cannot solve the problem alone – they need to be protected from themselves, as it were – and therefore need the external assistance that only the state can provide. Much like Thomas Hobbes' classic portrayal of the original state of nature (Hobbes 1991 [1651]), users would otherwise become entangled in a brutal struggle for scarce resources, with everyone losing in the long run and resources dwindling. So the state has a clear mission, which is to create order and moderation among the fishing ranks.

Social scientists have long disputed this assumption and the social analysis underpinning it. They argue that even though the state has a positive role to play in fisheries management, it is not always fully equipped to fulfil it. The state is often too weak to be effective. As Migdal points out (1988: 9): 'States are like big rocks thrown into small ponds: they make waves from end to end, but they rarely catch any fish'. Although they are fully able to penetrate society, they are often quite ineffective in generating social changes. Nor is the state a neutral arbitrator that user groups always accept. Rather, state structures and practices – like other structures and practices – tend to be biased; they select the issues, goals and interests that shall attain prominence and those that shall not (Cerny 1990). Thus, questions regarding the legitimacy and justice of state authority tend to be challenged, in fisheries affairs and in other sectors. The state is situated far from the daily problems of fishers and thus unable to fully grasp their situation, concerns, and aspirations. Durkheim's observation is a pertinent reminder: 'The state is too remote from individuals; its relation with them too external and intermittent to penetrate deeply into individual consciences and socialise them within. Where the state is the only environment in which men can live communal lives, they inevitably lose contact, become detached, and thus society disintegrates' (Durkheim 1964 [1893]: 28). The case studies of Mozambique, Nicaragua, and Senegal described above illustrate these points well.

So there is ample reason why disenchantment with the state is widespread and the focus of observers has shifted to markets and civil society. One of the issues with the state is that civil society is key to a sustainable democratic process 'and as a countermeasure against neo-corporatist arrangements that brought organised labour and its parties into institutionalised patterns of governance but afforded little access to other constituencies' (Elliot 2003: 2-3). But as Elliot also points out, supporters of civil society may go so far as to exalt civil society to 'mythic proportions as a tool of the social imagination, an ideological construct for good society'. Obviously, civil society also has its pitfalls. It can mean many things and may also have some limitations on what it can do in socio-political governance, in fisheries as in other industries. The same, of course, applies to markets. If drawn too far, the division between civil society and the state may be abolished and we end up with the stateless communist society envisaged in positive terms by Marxist theoreticians like Gramsci (cf. Keane 1988).

If the state has a necessary role in fisheries governance, but is not fit to take on all the responsibilities of governing fisheries in an efficient and just fashion and has to rely on the active support of other societal institutions such as the market and civil society, the question is what exactly the state role should be and how the division of labour between the state, the market, and society should be structured. This is one of the most basic governance issues and it also involves ethical and moral issues (Kooiman 2003). The question in fisheries is what needs to be done, what concerns are important and which instruments are preferable to others. Social and natural research has provided deep insight into these matters. What remains – and here we need more research, institutional experimentation, and learning – is to determine who should do whatever needs to be done. The partnership between the state, the market, and civil society needs an institutional foundation, basically in the form of a social contract (Jentoft 2004b). What the subsidiarity principle could possibly mean in the fisheries sector is an issue of great importance here. The principle notes that responsibilities should rest with the lowest possible organisation. It is hard to say unequivocally which organisations they are, since old organisations can be strengthened and new ones built.

One could argue that the state's only concern is, or should be, the public interest. The state has no other agenda than to be the ultimate guardian of what is common to its current and future citizens. What exactly the public interest is, however, is not all that clear. Are we only thinking of ecosystem health or should we also include social, cultural, and even spiritual items? People and states typically think differently on matters of this kind. The debate on the subsidiarity principle that has been going on under the auspices of the Catholic Church has centred on these issues. It has also focused on the agenda of the European Union. The answer largely depends on what the state's ambition is. At the outset this is a political issue for its citizens to decide in a democratic election. The state could confine itself to a reactive role and focus on establishing the legal and institutional framework within which the market and civil society freely operate. State interference in fisheries would then be restricted to providing and enforcing rules and regulations, and the market would determine matters of distribution. But the state can also adopt a more proactive, entrepreneurial role. Fisheries development could be a state task. The state would not intervene because it has to but because it wants to do what it deems best. Local communities, volunteer organisations, schools, women's groups, and so forth would also be targets for state initiatives and support. Where the state should operate on the reactive-proactive continuum is a major political governance issue, but there is no standard answer.

Challenges and Implications for Fisheries Institutions

One may conclude that there is, and will most likely always be, a role for the state in the governance of fisheries, as for instance where market competition will not survive without powerful policing by the state (Moran and Wright 1991). Even though the state as a structure is becoming increasingly complex, and the structural changes of the state and other societal institutions will continue, there is no reason to believe that the state will be superseded (Cerny 1990). Neither markets nor civil society can fully compensate for the state's governing capacities (Dror 2002), because the state commands resources such as information, expertise, legitimacy, financial resources, symbolic authority, and in the last instance, a considerable power apparatus that represent essential contributions to good governance (Moran and Wright 1991). The nature of this industry, and the exploitation of the natural resources on which it is based, will always need some form of steering, if not through hierarchical governance, then at least through a cooperative mix of institutions tuned to the particular problems and opportunities that are to be targeted. Thus, invoking the market and civil society in the governance equation is about shifting the division of labour, and not the abdication of state responsibility.

Here we are not necessarily talking about a leaner state as much as a state that works differently, and that builds partnerships in its affairs rather than doing it all alone in a top-down manner. This argument is also relevant within the context of globalisation. The common perception is that this means that the state is becoming increasingly obsolete as powers are transferred from national institutions to regional institutions like the EU. True, globalisation suggests 'a questioning of pre-existing institutional arrangements and behavioural patterns' (Djelic and Quack 2003: 8), but also within international institutions, people usually represent their nation of origin, which serves as their frame of reference. From here they draw their experiences, identities, interests, and resources. Globalisation means a re-figuration, sometimes even a reinvention, of the links that exist between national and international institutions, not their truncation. Globalisation is therefore also about governance, where the expected death of the nation state is highly exaggerated.

We may conclude that neither globalisation nor decentralisation of management responsibility would suggest state abdication from involvement in fisheries; it just means a different role in the division of governance labour. The state is still needed in a supportive, enabling, and steering role. Notably, the trend towards delegation and decentralisation, where the capacities of state and civil society are invoked, should not be seen as a zero-sum game. Rather, it should first be perceived as, and then actively turned into, a win-win situation through a process of mutual empowerment that makes the state, market, and civil society partnership concentrate on tasks where they have their unique strengths and comparative advantage. There is no need for the state to do things that the market and civil society can do better. Good governance requires a strong and competent state but not an omnipresent one. Good governance in the age of diversity, complexity, and dynamics requires a competent and democratic state, but is also dependent on a well-functioning and cooperative market and civil society.

Thus, with diversity, complexity, and dynamics, the state, market and civil society must share the burden of societal governance as none of the three can do it alone. Instead, together they need to find some *modus operandi*, a functional division of social responsibility and an interactive relationship. Partnership arrangements, such as co-management, have a great potential in principle, but are demanding in their organisation. For instance, they all depend on supportive legislation, which only the state can provide. They also depend on market actors to whom corporate social responsibility is not seen as an unnecessary burden but as a positive contribution in their own long-term interest. Last but not least, they depend on a moral constitution of trust and solidarity nurtured by civil society. Since the state, market, and civil society are institutions of very different constitutive elements and working principles, such partnerships will by themselves be diverse, complex, and dynamic. They need to be tailor-made for the particular context within which they shall exist. Such partnerships must also be able to produce legitimate decisions. If legitimacy is to be enhanced by participation, transparency, and accountability, it is not only the state that must change its ways. We would need to be equally as principled and demanding with regard to the market and civil society as we are with regard to the state. They would also have to be able to meet certain universal standards, for instance pertaining to democracy and human rights.

As coastal states are moving towards ecosystem-based management, a more holistic governance approach is required. Which governance institutions are able to address the complexity, diversity, and dynamics of interactive and overlapping ecosystems and the human extractive practices that benefit from them, is a major issue. Such governance institutions must work at multiple scales; local and regional, but also national and international. Pressmann and Wildavsky (1983: 208) say that 'the closer one is to the source of the problem, the greater is one's ability to influence it, and the problem solving ability to complex systems depends not on the hierarchical control but on maximising discretion at the point where the problem is most immediate'. However, their statement cannot be taken as an unqualified, *carte blanche,* support for decentralisation of governance – that decentralisation is always better. Problems that are felt at higher levels than the community cannot be left to the local level, as when the carrying capacity of resources is exhausted beyond a certain locality. Fisheries governance also concerns issues and principles of a general nature, such as those pertaining to social justice, where there is need for uniform solutions. Fisheries also need standardised regulations that apply to more than one locality. Notably, problems of scale may also be addressed through a governing process that is bottom-up rather than top-down, provided that there are integrative mechanisms in place to handle difficulties pertaining to aggregation.

Fisheries management problems are not always really fisheries management problems; they may reflect some deeper socio-political and institutional problems within a given society. For instance, overfishing may stem from unemployment in other sectors, enforcement problems may stem from a weak judiciary, and management impotence may result from 'community failure' (McCay and Jentoft 1998) or dysfunction. Solutions to the problem of overexploitation of marine resources may often be found outside the fisheries sector. Hence, a sector perspective is too limited. We need to move beyond fisheries management, outside the typical management 'tool-box', towards broader social reform involving the state, market and civil society at large. As our examples show, fishing peoples are occasionally victims of human rights and international labour law violations, and state agencies are often captives of powerful private interests. In fact, current developments are moving in the direction of private power increasing its power in relation with the state, and in many instances 'governing governance, rather than being governed by it' (Dror 2002). In many countries, corruption is rampant and therefore poses a severe hindrance to sound governance. All of these developments imply that before governments can help reform fisheries systems, they have to reform themselves. More often than not, such reforms would have to be initiated from the outside. That is why fisheries need global governance; i.e. institutions at the supra-national level that can exert pressures on national governments when they are unable to deliver. That is also why we argue that we need a governance approach to fisheries problems. In some situations, a major institutional overhaul is needed.

Institutional change does not always have to be revolutionary. Neither does it always have to start from scratch. Sometimes marginal reform will do, and reinventing the wheel is sufficient. Dormant or ineffective institutions might be invoked or recycled. Existing institutions may acquire new or additional mandates. Occasionally, more fine-tuning of existing institutions is what it takes.

10

International Institutions

Juan L. Suárez de Vivero, Juan C. Rodríguez Mateos, and David Florido del Corral

Introduction

Despite the drastic changes that property rights over fisheries resources have been subject to since the creation of exclusive economic and fishing zones and despite the crisis the United Nations system is currently experiencing, international institutions still continue to exert a marked influence on national and international policies. Access to resources (United Nations convention on the Law of the Sea – UNCLOS), trade (World Trade Organization – WTO), international co-operation (the UN and regional organisations), research, technical and scientific advisory bodies, international statistics (Food and Agriculture Organization – FAO), and supra-national political organisations (EU) are only a few examples of the dynamic and forceful role a wide range of organisations and institutions play with regard to fishing, fisheries management and policies.

The theory of governance specifically insists on new social and political agents in the decision-making process and on political control over new production and marketing practices. With this in mind, international institutions, particularly United Nations institutions and Regional Fisheries Organisations, traditionally devote efforts to strengthening institutions in less developed countries and regions and boosting public policies. To a certain extent the new trend towards greater roles for the market and civil society entails the risk of weakening public action and in more general terms state action as well. Although this is part of the logical evolution of more developed states, it renders less-developed ones more vulnerable, lacking as they do the institutional framework that allows public and private action to be balanced out.

Institutional Development in Ocean Governance

The institutional pillars of ocean governance have recently been drawn up around the Third United Nations Convention on the Law of the Sea (UNCLOS 1982) and its predecessors the First and Second Conferences, the United Nations Convention on Environment and Development (UNCED

1992) and more specifically Agenda 21, the seventeenth chapter of which is devoted to oceans and coastal areas.

UNCLOS (1982) in particular can be interpreted as the final phase of maritime tradition in the modern era with the oceans conceived as an issue for the international community ruled by the principle of *mare liberum* and inspired, prior to the reform of Part XI and the Agreement on Straddling Stocks and Highly Migratory Fish Stocks, by public action as a balance to the inequalities between states (the Area as the common heritage of mankind and the establishment of bodies such as Authority and Enterprise). Yet at the same time, UNCLOS opens the door to maritime nationalism by confirming wider jurisdictions with a consequent reduction in common areas (the high seas and the deep seabed), which in turn allow for the first national Oceans Acts (the Canadian Oceans Act 1997 and the US Ocean Act 2000). Along with national legislation, a new generation of public policies has also emerged, characterised by a recognition of integrated and all-embracing action in the oceans to allow multiple uses and interaction to be managed, while incorporating the principles confirmed at Rio 1992 such as sustainability, and managementbased on an ecosystem approach that includes human action and the precautionary principle.

Post-UNCLOS/UNCED marine policies include concepts of governance such as new public management and good governance. The state is less interventionist and there is greater prominence for various social agents (principles of representation, collaboration and legitimacy) and especially new values and principles of environmental ethics that are clear in the Canadian and US legislation. Maritime nationalism, fostered as a mechanism to safeguard resources in waters adjacent to developing countries, became the standpoint the most advanced countries founded their new marine policies on, directed at exercising world leadership and opposing the idea of marine internationalism, an argument timidly voiced in the post-colonial era. The notion of governance as international order pertaining to the international community's social and economic inequalities was supplanted towards the end of the twentieth century by tough environmental ethics that have introduced new property rights and a new redistribution of resources that are already beginning to transform some communities of fishermen into mere tenants or lease-holders on a par with landless peasants (Eythórsson 1996).

The beginning of the new millennium thus yields a confused and complex panorama as regards relations between public and private and nationalism and internationalism, notions contradictorily present in the new governance of the oceans.

Ocean Issues and the Role of Private Initiative at Rio+10

As far as the oceans are concerned, the Johannesburg Conference did not result in any significant changes or innovations regarding the greater soundness and ambition emerging from its predecessor, UNCED (1992), especially with regard to Agenda 21 and its Chapter 17. Trends can nevertheless be detected in the direction of thoughts with respect to mechanisms and principles of government on the main problems and challenges the conservation of the ocean and exploitation of its resources are facing.

Recognition of the key roles the ocean plays in the natural balance of the planet, feeding the world and economic prosperity (World Summit on Sustainable Development: Plan of Implementation) is a possibly necessary re-iteration of declarations made more than a decade ago. Recommended action such as the need for UNCLOS to be fully ratified not only bore witness to the validity of instruments that emerged over a decade earlier, but also to the slow pace they are being developed and implemented at. The same is true of recommendations for reinforcing regional co-operation, applying measures for ocean conservation and management, and for said measures to be applied in an integrated and co-ordinated way with a multidisciplinary focus.

This recommendation dwells on this very circumstance for fishing, i.e. the need to drive previously achieved and formulated accords, declarations and principles and an effort to implement them. As such, the Reykjavik Declaration on Responsible Fisheries in the Marine Environment (2001) should be implemented by 2010 by strengthening co-operation and co-ordination among the various regional fisheries organisations and between them and other scientific bodies and programmes (UNEP Regional Seas Programmes) and developing other kinds of measures to allow stocks to be conserved and even permit them to be restored or maintained by 2010.

The issue thus relates to giving continuity to objectives that in general terms, had already been formulated by 1992 (Agreement on Bio-diversity, Agenda 21) and implementing them. There are now however some new points of focus such as the elimination of fisheries subsidies, given that they are thought to encourage overcapacity and overfishing. In addition, there is the importance of applying measures agreed on by the WTO, which are generally designed to further market deregulation and the commercialisation of natural resources. In short, the above-mentioned trend becomes more patently obvious. There is a reversal of the principles advanced since the 1960s, characterised by a greater emphasis on social issues, common property, and co-operation. These are being replaced by thinking more in line with current neo-liberal trends: the defence of the priority of the market in the regulation and assignment of resources, the gradual erosion of the capacity of state and supra-state institutions and the privatisation of any spaces or resources that might yield economic benefits.

Other issues referred to in the Johannesburg Plan of Implementation relate to the opportunity globalisation presents for achieving sustainable development (Sustainable Development in a Globalising World). These involve the transfer of technology, financial cooperation, economic rationalisation by increasing productivity, boosting the private sector and making effective use of investment and international aid, recognising the essential role trade might play in achieving sustainable development and the fight against poverty in accordance with WTO guidelines through the deregulation of markets, the cooperation of the public sector, and technical and financial aid. To conclude, there is also an appeal for good governance to be the basis for political action and a combined strategy of theoretical and abstract principles (freedom, democracy, the democratic state, gender equality) and more practical principles, such as market-oriented policies. In this way, a certain amount of support is given to other actors such as civil society and the market, with the latter gaining greater influence in political affairs via big business.

The Governance of Fishing as Global Action: Aims, Tools and Institutions

Aspirations for co-ordinated global action designed to tackle the great problems facing fishing throughout the world are closely linked to the creation in 1965 of the Food and Agriculture Organization (FAO) as one of the United Nations specialist agencies and of the Committee on Fisheries (COFI) in the FAO itself. Four large domains can be distinguished (table 10.1) where the various initiatives have been developed over the past four decades along with the corresponding institutions, which are responsible for fisheries governance being implemented: i.e. 1) new ocean order, 2) sustainability, 3) the production of fish products with a view to food requirements, and 4) fishing communities.

The main contents of each of these four great domains are analysed below along with the historical context they emerged in, the social and ideological bases that inspired them and the power structures that support fisheries governance as defined by the typology of the players that drive them (states, governmental and non-governmental organisations, the market and so forth).

The United Nations Convention on the Law of the Sea (UNCLOS 1982) is, as noted above, the most relevant milestone in the evolution of marine policies on an international scale, with fishing occupying a core position in the creation of new rules of access to resources and for the first time, obligations regarding their conservation and management. UNCLOS contains a number of provisions related to fisheries governance, but always with the underlying principle of equity between the states in issues involving a marked sense of community in international society.

In this early phase of the emergence of fisheries governance, state aspirations to regulate and obligate can be detected in an effort to strengthen this institution rather than weaken it in favour of private interests (the market). This attitude is in part expressed in the transformation of international society after the end of the Second World War and the commencement of the decolonisation process. During this process the new greater influence acquired by developing countries (110 of the 150 who took part in UNCLOS III belonged to the Group of 77) seemed to turn the regulatory framework in the direction of positions dominated by common interests, facilitating indiscriminate access to the seas by all the states. In the following decades, the situation gravitated towards more individualistic positions and even the text of the Convention was modified in favour of states and business groups that own economic and technological resources.

Table 10.1 Main domains in fisheries governance

	New ocean order	Sustainability	Food supply	Fisheries communities
Subjects	– EEZ[a] Programme – Flagging – Vessels Register – ITQs[b]	– Fishing capacity – Drifting nets – Small island developing states – Bio-diversity – Multi-annual and multi-specific fisheries management – Ecosystem management approach	– Bycatch – Discards – MCS[c] – Food security	– Strategies for development and management – Women in fisheries – Subsidies – Investment
Tools	– Agreement to promote compliance[d] – UNCLOS[e] – Straddling and highly migratory fish stocks – Agenda 21	– UNCED[f] – Agenda 21 – CCFR (FAO)[g] – Rome Consensus[h]	– CCRF (FAO)[g] – Kyoto Declaration[i]	– CCRF (FAO)[g]
Institutions	– RFB[j] – United Nations	– United Nations – RFB[j] – Kyoto Declaration[i]	– WTO[k] – WB[l]	– FAO – WB[l]
Principles	– Free access to high seas – Equity between states – Sovereignty over resources in adjacent waters	– Protection and conservation of common resources – Precautionary principle – Principle of inter- and intragenerational equity	– Social justice – Fair trade – Transparency principle	– Right to development – Gender equality – Protection of ethnic minorities

Source: Authors of this chapter, based on Swan and Satia 1998; Lugten, 1999.

[a] EEZ: Exclusive Economic Zone
[b] ITQs: Individual Transferable Quotas
[c] MCS: Monitoring, Control and Surveillance
[d] Agreement to Promote Compliance: Agreement to Promote Compliance with International Conservation and Management Measures by Fishing Vessels on the High Seas
[e] UNCLOS: United Nations Conference on The Law of the Sea, 1982
[f] UNCED: United Nations Conference on Environment and Development, 1992
[g] CCRF (FAO): Code of Conduct for Responsible Fisheries (FAO), 1995
[h] Rome Consensus: Rome Consensus on World Fisheries (FAO/UNCED), 1995
[i] Kyoto Declaration: Kyoto Declaration and Action Plan on Sustainable Contribution of Fisheries to Food Security, 1995
[j] RFB: Regional Fishery Bodies
[k] WTO: World Trade Organization
[l] WB: World Bank

The Exclusive Economic Zone Programme initiated by COFI is designed to help developing states manage their extended fishing zones. Along with food security, it is a clear example of the mentality that drives this kind of international action and of the priority issues that emerged early in the 1960s. Technological development and the growing demand from a mushrooming population put pressure on the resources. Indications of their decline were already evident towards the end of the 1970s, turning into one of the priority subjects in the following decade, when the paradigm of sustainability was formulated. The situation worsened towards the end of the century and conservation measures were reinforced. Together with the collapse of high commercial value stocks, this began to endanger the survival of communities reliant on fishing. This process concurred with the development towards ideological standpoints dominated by neo-liberalism, the erosion of the welfare state and the discrediting of public interventionism and strong competition in an economy becoming increasingly global.

Fisheries governance is affected by these trends, as is witnessed by a reverse in social policies (a drastic reduction in the fishing effort with a consequent increase in unemployment and withdrawal of subsidies) and changes in private property rights. The activation of new principles (precautionary principle, inter- and intra-generational equity, fair trade, gender equality and the protection of ethnic minorities) was not effective enough to halt the de-structuring of developing countries and the consequent loss of political weight in international society and progress towards more individualistic positions. These positions have consistently weakened initiatives such as the Strategy for Fisheries Management and Development (1984), which included issues of highly charged social content such as artisanal fishing, rural fishing, agricultural communities, the contribution of fishing to the national economy and social and nutritional objectives, financial aid and so forth (Swan and Satia 1998).

At the same time these ideological trends and political economy were developing, there was a major deterioration and depletion of the prestige of the United Nations and other international institutions (especially the ones in the United Nations system) including the tools created in the heart of the United Nations itself (UNCLOS, UNCED) devoted to raising the edifice of global governance and of fisheries governance within it. Regional Fishery Bodies (RFB) have been one of the key tools of fisheries governance. Their origins can be traced back to the beginning of the twentieth century (ICES was created in 1902) and there are more than thirty of them in existence nowadays, nine of which are dependent upon FAO. Almost half of them were created in 1982 in the wake of UNCLOS. Although the effectiveness of these bodies is undergoing critical review (1997, 1999, 2000), what they do continues to be considered highly relevant for guaranteeing the conservation of resources and economic effectiveness of the fisheries sector. In their development since the mid-twentieth century, there have been clear signs of changes to adapt to new ideological paradigms and new ways that international society conceives governance (table 10.2).

Table 10.2 Priorities in fisheries management at the international level

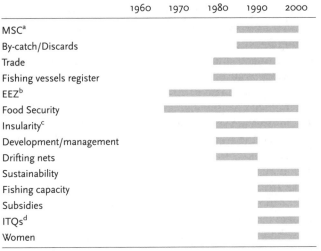

	1960	1970	1980	1990	2000
MSC[a]				▓▓▓▓▓▓	
By-catch/Discards				▓▓▓▓▓▓	
Trade			▓▓▓▓▓▓		
Fishing vessels register			▓▓▓▓▓▓		
EEZ[b]		▓▓▓▓▓▓			
Food Security		▓▓▓▓▓▓▓▓▓▓▓▓			
Insularity[c]			▓▓▓▓▓▓▓▓▓		
Development/management			▓▓▓▓		
Drifting nets			▓▓▓		
Sustainability				▓▓▓	
Fishing capacity				▓▓▓▓	
Subsidies				▓▓▓	
ITQs[d]				▓▓▓	
Women				▓▓▓▓	

Source: Authors of this article, based on Swan and Satia (1998), Lugten (1999)

[a] MCS: Monitoring, Control and Surveillance   [c] Insularity: Small island developing states
[b] EEZ: Exclusive Economic Zone   [d] ITQs: Individual Transferable Quotas

The RFBs were created under the aegis of the United Nations Charter to further co-operation as a tool to mitigate inequalities (Lugten 1999). In as much as the United Nations Charter emphasises the role of the state in tackling global problems such as fishing, the RFBs are essentially governmental organisations and their priorities after the Second World War (1951-1982) acquired a fundamentally social flavour (the contribution made by fishing to food security, help for developing countries' EEZs) in a context of world fishing still featuring growth and optimism. During the above-mentioned critical review of the RFBs, priorities became more technical with the emergence of issues of evident interest and importance (overfishing, overcapacity, discards, bycatch, trade and so on). They have become less focused due to the urgency and grave importance of these new problems, the enormity of the social issues and requirements of developing countries, in spite of which their circumstances worsened in many aspects compared to the 1951-1982 period. As part of the RFB review process, the participation of industry and NGOs has been encouraged and management responsibilities devolved to the private sector and to national and international non-governmental bodies. On the other hand, the crisis affecting most of the nine RFBs dependent on the FAO, due to the financial difficulties of the United Nations system, could lead to their being turned into independent bodies (Marashi 1996) financed by their own members. This implies the risk that the withdrawal from the FAO might hinder inter-state co-operation in developing regions. In the fisheries regions of the developed world (primarily the North Atlantic) and the developing world, the new forms of governance are inspiring a withdrawal from the public sector that is generally justified by the lack of effectiveness on the part of the institutions responsible for management, yielding ever more ground to the private sector and NGOs, or by encouraging changes in property rights as a result of turning fishing resources into merchandisable goods.

International fisheries organisations are beginning to play an equally significant role in the development of instruments and agreements to foster the conservation and sustainable use of resources on the high seas, especially since the 1993 Agreement (the Agreement to Promote Compliance with International Conservation and Management Measures by Fishing Vessels on the High Seas), the Agreement for the Implementation of the Provisions of the United Nations Convention of the Law of the Sea Relating to the Conservation and Management of Straddling Fish Stocks and Highly Migratory Fish Stocks (1995), and the Code of Conduct for Responsible Fisheries (1995). All of these agreements highlight the potentially important role of regional organisations.

In accordance with the Code of Conduct, these organisations have to be open and admit any state wishing to join and engage in the management of the resources in question. Nonetheless, as a result of the entrance conditions, three types of regional organisations can be identified in the organisations as a whole. They vary according to the conditions for membership (Vázquez Gómez 2002: 218-219) (see table 10.3):

Table 10.3 Regional fisheries organisations

Type of Organisation	List of Organisations
Open to all states	International Commission for the Conservation of Atlantic Tunas (ICCAT), General Fisheries Commission for the Mediterranean (GFCM), Northwest Atlantic Fisheries Organization (NAFO), South East Atlantic Fisheries Organisation (SEAFO), Regional Commission for Fisheries (RECOFI), Commission for the Conservation of Antarctic Marine Living Resources (CCAMLR), International Whaling Commission (IWC)
Membership conditional	Indian Ocean Tuna Commission (IOTC), Asia-Pacific Fisheries Commission (APFIC), North East Atlantic Fisheries Commission (NEAFC), International Council for the Exploration of the Sea (ICES), North Pacific Anadromous Fish Commission (NPAFC), Inter-American Tropical Tuna Commission (IATTC), North Pacific Marine Science Organization (PICES), International Baltic Sea Fishery Commission (IBSFC), The Commission for the Conservation of Southern Bluefin Tuna (CCSBT), North Atlantic Marine Mammal Commission (NAMMCO), North Atlantic Salmon Conservation Organization (NASCO), Forum Fisheries Agency (FFA)
Closed	International Pacific Halibut Commission (IPHC), Pacific Salmon Commission (PSC), Permanent Commission for the South Pacific (PCSP)

Source: Authors of this chapter.

INTERNATIONAL INSTITUTIONS

Through these organisations, especially the ones that impose entrance conditions or simply do not admit new members under any circumstances, some coastal states are able to create mechanisms involving a new phenomenon: progressive or creeping collective jurisdiction via the establishment of closed or semi-closed organisations in certain areas of the high seas. The 1995 Agreement, in so far as it is a framework agreement, has to be established on a regional scale. Within the bounds of the agreement, the interests of the coastal state have to be reconciled with the principle of freedom of the high seas. Regional management organisations can therefore be regarded as an instrument to drive coastal state jurisdiction outwards towards the high seas.

Institutionally speaking, RFBs fall under the concept of international regimes (with agreements, principles, norms, regulations and procedures) and their role in environmental and natural resource management policies is making them a focus of growing academic interest, with their formation addressed from three theoretical perspectives: neo-realism, neo-liberalism and constructivism (Sydnes 2001a). State action could be justified under one of these perspectives such as neo-realism which, assuming there was no supra-national authority within the international system (the high seas?), would lead to unilateral acts to extend rights of sovereignty beyond national jurisdiction or the exclusive economic zone.

International Institutions and Global Civil Society

The acceleration and permanent change brought about by new technologies and economic globalisation have resulted in two basic pillars of democracy, progress and social cohesion, being replaced by communication and the market, and a change in the meanings of some old geo-political concepts. The three main actors on a world scale are now state associations (the EU, NAFTA, MERCOSUR, ASEAN and so forth), global companies, and large media or financial groups and non-governmental organisations (NGOs) with global influence (Greenpeace, WWF, Amnesty International, etc.). These three actors follow their courses in a global, indeed a planet-wide framework established not so much by the UN as the WTO, the new global arbiter. As such, confronting the political power wielded by supra-national bodies and the economic power of huge transnational corporations, we encounter what is called global civil society (GCS).

From a freer point of view, in the fields of the environment and fisheries on a global scale, civil society can be viewed as representing the group of non-governmental bodies with direct influence on the management of fisheries resources (environmentalist NGOs, marketing and processing companies, trades union, professional associations, citizens' groups, etc.) and groups that perform duties of a scientific, advisory, assessment, critical and motivation nature (Gemmill and Bamidele-Izu n.d.; Dunn 2003). Nevertheless, from a more critical point of view, global civil society can be viewed as representing a genuine counter-power to official regional or supra-national bodies and large economic corporations, even though the NGOs it consists of do not always have the appropriate mechanisms for participation, expression and funding.

Be that as it may, and although there are people who doubt the existence of global civil society, various state and supra-state entities try to legitimise their political decisions on the basis of the participation and opinions of citizens' groups and organisations they consider representative.

Box 10.1 NGOs and fisheries issues

The Marine Stewardship Council (MSC) is an NGO whose aim is to encourage proper fisheries management as is understood by the term *governance* by means of a certification programme for fish products. This is done via a distinctive blue label assigned to products that comply with the MSC Standard, which now entails a number of internationally recognised environmental principles for the appraisal of fisheries management and sustainability: the state of fish reserves, the impact of the fishery on the marine environment and the management systems of the fisheries.

Its newness might be the main obstacle to its having a more widespread effect. It seems clear that its effectiveness depends on the degree to which social awareness of the social and environmental issues surrounding the highly industrialised fisheries model are raised and presented to the public. In other words, it hinges on responsible demand in an international market, one of the most prominent features of which is the lack of product differentiation. As such, its real effects on the suppression or harassment of bad practices in fisheries exploitation are limited.

Source: Authors of this chapter

Global Civil Society (GSC) plays a role in international institutions in an extremely wide range of ways. This is why it is difficult to arrive at a clear, ordered, and systematised typology. A first approach, at risk of oversimplification, shows how GSC acts at two levels: a political level (in the structures of the administration) and a civic level, as an authority complementary to government action or counter-power (although these are not always exclusive categories). One example in fisheries activity might be the EU's Advisory Committee on Fisheries (ACF), which is made up of professional organisations (fishermen, boat-owners) and citizens' associations (consumers' and environmentalist organisations).

Table 10.4 Advisory committee on fisheries organisations[1]

Type of Organisation	List of Organisations
Professional	Europêche, General Confederation of Agricultural Cooperatives in the European Union (COGECA), European Association of Producers Organisations (EAPO), Association des Industries du Poisson de la Communauté Économique Européenne/The Federation of National Organisations of Fish Wholesalers, Importers and Exporter of the European Economic Community (AIPCEE/CEP), European Farmers Union/General Committee of Agricultural Cooperation in the EU (COPA/COGECA)
Environmentalist	Greenpeace, World Wide Fund for Nature (WWF), Birdlife International
Consumer	European Community of Consumer Cooperatives (EUROCOOP), European Consumers' Organisation (BEUC), Consumers Associations (COFACE), Institute of European Inter-regional Consumer's Organisations (IEIC)
Scientific and sporting	European Anglers Association
Financial	European Association of Cooperative Banks
Trade union	Federation of Transport Workers Unions

Source: The examples of professional, environmental, consumers', sporting, financial and trade union organisations are taken from the EU's Advisory Committee on Fisheries (Report on Advisory Committee on Fisheries. Prepared for the DGXIV of the European Commission by Nautilus Consultants in collaboration with Cofrepêche in France, Gico in Italy, IFM in Denmark, LEI in Holland and the University of Seville in Spain, 1998).

At the same time, the complex role GSC plays in fisheries reveals various problems and a number of contradictions. The first one is geographical scope, since global institutions are essentially confined to a single more economically and politically advanced sector of societies. For example in the case of Greenpeace, 70% of its income comes from the EU and Germany provides almost half the amount it receives in European contributions. The adjective global thus requires more than one qualification. Are the only truly global organisations those that have no national base? Or those that are organised into supra-national structures (i.e. European federations)? Or the national or local organisations that perform on the global stage? Or perhaps the organisations or groups that act within global networks? A more detailed study of the NGOs would shed more light on these issues.

Geographical Inequalities in Access to the Sea

Inequality in the use of fishery resources is varied and impacts societies in a number of ways. One way to detect inequality is via the geographical factor, without it necessarily being interpreted as geographical determinism.

In the face of physical and natural adversity, developed societies can overcome their geographical constraints and gain access to fisheries resources through economic and political action (agreements with third-party countries). In the spirit of international co-operation that characterised part of the 1960s and 1970s, an effort was made to overcome geographical injustice during the discussion at UNCLOS. This led to oceans being declared part of the Common Heritage of Mankind. Efforts to facilitate access to the seas for all the states without discrimination were eventually thwarted.

Its access to stocks mainly depends on a state's relative geographical location and the morphological features of its territory, whether it has access to a coast or is land-locked, the length of its coastline, whether it lies alongside or opposite other states it has to delimit its jurisdictional waters with, whether it is an island or a continental state and so forth. In the case of a coastal state, coastal waters can either be very productive or of little biological interest, depending on the physical and natural factors regulating the marine productivity there. In addition to geographical and biophysical factors, political ones come into play, especially with regard to gaining access to localised stocks outside the national jurisdiction, since most stocks are subject to some coastal state's exclusive rights. Access to stocks falls within the political domain and more specifically within the scope of international relations, since they are regulated by agreements and accords made between states.

Geopolitical factors have emerged in the wake of the new legal order governing the seas resulting from the UNCLOS. There has been widespread redistribution of fish stocks throughout the world due to exclusive economic and fishing zones being established on a large scale. A combination of geographical (the territory belonging to a state and its relative location) and bio-physical factors (regulating productivity) means developed and developing countries alike are at the forefront of world fishing, with the latter overtaking the industrialised nations in the world ranking of fishing powers.

Another consequence of the new legislation covering the seas has been a wide-ranging transformation of property rights. The regime of free access that mainly operated throughout the marine areas has been limited to the high seas which, although greater in surface area, are low in biological productivity, providing only 10% of the world food resources. Since they are located within exclusive economic areas or the 200-mile fishing zones around coasts all across the globe, most stocks are classified as state property. Other property rights such as communal or private rights do not mean much on a global scale, although under a system known as Individual Transferable Quotas, private property rights may come to be more than isolated experiences applicable to certain species. Although fishing is still viewed as the last global activity carried out all over the planet today, political borders are fundamental in determining property rights over stocks in a general trend that is progressively widening legal rights on the basis of proximity and to the detriment of free access; the high seas are defined by exclusion. Apart from glaring inequalities regarding access to stocks, other inequalities are also caused by natural factors, such as the unequal distribution of biological productivity throughout the world.

The Influence of Markets on Fisheries Governance

The current market economy is characterised by numerous autonomous centres of political and economic decision-making and almost exclusive reliance on a single criterion for management and resource assignment: market mechanisms. Today's market is a kind of abstract entity where supply and demand come into contact, that seems to pervade all economic activities to the extent that it shapes production (or extraction) as well as consumption.

Fishing and associated economic activities are similarly caught up in these mercantilist dynamics, with the marketing of fish products now a phenomenon of the first order moving some US$115 billion, especially in countries that are either high producers or high consumers (FAO 2000a, FAO 2000b, FAO 2002) (table 10.5). It should not be forgotten that the market makes its presence most felt in fisheries via huge transnational marketing companies and, albeit indirectly, via the globalisation of other activities (industrial, financial, etc.).

Table 10.5 International trade in fishery commodities by 12 principal importers and exporters (2000)

Country	Imports (US $ 1000)	Country	Exports (US $ 1000)
Japan	15513059	Thailand	4367332
USA	10453251	China	3605838
Spain	3351670	Norway	3532841
France	2983618	USA	3055261
Italy	2535269	Canada	2818433
Germany	2262018	Denmark	2755676
UK	2183811	Chile	1784560
China, Hong Kong	1948824	China, Taiwan	1756133
Denmark	1806365	Spain	1599631
China	1795953	Indonesia	1584454
Canada	1388621	Vietnam	1480110
Korea	1371830	India	1405196

Source: FAO, 2000a.

So, despite the efforts of national and regional departments to impose some sort of management, fisheries have gradually come to be part of this huge globalising phenomenon that has progressively forced all kinds of markets (from fish products to employment) to become more flexible, and prompted a diversification in the range of fish products on offer. There has been a move in the fish-processing industry towards greater vertical integration, the take-over of small industries by large multinational companies and, in short, the control of prices and distribution by the large marketing chains (Friis 1994; OECD Committee for Fisheries 2000: 112; FAO 2000b). As such, grand declarations on sustainable fisheries management, constraints on the fishing effort, responsible fishing and other long-term good intentions contradict the objectives the market, as represented by big business, lays down with respect to the management of fisheries resources. This is especially true in developing countries, where development goals are more related to intensifying and diversifying the fishing effort than limiting it, where there is a logical preoccupation with social and economic development and the creation of employment (with social and economic rights being given precedence over environmental rights), and where a certain leeway is important in dealing with the deregulatory strategies of international capital.

Given that it is already complex for a local or domestic market to work in a rational and equitable way, it being almost certain that neither perfect competition nor market transparency or rational choice exists, we have to bear in mind that on a global scale, the market is being progressively tainted by monopolisation and oligopolisation processes that are turning the large chains and multinational companies into exclusive agents for production management, price setting and the marketing of numerous products (Friis 1994; Van Vliet and Friis 1999; FAO 2000b). Only these large companies have the actual ability to compete on markets on a global scale and have access to privileged information, as is the case with European lobbies. It is consequently these huge marketing companies that really benefit from fishing activity while the producers, especially the small-scale ones, find themselves increasingly ousted from the big economic circuits and deprived of the social and economic benefits they could otherwise derive from their activities.

Despite the highs and lows – often the result of the crisis in the economic system itself – trade figures for fish show it is a highly profitable business for big companies that have diversified and turned many fish products into food products that are of enormous interest to the average consumer in rich countries (Friis 1994; Van Vliet and Friis 1999). This huge rise in trade logically conditions extraction which, in order for it to be more profitable, requires greater effort and the progressive depletion of fish stocks (Arnason 1993: 334-335; Van Vliet and Friis 1999: 214) and creates deep social and economic rifts, leaving fishing communities very poor. It even puts deliberate and heavy pressure on fisheries management, propagating more flexible systems that would prefer to see state regulation progressively reduced to a minimum and where economic lobbies made their influence felt in fisheries decision-making political circles. As far as Europe is concerned, this is paradigmatic. In all probability, what is being witnessed today is a transitional period from a system where state institutions used to pass on the fisheries management stick to one where the market and big business increasingly impose their strategies (Apostle et al. 1998). In addition, trade in fish has often boomed as a result of biological or legal impositions, given that numerous countries whose fishing grounds are depleted or that have access to other countries' fishing grounds refused to them are beginning to become significant purchasers of fish products. This has led to vast distribution and marketing chains and to states previously on the fringes of the business now turning into producers and suppliers (FAO 2000a; FAO 2001). These processes change property and management structures and accommodate themselves to global strategies in such a way that processing and marketing activities, once adapted to global strategies, do not always leave profit at a local level. The global fish produce market can thus impose limitations on the social and economic development of communities dependent on fishing, giving rise to an increase in profit for big business at the expense of depleted stocks, flexibility of labour and re-siting activities.

Yet the market and its associated activities (deregulation, privatisation of common resources, deregulation of activities) imbue the current analyses of the fisheries sector and management measures with a new, more economic-ist and in all probability neo-liberal philosophy. As a result, despite deriving from a system that led to resource overexploitation and where David Ricardo's law of decreasing returns has clearly been fulfilled (Arnason 1993), the world fisheries crisis has basically been paraded as a problem arising from the existence of some common property (fish stocks) and a specific regime of use (free access). This has, since the 1980s, led to the proposal and justification of new methods of management based more on economic instruments such as restrictions on the fishing effort and the capital devoted to it, taxes and similar charges and instruments based on property rights (Arnason 1993; Sutton 2001; Hannesson 2001), to the use of trade measures designed to achieve a more sustainable use and consumption of resources (OECD Committee for Fisheries 2000: 92-94) and to the use of resource privatisation as a way to put a brake on stock depletion and select fishermen (individuals or companies) on the basis of their economic efficiency and productivity. Some scientists have nevertheless denounced this privatisatory method, this imposed system of Individual Transferable Quotas (ITQs) that seemingly increases economic efficiency, encourages sustainable resource exploitation and optimises the material and financial means invested in the fishing activity but does not go so far as to call itself true privatisation, perhaps because the term could provoke hostility from those affected and from others in defence of common or public property. However, if this kind of private property were to be made official, other and more critical experts would see it as a triumph for the commercialisation of rights of tenure and resource use, resulting in the concentration of the ITQs in the hands of big business and the emergence of undesirable social effects such as a drop in wages and a rise in unemployment (Eythórsson 1996). Together with the deregulation of the market and the end of subsidies, this could have grave negative effects on the communities that most rely on fishing. Thus yet another element has appeared on the fisheries stage, bearing witness to the growing influence of markets and deregulation and the rise of large business corporations controlling extraction and marketing, with a consequent reduction of the role of seafarers who see their capacity for political and economic negotiation severely reduced.

Fisheries Communities and Ethnic Minorities

There is a great deal of documented international legislation that recognises and protects the legitimate rights of local societies, be they ethnic minorities or not, to preserve their indigenous modes of territorialisation, including the exploitation and management systems they apply to natural resources. As such, the Office of the High Commissioner for the Rights of Minorities (1994) published a document stating that 'to enjoy a particular culture may consist of a way of life which is closely associated with territory and use of its resources. This may be particularly true of members of indigenous communities constituting a minority.' Point 7 of the same document notes that the social reproduction of a cultural system inevitably involves material and symbolic appropriation of the surroundings via the 'use of land resources, especially in the case of indigenous peoples. That right may include such traditional activities as fishing or hunting and the right to live in reserves protected by law.' Thus an effort was made to better define the ambiguous Article 27 of the Universal Declaration of Human Rights with respect to cultural rights.

Article 6.18 of the Code of Conduct for Responsible Fishing states that 'states should appropriately protect the rights of fishers and fishworkers, particularly those engaged in subsistence, small-scale and artisanal fisheries, to a secure and just livelihood, as well as preferential access, where appropriate, to traditional fishing grounds and resources in the waters under their national jurisdiction' (FAO 1995).

According to a recent publication, there have been various legal initiatives in international and state organisations supporting indigenous communities' property rights and natural resource management systems at the expense of various forms of intervention, especially by state agencies. Some cases in point are the Mayagna Awas Tingni in Nicaragua, the Maori, the Rama in Nicaragua, the Saami in Norway and the Nunavut Inuit in Canada (Jentoft et al. 2003). It has not gone unnoticed that this has been the International Decade for the World's Indigenous People (1995-2004).

However, these action principles have been historically obstructed by various control processes established by political, economic and scientific agencies. Current conventional economic theory seriously questions the communal model of exploitation implemented in numerous local or regional societies with varying degrees of ethnic homogeneity. Many empirical studies and theoretical analyses (Feeny et al. 1990) demonstrate that communal property is regulated in a number of different ways and via numerous institutions, i.e. through written rules, non-explicit customs or native and common or customary laws valid in a highly-defined social and local environment, handed down to a group of users who devise a kind of 'law by tradition' that regulates access to resources subject to social exploitation and the types of appropriation that are permitted or not.

As regards fishermen's societies, the most striking analyses are the ones conducted in the Asian Pacific and Australia (Dyer and McGoodwin 1994). Various types of territorialisation are put into practise in these areas. Various authors (Akimichi 1984; Kalland 1984 in Japan; Baines 1989 in Melanesia; Ruddle 1989) have analysed fishermen's villages where the resources are exploited by cooperatives in a maritime area regulated by norms and customs. There is a similar system in force in Papua New Guinea, where the affiliated groups have tenure on the maritime space and are responsible for the management of the fisheries there, and in Micronesia, where the social units significant for access to and exploitation of fisheries resources are families, blood lines and clans (Sudo 1984). In northern Australia, access to and exploitation of marine resources by Aborigine societies is similarly organised in strictly defined territorial terms (Davis 1984; Johannes and MacFarlane 1984).

Territorial practises that work on the basis of local logic have continued to work all over the world and are not at all limited to social and cultural minority groups. One paradigmatic case is the classic study of Maine lobster fishermen (Acheson 1979), but it is by no means the only one. Practices of this type and the customary forms of fishery resource exploitation and management should not be limited to ethnic groups or cultural minorities. The integration of ethnic groups into state societies is now the most significant social process in understanding the possibilities for social reproduction of indigenous systems of fisheries exploitation, and analysis should not only consider local forms of territoriality and resource exploitation but also how these communities are affected by the state framework in place. With state legislation and the bureaucratic rationality accompanying it becoming widespread, public property is a legal deed of title evident in almost all societies to regulate access to fisheries resources and their exploitation. As a result, the analyses on this issue draw attention to the difficulties the imposition of state logic has meant to the social collectives that are affected (see Campbell 1996 on Canada; the Finnish Sami Parliament 1997 on the Laplanders – Saami People – in Norway; Robinson and Osherenko 2001 for a comparative analysis of fishing rights and ethnic communities in the Circumpolar North). The issues of rights of access to and exploitation of certain resources that are collectively appropriated and the norms that secularly regulate the types of exploitation have thus been turned into a political arena for groups and ethnic minorities who have to assert their rights of access and use of fisheries resources. Any groups that are not adequately organised politically to defend their interests and forge links with international organisations might find their traditional rights endangered and their livelihoods seriously threatened.

The economic, political and social processes of the past twenty years, collectively referred to as globalisation, should be regarded as the reference framework in which the possibilities of historical reproduction of indigenous populations can be understood along with their territorial practises, appropriation of resources and vernacular socio-economic systems. 'What happens at the level of the community is not of less importance than what occurs at national and international levels. What occurs globally also has a great impact on what occurs locally' (Jentoft et al. 2003: 1).

Meanwhile, a number of economic processes linked to the expansion of the market as the central institution in contemporary societies have gained prominence over the past two decades and ended up affecting traditional forms of exploitation and territoriality. The dynamics to be highlighted include the impact of new and increasingly industrialised economic activities on land (e.g. tourism or recreational fisheries, see Robinson and Osherenko 2001) and at sea (large-scale fleets, aquaculture companies and the dependency of suppliers of raw materials on marketing chains that are increasingly hierarchical and expansive (see McGoodwin 1990; Symes 1996). Analyses of a number of localised places show how new business agents who enjoy a position of hegemony in the world economy are establishing new control mechanisms to subordinate local fishing societies via the market, especially in areas that are not central to the world market. Not only are the small artisanal fisheries of ethnically or non-ethnically homogenous societies of fishermen in developed countries caught up in this, so are ethnically differentiated communities in areas that are not at the hub of the world system. The social and cultural integrity of these collectives is at risk in the local or global conflict. This is the framework in which ethnic groups are obliged to socially reproduce their forms of fisheries resource management. Any political logic that includes social justice as a prime criterion and embodies cultural identity as a key aspect of social reality rather than economic optimisation from a capitalist point of view should take this into account.

One of the most outstanding issues which ethnic minorities and rural communities (who exert fishing activities and forestry practices) are to face is shrimp aquaculture. It could be understood as one of the local/global processes in which economic, social, political and cultural dimensions are concerned, so that the state, the market and social movements are involved. There are two distinct aspects to the problems surrounding this activity, which shows signs of increasing significantly during the first decade of the twentyfirst century, while its produce already floods the US, Japanese and European markets: community impacts and environmental impacts. These are expressed both in clashes between the social agents involved – there are many violent affairs between local communities, State agents and shrimp farm owners, as a result of the claim campaigns organised by concerned populations, and in the effects it has on vast coastal tracts. Some of these, such as tropical coastlines, wetlands and mangrove swamps, are of the highest environmental value, with the effects eventually impacting the populations that are dependent upon these resources. The implantation of shrimp farms in mangroves is eventually supported by governments, powerful industrial and trade companies and international institutions such as the International Monetary Fund and the World Bank, and the phenomenon is taking place world-wide, particularly throughout the tropical belt: Africa (Nigeria, Tanzania); Asia (India, Indonesia, Malaysia, Myanmar, Philippines, Sri Lanka, Thailand, China, Vietnam) and Latin America (Belize, Colombia, Ecuador, Guatemala, Honduras, Mexico, Venezuela, Brazil). In addition, different social movements and environmentalist groups are joining to take part actively in this political arena, on local, regional and international levels.

Conclusion

Since the middle of the twentieth century, there has been a great deal of progress in initiatives driven by organisations on the international front and they have exerted a significant influence on the spread of general principles designed to face new challenges, although the effectiveness of these principles and the compliance with them have not always been successful.

Some reflections can be deduced from this chapter on how international organisations are developing and whether they are valid for and have properly adapted to the profound and fast-moving social, economic, political and environmental changes that characterise the beginning of the new millennium. The issues that have been given attention in this chapter include organisations and governance, the role of global civil society, the emergence of the market as a widespread convention, the stagnation of some of the most ambitious initiatives to confront the problems of development and environmental balance, and the harmonising of the processes of decentralisation and globalisation.

It is safe to say the ocean environment and its associated problems, with fisheries at the core, are not only a precedent but one of the most consolidated experiments in global governance. The recent past bore witness to a valuable historical heritage that has been continually renewed and updated. The crowning achievement was UNCLOS III, although calls are already being heard for a new process to be launched to keep in touch with the changes that occurred at the end of the twentieth century. UNCLOS has played a decisive role in shaping the map of maritime jurisdiction and having rights of property over fishery resources recognised. Although this is no insignificant feat given the complexity of the matter and the moment in history when it was achieved, coinciding as it did with the huge expansion of the nation state in the wake of decolonisation, the outcome has been far from satisfactory in overcoming geographical inequality and unfair access to marine resources by different states.

The 1990s were a very fertile period for contributions to oceans and fisheries governance starting with the Cancun Declaration, followed by Agenda 21 and the Code of Conduct for Responsible Fisheries, and ending with the 95th Inter-Parliamentary Conference. Perhaps it is because this legacy is so great that so little progress was made in its development and implementation at further events (Rio+10), where the only occurrence of note was a drift towards statements whose contribution to advancing less prosperous societies is questionable, e.g. the role of free trade, the WTO guidelines and globalisation as opportune elements for achieving sustainable development. Market globalisation is bringing about a profound change in fishing, with the large extraction and marketing companies gaining more and more weight with regard to management policies. This is leading to state and public politics being sidelined and replaced by more flexible, open and de-statist (a system in which public politics no longer has a central role) focuses, with local structures weakened and the survival of barely protected minorities put at risk.

Fishing communities, especially the ones consisting of ethnic minorities, have thus had to contend with the hardship caused by global processes that seriously harmed the relations between society and the environment. With states widening their jurisdiction over marine areas and fishery resource management being turned into a marketable commodity, many communities have been divested of their rights of access and exploitation, with communal management being supplanted and even regarded as something exotic by political leaders and some scientists.

If more emphasis were placed on local fisheries management, it might be an answer to the impact of globalisation. In response to the crisis in centralised and state-controlled management systems, a whole school of political thought has emerged in favour of decentralisation and participation processes. Their effectiveness largely depends however on the degree of development of political organisations and their associated fabric, especially in less developed countries where a lack of finances could be a hindrance to local and regional initiatives. Geographical specificity may be a decisive motor for highly decentralised political and territorial models, but simply counteracting the impacts of globalisation by strengthening local and regional autonomy would not seem to be enough. Other more complex organisational models for political and territorial associations and new international bodies including RFBs to co-ordinate them in the inexorable process of globalisation are required to face the challenges posed by the conservation of resources, food security and the fostering of development.

11

Institutional Linkages

José J. Pascual-Fernández, Svein Jentoft, Jan Kooiman, and Abbie Trinidad

Introduction

In this chapter we address a variety of issues related to vertical and horizontal relationships and conflicts within the chain of fisheries governance related to fish distribution, fisheries policymaking and resource management. Diversity constitutes a central issue in this scenario, due to the multiple activities and uses developed in many coastal areas like tourism, artisanal or industrial fishing, aquaculture, or even housing. However, a typical consequence of this multiplicity of activities is a reduction in the diversity of affected ecosystems (see chap. 4). Furthermore, the relationships between these activities have originated, in the last decades, a system of increasing complexity, as pressures on the shoreline and the marine ecosystems intensify and intermix in a changing situation. In this sense, the dynamics of these processes may be completely different in Northern or Southern countries, or in areas where tourism, aquaculture, or industrial fishing have developed rapidly. The dependency on natural resources that are affected by global processes, such as climate change, only increases this dynamic, further augmented as a consequence of trade liberalisation and globalisation. All these specifics need to be taken into account in the design of institutions and governance policies.

What follows is a presentation of some of the key ideas and challenges concerning institutional linkages. Interdependence in dynamic and complex situations causes vulnerabilities that the actors involved need to somehow address. The institutional and organisational options available must, however, be fine-tuned to the particularities of the diverse circumstances in fisheries. There are hardly any standard institutional responses to the needs of co-ordination that exist in fisheries regardless of the context. With that in mind, we shall start by attempting to conceptualise these linkages, and how they tend to be addressed institutionally in fisheries.

Conceptualising Institutional Linkages

Industrial Organisation and Institutional Linkages

As described in Part II, the 'chain' of distribution from capture to consumption is a highly institutionalised interactive system, where relations are structured and governed according to various modes and principles, with markets and hierarchies as the two extremes of the continuum. Sometimes we are dealing with independent, self-employed, small-scale entrepreneurs who specialise in one activity such as fishing or fish processing and buy and sell their produce in the open market. In other instances, the actors are (multinational) corporations that comprise the entire chain and that internally run their operations almost like a Soviet planning economy (Galbraith 1973). In between we find a diversity of organisational forms, such as networks, coalitions, cooperatives, joint ventures, federations, and the like. In other words, various forms of integration and cooperation are sometimes preferred to free and autonomous exchange.

What makes vertical integration (hierarchy) in some situations preferable to markets has been subject to scholarly theorising since Coase raised this thought-provoking question in his seminal article on the 'The Nature of the Firm' (1937): Why do we have firms when we have markets? Both institutions are about co-ordination of interdependent activities and resource allocations. But whereas the market outside the firm employs the price-mechanism, the firm employs leadership and command-and-control as co-ordination devices when resources are put to alternative uses. There may be different explanations for why hierarchy is sometimes preferred – such as the power that comes with monopoly/monopsony positions or economics of scale. Coase, however, argued that hierarchies might be more efficient relative to markets if one considers the cost of transactions – something he criticises neo-classical economics for ignoring. Obviously, he insists, there are the costs of negotiating and securing contracts, of stabilising business relations. Firms (hierarchies) typically internalise these costs by bringing them under direct control and supervision by management. Dependency makes market actors vulnerable, whereas hierarchy brings loyalty and mutual commitment, hence security and reduced transaction costs. Williamson (1975) refined Coase's theory by specifying some further conditions that influence the choice of institutional alternatives. For instance, he pointed to the prevalence of limited rationality and opportunism among market actors as incentives for choosing hierarchy instead of the market mode. Also, he noted the degree of uncertainty and complexity involved in the transaction and the number of alternative transaction partners available. If stuck with only one alternative, with a complex product that binds you for a long period of time, you are obviously in greater danger than if the product is simple, the contract is short lasting, and the alternatives substitutes are many.

Nested Institutions

Institutions sometimes operate at multiple levels of jurisdiction linked together across scales (Jentoft 2004a; Scott 1995). For instance, as institutions firms are also embedded within markets that exert a considerable influence upon the firms' operations. Markets, in turn, are part of a larger regional, national, and global society represented and governed by state institutions such as a fisheries ministry or international bodies such as the World Trade Organization. These higher-level institutions impose rules and regulations, which actors at lower levels have to abide by. In many instances, institutions are designed to operate like Chinese boxes; institutions within institutions – with international, national, regional and local branches forming a joint organisation. States operate at different societal levels with management ties in between. Non-governmental Organisations (NGOs) often form a similar federative pattern. Private fisheries enterprises in the market sector are often structured in a 'parent-daughter' configuration, head-offices in central locations with national, regional and local subsidiaries.

Thus, institutions are linked to each other and form networks that are themselves institutions. Their functioning is then dependent on how these networks are structured and what flows within them. March and Olsen observe this:

> Institutional survival is also often related to their ability to match 'institutionalised' norms and beliefs of how institutions should be organised and run. Those norms are particularly compelling in highly developed social systems where an institution depends on a network of relations with other institutions that simultaneously depend on it... An institution survives because its structures, processes, and ideologies match what society finds appropriate, natural, rational, democratic or modern (March and Olsen 1995: 41-42).

Thus, institutions should be analysed as semi-open systems by emphasising intra- as well as inter-relational processes across scales. Institutions are not fully self-controlled because they never exist in a cultural and social vacuum. What flows within and between institutional entities, such as impacts, resources, information, norms, etc., is of particular interest to the researcher and governor alike. The dynamics surrounding the conflicts between internal sovereignty and external control are an issue of research as well as of governance. Notably, only in rare situations have the institutional networks been constructed as a 'grand scheme'. Rather, they have developed incrementally over time, often as local adaptations to environmental change, sometimes resulting from conflicts and unco-ordinated initiatives, therefore in many instances leaving inconsistencies and 'missing links' in the system as a whole. It is a governance question how these links could be improved, which suggests that governance is about coupling and co-ordination of linkages within institutional frameworks.

Interdependence and Inter-Penetration

Governance interactions and institutions not only fluctuate continuously in their diversity, dynamics, and complexity, they also continuously influence each other. These mutual influences can be called interdependence and inter-penetration. Interdependence can be conceptually located at the actor-level of governing interactions and inter-penetration at their structural level. These two forces, or movements, also influence each other: interdependency relations between governing actors or entities may evolve into inter-penetration at the structural level; or interdependence may be a consequence of inter-penetration.

In the literature, interaction – as distinct from other types of relations – is connected with concepts such as renewal, evolution, and growth. Luhmann (1982) and Münch (1988) distinguish interaction from other exchange relations. Mutuality is a central aspect of interactions. Entities contribute to each other's development: this applies to all parties involved in an interaction. The interaction of two entities implies that each has its own centre of autonomy, which serves as the point from which interrelations with others emanate. Entities interacting means that boundaries of one entity are accepted in the other's area or sphere of activity, and vice versa. Interdependence in interaction, therefore, is more than just exchange; it is deeper. It must also be distinguished from input and output relations. It refers to the constitution and reconstitution of actors or entities. Inter-penetration refers to tendencies in which the overlap or even disappearance of boundaries between interacting entities or institutions gets a semi-permanent character. New institutions are sometimes created on the basis of such processes.

The relation between the intentional and structural level of governing interactions is conceptualised in terms of enabling and controlling. The two levels are also seen as being mutually compliant, in the sense that at the intentional level the structural level is less influenced in the short term, while in the long term, structural aspects of those interactions will be changeable depending on efforts on the intentional level. What we might infer is that the two processes, distinguished as the enabling one and the controlling one, can also be seen as processes with 'cybernetic' qualities: the enabling process with positive feedback loops, reinforcing existing tendencies, while the controlling process is characterised by negative feedback loops, dampening such tendencies. Supposing a starting situation of recognised interdependence, the governing reaction might be a propensity to co-operate, which in time, would mean more inter-penetration. Though using other terms, Münch (1988) explains societal differentiation and integration in this perspective.

Mixes of Modes

In terms of second-order governance, this means that an important governance task is to organise or institutionalise mixes of three modes of governance: self-governing, co-governing and interventionist governing. Each society has enormous reservoirs of self-governing capacity, which, in its governance, should protect and reinforce where necessary. It is particularly from civil society or the non-profit sector that such initiatives can be observed in many parts of the world. Where this is the case, governments can restrict their activities in this direction and take care that necessary institutionalisation of such private initiatives takes place. It should not be forgotten that self-governing forces may often implicate some degree of de-stabilisation when things are stuck in a rut, or, to the contrary, self-organising capacity may have stabilising power in situations of rapid change. This requires a rather subtle balancing of societal needs and capacities. At the other end of the spectrum of governing modes interventions remain important as a corollary to self- and co-governing. Experience has shown that 'self-' and 'co-modes' of governance often need something of a 'stick' in the background, if not for other reasons than the well-known 'free-rider' who may threaten cooperative efforts in interventionist governance measures. Therefore, it maybe necessary to define the realm and the scope for self- and co-governing.

Our plea is definitely not for withdrawal or non-interventionism of public authorities in the governance of present-day societies; it advocates well-designed mixes of the three modes. Again, a balance needs to be struck for the scale and time conditions for such mixes. In practice, sectors of societal governing may be the best scale for the institutionalisation of certain mixes between the three modes in which the capacities of state, civil society, and market actors and institutions are balanced. Rules of thumb are hard to give; what is more important is a realisation that these mixes take time to become effective, but should not outlive their need.

Developments in Institutional Linkages in Fisheries Governance

Chains: Towards More Differentiation or Integration?

Fisheries fulfil some, but not all, of Williamson's conditions described in the previous section, although situations differ from fishery to fishery and from capture fisheries to aquaculture. Thus, as one would expect, there is a wide range of institutional forms linking one activity to another. The technology and production processes of small-scale coastal fisheries do not have the same complex and uncertain transactions, and hence vulnerability, as industrial large fisheries. Besides, social relations in community based, small-scale fisheries do not usually resemble those of the free market. Instead, exchange relations have a history, people often know each other intimately and feel mutually committed to the well-being of the community and its work force. Thus, Williamson's idea of opportunism that is characteristic of markets is replaced by trust. Clearly, Granovetter's point is of relevance to fisheries: Other things being equal, we should expect pressures toward vertical integration in a market where transaction firms lack a network of personal relations that connect them or where such a network eventuates in conflict, disorder, opportunism and malfeasance. On the other hand, where a stable network of relations mediates complex transactions and generates standards of behaviour between firms, such pressures should be absent (Granovetter 1985: 503).

If Granovetter is correct, formal and informal co-operation embedded in social relations that acquire network and partnership features of familiarity and trust (Thomson et al. 1991), should function well in fisheries – at least in the small-scale sector. In large scale, industrial ('Fordist') fisheries (Apostle et al. 1998), these qualities are rare and, hence, hierarchy is more common. But there are limits to hierarchy in large-scale fisheries as well. The flip side of centralised 'command-and-control' – the pivotal governance mode of hierarchy, inevitably, is less decision-making autonomy for its constituent units.

These are features that provide flexibility, responsiveness, and learning in an organisation, which in a complex and dynamic industry like fisheries are essential capabilities. Also, Richardson (1972) points to the fact that in some industrial chains more is required than just securing the right volume of produce to make supply meet demand; rather there is a need for the fine-tuning of resource flows, which calls for a detailed 'matching' of activities. Fishing, fish processing, and marketing are typically interdependent activities, which in a large-scale, technologically sophisticated operation need synchronisation, as timing is key, and quality is as important as quantity. Contrary to small-scale fisheries they cannot live with boom and bust, but need steadiness, predictability, and control. Yet, catching, processing, and marketing activities require totally different, specialised kinds of know-how. One kind of expertise is not easily converted into another. Therefore, one's skills as a fisher would be rather inadequate in processing and marketing – and vice versa. Thus, Richardson argues, when interdependent activities require different competencies, there is less to be gained from vertical integration. This, we believe, is one reason why both 'upstream' and 'downstream' vertical integration in fisheries have proved to be less than successful and why producer co-operatives in fisheries have met with mixed results (Jentoft 1985,1986). While solving some problems, co-operatives have also created new ones that they are not well-suited to handle. Fishing activities are rarely well-managed from the shore, while fish processing run as an extension of the fishing enterprise often fails.

State, Market, and Civil Society: Towards Interdependence and Inter-Penetration?

Interdependencies and inter-penetration between the main societal institutions may be defined in terms of handling the growing diversity, dynamics, and complexity of societal issues. In line with some other recent thinking, it may be observed that each of these institutions contributes to societal issues particularly in what it is 'good' at: civil society is well-placed to handle issues of diversity; the market handles the dynamic aspects, while the public sector (the state) confronts particular issues of complexity in modern societies. Different societal issues demand different combinations of interdependencies or inter-penetrations in terms of overlapping contributions of societal actors from these three institutions. A basic (second order) governance task, then, is to look critically at such 'overlaps' in terms of institutional requirements. As the authors of chapter 8 to 10 point out, fisheries institutions present a confused and complex panorama. Enormous assortments of organisations are engaged in fisheries management, at all levels and locations, and the number of rules, norms, and instruments applied to the field are overwhelming. Between institutions there are many variations in range and effectiveness, as well as in measures of agreement and cooperation – or disagreement and opposition.

Globalisation has made fisheries systems more open and permeable, less self-sufficient, and more incorporated. This poses new problems and opportunities for fisheries governance. It demands governors to adopt a broader focus as the number of variables and relationships multiply. In other words, globalisation brings new dynamics and additional complexity into the governance equation. When crises occur in the age of globalisation, one cannot always assume that they result from *aggregation*, i.e., of simultaneous but unrelated occurrences. The tragedy of the commons, as portrayed by Hardin and others, is one of overpopulation, overexploitation, and/or overcapitalisation. It is the total effect of too many resource users trying to do too much – as in the well-known phrase, 'too many fishers chasing too few fish'. The 'post-modern' crises are not so much an outcome of aggregation as of interdependencies; of events and forces that are interrelated, growing, and spreading. With globalisation, fisheries governance must emphasise the interaction, linkages, and relationships that extend beyond the local and national levels. It must address the cross-linkages that exist between the fishing industry and other industries and sectors of society. It must be equally as concerned with civil society as with state and markets and, most importantly, the interactions and interdependencies, and the potentials of mutual support that exist between the three. This means governance that goes both deeper and broader than current approaches, which have eyes for the fisheries industry and the state-market axis in particular (Jentoft and McCay 2003). The institutional implication of a governance procedure that goes both broader (involves other societal sectors) and deeper (involves civil society) is the theme of this chapter.

The new ocean regime established by the 1977 United Nations Convention on the Law of the Sea no doubt raised the ambitions and the expectations of the nation-state in fisheries management. As a result of assuming new responsibilities, however, the relationship between state, market and civil society took a new form. While the state and the market gained prominence, civil society lost – with the consequence that functional responsibilities in fisheries governance were largely 'lifted out' of communities and into distant government and private (multinational corporations) bureaucracies. Thus, fisheries provide a good example of what Giddens (1990) describes as the 'dis-embedding' consequence of globalisation. It can be argued that this has developed too far and that we are now at a point where the governance of fisheries also needs 're-embedding (Apostle et al. 1998). In the 1990s, we saw a new turn in the state-market-civil society relationship as state governments, inspired by neo-liberal ideologies and concepts such as New Public Management (cf. Pollitt and Bouckaert 2000); a leaner state, combined with the mobilisation of market mechanisms as governance tools, became popular, in fisheries most prominently demonstrated by Individual Transferable Quotes (ITQ's).

'Global governance' is in demand, in fisheries as in other social and economic spheres. Existing institutions at this level have had mixed success and their performance is highly contested (cf. for instance Keohane 2002; Drainville 2004; Wilkinson 2004). Fisheries are of course no exception. The issue is perhaps even more urgent than in most other industries, as fish is an important international commodity and countries often share marine resources. However, it is equally essential that governance is sensitive and appreciative to the concerns, interests, and roles of fishing peoples and their local communities where the impacts of governance failures are felt. Thus, a governance approach to fisheries must target and achieve many things at the same time, as there is no simple technical fix that fits all situations, problems, and demands (cf. chap. 2). For governance to deal with diversity, complexity, and dynamics it must, as Kooiman (2003) argues, be inherently complex, diverse, and dynamic. Such a governance model cannot only be layered at community, state, and global levels, as the three chapters of this section also suggest. It must cut across levels, establishing governance mechanisms that run vertically, but also diagonally as in the case of coastal zone management becoming involved in watershed management. It is a lesson from fisheries and societal sectors that modes of governance cannot be structured from the top-down or alternatively from the bottom-up, but that they are best handled through a combination of both. There are things that can only be done from a central position, but there are also things that are better handled at a lower level. Civil society can do things that the state and markets cannot do – and vice versa. This insight is captured in the well-known 'subsidiarity principle', now adopted by the European Union as a general governing principle for structuring the relations with the member states. Also, this is basically what the mode of 'co-governance' intends to implement, as it institutes broad participation of user-groups and stakeholders representing governments, the market, and civil society in decision-making processes that are based on a mutually binding partnership.

Vertical Linkages: Moving Towards Nested Arrangements?

The previous chapters dealt with institutions that operate at three societal levels: the local, the national, and the global. Together they revealed what seems to be an important 'mega-trend'. Institutions at the level of the fishing community have deep historical roots, are often informal in their structure and operation, and are not always specialised in dealing solely and directly with fisheries issues. They not only ensure a safe supply of food, but also keep order and integration among users and stakeholders. Still, there is a growing awareness within the research community and within international organisations of the potential they hold in assuming a greater role in fisheries management. Community-based management is now on the agenda of many governments and development agencies. From 1970 onwards, we have seen the increasing involvement of state institutions in fisheries governance.

Fishing is an activity heavily dependent on renewable resources, which may be overfished. Some prerequisites for this to happen are availability of technology, a market or consumption patterns that absorb all the produce, and, of course, the absence of adequate management. Over the past few years, we have had increasing evidence of historical overfishing (Pauly et al. 2002), yet, at the same time, we have found a great deal of evidence of populations that have made sustainable use of the resources for centuries (Ruddle and Johannes 1985; Ruddle 1988). In the literature about fisheries we find an enormous variety of management measures, and some of the modern instruments developed to organise the use of resources have parallels in the past. Perhaps the main difference is the strong position of the marine sciences (marine biology in particular) in recent models. During the 20th century, large research institutions responsible for assessing or determining how to use fish resources appeared in many Western countries. Their scientific language and models increasingly substituted traditional institutions and knowledge in many areas; these models were imposed as the state became increasingly involved in the daily management of fish resources.

Modern international fisheries management discourse originated in the early 20th century in the process of building up international institutions that would enable national states to develop their fishing industries and achieve 'rational fishing' (Graham 1948) of shared stocks. It was deeply rooted in the modern rationality of industrialised societies that it is not only desirable but also possible to manage the interaction between society and nature in a rational way, to achieve certain objectives. These objectives were, until the late 1980s, largely focused on variants of optimisation but have later had an increasing emphasis on variants of risk avoidance. The confidence in modern science and its ability to control and predict natural processes has spread to all areas of interaction between human populations and the environment, fisheries being only one instance of this general attitude.

The institutional set-up of modern fisheries management emerged in an interaction between national governments and science institutions. The main focus has been on objectives relating to the natural resource base for fisheries – whether it has been optimal capture or ecological sustainability. This has led to a perpetuation of natural science as the main contributor of knowledge as the basis for decision-making, produced in specialised research organisations at the national level and communicated through national and international organisations and regional fisheries commissions. The combination of an international emphasis, objectives primarily relating to fisheries resources and dependence on formal science has developed within and reinforced an institutional framework of centralised decision-making and top-down control. One of the best examples of those processes is the ITQ paradigm, linked to the management of single-species fisheries primarily in industrialised countries but also extended to many other areas in the world. In this case, the role of scientific institutions in charge of evaluating the allowable catch on the stocks, and the models designed by economists to minimise capital expenditures allocating transferable property rights, have changed the lifestyles of fishing populations in many areas of the world.

It is well-known that in many situations there is a conflict between individual and collective interests. What is rational from the view of the individual may well be irrational for the group. This is basically the dilemma portrayed by Hardin in his *Tragedy of the Commons* parable. It is also the case with the provision of collective goods in general, as explained by Olson (1977). The market does not by itself solve this problem. Such situations call for governance at the collective level, either from an external authority like the state, or through some form of binding cooperation (informal or formal) among the actors themselves (self- and co-modes of governance, see above). Thus, it is the linkages that structure the relationships between fisheries actors that need surveillance and mediation. If these mechanisms are not present, natural resources, communities, and markets run the real risk of overexploitation, inaction, and overload.

In ideal situations, as when systems for resource distribution and management are constructed from scratch, one would expect relationships between constituent parts to be streamlined and systematised. Institutions at different levels would acquire a 'nested' form – like in federative systems – with clarified divisions of labour, standardised procedures for decision-making, and with identical principles of organisational design at the root. In some countries, management systems come close to such a set-up. In other countries, the system is more arbitrary, segmented, and anarchic. In real life, governors seldom start with a clean slate, free to reorganise without institutional restraints. Instead they are bounded by institutional histories and cultures. As Holm (1995: 400) notes, '...new institutions are built upon older institutions and must replace or push back existing institutional forms'. Thus, one can argue that institutional change is always a combination of processes of de-institutionalisation and re-institutionalisation (Djelic and Quack 2003:8)

This is why institutional change can be such a slow process and why it is more easily accomplished in some situations than in others. It may also explain why institutional set-ups vary from country to country and from fishery to fishery even if the problems they are facing are identical. Governors may never acquire the ideal, their degrees of freedom are restricted, and their hands are tied – at least loosely so. Nevertheless, even though conditions for institutional design may vary from one situation to the next, good governors would (as they should) look for opportunities of smoothing out the linkages between existing institutional connections. In interdependent functional systems, such as fisheries, much would be gained if institutions could acquire federative forms. It is hardly likely, for instance, that community-based management would work without cooperative linkages to other communities sharing the same resource base. Linkages among different sectors, for instance between fisheries, aquaculture, and coastal tourism, would be transformed from competitive and frequently destructive relationships into cooperative and symbiotic ones. Today, in many countries, coastal zone management is hampered by fragmented and uncoordinated institutional structures (Cicin-Sain and Knecht 1998). Devolution of responsibilities for fisheries management functions, or 'co-management' (Wilson et al. 2003), requires that both vertical and horizontal linkages are clarified and institutionalised. For co-management arrangements to work at the local level, they must be nested within the community and its public and civic institutions; they must also be nested in co-management institutions at regional and national levels, as with the Spanish *cofradias* or the producer cooperatives found in the Japanese fisheries sector (Jentoft 1989).

Horizontal Linkages in Multiple Uses: Is Integrated Coastal Management a Solution?

Linkages between fishing activities, management institutions, and different economic sectors like tourism are much more pervasive than is usually recognised. In development agendas, different sectors are usually treated independently, but they share many elements: coastal areas, natural resources, and even people. In the literature about fishing activities, we find few references about the relationships it has with aquaculture, tourism, agriculture, or industry. Many of these links are also of a conflicting nature, and this makes the lack of analysis even stranger. Perhaps we can find some explanation for this scarcity in the specialisation of scientific communities in concrete topics, making it more difficult to analyse the crosscutting issues. This narrow focus makes it enormously difficult to cope with real situations, where not only interdisciplinary work is necessary (Pontecorvo 2003), but also inter-sector analysis. The integrated coastal zone management strategy was created to cope with these tasks, with its focus precisely on an integrated and interdisciplinary research and implementation strategy that has received relevant support from government institutions, such as the European Union. In this field, one frequent issue is the management of coastal impacts, produced by the tourism industry, that usually affect fishing populations in particular.

Fishing and Tourism: Impacts and Prospects for Development

The impacts of tourism may be divided into three fields: socio-economic, physical (environment, landscape) and socio-cultural (Santana Talavera 1997, 2003). All three continuously interact with one another, and are inextricably linked in real-world situations. The socio-economic impact of tourism development constitutes perhaps the most studied field. Until the 1970s, tourism was valued as a decisive contribution to economic development, not taking into account the implicit costs, frequently valuing only the economic benefits. One of the impacts is the diversion of resources (capital, spaces, people) from agriculture or fisheries to tourism. As a diversifying strategy, even small-scale fishing families may be interested in investing their surpluses into a non-fishing activity, obtaining complementary incomes, and thus reducing their need to exploit sea resources at the same level.

Also, many changes in work patterns arise with tourism development. The majority of the workforce needed for tourism is from the local area, but sometimes, especially for higher level positions, also from abroad. Local people frequently enter this activity as unskilled workers in infrastructure and hotel building, as maintenance personnel, waiters, or cooks. Women, especially, take up the roles of hotel maids and cleaning personnel, but they also work as shop assistants or in different service-related jobs. Their access to the higher level and better-paid jobs is limited as they usually lack the necessary qualifications. An inflationary tendency also accompanies this process, and the rise in property values constitutes one of the main economic indicators. If tourist development is fast and property is concentrated, local populations are frequently expelled from the best zones. Immigration processes, and a change in demography caused by new job opportunities accompanying this phenomenon result in increasing demands for land, water, and energy.

The physical impacts are no less relevant. Tourism usually requires major infrastructure. Hotels, apartments, resorts, roads, harbours, airports, artificial beaches, golf courses, and swimming pools – all of these contribute to the radical transformation of landscapes. In this process, local populations are often alienated from many of their traditional spaces, devoted now to new uses. For instance, in the Canary Islands many of the beaches where fishers used to land their beach-seines and repair their nets are now devoted exclusively to tourist uses. Also, many fishing harbours are overcrowded with leisure craft, obstructing landing or berth operations, and even impeding the access of fishing boats. With tourism development, infrastructure planning mainly takes the needs of the visitors into account, and even the fishing harbours may be constructed with the hidden agenda of future tourism uses. The overcrowding of space, in littoral but also maritime areas, is also a consequence. Maritime excursions on leisure and sport-fishing boats may transform the uses and perception of maritime spaces, even changing fishing habits of professional fishers due to congestion conflicts.

Socio-cultural impacts are caused by the effects of tourism-related economic transformations, but are also linked to contacts with foreign people with different behaviour patterns and values, which are no less important. The prestige associated with being a good fisher, the intergenerational processes of the transmission of knowledge and abilities, and the gender roles in economic and day-to-day activities, are all altered with the advent of tourism. New values associated with economic success deny the relevance of hard-acquired traditional environmental knowledge, and impede the process of transmitting this knowledge or fishing skills to the young, who are now more interested in entering the land-based job market. The best fishers in the community may no longer be considered as the reference models in these circumstances, being replaced instead by wealthy land-based entrepreneurs. Enculturation processes are similarly difficult for young women, who abandon traditional jobs related to fish processing or commercialisation.

Throughout this process it is very difficult to differentiate the impact of tourist development from general patterns of change in Western societies. The cultural impact of the media frequently pushes in the same direction as tourism-induced transformations, which may mean that giving each factor a specific causal weight may become impossible. Similar reasoning may be used in relation to economic or physical impacts, but evidently in all three cases, tourism may act as a catalyst in speeding up transformations. Tourism cannot be demonised so easily either, because living standards generally rise wherever it appears. Tourism and fishing activities may merge in some sense, improving the living standard of littoral populations and giving a new value to their knowledge and cultural heritage.

Fisheries and Aquaculture Development

Fisheries and aquaculture constitute two different sectors, even when they may capture or raise the same species and work in contiguous maritime spaces with similar target markets. Interactions between the sectors may differ greatly depending on several factors. Also, in some cases we can find linkages between the two activities that may even become complementary. For instance, in some areas of the developed world like Norway (Aarset and Foss 1996), cod captured by small-scale fishers may be fattened in cages until they reach optimum size and price, as dictated by market conditions, making the adaptation to fluctuations in demand and capture easier. Capture may be limited by climate conditions, closed seasons, etc., and in this case, aquaculture may increase the flexibility of productive units, fully using the workforce by avoiding the fluctuations typical of fishing cycles. It may also be a source of complementary income.

Models of aquaculture present huge differences (see chap. 5). The prerequisites of capital, knowledge, and expertise, the workforce needed, and the spatial competition with fishing activities differ considerably for cages in littoral areas, freshwater extensive installations, or intensive exploitations inland. Not taking into account the problems of targeting the same markets with similar products, one of the main sources of conflict in many areas is the competition for space. For instance, the cages used in the Canary Islands for rearing dorada compete in some areas with fishing activities, but mainly with tourist resorts.

In general, aquaculture facilities should be seen not strictly as a concession that vetoes any other use of marine space. The possibility of transforming the cages into tourist attractions may be considered; by integrating them into the tourist landscape they offer new experiences to the visitors. The possibility of seeing great quantities of fish in captivity, feeding them or receiving information on the breeding process could become a complementary source of revenues for the aquaculture companies and a way of inserting the activity into a wider social context. For instance, in the oyster camps in the area around Arcachon (France), visitor numbers have risen steadily in recent years, complementing the incomes of local producers.

Integrated Coastal Management

The relationship between fisheries and aquaculture, as we have seen, can be conflicting. They may compete for the same spaces, but this can also happen with other activities, like tourism. Conflicts between fisheries, tourism, aquaculture, infrastructure construction, housing, and many other activities developed along the coasts are spreading throughout the world. This is related to population growth, but also to tendencies common to recent human history. Cities have been located near the coast because of the food, transport, and ecological benefits. The evolution of world markets is related to maritime commerce, and cities located in coastal areas had many advantages in the flow of people, goods, knowledge, and money. Eight of the top ten largest cities are located along the coast, and in 2001 nearly half of the world's population lived within 200 km of a coastline. Pressure on space and resources, on land and sea, consequently increases with population growth. Problems concerning waste and sewage disposal also increase accordingly. Space that was previously used solely by fishers is now often overcrowded with people, harbours, tourists, and buildings.

Box 11. 1 Multiple-use conflicts in the Philippines

The Philippines is an archipelago consisting of 7,100 islands and 18,000 km of shoreline and its coastal resources provide food, livelihood, and development potential for a population rapidly reaching 80 million. Other important facts about Philippines coastal resources are:
- 832 municipalities out of 1,541, or 54%, are coastal;
- Almost all major cities are coastal;
- 62% of the population lives in the coastal zone;
- There are about 27,000 km² of coral reef but less than 5% is in excellent condition;
- The 120,000 hectares of mangrove are only about 25% of the area they covered in 1920;
- More than 50% of the animal protein intake is derived from marine fisheries.

As such, a host of economic activities occur in the coastal area. These range from resource extractive activities such as fishing, forestry, and mining, to non-extractive activities, such as agriculture, housing, and industrial development. Amongst all these many uses of coastal resources, there are intra- and intersectoral conflicts. In the fisheries sector alone, there are currently several intrasectoral conflicts that deal with spatial and proprietary use rights. For example, there is now a heated dispute between local and commercial fishers on the use of municipal waters. Meanwhile, other sectors such as agriculture and forestry cause decreasing productivity of mangroves, sea grass, and coral reefs through sedimentation. Likewise, specific activities such as aquaculture, human settlements, and the development of port facilities necessitate the clearing of mangroves and sometimes the dredging of coral reefs.

Author: Annabelle Cruz-Trinidad

Traditional sector-wise approaches to the management of those areas with conflicting activities are useless, because the real issue is the determination of priorities among all those conflicting interests. Integrated coastal management and its variants developed because of the need for a holistic and integrated approach to managing coastal resources. The challenge of addressing the myriad problems in the coastal area has been taken up by various types of strategies and approaches known collectively as coastal resource management. These approaches differ in many aspects, such as how they address participation, the scope of their activities, or the sharing of responsibilities. This perspective of analysis and management has grown in both developed and developing countries, with nearly all coastal states taking initiatives in this area (Belfiore, 2003). But this is not an easy question, and as usually happens in the management of human activities, defining priorities and designing indicators in order to analyse the success of these programmes may constitute an overwhelming task.

Modes of Governance: Towards Mixes?

A change of focus has begun to emerge mainly because of the critics of these traditional measures and the appearance of new models that explain the relationships between users and resources in alternative ways to the 'tragedy of the commons' paradigm. In addition, the ability of modern science to really model and control nature has been called into question. In this sense, the focus on the natural resource base has changed from optimisation (maximisation of biological or economic yield, as in the case of ITQs) to a requirement that addresses the increasingly complex issues related to risk aversion. The introduction of the precautionary approach through, *inter alia*, the UN Agreement on Highly Migratory and Straddling Stocks (UN 1995), was the first major step in this direction. The requirement that fisheries management integrates the Convention on Biodiversity is a further step, and the World Summit on Sustainable Development (WSSD) requirement that fisheries management implements an ecosystem approach to fisheries by 2010 is so far-reaching that it is difficult to imagine how the practical implementation will take place.

This change and expansion of scope has occurred in a situation where fishing fleets world-wide have outgrown the resource base to support them on a grand scale. This combination has put fisheries management institutions under heavy pressure – more and more complex issues need to be addressed while the political and economic pressures on the entire fisheries system are increasing.

The reaction to this pressure has generally been internalisation – trying to solve the problem through more of the same, by adding more technical adjustment buttons to the existing machinery. More detailed regulations are developed to address the widening scope of complexities, with the consequences that the requirements for similarly detailed science inputs to policy decisions are growing and that top-down control must be reinforced and expanded. However, the internalisation of expanding scopes and pressures is reaching its limits. It is becoming increasingly difficult to produce the research base needed to address complex issues through more detailed regulations, and the implementation through top-down control is similarly challenged.

The management set-up is also challenged on a more fundamental level. The consequences of development have also been that modern fisheries management has alienated the users from management, whether they are fishers or other citizens with an interest in fisheries or in the marine environment. The objectives are primarily related to nature and are defined on the basis of international agendas rather than on local needs, the knowledge base for decisions does not include users' knowledge, and users are only involved in implementation to a limited degree (Degnbol 2003). The requirements for increased user participation in the identification of objectives, in identifying relevant knowledge, and in implementation, have been articulated with increasing strength. Modern fisheries management is thus under triple pressure – a widening scope to address increasingly complex issues, a build-up of overcapacity in fishing fleets, and a requirement for management to be legitimate on the basis of user participation.

The responses to these pressures have been very different in different regions. In North America, one of the responses has been to develop fisheries councils with user participation both in knowledge production and management decisions. The European Commission (EC) has, in the latest reform of the Common Fisheries Policy, abstained from addressing the capacity problem but has started a process of more involvement of users by establishing advisory bodies on the regional level. Other countries have turned to market-based instruments with the understanding that such instruments will both solve the overcapacity problem and replace the need for complex control as discussed below. Each of these approaches has its own problems as indicated by the litigation in the US, the need for the EC to continue with ever more detailed regulations and the distribution problems associated with market-based approaches.

A different approach puts more emphasis on the notion of the community as the agent for fisheries management. This is based on the notion that the existence of local management systems in fisheries seems to have been the historical norm rather than the exception and that the community, because of its proximity to and dependence on the resource, will be in the best position to address management issues. This approach has been especially promoted in developing countries. Communities may, however, not always be in a position to handle conflicts of interest or have the authority to control access to resources. This is a problem in cases where the scale of the resource system is larger than the authority of the community.

Co-management has been suggested as a solution to these problems (Jentoft 1989; Pinkerton 1989a,b). Government can bridge scales by cooperating with users on the scale of the resource system and by giving authority to a management body. Extensive experiments with shared responsibilities between users and government have been implemented world-wide. The results indicate that for such arrangements to be effective, responsibilities must be shared in relation to objective identification, knowledge bases, and implementation (Raakjær Nielsen et al. 2002).

One sector of fisheries management where we find examples of top-down management vs. bottom-up strategies is in the marine protected areas. In some cases, these fulfil the prerequisites of taking into account local populations and knowledge in their design, implementation process, and management strategy. However, frequently they share the same top-down management schemes used in more traditional approaches, like ITQs.

Institutional Continuation and Change in Fisheries Governance

Global Development Agendas in Fisheries

National and international government and non-government development agencies have an important impact on fisheries governance in many developing countries. It is not unusual that a fisheries department may receive more funding through such agencies than it receives from local sources. Furthermore, it is commonplace that development agencies will tie quite restrictive policies to their co-operation. The net result is that fisheries governance in many developing countries comes under considerable pressure to conform to international development agendas presented by development agencies.

The international agenda of fisheries development agencies changed dramatically during the second half of the twentieth century. Some changes reflect general changes in development policies, and others are specific to the sector. In accordance with the general pattern for development assistance, the approach in the 1950s attempted to reproduce the development which had taken place in industrialised countries earlier, with emphasis on resource extraction and technological development. Small-scale fisheries came into focus later and were further emphasised when integrated community development became a mainstream approach to rural development. The expansive approach with strong technological components survived into integrated community development, although it was modified to address the needs of small-scale fisheries as perceived by development agencies.

Increasing awareness about the limitations of resources climaxed with the introduction of the 'sustainable development' concept in the late 1980s (see chap. 13). In fisheries, this resulted in a reorientation of existing programmes and in the formulation of new strategies. As a result, fisheries development co-operation became reoriented towards management from a sustainability perspective. One conclusion was that local capacity should receive much more attention as a precondition for longer-term sustainability. Fisheries management and institutional capacity building became the focus.

Development efforts in the last decade have focused on fisheries management and capacity building. However, some new trends have emerged. These trends relate to changing global agendas (see chap. 10) as well as to the globalisation of markets for fish products. The globalisation of markets has led to an increasing awareness of the need for, and the dilemmas involved in, both supporting development to meet immediate local needs for food supply and economic opportunities, and addressing the need to develop commercially viable and ecologically sustainable fisheries, which can be a net asset for national economies. The dilemmas involved relate, for instance, to the need to assist developing countries in utilising the commercial opportunities of increasingly globalised markets for fish products, which in the short term may be in conflict with local needs for supplies to local markets and economic opportunities in small-scale fisheries. Another aspect of this dilemma relates to the use of direct and indirect subsidies in subsistence-oriented small-scale fisheries and in the export-oriented part of the sector.

Globalisation and Institutional Challenges

The recent emphasis on globalisation has modified the tendency to dismiss the linkages between global and local realities, complementing micro and macro levels of analysis. The exchanges of people, goods, behaviour, and knowledge throughout the last five centuries have become increasingly important, modifying societies and cultures on a truly global scale. Such exchanges have led to the transformation of concepts, symbols, lifestyles, and signs of identity. Besides these exchanges, the different institutions that made the appropriation of resources, territories, or people possible constitute an essential element of these transformations. The concept of globalisation emphasises an increase in these interconnections (Hannerz 1996) resulting in qualitative transformations. The closely linked processes of economy, technology, culture, and even ethical or judicial models have been the subject of many analyses developed from this perspective. Nevertheless, interaction and the diffusion of ideas, objects, or behaviour have been a constant in the history of humanity. Many authors point out that globalisation has been a central aspect of capitalism from its origins (Martínez 1998: 607) and as such has been analysed from different theoretical perspectives in recent decades (Kearney 1995: 550). From this position, our situation today is simply seen as an intensification of such processes, modified and impelled by new technologies, but also by transcendental institutional transformations such as the liberalisation of capital markets or the power of supra-national institutions in the economy, and, with regards to fisheries, in the diverse regional or world agreements established after the 1970s (Thorpe and Bennett 2001). In the analysis of the relationships between the state and globalisation processes, we find two contradictory positions, one of these signalling a retreat of the state (Strange 1996) as market forces obtain new prerogatives, the other position (Weiss 1997; Phillips 1998; Pilger 2003) claiming that the nation-state is in a process of adaptation (Thorpe and Bennett 2001).

The impact of these processes on fisheries and agriculture is enormous. Centuries ago, some wide markets existed for certain foods, such as the salted fish of Newfoundland that reached large areas of America and Europe. However, with transport and conservation facilities so common nowadays, these markets have expanded, and perishable foods are shipped to the other side of the planet within a few hours. It is often difficult to obtain information about the origin of the foods we buy in supermarkets, and in the case of seafood, this is especially difficult. There are several special characteristics that distinguish the globalisation phenomenon in fisheries. Fish stocks constitute a wild resource, impossible to fence into territorial waters or exclusive economic zones, with ecosystems shared between different countries and international waters – where surveillance and enforcement of protective measures are extremely difficult. These factors make fish stocks especially vulnerable to globalisation forces. Market pressures and the inabilities of states or communities to design, regulate, and enforce sustainable measures make fishing resources easily susceptible to overexploitation and depletion (Thorpe and Bennett 2001). The picture in the international context is not very promising either.

The need to institutionalise linkages in fisheries governance at more than one level and in more than one aspect in a globalised world – recognising that its underlying processes will remain active in the foreseeable future – is imperative. Recent theory (Djelic and Quack 2003) suggests that those who believe the institutionalising of those processes has to take place either in a transnational context or at the national (state) level have extreme positions and are thinking in rather static terms. Global trends are complex, vary greatly, and are in constant flux. Changes taking place are the result of what we call trickle-up and trickle-down trajectories, where national actors and factors influence the adaptation or creation of transnational institutions (trickle-up), which change those at national levels (trickle-down). Views like these offer opportunities for fisheries governance: reforming, adapting, or creating 'inter'-governance institutions in their vertical and horizontal dimensions. Nesting, mixes of modes, ICMs, institutionalising interdependent interrelations between the state, market, and civil society, are examples. For a diverse, dynamic, and complex system such as fisheries, two major strategies are available: learning and innovation. Learning as an appropriate strategy where experiences exist; innovation where new institutional avenues have to be opened.

Towards Institutionalising Fisheries Governance Education

The diversity, complexity, and dynamics of governance institutions in fisheries – be they of the market, state, or civil society variety – create huge demands for the co-ordination of their interactions. These demands are no less when institutions are of the hybrid or the 'mixed' modes, as they redefine the nature of their interdependencies through a restructuring of their respective agendas, responsibilities, cultures, and working principles. Fisheries governance institutions that draw on the combined competencies and capacities of the state, market, and civil society have to go through a trial-and-error learning process. Unfortunately history is not generous in offering experiences in mixed forms of governance in fisheries, even though there are examples that may provide some important lessons.

We believe, for instance, that the Spanish cofradias, the French prud'homies, and other traditional management institutions that we today would label 'co-management', provide some important clues despite their deep history within a particular socio-cultural setting. Co-management and the devolution of management authority to institutions at regional and local levels involving user-groups and NGOs, is now on the political agenda of fisheries authorities in the North as well as the South, but no blueprint model can be applied regardless of context. Therefore, mixed governance models must be tuned to specific contexts and this tuning process will require some experimentation. In other words, institutional learning is needed. Mixed governance modes must not only allow for pooling of specialised competencies, but also for mutual, interactive learning and innovation. This should occur in all governing activities from innovative, practical problem-solving to the creation of effective and legitimate institutions, as well as in learning how to apply adequate meta-governing principles. Drawing on Bateson (1972), interactive institutional learning would also involve 'deutero-learning', or learning about learning.

Interactive learning is a process in which participants learn from each other, and from each other's learning. Interactive learning requires systematic recording and reflection on experiences made throughout an institution's developmental history. How governing institutions structure these exercises will determine the capacity of members to learn and to share what they learn. It is not only a question of how individual actors learn. The more challenging issue is how learning at the individual level penetrates the institution so that it is preserved over time despite personnel turnover. We can raise similar issues for fisheries as an entire industry. The problem of qualifying whole industries is structurally very similar to the common pool natural resources, such as fish. Sharing the natural common resource and sharing knowledge may be in the collective but not necessarily the individual interest. Knowledge enhances one's competitive position, and although the knowledge itself may gain from being shared, those individuals that hold it may suffer. If shared, knowledge may lose some of its value as a strategic resource for the stakeholder. How to overcome this problem by turning learning into a positive-sum game, in which people learn from each other, is therefore an important governance issue.

An understanding of learning opportunities within fisheries must start from the analysis of fisheries as a system of chains, within which social interaction occurs and relationships of exchange exist and are built. Governors need to remember that fisheries have a variety of subsystems, each with distinct features and dynamics. They must also search for those initiatives that may enhance or inhibit interactive learning at the individual, the organisational, and the chain level.

Conclusion

It is clear from the issues raised in this chapter that many, if not all, aspects of linkages between institutions in the governance of fisheries have an open-ended character. Not only do we raise more questions than we answer, but the subjects of our questions are conceptually not yet fully developed. Although there is a difference of opinion on what we mean by institutions, as shown in the introduction of this book, institutional linkages as a subject for scholarly work has not yet reached the debate stage. Thinking in terms of interactive governance as we do in this book, we see that linkages should become a major area of attention. This is because, conceptually, linkages can be seen as a structural expression of governing interactions, and because, empirically, the broad governance perspective we apply almost naturally looks at the involvement of multiple governing institutions and thus to the way these institutions are linked. This chapter should be seen as a contribution to the development of both these aspects, as well as to the mapping of what institutional linkages mean for fisheries governance.

At least three major areas of governance can be identified from what we have presented in this chapter. In the first place, the whole idea of institutional linkages as such. A central assumption of the approach underlying this book is that the world we live in is diverse, complex, and dynamic. Institutional linkages also have these features. This means that our theoretical approaches to such linkages should, in principle, reflect these characteristics; in practical terms it means that we probably need several theories (reflecting diversity), that they should be non-reductionist (reflecting complexity), and that they should be change-oriented (reflecting dynamics). Secondly, and more directed at fisheries themselves, the relation between interactions, linkages, and their institutions or institutionalising processes demands governance attention. The chain is a good start for thinking about these relations. Within fishing, aquaculture, fish processing, marine tourism, and marketing chains, we find all kinds of 'internal' linkages. How are these phases of chains linked? What roles do the market, the state and civil society play? What kinds of governance modes do we find for such linkages? Other major questions are: If such linkages are of an interactive nature, how are they institutionalised? Are they mainly conflict-oriented or aimed at consensus building? What are their governing capacities? Thirdly, the chapter has pointed to major empirical research areas and themes. Rough ideas concerning concepts such as nested institutions, mixes of modes of governance, and vertical and horizontal linkages, are not only starting points of further conceptual work, they also form the basis for collecting systematic empirical data and testing conceptual ideas.

PART IV

Principles for
Fisheries Governance

Introduction

Jan Kooiman

Introduction

In arguing that fisheries governance should be founded on certain basic principles, we are essentially asking for several things. We are saying fisheries governors should be obliged to make their analytical, ethical, and political convictions explicit to others as well as to themselves. When governors define the problems they think should be addressed and ascribe certain solutions to these problems, they inevitably draw on fundamental assumptions and worldviews that should be brought to the surface so they can be explained, defended, and examined.

Do the convictions hold up to logical and ethical reasoning? We believe communication and hence the democratic process of decision-making would be strengthened if governors and stakeholders were to agree on basic principles. Even if they cannot agree on what the principles should be, they should at least be able to understand which concerns and stakes are involved, including those of other parties. This can only happen if principles are made clear. Principles come before goals and means. They determine which goals are valid, ethical, and reasonable. Governors and stakeholders should start by identifying the fundamental principles and go on from there to deduce the goals to be pursued before they finally turn to the means.

Something else we ask of principles is that they serve as a yardstick, something to relate to when we evaluate and criticise current governance systems and practices and suggest reforms. Which conceptual and moral standards are we referring to when we make judgements? How do actual governance systems and practices compare with our deeper convictions and concerns? In addition, we are asking for consistency. The normative foundations that fisheries governors use should be consistent. It does not make sense to propose a fisheries policy on the basis of conflicting normative considerations. If principles turn out to be inconsistent, this should be made explicit to enable everyone concerned to follow the normative reasoning followed by governors and to help them deal with the contradictions and dilemmas they face.

Some normative and ethical principles are universal and supposedly apply to all mankind. Human rights are a good example. Other moral and ethical principles are highly contextual, such as those that underpin share systems in fishing. Universal principles are typically arrived at through introspection and philosophical reasoning. Contextual rules or codes of conduct are specific to a social community. They arise from social practice and do not necessarily apply anywhere else. These principles can only be discerned through empirical research and their meaning can only be understood within their own cultural context.

Fisheries governance should balance contextual and universal principles. It needs to be sensitive to the possibility that principles differ because social practices differ. Contextual and universal principles may well appear to be in conflict. What should happen then cannot be determined in advance. There are never any easy answers to how conflicts should be resolved. We should be prepared to accept the possibility that contextual principles and practices will have to yield to universal ones. There are limits, for example, to corporal punishment in regulatory enforcement. The individual has rights. We should not be oblivious, though, to the possibility of alternative ways of solving conflicts between universal and contextual principles that may minimise or eliminate conflicts altogether. Solutions ought not to be imposed on communities. Communication and diplomacy are always preferable to force, although situations are conceivable where force is called for as a last resort.

In this part of the book, we begin a systematic analysis of governance principles. Meta-governance is about making the values, principles, rules, norms, and arguments that govern fisheries as explicit as possible. We approach the principles of governing fisheries step by step. Kooiman and Bavinck (see chap. 1) explain the concept of *meta* in greater detail. We argue that a new perspective on governance is impossible in conceptual terms and ineffective in practical terms if meta-principles are not taken seriously. In other words, if we want fisheries governance to be more effective, we need to address its fundamental principles

Bavinck and Chuenpagdee (see chap. 12) review actual governing principles and practices and make it clear that although current governance is based on certain principles, the application is not systematic. Nor is governance always aware of its intellectual origins and contexts. Kooiman et al. (see chap. 13) and Kooiman and Jentoft (see chap. 14) revisit the earlier parts of the book from an analytical normative point of view, using a number of normative principles as yardsticks. These authors identify rules at three different governance levels: first, second, and meta-order governance. At the first level, we reflect on the issues of efficiency, legitimacy, and equity. At the second, we discuss sustainability, ecosystem health, and inclusiveness, and at the third, the most general principles of fisheries governance, social justice, responsibility, and caution. Although governing instruments such as the Code of Conduct for Responsible Fisheries have strong normative aspects, more attention should be devoted to the concept of responsibility as an ethical principle. The same applies to justice and caution. These concepts have a deep philosophical and cultural history that is usually overlooked in discussions about fisheries. In the last chapter and elsewhere in the book, we argue that values, ethical principles, rules, and norms are culturally bound, and the ones that apply to the North may not necessarily apply in the South. Sensitivity to cultural difference is indispensable to fisheries governance.

Meta-Governance of Fisheries

The building blocks for a meta-perspective on fisheries governance have been sketched in this book and now remain to be turned into a proper structure. A normative framework serves as the mortar to keep it all together. Normative preconceptions have frequently crept into the analysis. This can hardly be avoided in discussing a theme like governance, as it is value-loaded from top to bottom. In fact, socio-political or interactive governance is far more than just analytical concepts. They are normatively charged and driven. Many of these normative preconceptions will now be systematically brought together.

So far, we have identified two orders of governance. First-order governance is aimed at solving day-to-day problems and creating opportunities and second-order governance deals with institutions of fisheries governance. However, this is not the whole story. We can also speak of third-order or meta-governance, with the conceptual focus on the normative issues of fisheries governance. Meta-thinking is thinking about thinking, a meta-system is a system of systems, meta-governance is the governance of governance. An effective meta-theory establishes the link between epistemology and the objects of knowledge. At a meta-level, basic questions need to be addressed if there is to be conceptual consistency. Our ideas here are the first steps towards devising a meta-theory of fisheries governance. Meta-governance reflects on norms, ideas, and principles to improve governance at the first and second-order levels. People continuously redesign their social world. Meta-governance seeks to inform the process by which these changes are made by invoking normative principles.

In a democratic fishery, the people who govern and the ones who are governed exert influence on each other. A central meta-governance question asks which normative principles determine the relations between the two parties. Our ideas on fisheries meta-governance are innovative in two ways: we define the meta-concepts and we suggest how to apply them. We retain a meta-position on this discussion by reflecting on their ethical implications in the context of fisheries governance and on how the implications can vary from culture to culture. In this introduction and the following chapters, we address normative principles from the perspective of individual fishers and fisheries governors in their cultural contexts.

Ethical Interactions in Fisheries Governance

Diversity, complexity, and dynamics are key concepts in our theory of fisheries governance. Together, they are crucial to the consideration of governance at the first, second and meta-levels. All three notions have important normative implications that should not be overlooked in fisheries govern-ance. *Diversity* requires the recognition of a wide range of ethical and nor-mative systems that have a deep history. Social anthropology provides am-ple evidence of this. As is noted above, we should, however, avoid the extreme relativist and particularist position. *Complexity* implies a moderate pluralist position. As has been demonstrated in this book, fisheries involve social, economic, cultural, and natural systems that are inter-connected in ways that often exceed our perceptual abilities.

Governance practices often have unforeseen and irreversible conse-quences across systems. Each discipline has distinct ways of conceptually reducing this complexity, which has normative implications for fisheries governance. Each discipline has its specific notions of shortcomings in fisheries governance and the remedies that are called for. Biologists typi-cally favour reserved areas to accommodate the inherent complexities of ecosystems. Anthropologists propagate community-based management for user empowerment and economists champion individually-based incentive systems for promoting economic efficiency. Clearly, complexity requires an inter-disciplinary approach to overcome disciplinary blinders. An additional difficulty is the often-implicit nature of the values guiding the scholarly approaches. In an inter-disciplinary approach to fisheries governance, im-plicit paradigms need to be made explicit and interrelated.

Lastly, the normative framework should capture the *dynamics* of fisheries systems. Dynamics in general spring from tensions and conflicts, provok-ing new patterns of interaction. This also applies to normative expectations. Justice and equality are often depicted as static. In reality, they change with time and circumstances and they themselves stimulate change. The recent awareness of the plight of indigenous peoples and the need to redress the injustice perpetrated against them are examples of changes in normative understanding over time.

We conceptualise a meta-level approach to fisheries governance in terms of a moderate normative hierarchy with the most general principles guid-ing fisheries governance at the top. These principles relate to issues of jus-tice, responsibility, or caution. Although applications vary in different parts of the world and among religions, they can still serve as indications for the apex of this normative hierarchy.

12

Current Principles

Maarten Bavinck and Ratana Chuenpagdee

Introduction

Many current debates on fisheries, food security, and safety centre on issues of policy and management. Having a practical focus, debaters rarely
reflect on the norms and principles underlying their positions. It is clear,
however, to a thoughtful observer that normative positions, permeate the
proposed solutions and approaches, and contribute to both consensus and
miscommunication alike.

This chapter presents the principles underlying the international governance of fisheries today. The perspective is analytical rather than prescriptive, the objective being to find out what currently informs governance. In
subsequent chapters, where the norms for interactive governance are highlighted, the mood becomes prescriptive. There we aim to pinpoint what
governance should be about.

The discussion is structured around the fundamental concerns cited in
chapter 2 – ecosystem health, social justice, livelihood and employment,
and food security and safety. As many of the normative positions taken
with regard to issues of this kind originate from outside fisheries and have
a broader application, the chapter highlights a variety of international organisations and documents. In addition, an investigation about how the precepts in these documents have filtered into the fields of fisheries is presented.

One must remember that international organisations and agreements
constitute only one expression of current governance. Much of the governance that actually takes place in fisheries has different sources altogether. A
comprehensive overview of governance practices, and the principles that
underlie them, is, however, outside the scope of this volume.

Ecosystem Health

Ecosystem health has become a major theme of international debate, decision-making, and action. It figured prominently in the discussion on sustainable development at the Earth Summit in Rio de Janeiro (1992) and the
World Summit on Sustainable Development in Johannesburg (2002). It is
also the subject of numerous agreements, including some on fisheries, and
plays a role in adjacent realms such as the regulation of international trade.

All these discussions and the agreements they have resulted in are based on an awareness that environmental deterioration is linked to human activity. The human role in environmental issues is argued to confer moral responsibility, but it also grants opportunities for remedial action. Since human welfare, present and future, is considered to depend on the vitality of natural resource systems, ecosystem health is an important concern as well as a guideline for action.

Our starting point is the Code of Conduct for Responsible Fisheries (CCRF), the most authoritative and comprehensive framework for fisheries management today (FAO 1995). We subsequently consider a set of more specific issues, i.e., straddling and highly migratory fish stocks, aquaculture, and biodiversity. They are dealt with in the UN Agreement on Conservation and Management of Straddling Fish Stocks and Highly Migratory Fish Stocks (the UN Fish Stocks Agreement), the Agreement to Promote Compliance with International Conservation and Management Measures by Fishing Vessels on the High Seas (the Compliance Agreement), the Bangkok Declaration and Strategy for Aquaculture Development Beyond 2000, and the Convention on Biological Diversity (CBD) respectively.

Code of Conduct for Responsible Fisheries

The Food and Agriculture Organization (FAO) of the United Nations developed the CCRF in response to recent developments and concerns in world fisheries. The goal was to establish principles and international standards for responsible fisheries, defined in relation to 'the effective conservation, management and development of living aquatic resources, with due respect for the ecosystem and biodiversity'. The CCRF emphasises conservation, an activity closely linked to ecosystem health. At the onset of a section on general principles, the CCRF identifies the object of conservation as aquatic ecosystems and clearly states that fishing rights come with the responsibility to ensure the effective conservation and management of the ecosystems. The relation between conservation and ecosystem health is explained in Article 6.2, which states that 'fisheries management should promote the maintenance of the quality, diversity, and availability of fishery resources'. In addition to the consumption needs of present and future generations, the terms quality, diversity, and availability can be assumed to refer here to the functions of a healthy ecosystem. The ecosystem perspective is reinforced in the second part of Article 6.2, which emphasises that management measures 'should not only ensure the conservation of target species but also of species belonging to the same ecosystem or associated with or dependent upon the target species'.

The CCRF was shaped in conformity with the United Nations Convention on the Law of the Sea (UNCLOS, see below). It applies to all fisheries, whether on the high seas, within the exclusive economic zones (EEZs), in territorial waters or in inland waters. Its main target is the regulation of professional fisheries, though it also voices the intention to cover recreational fisheries.

The first six articles of the CCRF describe its scope and modes of implementation and nineteen general principles that are related to various topics and analytical orders and do not differ substantially from prescriptions in other parts of the CCRF. The second set of articles is more specific, covering details about fisheries management, fishing operations, aquaculture development, integration of fisheries into coastal area management, postharvest practices and trade, and fisheries research.

Here, we make an effort to distil the guidelines directly related to ecosystem health and conservation from the body of the CCRF. Three trends stand out:

a. *The movement toward ecosystem-based management.* Acknowledging the urgent world-wide problem of overfishing and excess in fishing capacity, Article 6.3 calls for management measures that balance the fishing effort with the productive capacity of fisheries resources. The CCRF also recognises, however, the need to protect and rehabilitate critical habitats (Article 6.8) and the importance of gear use to avoid collateral damage to ecosystems (Article 6.6).

b. *The broadening of the knowledge base and the emphasis on participatory decision-making.* Article 6.4 emphasises that fisheries decision-making should be based on the best available scientific evidence as well as on traditional knowledge. In other parts of the CCRF, the proclivity for a broad range of knowledge sources is reason for recommending stakeholder participation and a transparent process (Article 6.13). However, the CCRF also recognises that the available information may not be good enough, which is why it advocates a precautionary approach to conservation, management, and exploitation (Article 6.5).

c. *The integration of fisheries in coastal area management.* Fisheries have long been managed using sectoral approaches and traditional assessment techniques. In addition to an ecosystem-based management of fisheries, as described above, CCRF Article 6.9 recommends an integration of fisheries in the management of coastal areas.

Straddling and Highly Migratory Fish Stocks

The UN Fish Stocks Agreement was adopted in 1995 and went into effect in 2001. Its aim is to establish a conservation and management regime for fish stocks that extend beyond or move across national boundaries, in which case conservation and management only make sense as part of a cooperative effort by adjoining states. The agreement gives regional fisheries management organisations (RFMO) a pivotal position in its implementation (FAO 2004a). The principles of the UN Fish Stocks Agreement do not differ from those of the CCRF, which aims for long-term sustainability of fish stocks and a precautionary approach.

High Seas Fisheries

The Compliance Agreement was adopted by the 27th Session of the FAO Conference in 1994 and is an integral part of the CCRF. Its purpose is to extend the conservation and management of fish stocks beyond the boundaries of national jurisdiction to the high seas. The control of fisheries activities in this area is known to be particularly tricky and largely depends on the commitment of individual states to effectively exercise their powers over vessels flying their flags. The agreement is particularly mindful of the incidence of flagging or re-flagging vessels as a means of avoiding compliance with conservation and management measures. The Compliance Agreement does not present a set of principles for ecosystem health, but refers to other international agreements such as the CCRF. Its contents are largely technical. The agreement has been signed by enough states and is now in force.

Aquaculture

The CCRF recognises the increasing role of aquaculture in the world fish supply and the need for the responsible development of aquaculture (Article 9). CCRF Article 6.19 emphasises the need to minimise adverse impacts of aquaculture on the environment and local communities. Safeguards for responsible aquaculture development are amplified in a set of technical guidelines issued to aid compliance with the CCRF (FAO 1997a). The Food and Agriculture Organization (FAO) has also reviewed the state of world aquaculture and analysed production trends, future outlook, sustainability, roles in rural development, new technology, and farmer organisations (FAO 2003a).

In 2000, the FAO and the Network of Aquaculture Centres in Asia-Pacific (NACA) co-organised the Conference on Aquaculture in the Third Millennium in Bangkok, Thailand. At the conference, 540 delegates from 66 countries and more than 200 governmental and non-governmental organisations discussed priorities and strategies for developing aquaculture in the next two decades, taking into consideration future economic, social, and environmental issues, and technological advances in aquaculture. The resulting Bangkok Declaration and Strategy (NACA/FAO 2000) proposes aquaculture development based upon a lengthy set of principles and actions including investment in communication, education and research, environmental sustainability, food security and safety, and strong regional and interregional co-operation. It states that the goal of aquaculture development is to contribute to global food availability, household food security, economic growth, trade, and improved living standards. Moreover, it emphasises sustainable livelihoods for poor sections of the community, human development, and social well-being. In terms of management practices, the Bangkok Declaration stresses the importance of policies and regulations to promote environmentally responsible and socially acceptable practices. Corresponding with the CCRF principles, it recognises the need for transparent development processes in accordance with regional and international agreements, treaties and conventions, and cooperation among state and private sectors and stakeholders within a country and among the countries in the region.

A strategy for the sustainable development of European aquaculture is detailed in the communication from the Commission of the European Communities to the Council and the European Parliament (COM, 2002: 511). Its objectives are similar to those stated above. Actions proposed in the strategy include increasing production through research on new species, using organic and environment-friendly aquaculture, developing intensive production technology, promoting high quality and safety in products, and developing markets. Stakeholder participation and the role of women are stressed, as are efforts to mitigate environmental impacts. These actions are in accord with the principles for ecosystem health stated in the CCRF.

In addition to codes of conduct formulated by intergovernmental agencies, the aquaculture sector has begun to put its own house in order in terms of environmental and other safeguards. For example, the Global Aquaculture Alliance has drawn up a list of nine principles for companies and individuals engaged in shrimp farming (Boyd 1999b). They include responsible co-ordination with regulatory authorities, site selection and farming practices that minimise harm to biodiversity and the environment, and the responsible use of drugs. More recently, codes of conduct for aquaculture have begun to incorporate detailed Best Management Practices (BMP) to address environmental concerns (Boyd 2003). Examples of BMPs include conservative stocking, fertilisation and feeding, water reuse, and effluent treatment.

Convention on Biological Diversity

The CBD regards biological diversity as encompassing diversity within and between species and among ecosystems. According to its first article, the CBD aims are 'the conservation of biological diversity, the sustainable use of its components and the fair and equitable sharing of the benefits arising out of the utilisation of genetic resources' (CBD 1994). The CBD defines sustainable use in terms of an ecosystem's ability to meet the needs and aspirations of present and future generations.

In addition, the CBD notes the existence of social, economic, scientific, educational, cultural, recreational, and aesthetic values, as well as something it calls intrinsic value. The CBD is a response to the recent and continuing loss of and damage to biological diversity due to human activities including fisheries. It strives to 'anticipate, prevent and attack the causes' at the source. Unlike the CCRF, the CBD is legally binding and the 157 countries that have ratified it to date are obliged to implement its provisions. The governing body of the Convention is the Conference of the Parties

(COP), consisting of all the states and regional economic integration organisations that have ratified the treaty.

Convention on International Trade in Endangered Species

The Convention on International Trade in Endangered Species of Wild Fauna and Flora (CITES) is an international agreement launched by the International Union for Conservation of Nature (IUCN). It came into force in
1975 and has since been ratified by 164 nations (CITES 2004). Its overall
intention is similar to that of the CBD but its scope is more limited. The
purpose of CITES is to protect rare animals and plants from extinction due
to international trade. It acts primarily by regulating trade. In three appendices, CITES lists animals and plants according to the level of threat. The
appendices include whole marine groups such as cetaceans (whales, dol-
phins), sea turtles, and corals, and many different species and sub-species.
The preamble to the CITES text indicates the following points of departure:
- the irreplaceability of the earth's fauna and flora, in their many forms,
- their value from aesthetic, scientific, cultural, recreational, and economic points of view
- the urgent need to take action.

CITES is one of the largest conservation agreements in existence. Its website boasts that 'not one species protected by CITES has become extinct due
to trade since the Convention entered into force' (CITES 2004).

Social Justice

Social justice, our second concern, emerges as a principle in the international debate at various levels of scale. One might somewhat simplistically
argue that the issue of justice to nations resides at a higher level, while at
the micro-level the concern is for individual justice. In between these extremes there is a plethora of social justice issues and activities, e.g., with
regard to minorities or gender. We first discuss principles emerging from
UNCLOS and the Universal Declaration of Human Rights and then shift
the focus to social justice in fisheries.

United Nations Convention on the Law of the Sea

UNCLOS is the major expression of international attention for nations'
rights over oceans and their resources. The convention was the outcome of
a process of more intensified use and inter-state disputes. Reflecting on its
origins, the UN Division for Ocean Affairs and the Law of the Sea writes
(2005), 'A tangle of claims, spreading pollution, competing demands for
lucrative fish stocks in coastal waters and adjacent seas, growing tension

between coastal nations' rights to these resources and those of distant-water fishermen, the prospects of a rich capture of resources on the sea floor, the increased presence of maritime powers and the pressures of long-distance navigation and a seemingly outdated, if not inherently conflicting, freedom-of-the-seas doctrine – all these were threatening to transform the oceans into another arena for conflict and instability'.

In view of these pressures in the post-World War II period, states unilaterally began to extend their claims over the ocean. The Third United Nations Conference on the Law of the Sea, convened in 1973, marked a concerted effort of the international community to establish an ocean regime. This conference ended nine years later with the adoption of a constitution that eventually went into effect in 1994.

The UNCLOS is a package deal to be accepted as a whole. The states' signatures express their consent to be bound by its provisions and not to undertake any action contrary to its purpose. By 16 January 2004, 145 governments had signed the UNCLOS. According to the UN Division for Ocean Affairs and the Law of the Sea (2005: 4), 'the practice of states has in nearly all respects been carried out in a manner consistent with the Convention'.

The preamble of the UNCLOS establishes 'a legal order for the seas and oceans which will facilitate international communication and will promote the peaceful uses of the seas and oceans, the equitable and efficient utilisation of their resources, the conservation of their living resources and the study, protection and preservation of the marine environment'. This order is expected to contribute to 'the realisation of a just and international economic order' that takes into account the interests and needs of mankind as a whole as well as the special interests and needs of developing countries, whether coastal or land-locked. The UNCLOS points of departure are: a) the problems of ocean space are interrelated and can only be considered as a whole, b) sections of ocean space and resources fall under national jurisdiction, and c) the area and resources that lie beyond the limits of national jurisdiction are the common heritage of mankind.

The two provisions most relevant to fisheries are the de-limitations of territorial seas (up to 12 nm) and EEZs (up to 200 nm). Territorial seas are the areas where states are free in principle to enforce any law, regulate any use, and exploit any resource. With regard to an EEZ, coastal states have the right to exploit, develop, manage, and conserve all the resources found in the waters, on the ocean floor and in the subsoil.

The UNCLOS Article 3 states unequivocally that 'every state has the right to establish the breadth of its territorial sea up to a limit not exceeding 12 nautical miles'. Subsequent articles stipulate the rights following from possession of a territorial sea. Part 5 of the Convention deals with the EEZ and the rights it entails.

The natural injustice to land-locked or geographically disadvantaged states is pointedly addressed. The UNCLOS recognises that whereas territorial seas are the prerogative of the coastal state in question, land-locked and geographically disadvantaged states have a right to participate on an equitable basis in the EEZs of coastal states of the same subregion or region. The terms and modalities are to be established through negotiation.

Universal Declaration of Human Rights

No contemporary discussion of principles of social justice can fail to include the Universal Declaration of Human Rights adopted by the General Assembly of the United Nations in 1948. According to its preamble, it is rooted in 'barbarous acts which have outraged the conscience of mankind' and strives to emphasise the 'inherent dignity and ... the equal and inalienable rights of all members of the human family'. Rights, equality and inalienability are the three key terms. As Article 3 notes, the rights in this declaration pertain to core aspects of life, liberty, and security of person, and every person has them. Article 2 spells out the main dimensions of equality and denounces distinctions of any kind. Inalienability means that human rights cannot under any circumstances be withdrawn. Wherever these principles are violated, social justice would appear to be at stake.

Other UN agencies have continued along these lines. In its Philadelphia Declaration (1944), the International Labour Organization (ILO) states that 'all human beings, irrespective of race, creed or sex, have the right to pursue both their material well-being and their spiritual development in conditions of freedom and dignity, of economic security and equal opportunity'. The ILO is mainly concerned with labour rights and we return to it in greater detail below. It is important to note though that in its declaration, the ILO explicitly connects human rights to the need for social justice.

The social justice referred to in the declarations pertains to individuals and not groups or categories. However, collective ideas of social justice have since entered the international arena. Gender discrimination is a core topic that is included in the Millennium Development Goals (MDG) of the United Nations (2001a). MDG 3 aims to promote gender equality and empower women. Social justice is also the vantage point of many other corrective initiatives on the behalf of children, indigenous peoples, minorities, and other disadvantaged groups.

The CBD is a relevant example. In addition to concern for ecosystem health, the CBD addresses rights to genetic resources and their distribution. Trade-related aspects of intellectual property rights (TRIPS) are an important issue on the international agenda, with the rights of developing countries, indigenous peoples, and other groups being fervently debated (cf. Martínez Pratt 2003).

Social Justice and Fisheries

The CCRF contains some references to aspects of social justice. Their inclusion was hard-fought and in the view of some non-governmental organisations (NGOs), they need further strengthening (cf. ICSF 1995: 10). Two sections of CCRF Article 6 that discuss general principles are particularly important, bringing forward a broad and a more focused perspective on social justice respectively. Regarding the broad perspective, Article 6.2 states, 'Fisheries management should promote the maintenance of ... fishery resources in sufficient quantities for present and future generations in the context of food security, poverty alleviation and sustainable development'.

The term sustainable development, as it is generally applied, has social and economic as well as ecological connotations. It refers to alleviating poverty in two ways: poverty as the condition of segments of the world population in the present tense, and poverty as a possible condition of the future. Article 6 of the CCRF not only refers to the people who depend on fishing for a living, it refers to the human population in a more general sense. This includes consumers as well as producers, those directly dependent as well as everyone who might in some way benefit from fish resources or be deprived by their absence. Although Article 6 does not specifically mention the plight of developing countries, it is clear that the CCRF emphasises their needs. In this article, social justice has a broad reach indeed.

Article 6.18 takes the following, more focused view.

> 'Recognising the important contributions of artisanal and small-scale fisheries to employment, income and food security, states should appropriately protect the rights of fishers and fish-workers, particularly those engaged in subsistence, small-scale and artisanal fisheries, to a secure and just livelihood, as well as preferential access, where appropriate, to traditional fishing grounds and resources in the waters under their national jurisdiction.'

The target group here are fishers and fish-workers – a term used to denote the men and women employed in various parts of the fish chain, especially those linked to subsistence, artisanal, and small-scale fisheries. The suggested contrast is with workers in industrial fisheries who are not perceived as needing privileged treatment.

The protection and preferential access to be given to the weaker segment of the fishing population is argued to follow from their contributions to employment, income, and food security. Justice demands that their role be recognised and recompensed by a 'secure and just livelihood'. What this entails is left to the states, who are urged to take appropriate action.

Livelihood and Employment

Many international initiatives in the past century have a bearing on livelihood and employment, and for good reason. After all, these concerns constitute a meaningful element in the generally accepted norms of human dignity and equality and are thus also included in the Universal Declaration of Human Rights. Its Article 23 argues that 'Everyone has the right to work, to free choice of employment, to just and favourable conditions of work and to protection against unemployment'. Article 25 notes that 'Everyone has the right to a standard of living adequate for the health and well-being of himself and of his family...'. These principles pertain to 'all members of the human family' without exception. Although Articles 23 and 25 are not explicitly connected, their sequence suggests a link: work contributes to livelihood and everyone has a right to both.

The Earth Summit in Rio de Janeiro (1992) and the Johannesburg Declaration on Sustainable Development (2002) approach the issue from another angle. Here the elimination of poverty is a major ambition. This is repeated in the United Nations' MDGs. MDG 1 calls for the eradication of extreme poverty and hunger, and strives to reduce by half the proportion of people living on less than US$1 a day by 2015. This objective is clearly related to employment and livelihood.

Since income and livelihood are recognised as being closely connected to trade and the terms that regulate it, these concerns have permeated the deliberations of the World Trade Organization (WTO). At the Singapore Ministerial Conference (1996), a heated debate about core labour standards pitted developing against developed nations. The confrontation was finally defused by referring the issue to 'the competent body to set and deal with these standards', the ILO.

This section first discusses the ILO and its contributions in the field of fisheries, then shifts to the trade-related agreements that are of importance to our topic.

The International Labour Organization

The ILO is the UN authority on labour issues and is thus crucial to our review of principles on livelihood and employment. It was created in 1919 by the Treaty of Versailles and became the first specialised UN agency in 1946. In the decades after World War II, the number of member states expanded and the industrialised ones became a minority among a majority of developing countries. The organisation currently has 245 members.

An important feature of the ILO is its tripartite structure, which includes the states, the employers, and the workers. At the annual International Labour Conference, each member state is represented by two government delegates, one employer delegate and one worker delegate. The Conference establishes and adopts international labour standards and acts as a forum where social and labour questions are discussed. International labour standards are frequently manifested as Conventions and Recommendations or incorporated into less formalised resolutions and declarations. In the course of its history, the ILO has adopted more than 180 Conventions and 185 Recommendations on a variety of topics. Once Conventions have been ratified by the member states, the ILO follows their implementation with a system of regular reporting. It has also developed special supervisory mechanisms. However, the organisation has no means to impose sanctions for non-compliance.

In 1999, the ILO launched the notion of *decent work* as an appeal and a strategic compass for the organisation and its partners. As the ILO website points out, 'implicit in this appeal is the view that work is not decent everywhere' and that there is a need to close the gap between goals and reality. The campaign works towards four objectives:
a. the promotion of ILO's Declaration on Fundamental Principles and Rights at Work;
b. the generation of employment and income;
c. the expansion of social protection and social security;
d. the strengthening of social dialogue between societal parties.

The ILO is presently carrying out a pilot programme on decent work that is to be implemented in selected countries.

The ILO and Fisheries

The ILO devotes specific attention to the fisheries sector. Fisheries are usually dealt with by the Committee on Conditions of Work in the Fishing Industry, which has met five times since 1950. On various occasions, the International Labour Conference has adopted international labour standards on fishers. The seven current standards (five Conventions and two Recommendations) are a mixed bag related to minimum age, working hours, crew accommodations, vocational training, standards of competency, medical examinations, and articles of agreement between owners and crew. Recognising its incomplete coverage of labour issues in the fisheries sector, the ILO submitted a comprehensive standard (ILO 2003) to the International Labour Conference in June 2004. The text of this standard is now in the process of completion.

In 1999, the Governing Body of the ILO organised a Tripartite Meeting on Safety and Health in the Fishing Industry to review the standards and specify follow-up activities. On its front page, the preparatory report for this meeting contains an evocative quotation from Herman Melville's Moby Dick, cautioning the reader as to the 'tiger heart' and 'remorseless fang' that underlie the ocean's tranquil beauty. The reference is to the fact that fishing is one of the most dangerous occupations in the world, and one with very specific health hazards. The various safety and health issues and the ways they can be better addressed constitute the main body of this report and of the meeting's proceedings (ILO 2000).

Safety and health concerns emerge in other recent ILO activities as well. An ILO working paper (Tomoda 1999) considers the safety and health of workers in the rapidly growing global fish, meat, and poultry processing industries. The perspective is normative: safety and health are intrinsically related to values of human dignity and equality. Besides developing special standards for the fisheries sector, the ILO is investigating the expansion of ILO maritime labour instruments to the fishing sector.

Of course, the general ILO Conventions are also relevant to the fisheries sector, one of the most noteworthy being the ILO Convention on Freedom of Association and Protection of the Right to Organise (No. 87). This convention, which not only applies to fisheries but to all sectors, champions the rights of workers and employers to establish and join organisations of their own choosing. It obliges the member states to take the necessary and appropriate measures to ensure that these rights are available.

Occupational conditions are one of the ILO's main fields of concern, and one where it has made efforts to develop and elaborate principles for management, policy, and governance. It should be noted, however, that many of them apply more to industrial than to small-scale fisheries, which are largely in the informal sector, outside the reach of state regulatory agencies. Countries define the regulatory cut-off point in different ways. Japan regulates fishing vessels down to three gross tonnes, Norway has substantial requirements for vessels beginning at 10.67 metres in length, and in India the government has regulated occupational conditions for all fishing vessels above 20 metres in length. In Senegal, to give one more example, the state is considering a code of conduct aimed at improving the safety of pirogues. Whatever regulations have been introduced, there is a very substantial category of the fishing population whose occupational conditions are still not regulated. Their numbers are larger in the South than in the North. Recognising its neglect of the small-scale fishing industry, the ILO has recently begun to devote special attention to it.

The World Trade Organization and Trade-Related Agreements

The Marrakech Agreement in 1994 established the WTO as successor to the General Agreement on Tariffs and Trade (GATT). Its overriding purpose was 'to help trade flow as freely as possible – so long as there are no undesirable side-effects. That ... means removing obstacles' (WTO 2001: 4). The WTO, as well as its predecessor, promotes a less restrictive system that supporters argue would raise standards of living and levels of employment and increase production and trade in goods and services to mutual advantage. Importantly, the Marrakech Agreement adds that efforts to reduce trade barriers should be 'in accordance with the objective of sustainable development' (cf. Preamble Marrakech Agreement). The statement points in the direction of Article XX of GATT, which provides for exceptions to the rule of free trade. Article XX also allows governments to take measures to protect animal or plant life and conserve exhaustible natural resources.

Underlying the WTO's activities are a number of simple principles (WTO 2001: 5). The WTO is founded on the premise that it would be to the general benefit if the trading system were (a) discrimination-free, (b) freer, (c) more predictable, (d) more competitive and (e) more beneficial for less developed countries. Not everyone agrees with the WTO precepts, as the anti-globalisation movement has demonstrated. Some of the agreements it had sponsored have nevertheless had an important impact, also on fisheries.

The WTO and Fisheries

The Agreement on Subsidies and Countervailing Measures (SCM Agreement) of 1994 aims to curb state funding for economic enterprises in all fields. The SCM draws a distinction between prohibited and actionable subsidies and permissible subsidies, and indicates how countries might react to suspicions of unfair subsidising by other agencies. In fisheries, the SCM Agreement understands that subsidies play a role in the expansion of the fishing effort and the problem of overfishing. Fishing subsidies constitute a major issue in the FAO's International Plan of Action for the Management of Fishing Capacity (1999) and the WTO's Doha meeting (2001), where fisheries were singled out as requiring special efforts to control subsidies (cf. FAO 2003c: 46).

Other important measures are the Anti-dumping Agreement of 1994, which governs procedures in the event of a suspicion of dumped imports and harm to domestic industry, and the Agreement on Technical Barriers to Trade (TBT Agreement) of 1994, which strives to ensure that the treatment of foreign goods is no less favourable than the treatment of similar goods from the importing country.

Principles for Food Security and Food Safety

Food security is an ancient human concern that is now expressed in the Universal Declaration of Human Rights (1948). Article 25 proclaims that 'everyone has a right to a standard of living adequate for the health and well-being of himself and his family, including food, clothing, housing and medical care and necessary social services'. The post-World War II decades heralded an increasing international focus on food security. At first the problem was mainly conceived in global terms. How could the world continue to feed its rapidly growing population? The Green Revolution in agriculture and the Blue Revolution in capture fisheries and aquaculture were scientists' and policy-makers' answers to this pressing question.

The World Food Conference of 1974 was the first international event devoted specifically to the issue of food security. The declaration issued upon conclusion proclaimed that 'every man, woman and child has the inalienable right to be free from hunger and malnutrition in order to develop their physical and mental faculties' (WFC 1974). As a follow-up to its decisions, the Conference established a Committee on World Food Security (CFS). In 1996, the CFS mandate was expanded to monitor the implementation of a Plan of Action.

The 1974 Conference was followed up in 1992 by the International Conference on Nutrition and in 1996 by the World Food Summit, with almost

10,000 delegates and 112 Heads or Deputy Heads of State gathering for five days in Rome. According to the website (WFS 1996), the Summit's objective was 'to renew global commitment at the highest political level to eliminate hunger and malnutrition and to achieve sustainable food security for all people'. The Summit resulted in a Declaration and a Plan of Action. Five years later, the 28th Session of the Committee on World Food Security reviewed the progress and decided on supplementary measures.

The complexity of the concept of food security and its linkage to other international concerns are noted above. The pivotal position of food security is highlighted by the fact that many international agencies such as the Food and Agriculture Organization (FAO), the International Fund for Agricultural Development (IFAD), the United Nations Children's Fund (UNICEF), the World Bank (WB) and many NGOs have drafted their own definitions and programmes, each with different emphases.

The Rome Declaration on World Food Security (WFS 1996) provides an authoritative formulation of the principle involved. It reaffirms 'the right of everyone to have access to safe and nutritious food, consistent with the right to adequate food and the fundamental right of everyone to be free from hunger'. This objective of food security is diametrically opposed to the reality of food *in*security, which is the unacceptable situation that, according to the same Declaration, 'more than 800 million people throughout the world, and particularly in developing countries, do not have enough food to meet their basic nutritional needs'. In order to achieve its goal, people need to have access to a sufficient quantity of food and this food has to be safe and nutritious.

The use of the phrase 'have access' is worth noting. Access implies the possibility of obtaining food and includes at least two dimensions, i.e., physical and economic. The first refers to the physical availability of food at the right time and place, and the second to the economic opportunities of poor people to procure it. Economic access also pertains to price and income levels and has a bearing on poverty and inequality.

The international debate on food security also highlights the question of levels. In the 1960s and 1970s, the trend was to view food security from a global supply perspective. It soon became clear, however, that enough food at the global level does not guarantee food security at the national or the household level. In the 1980s, the focus shifted to the meso-level (national and sub-national) and in the 1990s to the micro-level (household and individual). This followed from an awareness that gender is an important dimension in food security. Generally, food security is now held to pertain to multifarious levels. The WFS Plan of Action distinguishes individual, household, national, regional, and global levels.

At the World Food Summit, delegates formulated seven commitments and drew up a Plan of Action detailing objectives and ways to achieve them. The commitments are comprehensive and ambitious and address the causes underlying food insecurity. The onus of implementation is on the state. The CFS is the monitoring agency.

As is the case with other sweeping international agreements, progress towards food security has been slow. Following its 28th session in 2002, the CFS issued a report noting 'the disappointingly slow rate of decline in the prevalence and numbers of undernourished, especially in the African region' (CFS 2002). Although the reasons for this condition are varied, the scope of the ambitions has certainly played a role.

Food safety is a partial exception to the rule of slow progress. The principle is simple: food is safe if eating it does not harm a consumer. In its elaboration, however, complications frequently emerge. Setting codes of practice in this field is the responsibility of the Codex Alimentarius Commission of the FAO/WHO Food Standards Programme. Its principal mechanism for ensuring food safety is the Hazard Analysis Critical Control Point (HACCP) system. The HACCP system has been put into effect in the countries of the North. Moreover, food safety standards now regulate much of the international North-North and South-North trade. Food safety standards are less thoroughly applied, though, in many countries of the South and do not influence South-South trade interactions in a meaningful way.

Food Security and Fisheries

Policy-makers frequently use food security concerns to legitimate the technical development of fisheries. The rapid expansion of capture fisheries after World War II was motivated by the fact that it could help feed the growing population. The fact that fish is a particularly nutritious food underscored this potentiality. Thus, the FAO website (2003b) boasts that 'Fish is food for the brain as well as good protein'.

More recently, the development of aquaculture has been linked to food security. The FAO report, *Aquaculture in the Third Millennium* (2001d) argues that over the next two decades, aquaculture will contribute more to global food fish supplies and help further reduce poverty and food insecurity. According to its website (FAO 2003b), aquaculture is 'not just an export industry', it shoulders 'an increasing burden in the effort to feed the world's poor and hungry'.

As a buzzword, food security is thus instrumental in justifying technological and economic innovation. The first serious effort to reflect on fisheries' contribution occurred in 1995 at the International Conference on the Sustainable Contribution of Fish to Food Security in Kyoto, Japan. Delegates from 95 countries attended this five-day conference, where a Declaration and a Plan of Action were formulated. Interestingly though, both documents exhibit more concern with maintaining the production of fisheries products and establishing responsible fisheries than with food security, which is generally considered a function of the total food supply. There is no mention in the Kyoto Declaration (1995) of the issue of access that figured so prominently in the general discussion on food security. In fact, the only substantial reference it makes to food security is in one of its last points, entreating states to 'ensure that trade in fish and fisheries products promotes food security' and does not 'adversely impact the nutritional rights and needs of people for whom fish and fisheries products are critical to their health and well-being'. Neither of these recommendations is made operational, and it remains unclear how they are to be put into effect.

Subsequent gatherings of the Committee on Fisheries (COFI) went a step further and brought the fisheries discussion on food security in line with the wider international debate. The 23rd session of the COFI in 1998 included a high-level panel of external experts who discussed fisheries' contributions in countries vulnerable to severe food insecurity. They highlighted the issue of access and the multifarious levels at which food security should be considered. The 25th session of the COFI in 2003 continued this effort, focusing on the contribution of small-scale fisheries to food security and poverty alleviation. The meeting concluded that small-scale fisheries already play a vital role with regard to food security in many countries and that their performance can be improved through selective strategies (COFI 2003).

Discussions on the issue of food safety in fisheries have been held by the Joint FAO/WHO Programme on Food Standards. The FAO and the WHO established this programme along with the Codex Alimentarius Commission in 1963 to develop and implement an international food code or Codex Alimentarius. One of the Commission's main aims is to prepare standards to protect the health of consumers and ensure fair practices in the food trade. Towards this end, it has formulated principles on the use of food additives, import and export inspection, certification, and the addition of essential nutrients to foods. It has also established principles of food hygiene, codes of practice for the use of veterinary drugs and pesticides, and codes for the processing, transport, and storage of foods.

The Codex Alimentarius has such an excellent reputation that the Commission (CAC 2003) boasts that 'it has become customary for health authorities, government food control officials, manufacturers, scientists and consumer advocates to ask first of all: What does the Codex Alimentarius have to say?' The availability of uniform food standards has facilitated international trade. Codex standards also constitute benchmarks against which national food measures and regulations are generally evaluated.

Although substantial progress has been made in developing standards for safe and healthy food and fisheries products, the implementation is uneven. Many countries in the South have no mechanisms to implement the food code for the internal market, leaving domestic consumers unprotected. In their fisheries sectors, it is only export produce that is subjected to strict controls.

Overarching Features

A number of international organisations and agreements of the past fifty years are introduced above, devoting special attention to developments in the field of fisheries. Although each international organisation and each declaration, agreement or convention occupies its own niche in international affairs, they have at least the following four features in common: interconnectivity, the central role of the state, acknowledgement of market and civil society, and reliance on voluntary compliance.

Interconnectivity

A summary reading of the international documents reveals what may seem self-evident to some: they are closely linked. Not only are the authors of various declarations, agreements and laws aware of each other's existence, there is a conscious effort to adapt, reinforce, and fill in gaps. An international edifice is slowly being erected with coherence and effectiveness as important goals. This kind of edifice has some common starting points. In the current set-up, the Universal Declaration of Human Rights and the Law of the Sea play a cornerstone role. Although UN organisations occupy crucial positions, other international organisations such as the ILO and the WTO also contribute in a meaningful way.

The CCRF clearly brings out the interconnectivity of international activities. Article 3 details the relations with other instruments, emphasising conformity with UNCLOS and with other rules of international law, including obligations following from international agreements. The article also emphasises that the CCRF is to be interpreted and applied in the light of relevant declarations and international instruments such as the 1992 Rio Declaration. Other international actors are also acknowledged. Clearly, the authors of the CCRF do not intend it to stand alone. Instead, the CCRF is to bolster and be reinforced by the surrounding institutional structure. It is part and parcel of a broader endeavour to harmonise and regulate what are perceived as common international concerns.

Other examples of interconnectivity are provided above in passing. The Singapore Ministerial Conference (1996) of the WTO refers the discussion on core labour standards to the ILO, though the Marine Stewardship Council consciously chooses to develop its programme in the framework of the CCRF. The advantage of interconnectivity is that it increases the efficacy of international action, but for people with other ideological positions based on other sets of principles, interconnectivity poses a major challenge.

Central Role of the State

However great the bustle of international organisations, most agreements relevant to our topic rely heavily on the cooperation of states. They are the ones that take action in line with international understandings and they are the ones implored to sign agreements and cajoled into following up on their many promises. One reason is that most international organisations are mandated by states. At a more ideological level, the international community still perceives the state as the core agent of governance and management.

The CCRF is a good example. Although the CCRF stands out for including non-state parties in the management process and is lauded for it, states play an overwhelming role. 'States should' is one of the most common phrases in the document in reference to all the various phases and dimensions of the fisheries management process. International organisations, governmental and non-governmental alike, play a supplementary role in the governance process.

States play a key role in most other agreements too, with some qualifying exceptions. Representatives of employers and employees play a role in the ILO in addition to state representatives. Here too, however, the states tend to dominate.

Market and Civil Society

Liberalisation has gone hand in hand with the recognition of other societal parties besides the state in governance and development. The market and civil society are now commonly acknowledged as playing important roles. This trend is similarly clear in the activities of international organisations in the fisheries field.

The WTO is the global proponent of free, non-discriminatory and predictable trade (cf. WTO 2001), and its points of view are endorsed by other international players. In its section on principles, the CCRF includes the fact that 'international trade in fish and fisheries products should be conducted in accordance with the principles, rights and obligations established in the World Trade Organization' (Article 6.14). This is reiterated in Article 11 under the heading 'responsible international trade'. However, Article 11.2.2 introduces a cautionary note on the detrimental effects of free trade: 'International trade ... should not compromise the sustainable development of fisheries and responsible utilisation of living aquatic resources'.

'States and all those involved in fisheries are encouraged to apply the Code and give effect to it.' This quote from the introduction to CCRF (FAO 1995: 1) sets the stage for the role of civil society in responsible fisheries management. Article 1.2 elaborates CCRF positions on a wide range of organisations, whether governmental or non-governmental, and on all the users of the aquatic environment in relation to fisheries. In view of these broad premises, it is surprising to note that the main body of the CCRF is devoted to state tasks, with the role of other parties only occasionally noted. At some points, civil society does come into view. Article 6.16 in the section on principles urges the states to 'ensure that fishers and fish farmers are involved in the policy formulation and implementation process'. Article 7.1.2 urges the states to work with 'relevant domestic parties' to create responsible fisheries. Consultative arrangements should be established to this end.

Implementation and Follow-Up

The follow-up on international agreements is generally recognised as an important problem. One explanation is the lack of enforcement instruments. Relying heavily on voluntary state implementation of agreements, international organisations can do little more than apply gentle pressure. By monitoring, regularly measuring performance, and publishing the results, these organisations urge the states to meet their obligations. In the case of the CCRF, which is not legally binding, the FAO monitors its implementation and its effects on fisheries and reports to the COFI.

UNCLOS is an important exception to the rule as regards deficient enforcement. Along with the Law of the Sea, its founders have established authorities such as the International Seabed Authority and the International Tribunal for the Law of the Sea for implementation and adjudication. In addition, they include a mechanism in the document for settling disputes. The dispute settlement process is similarly written into the various WTO agreements. This settlement system includes the option to impose sanctions.

Conclusion

In this chapter we have examined the various principles underlying the international laws and agreements that have developed since World War II. We focused on four concerns: ecosystem health, social justice, livelihood and employment, and food security and safety. Overlooking the field it is clear that every one of our concerns is covered, more or less completely, by international law and agreements. International agencies and gatherings have deliberated on each of these topics and endeavoured to devise appropriate guidelines for action. We also noted that the principles that figure in the general discourse have filtered into the fisheries field, defining governance efforts there, too.

13

Meta-Principles

Jan Kooiman, Svein Jentoft, Maarten Bavinck, Ratana Chuenpagdee, and U. Rashid Sumaila

Introduction

In this chapter we discuss a number of principles that we think should guide fisheries governance at the meta-, normative, level. To outline their use in a conceptual manner, we apply the governance perspective as our model. We start with principles to be applied normatively to governing elements, followed by principles by which to judge modes of governance. We then discuss principles to evaluate governing orders. In each category, we formulate a general principle derived from governance theory, and three principles for each of the three governance components derived from fisheries. This gives us a list of twelve principles as a solid basis for an overall appraisal of meta-considerations for fisheries governance. Recently, others have formulated comparable lists (Costanza et al. 1998); the main difference between our list and the other lists is that these twelve principles are part and parcel of our governance approach, and form the meta-level thereof.

Before we discuss the principles to be applied to the components of governance, we briefly present what we see as their foundations (elements, modes, and orders – see chap. 1). Most of them are grounded in moral or ethical thought, with long histories behind them. Our normative notions for fisheries governance are not new, but are rooted in philosophical and religious thinking of yesterday and today. To discuss some of these foundations, we make use of what is known as 'applied ethics'. This is a branch of ethical thinking that, in its approaches, comes closest to what meta-principles for fisheries governance might be about, and it is helpful in demonstrating how the principles can be put into practice. In the boxes in subsequent sections, we give a short overview of where to place the principles in the conceptual governance framework.

Applied Ethics and Meta-Governance

In the second half of the twentieth century, most ethical and philosophical scholarship was largely devoted to analytical or meta-philosophical matters (Almond 1995). In recent decades, however, interest in practical applications of ethics as a separate branch of philosophy has grown. Under the title of *applied ethics*, studies are now offered on socio-political topics that have strong ethical ramifications, such as 'life and death' issues. The philosophy of applied ethics partly returns to the roots of ethical thinking (Plato, Aristotle, Aquinas), and partly to more recent thinkers like Mill, Kant, Marx, and Dewey.

Box 13.1 Philosophy and principles of meta-governance

Recent European philosophers developed ethical theories partly with an original quality, partly building upon earlier traditions (Schroeder 1992). Two of these theories seem particularly relevant for fisheries governance: value realism and studies in the Marxist tradition. Value realists (Brentano, Scheler, Hartmann) try to define objective, intrinsic values and analyse emotions as media through which such values can be elucidated. Value realists also believe in the plurality of intrinsic goods, but they differ on how these goods relate. In the Marxist ethical tradition, Gramsci suggests that ethical principles play a significant role in creating the dominant ideology, which legitimates the current mode of production. Habermas represents a more humanistic Marxist tradition arguing that norms can be justified and be considered ethically valid when they receive the consent of those involved by rational communication. Recent Anglo-American philosophy has moved away from normative ethics (kinds of moral actions) to meta-ethical questions (nature of morality) (Donagan 1992). A key figure here is Rawls, who builds upon traditions in contract theory (Kantian ethics) and upon Aristotle (theory of the good). He sees reason as practical and social arrangements as fair when everybody is accorded the fullest set of basic rights, and when socially produced goods are distributed according to the 'difference principle' – the least advantaged are to be made as well off in possible (Rawls 1973). His theory, although immensely influential, was attacked by, among others, 'communitarians' who stressed the role of the community in formulating ethical principles and not, as Rawls claimed, the existence of certain universally applicable principles. This and other developments have also revived an interest in Kantian ethics (O'Neill 1993).

Source: Authors of this chapter

Applied ethics distinguishes itself from its more abstract counterpart by using 'rich' definitions of key concepts like justice, liberty, rights, virtue, individual, and community, instead of reductionist and 'hard' modalities such as utilitarian or (neo-)Kantian theories (Edel 1986). It also tries to build bridges between ethics on micro-concepts like individual good or preference and macro-concepts like public goods and communal values. Applied ethics goes in two directions, one focusing on domains of application, such as bio-technical ethics, 'life and death ethics', business ethics, and feminine ethics; and the other focusing primarily on ethical processes by defining sets of principles, rules, arguments, judgements, and even manners of reasoning. Both perspectives – domain and process, or a combination of them – are applicable to the meta-governance of fisheries. The process aspect highlights concepts like principles, rules, and judgements, while the domain aspect can help in formulating ethical applications for fisheries as a whole, for parts of the fish chain, for specific fisheries, or for fisheries in the North or South. For fisheries governance, several areas of applied ethical thinking are relevant (environmental ethics, business ethics, developmental ethics and others). However, environmental ethics seems the most important.

Environmental Ethics

Environmental ethics have philosophical as well as religious foundations. Environmental moral considerations are built on a great number of principles. For example, the extinction of a species is bad as such, or it is bad in relation to human welfare. These principles have to be made explicit, justified, and criticised, because they often compete in the environmental arena and because they may lead to different policy responses (Wenz 2001).

Human-centred environmental ethics may be based upon a variant of utilitarianism, claiming a surplus of maximum happiness over individual human happiness. In this set of ethics, only humans are considered morally relevant. In nature-centred ethics, all living organisms are seen as deserving moral recognition, although, apart from humans, they can be ranked according to their moral significance. In life-centred ethics, the complexity of nature, including humans as well as non-humans, is given moral consideration. The more complex a system, the more morally relevant. This set of ethics requires that we take into account the impact of actions on all living things in a system. There are many other ways of looking at environmental ethics, but all of them – except the pure anthropocentric version, face the challenge of coming to grips with non-human aspects. For this reason, environmental ethics may be considered as a distinct set of ethics that confronts special moral issues (Rolston III 1990).

Box 13.2 Religions and principles of meta-governance

Principles based upon religion are an important source for meta-governance of fisheries, because in the North as well as in the South they have strong foundations in which religious values and ethical principles play a major role.

Buddhist ethical principles go directly back to the Buddha himself (De Silva 1993; Keown 2000) The three central elements of Buddhist ethics are free will, the distinction between good and bad, and causation related to moral action with a great emphasis on the well-being and care for others. Ethics of care and ethics of rights play an important role, and in a deeper sense include all living beings, not only humans but animals and lower creatures as well.

Beliefs in Islam are founded on the messages revealed by God to the Prophet Muhammad (Nanji 1993; Naqvi 2001). Four basic concepts in Islamic ethical thought emerge. Unity showing the inter-relatedness of all that exists – human and non-human, material and spiritual, perceptible, and imperceptible. Free will

---

applying to the personal as well as the social dimension of freedom. Responsibility is the natural counter-balance of free will in Islamic thinking. Muslims have to strive for perfection, and because of the absolute character of free will, the entire responsibility for not ushering in a better future rests entirely on man's shoulders.

In classical Hindu ethical principles, four concepts occupy a central place: *ashrama* (life-cycle), *dharma* (duty), *karma* (action-effect) and *purusharthas* (ends) (McKenzie 1922; Bilimoria 1993). Social and moral codes have been developed on the basis of dharma systems, some with a specific audience, some of a more universal nature. In modern Hindu-Indian ethical practice, the Bhagavad Gita is a central concept, being a synthesis of ascetic and duty aspects. Jain ethics have a number of vows, of which *ahimsa* refers to not harming and not injuring any and all living beings, and thus can be said to be 'among the earliest protagonists of animal liberation' (Bilimoria 1993: 52).

The Christian faith is based on the assumed reality of God, and on his disclosure through the ministry of Jesus Christ, and so are its ethics. (Preston 1993). Two basic issues are central to this ethics, how to act from the right motive and how to find what is the right action in particular circumstances.

Judaism prescribes clear environmental ethics, emphasising that God's permission to humans to 'take dominion' over all living things requires recognition that 'the earth is the Lord's' and an acceptance of responsibility to 'live lightly, conserving earth's resources' (Fink 1998). Christianity assumes broadly the same position, though its multiple traditions have led to diverse attitudes to nature. Hessel (1998) finds that an ecological reformation is now on the agenda of Christian theology and ethics.

Source: Jan Kooiman and Roger Pullin

Rationality as a Meta-Principle for Governing Elements

Governors (public or private) in fisheries have to be able to underpin their interactive governing proposals with reasonable arguments. Governing must in some way be rational. That is, it should be based on verifiable facts and data, logical choices of instruments and defendable action routes, although doubts about it will always remain. There is nothing particularly 'good' about rationality, but it helps: to act rationally, relevant considerations are needed; otherwise it can be called irrational – which in democratic governance is not advisable (see Kooiman 2003). But what about rationality itself? It has strong roots in many sciences and is at the same time highly controversial within and between sciences. 'We certainly have not been able to build a general theory of rationality for today's world, not even to lay any firm foundation for such a theory' (Geraets, as quoted by Kooiman 2003: 173). Claims for an all-embracing rationality concept seem to be overstated, and we have looked for a modest interpretation of it. Our choice for rationality as a meta-principle derives from our own ideas on governance. We take the three elements of governing – image formation, choice of instruments, and action – and link each one to a principle that is relevant for fisheries. For each principle, we select a (sub-)rationality concept as yard-stick.

Sustainability and Image Formation

Sustainability is a concept of recent origin, and closely linked to the centre staging of environmental concerns in post-World War II history. Sustainability is a popular term, 'one of those motherhood concepts that is hard to oppose, but difficult to pin down' (Sumner 2002: 162). Not only does it have multiple dimensions; it is taken as a goal, a condition, a vision, an ethic, a process, or even a management practice. Two definitions of sustainability are in widespread use. It is seen as development, which 'meets the needs of the present without compromising the ability of future generations to meet their own needs' (Brundtland 1987: 8); and as 'a kind of development that provides real improvements in the quality of human life and at the same time conserves the vitality and diversity of the Earth' (IUCN 1991: 8). Whereas the first emphasises the need for intergenerational equity, the second highlights the blending of human developmental and conservation concerns.

Many academics feel uneasy about the scope and the vagueness of these descriptions. As Jacobs (1999) points out, sustainability is a political concept with two levels of meaning; the first of which is unitary but vague, and the second applied yet contested. The differences of opinion about the interpretation of the unitary 'slogan' are, in his view, not a reflection of 'remediable lack of precision over what sustainable development *means*: rather, they constitute the political struggle over the direction of social and economic development' (Jacobs 1999: 26, emphasis in the original). He also makes a case for two competing concepts, which he terms 'weak' (or 'conservative') and 'strong' (or 'radical'). The first is technocratic in nature and holds less stringent ideas of environmental conservation. The second posits a sweeping interpretation of sustainable development, and emphasises the importance of equity and participation. The intention is to fundamentally re-order society (Jacobs 1999).

Debates on sustainability are also reflected in fisheries. In 1989, the FAO drew up a definition of sustainable development that echoed the views of the Brundtland Commission. The FAO guidelines, *Indicators for Sustainable Development of Marine Capture Fisheries*, provide a justification for this policy direction that is familiar (FAO 1999d: 10): 'Human-induced changes in ecosystems, including changes by fishing, are jeopardising the welfare of current and future generations'. Environmental sustainability is the baseline and objective of many fisheries scientists. However, discussions have not stopped there. There is an ongoing debate on the sustainability of the fisheries system or fish chain, as a whole. In fisheries, the perspective is visionary and complex, with problems emerging particularly in the translation from science to policy and management practice. The FAO in particular has not shied away from this task, as the authors of chapter 12 show in their discussion of the Code of Conduct of Conduct for Responsible Fisheries.

> ## Box 13.3 Communicative rationality and image formation
>
> In the governance perspective, images have broad meanings. They cover goals, opinions, visions, norms, and values. The most important event in image formation for governance is to arrive at collective images, either shared or acknowledging where they differ. This comes about by communication in interaction between those involved in governing. Actors producing patterns of interactions use language to co-ordinate their actions. In this co-ordination, says Habermas, actors are oriented towards 'reaching an understanding' in concrete practical situations (Habermas 1984) Four demands fulfil this purpose: what actors say is comprehensible, a sincere expression of the speaker's feelings, it is true, and it is right – i.e., there is a normative basis for what is said. The essence of communicative rationality is striving for consensus based upon critical weighing of arguments. This may lead to acceptance of an argument by one party as given by another, or by mutual adaptation of views by all parties involved in a particular interaction. An important procedural guarantee of the practice of communicative rationality is checking and comparing each other's intentions with ensuing actions. Interactive discourses are a good example of how, in the last two decades, sustainability has become a central principle in environmental and also fisheries governance.
>
> *Source: Authors of this chapter*

Frugality (Efficiency) and Choosing an Instrument

Although there are probably as many definitions of efficiency as there are stakeholders in a given fishery, defining efficiency has long been among the goals of fisheries management. For many marine biologists, achieving maximum sustainable yield in fish capture would be considered efficient (see Hilborn and Walters 1992). For economists, fixing capture levels so as to achieve maximum economic rent would be considered efficient (Sumaila 1997). In the case of other social scientists, meeting some social objectives (e.g., equity among fishers) may be considered efficient management of a fishery (see Coward et al. 2000).

The quest for efficiency reflects a deeper principle of frugality and the broader cardinal rule: *Thou shall not waste what thou holds most dear about the fishery.* If money is what you hold most dear, avoid wasting it. If the biomass of fish in the ocean is what you care most about, then certainly do not waste it. If, on the other hand, what you do hold dear is some social object, such as sustaining fisheries as a way of life, ensure that the objective is met without waste. In reality, most people hold dear a combination of ecological, economic and social attributes of a fishery. The trick and challenge, then, is to ensure that 'waste' of the desired combination of attributes is minimised (see Charles 1992 on multi-criteria optimisation). More formally, one can express our generalised definition as maximising the following objective function:

$$PV = \int_{t=0}^{\infty} e^{-\delta t} R(x, E) dt$$

subject to the relevant constraints.

In the above equation, PV denotes the present value of what 'thou holds dear' from fishing; $\delta > 0$ is a constant denoting the discount rate; R is the net value of what 'Thou holds dear'; x is the stock biomass; and E denotes fishing effort. The equation says that the 'owner' of the fisheries resource should employ a capture rate that results in the highest possible discounted value of what one holds dear.

The above definition of (fishing) efficiency as an expression of frugality is flexible and practical enough to capture the complex nature of fisheries, in terms of both the natural and human aspects. Clearly, different stakeholders in different fisheries hold different things dear, or even if stakeholders in different fisheries have the same sets of attributes that they hold dear, the weights they may place on each attribute will differ, therefore requiring a flexible model, such as the one defined herein.

Box 13.4 Bounded rationality – An instrumental principle

Within the governing space created between images on the one hand and courses of action on the other, governors have to select instruments. Which principle can guide this selection to evaluate such processes in a meta-governance perspective? The bounded-rationality concept seems to be such a principle (Simon 1983). In contrast to perfect rational decision theory that locates all constraints in the context and not in the actor, Simon assumes that actors are severely limited, too, in particular cognitively. This causes them to act within what Simon calls limits of bounded rationality. According to Simon, rational actors 'satisfice' instead of optimise or even maximise. They aspire to acceptable costs versus benefits, simplified calculations, and routine searching for (new) information. The frugality principle is a good example of what the application of the bounded rationality concept means in practice for guiding and evaluating the choice of governing instruments.

Source: Authors of this chapter

Precaution and Taking Action

The European Commission (CEC 2000) considered the elements required for application of the precautionary principle. These include proportionality to the level of protection sought, non-discrimination, consistency, benefits and costs, ongoing review in the light of new scientific data, and assigning responsibility for producing scientific evidence. This last element determines, to a large extent, where to place the burden of proof that an intervention or product is safe or risky.

Fisheries management, whether based on stock parameters, social and economic targets, ecosystem productivity, or combinations of these, cannot avoid dealing with uncertainty (e.g., Ludwig et al. 1993; Seijo and Caddy 2000). Assessing and managing the risks of the future decline or collapse of fisheries therefore demands a precautionary approach, with safety factors that allow for uncertainties. This is not an easy approach for fishers and the public to accept. They want the supply of fish to increase, and many believe that this is possible – from resource systems and fish that they cannot actually see. If fish were more visible, like animals hunted on the open plains, the precautionary approach would probably be more easily accepted, at least by those seeking sustainability.

The same applies to aquaculture, particularly to its impacts on the ecology and biological communities of water bodies. The FAO has embraced the precautionary approach. Article 19 of the FAO guidelines on precaution and fisheries management states (FAO 1996): 'Management according to the precautionary approach exercises prudent foresight to avoid unacceptable or undesirable situations, taking into account that changes in fisheries systems are only slowly reversible, difficult to control, not well understood, and subject to change in the environment and human values'. Some reviewers, however, under-emphasise or oppose the precautionary approach. It is not a significant feature in the rights and trade-based perspectives on fisheries (WHAT 2000).

Box 13.5 Rationality of action in a particular situation

Nothing 'happens' in governance if no action is taken. So, one might say that action in governing interactions, as it were, 'binds' image formation and the choice of instruments. Can a (meta-) rationality norm be formulated that is able to evaluate this integrating step in governing? A promising one might be the concept of 'situational rationality', meaning: if I were in the same situation as the observed actor, pursuing the same goal with the same information available, having the same glasses on, would I do the same thing (see Boudon 1996, Kooiman 2003)? In this view, rationality of behaviour can be explained as a function of the structure of the situation of an actor, as an adaptation to this situation. Boudon adheres to a rational choice model in which cost-benefit considerations play a central role (Weber's instrumental rationality). At the same time, he is aware that in many important situations this model has little explanatory power, e.g., when actions are inspired by beliefs (Weber's value rationality). This situational rationality, I would do the same thing – *ceteris paribus* – is broad and at the same time precise enough to be applicable to the action element of governing, and the precautionary principle is a sound principle to base such action on in fisheries governance, with so many uncertainties involved.

Source: Authors of this chapter

Responsiveness: A Meta-Principle for Modes of Governance

In this section, the attention shifts from principles for the intentional level of governing to the structural component of governance interactions, or *modes of governance*. As a central concept for this exercise 'responsiveness' seems an appropriate one. In contrast to rationality, which is typically actor-bound, responsiveness has a more structural connotation. In the literature, examples of both orientations can be found, but several sources (see Kooiman 2003) give it an interpretation leaning towards the structural or institutional side.

With varying emphases, responsiveness is regarded as the quality to respond to wishes. Pitkin, discussing responsiveness, says: 'There need not to be a constant activity of responding but there must be a constant condition of responsiveness, of potential readiness to respond .... there must be institutional arrangements for responsiveness' (quoted in Kooiman 2003: 177). A broader concept of responsiveness is formulated by Etzioni, who sees it as an essential element of an 'active society' and puts it squarely in a meta-context by using phrases such as 'to be active is to be responsive', and 'as some mechanism for converting the aggregate demands of its members into collective directives, and it is its responsiveness to these directives that can be assessed' (quoted in Kooiman 2003: 177). Although interaction as such is not explicitly part of the examples mentioned, the two-way character of responsiveness is a key element of it.

Respect as a Principle for Self-Governance

When looking for a moral principle on which to base self-governance in fisheries from a meta-point of view, 'respect' naturally emerges. Respect, for people or things, is a common moral notion, but also a central element in ethical theory, in which it is frequently linked to ideas on autonomy (Hill 1991). It was the philosopher Emmanuel Kant who argued that all human beings have a dignity that is independent of rank and merit. One's respect for the autonomy of a person is mirrored in the idea of positive freedom, or the capacity of people to frame their own law. 'All moral agents, by virtue of their rationality and autonomy of will, are jointly "authors" of moral law, bearers of fundamental rights, and pursuers of ends that others may not ignore' (Hill 1991: 285).

Respect for individual autonomy does not differ essentially from respect for the autonomy of collections of individuals and their institutions. Because people can make their own laws, these laws can be made into laws applying to all. In the Kantian sense, autonomy thus becomes a constrained one 'bound by the requirement to identify principles that can be adopted by all' (Ingram 1994: 101-102). In other words, autonomy is not a principle people can claim, without also taking the autonomy of (all) others into consideration. This allows the concept of individual autonomy, and the respect for persons connected with it, to become a concept of political autonomy.

Respect for persons is more than an individual duty but also part of a collective responsibility in the meta-governance perspective.

Box 13.6 Self-governance, autonomy and responsiveness

Approaches to self-governance differ. One school of thought emphasises that all social systems have an inherent quality of self-referentiality and a tendency towards closing themselves off from their environments. To distinguish themselves from others they create self-identities. In this line of thinking responsiveness is by definition limited. A second theory stresses that social, political, and historical processes explain why societal (sub-)sectors show tendencies towards autonomy and self-governance. This school of thought sees responsiveness to outside influence as variable. Thirdly, the governance perspective considers societal self-governance as a governance mode embedded within the sphere of spontaneous and variable forms of governing interactions. In terms of responsiveness, it takes a middle position: autonomy as well as external dependencies play a role. No self-governing societal entity lives an isolated life, they are all part and parcel of other, broader societal contexts, also raising normative responsiveness demands. As long as self-governing societal entities fit within expectations or conditions in their environment, this self-governing nature will be respected and reinforced. Conceptually, such environments consist of other self-governing entities, 'equal among equals in self-governance'. It is to be expected that the two-way notion of responsiveness also applies to them, and the question then becomes what we can say about such 'mutual' responsiveness expectations. We expect that self-governing bodies will have a certain degree of respect for insights and interests of others, providing a normative direction for external responsiveness as a conditioning principle.

Source: Authors of this chapter

In the case of fisheries, the respect shown for the user management of resources may be based on Kantian notions of autonomy. The respect shown by one user group for the management regime of another user group has Kantian connotations, and is associated with ideas about primal rights: 'Because a particular group has fished in an area for so long (or whatever feature is judged important), it has the right to determine how resources are used. Consequently, it has a right to others' respect for its rules'.

The respect shown by other stakeholder categories, such as government officers, for the self-governing capacities of users may have different grounds. After all, government generally prefers not to recognise authority originating outside of itself. In this case, respect may follow from the acknowledgement of one's own inabilities and failures, in combination with the proven ability of user groups. For instance, this is the case in India where the government does not possess the means to implement its own management regime, and is faced with strong user management practices.

Respect in such cases is related to powerlessness and even fear. Respect may also reside in a calculation of the advantages of user-management, such as its lesser cost and its greater effectiveness and legitimacy. The prevalence of strong 'local knowledge' of the marine ecology among users may be another reason for giving respect.

Inclusiveness as a Principle for Co-Governance

Who are the actors in fisheries? Are some being included or excluded in fisheries governance? Fishers and people who rely on fisheries as their major sources of income are the first actor group generally considered in the discussion about fisheries governance. The movement from top-down, government-based, centralised approaches to management to bottom-up, community-based, decentralised approaches in many parts of the world (Jentoft and McCay 1995; Sen and Nielsen 1996) suggests the recognition of fishers and fishing communities as owners of the resources, whose concerns are to be taken seriously when making decisions about fisheries management. This movement also requires new institutional arrangements and strategies to deal with issues such as heterogeneity of user groups (Felt 1990), community representation (Jentoft et al. 1998), community support (Noble 2000), and the genuine devolution of power (Sandersen and Koester 2000).

Box 13.7 Responsiveness, co-governance and inclusiveness

Modes of co-governance are the structural arrangements for societal interactions with a 'horizontal' nature, in other words for collaborative and cooperative interactions aimed at pursuing a common goal. These usually have a (semi-)formalised character. The question now is if we can specify the general responsiveness principle for co-governance into a more specific one, and in our opinion inclusiveness serves this purpose quite well. Here internal and external orientations of responsiveness can be found, internal responsiveness being the way the partners in those arrangements are responsive to each other and external responsiveness the manner the arrangements are responsive to their environment, as co-governance might be a response to growing societal interdependencies and interpenetrations between societal institutions (state, market, and civil society). The more that a co-arrangement becomes independent from the parties involved, the more it becomes an entity of its own, and the more it can externally can be seen as a self-organising societal entity. So internal responsiveness is the more crucial normative expectation. Whatever the reason for creating and maintaining a co-arrangement, who will be part of it is a crucial question. To establish a norm answering this question inclusiveness seems an appropriate one: who is included or excluded?

Source: Authors of this chapter

The community-based management model encourages fishers, other resource users, and the community to be more engaged in the decision-making, and in some cases, in taking the leadership role in management. In this model, power is shared between the 'authorised' (i.e., government managers) and the community, and responsibility for management is jointly shared. One of the most important issues associated with this model is the 'inclusiveness' of the actors in the community, and their interactions, which can be either positive or negative. Positive interaction involves open dialogue, communication, negotiation, and transparency, which then result in conflict resolution and collaboration. The latter, on the other hand, is partly caused by marginalisation, when interaction is not considered just by all involved parties, and may consequently result in rejection of the interactions, or at least the creation of mistrust.

One of the main reasons for exercising the community-based management model is to alleviate the overfishing problem. While this problem is a core issue for food security, it is no longer adequate to deal with the overfishing problem without using an ecosystem-based approach that takes into consideration destruction of coastal habitats by both ocean and land-based activities. This premise offers an opportunity to re-examine whether the actors in ocean and fisheries governance should include other groups, such as those who do not benefit directly from fisheries and whose activities do not directly impact the resources, as well as those who generally have little interest in the resources. In effect, this second group of actors is the public at large. The underlying principle in suggesting its inclusion is the need for integration across disciplines, stakeholder groups, and generations in order to achieve sustainable governance (Costanza et al. 1998). This comprehensive view leads not only to an expansion of the actor groups in the current generation, but also to an inclusion of those of future generations.

Equity as a Principle for Hierarchical Governance

Equity is often used synonymously with concepts such as justice, fairness, and equality; even in dictionary definitions (Le Grand 1991). For our purposes, where justice is considered as a broad concept, equity and fairness point to rather similar principles or norms, not only in common usage but also in scholarly discussions. Equity has had, and still has, an important position in legal and philosophical thinking all over the world. It can be found in Greek, Chinese, Jewish, Hindu, and Islamic traditions, among others. (Rossi 1993). Equity has a place in national law, and increasingly, in international law in regards to the adjudication, arbitration and settling of international disputes, many of them with a distributional character. International (environmental) law theory and practice provide lessons from which – by analogy – equity principles with a more general scope and application can be derived. For example, principles such as 'more capable states shall accept more duties', 'more capable states shall assist others', and 'equal participation shall be guaranteed and participation shall be transparent' (Biermann 1999) can be easily transplanted into other situations. In international law equity principles are developed, applied, and tested and, as such, a body of experience and knowledge is built from which many conceptual and practical 'meta'-lessons can be drawn. Also, in other disciplines and societal fields, equity and fairness are becoming the subject of scholarly discourses and practical applications, such as in economics, politics, and environmental issues, including fisheries. It is a major concept, for example, in debates and treaties on climate change (Banuri et. al. 1995).

Box 13.8 Responsiveness, hierarchical governance and equity

Many discussions about hierarchical governance concern responsiveness among governors and the governed. Most of the literature on responsiveness deals with responsiveness in this context. Discussions on the lack of responsiveness of modern governments are particularly well-known. One way of looking at responsiveness as a norm for hierarchical governance is to see it in relation to interventions at the intentional level of hierarchical governance interactions. Hierarchical governance interventions are highly formalised, have a command-and-control character and are often associated with sanctions. Although they can be found in the market and in civil society, they are most characteristic of public authorities and the state. It is quite well-known that much hierarchical governing has a symbolic character, or if it has substance, is poorly controlled and seldom fully enforced. In the market sector, this lack of responsiveness may also be problematic, but in the long run competitive forces will give a normative answer to such defects. In the civil society domain, with its emphasis on voluntary participation, lack of responsiveness because of low-quality interventions is least pressing, although in the long run it may also have disintegrating effects. For the public sector, responsiveness issues are the most complicated and the most serious, because the state 'does not end'. However, the state may change from 'command' to 'regulation' and from 'procuring' to 'enabling'. These adaptations are usually a response to broader societal developments or demands, and they may make hierarchical governance more responsive to those governed.

Source: Authors of this chapter

A useful first encounter as a principle for fisheries governance is a distinction between two types of equity: procedural equity and outcome equity. The first tries to define rules for fair procedures and the second to assess outcomes or consequences of decisions or policies according to equitable criteria in the distribution of costs, benefits, hardships and burden-sharing (Banuri et al. 1995). In the practice of applying equity principles to governance issues, such as those in fisheries, procedural and substantive aspects of equity issues are linked together: substantive distributive problems translate into procedures, and procedural ones often hide matters of substance. To overcome this duality, Rayner et al. (1999) and Linnerooth-Bayer

(1999) argue for an integrated approach (in their case to climate change), based upon the assumption that outcome and procedural issues around equity are basically looked at from three ethical positions: libertarian, contractarian, and egalitarian. These can also be expressed in three basic institutional forms promoting particular forms of equity. In the libertarian approach, linked to market-based institutions, the priority version of equity plays an important role; in the contractarian view, linked to hierarchical institutions, proportionality criteria of equity or fairness are dominant, while in the egalitarian mode, linked to community or civil society, parity criteria for applying equity principles are crucial. This way of analysing, but at the same time integrating, different aspects of equity can play an important role in the governance perspective of fisheries.

Performance: Principles for Governance Orders

Meta-governance also applies to the three governance orders: problem solving/opportunity creation, institutions, and principles. The governing activities comprising these three governance orders differ substantively and consequently normative notions about them also differ. However, there is a binding element between them: together they form the core of what governance is about, and they cannot exist without each other. The search, then, is for criteria that cover norms relating to these three different types of governing activities. Performance appears to be a concept that might serve this purpose: it has an evaluative connotation, it can be applied to quite different settings – public and private – at different levels of governing (actor, inter-actor, organisational, and institutional) and it can be considered a multi-dimensional or composite normative concept. However, we have to realise that 'the tools we use and the calculations we make are only imperfect measures of performance that depend for their meaning upon shared communities of understanding and agreement' (Ostrom 1986: 242). This warning bears upon all of the norms applied, because there are no objective standards or criteria with which to operationalise meta-considerations. Our choice is to operationalise performance in dimensions or sub-norms, showing varying degrees of concreteness.

Effectiveness as a Principle for First-Order Governing

Effectiveness can be considered a relatively reliable normative meta-criterion for evaluating problem-solving and opportunity creation as first order governing activities. Literature on evaluation in the public sector is a rich source for developing conceptual ideas on how to apply effectiveness criteria to these activities. General concepts and theoretical notions used in this literature can, with certain modifications, be made usable for the purpose of meta-evaluating first order governance. There is much more available on problem-solving than on opportunity creation, but recently this aspect has also been the subject of scholarly attention, for what is called 'policy strategy'.

Research traditions on evaluation and effectiveness all have their specific contributions to make, such as emphasising more 'rationalistic' or more 'hermeneutic' values (Van Vught 1987). Rationalistic approaches rely heavily on deduction of causal relations, and ex-post evaluation research has developed a broad array of relatively simple to highly sophisticated methods, models, techniques, and tools to track down such causal relations. In the hermeneutic approach, relations are not deductively arrived at, but must be induced by observation and interpretation. To study effectiveness, we use concepts as understanding, intentionality, functionality, empathy, and detailed description (Van Vught 1987). The approach, combining substantive requirements (coping with diversity, complexity, and dynamics) and process aspects (interaction, participation, feedback) offers space for model and observation or interpretation types of evaluation methodologies, depending on the purpose of the normative exercise at hand.

Box 13.9 Performance, problems, opportunities and effectiveness

A problem-and-opportunity approach points at the need of an instrument to make the diversity, complexity, and dynamics of socio-political issues accessible and visible. The great challenges in modern societies are not only finding solutions to collective problems, but also creating collective opportunities. The 'classical' distinction of turning to government for problem-solving and to the private sector for creating opportunities is an inappropriate and ineffective point of view in modern societies. Collective problem-solving and collective opportunity creation in diverse, complex, and dynamic situations is a public as well as a private challenge. Problem-solving can be divided into four different stages: recognising diversity of interests and aspects, deciding on the complexity of the relation among different parts of the problem 'as a system', locating sources of tensions (dynamics), and tracing back to where these can be located. The process of opportunity creation runs the other way around. There are no experiences to be taken stock of and identified yet. Here it is the governor him- or herself who has the experience of an opportunity. After the defining process of problem-solution systems or opportunity-strategy space is completed, it is time to choose the appropriate instruments and to take action. These phases can also start earlier and run (partially) parallel to the process of image formation of the problem or the opportunity. Effectiveness seems to be an appropriate principle to evaluate problem-solving or opportunity creation.

Source: Authors of this chapter

Legitimacy as a Principle for Second-Order Governing

It is generally assumed that a management system that benefits from a high degree of legitimacy will have a greater chance of achieving its goals when compared to a management system that has less legitimacy. This is because legitimacy enhances respect and support among affected users, who will be willing to abide by the rules willingly and voluntarily without heavy enforcement. If all this is true, two questions must be answered: what is legitimacy really? and what can be done to promote it?

Box 13.10 Performance, institutions and legitimacy

Socio-political problem-solving and opportunity creation (first-order governing) do not take place in a void: theoretically and in practice both are embedded in institutional settings, which can be looked upon as frameworks that have to cope with the diversity, complexity, and dynamics of modern societies – second-order governing. We can say that in conceptual terms, most coping with these characteristics in problem-solving and opportunity creation has to do with governing in terms of processes. In second-order governing, attention is more focused on structural aspects of governing interactions. This is not only a question of analytical distinction and attention, because taking care of these institutional settings for first-order governing is a governing order by itself, with its own character and flavour.

In the opinion of many who stress normative aspects, institutions are particularly important because they focus on rights and obligations, neglected in much of the more behaviourally-oriented literature. Here it is important from a governing perspective to call attention to prescriptive, evaluative, and obligatory dimensions of institutions (Scott 1995)) in the form of values; these are broad indicators of what is preferred or unacceptable, norms that specify how things should be done. These 'logics of appropriateness' also structure institutions. Normative aspects of governing institutions are quite important at the 'borderlines' between the social and the political, and between public and private.

Source: Authors of this chapter

Max Weber asked: When is power legitimate? Since any management regime ultimately rests on power, the question is also relevant to fisheries. First, it must be stressed that legitimacy is to be distinguished from legality. Beetham (1991) argues that to be legitimate, rules and regulations must be in accordance with some overarching concerns and standards, for instance pertaining to rationality, reason, and justice. Hence, we can conclude that a management system that scores low on such variables lacks legitimacy and would most likely be opposed by those affected. In many instances, fisheries management systems do not conform to the norms and moral views characteristic of the communities in which they are supposed to work. In this instance, the legitimacy of the management system is low within the community.

Weber argued that legitimacy rests in the eye of the beholder. If those that are subject to power regard it as legitimate, power is indisputably legitimate. The same would apply to a fisheries management regime. For

Weber, the criteria of legitimacy are basically subjective. There are, however, problems with such a concept of legitimacy. One issue concerns the relationship between legitimacy and truth. Through effective propaganda people can be led to believe, contrary to fact, that the management system works in their interests. It can be argued that for a management system to be legitimate it must fulfil some general standards pertaining to justice, fairness, equity, efficiency, rationality, etc. Thus, people's perceptions cannot alone determine whether or not a management system is legitimate. Rather, legitimacy is intrinsic to the system itself.

The second question regarding ways to promote legitimacy in fisheries management pertains to the processes through which management systems are developed. It is common to talk about this as 'procedural legitimacy'. Here, it is generally held that democracy is a significant contributor. Active participation by affected user-groups and stakeholders, other conditions remaining equal, makes management systems more legitimate, in part because it provides participants with a sense of 'ownership' of the system. They are not simply passive receivers of a regime imposed on them from the top down. Rather, they hold a hand on the pen when rules and regulations are written. This calls for decentralisation and delegation of management responsibilities, in other words co-management, which allows participants to deliberate and decide on basic standards that the management system should endorse.

Moral Responsibility as Principle for Third-Order (Meta-)Governance

Finally, we come to norm-setting for meta-governance itself. How we want meta-governance itself to be governed, and by what, are the questions to be answered in this setting. How do we conceptualise the process to get answers on questions like these? We speak here about governing norms, governance processes, and those responsible for governing interactions as a whole. Phrasing and answering such meta-issues is not something to be left to discussions between moral specialists or to the exclusive agenda of ethical institutions. To the contrary, ethical and moral questions are the essence of the governance domain. They are not only part of meta-socio-political interactions, but in a final sense, they are also the foundations of these interactions.

Our purpose is to make a plausible argument for looking at aspects of meta-governance at the individual and the collective level as part of normal and continuous governing interactions, and as part of our roles in those interactions. Moral dilemmas may arise when these governing roles are taken seriously. It is widely assumed in moral theory that 'the existence of moral dilemmas is evidence of the inconsistency in the principles or obligations giving rise to the dilemma' (Mason 1996: 5). It is exactly from the conflicts and inconsistencies between principles and obligations of interactive governance at and between the different governance levels, and the moral dilemmas they may give rise to, that meta-governance derives its importance. Taking responsibility for such governing interactions seems to be the most fundamental normative principle present in meta-governance.

> ### Box 13.11 Performance and moral systems
>
> Moral systems are practice-oriented imperative answers to the question '[h]ow should we live... they are multifaceted: they address problems of the possible rea-lisation of ethical projects: they set priorities among aims and provide principles for coordinating a range of primary ideals and values' (Oksenberg-Rorty in Kooi-man 2003: 185-187). This definition of a moral system is the general description of what we mean when we speak about a set of norms and values which might be able to 'govern governance'. According to Oksenberg-Rorty, there are advantages in the diversity of these moral systems; they are often organised in dynamic sys-tems of checks and balances, and the complexity of most communities with dis-tinct and layered sub-communities sets the stage for negotiation and sometimes conflict among a range of moral systems, each attempting to define a dominant configuration of ethical projects (Oksenberg-Rorty in Kooiman 2003).
>
> Meta-governance questions and answers of such an ethical nature cannot be separated from the general moral culture of which they are part. Recently, there has been a growing interest in the discussion of governance issues with a moral character. There is a call for the 'restoration' of a public morality, which empha-sises that societal developments ask for a redefinition of what a concept like pub-lic morality might mean.
>
> *Source: Authors of this chapter*

There is a tradition in ethical discourses on 'taking responsibility for', and its relevance for (meta-)governing seems to be beyond doubt. 'The links between representation, legitimacy, authority and power provide the basis for a deepened analysis of responsibility' (Friedrich 1963: 309-310). The same can be said of ethical/philosophical literature in which 'to be respon-sible for' is ascribed to individuals, members of groups or organisations, and also to collectivities. All these ascriptions have raised moral questions that have been the subjects of philosophical and ethical debates (Duff 2000). 'Ultimately moral responsibilities are by their nature shared by all those who themselves count as moral agents, notwithstanding the fact that (collectively) we may assign special responsibilities to particular people' (Goodin as quoted by Kooiman 2003: 186).

Conclusion

In this chapter we have tried to conceptualise a meta-perspective on govern-ance. To keep this survey manageable, we reduced the scope of the subject by searching for a particular principle for each of the major aspects of the perspective, serving as an exemplar for the normative dimensions of governance as a whole. These principles have dual purposes. On the one hand, they guide the behaviour of actors in fisheries involved directly in governing interactions. In this regard, the principles form the meta-normative framework that directs and sets boundaries for actual governing at the first and second governance orders, and for meta-governing itself. This is the world of governance-as-practice in which meta-norms are followed or neglected, tested out or changed in governing interactions. On the other hand, these principles, either practical or distanced, should be the subjects of governance debates. This is the use of 'meta' as a kind of aerial view scrutinising these principles for appropriateness, relevance, and applicability. This critical review at the meta-governance level addresses individual norms, but also looks at them in their mutual relations. This, as we explained, pertains to both governors and governed alike, and belongs to their 'taking responsibility for' governing role.

We have tried to show in this chapter that phrasing norms for each of the dimensions of governance serving these two purposes is possible. Of course, one can debate about which norms apply to which dimensions, about other norms, or about other definitions of them. We tend to believe that this is exactly the sphere or level of governance where such differences of opinion should find their greatest freedom of expression. Individuals and societies have invested energy and power in such principles and in other parts of normative systems that guide their governance.

14

Hard Choices and Values

Jan Kooiman and Svein Jentoft

Introduction

Fisheries governance is multidimensional. As pointed out in previous chapters, fisheries governors must address a number of concerns, principles, and goals that are all laudable but frequently also in conflict with one another. Resource conservation, securing jobs in the fishery, sustaining communities, feeding the poor, increasing export earnings, etc. are all worthy objectives for fisheries. However, they are not easily reconciled but confront decision-makers with dilemmas that require hard choices (Bailey and Jentoft 1990). Hard choices are always controversial and politically painful; they always come with a cost.

In this chapter we address the question of what a choice is, and what makes choices 'hard'. These rather simple questions have given rise to extensive scholarly debates, which we will draw on. How rational are individual actors? What is the relation between individual and collective choice: Is collective choice simply the aggregation of individual choices or not? Is a hard choice just more difficult than other choices or is it of a qualitatively different nature? What are typical hard choices in fisheries, and what can we, from a governance perspective, say about their resolution?

In all governance choices, values play a part. What makes some hard and others less hard is the fact that the values confined in them are in conflict. Many governance issues imply such conflicts. This is the reason that we deal with hard choices in fisheries governance in the context of the values implied in them. The cases presented are illustrations of what we feel are typical hard choices fisheries governance faces.

Choosing and Deciding

Choice and decision, or choosing and deciding, are concepts that are rather close. In the literature we often find decision-making as having a somewhat broader meaning, including a whole process from defining a problem to implementing a chosen alternative solution. Thus, choice is related to alternative courses of action, from which one is considered the best in relation to a particular purpose or goal. Choosing is also always related to a particular decision-maker, an individual, group or another form of collective actor, at a particular moment in time. Choices are place and time bound, and they are uniquely related to a particular actor or set of actors, based as they are on their specific experiences and competencies. As Schackle points out (Schackle 1969: 13): 'Decision is choice amongst available acts, and this choice is aimed at securing a preferred combination of experiences'. Furthermore, choosing means creating something new: '... if nothing new can enter the scheme of things ... nothing is created by choice and choice is empty' (Schackle 1969: 6). And what is 'new' is constantly surrounded by uncertainties, for instance with regard to 'complexity' and 'partial ignorance' (Loasby 1976). In this view economic and social systems are often too diverse, complex, or dynamic to ensure the decision-maker that his choice of alternatives is complete. Decision-makers are always 'partially ignorant' because even if they have a complete overview of all possible courses of action, they can never know the full range of possible outcomes. So decisions can be seen as choice, choice not in the face of perfect knowledge or in the face of total ignorance (Schackle 1969: 5; Loasby 1976: 9). In the real world, when decision-makers make a choice, they move between these two 'faces'.

However, not all approaches to choice start from images and acknowledgements of the real world. To the contrary, important theories of choice have their starting point in an ideal rather than the real world. This is a source of much debate and confusion. In many areas of research, this poses methodological and analytical restrictions, in fundamental as well as applied research, by limiting our understanding of what empirically motivates choice and the range of activities that surrounds it (cf. Fine 1998).

Box 14.1 Small-scale vs. large-scale fisheries

Development may include choices between allocation resources to either small-scale or large-scale (fish) capture subsectors. This may be either via total available catch or zoning. Often, the resource cannot be fully utilised by either group; small-scale fisheries cannot operate offshore, and large commercial vessels cannot operate without serious environmental consequences. So the question is often one of a dynamic balance between the two groups.

The relative merits of going either way are numerous. Small-scale fishers often represent more votes, but have less bargaining power. Opportunities for direct revenue recovery are fewer with small-scale fisheries and management costs are often higher. However, small-scale fisheries are often more efficient and may thus represent less drain of foreign exchange for inputs. On the other hand, commercial fisheries may be more likely to export and earn foreign exchange. But exports may be at the expense of local food security, unless they can be offset with cheaper imported substitutes.

The issues related to this policy question may appear to be largely economic, but they have a large element of social impact, too. Small-scale fisheries may be located in rural areas with fewer alternative forms of employment, and may employ persons who lack the skills for other employment. Accessibility of protein in rural areas may be an important health consideration. Less tangible issues, such as threats to traditional ways of life and diets, also arise.

Author: Robin Mahon

HARD CHOICES AND VALUES

Our lead principle for positioning ourselves is looking at the real world of choices in fisheries, simple or hard, and touching upon the ideal where it seems fit. We do this primarily by examining the relation between rationality and choice. Most if not all theories of choice in one way or another see choosing as being guided by rationality concepts. This seems a logical choice in itself: which fisheries governor wants to be painted as irrational in the making of his or her choices? But limiting choices to being rational, or looking at rational choice behaviour, does not help much, because there are many contradictory theories and concepts trying to explain choice as rational. This has not only to do with the multitude of rationality concepts utilised, but also with the ways in which the relation between rationality and choice is conceptualised.

Actor-Bound Conceptions of Rational Choice

Simon (1957) conceived the idea of 'bounded-rationality' (see chap. 13, box 13.4). According to Simon, bounded, rational actors are rational within limits, and 'satisficing' behaviour is rational in that it responds to finite means towards a particular end. The bounded, rational actor overcomes his limitations by setting out procedures, or follows operating rules to reach a satisfactory outcome. With the advent of the information revolution overcoming limits of information collection and processing, and the modelling techniques based upon them for aiding choices governors have to make, it seems that the boundaries as assumed by Simon have not disappeared, but that they are opening up and widening.

> **Box 14.2 Short-term vs. long-term development**
>
> Short-term economic gain versus long-term sustainability is a classic and basic dilemma in fisheries. In the modern variant this is redefined for long-term sustainability to include the precautionary principle, biodiversity considerations and an ecosystem approach. In developing countries, this involves hard choices, as these concerns may not, or only very indirectly, relate to local productivity – even in the long term. For food security, this dilemma becomes even tougher as it can become an issue of survival – there is no such choice as between short-term non-survival vs. long-term survival! In the European Union, the scope for fisheries is to restore single stocks to above depletion. The hard choice in developing countries may present itself as the conflict and trade-off between maintaining high exploitation in spite of biodiversity and ecosystem considerations or maintaining good relations with the international community, including important donors.
>
> *Author: Poul Degnbol*

Another approach to rationality on the individual actor's level puts reasoning in a central place. Governors (public and private) at least in liberal democratic societies, with all their goals, ambitions, emotions, and intuitions, have to be able to underpin their governing activities with verifiable facts and data, logical selection of instruments and defendable action routes. Giving reasons for one's choices is considered to be the most common denominator of all conceptual perspectives on rationality. As stated by Simon: 'Virtually all human behaviour is rational. People usually have reasons for what they do, and when asked, can opine what these reasons are' (Simon quoted by Lupia et al. 2000: 6). In real life, however, decision-makers often rationalise: the reasons follow rather than precede action. A 'weak', if not the 'weakest', form of rationality to be applied in governance might be a rational choice 'based upon reasons, irrespective of what these reasons may be' (Lupia et al. 2000: 7). To find out what this form of rationality might mean one must go deeper into the analysis of how people reason. In this perspective, 'choice must be regarded as an individual's contemplation of plausible reasons for action, and then taking that action (choice) for which the individual can muster best reasons', and 'preferences or utility do not count as reasons' (Bromley and Paavola 2002: 265). Cognitive sciences indicate that people follow certain 'heuristics' (procedural shortcuts) in the reasoning for the (political) choices they make. Also at play are institutional factors, which 'mould' the mental models or belief systems people share in their choosing behaviour, and underpin the reasons they give for making choices (Sniderman et al. 1999; Lupia et al. 2000).

Interactive Perspectives on Rational Choice

Actors producing patterns of interactions use language to co-ordinate their actions. In this co-ordination, says Habermas, actors are oriented towards 'reaching an understanding' in concrete, practical situations. 'Communicative rationality' characterises interactions between social actors striving for a common definition of reality by means of communicating (see White 1995: 36-43). The essence of communicative rationality is striving for consensus based upon the critical weighing of arguments. This may lead to acceptance of an argumentation by one party as given by another, or by mutual adaptation of views by all parties interacting. Even if no agreement is reached there is always the opportunity for a new sequence of argumentation resulting in better and more convincing arguments. Legitimacy is the norm regulating communication. Legitimacy is based on the acceptance of the justification of the agreement by those involved. Here an important procedural guarantee is checking and comparing each other's intentions with ensuing actions. Communicative rationality, as phrased by Habermas and the debate it provoked, is a prime source for testing arguments and reasons given in the collective processes of making choices and decisions.

A more dynamic analytical approach is to conceptualise collective choice as interactive learning. Learning is the process in which information becomes knowledge (cf. Jentoft et al. 1999). Governance allows for mutual, interactive learning for decision-making. Learning occurs throughout the governing process, from practical problem-solving, to institutional learning and learning at the 'meta'-level of governance. Learning can take two different forms, single-loop learning, and double-loop or meta-learning (what Bateson (1972) called 'deutero' learning; see chapter 11). Single-loop learning is considered to be learning of the common type at the level of problem-solving, i.e., first-order governing, while double-loop learning occurs at the institutional level, i.e., second-order governing, while meta-learning is 'learning how to learn'.

In governing, logical reasoning, empirically verifiable facts, controllable experiences and interpretations open for discussion are important single-loop learning elements. However, actors may also express different forms of rationality with high chances that different insights and perspectives are deemed irrational, thus blocking learning and communication in the formation of governing images.

Double-loop learning happens when the basic variables and conditions that create disparity at the first level are identified and changed. Argyris (1992) argues that greater emphasis should be placed on double rather than on single-loop learning.

> Although single-loop actions are the most numerous, they are not necessarily the most powerful. Double-loop actions, i.e., the master programmes, control the long-range effectiveness, and hence, the ultimate destiny of the system (Argyris 1992: 10).

However, what Argyris suggests is easier said than done. Learning of the double-loop kind requires us to question and scrutinise fundamental assumptions and values. Such an exercise may be experienced as threatening for actors who may be inclined to evade or resist it. Interactive learning is a process in which participants learn from each other and from each other's learning. How learning proceeds throughout an institutional process as a cause and effect and as a force shaping the change process itself is also an important governance question. Is the range of options broadened or narrowed as a consequence of learning? At first glance, one would expect the former because learning is supposed to broaden our perspectives. However, as in the case of changes in scientific paradigms, learning may often have the opposite effect: discarding what we already know.

Box 14.3 Innovation vs. precaution

Biosafety means safeguarding the natural environment and its biodiversity, the sectors that depend upon these (including agriculture, aquaculture, and capture fisheries and their biodiversity), and humans, against risks from biotechnology. Precaution demands prior and thorough appraisal of possible risks before introducing and distributing alien aquatic species and farmed organisms. This applies especially to first time introductions of alien species and to their subsequent transfers to different ecological zones and habitats, especially those that contain wild biodiversity and genetic resources of national or international importance and those that support aquaculture and fisheries. Their potential ecological and genetic impacts, when accidentally or intentionally introduced or distributed into open waters and wetlands, are serious concerns. They are far less visible and controllable than terrestrial organisms and, once established, are usually impossible to eradicate.

In principle, whether to introduce an aquatic alien species or farmed organism and where to distribute it among aquatic resource systems are very hard choices. The consequences can change that resource system forever, as lakes all around the tropics covered in water hyacinth bear witness. However, the conditions for making this a hard, well-considered choice rarely exist. Proposals to introduce and to distribute 'new' organisms for aquaculture are often accompanied by promises of wealth generation, livelihood opportunities, export potential, etc.

Author: Roger Pullin

While Argyris stresses the need for double-loop learning, from a governance perspective it is equally important to emphasise the need for meta-learning. This is partly for the simple reason that the latter is a condition for the former. In other words if the diversity, complexity, and dynamics of fisheries require management systems that are adaptive and flexible, learning how to learn becomes an essential condition. One issue is how institutions remember, how they can accumulate lessons by drawing on previous successes and failures when they are faced with new situations that require hard choices. Hersoug (2004), for instance, claims that when donor organisations involved in fisheries development tend to make the same mistakes over and over again, it is largely due to their inability to learn from their own and others' experiences.

Rationality and Choice

The different approaches to rationality create an opportunity to locate and conceptualise various kinds of choices related to different kinds of rationality. This is important because – as we already mentioned – it is generally assumed that making choices is a rational activity, whatever rationality might mean in a particular situation. In other words, rationality and choice 'meet' when an occasion arises and asks for a decision to be taken.

Box 14.4 Domestic vs. foreign markets

There are at least two reasons to question the liberalisation of marine produce markets and the increasing internationalisation of trade. The first is that the world's poor, mostly living in the South, depend on the availability of seafood at cheap prices on the local market. With the range of export products increasing all the time, it is not illogical to assume (although I have not seen evidence confirming it) that internationalisation negatively affects the chances of the poor to sustain themselves through seafood. After all, more and more effort, and produce, goes toward providing the international market, where prices are better. To ensure food security, managers will need to address the needs of the local market, too.

The second reason to question the internationalisation of trade is the fact that higher prices encourage fishers to overexploit local fishing grounds. Markets are in principle insatiable, and there are many examples of how fisheries that have tried to meet their demands have crossed ecological thresholds. If one wants to address the problem of overfishing, one must therefore also consider the market. In this era of liberalisation and World Trade Organization Agreements, the 'closing' of markets is not on the political agenda. However, fisheries governors are faced with the dilemma and hard choice of how to balance liberalisation with the regulation of markets.

Author: Maarten Bavinck

A way to establish this relation between different types of choice and the kind of rationality belonging to them is to distinguish four types of decision situations, each asking for their particular type of choice based upon a fitting type of rationality. Table 14.1 illustrates these four situations.

Table 14.1 Types of rationality applied in different choice situations

Choice context\Rationality	*Information*	*Knowledge*
Individual	Situation 1	Situation 2
Collective	Situation 3	Situation 4

The horizontal axis indicates that in all decision-making models (individual or collective) processing information or the creation of knowledge is crucial for making choices. Decision-makers may see this primarily as a matter of processing information or they may consider the decision situation they face primarily as something they need to understand first. With information processing the decision-maker builds, as it were, a rational picture from bits of information, a process in which technical means and modelling operations might be used. In the second form, the decision-maker is rational in an interpretative way. In dealing with uncertainties, it is not so much information but knowledge-building he or she is after. As O'Connor (2002: 185) remarks:

> The space of 'feasible outcomes' is characterised ex ante by an inherent indeterminacy, and ex post by irreversibilities. Knowledge in the sense of insight and understanding is not synonymous with the capacity for predictions.

An important and oft-used distinction made by Max Weber between instrumental and value-oriented rationality might serve to indicate roughly the difference between the two: information-processing with instrumental rationality and knowledge creation with value rationality. It should be clear that this is our 'short-hand' for summing up a whole world of sophisticated approaches to rationality.

On the vertical axis, two choice situations are conceptualised, the level of an individual actor and at the collective level. In the literature much is made of this, and – again to summarise – at the actor level we locate choice situations in which all kinds of ideas on how an individual actor arrives in a rational way at her or his choice. At the collective level we have a decision situation in which together – in concert – a number of actors have to make a choice. In other words, in collective decision-making the participating actors are supposed to influence each other's choice ideas and behaviour through communication and interactive learning and thereby arrive at a joint decision to choose between alternatives.

With these two axes we create a matrix of four cells, each representing one of the rationality concepts discussed above. This is a typology that 'hints' at different ways in which actors either individually or collectively underpin their choices with a particular form of rationality. In the individual information cell we find the bounded-rational decision-maker; in the individual knowledge cell we find the reasoning actor. At the collective level we find the situation where actors by communicating together come to a rational choice, either through rational communication or by interactive learning. This matrix also offers the possibility to conceptually differentiate types of choices, varying from 'light' and 'moderate' to 'hard'. The upper left part of the matrix (situation 1) contains choices that are relatively 'easy', cells 2 and 3 choices of the 'moderate' kind, while in cell 4 (situation 4) the choice is 'hard'. From a governance perspective, cell 1 choices are not particularly interesting. For the policy-oriented choice situations presented in cells 2 and 3, there is an extensive literature of relevance. One debate is whether or not individual choice models can be applied to collective choice. An argument is that collective choice is not simply an aggregation of individual ones. The idea here is that the relation between individual and collective choices is to be found in values, and in particular in value pluralism. When there is a plurality of values, it is impossible to conclude that the individuals in the same choice situation express the same preferences. As Paavola (2002: 91) argues: 'Choices do not and cannot reveal preferences when agents are motivated by plural values'.

Now we move to the collective level of choice – such as policy choices. Only in an ideal situation can standard neo-classical economic theory explain collective welfare maximising. Thus, in the practice of fisheries governance, it is not sufficient as a basis for collective hard choice making. Recent introductions of transaction costs into the equation of collective choice making has brought the theory a step forward. However, introducing those costs means that basically we do not speak any longer of uniquely optimal outcomes but of outcomes with a distributive character, because transaction costs (and other costs) are not evenly distributed in societies. Again, Paavola holds:

> The resources commanded by agents, the transaction costs they face, and the institutional rules that structure decision-making in collective choices determine whose values will be translated into public policy ... Collective choices simply involve deliberation to choose between the values that inform public policy (Paavola 2002: 95).

We also have the third type of choice, which conceptually might be seen as the 'real' hard one. It might be related to the typical governance issues we speak about in this book. Before we go into discussing this kind of choice in more detail a short detour is needed. We will discuss the choice situations that the literature terms as situations where there are incommensurable, incompatible, or incomparable values at play.

Values

To distinguish the factors that make choices 'easy', 'moderate', or 'hard', we draw on a literature (partly philosophical) addressing what is called the (in)compatibility, (in)comparability, or (in)commensurability of values. The relevance of this body of thought is expressed in quotes such as: 'Every choice situation is governed by some value' (Chang 1997: 7) and 'All environmental policy instruments require a moral choice as to whose interests count' (Schmid 2002: 133). In other words, choices always have, in one way or another, to do with values, be they implicit or explicit, obvious or hidden, technical or instrumental.

'Easy' choices are characterised by values that are basically comparable, commensurable and compatible. 'Moderate' choices involve mixes of comparable and commensurable values. 'Hard' choices are those where basically values at stake are incomparable, incommensurable and incompatible. Or, put differently, easy choices can be dealt with on the basis of exchanges between or within the scope of one value, while moderate choices make trade-offs between different but comparable or commensurable values. In hard choices, on the other hand, these 'ways out' are not available: choices are basically of the 'either-or' type.

Depending somewhat on the discipline, there is confusion as to definition: some see (in)commensurability as a narrower concept than (in)comparability, which has to do with measurement and scales. (In)comparability means that items cannot be compared, they simply are of a different kind (Chang 1997: Introduction). Some see it the other way around: 'Incompatible moral claims become incommensurable when trade-offs become unavailable because there is no common currency' (Lukes 1991: 11). Raz uses them synonymously (quoted by Chang 1997: 1). There is also the use of (in)comparability; values are not only of different kinds, but attempts to compare them 'may break down' (MacLean 1998). For our purposes, we prefer to use (in)comparability and (incompatibility) synonymously as they both certainly belong in category 4 of the four-square table, where the hard choices are. In contrast, we see incommensurability as the shallower concept, thus belonging more in the 'moderate' choice category.

Besides this classification of what in fisheries and elsewhere the basic qualities of choices might be, there is also the question of what values are at stake. This is of importance, particularly in the discussions on the pros and cons of the application of techniques such as cost-benefit analyses and the reasoning behind them. There are those who hold the opinion that there are no incompatible or incomparable values. In the words of Chang, there are no easy arguments for incomparability. In her view (and that of others) 'comparability is essential', because without comparability no trade-offs between costs and benefits, no maximisation of utility, nor the possibility that practical reason might guide choices if alternatives are incomparable (Chang 1997: 2-3)? Positioning (in)commensurability and (in)compatibility in these terms already hints at the essence of the debate on them, because they play an essential role in the economic and politico-economic use of concepts like utility, cost-benefit, and trade-offs, and the theoretical (and normative) basis for them. In one way or another, they all rely on comparability, commensurability, and compatibility, as Chang expressed so clearly.

Therefore, it is understandable that opponents of an all too general and broad use of these economic and political-economic concepts challenge their theoretical basis. For example, Radin (1996) argues that commensurability is central to what is called 'commodification', and in particular to universal commodification. According to this view, all human or social and political interactions are 'conceived of as exchanges for monetizable gains', are 'characterizable as trades' (Radin 1996: 5). She vehemently challenges this as unduly reductionist and also points at the danger that this 'market rhetoric' is being expanded to real political-economic life, in other words 'commodification as a worldview'.

Box 14.5 Aquaculture development vs. capture fishery restoration

Aquaculture development is usually more politically attractive than fisheries restoration, because of its high visibility and promise of rapid results. There are, however, limits to the growth of aquaculture and its contributions to fish supply. Resource constraints (limited availability of good sites, user conflicts, and the cost and availability of feeds and fertilisers) are major limiting factors. There are also risks. Stand-alone (as opposed to integrated) aquaculture operations commonly experience serious losses of profits about twice per every ten years: from adverse weather, plant failure, operator error, disease, fickle markets, etc. Aquaculture must also meet increasingly strict environmental and ethical criteria to be considered responsible.

Fisheries restoration is often more difficult than aquaculture expansion. It usually requires reduction of fishing effort; i.e., taking fishers out of fishing and/or restricting where, when, and how much those who remain can fish, usually with the establishment of protected areas, closed seasons, or complete moratoria, etc. The application of these tools is not an exact science, and their results are not easily predictable and are sometimes discouraging. Attempts to rehabilitate some of the world's large and overfished salmon and cod fisheries have met with little success so far. However, some interventions in smaller-scale fisheries, particularly the use of community-managed protected areas in tropical reef fisheries, have shown almost immediate and very substantial benefits to fishers and to their communities. Moreover, adoption of ecosystem-based management of large-, medium- and small-scale fisheries holds much greater promise for their successful restoration. The reward is a large, diverse, and sustainable fish capture from healthier ecosystems.

The hard choices here are how to make balanced policies for aquaculture and capture fisheries restoration against limited budgets and human resources, short-term needs vs. longer-term consequences, vested interests and current livelihoods vs. the reality of declining natural resources. The choices affect directly food security, employment, and environmental health, and also have impacts on non-fisheries sectors, such as agriculture and tourism. They also determine investments in aquaculture and capture fisheries education and research, the strengths and weaknesses of the organisations that carry out those functions, and the future human resources available for management of aquaculture and fisheries.

Author: Roger Pullin

In a similar vein we find argumentation on a more applied level. In a study on environmental policy, Bromley and Paavola (2002) discuss the issue of treating choices as simple trade-offs. In their opinion, the tendency is to consider values expressed in environmental policies as commensurable. They challenge the assumptions that in environmental policies hard choices are merely trade-offs. Holland (2002: 17) argues against the tendency to equate choice making with trade-offs and even more against the claim that 'only if our choices have the form of a trade-off will they be rational'. He shows that the assumption of comparability, which underlies these pleas for trade-offs, no longer goes unchallenged and that not seeing trade-offs as the major form of rational choice-making does 'not deny the existence of tough decisions – to the contrary ... the exchange or trade-off model fails utterly to explain the toughness of tough decisions. They only conceal the toughness of choice' (Holland 2002: 25).

There is also a tendency to push the instrumental side of dealing with plural values in choice situations. This might be an attempt to shove a plurality of values into a mould, or to misrepresent them, in order to 'make' them commensurable with a particular purpose, for example, for the practice of cost-benefit analysis (MacLean 1998: 110). If the alternatives in a choice situation can be phrased in terms of one overriding criterion or comparable value, then a trade-off might be possible and the conflict lessened – for instance, when export of fish versus fish for domestic consumption is defined as part of a combined strategy for fisheries development. Generally, in environmental-economic theories, this is a common way of looking at choices. But how representative are the situations in which trade-offs seem a feasible way of rational choice making?

Box 14.6 Centralisation vs. decentralisation

Community-level management has received a great deal of interest in fisheries, as have co-management and forms of participatory management. At the same time, there are important efforts at the other end of the scale – the international one – to achieve more sustainable fisheries, based on agreements between countries. At national levels too, governments are involved in regulation that is becoming more complicated all the time. The urge, for example, to work toward integrated coastal zone management reinforces central planning. There is, therefore, a tension between decentralisation and the participation of stakeholders on the one hand, and the centralisation of decision-making on the other. Policy-makers have to decide, within the constraints imposed by broader governmental structure and practice, how to structure the policy-making process and what to structure.

Author: Maarten Bavinck

But what about a choice situation where many values compete for attention, and especially when they are considered to be incommensurable? Then, 'whatever we do would be wrong ... and in part precisely from the absence of a yardstick, a circumstance that leaves us confused...' (Holland 2002: 25). This is exactly the sort of choice where models based upon calculating and aggregating do not work, when we have to look for other ways and means to bring conflicting values together, and come to reasoned instead of calculated outcomes in cost and benefit terms or in other technical or political-economic terms. As Bailey and Jentoft argue, many basic issues in fisheries development are not of these kinds, but are 'hard choices which are fundamentally moral and political rather than economic and technical' (Bailey and Jentoft 1990: 333).

One might say: Follow what has been said about the rationality of dealing with choices of a more simple nature, in other words, apply whatever is known about bounded rationality; stretch those boundaries and broaden the models fit for simple choices to make them also applicable for more difficult or hard choices. However, this seems to be a path that cannot be followed. Denzau and North (2000) argue that this model of substantive rationality does not apply to situations of hard choices. Substantive rationality can be characterised in terms such as minimum modelling, good information, and direct feedback. According to these authors, competitive markets provide the setting for such choices. In their opinion, when dealing with hard choices the false assumption is often made that we can extend the scope of substantive rationality. For those choices 'we must be using some procedure that differs fundamentally from the deductive rational procedure' (Denzau and North 2000: 31). This procedure, in their eyes, is essentially about learning – not direct learning on an individual level, 'because the world is too complex for a single individual to learn directly how it all works' (ibid.: 34), but collective or cultural learning in which ideology and institutions play a crucial role. Institutions and ideology provide human beings with shared mental models that are, according to the authors, needed to interpret and bring order into their environment. (ibid.: 40). This is exactly why we think interactive learning is of such great importance in dealing with hard choices, as the positioning of this way of 'rational' acting at the collective level shows (see figure 14.1). There are models available weighing alternatives based upon different and even incompatible value systems. However, in the last resort, 'socio-political' processes guided by the proper governing institutional arrangements must decide upon which values and whose values should have priority. In order to cope with hard choices, it seems wise that the bearers of the various value systems are allowed to participate in one way or another, in some form of co-governance.

Conclusion

The governance of fisheries needs a thoughtful debate on basic values or principles. Too often attention is concentrated on goals and means, as if there are no real dilemmas and hard choices that cannot be reduced to simple calculation. The underlying and implicit values, norms, and concerns that are always involved in fisheries are therefore concealed, not brought out in the open so that they can be deliberated rationally and democratically. This is, of course, not unique to fisheries. Neither is it something that should be regarded as a personal deficiency of decision-makers. Rather it should be perceived as a consequence of the inherent diversity, complexity, and dynamics of fisheries, the limitations of the rational model in decision-making in dealing with incommensurable values, concerns and principles, and the institutional insufficiency that characterise this industry. Basic principles and concerns, and the more abstract values behind them, require thorough investigations into issues that have no easy answers and where practical applications do not follow clearly. However, when these basic issues are not communicated in a rational fashion, fisheries governance becomes a 'special case', something that is not informed by basic intellectual reasoning, and thus the easy victim of opportunism and strife among special interests.

We argue that the shortcomings of current governance practices in fisheries have much to do with the fact that too much attention is concentrated on the last element of the decision-making process, i.e., means, and too little effort is spent on the basic values, concerns, and principles, which is where any rational decision-making process should start. What makes our governance approach different from any other approach to fisheries problem-solving and opportunity creation is its insistence on the precedence of basic social, economic, political, and environmental values, and on the concerns and principles to be derived from them. Moreover, this governance approach also prescribes some principles and guidelines as to the process through which these basic values, concerns, and principles can be deliberated – a process of inclusion, communication, and cooperation. We will elaborate on this aspect of governance in chapter 16.

A rational approach to fisheries governance would insist that the order of attention should be as follows: 1. values, 2. concerns, 3. principles, 4. goals, and 5. means. Values are the normative and ethical cornerstones on which the working of the fish chain and the institutions regulating and enabling the chain are built. Concerns are the basic problems and opportunities of what fisheries governance wants to realise. Principles are the moral ramifications within which fisheries governance operates and which it should not violate. Goals are the particular ambitions of fisheries governance that may or may not be quantified and specified according to time and place, while means are the technical instruments that governance institutions employ in order to reach goals.

The process through which values, concerns, principles, goals, and means are determined must be open, transparent, and participatory because it is ridden with hard choices all the way. (Examples of hard choices in fisheries are included in the boxes in this chapter.) Should the process at one stage halt because hard choices are too tough, rather than moving ahead with the problem unresolved but suppressed, one should step back by moving the deliberation to the (higher) value level. Thus, the attention of decision-makers should be reversed. Once decision-makers can agree on the basics, they should move forward again.

The governance approach would also emphasise the importance of learning that is inclusive and interactive. This is particularly important in an industry characterised by diversity, complexity, and dynamics. Sometimes means prove ineffective and must be corrected (first-order governance). In other instances, institutional arrangements prove inadequate and need to be changed (second-order governance). In some instances, the concerns and moral values are inadequate and need to be redefined (meta-governance).

The degree of citizen democracy must be larger when the hard choices that confront decision-makers pertain more to values, principles, and concerns than goals and means. In other words, the more basic and normative the issue, the more essential is participation in the broadest sense. The less basic and more derived the issues are, the easier they are to devolve to regulatory agencies and stakeholder groups within a particular sector. When values, concerns, and principles apply not only to fisheries but to other social sectors and industries as well, stakeholder democracy cannot replace citizen democracy, but stakeholder democracy can add to and broaden the democratic process if it involves both market and civil society.

PART V

Prospects for
Fisheries Governance

15

Challenges and Concerns Revisited

Maarten Bavinck, Ratana Chuenpagdee, Poul Degnbol, and José J. Pascual-Fernández

Introduction

In chapter 2, the challenges facing fisheries and aquaculture were briefly described. The crucial issue pointed out is that the drivers for increasing fish production are ubiquitous, multifarious, and strong and that they surpass the capacity of available management systems. The result is a consistent over-demand on natural and social systems and a crisis in fisheries as well as in fisheries governance.

We connected the drivers in fisheries to the globalisation that has been accelerating since 1950. With the sharp rise in the international demand for fish products and the growing connection between local producers and global markets, the pressure to increase production has also grown and new market players have emerged in response. This has resulted in investments and industrialisation in capture fisheries in the North and South alike, and in the growth of aquaculture.

We then identified four concerns that have emerged from the societal debate on fisheries across the globe. Concerns differ from principles in that they do not materialise from systematic top-to-bottom analyses but from political discussions from the bottom up – they constitute fields of attention as well as measuring devices for the results of governance effort. The concerns we presented are 1) ecosystem health, 2) social justice, 3) livelihood and employment, and 4) food security and safety. Each is important to large categories of people now and in the future. Significantly, most of the people affected by the failure to address these concerns live in the South. It is important to note that concerns are related to different population categories in time as well as in space. Ecosystem health is of special importance to future generations, but livelihood and employment and food security are relevant to present ones. Livelihood and employment pertain to people who work in and obtain their income from the fish chain, and food security and safety to the much broader category of the rural and urban poor. Social justice has implications for people at all scale levels, both present and future alike.

We have examined fisheries governance in this volume from many perspectives, dividing the analysis into three parts. The first addresses the constitution and workings of the fish chain, the second the regulatory institutions at various levels from local to international, and the third the principles that actually and those that should underlie fisheries governance. Now we shall link and explicitly explore the relation between the three parts and the concerns voiced earlier. Our key questions are:

- What consequences emerge from our study of the fish chain for *understanding* the concerns (chapters 3-7)?
- How do our principles and ethics affect our *judgement* of the concerns (chapters 12-14)?
- What consequences does our analysis of institutions have for *handling* the concerns (chapters 8-11)?

Note the italicised objective in each question. The first question inquires into a state of knowledge and insight, the second focuses on valuation, and the third on action and control. The sequence of questions differs slightly from the ordering of the parts, with the inquiry into principles preceding the study of institutions. Because of our interest in their potential for addressing the challenges facing fisheries in light of the key principles, we focus on institutional issues last. Sections 2 and 3 discuss our understanding and judgement of the concerns. Section 4 focuses on institutions and consists of three parts. The first considers our understanding of the role of institutions in fisheries, the second the strengths and weaknesses of some of the institutional solutions to fisheries problems currently in vogue, and the third the gaps between disciplinary approaches to fisheries and the possibilities of bridging them.

Understanding the Concerns

Developments in the Fish Chain

Our point of departure is not the present state of knowledge but quite the opposite, the severe lack of information and insight characterising our understanding of the fish chain. What we do not know is sometimes more striking than what we do, and this basic deficiency in our understanding of the system to be governed figures strikingly in chapters 3 to 7. It starts with basic facts. Kulbicki (see chap. 3) notes that there are serious gaps in our knowledge of fish species and their distribution and position in the marine ecosystem, particularly in tropical waters. The dearth of reliable information continues up the chain, also affecting the catch and effort statistics. Figures on catch and effort may be either non-existent or very basic and even if they do exist, they are frequently unreliable. The unreliability of the data is demonstrated by the recent upheaval with regard to Chinese catch statistics (cf. Watson and Pauly 2001).

The lack of reliable data on production is replicated in the figures on employment and income, particularly with regard to the labour-intensive fisheries of the South. Despite the tables that suggest the contrary, the numbers of people working directly in capture fisheries and aquaculture often prove very difficult to estimate. In addition, some of them are indirectly employed, e.g., in the post-harvest system. The very first serious assessment of employment in fish processing and trade was only conducted in 1999 by the International Labour Organization (ILO), and the authors admit the figures are tentative indeed (Tomoda 1999).

The Food and Agriculture Organization (FAO) is aware that the lack of reliable statistics is a serious problem for fisheries management. The matter is all the more urgent because 'as capture fisheries approach maximum yields, scientists require more, and more accurate, data on which to base their analyses' (FAO 2002a: 61). As a consequence of this deficiency and the effects of environmental variability and long-term changes, the organisation concludes that 'there is thus far more uncertainty and risk in fisheries management than there is in the management of almost any other food sector or industry' in the world (ibid.: 59).

Information deficiency carries forward into the understanding of processes and relationships. Kulbicki points out the complexity of aquatic ecosystems and our summary understanding of their workings. Similarly, Johnson et al. (see chap. 4), Pullin and Sumaila (see chap. 5), and Thorpe et al. (see chap. 6) emphasise the complexity and diversity of capturing and post-harvesting systems. The embeddedness of fisheries in a wider economic, social, political, and physical setting and the relations across sector boundaries contribute to the difficulties of knowledge formation.

We have made some inroads in the context of general knowledge deficiency. The key assumption in Part II of this book is that there is something like a fish chain, a linkage between segments of the fisheries sector, with each part adapted to and influencing the others and being influenced in turn. This chain is conceived in a vertical sense, connecting aquatic ecosystems to capture fisheries and aquaculture and subsequently, through a sequence of processors and market intermediaries, to the consumer. The unit moving through the chain from bottom to top is a certain species or category of fish. The unit moving the other way around, from top to bottom, is generally money. Chains have strong geographical connotations, with fish originating in specific aquatic ecosystems in defined parts of the world and proceeding to equally specific processing outfits or fishmeal factories, retail markets, and homes. Likewise, chains are closely connected to people as agents and as part of social structures: fishers and aquaculture workers, men and women, traders and processors, and many others. Many of these people participate in more than one fish chain, shifting back and forth with the flow of events. In many cases, they also take part in economic sectors other than fisheries. The conclusion is that although the fish chain is a concept developed for the purpose of analysis, it has a firm basis in reality.

It is clear that at each level in the fish chain – the ecosystem (pre-harvest), the capture or capturing system, and the post-harvesting system – people and organisms, activities, and events are also interconnected. Ecosystems are assumed to be functional wholes whose workings can be analysed and compared in a horizontal fashion. Capturing systems and post-harvest systems can also be studied from this angle. Diversity, complexity, and dynamics characterise fish chains as well as their constituent elements. Scale is an important dimension, manifesting itself in time, space, and technology.

In our analysis of aquatic ecosystems, we highlight the role of diversity (see chap. 3). There is a strong positive correlation between species diversity and density or biomass in each biotope. As this is the stock or resource potential that fishing is based on, high species diversity raises capturing potential and indirectly contributes to livelihood, employment, and food security. Moreover, species diversity is a major factor in ecosystem health and may serve as an indicator of the condition of a particular ecosystem.

Fishing is defined as a major disturbance affecting aquatic ecosystems. Although there is still a great deal that scientists do not know, no matter how fishing is done it has been demonstrated to have direct and indirect effects on fish as well as on the benthic environment. At a global level, fishing reduces species diversity, sometimes inducing irreversible phase changes. Evidence of stock collapse and fishing down the food web has caused widespread alarm and triggered new projects, such as this book.

However, not all ecosystems are equally disturbed, not all disturbance is bad, and some fishing methods, gear, or activities have more negative consequences than others. One important lesson is to allow for variation according to geographical locale and ecosystem and adjust the governance approach accordingly. Our lack of knowledge on basic ecological processes and the lack of consensus on what actually constitutes ecosystem health are other conditioning factors for governance.

Johnson et al. (see chap. 4) note that diversity is a characteristic of capture fishing systems and a residue of varying historical trajectories and adaptations to the conditions of particular locales. Globalisation has precipitated a reduction in the variety of fishing gear and methods used and a dramatic increase in the fishing effort. Here again, there are differences from one place to another. A core feature of fisheries development since the 1950s is industrialisation, which pertains to the rise of capital-intensive fishing fleets in the North, and, on a different scale, in the South as well. It also pertains to the gradual modernisation of small-scale fishing through new factory-produced fishing gear and methods of propulsion. Both these manifestations of industrialisation have contributed to the overall increase in the fishing effort.

In combination with market globalisation, industrialisation has had important social consequences. In many countries in the North, the fishing sector has shrunk dramatically in terms of employment. In the South, however, small-scale fishing is still pervasive, with major confrontations between industrial and small-scale fishers. Below the surface, the small-scale sector is also changing and new arrangements and divisions are replacing old ones. The primary bone of contention in all the changes is the allocation of benefits. Fishers who have no choice but to use simple technology dispute the rights of more fortunate fishers to what they view as a disproportionate part of the catch. Conflicts of this kind frequently have an intergenerational dimension, with some fishers having larger stakes in the long-term continuity of fishing activities than others. Livelihood, employment, and social justice are crucial concerns here.

The form and structure of capture fishing have changed substantially since the 1950s. The most striking development of the past decade and a half, however, is the leap made by aquaculture (see chap. 5). Its expansion has been so vast that people now often assume aquaculture will play a key role in meeting the market's ever-increasing demand. In terms of food security, however, this assumption is conditional on the development of aquaculture that does not rely on feed from sources that could otherwise have been used for human food. Aquaculture based on fish including fishmeal as feed thus represents a net loss of protein and calories and the market outlets for capture fisheries provided by aquaculture that relies on fish for feed will contribute to increased pressure on marine resources rather than the other way around.

Production in aquaculture continues to mount year by year, with areas of aquatic farming growing and the number of people directly or indirectly involved also increasing. It is important to note that aquaculture generally attracts a different segment of the population than capture fisheries and the benefits go to different categories. Like any other economic activity, aquaculture creates winners and losers at various scale levels.

Aquaculture has any number of implications for the health of inland, coastal, and marine ecosystems. In the course of its short history, it has had negative impacts through pollution, the introduction of alien species, the cutting of mangroves, and the demand for feed from capture fisheries. There are also various kinds of interaction at different scale levels with other economic sectors such as agriculture and tourism, and societal objectives such as conservation. In some developing countries, aquaculture is now bifurcating into two sub-sectors – one producing food for the household or serving local markets and the second targeting the upmarket and taking increasing advantage of global market opportunities. This is to some extent also a division between freshwater and marine aquaculture, although there are exceptions each way. The dynamics, the benefits to society, and the governance challenges of the two sub-sectors are very different. As the fish production in the upmarket sub-sector largely relies on carnivores, its development is presently dependent on feed extraction by capture fisheries.

Post-harvest systems link capture fishing and aquaculture to the market in many intricate ways. For Thorpe et al. (see chap. 6) the key variable is scale, with different chains serving markets at different scale levels. For countries in the South, the distinction between domestic and international markets is currently the most important one, as it has created different patterns of demand. In combination with a priority for food safety, the international demand for luxury fish products appears to exert a decisive influence down the food chain, influencing the activities of individual fishers and fisheries sectors as a whole. The dynamics of the international fish market have implications for the food security of the domestic poor. The drive for efficiency and food quality also causes capital concentration in fish capture and production, as well as in the post-harvest chain. This process may have consequences for employment and social justice.

The Fish Chain and the Four Concerns

Having sketched the total picture, what are the trends in our four concerns? The first concern, ecosystem health, is the key issue in all capture fisheries. Attention is now focused on halting the decline of target species, as well as on marine ecosystems as a whole. Fishing is considered a major factor in their downfall. The growing global fishing effort follows from an absolute increase in the number of fishers as well as the use of more efficient gear. Behind these developments in the capture system loom increased demands for fish products in a globalising market and an inflow of workers to fisheries due to the shortage of alternative job opportunities. Changes in capture and market structures can thus be related to ecosystem health. There are, however, other factors such as pollution, habitat destruction, and climate change that influence aquatic ecosystem health. As is noted in this book, their origin and their solution lie outside the fisheries sector. Ecosystem health is an important concern in aquaculture as well. The externalities caused by aquaculture operations and development are the main issue here. In addition, there is the connection between capture fisheries and aquaculture, mainly through the feed industry.

Social justice, our second concern, comes up repeatedly in any consideration of the capture and post-harvest system or the relation between fisheries and other economic sectors. In fact, there are various social justice concerns at different scale levels. Concern about inequality in the division of labour between the North and the South, which continually manifests itself in new ways, is at the high-end of the scale, as are claims pertaining to inter-generational justice. In the middle there are conflicts between industrial and small-scale fishers about the allocation of resources, and gender-related confrontations between large and small market parties. Communities also pursue social justice and are affected by new developments, such as the reallocation of fishing rights. Lastly, there are numerous justice issues at the individual or household level. From this wider perspective, it is difficult to estimate whether social justice is declining or increasing, with the answer depending on perspective as well as scale level.

The third concern is livelihood and employment, which is different in each situation. The FAO (2002a) indicates that the number of fishers and fish farmers has increased from 1970 to 2000 across the globe. The rate of employment growth is extremely variable though, with European fisheries demonstrating the least development (<20% on average, with the workforce in some developed countries even shrinking) and Asian fisheries the most (>300% on average). Similar timelines are not available for the post-harvest sector, though it is also likely to have witnessed substantial growth in the rate of employment.

In the future, the FAO (2002a) argues that in rich economies with steady economic growth, the fisheries labour force will shrink. In poor countries with more stagnant economies and insufficient employment alternatives, however, capture fisheries will probably continue to absorb large numbers of newcomers. Their situation may come to resemble the involution characteristic of Indonesian farmers in the 1960s, making do with smaller and smaller parcels of land and diminishing overall returns (Geertz 1966).

There are also indications of changes in the nature of livelihoods in fisheries. The industrialisation of fisheries noted in chapter 4 has had major effects on the use of labour and will probably continue to do so. The changes in the post-harvest sector, especially the globalisation of trade and the movement towards consumer-driven, food safety-oriented markets, also have implications for the nature of livelihoods in the sector.

The last concern is food security and safety, which is defined as the contribution of fisheries to the availability of sufficient, safe, and nutritious food for the world's non-fishing poor (in contrast to the world's fishing poor, who are discussed under the heading of employment and livelihood). Recent documents note the continued relevance of under-nourishment and food security in the world. According to *The state of food insecurity in the world 2003* (FAO 2003h), the number of undernourished people across the developing world as a whole is again rising to an estimated 798 million (figures 1999-2001). The number of chronically hungry people fell in some countries, but in many others it rose.

Although a great deal has been written about the real and potential role of fisheries in providing food security, the evidence of actual trends has been scarce. Do the poor have more access to seafood than before or less? It is argued that globalisation and the orientation of fishers towards the international market may have reduced the availability of cheap fish for the non-fishing poor in the South. However, the development of aquaculture is sometimes considered relevant to domestic markets, thus contributing to food security. A recent study of fish supply and demand in changing global markets until 2020 (Delgado et al. 2003) projects that global per capita fish consumption in 2020 will range from 14.2 kg per capita in a scenario of extreme ecological collapse in capture fisheries to 19.0 kg per capita in a scenario with faster investment in aquaculture, while a baseline scenario indicates 17.1 kg per capita. This compares with an estimated 15.7 kg per capita in 1997. The study concludes that

> 'growth in fish consumption will very likely continue, but it will be driven primarily by the developing countries. Moreover, growth will occur slightly more in high-value than in low-value items, except in India and the rest of South Asia. Overall consumption of food fish will overwhelmingly occur in developing countries, where the effects of population growth will combine with consumer desire for a larger, diversified food basket'.

Urbanisation is identified as an important factor in the growth of developing country fish consumption. The supply for this increase is expected to come from aquaculture, mainly in developing countries. Real prices for fish products, including prices for low-value fish, are expected to rise and generally become more expensive relative to meat and other food products. The implications are heavy pressure on capture fisheries, a link between aquaculture and capture fisheries leading to increased prices for low-value capture fish, and a shift in 'fishing pressure from output fish (such as salmon) to input fish (such as capelin)'. Concerning the outlook for the poor, the study concludes that

> 'the outlook is not especially good ... On the consumption side, it seems likely that over time the poor who used to get small amounts of animal protein from small fish are likely to substitute milk and meat as meat and milk calories become cheaper relative to fish. The nutritional impact of this is not known, but at minimum it will be necessary for the poor in question to increase their total consumption of animal protein despite rising prices of fish'.

Judgement of the Concerns

Bavinck and Chuenpagdee (see chap. 12) describe the current international principles in terms of how they address the concerns of ecosystem health, social justice, livelihood and employment, and food security and food safety. The next step is to relate the principles to the governance approach prescribed in this book and discuss the connections. Following the division introduced in chapter 1, we distinguish first-order, second-order, and meta-order governance. The principles we suggest should structure them are discussed more fully in chapter 13.

First-Order Governance Principles

First-order governance focuses on the resolution of day-to-day problems and the realisation of fisheries management goals. Rationality of action is a key principle and sub-principles deal with sustainability, precaution, and the economic efficiency of fisheries operations. There is an obvious link between these first-order principles and the ones currently prescribed. The precautionary approach in the Code of Conduct for Responsible Fisheries (CCRF) and other principles promoting ecosystem health are complementary. At this level of governance, the precautionary approach in fisheries management directly promotes sustainability and results in food security. However, there are some complications as efforts are made to achieve social justice, good livelihoods, and food security at the same time. In fact, the problems with fisheries today, whether related to ecosystem health, such as overfishing and habitat degradation, or to unequal access to food, suggest we have not been able to effectively adopt the principles that can lead to economic efficiency and sustainability. So, although balancing between environmental, economic, and social considerations is evidently one of the fisheries management objectives, mechanisms to facilitate it are not clearly identified.

At the basis of economic efficiency, the total market and non-market values of resources need to be properly incorporated. This involves traditional monetary valuation techniques as well as innovative valuation approaches such as generational cost-benefit analysis (Sumaila 2001) and the non-monetary damage schedule approach (Chuenpagdee et al. 2001). Unfortunately, only generational cost-benefit analysis has been widely practiced despite its shortcomings, and often results in the promotion of unsustainable fishing practices. Moreover, the use of inappropriate incentives in many fishing nations, such as subsidies on fuel prices and for the development of fisheries using destructive gear (e.g., trawlers in the Gulf of Thailand) widens the gap between economic efficiency, sustainability, and precaution. Subsidies counteract sustainability by promoting catch capacity beyond the carrying capacity of the resources and have been shown to mainly benefit large-scale operators. They are thus the sources of equity issue concerns as discussed below in the second-order principles section.

On the positive side, many of the principles for ecosystem health, particularly the CCRF principles on sound fisheries management and good fishing practices that minimise waste, improve product quality and extend to sustainable aquaculture development, are supportive of this level of governance. Initiatives by the Marine Stewardship Council for certifying seafood products and the whole process encourage economic efficiency, particularly when they are conducted to achieve conservation and the wise use of fisheries and marine resources and are not used as a marketing tool by industries. Efforts to raise awareness and build capacity at the local level as prescribed in many principles can also lead to sustainability in the long run. It should be noted, however, that while the need for ecosystem-based research and training is recognised in the CCRF, training on economic and social research is not yet emphasised.

Second-Order Governance Principles

Second-order governance relates to institutions and is particularly concerned with their responsiveness. It has three aspects, respect, inclusiveness, and equity. These are critical to the pursuit of social justice, livelihood and employment, and food security. Here, things seem to be more consistent than in the first-order level, at least in principle. For example, the United Nations Convention on the Law of the Sea (UNCLOS) aims to give the use of the seas and the oceans legitimacy, peace, and order. The ILO Conventions and Declarations aim to promote equitable rights for everyone. The notion of rights in these statements is noteworthy since they include the rights of small-scale fishers to engage in fishing activities, rights to a healthy lifestyle, and rights to adequate, safe, and nutritious food. It is not surprising that access is an important aspect of the discussion related to these principles. Recent debates on access and property rights in fisheries suggest a need for revolutionary thought involving a different system of rights, such as community fishing rights allocated through an open-bid system (Bromley and Macinko 2002). In some ways, this is a mechanism to ensure that the allocation of rights does not favour large-scale operators, as is often the case.

Another interesting emphasis in the CCRF is on ensuring food security and poverty alleviation for present and future generations. While this is an admirable initiative, its implementation is extremely difficult, considering that even in the current generation, the societal gap between those who have and those who have not is large. More often than not, consideration for future generations is explicitly stated as a principle, and we tend to believe that what we express in terms of our choices and actions is for the benefit of our children and grandchildren. However, incorporating the values of future generations requires serious re-interpretation of current economic theory, which not too many economists are prepared or pleased to do.

Incorporating all the stakeholders in management and decision-making, i.e., others in the coastal areas as well as fishers and fisheries-related people, is equally challenging. Integrating fisheries into coastal area management simply means multiplying the numbers of actors and issues as well as management conflicts. Integrated coastal zone management (ICZM), widely accepted as an approach to deal with such complexity, also involves a thorough understanding of coastal resource systems, the impacts of human activities on these systems, and the social, cultural, and economic values of the resources. Needless to say, these are daunting tasks and there are very few good examples of ICZM around the world.

The inclusiveness principle, requiring the involvement of all the stakeholders and the integration of local and scientific knowledge, can help facilitate our understanding of the systems and minimise the conflicts. More importantly, it can lead to an exploration of alternative jobs outside fishing. This trend is observed in several fishing communities where tourism is bringing additional income to fishing households that participate in the activities, such as adapting fishing boats to serve tourists and providing lodging in their homes.

Many principles encourage regional and international collaboration in the conservation and management of fisheries and coastal resources. These initiatives enhance the overall management capability of coastal states and help provide a level playing field for everyone. It should be noted, however, that the equity principle needs to be rigorously practiced to ensure fair opportunities for countries of different sizes and economy scales.

Meta-Governance Principles

Meta-governance is related to ethics and its main principle is responsibility. While it is not directly addressed by any of the initiatives for ecosystem health, the Convention on Biological Diversity's (CBD) aim of maintaining biological diversity is founded on ethical issues and responsibility and suggests harmonising man and the ecosystem (CBD 1994). Together with the precautionary principle, this can result in greater ecosystem health and food security at all levels. The principles that support social justice, livelihood and employment, and food security address ethical issues more directly. In particular, the fundamental rights of people to access safe and nutritious food are based on high ethical grounds. This is the most challenging principle, especially in a modern society that relies heavily on the market economy and in a world where many people may feel threatened and insecure.

As is noted in *Global Environmental Outlook* (UNEP 2002), when a lack of security is a real prospect in the world, people do not care much about each other and most of them tend to withdraw into their own secure world, as is already clear from gated communities in various parts of the world. At this level of principle, it might also be wise to revisit gender roles and conservation issues and the protection of ecosystems in promoting social justice and improving everyone's livelihood and food security.

Searching for Institutional Solutions

Institutions to Address the Concerns

Institutions, i.e., the organisations as well as the rules, norms, values, and knowledge that facilitate communication, are crucial to fisheries problems. They have been discussed at length in Parts II and III of this book. In this section, we gather some of the threads of the argument and explore the consequences of the institutional state of affairs in addressing our four concerns. In doing so, we leave the institutional design and best fit, which are so important to policy-makers, to the side.

As Suarez de Vivero et al. (see chap. 10) point out, fisheries institutions present 'a confused and complex panorama'. An enormous assortment of organisations engages in fisheries management at all levels and locations, and the number of rules, norms, and instruments is overwhelming. There are many variations in the range and effectiveness of the institutions and in the measures of agreement and cooperation or disagreement and opposition.

The institutions are divided in this volume into those of the state, the market, and civil society. Depending on the perspective of the observer, the values attributed to these parties and the contributions they are expected to make to fisheries governance differ.

Despite the criticism of its functioning, the state continues to occupy a major position in most fisheries management perspectives. The political reality of power is a major rationale. Although international institutions have obviously become stronger in recent decades, in the field of fisheries they continue to rely heavily on state support. Suarez de Vivero notes that the state has actually seen its authority over fisheries increase with the ratification of UNCLOS and the extension of its jurisdiction to 200 nm. Another reason to emphasise the state is because it is the only authority with sufficient legitimacy (see chap. 9).

All authors in Part III of this volume note however that the state is a complex body with parts pointing in various directions. Departments of Fisheries and Aquaculture may have different goals than Departments of the Environment or Economic Affairs. What is more, local bodies may have different agendas than provincial or national ones. States vary greatly in their responsiveness to public issues and demands. There are autocratic states and states run by the few and powerful for their own interests. Other states are singularly weak and incapable of any action at all. Some states are genuinely interested in devolution and the promotion of participation, and others are centralised to the extreme. Flexibility and strategic thinking with regard to the role of the state thus emerge as central elements in any governance approach.

Market forces are among the main drivers for globalisation and the ever-increasing exploitation of marine resources. They are an essential part of the problem, and in as far as problems are tackled at their roots, they are a necessary ingredient of any solution. It is not surprising that market reforms should figure in most governance approaches, including those of the World Trade Organization and the anti-globalisation movement. In contemporary fisheries management, market considerations play a significant role, e.g., in the promotion of transferable property rights and certification, or in coming to grips with subsidies.

Alluding to the supposed limitations of the state, the market is promoted as a management mechanism. Rather than the state applying itself to fisheries management, for example through subsidies, the market is presented as a way to find an optimal solution. Individual Transferable Quotas (ITQs) are an example of market-based regulations primarily based on an understanding of the optimal solution, defined as economic efficiency. But some authors in this volume, especially Suarez de Vivero et al. (see chap. 10), are fervent opponents of this tendency, which contributes to the growth of multinationals and capitalism and the impoverishment of some segments of society. The debate reveals how many competing criteria there are for the optimal solution, including equity, sustainability, and governance issues, in addition to economic efficiency. The basic concerns discussed in this volume can also be seen as a discussion of multidimensional optimality. Solutions based exclusively on the market cannot automatically be expected to address this multidimensional optimum. In many cases, the situation differs in the South and the North. Rather than leading to economic efficiency, in some cases in the South a reduction of the role of the state has led to a political vacuum, banditism, and monopolisation, which has proven suboptimal, even from a strictly economic perspective. The failure of privatisation in the North in relation to equity and sharing the resource rent of common resources with the greater society once again reveals the importance of the state versus the market.

Although civil society manifests itself in various ways and exists at all levels of society, in this book it features most prominently in the discussion of communities and the local level of fisheries governance (see chap. 8). Community institutions frequently play a constructive role in managing common pool resources such as capture fisheries and in providing social justice, employment, and food security. More generally, we argue that fishers' organisations and non-governemental organisations embody expertise, capabilities, and insights that are valuable for fisheries governance. These inputs have often been overlooked in the past, with distrust prevailing between government and science-based organisations on the one hand and user groups and their representatives on the other. Slowly, however, bridges are being built. Co-management has emerged as one of the useful frameworks for this process.

Means to Address the Concerns – Remedies

The concerns need to be addressed within the governance principles and through the institutions of the state, the market, and civil society. The governance principles and institutions addressed so far at the abstract level apply generally, but it is impossible to derive specific solution models that apply universally. Each case has to be judged on its own merits within the boundaries of governance principles and based on the institutions' own experiences. In identifying ways to address the concerns, issues of nestedness, horizontal and vertical problems of agreement (diversity of goals and values), and problems of cooperation (unwillingness to work together, recognising each other's contribution) all need to be addressed.

Nestedness, Agreement and Co-operation

The contradictions that emerge between governance principles as they are applied, and the varying political discourses to which actors in their choice of solutions refer, constitute major challenges. The solution is to focus on processes rather than outcomes. There is no automatic optimal balance between what may seem to be contradictory principles. Political discourses can only arrive at compromises through dialogue and a willingness to compromise.

In specifying ways to address the concerns, we should start by identifying the stakeholders, their interests, and the scale of the issues to be addressed. Scale is a major determinant of institutional solutions because institutions are set up very differently if the scale of the issue is such that it can be addressed entirely at the local level with direct participation of the parties involved. It is a very different matter if the scale is global and requires interaction among governments. The scale of an issue relates to the scale of the underlying biological resource system, the social organisation of the fish chain and the norms that apply. Fisheries management in a small lake supporting subsistence fisheries would merit local management with direct participation. Even in this case, though, there would be a need to develop mechanisms to relate to norms at a larger scale. After all, an international agreement such as the Convention on Biological Diversity would also apply in this local context if the government of the country where the lake is located has signed it. In practice, this means there will always be an element of state involvement, even in local management arrangements.

The management of larger-scale systems where direct participation is no longer possible can be addressed through representation and nested institutions. A hierarchy of management institutions is developed and stakeholders participate indirectly through representation. In systems of this kind, accountability and transparency are crucial to positive outcomes in terms of legitimacy, inclusiveness, and equity (second-order governance principles). There is a risk in nested institutions of the direct discussion of knowledge and interests being replaced by coercion and power plays. This can be counteracted through responsibility (meta-governance principle) on the part of everyone involved, checked by institutionalised accountability and transparency.

The development of solutions does not start from a blank slate. All fisheries operate through existing institutions, involving various blends of the state, the market, and civil society. The people who advise on solutions and the ones who make the decisions each have their own perceptions of the causes of problems and their own experiences with various types of solutions. The situation and the perceptions thereof influence and limit the choice of solutions to be decided upon and prescribed.

The starting point is the present situation, and it will induce path dependence in the process. Transitions are always required, but path dependence may also develop into a long-term limitation on management options. There are, for example, the long-term consequences of decisions pertaining to the distribution of access rights. They may be the most fundamental decisions made in a fisheries management system and can be very difficult to change once they have been made. If access rights are defined as a percentage of the quantities of each species caught, the management system is bound to rely mainly on single species catch quotas. If access rights are defined as territorial user rights, area-based management tools will play a key role. This may seem trivial but it has far-reaching consequences if and when fisheries are affected by internationalisation, technological advances, or the exploitation of new species or areas. Management tools that seemed reasonable in the starting situation may prove counterproductive or even disruptive, but may be very difficult to abandon because of the distribution implications.

An example is the European Union's policy of relative stability. The distribution of fishing access among nations in the first common fisheries policy starting in 1983 was locked into a percentage of the annual total available catch (TAC) for each stock separately, based on historical catches. To-day, a single stock TAC-based management system has demonstrated its inability to manage the mixed fisheries characterising most European de-mersal fisheries. Because of the path dependency originating from the de-cision on the distribution key in 1982, it has proven very difficult to develop more adequate solutions.

Perceptions of the problems to be addressed and experiences from other fisheries systems are increasingly globalised via the debate on fisheries in international political and technical circles and the media. Specific solu-tions may be promoted across the globe as panaceas on the basis of real or perceived positive experiences in some specific situations. Panaceas of this kind may represent an imbalanced focus on the problems in other situa-tions. Solutions with a strong emphasis on increased state intervention may be relevant in cases where the market functions well but where effects outside the market need to be addressed. However, solutions with a strong emphasis on market forces may be relevant in cases where distortions of the market such as subsidies lead to overinvestment, ecological unsustain-ability or low economic efficiency. Solutions of this kind cannot automati-cally be transferred to other situations where the local problems are very different. Individual transferable quotas and marine protected areas are two examples of solutions that are relevant in specific situations, but are also being promoted as global panaceas.

Example 1: Individual transferable quotas

One of the best examples of the global extrapolation of an unbalanced man-agement focus is the ITQ paradigm. It is linked to the management of sin-gle-species fisheries, primarily in industrialised countries, but also extends to many other areas in the world. In this case, the role of scientific institu-tions in charge of evaluating the allowable catch in the stocks and the mod-els designed by economists to minimise capital expenditures allocating transferable property rights have changed the lifestyle of fishing popula-tions in many areas of the world.

In fisheries, the system was invented by resource economists at the University of British Columbia in the early 1970s, exported to the rest of Canada, Australia, and New Zealand by the early 1980s, and then adopted by Iceland, the Netherlands, the United States and other countries. There are several reasons why this model has become so popular. Firstly, the ana-lysis is simple and the solution concrete. The solution follows logically from the premises of the analysis. If open access is the problem, then some form of access restriction is needed. This simple answer led to licen-sing programmes, but by the 1980s they were doing poorly in promoting more efficiency, hence the shift to ITQs, which allot specific and transfer-able amounts or shares of a quota to participants in a fishery. Secondly, ITQs provide an answer to a serious problem in fisheries, i.e., overcapitali-sation. Today, there is far too much fishing capacity for the resources available. As has been shown in the surf clam and ocean quahog ITQ system of the United States (McCay and Brandt 2001), once ITQs are implemented, fleet tonnage, a measure of capacity, can decline significantly as vessel owners economise. These are the two most widespread reasons for the popularity of ITQs. Thirdly, ITQs are in perfect harmony with current neo-liberal economic policies and the belief in the supremacy of the market. Fourthly, the popularity of ITQs may also be related to the much stronger involvement and prestige of economists in state bureaucracies compared to other social scientists, such as anthropologists or sociologists who prefer other solutions to the commons problems and who tend to see the tragedy as neither natural nor inevitable, but as a result of the erosion of community (McCay and Jentoft 1998).

Criticism has been voiced on the feasibility and social impact of ITQs. For instance, ITQs are more feasible in temperate waters, where there is less biodiversity, than in tropical waters. ITQs may work well in single-species fisheries, but are useless if fishing cannot target specific stocks, as is noted by the economist Hanneson in the case of Kerala (Kurien 2002). But ITQs are also controversial in developed Northern countries, partly because of their distributional impacts. As the economist Copes, whose research mainly draws on the Canadian experience, notes, 'The problem is that this theoretical case for superiority [of ITQs] is highly dependent on gross simplifications embedded in the implicit or explicit assumptions, which remove the ITQ mode from the real world of fisheries'. He further claims that 'ITQs are prone to external diseconomies that impose a variety of costs on society, invalidating in large measure the theoretical claims of efficiency' (Copes 1997: 65). Copes is troubled by the social inequities that ITQs tend to create between small and large scale, between license holders and crew, and between generations of fishers. Over time, ITQs also tend to become geographically concentrated, removing the only conditions some coastal communities have for survival. This has been well documented in the case of Iceland. Helgason and Pálsson (1998) express fundamental criticism of the use of the ITQ model in fisheries, arguing that ITQs fall within the tendency to regard the world in idealised terms, and then act to make the ideal real. In Carrier's words, 'the virtual becomes a blueprint for the real' (Carrier 1998: 8). Then, the tragedy of the commons becomes a self-fulfilling prophecy. If fishers are not *homo economicus* in the narrow sense of the term at the outset, i.e., atomised, ego-centred profit-maximisers, ITQs turn them into precisely that. Helgason and Palsson see the alternative as a management model firmly embedded in empirical reality, a model that fits the social and cultural context in which it is supposed to operate. These critics propose an alternative perspective that addresses a complex reality and reject the advantages of oversimplifying models that only try to optimise some variables such as capital investment or fleet tonnage. The social consequences of divesting coastal communities and their residents of access rights to the resources can be extremely significant in the long term. The concentration of boats with fishing rights in some harbours can even lead to the depopulation of large coastal areas. Since they are considered externalities, the costs of these processes are often not taken into account in the economic analysis of the efficiency of these measures.

Example 2: Aquatic protected areas[1]

Aquatic protected areas, such as marine reserves or marine protected areas (MPAs), constitute one of the emergent measures developed to guarantee the conservation and viability of many fisheries. At the first World Conference on National Parks held in Seattle, Washington (US) in 1962, a recommendation was passed to advise the governments of the world to establish marine parks or marine reserves to protect endangered habitats in their shallow waters (Bacallado et al. 1989: 17). The recommendation has been taken into account all over the world, especially in recent years (Munro and Willison 1998; Shackell and Willison 1995). In 1970, there were 118 marine protected areas in 27 nations, by 1980 the figure had increased to 319 (Silva et al. 1986), and in 1995 there were more than 1,300 (Boersma and Parrish 1999; Kelleher et al. 1995). This number has probably increased substantially since then.

The decline in biological diversity and productivity in many areas due to fishing, alterations of coastal spaces, tourism, and so forth has led to the promotion of alternative management approaches geared towards conserving and restoring biological diversity and productivity, especially in critical ecosystems (National Research Council 2001). Generally speaking, aquatic protected areas have a 'fundamental role as a common-sense and flexible tool for providing holistic protection to marine species, habitats, and ecological processes' (Kelleher and Recchia 1998: 2), avoiding the risks of traditional fisheries resource management measures for ecosystems and seabeds. Another reason these areas are created is to allow the fish populations to reach their full reproductive age in the protected area so as to enhance recruitment. The surrounding areas are the immediate recipients of fish spill-over from the reserves (Kelly et al. 2002). The conservation measures intend to preserve ecosystems as a whole in all their complexity and diversity and to reduce the interference of human activities, especially fishing.

There is a great deal of variety in the design of these conservation measures. In the Canary Islands, the reserve core is an area of integral protection, an ecological reserve in the typology of the National Research Council (2001), where almost any human activity is forbidden except for strictly research purposes, and even in that case only under the supervision of the authorities. On the margins of this no-take zone, there is frequently a cushion area with many restrictions. Lastly, in the remaining zone professional fishing is allowed under certain conditions, along with recreational activities such as scuba diving or even sports fishing, also with many restrictions.

Protected zones have advantages and disadvantages for fishers who work in the area. One advantage may be the increase in captures due to the spill-over effect in the surrounding areas. In this sense, protected areas are useful if they somehow increase the total fisheries production of the region. There is virtual unanimity in the biological sciences about the benefits of these measures, but some critics note that it may not be the definitive solution to overfishing problems (cf. Shipp 2002, 2003). From an economic point of view, several authors tend to be sceptical of the aggregate benefits in the fisheries sector of the protected areas (Farrow and Sumaila 2002), no matter how many other benefits may derive from them. One consequence of the creation of protected areas is the increased flow of tourists attracted by the natural values of the area, assured by the classification as marine reserve. The tourists' activities may generate relevant impacts on the protected areas, but they also constitute an economic alternative for the fishers, who have been restricted in their activities. However, in many cases, and in the MPAs of the Canary Islands in particular, it is frequently not the local people who take advantage of these new economic opportunities, it is non-fishing or even foreign people who have an important role in the diving clubs, restaurants, hotels, boat trips, and so on. Economic models of protected areas usually take into account extractive activities, but in many areas, as in the Canary Islands, tourism-related activities need to be taken into account since the winners and losers may be different groups. In this context, the opportunity for local fishing populations to participate in eco-tourism activities related to the reserve may constitute an interesting alternative for maintaining their income levels (Boncoeur et al. 2002).

Up to now, tourism has received only marginal attention from most scientists collaborating in the design of MPAs. However, it is not uncommon for the politicians who demand the installation of these areas to clearly consider the effects of an increasing influx of quality tourism focused on nature. Marine reserves receive the same kind of attention from tourists as inland national parks (Roberts and Hawkins 2000), since people assume that the marine life will be interesting or unusual.

The protected areas could offer fishers important opportunities to improve their standards of living, but in fact they are frequently limited by specific regulations. Fishers in Spain are prohibited by law from using their fishing boats to take tourists to visit or even fish in some areas. This limits their chances of improving their standard of living and reducing their fishing effort. If the MPAs were linked to part-time alternative activities that valued the fishers' knowledge and abilities, reducing the necessity to extract marine resources, the effects of these measures would probably be much more adapted to the needs of the local populations (Pascual-Fernández et al. 2001; Roberts and Hawkins 2000).

This means the design of protected areas not only affects the fish populations, in a very relevant way it also affects the human communities that depend on those areas. Frequently, the design efforts focus on the non-human populations in an area, overlooking the fact that local communities may depend on these resources and it may even be essential to get their consent and participation in the implementation process. Surveillance and enforcement costs are one of the main difficulties in setting up these measures in a top-down scheme, but if they are created in collaboration with local institutions and communities, local people may assume some of these duties.

Management models of aquatic protected areas oscillate between top-down schemes linking their implementation and administration to state institutions that constantly monitor the protected territory, and community-based systems that place resource control in the hands of the local population, which has many advantages and also some possible inconveniences (Roberts and Hawkins 2000). The effectiveness of protection measures increases with user collaboration in administration and surveillance duties.

However, this model is not always feasible, as Robert Wade outlined some years ago. There are preconditions of collective action that may vastly facilitate common property regimes and community administration (Wade 1992 [1987]). For example, a bounded and not too large population with a sense of community and with institutions already in charge of solving problems related to natural resources may facilitate the co-management of protected areas. Top-down state management of these institutions does not guarantee the sustainable use of the resources (Pascual-Fernández 1993).

In general, aquatic protected areas are included on the global agendas of international institutions and decision makers and in the plans of development agencies and environmental groups. Even in the scientific arena, there is a growing tendency to consider the creation of protected areas a holy grail in fishing management. Further social and natural science research may lead to greater understanding of the practical benefits of these measures and the consequences of their implementation for various user groups. In many cases, they may constitute examples of good governance measures, but they can sometimes lead to conflicts due to a lack of local participation in the creation process or in the institutions devised for their management.

One of the polemic issues pertains to how large these protected areas need to be for them to be effective in a local and global perspective (see chap. 4). In this sense, the scale aspect constitutes a crucial element in the implementation of these measures. In the short run, the transformations induced in global or local fisheries by these new institutions may produce new tensions, increasing the global dynamics in the system. In the long run, however, they may be diminished as a result of better management of the resources and ecosystems.

The Cognitive Remedy – Crossing the Interdisciplinary Divide

There are many things we do not know about the fish chain and institutional options. This should not lead to the conclusion, though, that this lack of knowledge is the main impediment to action. There is enough natural science knowledge of the ecological problems of fisheries to identify the specific action required and to move in a more ecologically sustainable direction, which would also serve the food security of future generations. In most fisheries world-wide, a reduction in the overall fishing pressure is called for and can be achieved by combining reduced fishing capacity and effort with fishing practices that have fewer impacts on habitats.

Improved knowledge on the fish chain and institutional options may not be needed to guide immediate action, but in the longer term it is crucial to ensure that whatever processes are initiated are monitored and adapted according to the lessons learnt underway. The major gap is in the integration of various types of knowledge which, when used in isolation, may lead to poorly advised solutions or even conflicts. In the past, extreme consequences of disciplinary isolation could be observed when biologists advised closed areas or quota control in certain situations without the institutional capacity to decide and implement the measures.

Social scientists have similarly advised community-based resource management systems to deal with resources that are steered by ecological processes on a much larger scale than can be handled on the local scale. It is easy to ridicule extreme cases along these lines, but less extreme advice that still exhibits the same kind of blindness to other aspects than the ones addressed by the advisor's discipline is still ubiquitous and can be an obstacle.

Another reason knowledge needs to be integrated is related to legitimacy and inclusiveness. To achieve legitimacy, and as a necessary component of a co-management institution where fishers take responsibility for implementation, it is often noted that fishers' and other users' knowledge should serve as a basis for decisions. However, it is difficult in actual practice to find a way to achieve this kind of inclusion. This is a reflection of the considerable discourse differences resulting from the differing practices of fishers and researchers. It has proven difficult to incorporate fishers' knowledge in management institutions based on the knowledge requirements formulated and rationalised in the language of research. Efforts to incorporate local knowledge may be rather extractive and alienated from the users if local knowledge is selected and re-rationalised to meet the formal criteria of management institutions.

So, in terms of knowledge, it is hard to include fishers in management institutions by simply allowing biologists to extract and translate fishers' knowledge. Social scientists need to help identify the conditions for the common ground between research-based and local knowledge and respect the local as well as the research discourse. Social scientists also have a responsibility to assist in identifying management institutions that are able to absorb multiple sources of knowledge without needing them all interpreted and translated. In itself, including users in management institutions is an example of the need for interdisciplinary co-operation.

Conclusion

In this chapter we have discussed developments in fisheries and aquaculture from the perspective of real-life concerns that affect people all across the globe presently and in the future. It is precisely because of real or perceived impacts on people's lives and conflicting valuations that alternate courses of action have become highly politicised. Policy-makers consequently face hard choices (see chap. 14).

From a governance perspective, the diversity, complexity, and dynamics of the system to be governed are striking. Fish chains are so varied, complex, and in flux that in order to be effective, governing systems can only adapt and take on similar characteristics. The scale levels where governance takes place are of particular importance. We have pointed out the need to determine the appropriate scale level for governance in any situation and the need for connections between the governance at various scale levels.

The fact that fish chains involve so many actors has special implications for governance. At various points in this volume, we note that governance is not the prerogative of government, it is also carried out by market and civil society actors. It is only by considering the interaction between the various actors that governance can potentially become more effective. But for this to occur, there has to be some notion of partnership. Mahon et al. (see chap. 17) further explore this topic. Partnership would seem to be especially important if and when the system to be governed is undergoing a major transition. This is clearly the case in contemporary capture fisheries and aquaculture, where crisis and opportunity alternately emerge.

Note

1. This section is partially based on findings of the project entitled 'Marine reserves and littoral fishing populations: impacts and strategies for sustainable development' (REN 2001-3350/MAR), funded by the Ministry of Science and Technologie of Spain and the European Regional Development Fund, and directed by José J. Pascual-Fernández.

16

Governance and Governability

Jan Kooiman and Ratana Chuenpagdee

A Synthesis

This entire book is based on a governance perspective. In the previous chapters, this perspective has been used to structure many ideas and findings on fisheries governance. The present chapter will try to show that experiences with governing fisheries, although still being played out in different parts of the world and in varying social and economic settings, can still be looked at in a coherent manner. This coherence can be implicitly or explicitly demonstrated in activities at the fish chain level, in the institutions supporting or limiting those activities, and in the principles guiding fisheries and its governance. It can also be expressed in the ways in which activities, institutions, and principles are linked. In other words, the governance perspective that has been an analytical tool up to this point in this book can also be used in a synthesised manner. That is the goal of this chapter.

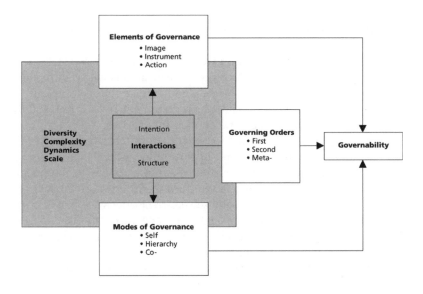

Fig. 16.1 A synthesised scheme for governance.

Governance and the Fish Chain

The governance approach applies to fisheries throughout the entire fish chain – from pre-capture (i.e., fish in its natural ecosystem), capture (i.e., capture and culture of fish), to post-harvest (i.e., processing and distributing fish and fish products to consumer). The phrase 'fish chain' is used here to emphasise the inter-connection between its parts, acknowledging that the three features operating within and between components would earn them the phrase 'fish web'. In ecosystems, they represent natural phenomena, in capture and aquaculture their emphasis is on human-nature interfaces, while in post-harvest they stand mostly for human-human inter-relations.

Knowledge of fish chains and their interactions varies since some have been studied thoroughly, while others scarcely. For example, we know much about interactions within and among households as pivotal entities in catching or farming fish, and about communities as their contexts. Interactions in other parts of chains are, however, less known, such as interactions in the global market place and the systems they are part of. Governance of fisheries starts with paying systematic attention to the primary and governing interactions at and among all levels. Lack of such attention accounts for poor results of many management practices in fisheries.

> It is not the actions of those involved in fish chains and their governance per se that need attention, but rather the interactions in the systems that they comprise.

Governance Features: Diversity, Complexity, and Dynamics

Diversity, complexity, and dynamics are useful notions to describe, analyse, and govern fisheries chains. Diversity is seen as qualitative differences within and between interacting societal and natural entities, complexity as the multiple relations within and between these entities or actors, and dynamics as tensions within and between their interactions.

Present-day fisheries derive their strengths from these features, as they continuously present problems and opportunities, which themselves are diverse, complex, and dynamic. Further, the same applies to the institutional conditions under which opportunities in fisheries are created and seized, and problems formulated and solved. To be effective – that is to say, up to standards such as efficiency, legitimacy, and fairness – fisheries governance itself has to reflect the diverse, complex, and dynamic character of the challenges it faces. Often, problem definitions in fisheries are too simple, policies too static, and audiences too generalised. This might be one of the primary reasons why so much governing seems inefficient, governance unjust, and governability weak.

The diversity of marine ecosystems is a rich source for formulating governance issues, not only because of its central role in the study of those systems, but also for its strong relations with the dynamics of their stability, resilience, and resistance. Diversity of chains, partly built on such ecosystem diversity, is also an important variable in governing fisheries. In accordance with a well-known (cybernetic) law, saying that 'only variety can deal with variety', governing diversity asks for interactive governance that takes a broad and long-term view on fisheries and incorporates fine-tuning and feedback into its processes. Complexity of aquatic ecosystems raises other sets of governance challenges. Handling the infinite complexity of natural and social systems is a perennial issue that needs to be dealt with and should not be left to chance, especially not to those who have the power to reduce it in light of special interests. Diversity and complexity in fisheries are reinforced by dynamics and the propensity towards changes, which apply to tensions within a system and between systems.

The diversity, complexity, and dynamics of fish chains and their parts will be couched in different terms, but their utility as variables explaining main features of pre-harvest, capture, aquaculture, and also post-harvest is quite apparent. A strong point of governance purposes is that they offer a conceptual language not only understandable by analysts from different backgrounds, but also helpful in bridging gaps between scholars and between scholars and practitioners.

> Although much knowledge on the diversity, complexity, dynamics, and scales of fish chains is available, the importance of these features for governance purposes is poorly recognised.

Interactions and Scales

Interactions abound in fisheries and fisheries governance, and our understanding of these interactions is far from complete. The ecosystem-based approach to fisheries is a fairly new concept, for example, and requires thorough understanding of the various components and their interactions. Interactions of fishing households and communities are relatively better studied than interactions in the market sphere. From a governance point of view, these primary interactions are much more visible than actions by themselves. Take scale, for example. Insights into primary interactions in small, medium and large (or industrial) scale and the structural constraints for those interactions are needed for effective governance. The lack of fit between many management practices and the scales they apply to in fisheries has much to do with their perceived lack of expected effects.

The chains of interactions are greatly lengthened when the scale is expanded to the global level, as in the case of globalisation. Fisheries and fisheries governance become far more complex with larger number of actors, higher interdependency, and greater geographical distance. Globalisation has, in effect, created new fisheries and changed existing ones in smaller and bigger ways. It has led to a lengthening of the interaction chains between parties to the fisheries, and muddled any single actor's view. More importantly, it contributes to a highly diverse system, with fishers from different background and locations exercising their professions in widely divergent ways. They hunt or culture different fish, using a range of methods and techniques, resources, and bodies of knowledge. Their understandings of, and meanings attributed to fisheries, also differ from one location to another. Globalisation has tended to further the existing division of labour, creating a rich plethora of specialised niches and activities. Differences also emerge between countries and regions, for example, what is termed small-scale in one context is termed large-scale in another.

The dynamics affecting global fisheries derive from various sources, affecting disparate moments in the fish chain. The origin of change may be the aquatic ecosystem, the market, the wider social, cultural, and political environment, or the regulatory regime. The pace of dynamics is argued to be increasing because of the vigour of modern society, in combination with a lengthening of the chains of interaction. When chains extend and include more actors, changes in any one aspect have a broad series of consequences.

All of the above indicate that the governing system and the framework of actors engaged in governing are often as diverse, complex, and dynamic as the system to be governed. There is no reason to assume that fisheries and aquaculture are exceptions. In fact, scholars and policy-makers repeatedly point out how intricate, variegated, and vigorous governing efforts in these fields often are. These qualities are enhanced when governance takes place at different spatial, temporal, and organisational scales.

Problems frequently arise when systems are scaled up or down without careful consideration of the consequences for functionality. For example, many small, developing countries have attempted to replicate large-country fisheries department capacity in small departments with the result that few functions are carried out effectively. A small fisheries department cannot just be a small version of a large one. It needs to be qualitatively different, with less emphasis on technical capacity and more attention to co-ordination, project development and management, and people-based approaches. Scaling up from local to global, or down from global to local, is also problematic, as observed in the implementation of the Code of Conduct for Responsible Fisheries (CCRF). Although agreed upon by virtually all countries, and despite the production of several guidelines, national level implementation is slow, often because there is great difficulty in translating the concepts and required actions to the local level.

> Globalisation and global developments clearly affect fisheries to various extents, depending on scale, but the consequences for governance are far from clear.

Governing Elements: From Images to Instruments to Action

Three elements, i.e., images, instruments, and action, are required for each of the orders of activities. To be able to govern, governors need ideas on where the fisheries system is, where it needs to be, and how to get there. For all these ideas the term images is used, which is broader than the concepts such as goals, intentions, and purposes. To achieve the desired situation, governors need a set of tools; thus the 'toolkit' containing existing instruments or measures yet to be invented. This is called the 'instrumental condition'. Finally, governors need support for applying their toolkits. This is called the 'action condition' for governing.

All these elements needed for governing imply interactions, and the governance perspective requires that such interactions are organised systematically and with transparency according to the situation. Further, governors (public or private) in fisheries have to be able to underpin their interactive governing proposals with reasonable arguments. Governing has in some way to be rational, i.e., based upon verifiable facts and data, logical choice of instruments, and defendable action routes.

Images

Images of fisheries come in many types: visions, knowledge, facts, judgements, presuppositions, hypotheses, convictions, ends, and goals. They do not only relate to the specific issue at hand, such as capturing or food security, but also contain assumptions on fundamental matters such as the relation between man and nature, and the role of government in modern society. The main question is not whether actors involved in governance possess images – because everyone does – but how explicit and systematic they are and how to use them in actual governing. By checking governing images and the processes in which these are formed, we can control and criticise them. In the governance approach, it is important that images used are open and flexible enough to cope, among other things, with the diversity, complexity, and dynamics of governing objects.

> **Box 16.3 Images of the fish chain differ**
>
> The advantage of disassembling the chain into parts, besides allowing the more detailed examination of its components, is that doing so gives a better sense of how the chain looks from the perspectives of different places within it. A perfect, complete view of the fish chain is impossible. At the same time, the movement between different perspectives and scales in relation to fish chains can allow for a more appropriate approximation of their diversity, complexity, and dynamics. Such an adaptive approach to understanding the chain mirrors the dynamism of the interactive approach advocated in this book.
>
> *Source: Chapter 7 of this volume*

It is generally accepted that there is a strong trend towards overfishing, but is it also generally accepted what is behind this tendency or which forces are driving it? Can facts be separated from values? Can knowledge be combined with judgement? In other words: what do the images governing fisheries look like and how do they emerge? These questions are critical because of the potential consequences of the images. For example, one of the most influential images in fisheries management in the last decades has been the 'tragedy of the commons', coined by Hardin (1968). This image, suggesting humans as relatively short-sighted, non-communicative, and profit-maximising beings, has exerted substantial influence on management theory and practice, and provided an impetus to the movement for the privatisation of fishing rights. Not only are the results of privatisation in fisheries mixed, but there has also been much debate about whether such an image has been misused and led to undesirable outcomes.

Another, more recent, popular concept is 'sustainability', which has taken centre stage in environmental concerns. Sustainability is 'one of those motherhood concepts that is hard to oppose, but difficult to pin down' (Sumner (2002: 162). Two definitions of sustainability are in widespread use. It is seen as development, which 'meets the needs of the present without compromising the ability of future generations to meet their own needs' (Brundtland 1987); and as 'a kind of development that provides real improvements in the quality of human life and at the same time conserves the vitality and diversity of the Earth' (IUCN 1991: 8). Whereas the first emphasises the need for intergenerational equity, the second highlights the blending of human developmental and conservation concerns. Fisheries sustainability is a visionary but complex image, which has difficulty emerging, particularly in the translation to instruments (policy) and actions (management practice).

In conventional top-down management, images are developed by individuals or small groups and are seldom communicated to those who are affected. Recent trends towards developing 'shared images' require the involvement of many more actors to assess the validity of the image from their perspectives and to add to it, or suggest modifications. This leads to methodological and logistical problems of how to engage them all in a single transparent process, and to avoid being perceived as biased based on the lead agency that 'puts it all together'. Group process methodology is needed especially when the image is perceptual rather than technical.

> In fisheries, the inability or unwillingness of those producing images to interact with others is a major hindrance to governance.

Instruments

The range of instruments available in governance is extremely wide. They may be 'soft' in nature, as in the cases of information or peer pressure. They may also have roots in the legal or financial realms, and involve court cases, taxes, permits, or fines. Finally, there are the 'hard' instruments of physical force. It is clear that the choice of instruments is not free; one's position in society determines the range available. In addition, instruments have a varying range of applicability, some being general and others specific.

All instruments have their advantages and disadvantages, some work better in certain situations than others. One can even say that instruments have a lifecycle: older ones go out, and new ones come in. In the governance approach, it is not so much instruments themselves that require attention, but their context: e.g., what problem is an instrument supposed to solve, whose problem is it, and how has it been defined? Why was a particular instrument chosen, and not another one? Who are the winners and losers? Was it an interactive, or a unilateral choice process?

A fisheries management plan is recognised as a powerful instrument for drawing the actors into a commonly agreed system. Traditionally, there has been a strong emphasis or even bias on managing by 'technical' instruments. Gear controls, licensing, quota systems, to mention a few, are found in the toolkit of fisheries managers all over the world. However, effective governance requires that fisheries management goes beyond the scope of many conventional management plans, and emphasises the importance of information. Similar to image, sharing information is an essential interaction in governance, which must be clearly specified and built into fisheries institutions.

> In fisheries governance, in the face of its diversity, complexity, dynamics, and scales, innovation and combinations of instruments remain underdeveloped.

Action

The last element of interactive governance is action – putting instruments into effect. This includes the implementation of policies according to set guidelines, which is a relatively dry and routine affair. Action may also, however, consist of mobilising other actors in a new and uncharted direction. In this case, the actors rely upon convincing and socially penetrating images and sufficient socio-political will or support. Here the interactive aspect of governance clearly emerges.

Box 16.4 The role of women in African fisheries

In Ghana, where pirogue fisheries constitute an exclusively male task, the women are in charge of selling and processing fish, and for this reason own an important source of capital that is used for credit. It was the women who believed in the positive effects of using outboard engines to catch the pirogues and who provided the credits to fishers to install this innovation. The fishers increased their production and the women who loaned the capital to acquire the engines got preferential access to the captures. For this reason, some of the women have considerable wealth and social prestige. Their capacity to manage and control their money allows them to join the world of men. In Togo, a group of women is called 'Nana Benz' – the French word nana (girls) and Benz because they drive Mercedes-Benz cars. They are the main actors in the fisheries sector in Togo because they control both fish commercialisation and credit.

Source: Chapter 8 of this volume

Fisheries governors, public and private, take action in all parts of the chain and at all governing levels. Locally, fisher families or fisher organisations have, as private actors, the lead in day-to-day governing matters, although the role of the community as an institutional structure for such actions, not to overstate or romanticise it as such, is on the decline in many parts of the world. The state, which has had semi-monopolist powers in policy and rule making at the national level, is reaching its acting limits as the primary public governor in fisheries governance. Internationally, the acting scene is shifting: the influence of public actors is decreasing, and the role of the market and civil society (NGOs) growing. The question is how such events and developments affect the overall societal action potential in fisheries governance. Answers might be found by differentiating between three forms of action: leadership, mobilisation, and co-ordination. None of these are well advanced in fisheries governance, although many initiatives are taken and good intentions shown. At the international level, mobilising support and willpower in implementation is clearly lacking, despite the ratification of many principles. At the national level, the state rarely serves as the co-ordinator it could be (for example, on issues of indigenous rights), and at the local level, there is too little leadership to motivate and create or develop new initiatives (thus, the marginal recognition for gender roles).

It is important to distinguish between two types of action – enabling action and implementing action. Examples of enabling action include engendering political will, building organisational capacity, promoting leadership, drafting regulations, etc. For civil society, this may include establishing mechanisms to influence the government or the private sector. Lack of political will is often cited as a main factor contributing to the failure of fisheries management. Top-down exclusion of stakeholders from the benefits of a publicly owned resource, the status of which is often highly uncertain, requires strong political conviction. This is so whether the stakeholders are large private companies providing employment, or the rural poor.

For implementing action, principles such as the precautionary principle are required. Application of the precautionary principle include aspects such as proportionality to the level of protection sought, non-discrimination, consistency, benefits and costs, ongoing review in light of new scientific data, and assignments of responsibility for producing scientific evidence. This last element deals, to a large extent, with risk and uncertainty, acknowledged as part of fisheries management, whether based upon stock parameters, social and economic targets, ecosystem productivity, or combinations of these.

> In fisheries governance, action potential is dispersed and can be greatly enhanced by pooling leadership, creative social capital, and willpower.

Governance Modes: Self-, Hierarchical, and Co-Governance

In modern fisheries, an enormous range of interactions can be observed, varying from informal ones in small groups to formalised ones between states. Three types serve us well: the spontaneous, least formal interactions, called 'interferences'; the most formal, vertically organised interactions, labelled 'interventions'; and the horizontal, semi-formalised interactions, referred to as 'interplays'. These three types can be institutionalised into recognisable patterns or styles, and for governing purposes can be referred to as three modes of governance: self-governance, hierarchical governance, and co-governance modes, respectively.

Self-Governing Interactions

The most informal and fluid mode of governing interactions are clearly of a self-governing nature, embedded within the societal realm of societal interferences, with individuals, families, groups, organisations, and even societal sectors governing themselves. This is often not fully recognised in the governance of modern societies, because governing is easily equated with what formal authorities do, and not with what individuals, groups, and organisations contribute to societal governance. A full-grown governance theory has to give a proper place to self-governing capacities and the interactions on which this capacity is built.

Self-governing is predominantly not a favour handed down by public authorities, but an inherent societal quality, which greatly contributes to the governability of modern societies. Certainly, many sectors in present-day societies largely govern themselves. Self-governance reflects the situation in which actors take care of themselves, outside the purview of government. This is a ubiquitous phenomenon, quite distinct from government intention or policy. Indeed, liberal governments will highlight societal self-governing capacities, and socialist ones may downplay them. Governments may choose to deregulate or privatise, withdrawing the public sector or incorporating self-regulatory capacities in their governance frameworks. It is emphasised, however, that self-governance is not a government-created capacity, but comes about of its own accord. In fact, without sustaining a capacity for self-governance, societal governance is an impossible task.

The collective-action school has made the most systematic analysis of self-governance with regard to the exploitation of common pool natural resources, such as capture fisheries. Studies have been made about the circumstances under which actors join to construct rules and organisations for long-term resource use, and identified conditions that facilitate or hinder collective action. These include the size and heterogeneity of the social group, and the boundedness of the resource in question.

Self governance in fisheries has been a common feature world-wide, with their bases usually in local communities, contrary to many other branches of economic and social activity. The main reason is the use of the resource as a commons, and the need to regulate its use, either for technical reasons or to avoid conflicts. In the North, this governing mode in its purest form has become a rare phenomenon, but remnants are still in operation in some parts of southern Europe. In the literature, self-governance of fisheries as a specific form of collective action receives much attention, partly because alternative forms of governance, such as the state controlling the use of the resource, have had mixed results.

> Theoretically and empirically there are strong arguments favouring self-governing modes of governance.

Hierarchical Governing Interactions

Hierarchical governance is the most classical of the governance modes, characteristic for the interactions between a state and its citizens. It is a top-down style of intervention, with steering and control as key concepts; it expresses itself in instruments such as laws and policies. Although the metaphor 'steering the ship of state' has now become old-fashioned, the act of steering societal dynamics is still commonplace. The key element of steering is direction. Although the state creates the illusion of goal-setting, in practice this is done in interaction with societal parties. Hierarchical modes of governance are the most formalised forms of governing interactions, but of the interventionist type. Rights and obligations are organised according to super-ordinate and subordinate responsibilities and tasks. In particular, positive and negative sanctions attached to interventions have a formalised character and are surrounded by all kinds of guarantees. In addition to laws and policies, financial means such as taxes and subsidies are important ways of interacting in hierarchical governing.

In fisheries, hierarchical governance is widespread, particularly in the North where interventionist interactions by the state are the order of the day. However, this involvement by the state does not go unchallenged. Discussions focus on matters such as the assumptions underlying its supposed role in the 'tragedy of the commons', or on theoretical as well practical reasons why so many efforts in managing the resource either fail or have other negative side-effects. One of these side-effects is the erosion of traditional self-governing modes as described above and their replacement with management approaches that either do not fit or do not work. It is also argued that the state even contributes to the poor state of the resource by promoting and subsidising the capacity to fish on a world-wide scale. It is also important to mention that although hierarchical governance is mainly connected with the state, it is also a common governing mode in the market sector. Because of tendencies where the state is retreating, e.g., because of liberal-economic reasoning, the market takes over, often in the form of multinational companies. In those cases, and they are not marginal ones, hierarchical governance by the state is replaced by hierarchical governance by the market.

Despite the flaws in its traditional mechanisms, the hierarchical governing mode remains important in fisheries.

Co-Governing Interactions or Partnerships in Governance

The final and most recently pursued governance style, at least in fisheries, is co-governance, where societal parties join hands with a common purpose in mind, and stake their identity and autonomy in the process. Co-governance implies the use of organised forms of interaction for governing purposes. A key assumption is that no single actor is in control; instead, interactions are of a horizontal kind.

There is a certain degree of equality in the structure within which participating entities relate to each other. Autonomy of those entities remains an important characteristic of these modes of governance. Ceding autonomy is always only partial and contains mutual agreements, common rights, and duties. In the governance perspective, parties cooperate, co-ordinate, and communicate 'sideways', without a central or dominating governing actor. It is in particular these forms of governing that seem better equipped than other modes to cope with diverse, complex, and dynamic governing situations. Networks, public-private partnerships and communicative governance schemes are prime examples of this mode or style of governance.

The emergence of mixed networks of public and private actors has to do with broad social developments. Growing social differentiation engenders increasing dependencies. In this context, the emergence of policy networks is an important change in the political decision-making structure. Concepts like 'negotiation by governments' in the context of networks as a new model of social ordering between 'market' and 'state' are bandied about; or as governance in a centre-less society with complex configurations of horizontal co-ordination and synchronisation. Others consider the development of mixed public-private networks in terms of the need to solve social-political problems.

The public-private partnership (PPP), a specific form of social-political governance, has been at the centre of interest for some years. The growing interest in co-operation between public and private parties has been at least partially influenced by economic, social, political, and cultural changes. As a consequence, the question is increasingly voiced whether certain issues could not be dealt with more effectively and efficiently by joint action of public and private parties, rather than their acting in isolation. Essential to this is the synergetic effect actors expect in interactions, thus enabling greater effectiveness and/or efficiency than acting separately, given that their objectives are not incompatible. It is only then that private means can contribute to the solution of public problems, or public means be used to react to commercial opportunities and threats. Likewise, PPPs set themselves apart from similar organisations by the preservation of the identities of the parties involved. It is obvious, then, that PPPs are considered specific governing interplays.

New patterns of governance stimulate learning processes that will lead to co-operative behaviour and mutual adjustment, so that responsibility for managing structural changes is shared by all or most involved actors. One such alternative form of governance, described as communicative governing, is based on the image of complex problems in which problem-resolving capacities are distributed across autonomous but interdependent actors. In this type of governing, a form of rationality is presented in which social actors are considered 'reasonable citizens'. This is another kind of rationality than the selfish, opportunistic, profit- or benefit-maximising kind used in economic or public-choice theory. This call upon the 'reasonable citizen' corresponds with the concept of *communicative rationality* which is considered appropriate in complex problem-solving as a substitution for instrumental, functional, or strategic forms of rationality.

> Co-governance modes have the potential to address fisheries concerns, as indicated by experiences with co-management.

Three Orders of Governance

In governance, all kinds of governing activities take place, varying from short-term routine decisions aimed at small matters to the development of strategic plans pertaining to major issues and long-term developments. In the governance perspective, governing activities are brought together in three categories, called orders of governance. The issue here is not geographical or temporal scale, but levels or rings, as in the construction of an onion. Three concentric circles are distinguished: first-order, second-order, and meta-governance.

First-order governing takes place wherever people, and their organisations, interact in order to solve societal problems and create new opportunities. Second-order governance deals with the maintenance and design of institutions necessary to solve problems and create institutions. In third-order, or meta-governance, the main normative principles are articulated, which guide first- and second-order governing actions. All three orders of governance are needed for effective and legitimate governance of fisheries, in the short-term and the long-term, in the South and in the North. For all governing activities, guiding principles or evaluating criteria can be formulated, some of which are described below.

First Order: Problem-Solving and Opportunity Creation

The great challenges in present-day societies involve not only finding solutions to collective problems, but also the creation of collective opportunities. The 'classical' distinction of turning to government for problem-solving, and to the private sector and the market for creating opportunities, is proving an inappropriate and ineffective point of view in modern societies.

Societal problem-solving and opportunity creation is a public as well as a private concern, a governmental as well as a market and civil-society concern. In one situation one sector takes the lead, in another situation the other takes the lead, and there seem to be a growing number of social-political challenges that call for shared responsibilities and 'co-arrangements'.

In the governance of fisheries, problems with fish capture receive the most attention these days, as the crisis in fisheries is related to, among other things, 'too many boats, too few fish'. Is this a world-wide crisis? Are aspects of the problem the same everywhere? Who are the problem-makers, small- or large-scale fishers? Does the problem only concern the capture part of the fish chain, or also other parts, even those outside the chain, such as globalisation? In the governance perspective, questions like these require an approach that takes not only the diversity, complexity, and dynamics of fisheries itself into account, but also the technological, economic, and political factors influencing fisheries.

In searching for solutions to problems, opportunities are created. An opportunity can be said to be a positively evaluated experience from a future-orientated perspective. What are the relevant tensions that bring about the opportunity experience? Which kinds of interactions are potentially involved in the opportunity? The entities participating in these interactions can be identified, and opportunity-creating and opportunity-exploiting strategies can be developed from there. Once the opportunity space has been defined, the opportunity-strategy system can be defined and its boundaries drawn. Then the instrumental, action phases can begin. The diversity of participants, the complexity of aspects taken into account, and the dynamics of tensions among interactions are central elements in the (first-order) governing processes of social-political problem-solving as well as opportunity creation.

Problem definition and opportunity creation require that participating actors have similar vantage points for temporal and spatial comparisons. Local fishers are seldom aware of the broader spatial picture, especially when it includes other countries, but they often have a longer temporal perspective than government technocrats, particularly where there is rich traditional knowledge. The latter are most vulnerable to the problem of 'shifting baselines' where each generation of technocrat sees only as far back as the government institutional memory, which is often short. The governance perspective provides guidance on how to define problems by starting with the key actors and gradually expanding the circle to include all actors, and on how to create opportunities along somewhat different lines. These require stakeholder assessment that includes both identification of roles and interests in relation to the problem to be defined, as well as appraisal of stakeholders' abilities to interact on equal terms and to communicate with each other effectively. Much of this may not become clear until they are brought together and begin to interact. Equitable participation may then take a long time to achieve. Other issues at the problem definition stage relate to who is to be included. In the broadest sense for fisheries, where the resource is usually publicly owned, all citizens of a country may be seen as stakeholders with an interest. Typically, there is an escalating scale to determine who participates: consensus > > voting > > mediation > > arbitration > > top-down. Ideally, these hard choices regarding legitimacy, inclusiveness, and representation are determined, or guided, by principles elaborated at a higher governance level.

Problem definition is an iterative process. Fisheries managers will recognise this as the typical management planning cycle. The problem is first outlined in rough form, then its complexity is explored and its dynamics are assessed. Technical approaches, such as root cause analysis, often require special expertise. Issues often arise in relation to the principle of using the best available information and to the question of who possesses that information. Technocrats may dominate at this stage, but recent thinking suggests that local knowledge (LK) and traditional knowledge (TK) can be important inputs. At a certain point in the problem-definition process, the problem may seem too complex to manage and there may be a need to reduce its complexity. This simplification, when required, should be done through agreements with all of the stakeholders, and problem definitions revisited as part of the iterative process.

> In terms of problem solving and opportunity creation in fisheries, there are insufficient systematic and cyclic interactions among all concerned.

Second Order: Building Governing Institutions

Governing institutions in fisheries are, among other things, supposed to enable or control the processes with which societal problems are solved or opportunities created. It is a widespread notion that this is the responsibility of public bodies, from local to international. However, in the governance perspective, private organisations, such as businesses and non-profit organisations, also play such roles. As societal institutions, they govern directly or indirectly, although their degree of institutionalised participation in governance will vary a great deal. In the governance perspective, institutions, i.e., state, market, and civil society, separately and in their interrelations, shape and influence patterns of governing interactions. An important second-order governance activity is to design, maintain, and change governing institutions as a framework for (first-order) governing interactions in problem-solving and opportunity creation.

In fisheries, the state has major responsibilities in the capture sector, mainly through controlling or enabling fishing efforts. At one end of the fish chain, market institutions govern the way fish and fish products move from natural ecosystems to consumers. On the other end, civil society, and in particular NGOs, act as guardians of natural ecosystems, through efforts to minimise environmental consequences of fisheries activities, and by raising public awareness of the risks and damages associated with these activities. Two major questions about these institutions are, one, if they indeed form a proper framework for problem-solving and opportunity creation, and two, what a division of tasks and responsibilities for each of them, or in combination between them, might look like. As to the first question, it is doubtful if such a framework exists in an appropriate manner, as most activities in governing chains are unilateral and concern only parts of chains, with little integration and without considerations for side-effects. Where more than one governing level is required, interactions are piecemeal, often caused by crises or other incidents.

As to the second question on institutionalisation of required responsibilities or tasks, some differences are found between the South and the North, although changes are ubiquitous. In the South, major governing roles are played by market parties themselves, both locally and in connection with international partners. Where the state is involved, it is usually marginal, aimed at increasing catch, and often based on self-, instead of common, interest. Civil society (e.g., communities) still plays a role in local fisheries affairs. There are few attempts to consciously and systematically look at tasks and responsibilities. Institutional models of the North are replicated, although often not appropriate to situations in the South, and one can hardly speak of serious governing interactions. In the North, institutions govern more systematically, and occasionally we find divisions of tasks between them. Internationally, changes of and between governing institutions are the most prominent, although a proper balance of the responsibilities between public and private (market and civil society) actors is still far away.

Typically, there is much interplay between institutions and organisations as they form. However, over time organisations often become most occupied with reactive activities that are outside the scope of the originating institutional arrangements, rather than pro-actively seeking to give expression to them. This weak coupling of institutions and problem-solving through effective organisations is most likely to occur when institutional arrangements do not adequately meet the governance needs of fisheries. Mechanisms and organisations for implementing institutions find that they are faced with a whole host of issues that the institutional arrangements do not provide for. This can happen for a number of reasons. One is that the circumstances may be changing faster than the institutions can adapt. For example, changes in mobility of fishers, in opportunities for trade, or in competition for ocean space may take the system outside of the present scope of the institutions, leaving the organisational, problem-solving level with *ad hoc* measures as the only available solution. Alternatively, institutions may be unresponsive to problems identified at the organisational level, due to poor communications.

Another reason for weak coupling of institutions and problem-solving mechanisms is that the institutions may have arisen, or may even have been imposed, outside of a broad, principle-based, context. This can be the case when the institutions do not include all affected parties and there are internal changes in the power structure. Thus, for fisheries management institutions and organisations to be flexible and adaptive to external changes, they should be structured with reference to a higher level of principles and embedded within a broader perspective on good governance.

When institutions and organisations are poorly matched with the problems that they are intended to address, they may hamper more so than enable problem solving. This is in part because institutions may take on a life of their own with much of their energy going into self-perpetuation, often accompanied by resistance to change and inability to adapt. Therefore institutional relevance should be evaluated periodically and reforms carried out where necessary. Alternatively, adaptive processes can be institutionalised and built into the organisation, thus creating a 'learning organisation' where change is continuous and integral.

> The many institutions in fisheries, from local to global, fail to provide a coherent governance framework.

Third Order (Meta-Governance): Setting Principles as Yardsticks

In the meta-governance of fisheries, principles, norms, and criteria are advanced according to which existing practices are evaluated. In meta-governance, new directions are also suggested and new goals formulated and pursued. These principles guide the actors who are directly involved in governing interactions, and they also direct governance from a distance, scrutinising governance itself, with both governors and governed, 'taking responsibility for governing how to govern'. Meta-governing is thus an essential part of fisheries governance. Articulation of meta-governance is essential to guide the institutional and problem-solving levels. It provides transparency and makes underlying principles clear to all actors.

The need for fisheries governance to be based on certain basic principles is three-fold. First, fisheries governors should be obliged to make the origin of their ideas explicit – analytically, ethically, and politically. When governors select and define problems and when they ascribe certain solutions to these problems, they inevitably draw on some fundamental assumptions and worldviews, which should be brought to the surface so that they can be explained, defended, discussed, and evaluated. Second, there is a need for a 'yardstick', something to relate to when we evaluate and criticise current governance systems and practices. Where do we come from conceptually, morally, and politically when we pass judgements? How do actual management systems and governance practices compare with our deeper convictions and concerns? Third, the argument is for consistency. It does not make sense to discuss a policy on the basis of normative considerations which are at odds with each other. Values are always embedded in social practices, thus we need to be sensitive to the possibility that values differ because social practices differ; and that consequently principles or norms applying to fisheries governance may differ. Governors and governed alike must be able to identify what these values are, bring them into the discourse on governance, and decide how, in practical terms, they should inform collective decision-making and managing practices.

As with all aspects of governance, these principles also have a diverse, complex, and dynamic nature. They are diverse because, for fisheries, no one universal normative measuring rod for evaluating its governance can do right to the great variety of ethical and other normative expectations governing it. The complexity of fisheries has to be represented in the normative aspects of its governance, as opposed to trying to reduce and simplify this complexity and represent it using only one or even a few normative notions. Finally, dynamics include the normative expectations for fisheries – concepts like justice, responsibility, and equity are not only constantly changing due to external circumstances and contexts, but they are also sources of tensions and conflicts that give rise to new definitions, substance, and effects in their application.

Box 16.5 Social justice and fisheries

The CCRF contains some references to aspects of social justice. The protection and preferential access to be given to the weaker segment of the fishing population is argued to follow from their contributions to employment, income, and food security. Justice demands that their role be recognised and recompensed by a 'secure and just livelihood'. What this should entail is left up to the judgement of governments, who are urged to take 'appropriate' action. The CCRF mentions state responsibilities vis-à-vis social groups and categories in other principles too, suggesting that such attitudes are morally worthy.

Source: Chapter 12

In actual governance terms, not all these normative notions are backed by equally powerful actors and the interests they represent. However, neglecting the normative notions guiding the less powerful regions and communities in fisheries in the North and in the South would not only be grossly neglectful of the attention they deserve, but it would also be a loss in terms of normative insights and ethical experiences for the development of a new meta-governance perspective for fisheries world-wide.

> There is a scope in fisheries for more debate on and application of meta-governance and its guiding principles.

Governability

Governability is left until the end because it can be seen as an overarching concept and a property of fisheries systems as a whole. Governability of fisheries is not static. On the contrary, it is always changing, depending on external and internal factors and other developments. The role of governance in fisheries in relation to its governability should neither be exaggerated nor underestimated. What may be high governability at a particular time may be low at another; similarly, what may be effective governance in one place may be quite ineffective in another. Since many of the factors influencing the governability of fisheries, or any of its components, are of an external nature, they can hardly be influenced by fisheries governors, who govern only indirectly and have little ability to change them. All features, elements, modes, or styles and orders so far described contribute to the governability of a particular fisheries chain at a particular moment in time. All these aspects play a role, each by itself, but especially in their inter-relations. Together they give a picture of what governability is about, partly based on history and heritage, and partly on actual internal and external circumstances.

Diversity, complexity, and dynamics are crucial not only to the understanding of what governability is about, but also how to evaluate and eventually improve it. These qualities not only apply to the objects to be governed, but also to those who govern, and to the relation between them. That is to say: governing, governance and governability themselves have highly diverse, complex, and dynamic qualities of their own. The lack of this insight might be one of the major reasons why so much present-day governance in fisheries is ineffective.

Each of the three societal features of fisheries has specific consequences for their governance and governability. Diversity is a source of creation and innovation, but also carries the danger of disintegration. Complexity is a condition for re-combining existing inter-dependencies, but has to be reduced in responsible ways. Dynamics are the potential for change in modern fisheries, but can have disruptive consequences. All these aspects can be differentiated into areas of governance attention and activities. The governability of fish chains, as an input and an output of their governance, is largely dependent on the way their diversity, complexity, and dynamics are handled in governance tasks. The responsibility for these tasks is not to be allotted to either public or private actors, but to both, and often with mixed task areas.

Separately, but in relation to each other, diversity, complexity, and dynamics at different scales are among the key building blocks of our perspective on governance and governability of fisheries. If we take these basic characteristics seriously, we can begin to conceptualise how they can be used in governance in terms of interactions, elements, modes and orders; in other words, in terms of governability. To apply these abstract notions to the governability of fisheries, we outline a number of necessary steps, as described below.

Governability in the Framework of Interactions

Since governance theory emphasises interactions and, particularly, governing-as-interaction(s), it is essential not to lose sight of the *actors*. In fact, they cannot be separated from the interactions among them. Actors and interactions mutually influence each other. Individuals and organisations are often considered independently of the interactions they participate in. Yet actors are continuously formed by (and in) the interactions through which they relate to each other. They interact and, seemingly, can stop their interactions at will. They constitute, as it were, intersections in interaction processes. Taking a closer view, it appears the actors themselves consist of interactions, and the boundaries from which they derive their identities are relative and often fuzzy. This applies to social systems such as the fish chains, but also to organisations, groups, and other actors involved in them.

Insight into the diversity of participants in interactions in fisheries governance can be gained only by involving them in the governing process, giving them the opportunity to act out their identities. In the development of the interaction concept in fisheries governance, the tension between the action and the structural level of each interaction can be considered the main source of the dynamics of governing. This tension is decisive for the nature and direction of the interactions involved, of the tensions within interactions and within the structural level. Finally, the complexity of fish chains as socio-economic systems is primarily expressed as multitude of interactions taking place in many different forms and intensities. Such interactions can only be influenced if these aspects of complexity are sufficiently understood.

Governing the problems and opportunities of fish chains requires clarity about the nature of interactions involved in a problem to be tackled or an opportunity to be created, and about the way these interactions are related to each other and their characteristic patterns. The basic relationships among diversity, complexity, and dynamics are the interactions we see in the socio-political world. Interactions should be considered relational elements of systems and the relational elements between parts of systems and systems as wholes.

The more space an interaction creates in fish chains, the more freedom there will be for actors to select their values, goals, and interests. A space-creating interaction is characterised by a large action space and a large degree of flexibility. Conversely, controlling interactions leave little space for actors and their aspirations. In strongly controlling interactions, the values, goals, and interests of actors, and the degree to which they can aspire towards something are influenced by structural components of the interactions rather than the actors exerting influence on these interactions. In space-creating interactions, the structure is more open, and new impulses can enter to countervail the tendency for entropy.

> Governability of fish chains is a strong synthesising construct for analysing the diversity, complexity, dynamics, and scale of fisheries and expressing the interactions representing these features for governance.

Governability and the Relation between Images, Instruments, and Action

In fisheries management, an image, or set of images, might unilaterally be developed to rationalise the managerial choice of a particular instrument, or an instrument might be chosen only because it gets sufficient political or user support. Sometimes these instruments may generate the anticipated results; often, however, their effects will be minimal or even counter-productive in the long term. In interactive governance, the aim is for choice of instruments to be based upon images considered as accurate and legitimate, and to provide the basis for effective action by users and governors alike. The same applies to the process for the formation of images. Again, diversity, complexity, and dynamics are useful features, serving as a starting point for instruments and potential actions based on images built upon these features. One way to approach this is to systematically scrutinise existing practices in fisheries governance and check for combinations in which images and actions 'fit'. The application of individual transferable quotas (ITQ) and marine protected areas (MPA) might be two examples.

Box 16.6 Governing fisheries with ITQ and MPA

The main weakness of ITQ systems might be that in their image component the complexities, diversity (probably less so the dynamics) and scale of the parts of the fish chains involved are underestimated. Their strong point is that there is a certain coherence between the images they are built upon (economic theory), the instrument (ITQ) and its action potential (neo-liberal politics). In MPA governing systems, the images in terms of dealing with diversity, complexity, and dynamics of the resource (ecosystems) and how to use it are well taken care of (interaction between experts and users). However, they seem weak in the action component, in terms of the sufficiency of will between governors and governed to establish them and put them into action.

Source: Chapter 11

Governability of fish chains requires conceptualising images, instruments, and actions as interdependent elements of interactive governance.

Governability and Mixes of Governance Modes

In governing practice, interventionist interactions in fisheries and hierarchical governance arise mainly in terms of the state. In similar terms, self governance may be seen more in the realm of market and civil society, and co-governance as appearing on the borderlines between them. In the governance perspective, interactive governance in the diverse, complex, and dynamic governing situations in fisheries is seen as a mix: of public and private and of state, market, and civil society. A growing number of challenges in fisheries governance evoke shared responsibilities and 'co-arrangements', next to the responsibilities and tasks of each of the partners themselves. In fisheries, this is expressed in a growing interest in co-management as a governance mode.

However, there is a theoretical as well as a practical reason to think beyond this in terms of mixes of public, public-private and private interactions, organised in three modes. Little is known about the quality of such mixes, not only in fisheries practice but also conceptually. Self- and co-governing in fisheries are being explored, but hardly in relation to each other or to the hierarchical version.

> The governability of fish chains depends to a large extent on the ways in which the three governance modes are developed and attuned to each other.

Governability and the Ways Governing Orders Relate

The three governing activities, distinguished in terms of three orders, i.e., problem-solving and opportunity creation, design and maintenance of institutions, and meta for setting and applying governance principles, also work together. In chapter 1, we expressed this as the rings of an onion. One might also see them more dynamically as three interdependent and interacting mutually conditioning activities. In looking at the governability of fisheries, it is important to realise that these three governing activities cannot survive without each other. If no problems are solved or no opportunities created, governing institutions become empty shells. If institutions do not renew and adapt, they will hamper rather than help in meeting new governance challenges. If these two different sets of governing activities are not put against the light of normative standards, such as ethical principles, in the long run they will become pillars without foundations, blown away or falling apart in stormy weather or chaotic times. At the same time, such principles have to be tested time and again with on-going problem solving and the realities of how institutions operate, in order to become or remain living and creative sources for governance. The need to make hard choices in fisheries (see chap. 14) is a good example of this. Without a culture of living values or principles such choices will be very difficult or even impossible to make. Without the capacity to make such choices and the institutions to support and apply them, these values or principles can only be academic or philosophy 'up in the air'.

> The present state of the governability of fish chains asks for hard choices to be made, ultimately to be based upon ethical principles and long-term visions.

Governability of Capture Fisheries and Aquaculture

Completing this overview of fisheries from a governance point of view, one question remains: what can we say about the governability of fisheries, keeping in mind that governability is not a quality of governments. In the governance perspective it is a quality of fisheries as a whole, that is to say a quality of its governing system in relation to the system to be governed. All of the aspects described above, and summarised in the statements at the end of each section, contribute to such an assessment. It is tempting to try to transform these findings into a set of coherent conclusions about the governability of fisheries based upon the insights from this exercise. However, we have stated several times that the diversity, complexity, dynamics, and scales of fisheries as a governed and a governing system are such that there is not one answer to this question. Conclusions about the level of governability, of the governing capacities, and the state of governability cannot be expected as an outcome of this exercise as they would surpass the boundaries of the synthesis to such an extent that they would become empty generalisations.

What we can do instead is suggest a framework on which some of these governance qualities can be assessed on a systematic and composite basis. This is a continuation of bringing together the discussed aspects and combining them into the four major categories distinguished: features (diversity, complexity, dynamics, and scale), elements (images, instruments, and action), modes or styles (self, hierarchical, and co-), and orders (first, second and meta).

For features, we suggest *representation* as an evaluation criterion. Representation is the manner and degree to which the features of a fisheries system correspond with those in its governing system. For example, does the governing system reflect the diversity of the ecosystem it is supposed to govern, and of those exploiting it? For elements, we propose *rationality* to evaluate the way in which the three elements are in tune with, or mutually supportive of, each other. In other words, does an action apply to an appropriate instrument or set of instruments, and are they chosen on the basis of an adequate image formation process? For modes or styles, we use *responsiveness* to assess these modes and their mix in the practice of governing fisheries, whether those in governing roles respond to the needs of those they govern, or whether they have other interests in mind or just their own. For instance, if a fisheries system consists of a great variety of fishing types, does the mix of governing modes respond to the varying governing needs of those varying types? Finally, for orders of governing, we choose *performance* as a major evaluating norm. Performance means different things when we talk about problem-solving, opportunity creation, institutional design, or making governing principles explicit and operational. One way to judge a particular fisheries system is based on responsibilities as expressed in the CCRF. The question is whether the CCRF is being applied as a serious set of norms in its governance.

The framework to build pictures of governability of fisheries and aquaculture or certain fish chains, which can be considered as systems to be governed with a governing system to be identified, and where data might be available or collected, is a composite one. A simplified version of the evaluation framework can be presented as a matrix (see table 16.1), where each criterion is evaluated using 'high' (H), 'medium' (M), and 'low' (L). The composite quality of governability, in this case, is a simple aggregation of scores from all four criteria.

Table 16.1 Scoring governability for imaginary examples of Northern and Southern fisheries and aquaculture enterprise

Criteria	A 'Northern' fishery	A 'Southern' fishery	Aquacultural enterprises
Representation of DCD*/scale	L	H	M
Rationality of fits of elements	M	L	H
Responsiveness of modes	M	H	L
Performance of orders	L	M	M
Overall	L	H	M

DCD = Diversity, complexity, dynamics

It is worthwhile to experiment with a methodology to understand, evaluate and measure the governability of fisheries and aquaculture.

Governance in Practice

The application of the governance perspective to fisheries and aquaculture requires a next step. From where we are now, we need to advance the concepts used in the direction of measurable terms and develop concrete indicators for them, as well as to find empirical cases to test and modify them. In the discussion of governability quality, it is useful to draw attention to some of the strengths and weaknesses, and the differences and similarities, in the application of governance to capture fisheries and aquaculture in North and South. Doing so can then lead to the exploration of options for improving their governability.

One of the main strengths of the application of governance to fisheries is related to their importance as sources of food and livelihood, which are widely recognised by policy-makers, resource users, and fishing communities. Fisheries in many countries have attained a high profile in political agendas, and there has been an increased interest in ensuring a level playing field for all participants. The situation is similar in the North and the South, particularly because of the poor state of health and productivity of ecosystems, despite the fact that fisheries in the North tend to be less diverse and less complex than those in the South, and thus more resilient. The level of interactions and scales depends on, among other things, factors such as the multiplicity of stakeholders, alternative employment options and opportunities, complexity of market systems, diversity of fisheries products, and consumer preferences. To the extent that these characteristics differ between North and South, the degree of correspondence of governing systems in these fisheries, as well as the limitations and constraints in governability, vary. Given the amount and flow of information and scientific knowledge about fisheries of the North, the accessibility of modern technology, and the close link to international associations and regional decision-making bodies, Northern states tend to be more capable of setting up governing systems that represent diversity, complexity, and dynamics. An importance feature of the South is the existence of local ecological knowledge and traditional management systems, which can either facilitate or hinder governability depending on how they are incorporated in the governance framework.

As aquaculture is considered one of the most promising solutions to shortage of food supply and increasing global demand for fish and fisheries products, there is a need and opportunity to create governable systems that ensure responsible, sustainable, and equitable expansion. Governance effectiveness may increase considering its high profile in global development agendas and strong potential in forming synergistic partnerships with other sectors that rely on the same resource bases (e.g., land, water, nutrient processing, etc.). The rapid development in some aquaculture results, however, in irresponsible and inequitable uses of these resources, often well above their natural carrying capacity. This causes the systems to become more vulnerable to changes caused by climatic effects, introduced species, pollution, and the spread of diseases. The challenges of creating a governance system that keeps pace with these development are faced in North and South alike, although the North may enjoy the advantages of longer production cycles that reduce capital and time requirements, and access to modern post-harvest equipment and processing technology.

Considering the strengths, weaknesses, and challenges outlined above, options for improving governability seem vast. The underlying effort is on matching the scale and scope of governance, governing institutions, governors, and the governed with the features of fisheries systems. At the international and national levels, this involves enhancing interactions and partnerships within governing institutions, across geographical boundaries and fish chains. At the local level, the focus is on increasing effective participation of all actors in the governing process, improving knowledge and communication, and offering training for non-fisheries occupations.

To ascertain governance of fisheries as an activity and its governability as a composite quality is not an illusion. It needs imagination and perseverance to translate such an exercise into governing action. This is what the next chapter takes up.

17

Governance in Action

Robin Mahon, Maarten Bavinck, and Rathindra Nath Roy

Introduction

In this final chapter we explore what governability is for fisheries and how this can guide the ways forward. We take governability as conceived in chapter 16 as our starting point. A fisheries governor aiming to put governance into action should first examine the governability of the fishery. Then we proceed with several ideas on how to enable and enhance governability, concluding with some issues faced by fisheries governors when changing governance.

We try to communicate a perspective of how to undertake the journey towards improving governance, rather than a road map. We urge practitioners to set out on this journey, to make a start even if the way is not entirely clear. Reform is an iterative, adaptive process promoted by change agents. Often the next steps reveal themselves only after the process has reached an appropriate stage. Those who would promote better governance of fisheries may not have a clear view of the target, which will be different for each situation, but should have a strong sense of which direction to go in order to get a better view of the target.

The Concept of Governability

The concept of governability introduced in chapter 16 is central in the process of change towards better governance. Fish chains will differ regarding the extent to which they are governable, i.e., have characteristics that facilitate or hamper governance. Chains with low diversity, complexity, and dynamics may be inherently more governable than those for which these characteristics are high. This may influence the approach that actors agree to take. For example, a large commercial fishery that uses a few large vessels to exploit a few relatively stable resources with outputs that are processed and sold in supermarkets may be more governable than a widely dispersed, small-scale fishery from which products are distributed fresh by a large number of middlemen with little organisation of either fishers of distributors.

Ideally, a change agent would evaluate a fishery in terms of the characteristics that determine its governability – whether the governance is matched with the system to be governed regarding diversity of actors, levels of organisation and capacity, channels and networks for information flow, inequities in actor group empowerment – and determine where inputs would be most likely to improve governability. These inputs can then be the focus of attention. We emphasise that governability is not about governing but about the properties that lead to good governance. The difference can be likened to that between a theatrical production where the actors' lines are predetermined and the director oversees the interplay, and improvisational theatre where the director is sure that the actors are capable and sets the stage for their interchanges, without knowing what they will be.

Governance has been described (see chaps. 1 and 16) as comprising three interrelated orders of human activity. The order most proximate to the fisheries action is problem-solving or day-to-day management, followed by the institutional framework for problem-solving, and finally, overarching meta-governance, which is about the principles and values that underlie the institutional frameworks. Consider briefly how conventional perspectives on fisheries management might map onto these orders. For some, the term 'management' encompasses all three orders, for others it is mainly the day-to-day activities. For some, policy is a very practical term that should translate with little variability into implementation, whereas for others, policy has a strong component of principles and concepts.

It is important to remain aware that governance is not only about solving problems but also about enhancing the capacity to recognise and take advantage of opportunities. Tension between fisheries management and the fishing industry arises when conventional control-based approaches limit opportunities. This often happens because the opportunity takers and problem solvers are different groups of people and opportunities are taken with minimal attention to the problems that may result. There is usually a time-lag between the origin of the problem and its recognition by the problem solvers. Increasing the problem-solving role and capacity of the opportunity takers could reduce this.

Interactions

The importance of interactions among stakeholders in governance is emphasised in earlier chapters. Different types of interactions characterise the different orders of governance. Interactions take place at different levels of complexity. Among interactions, one might see the exchange of information as most basic, decision-making and strategising as more complex, and the formulation of shared vision and mental models as most complex. Facilitating governance will be largely about setting the stage for effective interaction through rules and processes. The diversity, complexity, and dynamics of the fish chain coupled with the fact that individuals and organisations in different parts of the chain may be only indirectly connected through several other actors increases the need for clearly defined rules and processes for interactions. Actors in one part of the chain need to know how actors in another part are interfacing with it. They also need to know that there are linkages through which their inputs can be seen by other actors and can influence the chain.

In effective governance, the roles, interaction rules, and processes will be clear to all actors. The question remains, however, as to what drives chains, causing actors to play their roles and participate in interactions according to the agreed processes and rules. There is a clear perspective on the benefit of participating, or the costs of not participating. Mechanisms for peer pressure, economic sanctions, or whatever measures are agreed, must be functional. Again this emphasises the importance of information and communication. Initially, participation in governance systems may fall to a few individuals who participate on behalf of others. They may do so as true representatives, with the knowledge and endorsement of those whom they represent, or as individuals from whose participation the others in their actor group benefit as 'free-riders'. Moving from the latter situation towards the former would be an objective of interactive governance.

Governability will be enhanced by developing and implementing efficient and transparent processes for interaction among all actor groups. These processes must be iterative on time periods that are appropriate to the rates of change at relevant levels in the fish chain. These will differ. Harvest sector periodicity will be related to the life-cycles of the target species, as well as to rates of innovation and technology transfer. Post-harvest periodicity will be related to demand cycles (especially in tourism-driven markets) and to trends for which there is much less fisheries specific documentation to guide governance than is the case for the harvest sector and resource base. Institutional review periodicity may be longer yet, especially at international scales where diplomacy is an important component. At local levels, it may be related, for example, to rates of change in the capacity of actor groups or the trends in principles, such as the involvement of women or reduction in child labour.

Governability of the Fish Chain

Diversity, Complexity, and Dynamics

Effective fisheries governance will as fully as possible reflect its operating context. Clearly, fisheries score high in diversity, complexity, and dynamics. These features arise at all stages in the fish chain and at many spatial and temporal scales. The diversity in types of fisheries mirrors the combined diversity of resource types and the human systems that exploit them. This carries through into the diversity of post-harvest arrangements, depending on the local, national, and export demands for various types of products. For example, artisanal or small-scale, rural fisheries using small vessels and simple gear may serve local food demand, or they may contribute to a larger system that collects and processes the product for export. Much material is available on the biophysical diversity of fisheries and its supporting ecosystems. There is also much information on the diversity in human aspects of fisheries systems. Assessing these as they relate to management will be familiar territory for most fisheries managers. Although the emphasis in fisheries has been primarily on the resources (stock assessment), the importance of the broader perspective obtained by assessing the entire fish chain is increasingly being recognised (Berkes et al. 2001; Charles 2001).

Fisheries analysis has typically focused mainly on the local level and close to the bottom of the fish chain. Moving up the chain to national and global levels we continue to encounter diversity and complexity in human systems. Conventional businesses, trading nationally and internationally, with investors to satisfy, may have vastly different value systems than those at the local level. Yet these interact dynamically through formal and informal linkages with which governance must contend.

Complexity and dynamics arise from the multiple linkages that occur laterally within the fish chain, or between fisheries and non-fisheries activities, as well as through vertical linkages, up and down the chain. These must be made known in order to be accommodated. Complexity and dynamics may also emanate from uncertainty due to unpredictable external factors ranging from environmental effects on fish stocks to global markets. This propagates up and down the chain as humans adapt and respond to this variability. Actors continuously change their behaviour to dampen negative effects and to take advantage of opportunities. Actor behaviour may also be uncertain. Fishers are notorious for finding innovative, legitimate ways around regulations. Like its drivers, much of the dynamics are unpredictable, and governance systems must also be dynamic to adapt to such uncertainty.

In local human systems, there is increasing appreciation of the importance of understanding how fishers interweave fisheries activities with other livelihood components. Complex livelihood strategies incorporate activities such as foraging for firewood, taxi driving or providing labour for construction and agriculture. Recent attention to livelihood strategies has sharpened awareness of gender issues. Past development planning in fisheries and aquaculture generally concentrated on the roles and capacities of men. Prior to the 1970s, women's roles and contributions were neglected and remained invisible, but in recent years, these have increasingly been documented and emphasised.

Scale Issues

Much of the diversity, complexity, and dynamics of fisheries arise from scale-related issues that can be found everywhere in fisheries and that must be reflected in governance. At all points in the fish chain there are processes taking place on different spatial, temporal, and organisational scales. The implementation of governance at the appropriate scales is one of the 'ocean governance principles' proposed by Costanza et al. (1998). Governance at multiple scales may be required for a single resource type.

For example, marine protected areas may require local-scale governance, possibly through co-management, but should also be consistent with a national level management plan and may also be much more effective if implemented as part of a regional network. Similarly, unless all interested states participate in the management of migratory tunas within a region, management is likely to fail. However, localised spawning areas may require special attention at the national or even local level for protection from fishing and/or pollution. In both cases, action at only one scale level is unlikely to be successful, therefore upward and downward linkages among the scales are essential.

Recent emphasis on ecosystem health has led academics and policy-makers to focus on the scale of ecosystems and how to manage different scales so as to minimise mismatches between ecological and jurisdictional boundaries (see chap. 4). Taking ecosystems as the point of departure, attempts are made to identify the most appropriate political and administrative scale, and the measures needed. In view of the current severity of the resource problem, the ecosystem perspective may be the most relevant. However, social, economic, technical, administrative, and political units also have scale dimensions that are relevant for governability. Ethnic boundaries may, for example, be just as important for governance as the boundaries of ecosystems, as they define the parameters of the group willing to cooperate. The 'matching' of scales is thus an important consideration in any fisheries governance effort.

Another scaling issue for governance is the distribution of responsibility and functions among national and regional organisations (Sydnes 2001b, 2002; Haughton et al. 2004). There may be tension as well as collaboration in the linkages between these levels, because regional institutions must be supported from national funds, usually at the expense of national institutions. Scaling of governance initiatives up from local to global, or down from global to local, is often also challenging owing to weak inter-scale linkages and scalability of concepts. The FAO Code of Conduct for Responsible Fisheries (CCRF) is a powerful tool for fisheries governance reform, agreed upon by most countries (FAO 1995). Despite the production of several guidelines, national level implementation is slow, however, owing to difficulty in translating the concepts and required actions to the local level.

There are many other examples of scale-related problems in fisheries, for example, between national fisheries management, which usually operates at the scale of the entire country, and conservation initiatives, e.g., protected areas, which are usually local. The resulting mismatch in scale of planning and implementation often leaves these two activities disconnected, or even in conflict. Classically, time-scales of political, biological, and developmental processes are mismatched. Politicians typically operate on a four- to five-year time-scale whereas horizons for resource recovery from depleted states and results from people-based approaches to development are usually much longer.

It is 'All or Nothing' – Holism and Balance

Effective governance requires attention to the part that each of the three orders – day-to-day management, institutional governance and meta-governance – plays in the whole. Upward and downward linkages between the orders are essential to integrate them into a governance system. Meta-level principles and concepts that are not supported by institutional arrangements and problem-solving processes are only an intellectual exercise. Unless informed by real institutional issues and practical problems, the meta-level may be irrelevant to the lower levels. It has already been made clear that a problem-solving level that is uncoupled from principles and institutions is largely reactive and may even on different occasions react differently to the same problem.

Governability of the Governance System

The overarching message of this volume is that a governance system has many dimensions and linkages, both internal and external to the system, and that effective governance must examine and accommodate these dimensions and linkages. This should be explicit and systematic where possible, but governance in the context of the diversity, complexity, dynamism, and unpredictability of the fish chain requires more. It requires systems that are resilient and that can self-adapt by learning through interaction. For many, the terms 'fisheries management' and 'fisheries governance' may be synonymous. One important message of this book is that fisheries governance is conceptually broader in many ways than fisheries management as commonly practiced and written about. The difference between the two may account for much of the failure of conventional fisheries management. Two key aspects of the difference are highly interactive stakeholder partnership and self-adaptation through learning oriented feedback.

Problem-Solving Capacity

Problem-solving should start with problem perception, definition, and communication. Making this first step explicit is important, as it widens the opportunities for input into solutions. Communication among actors is essential for this process and differences in capacity and perspective will require special attention (see box 17.1). Kooiman (2003) provides guidance on how to define problems by starting with the key actors and gradually expanding the circle to include all actors. Stakeholder analysis is an important tool in this process. The governance approach builds on stakeholder analysis, but takes it a step further. Using the concept of the fish chain it first identifies actors with a stake in fisheries, then goes on to determine if these stakeholders are also governors, i.e., whether their actions have governance implications, and the extent to which they have partnerships and interact. Stakeholder analysis is thus expanded to become 'governor analysis'.

Box 17.1 Problem perception is problem-solving

Perceptions are inevitably comparative and relative to vantage point. Therefore, problem definition is greatly facilitated when participating actors have similar vantage points for temporal and spatial comparisons. Local fishers are seldom aware of the broader spatial picture, especially when it includes other countries, but often have a longer temporal perspective than government technocrats, particularly where traditional knowledge is rich. Technocrats are vulnerable to the problem of shifting baselines as each generation sees only as far back as the government institutional memory, which is often short (Pauly 1995). This is problematic when, as at the World Summit on Sustainable Development, ecosystem principles come to the fore in fisheries governance and ecosystem restoration becomes a target. In most cases, we can only guess at the target state (Jackson et al. 2001). Traditional knowledge may be critical in setting appropriate ecosystem restoration targets.

Source: Authors of this chapter

Problem definition is an iterative process. Fisheries managers will recognise this as the typical management planning cycle (McConney and Mahon 1998; Die 2002). The problem is first outlined in rough form, then its complexity and dynamics are assessed before returning to refine the definition. We have spent considerable time on problem-definition because it is often downplayed in the problem-solving process, due to the desire to move quickly to solutions. The issues discussed in problem definition set the stage for the rest of the process. Therefore, issues of different perceptions of time and space, power differences, empowerment and power levelling must carry through to the stage of identifying solutions.

The second stage of problem-solving is identifying alternative solution options. It is important to remain open to the possibility that solutions may emerge from group process when each actor is seen to have a unique contribution, or part of the puzzle. This part of the process will be guided by principles such as those in the CCRF calling for the use of 'best available information' and stating that action should not be 'delayed due to lack of information'. The latter precludes the no-action option. Precaution is also expected to be an important principle in developing solutions. These ideas indicate that hard choices in fisheries governance will often have to be made in situations where there is low information availability or where information is not agreed upon by all parties. When the way forward is not clearly defined by technical information, choices are best made by consensus, as this increases the likelihood of compliance. But the time required to reach consensus involves compromise and takes longer to achieve.

Images, Instruments, and Action

The governance elements – images, instruments, and action – provide a structured way of looking at problem-solving and opportunity creation. *Images* are an essential component of structured human activity. Without them, governability can be substantially diminished. Images are mental models of how the world or some part of it presently functions, or of how the world should be – often referred to as visions. In conventional control-based management, images are developed by individuals or small groups and are seldom communicated to those who are affected. For instruments and actions based on images to be effective, the images should be articulated as fully as possible and should be communicated among all actors so as to be commonly understood. Images are abstractions that will usually be from the perspective of a particular actor. Therefore, sharing allows other actors to assess the validity of the image from their perspective and to add to or modify it. Then it becomes a shared image. A shared vision is a very powerful image that can inspire change (Harrison 1995). Recent trends towards developing shared images require the involvement of many actors. This leads to methodological and logistical problems of how to engage them all in a single transparent process (see box 17.2).

Box 17.2 Working with many actors using group process (participatory) methodology

Working in groups with many actors that have various perceptions is an important issue for the governance of complex systems. When actors are engaged individually or in small groups by a lead agency that then 'puts it all together', there is the danger that the outcome will be biased, or seen as biased, by the perception of that agency. Image formation in groups of more than a few people requires group process methodology, especially when the image is perceptual rather than technical. Each actor is seen as having a piece of the picture and the process is to assemble the pieces to reveal a complete image.

Group process methodology is developing steadily (Holman and Devane 1999). Practitioners, referred to as facilitators, are professionals in their own right (Schwarz 1994). Their role as custodians of process who are impartial to content is increasingly appreciated. The literature on this topic is growing rapidly and organisations such as the Institute of Cultural Affairs (www.icaworld.org) and the International Association of Facilitators (www.iaf-world.org) are dedicated to group process facilitation.

Professional facilitation can play an important role in reaching agreement on process and ensuring adherence to it. However, professional facilitation services can be costly and may be beyond the financial scope of day-to-day management problem-solving. A way around this is to build facilitation capacity and awareness among actors, both governmental and non-governmental. Actors can take turns at facilitating, while others remind them that in this role their focus is on process rather than content.

Source: Authors of this chapter

GOVERNANCE IN ACTION

Instruments include existing institutions, plans, and information, inter alia. Institutions provide a framework within which to realise goals as well as a toolbox to address situations, and are an essential component of governability. Institutions may be formalised or informal in nature. Formal institutions are most common in government/state activities. Informal institutions are most common in civil society. Market institutions tend to vary more in type depending on their size and on the purpose of the organisation. A national fisheries act is a dominant governmental instrument in fisheries. A good fisheries act gives effect to the major principles or images, but does not prescribe action in such detail as to pre-empt flexibility. Flexibility of action is achieved by giving an individual (usually the minister) or, less often, a group of individuals such as a fisheries management committee the power to regulate within parameters established by the act.

An issue for fisheries governance is whether institutions should be formalised. There are many arguments in favour of formal institutions with appropriate organisational support. Transparency is among the foremost of these. As the numbers of actors and levels of organisation that are meaningfully involved in fisheries governance increases, the importance of communication of the institutional and organisational arrangements and processes to all actors increases. Formal institutions facilitate communication with diverse actors, enable strengthening capacity to participate, and provide a basis for legitimate representation. They can be an important component of the power-levelling process.

Rules and organisations that are poorly matched with the problems that they are intended to address may hamper more so than enable problem-solving. This is in part because institutions may take on a life of their own, with much of their energy going into self-perpetuation, often accompanied by resistance to change and inability to adapt. Therefore, institutional relevance should be evaluated periodically and reforms carried out where necessary. Alternatively, adaptive processes can be institutionalised and built into the organisation, thus creating a 'learning organisation' where change is continuous and integral as will be elaborated upon later in this chapter.

State organisational structure and function are particularly important components of institutional design for interactive governance. There has been little attention to whether government organisational structures are appropriate to problem-solving in fisheries. The conventional fisheries department has developed to serve the needs of large-scale (centralised), usually temperate, developed country fisheries based on large unit stocks of high total value. It has a wide range of management and development functions that include fisheries technology, assessment, advice, and enforcement. Skills to meet these needs are assembled in units that interact according to standard processes: data are collected and analysed, advice is developed, and regulations are formulated, (or where necessary laws amended) made known, and enforced. Conventionally, the fisheries department has acted as the major, sometimes the only actor, in these processes.

Most fisheries are not of the type upon which the above structure has evolved. They are small-scale (decentralised), tropical, developing country fisheries based on numerous small unit stocks of relatively low individual value (but high aggregate value). For fisheries governance in such countries to better match the problems they must solve, technical solutions to fisheries problems need to be de-emphasised and more emphasis needs to be put on people-based approaches (Mahon and McConney 2004). Managers would be more oriented towards improving group dynamics and building effective processes, thereby bringing about the desired changes (Weaver and Farrell 1999).

It is questionable whether a conventional fisheries department structure is appropriate for problem-solving even in large-scale fisheries. An alternative fisheries department structure consistent with an interactive governance approach would be much less technically based (lower demand for data and analysis) and much more facilitative. The key skills would be planning, project development and management, mediation, and facilitation. These are seldom taught in natural science or technical training programmes (Allison and McBride 2003, Mahon and McConney 2004).

The fisheries management plan is recognised as a powerful instrument for drawing actors into a commonly agreed framework. Effective governance will require a plan that goes beyond the usual scope. It should reflect principles, outline strategies, identify roles, and specify actions and information flows at all relevant scales. The planning process is as important as the output. It is in the process that much information is shared, values communicated, and agreements reached. Here again, for interactions to be effective and actors to feel included, group process methodology can be important (see box 17.2).

Planning enables actors to participate appropriately, knowing what is expected of them, and also to address capacity deficiencies that may affect their ability to participate effectively. Although many developed countries have well established, sophisticated planning processes in place, documented guidance on how to approach planning for fisheries is only recently emerging (e.g., Berkes et al. 2001; Die 2002). This has left a fisheries governance gap in a large number of countries, mostly tropical and developing.

In planning, it is important to distinguish between enabling action and implementing action. Examples of enabling action include: engendering political will, building organisational capacity, promoting leadership, drafting regulations, etc. Lack of political will is often cited as a main factor influencing the failure of fisheries management. Considering its notoriety there has been surprisingly little analysis in fisheries of what it is and how to influence it. Such analysis is basic to assessing governability (box 17.3).

Implementing action may include a wide range of activities such as needs assessment, data gathering, analysis, quota-setting process, monitoring, and enforcement. We will spend the least time on this type of action, as it will be most familiar to readers who are involved in fisheries management. The literature on fisheries management is most comprehensive in the area of implementation. The many publications of the Food and Agriculture Organization (FAO), especially its series of guidelines for the CCRF, provide a wealth of information on implementing management (e.g., FAO 1997b, 1999d; Cochrane 2002). Numerous other volumes emphasise various aspects, such as the role of stock assessment (Hilborn and Walters 1992), management targets (Caddy and Mahon 1995) and co-management (Berkes et al. 2001).

Box 17.3 About political will

Typical perceptions are that enlightening politicians and intensive lobbying are the main means of influencing political will. Another perspective might place more emphasis on activities aimed at enlightening and empowering voters, whom politicians will seek to please, whether they are themselves enlightened or not. This channel for influencing political will is bottom-up through the electoral process. These approaches are the standard fare of democratic politics. There is another channel for influencing political will that has perhaps not been explored as fully as it should be. This is the role of the government fisheries department. Appropriately structured fisheries departments adopting a serious, documented, custodial approach to participatory fisheries management planning with clear principles for guidance can serve to reduce much of the political expediency or inaction that presently characterises fisheries management. This burden can also be shared to some extent by non-governmental actors who participate in governance processes. Seen from this perspective, there is a substantial role for government departments in influencing political will with the support of other actors.

Source: Authors of the chapter

Improving Institutional Capacity

A major challenge in fisheries governance reform is to promote governability through the development of organisational forms that draw the organisations of all the actors into a commonly understood and agreed framework. Such integration is generally a slow process requiring commitment to structured participatory process, diversity programmes, capacity building and information transfer. Organisations are established for the implementation of institutional arrangements at the problem-solving level. Organisations such as government departments are formed within the conventional fisheries institutional framework. Others, such as non-governmental organisations (NGOs) and companies, may form within the framework, if it is progressive and comprehensive enough to accommodate them, or outside it, in another institutional framework, if it is not. When outside the fisheries framework they may form in reaction to it, if there are deficiencies in it, e.g., conservation NGOs or fisherfolk organisations, or independently in reaction to opportunities, e.g., private companies.

One of the important issues in bringing together organisations and institutions with different origins is the question of congruence. Congruence, or the lack thereof, may affect interplay in various ways. There may be in-congruence at the level of knowledge and perceptions. Incongruence may also emerge in goals or objectives, or in the methods to achieve a particular goal. In South India, fisher methods to ensure compliance with rules – such as corporal punishment and social ostracism – are incompatible with 'modern' governance (Bavinck 2001). Congruence, however, is not an abso-lute; it can be worked toward starting with an inventory of similarities and differences, and suspension of value judgements. Co-operation is smoth-ered from the inception if one organisation (such as government) or set of institutions (such as constitutional law) is considered to be 'better' than the other.

It is worth noting that there are many situations where the *de jure* ar-rangement for fisheries governance is government control, but the *de facto* arrangement is that for all intents and purposes control has been assumed by non-governmental stakeholders. Examples of the latter situation are found in remote rural areas and islands where the arm of government con-trol does not reach. This is more likely in places where there is traditional management and government control is relatively recent, perhaps originat-ing with colonial rule.

Although ultimate responsibility for governance of public resources usually lies with government, there is considerable scope for civil steward-ship involving both the private sector and civil society. A governance ap-proach to fisheries would de-emphasise government control while empha-sising civil stewardship and empowerment. It would recognise and promote the roles and responsibilities of the many different actor groups. The present view is one where many non-governmental actors perceive governance as largely being the domain of government.

An effective fisheries governance system will comprise a mosaic of gov-ernance styles. The problem facing those who would establish such a sys-tem is to determine and communicate which styles are appropriate in which circumstances. A hierarchical style may be appropriate within cer-tain types of organisations, e.g., government or private sector, but not others, e.g., civil society associations; and will seldom be effective between organisations, e.g., government to civil society. There is the need for agreed formal or informal rules regarding what styles are appropriate in various situations.

Meta-Governance

Meta-governance is where overarching principles and values about the aims of fisheries governance, and in particular about how it should be structured, arise and are explicitly articulated. As principles vary from dif-ferent actor perspectives, articulation is essential to guide the institutional and problem solving levels (Rayner 1999). It provides transparency and makes the underlying principles clear to all actors. Institutions and day-today management thus need to be structured within sets of meta-level principles that have been made explicit.

Chapter 12 and 13 discusses the available bodies of principles relevant to fisheries today. The CCRF is one of the most significant hereof. Principles relating to sustainability and conservation of the resource base are well represented in the CCRF. Principles pertaining to transparency and inclusiveness are less prominent. Equity principles and livelihoods are present only in regard to inclusiveness and the need to pay special attention to small-scale fishers and fish workers. The principles with relatively low emphasis in the CCRF, those pertaining to social justice, tend to be highly cultural and politically sensitive. Therefore, it is not surprising that an intergovernmental organisation might find it inappropriate to be overly normative in this respect. The CCRF is also relatively silent on the need for governmental organisational reforms in structure and function, probably for similar reasons. Thus, while the CCRF represents a major advance in establishing principles at the global level, it is not yet a comprehensive set of principles for fisheries governance.

The Ways Forward

The nature of the fish chain and the understanding of governability developed earlier in this chapter point to three major directions for implementing interactive governance in fisheries. For a policy-related elaboration of these directions see the companion volume of this book (Bavinck et al. forthcoming).

a. *The first way forward* is based on the view that the presence of widely understood and accepted values and principles promotes governability, especially when formulated into a vision.

b. *The second way forward* is the need to be inclusive and to share in the responsibility of governance. Including all actor groups, promoting active linkages within and among them, and enhancing their capacity to interact will enhance governability.

c. *The third way forward* is based on the view that the capacity of a governance system to learn and adapt will enhance governability. A learning approach is perhaps the only way to cope with uncertainty and change by repeatedly monitoring progress and quality and navigating accordingly.

In this section, we develop these three proposed directions. The aim, however, is to communicate a perspective about how to undertake the journey towards good governance, rather than to provide a how-to-do-it manual. Our hope is to encourage practitioners to set out on this journey, even if the way is not clear in its entirety. Improvements in governance, which includes institutional and organisational change, are iterative, adaptive processes during which change agents operate according to and are guided by certain principles or values. Often the next steps reveal themselves only after the process has reached an appropriate stage of maturity. The target or goal, which will be different for each situation, may not be in view. What is important is that those seeking to improve the governance of fisheries have a strong sense of the direction they need to go in, to get a better view of the target.

Principles and Values as a Foundation for Fisheries Governance

The first direction proposed by the interactive governance perspective highlights principles and values. It does so in the belief that principles and values structure governance, need to be articulated, and are essential elements in developing a vision for a fishery.

What are the obvious benefits or value added by placing values and principles centre-stage in fisheries governance?

- Principles and values give structure to governance. They provide a value structure guiding fisheries governors in assessing where fisheries are, where they should be and what means can be used to get them there.
- Values and principles, if agreed to and explicit, help make hard choices easier for governors. They provide a value frame that helps governors make choices between two acceptable but conflicting options by suggesting the preferred option on the basis of a higher level of logic. It also makes decision-making an institutional rather than a personal act, thus making avoiding hard choices unacceptable.
- Shared principles serve to increase the probability that partnership will evolve in the interest of all stakeholders, present and future. They serve to increase governability.

We recognise two types of principles and values: substantial and procedural. Substantial principles and values give direction to the development of images that drive problem solving and opportunity creation, and of visions that drive the building of institutions (box 4). Procedural principles and values guide the process of decision-making and interaction. The latter are crucial as interactive governance does not prescribe particular goals or objectives, but is largely about process.

Too often governance is concentrated exclusively on goals and means. This often follows from the urgent nature of events in fisheries and the need to act rapidly to resolve crises. The underlying and implicit values, norms, and concerns in fisheries are often concealed, not brought out in the open where they can be discussed rationally and democratically and then incorporated into a vision.

Chapter 13 posits a set of principles that we suggest are universal and should underpin governance in all times and contexts. At the same time,

Box 17.4 Some visions developed for fisheries

Articulated visions for fisheries are few, but one presented for small-scale fisheries by Berkes et al. (2001) and adapted by the FAO Working Party of Small-Scale Fisheries (FAO 2004b), provides a scenario for the benefits of a well-governed fishery:

'The vision for small-scale fisheries is one in which their contribution to sustainable development is fully realised. It is a vision where:
- They are not marginalised and their contribution to national economies and food security is recognised, valued and enhanced;
- Fishers, fish workers and other stakeholders have the ability to participate in decision-making, are empowered to do so, and have increased capability and human capacity, thereby achieving dignity and respect; and
- Poverty and food insecurity do not persist; and where the social, economic and ecological systems are managed in an integrated and sustainable manner, thereby reducing conflict' (FAO 2004b).

Clearly such a vision can readily be adapted to other types of fisheries and to community, national, or regional levels. It speaks loudly to the complexity, diversity, and interactions discussed in detail in previous chapters. It also reminds us that fisheries are integral to the fabric of the lives of many millions of individuals globally.

The vision for small-scale fisheries presented above illustrates the benefits of a well-governed fishery. It is general but clearly communicates a set of values, as does the vision for Canada's fisheries articulated by their Department of Fisheries and Oceans as one of 'Safe, healthy, productive waters and aquatic ecosystems, for the benefit of present and future generations, by maintaining the highest possible standards of service to Canadians, marine safety and environmental protection, scientific excellence, conservation and sustainable resource use'. At a more local level, Barbados' sea urchin fishers developed a vision of their fishery that communicates their value system for the fishery, including strong components of sustainability and cooperation (below).

The vision of Barbados' sea urchin (sea egg) fishers for their fishery

Vision element	Overview
Sea eggs back!!	A recovery to an abundance of sea eggs from year to year.
Laws and enforcement in place	Sea eggs to be protected through regulations and enforcement including options such as a five-year ban, shorter fishing season, licensing for fishers, and fines and penalties for violators.
Fisherfolk organisation in place	Fishers formally organised, working with stakeholders, and practicing co-management with government.
Pressure against polluters	Taking a stand against pollution.
Research and development	Using research to improve the industry.
Education and training organised	Providing education to fishers and the public about proper harvesting.

Source: FAO (2004b), Berkes et al. (2001), Mahon et al. (2003)

however, it is clear that these principles – like all others which may be added – are up for debate. Principles and values can only become the foundation of governance systems if all the actors agree and accept them, explicitly. Principles, unfortunately, are often implicit or assumed and are seldom brought to the fore, reviewed, and endorsed by stakeholders.

Dialogue is needed to help all stakeholders understand and adopt the principles that will guide their governance system. Participatory methodologies for developing a shared vision and principles are becomingly increasingly available. These methodologies are usually a component of an overall participatory strategic planning process. It is common to use a professional facilitator for these and other participatory processes. The facilitator is an impartial guide with knowledge and skill in selecting and applying the methodology that would be most appropriate for the situation. The partnership base must be built on principles that are pre-agreed. Enabling policy must be explicit about the underlying principles and must provide the platform from which stakeholders can discuss and decide on these principles with the assurance that they are supported at the highest levels.

Rather than start with a dialogue on the substantial principles that guide interactions and governance, however, it is sometimes useful to have an easier entry point. These are procedural principles that deal with the process of building and strengthening governance systems. Some common principles are included in box 17.5 below as an example.

Box 17.5 'TACIRIE' procedural principles

Transparent	- Everyone sees how decisions are made and who makes them
Accountable	- Decision-makers (both local and governmental) are procedurally and periodically answerable to those they represent
Comprehensive	- All interest groups are consulted from the outset in defining the nature of the problem or opportunity prior to any decisions about management being taken
Inclusive	- All those who have a legitimate interest are involved
Representative	- Decision-makers are representative of all interest groups
Informed	- All interest groups understand the objectives of the participatory process and have adequate and timely access to relevant information
Empowered	- All interest groups (women and men) are capable of actively participating in decision-making in a non-dominated environment

Source: Hobley and Shields (2000)

The purpose of the application of such principles is to assure that all stakeholders involved are treated as equals and have full access to the formulation of fisheries governance. Stakeholders may decide on various kinds of procedural principles. The acceptance of these procedural principles often paves the way by creating an environment wherein a proper dialogue of basic principles is possible and conducive.

Strengthening Capacity through Partnership, Inclusion, and Interaction

The second direction proposed by the interactive governance perspective to add value to and strengthen fisheries governance systems is to include the many actors and stakeholders involved through partnership. The challenges, concerns, and hard choices faced by fisheries governance are in good part generated by the large numbers of actors in the fish chain. These stakeholders, even if they are not formally involved in governance, already influence and impact on processes. Governments, who in most cases have seen themselves as the legitimate governors of fisheries, often consider the multiplicity of stakeholders as a bother and a nuisance to be dealt with through exclusion. On the other hand, the interactive governance perspective sees the many stakeholders as a potential resource to benefit governance and includes them in the process.

Some benefits of inclusion and partnership in a governance system are:
- the diversity and multiplicity of stakeholders increases the knowledge and experience available;
- involving stakeholders in governance ensures better problem definition and hence better images and visions;
- legitimacy of governance decisions is enhanced and could mean reduced costs of enforcement and compliance, which are usually the most expensive aspects of governance;
- the diversity and number of ideas and solutions have a higher probability of generating innovations;
- the diversity, interconnectivity and multiplicity of stakeholders working together may be better equipped to deal with the diverse, complex, and dynamic nature of fish chains;
- and, finally, it is just and it is the right of stakeholders to be heard and have the means to inform and influence processes that they are involved in or impact on.

Inclusiveness and partnership are not new to fisheries governance. In fact, they are propagated and practiced already in various forms: The CCRF emphasises that stakeholders should be included in the planning process; the Sustainable Livelihoods Approach insists on people-centredness and highlights the need to understand people's assets and livelihood strategies and to give them voice (DFID 1999); co-management of natural resources like fisheries strives to unite all stakeholders in an institutional framework; and Integrated Coastal Zone Management programmes emphasise the establishment of linkages and stakeholder participation. These attempts at broadening participation and promoting partnership are completely compatible with the interactive governance approach. Interactive governance strengthens these approaches by presenting an encompassing framework for understanding and addressing the problems and opportunities that take place in fisheries.

Stakeholder analysis is a tool that helps in identifying and understanding who the real actors and stakeholders are (Brugha and Varvasovsky 2000; Roy 2002). The understanding of stakeholders' involvement in the fish chain is important in bringing them into governance, using their competencies and capacities as necessary, and ensuring they are heard and have influence. Stakeholder analysis also seeks to determine the capacity of the groups and organisations to play their part in a participatory governance system as prescribed by the governance approach. This capacity or empowerment includes a number of facets: the extent to which they are informed, the level of membership in the organisation, the organisational strength of the group, leadership skills, problem-solving capability and the will to participate. There is a substantial literature on stakeholder assessment and several organisations that research and develop these methods such as the International Institute for Environment and Development (http://www.iied.org/forestry/tools), The World Bank (http://www.worldbank.org/participation/tn5.htm), and the UK Department for International Development (http://www.livelihoods.org).

Stakeholder analysis reveals where the system is deficient and points to a plan for addressing these deficiencies through capacity enhancement. It is not our intention to review or elaborate upon capacity building extensively here, but mainly to identify its importance in promoting the governance approach through enabling self-organisation. As such it should be a central component of policy aimed at promoting the interactive governance approach. As with any complex topic there are a variety of perspectives on capacity building. One perspective distinguishes between meta-, meso- and micro-capacity (CIDA website, capacity.org):

- Meta-capacity is the ability to develop a set of principles, a vision and a mission that guides the institution or organisation;
- Meso-capacity enhancement aims to bridge the gap between macro-policy levels and local communities (http://www.capacity.org Newsletter issue 22, July 2004) by addressing the capacity of the institutions and organisations that play an intermediate organising role in governance, translating meta-principles to their members and providing feedback from members into meta-capacity development (http://www.snvworld.org);
- Micro-capacity is associated with the ability of local organisations and individuals.

There is increasing emphasis on the multidimensional nature of capacity-building (Morgan 1998). It is perceived as much more than training involving a wide range of inputs that lead to the entrenchment of ways of doing business in the organisational culture (Krishnarayan et al. 2002). It also involves a substantial experiential component that can be referred to as 'learning by doing'.

The match between stakeholder capacity and responsibility is critical and should be approached iteratively so that stakeholders are not expected to assume unrealistic responsibilities. This can be addressed either by sharing the responsibility until it can be assumed fully, or by redesigning management systems to be simpler and appropriate to existing capacity. For example, where technical capacity is low and there is little chance that it will be possible to pursue conventional management effectively, simpler, less technical approaches that are consistent with stakeholder capacity should be explored. The assumption of inappropriate levels of responsibility and/or perpetually striving to achieve unattainable capacity levels condemns the organisation to perpetual failure. It is becoming increasingly evident that much can be achieved in fisheries management by consensus and the use of simple indicators (Berkes et al. 2001).

The governance approach has a strong emphasis on interactions among groups and organisations. Whereas there may be the capacity to interact meaningfully, processes for interaction may often be lacking. Stakeholder analysis has conventionally paid less attention to interaction processes, to understand what blocks interaction and what promotes it. Therefore, there is less in the literature to guide this aspect of stakeholder assessment, e.g., IIED Power Tools Series(see Stakeholder Power Analysis. IIED. Draft June 2001: james.mayers@iied.org). Assessment of interactions would seek to determine the presence of processes and channels that facilitate interaction, including the amount and type of interactions. Approaches could include social network analyses via the use of flow charts or matrices that allow the inventory and description of interactions e.g., formal or informal, positive or negative, strong or weak, etc.

Promoting interaction through networking is an important aspect of capacity building. Similar changes in operational style are taking place in the private sector. There may be much to learn about practical relationship building strategies from business approaches to forging collaborative networks with employees, customers, suppliers, and communities (Svendsen 1998). The diversity of networking or communication styles must match the diversity of stakeholders so that all groups have the opportunity to communicate in a style that is comfortable to them. Therefore, the burden of change for improved networking and interaction is distributed throughout the network, not just on a few stakeholder groups perceived as having low capacity to interact. Human diversity, which has been the source of much conflict and ranging from familial to global scales, is increasingly seen as a potential resource to be tapped rather than a problem to be solved (e.g., Baytos 1995). When the entire fish chain is considered, one sees considerable scope for enriching linkages among all levels through planned diversity awareness programmes and transfer of values, knowledge, and skills (e.g., Pollar and González 1994; Hetherington 1995).

Learning to Adapt and Assure Quality

The third direction suggested by the interactive governance perspective is to build learning into governance processes. Fish chains are by their very nature unpredictable. Dealing with unpredictable systems is like moving through uncharted territory. The only way to function in such systems is to constantly monitor where one has been and where one has reached, and then to reflect on the progress and to move forward guided by the learning. There is an increasing focus on integration of learning and knowledge management systems into sustainable development initiatives (http://www.infodev.org/, http://www.sdnp.undp.org, http://gkaims.globalknowledge.org).

A strong learning system is essential to the interactive governance approach, and yields substantial dividends:

- If fish chains are indeed uncertain and unpredictable, frequent feedback is essential.
- It provides the flexibility to adapt to changing conditions based on the best available information from the widest possible range of actors.
- It allows one to profit from the experiences of other governors in other times and places.
- It builds up an institutional memory, to fall back upon and learn from, as different from the memories of individuals in an institution (which are often not accessible to others).
- It increases the effectiveness and efficiency of processes and thus ensures quality.

Interactive governance is not unique in emphasising the importance of learning systems (e.g., Folke et al. 2002). Monitoring and evaluation are used in most organisations (although they are not necessarily utilised as learning instruments). Still, one could argue that most organisations in the fisheries sector can improve the extent to which they 'learn' from experience as well as from their surroundings. As in other areas of governance and institutional strengthening, much of the initial work in this area has been done with a view to improving the functionality of organisations, usually by private corporations (e.g., Senge 1990; Collison and Parcell 2001). Adapting and extending these concepts originally designed for commercial and business operations to a system as complex as the fish chain will be a substantial challenge, as it cuts across private, public, and civil organisations as well as local, national, and international scales. Consequently, there is need for careful attention to issues of intra-organisational (intra-group) learning as well as inter-organisational (inter-group), system-wide learning.

Here, rather than try to cover all that has been written on learning organisations and systems, we will attempt to give the reader a perspective on what it means to develop a learning organisation. In doing so we draw heavily on the work of Peter Senge, a leader in this area, and on a few key texts such as *Learning to Fly* (Collison and Parcell 2001). In describing the five 'learning disciplines' that are core to the learning organisation. Senge et al. (1994) explain that these are lifelong programmes of study and practice.

The challenge is how to activate and enhance these disciplines within organisations and indeed with an entire governance system. There are a variety of emerging perspectives on how this should be approached (e.g., Argyris 1991; Collison and Parcell 2001; Evans 2003; McElroy 2003) and a wealth of practical advice and methods (e.g., Belden et al. 1993 and Senge et al. 1994). Knowledge management, one practical perspective on developing a learning organisation, explores the wide range of styles and practices that can contribute to creating an effective learning organisation and emphasises that different styles are required in different situations (Collison and Parcell 2001). McElroy (2003) uses the 'knowledge life-cycle' to emphasise the dynamic nature of knowledge management. Collison and Parcell (2001) warn that knowledge management is '...not about creating an encyclopaedia that captures everything that everyone ever knew. Rather, it's about keeping track of those who know the recipe, and nurturing the culture and the technology that will get them talking'. Indeed, one may consider a knowledge management continuum ranging from knowledge capture at one end to connectivity at the other.

A focus on knowledge capture emphasises collection and codification of knowledge, databases, and access and distribution systems. There has been much emphasis on these types of systems in fisheries management, and they will continue to play an important role in increased availability of information to those who have previously had little access. Information 'capture' and distribution increase the 'informedness' of participating actors and empower them to participate.

At the other end of the continuum, connectivity emphasises investment of 'time and energy in the processes and technologies which stimulate connections between people' (Collison and Parcell 2001). This emphasis may include creating networks, building flexible teams to address specific issues, holding workshops, and developing and sharing a variety of tools for collaboration and group interaction. Emerging technologies make it increasingly easy to enhance connectivity and learning among people and organisations. The increased emphasis on facilitation of group processes also reflects the growing emphasis on connectivity as a significant component of a learning system.

A learning organisation should have processes in place to allow learning during all stages of implementation: before doing, while doing, and after doing. These three types of learning are different. *Learning before doing* involves asking the question 'has anyone else done this before'. Usually the answer is yes, or sufficiently close to it that there are lessons to be learned from what others have done. This provides the basis for a plan that adapts experience from others to the present circumstances using situation specific knowledge. *Learning while doing* involves asking questions about how the implementation is going and whether the plan needs to be adapted based on unforeseen circumstances. *Learning after doing*, involves active review of what was done, the ways in which it differed from what was planned or expected and why (Collison and Parcell 2001). A learning organisation has mechanisms to capture and share the knowledge acquired at all stages.

In order for the system to be a learning system there need to be indicators to measure system improvement and to check the learning feedback.

One aspect of assessment of these benchmarks is whether the system partners agree that they are improving (ideally the system would include all partners whose assessment matters). The learning loops need to be integral to the system, not an external check. When the learning system has become embedded in the system, there is a shift from unconscious incompetence to unconscious competence (Collison and Parcell 2001).

Implementation Issues

Fisheries governors who seek to put into practice the concepts and approaches described in this volume will find themselves having to address several issues with political decision-makers and other stakeholders. Prominent issues relate to generating the will for change and also to planning for change. They include evaluating how much risk there is in undertaking change, who is responsible for change, how long it will take and how much reorganisation to existing systems will be required for effective change. Here we provide some short answers to these issues. They are addressed more fully in the companion volume (Bavinck et al., 2005).

Diverse, complex, and dynamic systems are almost impossible to predict and control. It is increasingly clear that controllability of the fish chain is a fallacy, as evidenced by the numerous governance failures in fisheries (Charles 2001). Therefore, much of the apparent risk in moving from a command and control approach towards an interactive governance approach may be more perceived than real. This will be particularly so where the command and control approach is deeply ingrained. The perceived loss of control for governments that will accompany the process of encouraging and allowing stakeholders to take greater responsibility and to play a more active and decisive role in governance will naturally engender some reluctance to try interactive governance. However, the call for alternatives to the conventional command and control approach in fisheries is also increasingly frequent, strident, and difficult to ignore. In any change process, particularly one that involves sharing power, there will be wrong directions taken, and several iterations may be required to 'get it right'. However, the risks associated with pursuit of the interactive governance approach can be reduced by measures that enhance the governability of the system. There will be no guarantee of success, but an increased probability of success.

Knowing who is responsible for promoting and enabling interactive governance of fisheries systems is important given the number of stakeholders involved. In most countries, fish are public or common property and fisheries governance is perceived as the responsibility of the government. Although governments may have the greater responsibility to promote the interactive governance approach for fisheries, the scope of the task is too large for governments to adequately undertake on their own, and it is therefore the responsibility of all other actors to take leadership roles for implementing interactive governance. When governments lack the will, ability, or flexibility to change from the conventional command and control approach, non-governmental actors have an even greater responsibility to act as change agents.

Moving from present systems to strengthened governance will be a long-term effort requiring that people and organisations change the way they look at the world and think about problems. It requires a shift towards collective stewardship (Block 1996). Actors' approaches must then change to include new ways of doing and they must be convinced that they are empowered to change. This type of widespread responsibility or stewardship will take persistent extended nurturing to become culturally ingrained (Blanchard et al. 1998). Studies of participatory management of marine protected areas concluded that sustained assistance inputs for ten or more years are required for the concepts and processes to become an integral part of the organisational culture (Pomeroy et al. 1997). Clearly, even longer time-frames will be required to establish throughout the entire fish chain a comprehensive governance approach based on principles of inclusiveness, transparency, and sustainability. Note, however that the types of changes in governance being suggested in this volume are consistent with global trends towards inclusiveness and increasing involvement of civil society in governance (Burbidge 1997). This is fuelling and being fuelled by a rapidly growing, readily accessible literature on organisational change (Senge et al. 1994, Kotter 1996).

Convincing people and organisations that are comfortable and benefiting from the *status quo* to change will require dialogue, persuasion, the right circumstances, and a carefully chosen set of incentives and disincentives. New functions and ways of doing will clearly require the restructuring of institutions and organisations in the fish chain. This will have different implications and challenges for different stakeholders. At the level of fishers, there will be the need to get organised for collective, representative participation in governance (e.g., McConney 1999; Kurien and Paul 2000). This will, of course, necessitate the building of capacity and competencies. At the level of government organisations, changes towards greater emphasis on people-oriented skills will be required. Instilling stewardship and enhancing interactive governance will require a fundamental change in leadership style from the conventional leader who leads from a position of strength and charisma to the leader who is a facilitator or 'superleader' – a leader who helps others to lead themselves (Stanfield 2000; Manz and Sims 2003).

Conclusion

There is much yet to be done with regard to developing the interactive approach to governance. Structured approaches to assessing governability must be formulated, including easy-to-apply rapid appraisal techniques that encompass all its dimensions (e.g., Pitcher 1999). It is hoped that this volume will inspire a wide variety of fisheries governance interactions that will lead to a substantially increased body of knowledge and experience about fisheries governance. We are convinced that by starting with the three ways forward described above, fisheries governors will come to better grips with many of the factors that undermine and bedevil current efforts to achieve sustainable, productive fisheries.

Strategies that enable and enhance governability include: development of shared principles and values as a basis for self-organisation; inclusion of all stakeholders, particularly by strengthening their capacity to participate; and enhancing interactions, especially feedback for learning. Principles and values give structure to governance. If agreed to and explicit, they provide a value base that can make hard choices easier and transparent. Involving the full diversity and multiplicity of stakeholders in governance provides many benefits, notably legitimacy and ownership. In the face of the uncertainty and unpredictability that characterise fish chains, feedback interactions contribute to system learning and provide the flexibility to adapt to changing conditions based on the best available information from the widest possible range of actors.

The challenges presented and discussed in this chapter should not deter fisheries governors from engaging in the change process towards interactive governance. Change agents are increasingly appreciating that the horizons for societal change are distant ones. For changes of the magnitude and importance of fisheries governance reform to happen on a scale that will matter, it is important that they be started as soon as possible and that the necessary processes be sustained for long enough to become established and accepted. One thing is certain: unless new approaches are pursued, there will be widespread failure to realise the benefits from and achieve sustainability of a large proportion of the world's fisheries.

References

Aarset, B. and L. Foss 1996. Norway's cod farming industry: Adaptation, imitation or innovation? In: C. Bailey, S. Jentoft, and P. Sinclair (Eds.), *Aquacultural development: Social dimensions of an emerging industry.* Pp. 43-57. Boulder: Westview Press.

Abila, R.O. and E.G. Jansen 1997. *From local to global markets: The fish processing and exporting industry on the Kenyan part of Lake Victoria – Its structure, strategies and socio-economic impacts.* Working Paper 1997.8. Oslo: University of Oslo.

Abramovitz, J.N. 1996. *Imperiled waters, impoverished future: The decline of freshwater ecosysytems.* Worldwatch Paper 128. Washington DC: Worldwatch Institute.

Acheson, J.M. 1975. The lobster fiefs: Economic and ecological effects of territoriality in the Maine lobster industry. *Human Ecology* 3 (3): 183-207.

Acheson, J.M. 1979. Variations in traditional inshore fishing rights in Maine lobstering communities. In: R. Andersen (Ed.), *North Atlantic maritime cultures: Anthropological essays on changing adaptation.* Pp. 253-276. The Hague: Mouton.

Acheson, J.M. 1981. Anthropology of fishing. *Annual Review of Anthropology* 10: 275-316.

Acheson, J.M. 1988. *The lobster gangs of Maine.* Hannover: University Press of New England.

Achieng, A.P. 1990. The impact of the introduction of the Nile Perch, *Lates niloticus* (L.) on the fisheries of Lake Victoria. *Journal of Fish Biology* 37 (Supplement A): 17-23.

Ackefors, H. 1999. Environmental impact of different farming technologies. In: N. Svennig, H. Reinertsen, and M. New (Eds.), *Sustainable aquaculture. Food for the future?* Pp. 145-169. Rotterdam: A.A. Balkema.

Ackefors, H. and P. White 2002. A framework for declaring best environmental practices for aquaculture. *World Aquaculture* 33 (2): 54-59.

Acosta, M.L. 2002. *Condiciones laborales de los buzos miskitos en la Costa Atlántica de Nicaragua.* San José, Costa Rica: Oficina Internacional del Trabajo.

Afolabi, J.A. and O.A. Fagbenro 1998. Credit financing of coastal aquaculture in Nigeria. In: A. Eide and T. Vassdal (Eds.), *Proceedings of the 9th Biennial Conference of the International Institute of Fisheries Economics and Trade.* Vol. 1. Tromsø: University of Tromsø.

Agrawal A. and C.C. Gibson 2001. The role of community in natural resource conservation. In: A. Agrawal and C.C. Gibson (Eds.), *Communities and the environment: Ethnicity, gender, and the state in community-based conservation.* Pp. 1-31. New Brunswick: Rutgers University Press.

Ahmed, M. and M. Lorica 2002. Improving developing country food security through aquaculture development – Lessons from Asia. *Food Policy* 27:125-141.

Akimichi, T. 1984. Territorial regulation in the small scale fisheries of Itoman, Okinawa. In: K. Ruddle and T. Akimichi (Comps.), *Maritime institutions in the Western Pacific.* Pp. 37-88. Osaka: National Senri Ethnological Studies, Museum of Ethnology.

Aktea 2003. *Les femmes dans la pêche et les cultures marines en Europe. Journal of the "Femmes" European Thematic Network, No* 2:http://www.fishwomen.org/IMG/pdf/aktea2_net_uk.pdf. *Accessed 18-04-2005.*

Alegret, J.L. 1995. *Co-management of resources and conflict management: The case of the fishermen's confreries in Catalonia.* MARE Working Paper No. 2. Aarhus: Aarhus University.

Alegret, J.L. 1996. Ancient institutions confronting change: The Catalan fishermen's confradies. In: K. Crean and D. Symes (Eds.), *Fisheries management in crisis.* Pp. 92-98. Oxford: Blackwell.

Alegret, J.L. 1999. Space, resources and history: The social dimension of fisheries in the northwest Mediterranean. In: D. Symes (Ed.), *Europe's southern waters: Management issues and practice.* Pp. 55-65. Oxford: Blackwell.

Alegret, J.L. 2000. Economics and political anthropology of fisheries governance: The incipient failure of collective action in Catalan Cofradias. In: A. Hatcher and K. Robinson (Eds.), *Management institutions and governance systems in European fisheries. Proceedings of the 3rd Concerted Action Workshop on Economics and the Common Fisheries Policy, Vigo, Spain, 28-30 October 1999.* Pp. 179-195. Portsmouth: CEMARE, University of Portsmouth.

Alexander, P. 1977. Sea tenure in southern Sri Lanka. *Ethnology* 16 (3): 231-251.

Ali, S.A. 1964. Increased fish consumption through improved fish handling and distribution. *Contribution to Symposium on Increasing Fish Consumption Through Improved Fish Handling and Distribution, 16-31 October 1964.* Rome: FAO.

Allison, E.H. and R.J. McBride, 2003. Educational reform for improved natural resource management: fisheries and aquaculture in Bangladeshi universities. *Society and Natural Resources* 16: 249-264.

Almond, B. (Ed.). 1995. *Introducing applied ethics.* Oxford: Blackwell.

Amegavie, K. 1995. Outline of a fishery policy and action plan. *FAO Project TCP/Tog/3454.* Rome: FAO.

Anderson, E.N.J. 1987. A Malaysian tragedy of the commons. In: B.J. McCay and J.M. Acheson (Eds.), *The question of the commons – the culture and ecology of communal resources.* Pp. 327-343. Tucson: University of Arizona Press.

Anderson, J.L. 2002. Aquaculture and the future: Why fisheries economists should care. *Marine Resource Economics* 17: 133-151.

Anon. 2003. The promise of a blue revolution. *The Economist,* 9 August 2003: 19-21.

Apostle, R. and G. Barrett 1992. *Emptying their nets: Small capital and rural industrialization in the Nova Scotia fishing industry.* Toronto: University of Toronto Press.

Apostle, R., G. Barrett, P. Holm, S. Jentoft, L. Mazany, B.J. McCay, and K.H. Mikalsen 1998. *Community, state, and market on the North Atlantic Rim: Challenges to modernity in fisheries.* Toronto: University of Toronto Press.

Apostle, R., B.J. McCay, and K.H. Mikalsen 2002. *Enclosing the commons: Individual transferable quotas in the Nova Scotia fishery.* St. John's, Newfoundland: Institute of Social and Economic Research, Memorial University of Newfoundland.

Arbo, P. and B. Hersoug 1997. The globalization of the fishing industry and the case of Finnmark. *Marine Policy* 21 (2): 121-142.

Argyris, C. 1991. Teaching smart people to learn. *Harvard Business Review* May-June 1991.

Argyris, C. 1992. *On organizational learning.* Cambridge: Blackwell.

Armstrong, C.W. and D.J. Clark 1997. Just fishing? Equity and efficiency in fisheries management regimes. *Marine Resource Economics* 12: 203-220.

Arnason, R. 1993. Ocean fisheries management: Recent international developments. *Marine Policy* 17 (5): 334-339.

Arnason, R. 1995. *The Icelandic fisheries*. Oxford: Blackwell, Fishing News Books.

Asche, F. and P. Bernard 2000. Fisheries and the internationalisation of markets. In: U.R. Sumaila, R. Chuenpagdee, and M. Vasconcellos (Eds.), *Proceedings of the INCO-DC Workshop on Markets, Global Fisheries and Local Development, Bergen, Norway, 22-23 March 1999*. ACP-EU Fisheries Research Report No.7. Brussels: European Commission.

Asche, F. and R. Tveteras 2002. Economics of aquaculture. Special issue introduction. *Marine Resource Economics* 17: 73-75.

Bacallado, J.J., T. Cruz, A. Brito, J. Barquín, and M. Carrillo 1989. *Reservas marinas de Canarias*. Canarias: Consejería de Agricultura y Pesca de Canarias Secretaría General Técnica.

Bailey, C. and S. Jentoft 1990. Hard choices in fisheries development. *Marine Policy* 14 (4): 333-344.

Bailey, C., S. Jentoft, and P. Sinclair 1996. Social science contributions to aquacultural development. In: C. Bailey, S. Jentoft, and P. Sinclair (Eds.), *Aquacultural development: Social dimensions of an emerging industry*. Pp. 3-20. Boulder: Westview Press.

Baines, G.B. 1989. Traditional resource management in the Melanesian South Pacific: a development dilemma. In F. Berkes (Comp.), *Common property resources: Ecology and community based sustainable development*. Pp. 273-295. London: Belhaven Press.

Bakhayokho, M. and M. Kebe 1991. Problématique des relations entre la pêche artisanale et la pêche industrielle: Cas des ressources démersales. In: J.R. Durand, J. Lemoalle and J. Weber (Eds.), *La recherche face à la pêche artisanale*. Pp. 933-941. Orstom éditions, Montpellier.

Banuri, T.K., Göran-Mäler, M. Grubb, H.K. Jacobson, and F. Yamin 1995. Equity and social considerations. In: J.P. Bruce, H. Lee, and E.F. Haites (Eds.), *Climate change 1995*. Pp. 81-118. Cambridge: Cambridge University Press.

Barrett, G., M.I. Caniggia, and L. Read 2002. There are more vets than doctors in Chiloé: Social and community impact of the globalization of aquaculture in Chile. *World Development* 30 (11): 1951-1965.

Bartley, D.M. and R.S.V. Pullin 1999. Towards policies for aquatic genetic resources. In: R.S.V. Pullin, D.M. Bartley, and J. Kooiman (Eds.), *Towards policies for conservation and sustainable use of aquatic genetic resources. International Center for Living Aquatic Resources Management Conference Proceedings* 59: 1-16.

Basch, L.G., N.G. Schiller, and C. Szanton Blanc 1994. *Nations unbound: Transnational projects, postcolonial predicaments, and deterritorialized nation-states*. Langhorne: Gordon and Breach.

Bataille-Benguigui, M.C. 1999. Pêche et pêcheurs aux îles Tonga: Facteurs sociaux et culturelles du changement. In: G. Blanchet (Ed.), *Les Petites activitités de pêche dans le Pacifique Sud*. Paris.

Bateson, G. 1972. *Steps to ecology of mind: Collected essays in anthropology, psychiatry, evolution and epistemology*. Northvale: Jason Aronson.

Bavinck, M. 2001. *Marine resource management: Conflict and regulation in the fisheries of the Coromandel coast*. New Delhi: Sage Publications.

Bavinck, M., R. Chuenpagdee, M. Diallo, P. van der Heijden, J. Kooiman, R. Mahon, and S. Williams, 2005. *Interactive governance for fisheries – a guide to better practice*. Delft: Eburon.

Baytos, L.M. 1995. *Designing and implementing successful diversity programs*. New Jersey: Prentice-Hall.

Beamish, R.J. and C. Mahnken 1999. *Taking the next step in fisheries management. Ecosystem approaches for fisheries management.* Publication No. AK.SG. 99-01: 1-21. Fairbanks: Alaska Sea Grant College Program.

Beetham, D. 1991. *The legitimation of power.* Atlantic Highlands: Humanities Press International.

Begossi, A. 1996. The fishers and buyers from Búzios I.: Kin ties and modes of production. *Ciência e Cultura* 48: 142-147.

Begossi, A. 2002. Latin America fisheries: Local organization and management. In: *Proceedings of the 7th Biennal Conference of the International Association of Ecological Economics, 6-9 March 2002, Sousse, Tunísia.* Sousse Tunisia: International Society for Ecological Economics (ISEE).

Belden, G., M. Hyatt, and D. Ackley 1993. *Towards the learning organisation: a guide.* Toronto: Institute of Cultural Affairs (ICA).

Belfiore, S., 2003. The growth of integrated coastal management and the role of indicators in integrated coastal management: Introduction to the special issue. *Ocean & Coastal Management* 46 (3-4): 225-234

Bellwood D.R., A.S. Hoey, and J.H. Choat 2003. Limited functional redundancy in high diversity systems: Resilience and ecosystem function on coral reefs. *Ecology Letters* 6: 281-285.

Béné, C. 2003. When fishery rhymes with poverty: A first step beyond the old paradigm on povety in small-scale fisheries. *World Development* 31 (6): 949-975.

Berkes, F. 1985. Fishermen and the 'tragedy of the commons'. *Environmental Conservation* 12: 199-205.

Berkes, F. 1987. Common-property resource management and Cree Indian fisheries in sub-arctic Canada. In: B.J. McCay and J.M. Acheson (Eds.), *The question of the commons: The culture and ecology of communal resources.* Pp. 66-91. Tucson: University of Arizona Press.

Berkes, F. 2002. Cross-scale institutional linkages for commons management: Perspectives from the bottom up. In: E. Ostrom, T. Dietz, and N. Dolšak et al. (Eds.), *Drama of the Commons.* Pp. 293-321. Washington DC: National Academy Press.

Berkes, F., C. Folke, and J. Colding 1998. *Linking social and ecological systems: Management practices and social mechanisms for building resilience.* Cambridge: Cambridge University Press.

Berkes, F., R. Mahon, P. McConney, R. Pollnac, and R. Pomeroy (Eds.) 2001. *Managing small-scale fisheries: Alternative directions and methods.* Ottawa: International Development Research Centre.

Berting, J. 1996. Over rationaliteit en complexiteit. In: P. Nijkamp, W. Begeer, and J. Berting (Eds.), *Denken over complexe besluitvorming.* Pp. 17-30. The Hague: SDU.

Bharadwaj, A.S., W.R. Brignon, N.L. Gould, and P.W. Brown 2002. Evaluation of meat and bone meal in practical diets fed to juvenile hybrid striped bass *Morone chrysops* x *M. saxatilis. Journal of the World Aquaculture Society* 33 (4): 448-457.

Bianchi, G., H. Gislason, K. Graham, L. Hill, X. Jin, K. Koranteng, S. Manickchand-Heileman, I. Payá, K. Sainsbury, F. Sanchez, and K. Zwanenburg 2000. Impact of fishing on size composition and diversity of demersal fish communities. *ICES Journal of Marine Science* 57: 558-571.

Biermann, F. 1999. *Justice in the greenhouse.* In: F.L. Tóth (Ed.), *Fair weather.* Pp. 160-171. London: Earthscan.

Bilimoria, P. 1993. Indian ethics. In: P. Singer (Ed.), *A Companion to ethics.* Pp. 43-57. Oxford: Blackwell.

Binkley, M. 1995. *Risks, dangers, and rewards in the Nova Scotia offshore fishery.* Montreal: McGill-Queen's University Press.

Blaber, S.J.M. 1997. *Fish and fisheries of tropical estuaries*. London: Chapman &Hall.

Blaber, S.J.M., D.P. Cyrus, J.J. Albaret, Chong Ving Ching, J.W. Day, M. Elliott, M.S. Fonseca, D.E. Hoss, J. Orensanz, I.C. Potter, and W. Silvert 2000. Effects of fishing on the structure and functioning of estuarine and nearshore ecosystems. *ICES Journal of Marine Science* 57:590-602.

Blanchard, K., J. Carlos, and A. Randolph 1998. *Empowerment takes more than a minute*. San Francisco: Berrett-Koehler.

Block, P. 1996. *Stewardship: choosing service over self-interest*. San Francisco: Berrett-Koehler.

Boas, F. 1966. *Kwakiutl ethnography*. Chicago: University of Chicago Press.

Boersma, P.D. and J.K. Parrish 1999. Limiting abuse: Marine protected areas, a limited solution. *Ecological Economics* 31 (2): 287-304.

Bonanno, A. and D. Constance 1996. *Caught in the net: The global tuna industry, environmentalism, and the state*. Lawrence: University Press of Kansas.

Boncoeur, J., F. Alban, O. Guyader, and O. Thebaud 2002. Fish, fishers, seals and tourists: Economic consequences of creating a marine reserve in multi-species, multi-activity context. *Natural Resource Modeling* 15 (4): 387-411.

Bonfil, R., G. Munro, U.R. Sumaila, H. Valtysson, M. Wright, T. Pitcher, D. Preikshot, N. Haggen, and D. Pauly 1998. *Distant water fleets: An ecological, economic, and social assessment*. Vancouver: Fisheries Centre.

Boserup, E. 1970. *Women's role in economic development*. London: Allen &Unwin.

Botsford, W., J.C. Castilla, and C.H. Peterson 1997. The management of fisheries and marine ecosystems. *Science* 277: 509-514.

Boudon, R. 1996. The 'Cognivist Model', *Rationality and Society*, 8: 123-150.

Bouju, J. 1994. *De la bêche au filet. Étude anthropologique des populations littorales et des pêcheurs côtiers de Guinée*. Paris: Thèse d'Anthropologie Sociale et d'Ethnologie, EHESS, 2 Vols.

Bowen, B. 1999. Preserving genes species, or ecosystems? Healing the fractured foundations of conservation policy. *Molecular Ecology* 8: S5-S10.

Boyd, C.E. 1999a. Aquaculture sustainability and environmental issues. *World Aquaculture* 30: 10-13, 71-72.

Boyd, C.E. 1999b. *Codes of practice for responsible shrimp farming*. St. Louis: Global Aquaculture Alliance.

Boyd, C.E. 2003. The status of codes of practice in aquaculture. *World Aquaculture* 34 (2): 63-66.

Branch, G.M., J. May, B. Roberts, E. Russell, and B.M. Clark 2002a. Case studies on the socio-economic characteristics and lifestyles of subsistence and informal fishers in South Africa. *South African Journal of Marine Sciences* 24: 439-62.

Branch, G.M., M. Hauck, N. Siqwana-Ndulo, and A.H. Dye 2002b. Defining fishers in the South African context: Subsistence, artisanal and small-scale commercial fisheries. *South African Journal of Marine Sciences* 24: 475-88.

Brand, A.R., E.H. Allison, and E.J. Murphy 1991. North Irish Sea scallop fisheries: A review of changes. In: S.E. Shumway and P.A. Sandifer (Eds.), *An international compendium of scallop biology and culture world aquaculture society*. Pp. 204-218. Baton Rouge, LA: World Aquaculture Society

Brandt, A. 1984. *Fish catching methods of the world*. Farnham: Blackwell, Fishing News Books.

Bridger, C.J., B.A. Costa-Pierce, C.A. Goudey, R.R. Stickney, K.M. Fletcher, J.R. Gold, D.H. Lewis, J. Lotz, B.C. Posadas, E.W. Neyrey, R. Rayburn, T. Reid, C.A. Moncreiff, and D.L. Swann 2001. Sustainable offshore aquaculture development in the Gulf of Mexico. *World Aquaculture* 32 (3): 28-33, 60.

Britton, J.C. and B. Morton 1994. Marine carions and scavengers. *Oceanography and Marine Biology: An Annual Review* 32: 369-434.

Bromley, D.W. and S. Macinko 2002. *Who Owns America's Fisheries?* Center for Resource Economics, Covelo. CA: Island Press.

Bromley, D.W. and J. Paavola (Eds.), 2002. *Economics, ethics, and environmental policy.* Oxford: Blackwell.

Brugha, R. and Z. Varvasovsky, 2000. Stakeholder analysis: a review. *Health Policy and Planning* 15 (3),: 239-246.

Bruntland, G. (Ed.) 1987. *Our common future.* World Commission on Environment and Development. Oxford: Oxford University Press.

Burbidge, J. 1997. *Beyond prince and merchant; citizen participation and the rise of civil society.* New York: Pact Publications.

Bureau, D.P. 2000. Use of rendered animal protein ingredients in fish feeds. *International Aquafeed Magazine* (July).

CAC 2003. *Understanding the Codex Alimentarius.* Rome: Codex Alimentarius Commision. Available http://www.fao.org/docrep/w9114e/w9114e00.htm (Accessed 11 February 2005).

Caddy, J.F. 2000. Marine catchment basin effects versus impacts of fisheries on semi-enclosed seas. *ICES Journal of Marine Science* 57: 628-640.

Caddy, J.F. and R. Mahon 1995. *Reference points for fisheries management.* FAO Fish. Tech. Pap. 347. Rome: FAO.

Cadigan, S. 1991. *Economic and social relations of production in the Northeast coast of Newfoundland, with special reference to Conception Bay 1785-1855.* Ph.D. Thesis. St. John's, Newfoundland: Institute of Social and Economic Research, Memorial University of Newfoundland.

Campbell, T. 1996. Co-management of aboriginal resources. *Information North* 22 (1) Arctic Institute of North America. Available http://arcticcircle.uconn.edu/NatResources/comanagement.html.

Carrier, J.G. 1987. Marine tenure and conservation in Papua New Guinea: Problems in interpretation. In: B.J. McCay and J.M. Acheson (Eds.), *The question of the commons: The culture and ecology of communal resources.* Pp. 142-167. Tucson: University of Arizona Press.

Carrier, J.G. 1998. Introduction. In: J.G. Carrier and D. Miller (Eds.), *Virtualism: A new political economy.* Oxford and New York: Berg.

Cash, D.W. and S.C. Moser 2000. Linking global and local scales: Designing dynamic assessment and management processes. *Global Environmental Change* 10 (2): 109-120.

Caverivière A., M. Kulbicki, J. Konan, and F. Gerlotto 1981. Bilan des connaissances actuelles sur Balistes carolinensis dans le golf de Guinée. *Documents Scientifiques du Centre de Recherche Océanographique d'Abidjan* 12 (1) : 1-78

CBD 1994. *Convention on Biological Diversity. Text and annexes.* Châtelaine, Switzerland: Interim Secretariat for the Convention on Biological Diversity.

CBD 2000. *Cartagena Protocol on Biosafety to the Convention on Biological Diversity. Text and Annexes.* Montreal, Canada: Secretariat for the Convention on Biological Diversity.

CEC 2000. *Communication from the Commission on the precautionary principle. COM* (1. 02/02/2000). Brussels: Commission of the European Communities.

Cerny, P.C. 1990. *The changing architecture of politics: Structures, agency, and the future of the state.* London: Sage Publications.

CFS 2002. *Report of the 28th Session of the Committee on World Food Security, Rome, 6-9 June 2002*. Available http://www.fao.org/docrep/meeting/004/y707e.htm#p70_4078 (Accessed 11 June 2003).

Chamberlain, T. 2000. *Histamine in artisanal tuna fisheries of the Pacific Islands*. Marine Studies Technical Report 2000/06. Suva, Fiji: University of the South Pacific.

Chamberlain, T. 2001. Histamine levels in longlined tuna in Fiji: A comparison of samples from two different body sites and the effect of storage at different temperatures. *The South Pacific Journal of Natural Sciences* 19: 30-34.

Chang, R. (Ed.) 1997. *Incommensurablity, incomparability, and practical reason*. Cambridge: Harvard University Press.

Chapin, F.S., E.S. Zavaleta, V.T. Eviner, R.L. Naylor, P.M. Vitousek, H.L. Reynolds, D.U. Hooper, S. Lavorel, O.E. Sala, S.E. Hobbie, M.C. Mack, and S. Diaz 2000. Consequences of changing biodiversity. *Nature* 405: 234-242.

Charles, A. 1992. Fisheries conflicts: A unified framework. *Marine Policy* 16 (5): 376-393.

Charles, A. 2001. *Sustainable fishery systems*. Oxford: Blackwell.

Chauveau, J.P. and E. Jul-Larsen 2000. Du paradigme halieutique à l'anthropologie des dynamiques institutionnelles. In: J.P. Chauveau, E. Jul-Larsen, and C. Chaboud (Eds.), *Les pêches piroguières en Afrique de l'Ouest. Dynamiques institutionnelles: Pouvoirs, mobilités, marchés*. Pp. 9-86. Paris: Karthala, Institut de recherche pour le développement; Bergen: Christian-Michelsen Institute.

Chauveau, J.P., E. Jul-Larsen, and C. Chaboud (Eds.) 2000. *Les pêches piroguières en Afrique de l'Ouest. Dynamiques institutionnelles: pouvoirs, mobilités, marchés*. Paris: Karthala, Institut de recherche pour le développement; Bergen: Christian-Michelsen Institute.

Cheong, S.M. 2003. Privatizing tendencies: Fishing communities and tourism in Korea. *Marine Policy* 27 (1): 23-29.

Childs, W.R. 2000. Control, conflict and international trade (The internal and international fish trades of medieval England and Wales). In: D.J. Starkey, C. Reid, and N. Ashcroft (Eds.), *England's sea fisheries: The commercial sea fisheries of England and Wales since 1300*. Pp. 32-35. London: Chatham Publishing.

Christensen, V. 1998. Fishery-induced changes in a marine ecosystem: Insights for models of the Gulf of Thailand. *Journal of Fish Biology* 53 (Supplement A): 128-142.

Christensen, V. 2000. Indicators for marine ecosystems affected by fisheries. *Marine and Freshwater Research* 51: 447-450.

Christensen, V. and D. Pauly 1998. Changes in models of aquatic ecosystems approaching carrying capacity. *Ecological Applications* 8 (1) Supplement: S104-S109.

Christensen, V. and C. Walters 2002. Ecosystem-scale optimization policies: The nature of the beast. *Presentation at the 4th William R. and Lenore Mote International Symposium in Fisheries Ecology, Confronting Trade-offs in the Ecosystem Approach to Fisheries Management, 5-7 November 2002, Sarasota, Florida*.

Chuenpagdee, R., J.L. Knetsch, and T.C. Brown 2001. Coastal management using public judgments, importance scales, and predetermined schedule. *Coastal Management* 29 (4): 253-270.

Chuenpagdee, R., L.E. Morgan, S.M. Maxwell, E.A. Norse, and D. Pauly 2003. Shifting gears: Assessing collateral impacts of fishing methods in the US waters. *Frontiers in Ecology and the Environment* 10 (1): 517-524.

Chuenpagdee, R. and D. Pauly 2004. Improving the state of coastal areas in the Asia-Pacific region. *Coastal Management* 32 (1): 3-15.

Cicin-Sain, B., M.K. Orbach, S.J. Sellers, and E. Manzanilla 1986. Conflictual inter-dependence: United States-Mexican relations on fishery resources. *Natural Resources Journal* 26: 769-92.

Cicin-Sain, B. and R.W. Knecht 1998. *Integrated coastal and ocean management. Concepts and practices.* Washington DC: Island Press.

CITES 2004. Convention on International Trade in Endangered Species of Wild Fauna and Flora.. Available http://www.cites.org/eng/. (Accessed 9 April 2004).

Clark, B.M., M. Huack, J.M. Harris, K. Salo, and E. Russell 2002. Identification of subsistence fishers, fishing areas, resource use and activities along the South African Coast. *South African Journal of Marine Sciences* 24: 425-38.

Coase, R. 1937. The nature of the firm. *Economica* (Nov.): 386-405.

Cochrane, K.L. (Ed.) 2002. *A fishery managers guidebook: management measures and their application.* Fisheries Technical Paper No. 424. Rome: FAO.

COFI 2003. Strategies for increasing the sustainable contribution of small-scale fisheries to food security and poverty alleviation. *The 25th session of the Committee on Fisheries of the Food and Agriculture Organisation of the United Nations. Rome, Italy, 24-28 February 2003.* Available http://www.fao.org/docrep/meeting/005/Y8111E.HTM (Accessed 28 August 2003).

Cohen, M. 1989. The problem of studying 'economic man'. In: A.R. Miles and G. Finn (Eds.), *Feminism: From pressure to politics.* Pp. 147-159. Montreal: Black Rose Books.

Cole, S. 1991. *Women of the praia: Work and lives in a Portuguese coastal community.* Princeton: Princeton University Press.

Collet, S. 2002. Appropriation of marine resources: from management to an ethical approach to fisheries governance. *Social Science Information* 41 (4): 531-553.

Collison, C., G. Parcell, 2001. *Learning to fly: practical lessons form one of the world's leading knowledge companies.* Chichester: Capstone Publishing Ltd.

Comas d'Argemir, D. 1995. *Trabajo, género, cultura: La construcción de desigualdades entre hombre y mujeres.* Barcelona: Institut Català d'Antropologia.

COM (Commission of the European Communities) 2002. A strategy for the sustainable development of European aquaculture. *Communication from the Commission to the Council and the European Parliament. COM (2002) 511 final.* Available http://europa.eu.int/eur-lex/en/com/cnc/2002/com2002_0511en01.pdf (Accessed 11 February 2005).

Connell, J.H. 1978. Diversity in tropical rain forests and coral reefs. *Science* 199: 1302-1310.

Connelly, M.P. and M. MacDonald 1995. State policy: The household and women's work in the Atlantic fishery. In: D. Frank and G. Kealey (Eds.), *Labour and working-class history in Atlantic Canada: A reader.* St. John's, Newfoundland: Institute for Social and Economic Research, Memorial University of Newfoundland.

Conover, D.O. and S.B. Munch 2002. Sustaining fisheries yields over evolutionary time scales. *Science* 297: 94-96.

Cooper, F. 2002. *Africa since 1940. The past and the present.* Cambridge: Cambridge University Press.

Copes, P. 1997. Social impacts of fisheries management regimes based on individual quotas. In: G. Pálsson and G. Petursdottir (Eds.), *Social implications of quota systems in fisheries.* Copenhagen: TemaNord.

Copesino, W.C. 1997. *Supply chain management: The basics and beyond.* Eastborne, UK: Saint Lucie Press.

Cormier-Salem, M.C. 2000. Appropriation des ressources, enjeu foncier et espace halieutique sur le littoral ouest-africain. In: J.P. Chauveau, E. Jul-Larsen, and C.

Chaboud (Eds.), *Les pêches piroguières en Afrique de l'Ouest. Dynamiques institu-tionnelles: Pouvoirs, mobilités, marchés.* Pp. 205-230. Paris: Karthala, Institut de recherche pour le développement; Bergen: Christian-Michelsen Institute.

Costanza, R. 1992. Toward an operational definition of ecosystem health. In: R. Costanza, B.G. Norton, and B.D. Haskell (Eds.), *Ecosystem health: New goals for sustainable development.* Pp. 238-256. Covelo: Island Press.

Costanza, R., F. Andrade, P. Antunes, M. van den Belt, D. Boesch, D. Boersma, F. Catarino, S. Hanna, K. Limburg, B. Low, M. Molitor, J.G. Pereira, S. Rayner, R. Santos, J. Wilson, and M. Young 1998. Principles for sustainable governance of the oceans. *Science* 281: 198-199.

Costa-Pierce, B.A. 1998. Constraints to the sustainability of cage culture for resettle-ment from hydropower dams in Asia: An Indonesian case study. *Journal of En-vironmental Development* 7 (4): 333-363.

Costa-Pierce, B.A. 2002. Ecology as the paradigm for the future of aquaculture. In: B.A. Costa-Pierce (Ed.), *Ecological aquaculture: The evolution of the blue revolution..* Pp. 339-372. Oxford: Blackwell.

Côté, I.M. and J.D. Reynolds 2002. Predictive ecology to the rescue? *Science* 298: 1181-1182.

Cury, P., L. Shannon, and Y. Shin 2003. The functioning of marine ecosystems: a fisheries perspective. In: M. Sinclair and G. Valdimarsson (Eds.), *Responsible fish-eries in the marine ecosystem.* Pp. 103-123. Wallingford, UK: CABI Publishing.

Coull, J.R. 1996. *The sea fisheries of Scotland: A historical geography.* Edinburgh: John Donald Press.

Coward, H., R. Ommer, and T.J. Pitcher (Eds.) 2000. *Fish ethics: Justice in the Cana-dian fisheries.* St. John's, Newfoundland: Institute of Social and Economic Re-search, Memorial University of Newfoundland.

Creswell, R.L. and R. Flos 2002. *Perspectives on responsible aquaculture for the new millenium.* Baton Rouge: the World Aquaculture Society; Oostende, Belgium: the European Aquaculture Society.

Crozier, M. 1964. *The bureaucratic phenomenon.* Chicago: University of Chicago Press.

Crucible Group 2000. *Seeding Solutions: Policy options for Genetic Resources.* Vol. 1. Ottawa, Canada: International Development Research Centre.

CUTS (Consumer Unity and Trust Society) 2001. *Standards and market access.* Avail-able http://cuts.org/sps-analysis-sps_case_kny.htm (Accessed 15 July 2002).

Cyert, R.M. and J.G. March 1963. *A behavioural theory of the firm.* Englewood Cliffs: Prentice Hall.

Dahlberg, F. 1981. *Woman the gatherer.* New Haven: Yale University Press.

Davenport, J., K. Black, G. Burnell, T. Cross, S. Culloty, S. Ekaratne, B. Furness, M. Mulcahy, and H. Thetmeyer 2003. *Aquaculture: The ecological issues.* Oxford: Blackwell.

Davis, D.L. and J. Nadel-Klein 1992. Gender, culture and the sea: Contemporary theoretical approaches. *Society and Nature Resources* 5: 135-147.

Davis, S. 1984. Aboriginal claims to coastal waters in North Eastern Arnhem Land, Northern Australia. In: K. Ruddle and T. Akimichi (Comps.), *Maritime institu-tions in Western Pacific.* Pp. 231-251. Osaka: Senri Ethnological Studies, National Museum of Ethnology.

Dayton, P.K., S.F. Thrush, M.T. Agardy, and R.J. Hofman 1995. Environmental ef-fects of marine fishing. *Aquatic Conservation: Marine and Freshwater Ecosystems* 5: 205-232.

De Andrade, R. 1999. Fisheries disputes in Latin America. *ECLAC Environment and Development Series Paper No. 5*. Santiago: ECLAC.

Deere, C. 1999a. *Eco-labelling and sustainable fisheries*. Washington DC: IUCN.

Deere, C. 1999b. *Net gains: linking fisheries management, international trade and sustainable development*. Washington DC: IUCN.

Degnbol, P. 2003. Science and the user perspective: The scale gap and the need for co-management. In: D.C. Wilson, J.R. Nielsen, and P. Degnbol (Eds.), *The fisheries co-management experience: Accomplishments, challenges and prospects*. Pp. 31-49. Dordrecht: Kluwer Academic Publishers.

Degnbol, P., A. Eide, J.T. de Almeida, V. Johnsen, and J. Raakjær Nielsen 2002. *A study of the fisheries sector of Mozambique*. Oslo: NORAD.

Delgado, C.L., M.W. Rosegrant, S. Meijer, N. Wada, and M. Ahmed 2002. *Fish to 2020: Implications of global fish outlook for developing countries*. Washington DC: International Food Policy Research Institute; Penang, Malaysia: World Fish Center.

Delgado, C.L., N. Wada, M.W. Rosegrant, S. Meijer, and M. Ahmed 2003. *Fish to 2020: Supply and demand in changing global markets*. Washington DC: International Food Policy Research Institute; Penang, Malaysia: World Fish Center.

Denzau, A.T. and D.C. North 2000. Shared mental models: Ideologies and institutions. In: A. Lupia, M.D. McCubbins, and S.L. Popkin (Eds.), *Elements of reason*. Pp. 23-46. Cambridge: Cambridge University Press.

Des Clers, S. and C.E. Nauen (Eds.) 2002. *New concepts and indicators in fisheries and aquaculture/ Nouveaux concepts et indicateurs pour la peche et l'aquaculture/ Nuevos conceptos e indicadores para las pesquerias y la acuicultura*. Brussels: ACP-EU Fisheries Research Report No. 13.

De Silva, P. 1993. Buddhist ethics. In: P. Singer (Ed.), *A Companion to ethics*. Pp. 58-67. Oxford: Blackwell.

DeVorets, D. and K.G. Salvanes 1993. Market structure for farmed salmon. *American Journal of Agricultural Economics* 75 (2): 227-233.

DFID 1999. *Introduction, overview*. Sustainable Livelihoods Guidance Sheets 1.1. London: UK Department for International Development.

Diallo, M.M., V. Fautrel, R.P. Milimono, and K. Solie 1996. Fish marketing in Guinea: An overview of the main marketing player. *EC Fisheries Cooperation Bulletin* 9 (4): 16-17.

Die, D. 2002. *Design and implementation of management plans*. FAO Fisheries Technical Paper No. 424: 205-220. Rome: FAO.

Dierberg, F.E. and W. Kiattisimkul 1996. Issues, impacts, and implications of shrimp aquaculture in Thailand. *Environmental Management* 20 (5): 649-666.

Division for Ocean Affairs and the Law of the Sea 2003. *A historical perspective*. Available http://www.un.org/Depts/los/convention_agreements/convention_historical_perspective.htm (Accessed 11 February 2005).

Djelic, M.L. and S. Quack (Eds.) 2003. *Globalization and institutions. Redefining the rules of the economic game*. Cheltenham: Edward Elgar.

DOF (Thailand Department of Fisheries) 2002. *Thai fishing vessels statistics 2000*. Document No. 16/2002. Bangkok: Ministry of Agriculture and Cooperatives, Department of Fisheries.

Dollar, S.J. and G.W. Tribble 1993. Recurrent storm disturbance and recovery: A long-term study of coral communities in Hawaii. *Coral Reefs* 12: 223-233.

Donagan, A. 1992. Twentieth-century Anglo-American ethics. In: L.C. Becker and C.B. Becker (Eds.), *A history of Western ethics*. Pp. 142-154. New York: Garland Publishers.

Done, T.J. 1999. Coral community adaptability to environmental changes at scales of regions, reefs and reef zones. *American Zoologist* 39: 66-79.

Drainville, A.C. 2004. *Contesting globalization: Space and place in the world economy.* London: Routledge

Dror, Y. 2002. *The capacity to govern. A report to the Club of Rome.* London: Frank Class.

Duff, A.S. 2000. *Information society studies.* London: Routledge.

Dunn, E. 2003. The role of environmental NGOs in fisheries governance. *Paper presented to the Workshop on Fisheries Governance Politics, Newcastle, UK, 4-6 September 2003.*

Duplisea, D.E. and S.R. Kerr 1995. Application of a biomass size spectrum model to demersal fish data from the Scotian Shelf. *Journal of Theoretical Biology* 177: 263-269.

Durkheim, E. 1964 [1893]. *The division of labor in society.* London: The Free Press.

Durrenberger, E.P. 1996. *Gulf coast soundings: People and policy in the Mississippi shrimp industry.* Lawrence: University of Kansas Press.

Dwire, A. 1996. Paradise under siege: A case study of aquacultural development in Nova Scotia. In: C. Bailey, S. Jentoft, and P. Sinclair (Eds.), *Aquacultural development: Social dimensions of an emerging industry.* Pp. 93-110. Boulder: Westview Press.

Dyer, C.L. and J.R. McGoodwin (Eds.) 1994 *Folk management in the world's fisheries: Lessons for modern fisheries management.* Boulder: University Press of Colorado.

Eagle, J., R. Naylor, and W. Smith 2004. Why farm salmon outcompete fishery salmon. *Marine Policy* 28:259-270.

Eberlee, J. 2003. Assessing the benefits of bio-prospecting in Latin America. *Reports: Science from the Developing World.* Available http://www.idrc.ca/reports/read_article_english.cfm?article_num=609 (Accessed 15 April 2003).

Edel, A. 1986. Ethical theory and moral practice. In: J.P. Demarco and R.M. Fox (Eds.), *New directions in ethics.* Pp. 317-335. New York: Routledge & Kegan Paul.

Edwards, P. 1998. A systems approach for the promotion of integrated aquaculture. *Aquaculture Economics and Management* 2 (1): 1-12.

Edwards, P. 2000. Wastewater-fed aquaculture: State of the art. In: B.B. Jana, R.D. Banerjee, B. Conterstam, and J. Heeb (Eds.), *Waste recycling and resource management in the developing world.* Pp. 37-69. Kalayani, India: University of Kalayani; Geneva: International Ecological Engineering Society.

Edwards, P., R.S.V. Pullin, and J.A. Gartner 1988. Research and education for the development of integrated crop-livestock-fish farming systems in the tropics. *ICLARM Studies and Reviews 16.* Manila: International Center for Living Aquatic Resources Management.

Edwards, P., D.C. Little, and H. Demaine (Eds.) 2002. *Rural aquaculture.* Wallingford, UK: CABI Publishing.

Elliot, C.M. (Ed.) 2003. *Civil society and democracy. A reader.* Oxford: Oxford University Press.

Ellis, F. 2000. *Rural livelihoods and diversity in developing countries.* Oxford: Oxford University Press.

Ellis, R. 2003. *The empty ocean.* Washington DC: Island Press.

El-Saidy, D.M.S.D. and M.M.A. Gaber 2002. Complete replacement of fishmeal by soybean meal with dietary L-lysine supplementation for Nile tilapia *Oreochromis niloticus* (L.) fingerlings. *Journal of the World Aquaculture Society* 33 (3): 297-306.

Elvevoll, E.O. and D.G. James 2000. Potential benefits of fish for maternal, foetal and neonatal nutrition. *Food, Nutrition and Agriculture* 27: 28-39.

Erkoreka Gervasio, J. 1991. *Análisis histórico institucional de las cofradías de mareantes del país vasco.* Vitoria: Gobierno Vasco.

Escallier, C. 1995. *L'Empreinte de la mer: Identité des pêcheurs de Nazaré, Portugal. Ethnologie d'une communauté de pêcheurs.* Paris: Département d'Anthropologie, Université de Paris X-Nanterre.

Essuman, K.M. 1992. *Fermented fish in Africa: A study on processing, marketing and consumption.* T329. Rome: FAO.

European Commission 2003. The use of fish by-products in aquaculture. *Report of the Scientific Committee on Animal Health and Welfare.* Brussels: Health and Consumer Protection Directorate General, European Commission.

European Parliament 2003. *European Parliament resolution on aquaculture in the European Union: Present and Future (2002/2058 (INI)).* Brussels: European Commission.

Evans, C. 2003. *Managing for knowledge.* New York: Butterworth-Heinemann.

Eythórsson, E. 1996. Theory and practice of ITQs in Iceland. Privatization of common fishing rights. *Marine Policy* 20 (3): 269-281.

Fagbenro, O.A. 1997. A review of biological and economic principles underlying commercial fish culture in Nigeria. *Journal of West African Fisheries* 3 (2): 171-177.

Fairtrade Foundation. Available http://www.fairtrade.org.uk/about_standards.htm (Accessed 4 March 2005).

FAO 1985. Fish processing in Africa. *Proceedings of the FAO expert consultation on fish technology in Africa.* (R329 Suppl.). Rome: Food and Agriculture Organization.

FAO 1995. *Code of Conduct For Responsible Fisheries.* Rome: Food and Agriculture Organization.

FAO 1996. Precautionary approach to capture fisheries and species introductions. *FAO Technical guidelines for responsible fisheries No. 2.* Rome: Food and Agriculture Organization.

FAO 1997a. Aquaculture development. *FAO Technical Guidelines for Responsible Fisheries No. 5.* Rome: Food and Agriculture Organization.

FAO 1997b. Fisheries management. *FAO Technical Guidelines for Responsible Fisheries No. 4.* Rome: Food and Agriculture Organization.

FAO 1998. *The state of world fisheries and aquaculture.* Rome: Food and Agriculture Organization.

FAO 1999a. *Numbers of fishers 1970-1996.* Fishery Information Data and Statistics Unit. Rome: Food and Agriculture Organization.

FAO 1999b. *Yearbook of fisheries statistics: Commodities.* Rome: Food and Agriculture Organization.

FAO 1999c. *International plan of action for the management of fishing capacity.* Rome: Food and Agriculture Organization.

FAO 1999d. *Indicators for sustainable development of marine capture fisheries.* FAO Technical Guidelines for Responsible Fisheries No. 8. Rome: Food and Agriculture Organization.

FAO 2000a. *FAO yearbook of fisheries statistics.* Rome: Food and Agriculture Organization.

FAO 2000b. *El estado mundial de la pesca y la acuicultura-2000 (SOFIA).* Available http://www.fao.org/DOCREP/003/X8002S/x8002s04.htm.

FAO 2001a. *The state of food and agriculture.* Rome: Food and Agriculture Organization.

FAO 2001b. *Plan of action for women in development.* Rome: Food and Agriculture Organization.

FAO 2001c. *The state of food insecurity in the world 2001.* Rome: Food and Agriculture Organization.

FAO 2001d. Aquaculture in the third millennium. *Technical proceedings of the Conference on Aquaculture in the Third Millennium.* Rome: Food and Agriculture Organization.

FAO 2002a. *The state of world fisheries and aquaculture 2002.* Rome: Food and Agriculture Organization.

FAO 2002b. *World fisheries and aquaculture atlas.* CD-Rom. Rome: Food and Agriculture Organization.

FAO 2002c. *Community fishery centres: Guidelines for establishment and operation.* Rome: Food and Agriculture Organization.

FAO 2003a. *FAOSTAT: FAO statistical database.* Rome: Food and Agriculture Organization.

FAO 2003b. Farming fish for the future, sustainably. *Report of the FAO Sub-Committee on Aquaculture.* Rome: Food and Agriculture Organization. Available http://www.fao.org/english/newsroom/news/2003/21619-en.html.

FAO 2003c. *Supply utilisation accounts and food balance sheets in the context of a national statistical system.* Rome: Food and Agriculture Organization. Available http://www.fao.org/es/ESS (Accessed 3 January 2003).

FAO 2003d. Review of the state of world aquaculture. *FAO Fisheries Circular No. 886, Rev.2. FIRI/C886 (REV.2).* Rome: Food and Agriculture Organization.

FAO 2003e. *Fish is food for the brain as well as good protein.* Rome: Food and Agriculture Organization. Available http://www.fao.org/focus/e/fisheries/nutr.htm (Accessed 26 March 2003).

FAO 2003f. *Aquaculture: Not just an export industry.* Rome: Food and Agriculture Organization Available http://www.fao.org/english/newsroom/focus/2003/aquacutlre.htm (Accessed 17 September 2003).

FAO 2003g. Introducing fisheries subsidies. *FAO Fisheries Technical Paper 437.* Rome: Food and Agriculture Organization.

FAO 2003h. *The state of food insecurity in the world 2003.* Rome: Food and Agriculture Organization.

FAO 2004a. *Fisheries and aquaculture issues fact sheet, United Nations fish stocks agreement.* Available http://www.fao.org/figis (Accessed 9 April 2004).

FAO 2004b. *Report of the second session of the Working Party on Small-scale Fisheries.* Bangkok, Thailand, n18-21 November 2003. FAO Fisheries Reports No. 735: Rome: Food and Agriculture Organization.

FAO/DFID 2004. *Sustainable fisheries livelihoods programme.* Rome: Food and Agriculture Organization. London: Department For International Development. Available http://www.sflp.org/ (Accessed April 21, 2004).

Farrow, S. and U.R. Sumaila 2002. Conference summary: The 'new' emerging economics of marine protected areas. *Fish & Fisheries* 3: 356-359. Oxford: Blackwell.

Fay, C. 2000. Des poissons et des hommes: Pêcheurs, chercheurs et administrateurs face à la pêche au Maasina (Mali). In: J.P. Chauveau, E. Jul-Larsen, and C. Chaboud (Eds.), *Les pêches piroguières en Afrique de l'Ouest. Dynamiques institutionnelles: Pouvoirs, mobilités, marchés.* Pp. 125-166. Paris: Karthala, Institut de recherche pour le développement; Bergen: Christian-Michelsen Institute.

Fearne, A., S. Hornibrook, and S. Dedman 2001. The management of perceived risk in the food supply chain: A comparative study of retailer-led beef quality assurance schemes in Germany and Italy. *International Food and Agribusiness Management Review* 4: 19-36.

Feeny, D., F. Berkes, B.J. McCay, and J.M. Acheson 1990. The tragedy of the commons: Twenty-two years later. *Human Ecology* 18 (1): 1-19.

Felt, L. 1990. Barriers to user participation in the management of the Canadian Atlantic salmon fishery: If wishes were fishes. *Marine Policy* (July): 345-360.

Féral, F. 1990. *La prud'homie des pêcheurs de Palavas, droit et économie de l'environnement*. Lyon: Publications Périodiques Spécialisées.

Ferguson, A.R.B. 1999. The essence of ecological footprints. Letters to the Editor. *Ecological Economics* 31: 318-319.

Fine, B. 1998. The triumph of economics: Or, 'rationality' can be dangerous to your reasoning. In: J.G. Carrier and D. Miller (Eds.), *Virtualism: A new political economy*. Pp. 49-73. New York: Berg.

Fink, D.B. 1998. Judaism and ecology: A theology of creation. *Earth Ethics* 10 (1).

Finlayson, A.C. 1994. *Fishing for truth: A sociological analysis of northern cod stock assessments from 1977-1990*. St. John's, Newfoundland: Institute of Social and Economic Research, Memorial University of Newfoundland.

Finlayson, A.C. and B.J. McCay 1998. Crossing the threshold of ecosystem resilience: The commercial extinction of northern cod. In: F. Berkes and C. Folke (Eds.), *Linking social and ecological systems: Management practices and social mechanisms for building resilience*. Pp. 311-337. Cambridge: Cambridge University Press.

Finnish Sami Parliament 1997. Land rights, linguistic rights, and cultural autonomy for the Finnish Sami people. *Indigenous Affairs* 33/4.

Firth, R. 1966. *Malay fishermen: Their peasant economy*. Hamden: Archon Books.

Fishing News 2003. Get ready now for catch traceability. 9 May: 6.

Flyvbjerg, B. 2001. *Making social science matter*. Cambridge: Cambridge University press.

Folke, C. and N. Kaustky 1992. Aquaculture with its environment: Prospects for sustainability. *Ocean and Coastal Management* 17: 5-24.

Folke, C., S. Carpenter, T. Elmqvist, L. Gunderson, C.S. Holling, and B. Walker 2002. Resilience and sustainable development: building adaptive capacity in a world of transformations. *Ambio* 31: 437-440.

Folkerts, H. and H. Koehorst 1998. Challenges in international food supply chains: Vertical co-ordination in the European agribusiness and food industries. *British Food Journal* 100 (8): 385-388.

Fonseca, M.S., G.W. Thayer, and A.J. Chester 1984. Impact of scallop harvesting on eelgrass (Zoostera marina) meadows: Implications for management. *North American Journal of Fisheries Management* 4: 286-293.

Frangoudes, K. 1997. *Marine resource management in the French and Greek Mediterranean, final report*. MARE/EU, Contract EV5V-CT94-0386. Brest: OIKOS

Frangoudes, K. 2002. Fisherwomen in France: Role, organisations and claims. *Contribution to Workshop on Gender in Fisheries and Aquaculture, EC/INCO programme, Brussels, Belgium, 9-10 December 2002*. Unpublished manuscript.

Franquesa, R. 1993. *Le rôle des organisations professionnelles dans la gestion des pêches en Méditerranée: Étude de cas concernant de l'Espagne*. DGXIV, contrat 1/med/91/010. Barcelona: University of Barcelona.

Fraser, O. and S. Sumar 1998. Compositional changes and spoilage in fish – An introduction. *Nutrition and Food Science* 5: 275-279.

Friedrich, C.J. 1963. *Man and his government.* New York: McGraw-Hill.

Friis, P. 1994. Some outlines for the future of European fishing industry. *Contribution to EC/AIR Programme Workshop, Brussels, Belgium, 5-6 May 1994.*

Froese, R. and D. Pauly (Eds.) 1998. *FISHBASE 98: Concepts, design and data sources.* Manila: International Center for Living Aquatic Resources Management.

Froese, R. and D. Pauly (Eds.) 1999. *FISHBASE 99: Concepts, design and data sources.* Penang, Malaysia: World Fish Center.

Galbraith, J.K. 1973. *Economics and the public purpose.* London: Penguin Books.

Garcia, S.M. and R. Willmann 1999. Responsible marine capture fisheries: Main global issues and solutions. In: *Sustainable Agriculture Solutions: The Action Report of the Sustainable Agriculture Initiative.* Pp. 277-291. London: Novello Press Ltd.

Garcia, S.M. and D. Staples 2000a. Sustainability indicators in marine capture fisheries: introduction to the special issue. *Marine and Freshwater Research* 51: 381-384.

Garcia, S.M. and D. Staples 2000b. Sustainability reference systems and indicators for responsible marine capture fisheries: A review of concepts and elements for a set of guidelines. *Marine and Freshwater Research* 51: 385-426.

Garcia, S.M. and I.L. Moreno 2003. Global overview of marine fisheries. In: M. Sinclair and G. Valdimarsson (Eds.), *Responsible fisheries in the marine ecosystem.* Pp. 1-24. Wallingford, UK: CABI Publishing.

Garrison, L.P. and J.S. Link 2000. Fishing effects on spatial distribution and trophic guild structure of the fish communtiy in the Georges Bank region. *ICES Journal of Marine Science* 57: 723-730.

GATT 1947. *The General Agreement on Tariffs and Trade.* Available http://www.wto.org/english/docs_e/legal_e/gatt47_01_e.htm (Accessed 11 February 2005).

Geertz, C. 1966. *Agricultural involution: The process of ecological change in Indonesia.* Berkeley: University of California Press.

Gemmill, B. and A. Bamidele-Izu, n.d. The role of NGOs and civil society in global environmental governance. In: D.C. Esty and M.H. Ivanova (Eds.), *Global environmental governance: Options and opportunities.* Yale Center for Environmental Law and Policy. Available http://www.yale.edu/environment/publications/geg/gemmill.pdf.

Gibbon, P. 1997. *Of saviours and punks: The political economy of the Nile Perch marketing chain in Tanzania.* Working Paper 97.3. Copenhagen: Centre for Development Research.

Gibson, C.C., E. Ostrom, and T.K. Ahn 2000. The concept of scale and the human dimensions of global change: A survey. *Ecological Economics* 32: 217-239.

Gibson, C.C., M.A. McKean, and E. Ostrom 2000. Forests, people and governance: Some initial theoretical lessons. In: C.C. Gibson, M.A. McKean, and E. Ostrom (Eds.), *People and forests: Communities, institutions, and governance.* Pp. 227-242. Cambridge: MIT Press.

Giddens, A. 1990. *The consequences of modernity.* Oxford: Polity Press.

Gillespie, S. and L. Haddad 2001. *Attacking the double burden of malnutrition in Asia and the Pacific.* ADB Nutrition and Development Series No. 4. Manila: Asian Development Bank.

Glencross, B., J. Curnow, W. Hawkins, and M. Felsing 2002. Evaluation of yellow lupin *Lupinus lutens* meal as an alternative protein resource in diets for sea-cage reared rainbow trout *Oncorhynchus mykiss. Journal of the World Aquaculture Society* 33 (3): 287-296.

Globefish 1994. Fish trade in West Africa. *Globefish Research Programme.* Vol. 29. Rome: FAO.

Gordon, D.V. and R. Hannesson 1996. On prices of fresh and frozen cod fish in European and U.S. markets. *Marine Resource Economics* 11: 223-238.

Goulding, I. 2002. Health conditions and trade in fishery products. *Contribution to the 14th Annual Conference, European Association of Fisheries Economists, University of the Algarve, 25-27 March 2002.* Alfeizerão, Portugal: Megapesca.

Graham, M. 1948. *Rational fishing of the cod of the North Sea. Being the Buckland Lectures for 1939.* London: Edvard Arnold.

Graham, P., N. Klijn, A. Cox, A. Stokes, and J. Hartmann 1998. Modelling seafood trade liberalism in the APEC region. In: A. Eide and T. Vassdal (Eds.), *Proceedings of the 9th Biennial Conference of the International Institute of Fisheries Economics and Trade.* Vol. 2. Tromsø: IIFET.

Granovetter, M. 1985. Economic action and social structure: The problem of embeddedness. *American Journal of Sociology* 91 (3): 481-510.

Graz, M. 2002. *Realizing new tracing technology in food safety manufacturing systems: A case study in the fishing industry* (Mimeo). Cape Town, South Africa: Irvin and Johnson.

Greenstreet, S.P. and S.J. Hall 1996. Fishing and groundfish assemblage structure in the north western North Sea: An analysis of long term and spatial trends. *Journal of Animal Ecology* 65: 577-598.

Grzetic, B., M. Shrimpton, and S. Skipton 1996. *Women, employment, equity and the Hibernia construction project: A study of women's experiences on the Hibernia construction Project, Mosquito Cove, Newfoundland.* St. John's, Newfoundland: WITT Newfoundland.

GWP 2002a. *Dialogue on effective water governance.* Stockholm: Secretariat for the Global Water Partnership.

GWP 2002b. *Toolbox. Integrated Water Resources Management. Policy Guidance and Operational Tools.* Version I. Stockholm: Global Water Partnership.

Habermas, J. 1984. *The theory of communicative action.* Boston: Beacon Press.

Hahn, M.H. and R.V. Ribeiro 1999. Heuristic guided simulator for the operational planning of the transport of sugar cane. *Journal of the Operational Research Society* 50 (5): 451-460.

Hall, S. 1994. Physical disturbance and marine benthic communities: Life in unconsolidated sediments. *Oceanography and Marine Biology Annual Review* 32: 179-239.

Hall, S. 1999. *Effects of fishing on marine ecosystems and communities.* Oxford: Blackwell.

Handfield, R.B. and E.L. Nichols, Jr. 1996. *Introduction to supply chain management.* New Jersey: Prentice Hall.

Hannerz, U. 1996. *Transnational connections: Culture, people, places.* London and New York: Routledge.

Hannesson, R. 1996. *Fisheries mismanagement: The case of the Atlantic cod.* London: Blackwell.

Hannesson, R. 2001. The role of economic tools in redefining fisheries management. In: T.J. Pitcher, P.J.B. Hart, and D. Pauly (Eds.), *Reinventing fisheries management.* Pp. 251-260. Dordrecht: Kluwer Academic Publishers.

Haraway, D. 1994. *Simians, cyborgs and women: The reinvention of nature.* New York: Routledge.

Hardin, G. 1968. The tragedy of the commons. *Science* 162: 1243-1248.

Hardy, R.W. and J.A. Green 1999. How much feed does the world need? *Aquaculture Asia* IV (1): 4-8.

Harrison, R. 1995. *The collected papers of Roger Harrison*. San Francisco: Jossey-Bass Publishers.

Hart, M.W. and R.E. Scheibling 1988. Heat waves, baby booms and the destruction of kelp beds by sea urchins. *Marine Biology* 99: 167-176.

Harvey, B., C. Ross, D. Greer, and J. Carolsfeld (Eds.) 1998. *Action before extinction: An international conference on conservation of fish genetic diversity*. Victoria, Canada: World Fisheries Trust.

Harvey, D. 1989. *The condition of postmodernity*. Oxford: Basil Blackwell.

Haskell, B.D., B.G. Norton and R. Costanza 1992. What is ecosystem health and why should we worry about it? In: R. Costanza, B.G. Norton, and B.D. Haskell (Eds.), *Ecosystem health: New goals for sustainable development*. Pp. 3-20. Covelo: Island Press.

Hatcher, B.G. 1997. Coral reef ecosystems: How much greater is the whole than the sum of the parts? *Coral Reefs* 16 suppl.: S77-S91.

Haughton M.O., R. Mahon, P. McConney, G.A. Kong, and A. Mills 2004. Establishment of the Caribbean Regional Fisheries Mechanism. *Marine Policy*, 28: 351-359.

Hawkins, J.P., C.M. Roberts, and V. Clark 2000 The threatened status of restricted-range coral reef fish species. *Animal Conservation* 3: 81-88.

Helgason, A. and G. Pálsson 1998. Cash for quotas: Disputes over the legitimacy of an economic model of fishing in Iceland. In: J.G. Carrier and D. Miller (Eds.), *Virtualism: A new political economy*. Pp. 117-135. Oxford and New York: Berg.

Henson, S., A.M. Brouder, and W. Mitullah 2000. Food safety requirements and food exports from developing countries: The case of fish exports from Kenya to the European Union. *American Journal of Agricultural Economics* 82 (5): 1159-1169.

Hernes, H.K., S. Jentoft, and K.H. Mikalsen 2005. Fisheries governance, social justice and participatory decision-making. In: T. Gray (Ed.), *Participation in fisheries governance*. Dordrecht: Kluwer Academic Publishers.

Hersoug, B. 2004. Exporting fish, importing institutions – Fisheries development in the Third World. In: B. Hersoug, S. Jentoft, and P. Degnbol (Eds.), *Fisheries development: The institutional challenge*. Pp. 21-93. Delft, the Netherlands: Eburon.

Hersoug, B., S. Jentoft, and P. Degnbol 2004. *Fisheries development: The institutional challenge*. Delft, the Netherlands: Eburon.

Hessel, D.T. 1998. Christianity and ecology: Wholeness, respect, justice, sustainability. *Earth Ethics* 10 (1):

Hetherington, C. 1995. *Celebrating diversity*. Duluth, Minnesota: Whole Person Association.

Hilborn, R. and C.J. Walters 1992. *Quantitative fisheries stock assessment: Choice, dynamics, and uncertainty*. London: Chapman and Hall.

Hill, T.E., Jr. 1991. *Autonomy and self-respect*. Cambridge: Cambridge University Press.

Hillery, G.A.J. 1955. Definitions of community: Areas of agreement. *Rural Sociology* 20: 111-123.

Hites, R.A., J.A. Foran, D.O. Carpenter, M.C. Hamilton, B.A. Knuth, and S.J. Schwager 2004. Global assessment of organic contaminants in farmed salmon. *Science* 303: 226-229.

Hobbes, T. 1991 [1651]. *Leviathan*. Tuck R. (Ed.). Cambridge: Cambridge University Press.

Hobley, M. and D. Shields 2000. *The reality of trying to transform structures and processes: Forestry in rural livelihoods.* Working Paper 132. London: Overseas Development Institute.

Hoegh-Guldberg, O. 1999. Climate change, coral bleaching and the future of the world's coral reefs. *Marine and Freshwater Research* 8: 839-866.

Hoffman, J.M. and S. Mehra 2000. Efficient consumer response as a supply chain strategy for grocery businesses. *International Journal of Service Industry Management* 11 (4): 365-374.

Holland, A. 2002. Are choices tradeoffs? In: D.W. Bromley and J. Paavola (Eds.), *Economics, ethics, and environmental policy.* Pp. 17-33. Oxford: Blackwell.

Hollingworth, C. (Ed.) 2000. *Ecosystem effects of fishing.* ICES Journal of Marine Science 57 (3), special issue 465-792.

Holm, P. 1995. The dynamics of institutionalization: Transforming processes in Norwegian fisheries. *Administrative Science Quarterly* 40: 398-422.

Holman, P. and T. Devane (Eds.) 1999. *The change handbook: group methods for shaping the future.* San Francisco: Berrett-Koehler Publishers Inc.

Horemans, B.W. and A.M. Jallow (Eds.) 1997. *Report of the Workshop on Gender Roles and Issues in Artisanal Fisheries in West Africa, Lomé, Togo, 11-13 December 1996. IDAF/WP/97.* Cotonou, Benin: Programme for the integrated development of artisanal fisheries in West Africa.

Hoza, R.B. 1999. *Study on the impact of the EU-ban of 1999 to Nile Perch fish exports from Lake Victoria.* Lake Victoria Environmental Management Project. Available http://www.lvemp.org/L_News-articles-events/Tanzania/articles/eu_fish_ban 1999.htm (Accessed 19 August 2002).

Hubbell, S.P. 2001. *The unified neutral theory of biodiversity and biogeography.* Princeton: Princeton University Press.

Hughes, T.P. 1994. Catastrophes, phase shifts and large scale-degradation of a Caribbean coral reef. *Science* 265: 1547-1551.

Hutchings, J.A. 2000. Collapse and recovery of marine fishes. *Nature* 406: 882-885.

Hutchings, P. 1990. Review of the effects of trawling on macrobenthic epifaunal communities. *Australian Journal of Marine and Freshwater Research* 41 (1): 111-120.

ICLARM 1992. *ICLARM's strategy for international research on living aquatic resources management.* Makati, Philippines: International Center for Living Aquatic Resources Management.

ICSF 1995. NGOs and the FAO: Collaboration on the Code of Conduct. *Responsible Fisheries, Development Education Exchange Papers (DEEP).* Rome: International Collective for the support of fishworkers and Food and Agriculture Organization.

ICSF 2004. *Home page* International Collective in Support of Fishworkers. Available: http://www.icsf.net/jsp/english/index.jsp. (Accessed 22 April 2004).

ILO 1944. *Declaration concerning the aims and purposes of the International Labour Organization.* ILO General Conference 26th Session. Available http://www.ilo.org/public/english/about/iloconst.htm (Accessed 11 February 2005).

ILO 1948. *Freedom of association and protection of the right to organize* (No. 87). International Labour Organization, General Conference 31st Session. Available http://www.unhchr.ch/html/menu3/b/j_ilo87.htm (Accessed 11 February 2005).

ILO 2000. *Safety and health in the fishing industry. Report for discussion at the tripartite meeting on safety and health in the fishing industry, Geneva, Switzerland, 13-17 December 1999.* Geneva: International Labour Organization.

ILO 2003. *Conditions of work in the fishing sector. A comprehensive standard (a Convention supplemented by a Recommendation) on work in the fishing sector.* Report V (1) for the International Labour Conference, 92nd Session 2004. Available http://www.ilo.org/public/english/standards/relm/ilc/ilc92/pdf/rep-v-1.pdf (Accessed 11 February 2005).

Indicello, S., M. Weber, and R. Wieland 1999. *Fish, markets and fishermen. The economics of overfishing.* Washington DC: Island Press.

Ingram, A. 1994. *A political theory of rights.* Oxford: Clarendon Press.

Innis, H.A. 1954. *The cod fisheries: The history of an international economy.* Toronto: University of Toronto Press.

IUCN 1991. *Caring for the Earth.* Published in co-operation with UNEP and WWF. Gland (Switzerland): IUCN – The World Conservation Union.

IUCN 1994. *Guidelines for protected area management categories.* Gland, Switzerland and Cambridge, UK: IUCN and the World Conservation Monitoring Centre.

Jackson, J. 2001. What was natural in the coastal oceans? *Proceedings of the National Academy of Science* 98 (10): 5411-5418.

Jackson, J., M.X. Kirby, W.H. Berger, K.A. Bjorndal, L.W. Botsford, B.J. Bourque, R. H. Bradbury, R. Cooke, J. Erlandson, J.A. Estes, T.P. Hughes, S. Kidwell, C.B. Lange, H.S. Lenihan, J.M. Pandolfi, C.H. Peterson, R.S. Steneck, M.J. Tegner, R. R. Warner 2001. Historical overfishing and the recent collapse of coastal ecosystems. *Science* 293: 629-638.

Jacobs, M. 1999. Sustainable development as a contested concept. In: A. Dobson (Ed.), *Fairness and futurity: Essays on environmental sustainability and social justice.* Oxford: Pp. 21-45. Oxford University Press.

Jallow, A.M. 1994. Utilization of Bonga (*Ethmalosa Ffimbriata*) in West Africa. FAO Fisheries Circular. No. 870. Rome: Food and Agriculture Organization.

Jansen, E.G. 1999. Out of a Lake. *Samudra* (Sept.): 7-8.

Jansen, E.G., R.O. Abila, and J.P. Owino 1999. *Constraints and opportunities for community participation in the management of the Lake Victoria fisheries.* IUCN Eastern Africa programme. Available http://www.iucn.org/places/lakevictoria/6.htm (Accessed 19 August 2002).

Jennings, S. and N.V.C. Polunin 1997. Impacts of predator depletion by fishing on the biomass and diversity of non-target reef fish. *Coral Reefs* 16: 71-82.

Jennings, S. and M.J. Kaiser 1998. The effects of fishing on marine ecosystems. *Advances in Marine Biology* 34: 2-27.

Jennings, S., J.D. Reynolds, and N.V.C. Polunin 1999. Predicting the vulnerability of tropical reef fishes to exploitaiton with phylogenies and life histories. *Conservation Biology* 13 (6): 1466-75.

Jennings, S., J.K. Pinnegar, N.V.C. Polunin, and K.J. Warr 2001. Impacts of trawling disturbance on the trophic structure of benthic invertebrate communities. *Marine Ecology Progress Series* 213: 127-142.

Jentoft, S. 1985. Models of fishery development: The cooperative approach. *Marine Policy* 9 (4): 322-331.

Jentoft, S. 1986. Fisheries co-operatives: Lessons drawn from international experiences. *Canadian Journal of Development Studies* 7 (2): 197-209.

Jentoft, S. 1989. Fisheries co-management: Delegating government responsibility to fishermen's organizations. *Marine Policy* 13 (2): 137-154.

Jentoft, S. 2000a. The community: A missing link of fisheries management. *Marine Policy* 24 (1): 53-60.

Jentoft, S. 2000b. Legitimacy and disappointment in fisheries management. *Marine Policy* 24 (2): 141-148.

Jentoft, S. 2004a. Institutions in fisheries: What they are, what they do, and how they change. *Marine Policy* 28 (2): 137-149.

Jentoft, S. 2004b. Public-private management in European fisheries. *Samudra* 37:14-16.

Jentoft, S. and B.J. McCay 1995. User participation in fisheries management: Lessons drawn from international experiences. *Marine Policy* 19 (3): 227-246.

Jentoft, S., B. McCay, and D.C. Wilson 1998. Social theory and fisheries co-management. *Marine Policy* 22 (4-5): 423-436.

Jentoft, S., P. Friis, J. Kooiman, and J.W. van der Schans 1999. Knowledge-based fisheries. In: J. Kooiman, S. Jentoft, and M. van Vliet (Eds.), *Creative governance: Opportunities for fisheries in Europe.* Pp. 239-258. Aldershot, UK: Ashgate.

Jentoft, S. and B.J. McCay 2003. The place of civil society in fisheries management: A research agenda. In: D.C. Wilson, J. Raakjær Nielsen, and P. Degnbol (Eds.), *The fisheries co-management experience. Accomplishments, challenges, and prospects.* Pp. 293-307. Dordrecht: Kluwer Academic Publishers.

Jentoft, S., H. Minde, and Ragnar Nilsen (Eds.) 2003. *Indigenous people. Resource management and global rights.* Pp. 1-18. Delft, the Netherlands: Eburon.

Jentoft, S. and K.H. Mikalsen 2004. A vicious circle? The dynamics of rule production in Norwegian fisheries management. *Marine Policy* 28: 127-135.

JICA (Japanese International Cooperation Industry) 1994. *The development study on improvement of nationwide fish marketing system in Solomon Islands: Final Report,* Mimeo.

Johannes, R.A. and J.W. MacFarlane 1984. Traditional sea rights in the Torres Straits Islands, with emphasis in Murray Island. In: K. Ruddle and T. Akimichi (Comps.), *Maritime institutions in the Western Pacific.* Pp. 253-366. Osaka: Senri Ethnological Studies, National Museum of Ethnology.

Johannes, R.E. 1978. Traditional marine conservation methods in Oceania and their demise. *Annual Review in Ecology and Systematics* 9: 349-364.

Johnson, D. 1999. Merchants, the state and the household: Continuity and change in a 20th century Acadian fishing village. *Acadiensis* 29 (1): 57-75.

Johnson, D. 2001. Wealth and waste: Contrasting legacies of fisheries development in Gujarat since the 1950s. *Economic and Political Weekly* 36 (13): 1095-1102.

Johnson, D. 2002. *Emptying the sea of wealth: Globalisation and the Gujarat fishery, 1950 to 1999.* Unpublished Ph.D. Thesis Guelph: Department of Sociology and Anthropology, University of Guelph.

Johnston, R. 1995. Developments in seafood markets and marketing research. In: D.S. Liao (Ed.), *International cooperation for fisheries and aquaculture development: Proceedings of the 7th Biennial Conference of the International Institute of Fisheries Economics and Trade.* Vol. 3. Taipei: IIFET.

Johnston, R.S. and J.R. Wilson 1987. Interdependencies among fisheries management, fisheries trade, and fisheries development: Experiences with extended jurisdiction. *Marine Fisheries Review* 49 (3): 45-55.

Jones, E. 2000. England's Icelandic fishery in the early modern period. In: D.J. Starkey, C. Reid, and N. Ashcroft (Eds.), *England's sea fisheries: The commercial sea fisheries of England and Wales since 1300.* London: Chatham Publishing.

Jones, G.P., P.L. Munday, and M.J. Caley 2002. Rarity in coral reef fish communities. In: P. Sale (Ed.), *Coral reef fishes.* Pp. 81-102. San Diego: Academic Press.

Jul-Larsen, E. 2000. Prolifération des institutions et performance économique: L'accès au ressources des pêcheurs migrants à Pointe Noire (Conco). In: J.P.

Chauveau, E. Jul-Larsen, and C. Chaboud (Eds.), *Les pêches piroguières en Afrique de l'Ouest. Dynamiques institutionnelles: Pouvoirs, mobilités, marchés.* Pp. 167-204. Paris: Karthala, Institut de recherche pour le développement; Bergen: Christian-Michelsen Institute.

Kaczynski, V.M. and D.L. Fluharty 2002. European policies in West Africa: Who benefits from fisheries agreements? *Marine Policy* 26 (2): 75-93.

Kalland, A. 1984. Sea tenure in Tokugawa Japan: The case of Fukuoka domain In: K. Ruddle and T. Akimichi (Comps.), *Maritime institutions in the Western Pacific.* Pp. 11-36. Osaka: Senri Ethnological Studies, National Museum of Ethnology.

Kamphorst, B. 1994. *A socio-economic study on the distribution and marketing pattern of marine fish products in Ndian Division, South West Province, Republic of Cameroon.* FAO/DANIDA Programme for Integrated Development of Artisanal Fisheries in West Africa. Cotonou, Benin: Food and Agriculture Organization.

Kassibo, B. 2000. Pêche continentale et migration: contrôle politique et contrôle social des migrations de pêche dans le Delta central du Niger. In: J.P. Chauveau, E. Jul-Larsen, and C. Chaboud (Eds.), *Les pêches piroguières en Afrique de l'Ouest. Dynamiques institutionnelles: Pouvoirs, mobilités, marchés.* Pp. 231-246. Paris: Karthala, Institut de recherche pour le développement; Bergen: Christian-Michelsen Institute.

Kaufman, L. 1992. Catastrophic change in species-rich freshwater ecosystems: The lessons from Lake Victoria. *Bioscience* 42 (11): 846-858.

Kaufmann, F.X., G. Majone, and V. Ostrom (Eds.) 1986. *Guidance, control, and evaluation in the public sector.* Berlin: de Gruyter.

Kay, R. and J. Alder 1999. Coastal planning and management. New York: E & FN Spon.

Kazmierski, K.J. and M.K. Formela 1964. *The organisation of the distribution of fish in Poland.* Meeting on business decisions in fishery industries, R22, Vol.2 Paper 2.5. Rome: FAO.

Keane, J. (Ed.) 1988. *Civil society and the state.* London: Verso.

Kearney, M.M. 1995. The local and the global - The anthropology of globalisation and transnationalism. *Annual Review of Anthropology* 24: 547-565.

Kelleher, G. (Ed.) 1999. *Guidelines for marine protected areas.* Gland, Switzerland: IUCN.

Kelleher, G., C. Bleakley, and S. Wells 1995. *A global representative system of marine protected areas.* Canberra, Australia: Great Barrier Reef Marine Park Authority; Washington DC: The World Bank; Gland, Switzerland: IUCN.

Kelleher, G. and C. Recchia 1998. Lessons from marine protected areas around the world. Editorial. *Parks* 8 (2): 1-4.

Kelly, S., D. Scott, and A.B. MacDiarmid 2002. The value of a spillover fishery for spiny lobsters around a marine reserve in northern New Zealand. *Coastal Management* 30: 153-166.

Kempf, E., M. Sutton, and A. Wilson 1996. *Wanted alive! Marine fishes in the wild.* Gland, Switzerland: World Wide Fund for Nature.

Keohane, R. 2002. *Power and governance in a partially globalized world.* London: Routledge.

Keown, D. (Ed.) 2000. *Contemporary Buddhist ethics.* Richmond: Curzon.

Kirman, A. 1994. Market structure and prices: The Marseille fish market. *Proceedings of the 6th Biennial Conference of the International Institute of Fisheries Economics and Trade.* Vol 2. Paris.

Kolar, C.S., D.M. Lodge 2002. Ecological predictions and risk assessment for alien fishes in North America. *Science* 298: 1233-1236.

Kooiman, J. 2003. *Governing as governance.* London: Sage Publications.

Kooiman, J., M. van Vliet, and S. Jentoft (Eds.) 1999. *Creative governance: Opportunities for fisheries in Europe.* Aldershot, UK: Ashgate.

Koslow, J.A., G.W. Boehlert, J.D.M. Gordon, R.L. Haedrich, P. Lorance, and N. Parin 2000. Continental slope and deep-sea fisheries: Implications for a fragile ecosystem. *ICES Journal of Marine Science* 57: 548-557.

Kotter, J.P. 1996. *Leading change.* Boston: Harvard Business School Press.

Kowaleski, M. 2000. The internal fish trade (The internal and international fish trades of medieval England and Wales). In: D.J. Starkey, C. Reid, and N. Ashcroft (Eds.), *England's sea fisheries: The commercial sea fisheries of England and Wales since 1300.* Pp. 29-31. London: Chatham Publishing.

Krishnarayan, V., T. Geoghegan, and Y. Renard 2002. *Assessing capacity for participatory natural resource management.* Guideline Series No. 3. Vieux Fort: Caribbean Natural Resource Institute

Kronen, M. 2002. *Gender in fisheries and aquaculture: Case studies from Tonga and Fiji -South Pacific.* Contribution to Workshop on Gender in Fisheries and Aquaculture, Brussels, Belgium, 9-10 December 2002. EC/INCO programme. unpublished.

Kulbicki, M. 1992. Present knowledge of the structure of coral reef fish assemblages in the Pacific. Coastal resources and systems of the Pacific Basin: Investigation and steps toward protective management. *UNEP Regional Seas Report and Studies* 147: 31-54.

Kulbicki, M., P. Labrosse, and J. Ferraris, 2004. Basic principles underlying research projects on the links between the ecology and the uses of coral reef fishes in the Pacific. *MARE* 3: 28.

Kurien, J. 1985. Technical assistance projects and socio-economic change: Norwegian intervention in Kerala's fisheries development. *Economic and Political Weekly* 20: A71-A88.

Kurien, J. 2002. People and the sea: A 'tropical-majority' world perspective. *Maritime Studies (MAST)* 1 (1): 9-26.

Kurien, J. 2004. *Fish trade for the people. Toward understanding the relationship between international fish trade and food security.* Rome: FAO. Available http://www.tradefoodfish.org/ (Accessed 7 July 2004).

Kurien, J. and A. Paul 2000. *Nets for social safety – An Analysis of the growth and changing composition of social security programmes in the fisheries sector of Kerala State, India.* Samudra Monograph. Chennai: International Collective in Support of Fishworkers.

Kurlansky, M. 1997. *Cod: A biography of the fish that changed the world.* London: Jonathan Cape.

Landsbergh, J.H. 2002. The effects of harmful algal blooms on aquatic organisms. *Reviews in Fisheries Science* 10 (2): 113-390.

Law, R. 2000. Fishing selection and phenotypic evolution. *ICES Journal of Marine Science* 57: 659-668.

Lee, R.B. and I. DeVore 1969. *Man the hunter.* Chicago: Aldine Publishing Company.

Leeuw, F.L., R.C. Rist, and R.C. Sonnichsen 1994. *Can governments learn? Comparative perspectives on evaluation & organizational learning.* New Brunswick: Transaction Publishers.

Legendre, P. and L. Legendre 1998. Numerical ecology. Developments in Environmental Modelling 20. 2nd English Edition. Amsterdam: Elsevier.

Le Grand, J. 1991. *Equity and choice*. London: Harper.

Lenin, V.I. 1964. *The development of capitalism in Russia*. Moscow: Progress Publishers.

Le Sann, A. 1998. *A livelihood from fishing*. London: Intermediate Technology Publications.

Lightfoot, C., M.A.P. Bimbao, J.P.T. Dalsgaard, and R.S.V. Pullin 1993. Aquaculture and sustainability through integrated resources management. *Outlook on Agriculture* 22:143-150.

Lightfoot, C. and R. Noble 2001. Tracking the ecological soundness of farming systems. *Journal of Sustainable Agriculture* 19 (1): 9-29.

Linnerooth-Bayer, J. 1999. Climate change and multiple views of fairness. In: F.L. Tóth (Ed.), *Fair weather*. Pp. 45-64. London: Earthscan.

Loasby, B.J. 1976. *Choice, complexity and ignorance*. Cambridge: Cambridge University Press.

Lobe, K. and F. Berkes 2004. The *padu* system of community-based fisheries management: Change and local institutional innovation in South India. *Marine Policy* 28: 271-281.

Lögfren, O. 1979. Marine ecotypes in preindustrial Sweden: A comparative discussion of Swedish peasant fishermen. In: R. Andersen (Ed.), *North Atlantic maritime cultures: Anthropological essays on changing adaptations*. Pp. 83-109. The Hague: Mouton.

Lokshin, M. and R. Yemtsov 2000. *Household strategies for coping with poverty and social exclusion in post-crisis Russia*. Washington DC: World Bank.

Lomborg, B. 2001. *The skeptical environmentalist*. Cambridge: Cambridge University Press.

Long, N. 2001. *Development sociology: Actor perspectives*. London: Routledge.

Ludwig, D., R. Hilborn, and C. Walters 1993. Uncertainty, resource exploitation, and conservation. *Science* 260: 17-36.

Lugten, G.L. 1999. A review of measures taken by Regional Fishery Bodies to address contemporary fishery issues. *FAO Fisheries Circular No. 940*. Rome: FAO.

Luhmann, N. 1982. *The differentiation of Society*. New York: Columbia University Press.

Lukes, S. 1991. *Moral conflict and politics*. Oxford: Clarendon Press.

Lupia, A., M.D. McCubbins, and S.L. Popkin (Eds.) 2000. *Elements of reason*. Cambridge: Cambridge University Press.

Lupin, H.M. 1999. Producing to achieve HACCP compliance of fishery and aquaculture products for export. *Food Control* 10: 267-275.

MacAlister, E. 2002. *The role of women in the fisheries sector*. EC/DG Fisheries, Final Report, 1443/R.03/C. Brussels: European Commission.

MacDonald, M. and P. Connelly 1990. Class and gender in Nova Scotia fishing communities. In: B. Fairley, C. Leys, and J. Sacouman (Eds.), *Class and Gender in Nova Scotia Fishing Communities*. Pp. 151-170. Toronto: Garamond.

MacFadyen, G. 2002. *Poverty alleviation in small-scale fishing communities*. Mimeo.

Macinko, S. and D.W. Bromley 2002. *Who owns America's fisheries?* Center for Resource Economics. Covelo: Island Press.

MacLean, D. 1998. The ethics of cost-benefit analysis: Incommensurable, incompatible and incomparable values. In: M.M. Carrow, R.P. Churchill, and J.J. Cordes (Eds.), *Democracy, social values, and public policy*. Pp. 107-121. Westport: Praeger.

Maclean, J.L. 1988. Thanks for using Naga. *Naga, The ICLARM Quarterly* 11 (3): 16-17.

Maclean, J.L. 1993. Developing-country aquaculture and harmful algal blooms. In: R.S.V. Pullin, H. Rosenthal, and J.L. Maclean (Eds.), Environment and aquaculture in developing countries. ICLARM Conference Proceedings 31:252-284. Makati, Philippines: ICLARM.

Mahon, R., S. Almerigi, P. McConney, C. Parker, and L. Brewster 2003. Participatory methodology used for sea urchin co-management in Barbados. *Ocean and Coastal Management.* 46 (1-2): 1-25.

Mahon, R. and P. McConney, 2004. Managing the managers: improving the structure and operation of small fisheries departments, especially in SIDS. *Ocean and Coastal Management.* 47 (9-10): 529-535 .

Malakoff, D. 2002. Mixed schools a must for fish. *Science* 297: 31-32.

Malinowski, B. 1922. *Argonauts of the western Pacific: An account of native enterprise and adventure in the archipelagoes of Melanesian New Guinea.* London: Routledge and Keegan Paul.

Maltby, E. 1999. Ecosystem approach: from principles to practice. In P.J. Schei, O.T. Sandlund, and R. Strand (Eds). *The Norway/UN Conference on the Ecosystem Approach to sustainable use of biological diversity.* Proceedings of the Trondheim Conference, September. Pp. 30-40. Trondheim, Norway: International Institute for Sustainable Development (IISD).

Mann, K.H. 1982. *Ecology of coastal waters: A systems approach.* Oxford: Blackwell.

Manz, C.C. and H.P. Sims 2003. *The new superleadership: leading others to lead themselves.* San Francisco: Berrett-Koehler.

Manzany, L., N. Roy, and W.E. Schrank 1996. Multi-product allocation under imperfect raw material supply conditions: The case of products. *Applied Economics* 28: 387-396.

Maragos, J.E., M.P. Crosby, and J.W. McManus 1996. Coral reefs and biodiversity: A critical and threatened relationship. *Oceanography* 9 (1): 83-99.

Marashi, S.H. 1996. *The role of FAO regional fishery bodies in the conservation and management of fisheries.* Fisheries Circular n° 916. Rome: FAO.

March, J.G. and J.P. Olsen 1995. *Democratic governance.* New York: The Free Press.

Mariojouls, C. and K. de Lesquen 1997. Recent evolutions in the fisheries chain in France. *Proceedings of the 9th Annual Conference of the European Association of Fisheries Economists, Quimper, France, 28-30 April.* Quimper, France: EAFE.

Mariojouls, C. and C.R. Wessells 2002. Certification and quality signals in the aquaculture sector in France. *Marine Resource Economics* 17: 175-80.

Marsden, T., J. Banks, and G. Bristow 2000. Food supply chain approaches: Exploring their role in rural development. *Sociologia Ruralis* 40 (4): 424-38.

Martinez, N.D. 1996. Defining and measuring functional aspects of biodiversity. In: K.J. Gaston (Ed.), *Biodiversity: A biology of numbers and difference.* Pp. 114-148. Oxford: Blackwell.

Martínez, R.O. 1998. Globalisation and the social sciences. *The Social Science Journal* 35 (4): 601-610.

Martínez Pratt, A.R. 2003. *The impact of TRIPS and the CBD on coastal communities.* ICSF Occasional Paper. Chennai: International Collective in Support of Fishworkers.

Martino, R.C., L.C. Trugo, E.P. Cyrino, and L. Portz 2003. Use of white fat as a replacement for squid liver oil in practical diets for surubim *Pseudoplatystoma coruscans. Journal of the World Aquaculture Society* 34 (2): 192-202.

Mason, H.E. (Ed.) 1996. *Moral dilemmas and moral theory.* New York: Oxford University Press.

Mathew, S. 2003. Small-scale fisheries perspectives on an ecosystem-based approach to fisheries management. In: M. Sinclair and G. Valdimarsson (Eds.), *Responsible fisheries in the marine ecosystem.* Pp. 47-63. Wallingford, UK: CABI Publishing.

Maxwell, S. 1996. Food security: A post-modern approach. *Food Policy* 21 (2): 155-170.

McCann, K.S. 2000. The diversity-stability debate. *Nature* 405: 228-233.

McCay, B.J. 1981. Development issues in fisheries as agrarian systems. *Culture and Agriculture* 11: 1-8.

McCay, B.J. and S. Jentoft 1998. Market or community failure? Critical perspectives on common property research. *Human Organization* 57 (1): 21-29.

McCay, B.J. and S. Brandt 2001. Changes in fleet capacity and ownership of harvesting rights in the United States surf clam and ocean quahog fishery. In: R. Shotton (Ed.), *Case studies on the effects of transferable fishing rights on fleet capacity and concentration of quota ownership. FAO Fisheries Technical Paper 412.* Pp. 44-60. Rome: FAO.

McClanahan, T.R. 1994. Kenyan coral reef lagoon fish: Effects of fishing, substrate complexity, and sea urchins. *Coral Reefs* 13: 231-241.

McConney, P.A. 1999. Organising fisherfolk in Barbados without completing a clean round. *Proceedings of the Gulf and Caribbean Fisheries Institute* 52: 290-299.

McConney, P.A. and R. Mahon 1998. Introducing fisheries management planning to Barbados. *Ocean and Coastal Management* 39: 189-195.

McElroy, M.W. 2003. *The new knowledge management: Complexity, learning and sustainable innovation.* New York: Butterworth-Heinemann.

McEvoy, A.F. 1986. *The fisherman's problem: Ecology and law in the California fisheries, 1850-1980.* Cambridge: Cambridge University Press.

McGoodwin, J.R. 1990. *Crisis in the world's fisheries: People, problems, and policies.* Stanford: Stanford University Press.

McGoodwin, J.R. 2001. *Understanding the cultures of fishing communities: a key to fisheries management and food security.* Fisheries Technical Paper. No. 401. Rome: FAO.

McIntosh, D. 2002. The tragedy of the commons: Perspectives on sustainable aquaculture. *World Aquaculture* 33 (4): 21-22, 64.

McKenzie, J. 1922. *Hindu ethics.* Oxford: Oxford University Press.

McManus, J.W., L.A.B. Menez, K.N. Kesner-Reyes, S.G. Vergara, and M.C. Ablan 2000. Coral reef fishing and coral-algal phase shifts: Implications for global reef status. *ICES Journal of Marine Science* 57: 572-578.

Megapesca 1997. *Nile Perch – Marketing success or ecological disaster?* Available http://www.gisl.co.uk/Megapesca/nileperch.html (Accessed 19 August 2002).

Mehra, R. and S. Esim 1998. What gender analysis can contribute to irrigation research and practice in developing countries: Some issues. In: D. Merry and S. Baviskar (Eds.), *Gender analysis and reform of irrigation management: Concepts, cases, and gaps in knowledge. Proceedings of Workshop on Gender and Water, Habarana, Sri Lanka, 15-19 September 1997.* Pp. 265. Colombo, Sri. Lanka: International Water Management Institute.

Meltzoff, S.K. 2000. Nylon nets and national elites: Alata system of marine tenure among the Lau of Fanalei village, Port Adam passage, Small Malaita, Solomon Islands. In: T.D. King and E.P. Durrenberger (Eds.), *State and community in fish-*

eries management: Power, policy, and practice. Pp. 69-81. Westport: Bergin &Garvey.

Migdal, J.S. 1988. *Strong societies and weak states: State-society relations and state capacities in the Third World.* Princeton: Princeton University Press.

Miki, K. and T. Yamamoto 1992. Fish marketing system developed in Japan and price maintenance system. In: M. Antona, J. Catanzano, and J.G. Sutinen (Eds.), *Proceedings of the 6ᵗʰ Biennial Conference of the International Institute of Fisheries Economics and Trade.* Paris.

Milazzo, M. 1998. *Subsidies in world fisheries: A re-examination.* World Bank Technical Paper (Fisheries Series) No. 406. Washington DC: World Bank.

Mitchell, B. 1999. *La gestión de los recursos y del medio ambiente.* Madrid: Mundi-Prensa.

Mora, C., P.M. Chittaro, P.F. Sale, J.P. Kritzer, and S.A. Ludsin 2003. Patterns and processes in reef fish diversity. *Nature* 421: 933-936.

Moran, M. and M. Wright 1991. *The market and the state. Studies in interdependence.* London: MacMillan.

Moran, M.J. and P.C. Stephenson 2000. Effects of otter trawling on macrobenthos and management of demersal scalefish fisheries on the contiental shelf of northwest Australia. *ICES Journal of Marine Science* 57: 510-516.

Morgan, P. 1998. *Capacity and Capacity Development – Some Strategies.* Note prepared for the Political and Social Policies Division. Quebec: Canadian International Development Agency.

Muir, J.F. and J.A. Young 1998. Aquaculture and marine fisheries: Will capture fisheries remain competitive? *Journal of Northwest Atlantic Fishery Science* 23: 157-74.

Münch, R. 1988. *Understanding modernity.* London: Routledge.

Munro, N. and J.H.M. Willison 1998. Linking protected areas with working landscapes conserving biodiversity. *Proceedings of the 3ʳᵈ International Conference on Science and Management of Protected Areas, 12-16 May 1997.* Wolfville, N.S.: Science and Management of Protected Areas Association.

Myers, R.A and B. Worm 2003. Rapid worldwide depletion of predatory fish communities. *Nature* 423: 280-283.

Myrdal, G. 1968. *Asian drama. An inquiry into the poverty of nations.* London: Allen Lane.

NACA/FAO 2000. *Aquaculture development beyond 2000: The Bangkok declaration and strategy.* Bangkok: Network of Aquaculture Centres in Asia (NACA); Rome: Food and Agriculture Organization.

Nadal Egea, A. 1996. *Esfuerzo y Captura.* Mexico D.F.: El Colegio de Mexico.

Nadel-Klein, J. and D.L. Davis (Eds.) 1988a. *To work and to weep: Women in fishing economies.* St. John's, Newfoundland: Institute of Social and Economic Research, Memorial University of Newfoundland.

Nadel-Klein, J. and D.L. Davis 1988b. Introduction: Gender in the maritime arena. In: J. Nadel-Klein and D.L. Davis (Eds.), *To work and to weep: Women in fishing economies.* Pp. 1-17. St. John's, Newfoundland: Institute of Social and Economic Research, Memorial University of Newfoundland.

Nanji, A. 1993. Islamic ethics. In: P. Singer (Ed.), *A companion to ethics.* Pp. 106-118. Oxford: Blackwell.

Naqvi, S.N.H. 2001. The Islamic ethical system. In: K. Ahmad and A.M. Sadeq (Eds.), *Ethics in business and management.* Pp. 25-39. London: Asean Academic Press.

Narotzky, S. 1988. *Trabajar en familia: Mujeres, hogares y talleres.* Valencia: Edicions Alfons El Magnánim Institució Valenciana d'Estudis i Investigació.

Narotzky, S. 1995. *Mujer, mujeres, género: Una aproximación crítica al estudio de las mujeres en las Ciencias Sociales.* Madrid: Consejo Superior de Investigaciones Científicas.

National Research Council 2001. *Marine protected areas: Tools for sustaining oceans ecosystems.* Washington DC: National Academy Press.

Nautilus Consultants (1998) *Report on Advisory Committee on Fisheries Organisations.* Prepared for the DGXIV of the European Commission by in collaboration with Cofrepêche (France), Gico (Italy), IFM (Denmark), LEI (Netherlands) and the University of Seville (Spain). Edinburgh, UK: Nautilus Consultants.

Naylor, R.L., R.J. Goldburg, H. Mooney, M. Beveridge, J. Clay, C. Folke, N. Kautsky, J. Lubchenco, J. Primavera, and M. Williams 1998. Nature's subsidies to shrimp and salmon farming. *Science* 282: 883-884.

Naylor, R.L., R.J. Goldburg, J. Primavera, N. Kautsky, M.C.M. Beveridge, J. Clay, C. Folke, J. Lubchenco, H. Mooney, and M. Troell 2000. Effect of aquaculture on world fish supplies. *Nature* 405: 1017-1024.

Naylor, R.L., J. Eagle, and L.S. Whitney 2003. Salmon aquaculture in the Pacific Northwest: A global industry. *Environment* 45 (8): 18-39.

Nielsen, J.L. and D.A. Powers (Eds.) 1995. *Evolution and the aquatic ecosystem: Defining unique units in population conservation.* American Fisheries Society Symposium 17. Bethesda: American Fisheries Society.

Neilsen, M. 2000. *A review of research of market outlets for Nordic fishermen.* Copenhagen: TemaNord.

New, M.B. 2003. Responsible aquaculture: Is this a special challenge for developing countries? *World Aquaculture* 34 (3): 26-30, 60-68, 72.

New, M.B. and U.N. Wijkström 2002. Use of fishmeal and fish oil in aquafeeds. Further thoughts on the fishmeal trap. *Fisheries Circular 975. FIPP/C975.* Rome: Food and Agriculture Organization.

Noble, B.F. 2000. Institutional criteria for co-management. *Marine Policy* 24 (1): 69-77.

North, D.C. 1990. *Institutions, institutional change, and economic performance.* Cambridge: Cambridge University Press.

Novaczek, I., I.H.T. Harkes, J. Sopacua, and M.D.D. Tathuey 2001. *An institutional analysis of Sasi Laut in Maluku, Indonesia.* Penang, Malaysia: International Center for Living Aquatic Resources Management.

NTAS 1998. *Holmenkollen guidelines for sustainable aquaculture 1998.* Oslo: Norwegian Academy of Technological Sciences.

Nyström M., C. Folke, and F. Moberg 2000 Coral reefs distubance and resilience in a human dominated environment. *Trends in Ecology and Evolution.* 15 (10): 413-417

O'Connor, M. 2002. Social cost and sustainability. In: D.W. Bromley and J. Paavola (Eds.), *Economics, ethics, and environmental policy.* Pp. 181-201. Oxford: Blackwell.

Odaka, N. and T. Yamamoto 1992. Fishery cooperative association in Japan and its vital role in fish marketing. In: M. Antona, J. Catanzano, and J.G. Sutinen (Eds.), *Proceedings of the 6th Biennial Conference of the International Institute of Fisheries Economics and Trade.* Paris.

Odum, E.P. 1969. The strategy of ecosystem development. *Science* 104:262-270.

OECD Committee for Fisheries 2000 *Transition to Responsible Fisheries. Economic and Policy Implications*. Paris: Organisation for Economic Co-operation and Development.

Offe, C. 2000. Civil society and social order: Demarcating and combining market, state and community. *Archives Européennes de Sociologique* 41 (1): 71-94

Office of the High Commissioner for Minorities Rights 1994. *The rights of minorities (Art. 27). CCPR General Comment 23 (General Comments)*. New York: United Nations.

Olson, M. 1977. *The logic of collective action. Public goods and the theory of groups*. Cambridge: Harvard University Press.

Ommer, R.E. 1989. Merchant credit and the informal economy: Newfoundland, 1919-1929. Historical Papers 1989. Pp. 167-189. Ottawa: Canadian Historical Association.

O'Neill, O. 1993. Kantian ethics. In: P. Singer (Ed.), *A companion to ethics*. Pp. 175-185. Oxford: Blackwell.

Ostrom, E. 1986. A method of institutional analysis. In: F.X. Kaufmann, G. Majone, and V. Ostrom (Eds.), *Guidance, control, and evaluation in the public sector*. Pp. 495-510. Berlin: de Gruyter.

Ostrom, E. 1990. *Governing the commons: The evolution of institutions for collective action*. Cambridge: Cambridge University Press.

Ostrove, J. and N. Adler 1998. The relationship of socio-economic status, labor force participation, and health among men and women. *Journal of Health Psychology* 3 (4): 451-463.

Overaa, R. 2000. Les femmes chefs d'entreprise dans la pêche piroguière au Ghana. Le cas de la ville de fante de Moree. In: J.P. Chauveau, E. Jul-Larsen, and C. Chaboud (Eds.), *Les pêches piroguières en Afrique de l'Ouest. Dynamiques institutionnelles: Pouvoirs, mobilités, marchés*. Pp. 299-324. Paris: Karthala, Institut de recherche pour le développement; Bergen: Christian-Michelsen Institute.

Oyewumi, O. 1997. *The invention of women: Making an African sense of western gender discourses*. Minnesota: University of Minnesota Press.

Paavola, J. 2002. Rethinking the choice and performance of environmental policies. In: D.W. Bromley and J. Paavola (Eds.), *Economics, ethics, and environmental policy*. Pp. 88-101. Oxford: Blackwell.

Pálsson, G. 1991. *Coastal economies, cultural accounts – human ecology and Icelandic discourse*. Manchester, UK: Manchester University Press.

Pardey, P.G., B.D. Wright, C. Nottenburg, E. Birenbaun, and P. Zambrano 2003. Intellectual property and developing countries: Freedom to operate in agricultural biotechnology. *Biotechnology and Genetic Resources Policies Brief*. No. 3. Washington DC: International Food Policy Research Institute.

Parsons, T. 1968. *The structure of social action*. Vol. 2. New York: The Free Press.

Pascual-Fernández, J.J. 1991. *Entre el mar y la tierra: Los pescadores artesanales canarios. Santa Cruz de Tenerife:* Ministerio de Cultura-Interinsular Canaria.

Pascual-Fernández, J.J. 1993. Apuntes para el debate en torno a la tragedia de los comunes. In: J.J. Pascual-Fernández (Ed.), *Procesos de apropiación y gestión de recursos comunales*. Pp. 23-45. Santa Cruz de Tenerife: Asociación Canaria de Antropología, VI Congreso de Antropología.

Pascual-Fernández, J.J. 1999. *Participative management of artisanal fisheries in the Canary Islands*. In: D. Symes (Ed.), *Southern waters: Issues of management and practice*. Pp. 66-77. London: Blackwell.

Pascual-Fernández, J.J. 2001. Littoral fishermen, aquaculture and tourism in the Canary Islands: Attitudes and economic strategies. *Proceedings of the International Conference People and the Sea: Maritime research in the social sciences, an agenda for the 21st century, Amsterdam, the Netherlands,* (cd-rom) Amsterdam Centre for Maritime Research.

Pascual-Fernández, J.J. 2004. Littoral fishermen, aquaculture and tourism in the Canary Islands: Attitudes and economic strategies. In: J. Boissevain and T. Selwyn (Eds.), *Contesting the foreshore: Tourism, society and politics on the coast.* Pp. 61-82. Amsterdam: Amsterdam University Press.

Pascual-Fernández, J.J., A. Santana Talavera, J.A. Batista Medina, C. Dorta Morales, R. Hernández Armas, A. Díaz de la Paz, B. Martín de la Rosa, and J. Macías González 2001. *Pescatur: Un modelo de desarrollo integral de poblaciones litorales.* La Laguna: Instituto U. de Ciencias Políticas y Sociales, Viceconsejería de Pesca del Gobierno de Canarias. unpublished.

Paulson, J.A. (Ed.) 1999. *African economies in transition.* Vol. 1. *The changing role of the state.* Oxford: MacMillan Press.

Pauly, D. 1995. Anecdotes and the shifting baseline syndrome of fisheries. *Trends in Ecology and Evolution* 10 (10): 430.

Pauly, D. and R. Chuenpagdee 2003. Development of fisheries in the Gulf of Thailand large marine ecosystem: Analysis of an unplanned experiment. In: G. Hempel and K. Sherman (Eds.), *Large marine ecosystems of the world: Trends in exploitation, protection, and research.* Pp. 337-354. The Hague: Elsevier.

Pauly, D. and J.L. Maclean 2003. *In a perfect ocean: The state of fisheries and ecosystems in the north atlantic ocean.* Washington DC: Island Press.

Pauly, D. 2001. Importance of the historical dimension in policy and management of natural resources systems. In: E. Feoli and C. Nauen (Eds.), *Proceedings of the INCO-DEV International Workshop on Information Systems for Policy and Technical Support in Fisheries and Aquaculture.* ACP-EU Fisheries Research Report No. 8. Pp. 5-10. Brussels: European Commision.

Pauly, D. and V. Christensen 1995. Primary production required to sustain global fisheries. *Nature* 374: 255-257.

Pauly, D., V. Christensen, and C. Walters 2000. Ecopath, ecosim and ecospace as tools of evaluating ecosystem impacts on fisheries. *ICES Journal of Marine Science* 57: 697-706.

Pauly, D., V. Christensen, R. Froese, and M.L. Palomares 2000. Fishing down aquatic food webs. *American Scientist* 88: 46-51.

Pauly, D., V. Christensen, S. Guénette, T.J. Pitcher, U.R. Sumaila, C.J. Walters, R. Watson, and D. Zeller 2002. Towards sustainability in world fisheries. *Nature* 418: 689-695.

Pauly, D., J. Alder, E. Bennett, V. Christensen, P. Tyedmers, and R. Watson 2003. The future for fisheries. *Science* 302: 1359-1361.

Peterson G., C.R. Allen, and C.S. Holling 1998. Ecological resilience, diversity, and scale. *Ecosystems* 1: 6-18.

Phasuk, B. 1994. Fishing effort regulations in the coastal fisheries of Thailand. In: *Proceedings of the IPFC Symposium on Socio-economic issues in coastal fisheries management. Bangkok, Thailand. 23-26 November 1993.* RAPA Publication 1994/8. Bangkok: Regional Office for Asia and the Pacific, Food and Agriculture Organization.

Phillips, N. 1998. *Globalisation and the 'paradox of state power': Perspectives from Latin America.* Coventry: Centre for the Study of Globalisation and Regionalisation (CSGR), University of Warwick.

Phyne, J. 1996. Along the coast and the state: Aquaculture and politics in Nova Scotia and New Brunswick. In: C. Bailey, S. Jentoft, and P. Sinclair (Eds.), *Aquacultural development: Social dimensions of an emerging industry.* Pp. 69-92. Boulder: Westview Press.

Pilger, J. 2003. *Los nuevos gobernantes del mundo.* Barcelona: RBA Group.

Pinkerton, E. (Ed.) 1989a. *Cooperative management of local fisheries: New directions for improved management and community development.* Vancouver: University of British Columbia Press.

Pinkerton, E. 1989b. Introduction: Attaining better fisheries management through co-management: Prospects, problems and propositions. In: E. Pinkerton (Ed.), *Co-operative management of local fisheries.* Pp. 3-33. Vancouver: University of British Columbia Press.

Pinkerton, E. 1994. Summary and conclusions. In: C.L. Dyer and J.R. McGoodwin (Eds.), *Folk management in the world's fisheries: Lessons for modern fisheries management.* Pp. 317-337. Boulder: University Press of Colorado.

Pitcher, T.J. 1999. *Rapfish, a rapid appraisal technique for fisheries, and its application to the Code of Conduct for Responsible Fisheries.* Fisheries Circular No 947. Rome: Food and Agriculture Organization.

Pitcher, T.J. and D. Pauly 1998. Rebuilding ecosystems, not sustainability, as the proper goal of fisheries management. In: T.J. Pitcher, P.J.B. Hart, and D. Pauly (Eds.), *Reinventing fisheries management.* Pp. 311-329. London: Chapman and Hall.

Plahar, W.A., G.A. Nerquaye-Tetteh, and N.T. Annan 1999. Development of an integrated quality assurance system for the traditional Sardinella sp. and anchovy fish smoking industry in Ghana. *Food Control* 10: 15-25.

Platteau, J.P. 1989a. Penetration of capitalism and persistence of small-scale organisational forms in third world fisheries. *Development and Change* 20 (4): 621-651.

Platteau, J.P. 1989b. The dynamics of fisheries development in developing countries: A general overview. *Development and Change* 20 (4): 565-599.

Platteau, J.P. 1993. The free market is not readily transferable: Reflections on the link between market, social relation, and moral norms. *New institutional economics and development theory.* Pp. 71-178. Roskilde, Denmark: International Development Studies Roskilde University.

Platteau, J.P and J. Nugent 1992. Share contracts and their rationale: Lessons from marine fishing. *The Journal of Development Studies* 28 (3): 386-422.

Platteau, J.P. and J.M. Baland 1998. *Halting degradation of natural resources: Is there a role for rural communities?* Oxford: Clarendon Press; Rome: Food and Agriculture Organization.

Poirier, C.C. 1999. *Advanced supply chain management: How to build a sustained competition.* San Francisco: Publishers Group West.

Poli, B.M., G. Parisi, G. Zampacavallo, M. Mecatti, P. Lupi, M. Gualtieri, and O. Franci 2001. Quality outline of European Sea Bass (*Dicentrarchus labrax*) reared in Italy: Shelf life, edible yield, nutritional and dietetic traits. *Aquaculture* 202 (3-4): 303-15.

Pollar,O. and R. González 1994. *Dynamics of diversity: strategic programs for your organisation.* California: Crisp Publications.

Pollitt, C. and G. Bouckaert 2000. *Public management reform.* Oxford: Oxford University Press.

Pomeroy, R.S., R.B. Pollnac, B.M. Katon, and C.D. Predo 1997. Evaluating factors contributing to the success of community-based coastal resource management:

the Central Visayas Regional Project-l, Philippines. *Ocean and Coastal Management* 36: 97-120.

Pontecorvo, G. 2003. Insularity of scientific disciplines and uncertainty about supply: The two keys to the failure of fisheries management. *Marine Policy* 27 (1): 69-73.

Powles, H., M.J. Bradford, R.G. Bradford, W.G. Doubleday, S. Innes, and C.D. Levings 2000. Assessing and protecting endangered marine species. *ICES Journal of Marine Science* 57: 669-676.

Prein, M. and M. Ahmed 2000. Integration of aquaculture into smallholder farming systems for improved food security and household nutrition. *Food and Nutrition Bulletin* 21 (4): 466-471.

Pressman, J. and A. Wildavsky 1983. *Implementation*. Berkeley: University of California Press.

Preston, R. 1993. Christian ethics. In: P. Singer (Ed.), *A companion to ethics*. Pp. 91-105. Oxford: Blackwell.

Prins, H.H. 1999. The Malawi Principles: Clarification of the thoughts that underlay the ecosystem approach. *Proceedings of the UN Conference on the Ecosystem Approach to Sustainable Use of Biological Diversity*. Pp. 23-29. Trondheim: Norwegion Institute for Nature Research.

Pullin, R.S.V. 1981. Fish pens of Laguna de Bay; Philippines. *ICLARM Newsletter 4 (4)*: 11-13.

Pullin, R.S.V. 1993. *An overview of environmental issues in developing country aquaculture*. In: R.S.V. Pullin, H. Rosenthal and J.L. Maclean (Eds.), *Environment and Aquaculture in Developing Countries*. Pp. 359. ICLARM Conference Proceedings 31. Makati, Phillipines: ICLARM.

Pullin, R.S.V. 1998. Genetic resources for aquaculture: ownership and access. In: J.-F. Agnèse (Ed.), *Genetics and aquaculture in Africa*. Pp. 21-31. Paris: ORSTOM.

Pullin, R.S.V. 2000. Management of aquatic biodiversity and genetic resources. *Reviews in Fisheries Science* 8 (4): 379-393.

Pullin, R.S.V. 2002. *FISHGOVFOOD: Principles group, draft discussion paper*. Amsterdam: Centre for Maritime Research (MARE)

Pullin, R.S.V. and D.M. Bartley 1996. Biosafety and fish genetic resources. In: R.S.V. Pullin and C.M.V. Casal (Eds.), *Consultation on fish genetic resources.*Pp. 33-35. Manila: International Center for Living Aquatic Resource Management/CGIAR System-wide Genetic Resources Programme (SGRP); Rome: International Plant Genetic Resources Institute (IPGRI).

Pullin, R.S.V., H. Rosenthal, and J.L. Maclean (Eds.) 1993. *Environment and aquaculture in developing countries. ICLARM Conference Proceedings* 31. Makati, Phillipines: ICLARM.

Pullin, R.S.V., D.M. Bartley, and J. Kooiman (Eds.) 1999. *Towards policies for conservation and sustainable use of aquatic genetic resources*. ICLARM Conference Proceedings 59. Makati, Phillipines: ICLARM.

Pullin, R.S.V., R.F. Froese, and D. Pauly, forthcoming. Indicators for the sustainability of aquaculture. In: T.M. Bert (Ed.), *Ecological and genetic implications of aquaculture activities*. Dordrecht: Kluwer Academic Publishers.

Raakjær Nielsen, J., P. Degnbol, K. Viswanathan, and M. Ahmed 2002. *Fisheries co-management – An institutional innovation. IIFET Conference 2002*: Paper no 216.

Radin, M.J. 1996. *Contested Commodities*. Cambridge (Mass.): Harvard University Press.

Ram, K. 1992. *Mukkuvar women: Gender hegemony and capitalist transformation in a South Indian fishing community.* New Delhi: Kali For Women.

Randall, J.E. 1985. *Guide to Hawaiian reef fishes.* Newton Square: Harrowood Books.

Randall, J.E. 1987. Introduction of marine fishes to the Hawaiian Islands. *Bulletin of Marine Science* 41: 490-502.

Rapport, N. 1996. Community. In: A. Barnard and J. Spencer (Eds.), *Encyclopedia of social and cultural anthropology.* Pp. 114-117. London and New York: Routledge.

Rawls, J. 1973. *A theory of justice.* Oxford: Oxford University Press..

Rayner, S. 1999. Mapping institutional diversity for implementing the Lisbon principles *Ecological Economics* 31: 259–274.

Rayner, S., E.I. Malone, and M. Thompson 1999. Equity issues and integrated assessment. In: F.L. Tóth (Ed.), *Fair weather.* Pp. 12-43. London: Earthscan.

Redfield, R.R. 1971 [1955-6]. *'The little community' and 'Peasant society and culture'.* Chicago: University of Chicago Press.

Reid, C. 1998. Managing innovation in the British herring fishery: The role of the Herring Industry Board. *Marine Policy* 22 (4): 281-295.

Reid, C. 2000. From trawler to table: The fish trades since the late 19th century. In: D.J. Starkey, C. Reid, and N. Ashcroft (Eds.), *England's sea fisheries: The commercial sea fisheries of England and Wales since 1300.* London: Chatham Publishing.

Reid, C., forthcoming. A common delicacy: UK fish consumption in the 20th century. In: D.J. Starkey, P. Holm, J. Thór, and B. Andersen (Eds.), *Politics and people in the North Atlantic fisheries since 1485: Studia Atlantica.* Vol. 6. Hull: University of Hull Press.

Reid, C. and C. Robinson, forthcoming. Fish processing in the UK, 1907-1994: Evidence from the Census of Production. In D.J. Starkey, P. Holm, J. Thór, and B. Andersen (Eds.), *Politics and people in the North Atlantic fisheries since 1485: Studia Atlantica.* Vol. 6. Hull: University of Hull Press.

Revenga, C., J. Brunner, N. Henninger, K. Kassem, and R. Payne 2000. *Pilot analysis of global ecosystems: Freshwater Systems.* Available http://www.wri.org/wr2000/freshwater (Accessed 16 July 2002).

Reynolds, J.E. and D.F. Greboval 1988. *Socio-economic effects of the evolution of Nile Perch fisheries in Lake Victoria: A review.* CIFA Technical Paper No. 17. Rome: Food and Agriculture Organization.

Richardson, G.B. 1972. The organisation of industry. *The Economic Journal* (Sept.): 883-896.

Rijnsdorp, A.D. 1993. Fisheries as a large scale experiment on life-history evolution: Disentangling phenotypic and genetic effects in changes in maturation and reproduction of North Sea plaice Pleuronectes platessa. *Oecologia* 96: 391-401.

Roberts, C.M. 1997. Connectivity and management of Caribbean coral reefs. *Science* 278: 1454-1457.

Roberts, C.M. and N.V.C. Polunin 1992. Effects of a marine reserve protection on northern Red Sea fish populations. *Proceedings of the 7th International Coral Reef Symposium, Guam, 22-26 June 1992.* Pp. 969-977. Guam: International Association of Biological Oceanography (IABO).

Roberts, C.M. and N.V.C. Polunin 1993. Marine reserves: Simple solutions to managing complex fisheries. *Ambio* 22: 363-368.

Roberts, C.M. and J.P. Hawkins 2000. *Reservas marinas totalmente protegidas: Una guía.* Washington: WWF; York: University of York.

Robertson, D.R. 2001. Population maintenance among tropical reef fishes: Inferences from small island endemics. *Proceedings of the National Academy of Science* 98 (10): 5667-5670.

Robinson, D. and G. Osherenko 2001. Comparative analysis of fishing rights and resource management arrangements in the Circumpolar North. In: Chapter 7 of the *Ponoi river report: Sport fishing on the Kola Peninsula. A project of the Circumpolar Conservation Union.* Available http://www.dartmouth.edu/~arctic/Fishcomparanalysis.pdf.

Rodríguez Guerra, R. 2000. Sociedad civil: Aventuras clásicas, arquetipos contemporáneos y una propuesta teórica. *Laguna, Revista de Filosofía* 7: 39-61.

Roest, F., P. Spliethoff, and V. van der Knaap 1995. *Fisheries in developing countries: Towards sustainable use of living aquatic resources.* The Hague: Ministry of Foreign Affairs, Development Co-operation Department.

Roheim, C.A. 2003. Early indications of market impacts from the Marine Stewardship Council's ecolabeling of seafood. *Marine Resource Economics* 18: 95-104.

Rolston III, H. 1990. Science-based vs. traditional ethics. In: J.R. Engel and J.G. Engel (Eds.), *Ethics of environment and development.* Pp. 63-72. London: Belhaven.

Roos, N. 2001. *Fish consumption and aquaculture in rural Bangladesh.* Unpublished Ph.D. Thesis. Frederiskberg, Denmark: Research Department of Human Nutrition, Royal Veterinary and Agricultural University.

Rosendahl, R.W. 1984. The development of Mexican fisheries and its effect on United States-Mexican relations. *Pacific Basin Law Journal* 3 (1): 1-20.

Ross D.J., C.R. Johnson, C.L. Hewitt, and G.M. Ruiz 2004. Interactions and impacts of two introduced species on a soft sediment marine assemblage in SE Tasmania. *Marine Biology* 144(4): 747-756

Rossi, C.R. 1993. *Equity and international law.* New York: Transnational Publishers.

Roth, E. and 36 co-authors 2001. *An intellectual injustice to aquaculture development: A response to the review article, 'Effects of aquaculture on work fish supplies'.* Available http://ciencia.silvert.org/eim/response/draft.htm (Accessed 2 March 2005).

Roth, G. and C. Wittich (Eds.) 1978. Max Weber: *Economy and Society.* Pp. 3-38. Berkeley: University of California Press.

Roy, R.N. 2002. *Coming together to manage fisheries – a field guide to stakeholder analysis.* BOBP/MAG No 24. Chennai: Bay of Bengal Programme.

Ruckes, E. 1972. Fish marketing systems and their development: A cross-country comparison. *Zeitschrift fur Ausländische Landwirtschaft* 11 (3-4): 335-352.

Ruckes, E. 1995. World trade in fish and fishery products: Review and outlook, international cooperation for fisheries and aquaculture development. In: D.S. Liao (Ed.), *Proceedings of the 7th Biennial Conference of the International Institute of Fisheries Economics and Trade.* Pp. 1-16. Keelung, Taiwan: National Taiwan Ocean University.

Ruddle, K. 1988. The organization of traditional inshore fishery management systems in the Pacific. In: P.A. Neher, R. Arnason, and N. Mollett (Eds.), *Rights based fishing: Proceedings of the Workshop on the Scientific Foundations for Rights Based Fishing, Reykjavik, Iceland, June 27-1 July 1988.* Pp. 73-85. Dordrecht: Kluwer Academic Publishers.

Ruddle, K. 1989. Solving the common-property dilemma: Village fisheries rights in Japanese coastal waters. In F. Berkes (Comp.), *Common property resources: Ecology and community based sustainable development.* Pp. 168-184. London: Belhaven Press.

Ruddle, K. 1996. The potential role of integrated management of natural resources in improving the nutritional and economic status of resource poor farm households in Ghana. In: M. Prein, J.K. Ofori, and C. Lightfoot (Eds.), *Research for the future development of aquaculture in Ghana.* ICLARM Conference Proceedings 42: 57-85. Makati, Phillipines: ICLARM

Ruddle, K. and T. Akimichi (Eds.) 1984. *Maritime institutions of the Western Pacific.* Osaka: National Museum of Ethnology.

Ruddle, K. and R.E. Johannes (Eds.) 1985. *The traditional knowledge and management of coastal systems in Asia and the Pacific.* Jakarta, Indonesia: UNESCO, Regional Office for Science and Technology for Southeast Asia.

Ruddy, M. and T. Varley 1991. Sea farming and development in North Connemara. In: T. Varley, T.A. Boylan, and M.P. Cuddy (Eds.), *Rural crisis: Perpectives on Irish rural development.* Galway: University College Centre for Development Studies.

Ruffier, P. 1999. *Fumeuses de poisson à Abidjan. Entre pirogues et sardines: Les nouvelles dynamiques de la filière sardinière.* Rennes: Ensar.

Russell, S.D. and R.T. Alexander 2000. Of beggars and thieves: Customary sharing of the catch and informal sanctions in a Philippine fishery. In: T.D. King and E. P. Durrenberger, (Eds.), *State and community in fisheries management: Power, policy, and practice.* Pp. 19-40. Westport: Bergin & Garvey.

Ryman, N., F. Utter, and L. Laitke 1995. Protection of intraspecific diversity of exploited fishes. *Reviews in Fish Biology and Fisheries* 5: 417-446.

Sadovy, Y. 1993. The Nassau grouper, endangered or just unlucky? *Reef Encounter* 13: 10-12.

Sadovy, Y. 1996. Reproduction of reef fishery species. In: N.V.C. Polunin and C.M. Roberts (Eds.), *Reef fisheries.* Pp. 15-59. London: Chapman and Hall.

Sagdahl, B. 2000. *Norwegian fishery management: Learning by doing and 'fishing' for solutions.* ELSA Working Papers, Rennes.

Sainsbury, K.J. 1987. Assessment and management of the demersal fishery on the continental shelf of northwestern Australia. In: J.J. Polovina and S. Ralston (Eds.), *Tropical snappers and groupers – Biology and fisheries management.* Pp. 465-503. Boulder: Westview Press.

Sainsbury, J.C. 1996. *Commercial fishing methods: An introduction to vessels and gears.* Oxford: Blackwell.

Sale, P.F. and J.A. Guy 1992. Persistence of community structure: What happens when you change taxonomic scale? *Coral Reefs* 11: 147-154.

Sandersen, H.T. 1999. Organization and social capital as a prerequisite for participatory fisheries management - The case of Trinidad & Tobago and St. Lucia: Fisheries research in developing countries. *Proceedings from the Soria Moria conference, October 1998.* Pp. 98-127.Oslo: Division of Environment and Development, Research Council of Norway.

Sandersen, H.T. and S. Koester 2000. Co-management of tropical coastal zones: The case of the Soufrière marine management area, St. Lucia, WI. *Coastal Management* 28: 87-97.

Santana Talavera, A. 1997. *Antropología y turismo: ¿Nuevas hordas, viejas culturas?* Barcelona: Ariel.

Santana Talavera, A. 2003. Mirando culturas: La antropología del turismo. In: Á. Rubio Gil (Ed.), *Sociología del turismo.* Pp. 103-125. Barcelona: Ariel.

Sarch M.T. and E.H. Allison 2000. *Fluctuating fisheries in Africa's inland waters: Well adapted livelihoods, maladapted management.* Available http://oregonstate.edu/dept/IIFET/2000/papers/sarch.pdf. (Accessed 29 June 2004).

Satia, B.P. 1990. National reviews for aquaculture development in Africa, Nigeria. *Fisheries Circular* No. 770. 29. Rome: Food and Agriculture Organization.

Schlager, E. and E. Ostrom 1993. Property-rights regimes and coastal fisheries: An empirical analysis. In: T.L. Anderson and R.T. Simmons (Eds.), *The political econ-*

omy of customs and culture: Informal solutions to the commons problem. Pp. 13-41. Lanham: Rowman & Littlefield.

Schmid, A.A. 2002. All environmental policy instruments require a moral choice as to whose interest count. In: D.W. Bromley and J. Paavola (Eds.), *Economics, ethics, and environmental policy.* Pp. 134-145. Oxford: Blackwell.

Schroeder, W.R. 1992. Twentieth-century continental ethics. Part 2. In: L.C. Becker and C.B. Becker (Eds.), *A history of Western ethics.* Pp. 129-141. New York: Garland Publishers.

Schutter, O.D. 2002. Europe in search of its civil society. *European Law Journal* 8 (2): 198-217.

Schwarz, R.M. 1994. *The skilled facilitator: practical wisdom for developing effective groups.* San Francisco: Jossey-Bass Publishers.

Schwinghamer, P., J.Y. Guigné, and W.C. Siu 1996. Quantifying the impact of trawling on benthic habitat structure using high resolution acoustics and chaos theory. *Canadian Journal of Fisheries and Aquatic Sciences* 53: 288-296.

Scoffin, T.P. 1993. The geological effects of hurricanes on coral reefs and the intepretation of storm deposits. *Coral Reefs* 12: 203-221.

Scott, A. 1999. Introducing property in fishery management. In: R. Shotton (Ed.), *Use of property rights in fisheries management. Proceedings of the FishRights 99 Conference, Fremantle, Western Australia,* Fisheries Technical Paper 404/1. Rome: Food and Agriculture Organization.

Scott, W.R. 1995. *Institutions and organizations.* London: Sage Publications.

Seijo, J.C. and J.F. Caddy 2000. Uncertainty in bioeconomic reference points and indicators in marine fisheries. *Marine and Freshwater Research* 51: 477-483.

Seitzinger, S.P. and C. Kroeze 1998. Global distribution of nitrous oxide production and N inputs in freshwater and coastal marine ecosystems. *Global Biochemical Cycles* 12 (1): 93-113.

Sen, S. and J.R. Nielsen 1996. Fisheries co-management: A comparative analysis. *Marine Policy* 20 (5): 405-418.

Senge, P.M. 1990. *The fifth discipline. The art and practice of the learning organisation.* New York: Doubleday.

Senge, P.M., A. Kleiner, C. Roberts, R. Ross, and B. Smith 1994. *The fifth discipline fieldbook: strategies and tools for building a learning organisation.* London: Century Business.

Shackell, N.L. and J.H. Martin Willison (Eds.) 1995. *Marine protected areas and sustainable fisheries.* Wolfville, N.S.: Science and Management of Protected Areas Association.

Shackle, G.L.S. 1969. *Decision, order and time in human affairs.* Cambridge: Cambridge University Press.

Shein, E. 2000. Web-Based OLAP Tools Peel Back Data. *Managing Automation* 15 (8): 56-59.

Shiganova, T.A. and Y.V. Bulgakova 2000. Effects of gelatinous plankton on Black Sea and Sea of Azov fish and their food resources. *ICES Journal of Marine Science* 57:641-648.

Shipp, R.L. 2002. *No take marine protected areas (nMPAs) as a fishery management tool, a pragmatic perspective: A report to the Fish America Foundation.* Available http://www.asafishing.org/images/gais_shipp.pdf. (Accessed 30 March 2003).

Shipp, R.L. 2003. A perspective on marine reserves as a fishery management tool. *Fisheries* 28 (12): 10-21.

Shiva, V. 1991. *Ecology and the politics of survival, conflicts over natural resources in India.* New Delhi: United Nations University Press and Sage Publications.

Sider, G. 1986. *Culture and class in anthropology and history: A Newfoundland illustration*. New York: Cambridge University Press.

Silva, M.E., E.M. Gately, and I. Desilvestre 1986. A bibliographic listing of coastal and marine protected areas: A global survey. *Technical Report WHOI-86-11.* Woods Hole Oceanographic Institution.

Simchi-Levi, D. and E. Philip-Kaminsky 1999. *Designing and managing the supply chain: Concepts, strategies and case studies.* Boston: Irwin/McGraw Hill.

Simon, H.A. 1957. *Models of man: social and rational.* New York: Wiley.

Simon, H.A. 1983. *Reason in human affairs.* Stanford: Stanford University Press.

Sinclair, P.R. 1985. *From traps to draggers: Domestic commodity production in northwest Newfoundland, 1850-1982.* St. John's, Newfoundland: Institute of Social and Economic Research, Memorial University of Newfoundland.

Sinclair, P.R. 1992. Atlantic Canada's fishing communities: The impact of change. In: D.A. Hay and G.S. Basran (Eds.), *Rural sociology in Canada.* Pp. 84-98. Don Mills, Canada: Oxford University Press.

Sinclair, P.R. 1996. Sustainable development in fisheries dependant regions? Reflections on Newfoundland cod fisheries. *Sociologia Ruralis* 36 (2): 225-235.

Skytte, H. and N.J. Blunch 1998. An analysis of retail buying behaviour in various European countries. *Proceedings from the 3rd International Conference on Chain Management and the Food Industry.* Aarhus: Aarhus School of Business.

Smith, P.J., R.I. Francis, and M. McVeagh 1991. Loss of genetic diversity due to fishing pressure. *Fisheries Research* 10: 309-316.

Sniderman, P.M., R.A. Brody, and P.E. Tetlock 1999. *Reasoning and choice.* Cambridge: Cambridge University Press.

Soutar, A., and J.D. Isaac 1974. Abundance of pelagic fish during the 19th and 20th centuries as recorded in anaerobic sediment off California. *Fishery Bulletin* 72: 257-274.

Stanfield, B. 2000. *The courage to lead: transform self, transform society.* Toronto: Canadian Institute of Cultural Affairs.

Stank, T., M. Crum, and M. Arango 1999. Benefits of inter-firm co-ordination in food industry supply chains. *Journal of Business Logistics* 20 (2): 21-24

State Secretariat of Fisheries 1995. *Master Plan.* Maputo: Government of Mozambique.

Steele, J.H. 1991. Marine functional diversity. *BioScience* 41: 470-474.

Steen, F. 1995. *Testing for market boundaries and oligopolistic behaviour: An application to the European Union market for salmon.* SNF Working Paper No. 3. Bergen: Institute for Research in Economics and Business Administration

Stevens, J.D., R. Bonfil, N.K. Dulvy, and P.A. Walker 2000. The effects of fishing on sharks, rays and chimaeras (Chondrichthyans) and the implications for marine ecosystems. *ICES Journal of Marine Science* 57: 476-494.

Stewart, H. 1977. *Indian fishing: Early methods on the northwest coast.* Vancouver: Douglas and McIntyre.

Steyn, N.P., J.H. Nel, J.F. Prinslao, H.Y. Tichelaar, M.A. Dhansay, J. Theron, L.C. Hoffman, and A.J.S. Benadé 1995. Nutritional status of preschool children consuming a diet rich in Clarias gariepinus. *The South African Journal of Food Science and Nutrition* 7 (4): 158-162.

Stickney, R.S. 2000. *Encyclopedia of aquaculture.* New York: John Wiley and Sons, Inc.

Stokes, T.K., J.M. McGlade, and R. Law (Eds.) 1993. *The exploitation of evolving resources.* Berlin: Springer-Verlag.

Storey, K. and B. Smith 1995. Collapse in the Newfoundland groundfish fishery: Responses, constraints and opportunities. In: S.T.F. Johansen (Ed.), *Nordiske fiskersamfund i fremtiden: Fiskeri og fiskersamfund.* Vol 1. Pp. 163-188. Copenhagen: TemaNord, Nordisk Ministerrad.

Strange, S. 1996. *The retreat of the state: The diffusion of power in the world economy.* New York: Cambridge University Press.

Strathern, M. 1991. *Partial connections.* Savage: Rowman and Littlefield.

Sudo, K.I. 1984. Social organization and types of sea tenure in Micronesia. In: K. Ruddle and T. Akimichi (Comps.), *Maritime institutions in the Western Pacific.* Pp. 203-230. Osaka: Senri Ethnological Studies, National Museum of Ethnology.

Sumaila, U.R. 1997. Strategic dynamic interaction: The case of Barents Sea fisheries. *Marine Resource Economics* 12: 77-94.

Sumaila, U.R. 1999. A review of game theoretic models of fishing. *Marine Policy* 23 (1): 1-10.

Sumaila, U.R. 2001. Generational cost benefit analysis for evaluating marine ecosystem restoration. In: T.J. Pitcher, U.R. Sumaila, and D. Pauly (Eds.), *Fisheries impacts on North Atlantic ecosystems: Evaluations and policy exploration.* Fisheries Centre Research Reports 9 (5). Vancouver, Canada: Fisheries Center, University of British Columbia.

Sumaila, U.R. and Bawimia 2000. Ecosystem justice and the marketplace. In: H. Coward, R. Ommer, and T.J. Pitcher (Eds.), *Fish ethics. Justice in the Canadian fisheries.* Pp. 140-153. St. John's, Newfoundland: Institute of Social and Economic Research, Memorial University.

Sumaila, U.R., Y. Liu, and P. Tyedmers 2001. Small versus large-scale fishing operations in the North Atlantic. *Fisheries impacts on north atlantic ecosystems: evaluations and policy exploration.* Vancouver: Fisheries Centre, University of British Columbia.

Sumner, J. 2002. *Sustainability and rural communities in the age of globalization: Can we learn our way out?* Unpublished. Ph.D. dissertation. University of Guelph, Canada.

Sutton, M. 2001. Harnessing market forces and consumer power in favour of sustainable fisheries. In: T.J. Pitcher, P.J.B. Hart, and D. Pauly (Eds.), *Reinventing fisheries management.* Pp. 125-135. Dordrecht: Kluwer Academic Publishers.

Suvapepun, S. 1997. Environmental aspects of responsible fisheries in the Gulf of Thailand. *Proceedings of the APFIC Symposium Seoul, South Korea, October 1996.* FAO-RAPA Publication 1997/32: 168-183.

Svendsen, A. 1998. *The stakeholder strategy: Profiting from collaborative business relationships.* San Francisco: Berrett-Koehler.

Swan, J. and B.P. Satia 1998. *Contribution of the Committee on Fisheries to global fisheries governance 1977-1997.* FAO Fisheries Circular n° 938. Rome: Food and Agriculture Organization.

Sydnes, A.K. 2001a. New regional fisheries management regimes: Establishing the South East Atlantic fisheries organisation. *Marine Policy* 25 (5): 353-364.

Sydnes, A.K. 2001b. Regional fishery organizations: how and why organizational diversity matters. *Ocean Development & International Law,* 32: 349-72.

Sydnes, A.K. 2002. Regional fishery organisations in developing regions: adapting to changes in international fisheries law. *Marine Policy,* 26 (5): 373-381.

Symes, D. 1996. Fishing in troubled waters. In: K. Crean and D. Symes (Eds.), *Fisheries management in crisis.* Pp. 3-16. Oxford: Blackwell, Fishing News Books.

Symes, D. 1998. *The integration of fisheries management and marine wildlife conservation.* Report, No. 287. Peterborough, UK: JNCC.

Tacon, A.G.J. 2001. Increasing the contribution of aquaculture for food security and poverty alleviation. In: R.P. Subasinghe, P. Bueno, M.J. Phillips, C. Hough, S.E. McGladdery, and J.R. Arthur (Eds.), *Aquaculture in the Third Millennium. Technical proceedings of the Conference on Aquaculture in the Third Millennium, Bangkok, Thailand, 20-25 February 2000.* Pp. 63-72. Bangkok: Network of Aquaculture Centres in Asia; Rome: Food and Agriculture Organization.

Tacon, A.G.J. (Ed.) 2003. Aquaculture production trends analysis. In: Review of the State of World Aquaculture. *FAO Fisheries Circular No. 886.* Rev 2. FIRI C886 (Rev. 2): 5-29.

Tall, A. 2002. Small scale fish trade in West Africa – Prospects for expansion. *Infofish International* 2: 12-16.

Tasker, M.L., C.J. Camphuysen, J. Cooper, S. Garthe, W.A. Montevecchi, and S.J.M. Blaber 2000. The impacts of fishing on marine birds. *ICES Journal of Marine Science* 57: 531-547

Tayamen, M.M., R.A. Reyes, J. Danting, A.M. Mendoza, E.B. Marquez, A.C. Salguet, R.C. Gonzales, T.A. Abella, and E.M. Vera-Cruz 2002. Tilapia broodstock for saline water in the Philippines. *Naga, The ICLARM Quarterly* 25 (1): 32-36.

Trade & Environment Database (TED) 1996. *Shrimp aquaculture in India.* Available http://www.american.edu/TED/INDSHRMP.HTM, (Accessed 6 June 2003).

Tegner M.J., and P.K. Dayton 2000. Ecosystem effects of fishing on kelp forest communities. *ICES Journal of Marine Science* 57: 579-589.

Tempier, E. 1986. Prud'homie et régulation de l'effort de pêche. *Economie Méridionale* 34 (133-4): 41-50.

Thiebaux, M.L. and L.M. Dickie 1993. Structure of the body size spectrum of the biomass in aquatic ecosystems: A consequence of allometry in predator-prey interactions. *Canadian Journal of Fisheries and Aquatic Science* 50: 1308-1317.

Thilsted, S.H., N. Roos, and N. Hassan 1997. The role of small indigenous fish species in food and nutrition security in Bangladesh. *Naga, The ICLARM Quarterly* July-December 1997 Supplement: 13-15.

Thollot, P. 1992. Importance of mangroves for Pacific reef fish species, myth or reality? *Proceedings of the 7th International Coral Reef Symposium, Guam, 22-26 June 1992.* Vol. 2. Pp. 934-941. Guam: International Association of Biological Oceanography (IABO).

Thomson, D. 1980. Conflict within the fishing industry. *ICLARM Newsletter* 3 (3): 3-4.

Thompson, P. 1983. *Living the fishing.* London: Routledge and Kegan Paul.

Thompson, R. and J.L. Munro 1983. The biology, ecology and bionomics of the hinds and groupers, Serranidae. *ICLARM Studies and Reviews* 7: 59-81.

Thompson, G.J., F.R. Levacic, and J. Mitchell 1991. *Markets, hierarchies and networks: The coordination of social life.* London: Sage Publications.

Thorner, D. 1966. Chayanov's concept of peasant economy. In: A. Thorpe, B. Kerblay, and R.E.F. Smith (Eds.), *The theory of peasant economy.* Pp. xi-xiii. Homewood: Richard D. Irwin.

Thorpe, A. and E. Bennett 2001. Globalisation and the sustainability of world fisheries: A view from Latin America. *Marine Resource Economics* 16: 143-164.

Thorpe, A., A.A. Ibarra, and C. Reid 2000. The new economic model and fisheries development in Latin America. *World Development* 28 (9): 1689-1702.

Thurow, F. 1997. Estimation of the total fish biomass in the Baltic Sea during the 20th century. *ICES Journal of Marine Science* 54: 444-461.

Tidwell, J.H. and G.L. Allan 2002. Fish as food: aquaculture's contribution. *World Aquaculture* (Sept.): 44-48.

Tobor, J.G. 1984. A review of the fish industry in Nigeria. *NIOMR Technical Paper.* Lagos: Nigerian Institute for Oceanography and Marine Research (NIOMR).

Tobor, J.G. 1990. The fishing industry in Nigeria: Status and potential for self-sufficiency in fish production. *NIOMR Technical Paper No. 54.* Lagos: Nigerian Institute for Oceanography and Marine Research (NIOMR).

Tobor, J.G. and F.O. Ajayi. 1979. Identification of marine fishes found in Nigerian coastal waters. *NIOMR Technical Report.* Lagos: Nigerian Institute for Oceanography and Marine Research (NIOMR).

Tomoda, S. 1999. *Safety and health of meat, poultry and fish processing workers.* ILO Working Paper. INDCOM/19-1.E97/fv2. Geneva: International Labour Organization.

TPI (Tropical Products Institute) 1977. *Proceedings of the Conference on the handling, processing and marketing of tropical fish. London, 5–9 July 1976.* London, Tropical Products Institute.

Tuominen, T.R. and M. Esmark 2003. *Food for thought: The use of marine resources in fish feed.* Oslo: World Wildlife Fund.

UC Atlas 2003. *UC atlas of global inequality.* Available http://ucatlas.ucsc.edu/income.php (Accessed June 11, 2003).

UN 1948. *Universal Declaration of Human Rights.* Available http://www.un.org/Overview/rights.html (Accessed 11 February 2005).

UN 1982. *Law of the Sea Convention.* Available http://www.globelaw.com/LawSea/lsconts.htm (Accessed 11 February 2005).

UN 1992. *Conference on Environment and Development, Rio de Janeiro, Brazil, 3-14 June 1992: Convention on Biological Diversity.* Available: http://www.biodiv.org/doc/legal/cbd-en.pdf (Accessed 28 March 2003).

UN 1994. *Agreement for the implementation of the provisions of the United Nations Convention on the Law of the Sea of 10 December 1982 relation to the conservation and management of straddling fish stocks and highly migratory fish stocks.* Available http://www.oceanlaw.net/texts/unfsa.htm (Accessed 11 February 2005).

UN 1995. *United Nations Conference on Straddling Fish Stocks and Highly Migratory Fish Stocks.* Available: http://www.iisd.ca/fish.html (Accessed 2 March 2005)

UN 2001a. *Millenium Development Goals.* Available http://www.un.org/millenniumgoals/ (Accessed 11 February 2005).

UN 2001b. *The right to food.* Note by the Secretary General. UN 56th Session. Item 131(c) Provisional Agenda. Ref. A/56/210. New York: United Nations.

UN 2002a. *World Summit on Sustainable Development. Plan of Implementation.* Available http://www.johannesburgsummit.org/html/documents/summit_docs/2309_planfinal.htm (Accessed 29 March 2003).

UN 2002b. *World Summit on Sustainable Development. The Johannesburg Declaration on Sustainable Development.* Available http://www.johannesburgsummit.org/html/documents/summit_docs/1009wssd_pol_declaration.htm (Accessed 29 March 2003).

UN, UNCED 1992. *Agenda 21, Chapter 17: Protection of the oceans, all kinds of seas, including enclosed and semi-enclosed seas, and coastal areas and the protection, rational use and development of their living resources.* Available: http://www.oceansatlas.com/world_fisheries_and_aquaculture/html/govern/instit/intlagr/unced.htm (Accessed 2 March 2005)

UNDP 1986. *Fisheries development: Review of support by UNDP.* New York: United Nations Development Program.

UNEP 2002. *Global environmental outlook 3: Past, present and future perspectives.* London: United Nations Environment Programme and Earthscan Publications.

UN Division for Ocean Affairs and the Law of the Sea 2005. A historical perspective. Available http://www.un.org.Depts.los.convention_agreements/convention_historical_perspective.htm (accessed 20 May 2005).

Ursin, E. 1982. Stability and variability in the marine ecosystem. *Dana* 2: 51-67.

US Bureau of Labor Statistics 1998. Fishing for a living is dangerous work. *Census of Fatal Occupational Injuries.* Available http://stats.bls.gov/iif/oshwc/cfar0025.txt (Accessed 2 March 2005).

Van den Bergh, J.C.J.M. and H. Verbruggen 1999. Spatial sustainability trade and indicators: An evaluation of the 'ecological footprint'. *Ecological Economics* 29: 61-72.

Van der Schans, J.W. 1999. Governing aquaculture: Dynamics and diversity in introducing salmon farming in Scotland. In: J. Kooiman, M. van Vliet, and S. Jentoft (Eds.), *Creative governance: Opportunities for fisheries in Europe.* Pp. 95-118. Aldershot, UK: Ashgate.

Van der Schans, J.W., K.I. Metuzals, N. Venema, and C.I. Malvido 1999. Adding quality to the fish chain: How institutions matter. In: J. Kooiman, M. van Vliet, and S. Jentoft (Eds.), *Creative governance: Opportunities for fisheries in Europe.* Pp. 119-140. Aldershot, UK: Ashgate.

Van der Voorst, J.G.A.J., A.J.M. Beulens, and P. van Beek 2000. Modelling and simulating multi-echelon food systems. *European Journal of Operational Research* 122 (2): 354-367.

Van Duijn, A.P. 2004. The rich eat fish, the poor eat pork: The decline of livelihoods of handpickers of aquatic organisms in North Vietnam. In: L. Visser (Ed.), *Challenging coasts: Transdisciplinary excursions into coastal zone development.* Pp. 211-238. Amsterdam: Amsterdam University Press.

Van Vliet, M. and P. Friis 1999. Creating co-operation in the chain. Options for integrating 'catch' and 'market'. In: J. Kooiman, M. van Vliet, and S. Jentoft, (Red.), *Creative governance. Opportunities for fisheries in Europe.* Pp. 207-226. Aldershot, UK: Ashgate.

Van Vught, F.A. 1987. Verklaringsmodellen bij beleidsevaluatie: De keuze tussen de rationalistische en de hermeneutische evaluatiemethodologie. In: P.B. Lehning and J.B.D. Simonis (Red.), *Handboek beleidswetenschap.* Pp. 154-176. Meppel: Boom.

Vázquez Gómez, E.M. 2002. *Las organizaciones internacionales de ordenación pesquera. La cooperación para la conservación y gestión de los recursos vivos de la alta mar.* Sevilla: Junta de Andalucía, Consejería de Agricultura y Pesca.

Vecchione, M., M.F. Mickevitch, K. Fauchald, B.B. Collette, A.B. Williams, T.A. Munroe, and R.E. Young 2000. Importance of assessing taxonomic adequacy in determining fishing effects on marine biodiversity. *ICES Journal of Marine Science* 57: 677-681.

Vitalis, V. 2002. *Private voluntary eco-labels: Trade distorting, discriminatory and environmentally disappointing.* Paris: OECD. Available http://www.oecd.org/oecd/pages/documentredirection?paramID=37686&language=EN&col (Accessed 23 June 2003).

Wackernagel, M. 1994. *How big is our ecological footprint? Using the concept of appropriate carrying capacity for measuring sustainability.* Vancouver: Task Force on

Healthy and Sustainable Communities, Department of Family Practice, University of British Columbia.

Wackernagel, M. 1999. An evaluation of the ecological footprint. Letters to the Editor. *Ecological Economics* 31: 317-318.

Wade, R. 1987. The management of common property resources - Collective action as an alternative to privatisation or state-regulation. *Cambridge Journal of Economics* 11 (2): 95-106.

Wade, R. 1992 [1987]. La gestión de los recursos de propiedad común: La acción colectiva como alternativa a la privatización o a la regulación estatal. In: F.C. Aguilera Klink (Ed.), *Lecturas sobre economía del agua.* Pp. 403-425. Madrid: MAPA.

Walters, C. 1998. Designing fisheries management systems that do not depend upon accurate stock measurement. In: T.J. Pitcher, P.J.B. Hart, and D. Pauly (Eds.), *Reinventing fisheries management.* Pp. 279-288. Dordrecht: Kluwer Academic Publishers, Fish and Fisheries Series 23.

Walzer, M. 1983. *Spheres of justice. A defense of pluralism and equality.* Oxford: Basil Blackwell.

Walzer, M. 2003. The idea of civil society: A path to social reconstruction. In: C.M. Elliot (Ed.), *Civil society and democracy. A reader.* Pp 63-83. Oxford: Oxford University Press.

Ward, B.E. 1985. A Hong Kong fishing village. In: B.E. Ward (Ed.), *Through other eyes: Essays in understanding 'conscious models' – mostly in Hong Kong.* Pp. 3-21. Boulder: Westview Press.

Watling, L. and E.A. Norse 1998. Disturbance of the seabed by mobile fishing gear: A comparison with forest clear-cutting. *Conservation Biology* 12: 1189–1197.

Watson, M. and R.F.G. Ormond 1994. Effects of an artisanal fishery on the fish and urchin populations of a Kenyan coral reef. *Marine Ecology Progress Series* 109: 115-129.

Watson, R. and D. Pauly 2001. Systematic distortions in world fisheries catch trends. *Nature* 414: 534-536.

Weaver, R.G. and J.D. Farrell 1999. *Managers and facilitators.* San Francisco: Berrett-Koehler.

Weber, M. 1964 (1925). *The theory of social and economic organization.* New York: The Free Press.

Weigel, J.Y. 1987. Nana et pêcheurs de port de Lomé: Une exploitation de l'homme par la femme? *Politique Africaine* 27: 37-46.

Weiss, L. 1997. Globalisation and the myth of the powerless state. *New Left Review* 225: 3-27.

Wenz, P.S. 2001. *Environmental ethics today.* New York: Oxford University Press.

Wessells, C.R. and J.L. Anderson 1992. Innovations and progress in seafood demand and market analysis. *Marine Resource Economics* 7 (4): 209-28.

WFFP Secretariat 2004. *World forum of fisher peoples.* Available http://www.wffp.org/ (Accessed February 24, 2004).

WFS 1996. *World Food Summit, 13-17 November 1996, Rome, Italy.* Available http://www.fao.org/wfs/main_en.htm. (Accessed 11 June 2003).

WHAT 2000. *Governance for a sustainable future.* Part 2. *Fishing for the future.* London: World Humanity Action Trust.

White, S.K. 1995. *The Cambridge companion to Habermas.* Cambridge: Cambridge University Press.

Wilkinson, R. (Ed.) 2004. *The global governance reader.* London: Routledge.

Williams, M. J., S. B. Williams and P. S. Choo 2002. From Women in Fisheries to Gender and Fisheries. In M. J. Williams et. al (Eds). *Global symposium on women in fisheries*. Sixth Asian Fisheries Forum. 29 November 2001, Kaohsiung, Taiwan. Pp. 13-20. Penang, Malaysia: ICLARM – The World Fish Center. Available www.worldfishcenter.org.

Williams, S.B. 1998. Women's participation in the fish industry in Nigeria: A review. *African Note*. Women's Research and Documentation Center (WORDOC), Institute of African Studies, University of Ibadan.

Williams, S.B. 2000. *Economic potentials of women in small-scale fisheries in West Africa*. Paper presented at International Institute of Fisheries Economics and Trade (IIFET) Conference, Corvalis, Oregon.

Williams, S.B. 2002. Making each and every African fisher count: Women do fish. In: M.J. Williams, N.H. Chao, P.S. Choo, K.I. Matics, M.C. Nandeesha, M. Shariff, I. Siason, E. Tech, and J.M.C. Wong (Eds.), *Global symposium on women in fisheries*. Penang, Malaysia: World Fish Center.

Williamson, O.E. 1975. *Markets and hierarchies: Analysis and antitrust implications*. New York: The Free Press.

Wilmsen, E.N. 1989. *Land filled with flies: A political economy of the Kalahari*. Chicago: University of Chicago Press.

Wilson, D.C., J. Raakjær Nielsen, and P. Degnbol (Eds.) 2003. *The fisheries co-management experience. Accomplishments, challenges and prospects*. Dordrecht: Kluwer Academic Publishers.

Wilson, E.O. 1998. *Consilience: the unity of knowledge*. New York: Knopf.

Witte, F., T. Goldschmidt, J. Wanink, M. van Oijen, K. Goudswaard, E. Witte-Mass, and N. Bouton 1992. The destruction of an endemic species flock: Quantitative data on the decline of the *Haplochromine Cichlids* of Lake Victoria. *Environmental Biology of Fishes* 34: 1-28.

Wolf, E.R. 1982. *Europe and the people without history*. Berkeley: University of California Press.

Wolfe, A. 1989. *Whose keeper? Social science and moral obligation*. Berkeley: University of California Press.

Wonham M.J., J.T. Carlton, G.M. Ruiz, and L.D. Smith 2000 Fish and ships: relating dispersal frequency to success in biological invasions. *Marine Biology* 136(6): 1111-1121.

Woolston, J. 2000. Food irradiation in the UK and the European Directive. *Radiation Physics and Chemistry* 57 (3): 245-247.

World Bank 1984. *Harvesting the waters: A review of bank experience with fisheries development*. Washington DC: World Bank.

World Bank 1986. *Poverty and hunger: Issues and options for food security in developing countries*. Washington DC: World Bank.

World Bank 1989. *A framework for capacity building in policy analysis and economic management in Sub-Saharan Africa*. Washington DC: World Bank.

World Bank 1992. A study of international fisheries research. *Policy and Research Series No. 19*. Washington DC: World Bank.

World Bank 1997. The state in a changing world. *World Development Report 1997*. Washington DC: World Bank.

World Bank 2001. *World Development Report 2000/2001. Attacking poverty*. Oxford: Oxford University Press.

World Bank 2004. *Saving fish and fishers*. Washington DC: World Bank.

World Food Conference 1974. *Universal declaration on the eradication of hunger and malnutrition, 16 November 1974.* Available http://www.unhchr.ch/html/menu3/b/69.htm (Accessed 11 February, 2005).

WTO 1994. *Marrakesh Agreement.* World Trade Organization. Available http://www.jurisint.org/pub/06/en/doc/02.htm (Accessed 9 April 2004).

WTO 1996. *Singapore Ministerial Declaration.* World Trade Organization. Available http://www.wto.org/english/thewto_e/minist_e/min96_e/wtodec_e.htm (Accessed 11 February 2005)

WTO 2001. *Trading into the Future. 2nd Edition, revised.* World Trade Organization. Available http://www.wto.org (Accessed 1 September 2003).

WTO *Agreement on Technical barriers to trade* (TBT Agreement). World Trade Organization. Available http://www.worldtradelaw.net/uragreements/tbtagreement.pdf (Accessed 11 February 2005).

WTO *Agreement on implementation of Article VI of the General Agreement on Tariffs and Trade 1994* (The anti-dumping agreement). World Trade Organization. Available http://www.wto.org/english/docs_e/legal_e/19-adp.pdf (Accessed 11 February 2005).

WTO *Agreement on subsidies and countervailing measures* (SCM Agreement). World Trade Organization. Available http://www.wto.org/english/docs_e/legal_e/24-scm.pdf (Accessed 11 February 2005).

Yanagisako, S.J. and J.F. Collier 1987. Toward a unified analysis of gender and kinship. In: J.F. Collier and S.J. Yanagisako (Eds.), *Gender and kinship: Essays toward a unified analysis.* Pp. 14-50. Stanford: Stanford University Press.

Young, J.A. 1986. Marketing in a dynamic environment: An overview of the UK fish processing industry. *Contribution to Marketing in the Food Chain Conference, Sheffield City Polytechnic, 24-25 September 1986.* Sheffield, UK: Sheffield Hallam University.

Young, J.A. and J.F. Muir 2002. Tilapia: Both fish and fowl? *Marine Resource Economics* 17: 163-173.

Zaibet, L. 2000. Compliance to HACCP and competitiveness of Oman fish processing. *International Food and Agribusiness Management Review* 3: 311-321.

Zalewski, N.G., A. Januaer, and G. Jolánski 1997. Ecohydrology: A new paradigm for the sustainable use of aquatic resources. *International Hydrological Programme IHP-V Technical Documents in Hydrology No. 7.* Paris: United Nations Educational, Scientific and Cultural Organization. (UNESCO).

Zohar, I., T. Dayan, E. Galili, and E. Spanier 2001. Fish processing during the early Holocene: A taphonomic case study from Coastal Israel. *Journal of Archeological Science* 28 (10): 1041-1052.

Zwanenburg, K.C. 2000. The effects of fishing on demersal fish communities of the Scotian Shelf. *ICES Journal of Marine Science* 57: 503-509.

List of Contributors

Maria Luisa Acosta is Director of the Center for Legal Assistance to Indigenous Peoples (CALPI) in Nicaragua.
calpi@ibw.com.ni

Maarten Bavinck is Senior Lecturer at the Department of Human Geography of the Universiteit van Amsterdam (the Netherlands) and Director of the Centre for Maritime Research (MARE).
j.m.bavinck@uva.nl

Ratana Chuenpagdee is Co-director of the Coastal Development Centre at Kasetsart University (Bangkok, Thailand), and Senior Research Fellow, International Ocean Institute in Halifax (Canada).
Ratana.chuenpagdee@dal.ca

Poul Degnbol is Director of the Institute for Fisheries Management (IFM) in Hirsthals (Denmark).
pd@ifm.dk

David Florido del Corral is Lecturer in Social Anthropology at the Universidad de Sevilla (Spain).
dflorido@us.es

Katia Frangoudes is Senior Researcher in the Center for the Law and Economics of the Sea (CEDEM) at the University of Western Brittany (Brest, France).
Katia.Frangoudes@univ.brest.fr

Svein Jentoft is Professor of Sociology at Norwegian College of Fishery Science, University of Tromsø (Norway).
sveinje@nfh.uit.nl

Derek Johnson is Senior Researcher with the Centre for Maritime Research (MARE) at the Universiteit van Amsterdam (the Netherlands).
dsjohnson@marecentre.nl

Jan Kooiman is Professor Emeritus of Public Management at Erasmus University (the Netherlands).
jkooiman@xs4all.nl

Michel Kulbicki is a Marine Biologist connected to the Institut Rechêrche en Développement (IRD), in Perpignan (France).
michel.kulbicki@univ-perp.fr

Robin Mahon is Acting Director of the Centre for Resource Management and Environmental Studies (CERMES) at the University of the West Indies (Barbados).
rmahon@caribsurf.com

Jose J. Pascual-Fernández is Senior Lecturer of Social Anthropology at the Instituto Universitario de Ciencias Políticas y Sociales, University of La Laguna (Canary Islands, Spain).
jpascual@ull.es

Roger Pullin is an Aquatic Biologist associated with the Manx Wildlife Trust (Isle of Man, Great Britain) and currently based in Manila, Philippines.
karoger@pacific.net.ph

Juan C. Rodríguez Mateos is Lecturer in Human Geography at the Universidad de Sevilla (Spain).
juancarlos@us.es

Rathindra Nath Roy is a Fisheries Consultant and Communications Expert based in Chennai (India).
yarish@vsnl.com

Juan L. Suárez de Vivero is Professor and Head of the Department of Human Geography at the Universidad de Sevilla (Spain).
vivero@us.es

Rashid Sumaila is Director of the Fisheries Economics Research Unit, Fisheries Centre at the University of British Columbia (Canada).
r.sumaila@fisheries.ubc.ca

Andy Thorpe is Principal Lecturer with the Department of Economics at the University of Portsmouth (United Kingdom).
Andy.Thorpe@port.ac.uk

Annabelle Cruz-Trinidad is a Consultant with the Pacific Rim Innovation and Management Exponents (PRIMEX) in Pasig City (the Philippines).
abbie@trinidad.com.ph

Joeli Veitayaki is Senior Lecturer in the Marine Studies Programme of the University of the South Pacific (Fiji Islands).
veitayaki_j@usp.ac.fj

Stella Williams is Senior Lecturer in the Department of Agricultural Economics at the Obafemi Awolowo University, Ile-Ife, Osun State (Nigeria).
swilliam@oauife.edu.ng

Jacques van Zyl is a Fisheries Economist employed by the Department of Marine and Coastal Management (South Africa).
Jacques@mcm.wcape.gov.za

Index